JOHN REVELL REINHARD

Mediaeval Pageant

HASKELL HOUSE PUBLISHERS LTD.
Publishers of Scarce Scholarly Books
NEW YORK, N. Y. 10012
1970

First Published 1939

HASKELL HOUSE PUBLISHERS LTD.
Publishers of Scarce Scholarly Books
280 LAFAYETTE STREET
NEW YORK, N. Y. 10012

Library of Congress Catalog Card Number: 75-129969

Standard Book Number 8383-1166-0

Printed in the United States of America

Hit is a noble and faire thinge for a man or a woman to see and beholde hemself in the mirrour of auncient stories, the which hath ben wretin bi oure aunsetters for to shewe us good ensaumples that thei dede, to leve and to eschewe the evell.

—KNIGHT OF LA TOUR LANDRY

Preface

BY IMMEMORIAL CONVENTION this space is reserved for the maker of the book so that he may tell the reader what he intended to do and why he failed to do it. This places me in a rather awkward position, for I am unable to take advantage of a Black Death, a Pilgrimage to Canterbury, or a Sack of Rome. Perhaps it would be best to say frankly that in collecting, translating and publishing these tales I have had no other purpose than to share with the Gentle Reader my own interest and pleasure. Though I think they are all good stories, and most of them as interesting now as they were in their own time, it is for him to judge.

But if I have no excuses to make, I can at least save the Learned Friend some trouble and irritation by candidly confessing my various crimes. First of all, I have made use of existing translations, some of them so well known that the Learned Friend will recognize them subconsciously; but I have not always felt obliged to follow them to the letter. If, by reference to the original, or even to a different version of the story, I could improve the effect for the Gentle Reader, I have not hesitated either to excise or conflate. In some cases, perhaps, an author would have a little difficulty in recognizing the work here attributed to him. For this my only justification was the desire to set forth as good a story as I could. Art, like truth, needs many witnesses.

In a similar manner have I tampered with some of the texts translated by myself. Occasionally, when it fell to my lot to retell a story in English, I have been faithful to the original, as with Boccaccio or Machiavelli. At other times I have taken such liberties as seemed to me necessary to convey to the Gentle Reader of the twentieth century the same impression or idea as that received by the Gentle Auditor of the eleventh, twelfth or thirteenth. The statement—

> When we shall be—story without weariness—in our
> house in our singleness we two, there is to us limitless in
> feat something against which we can put our keenness

is, of course, just as intelligible to the Learned Friend of today as it was to the Irishmen of the tenth century. But I think, and hope, that most readers will prefer the interpretation given in No. 30, since those who can read these tales in their original languages will probably not be reading them here.

As for the Gentle Reader, however, I expect him to read every word —if he is interested in people. In these pages he will find gathered a hundred men and women—kings and usurers, heroes and churls, learned clerks and lovely ladies. Among them are those who understand the problems of science and of letters, those who are able to expound the law between man and man, and between man and God; conquerors of men, conquerors of time, conquerors of evil, conquerors of themselves; here are thinkers and poets, explorers of the heavens and of the seas, and of the dark recesses of ignorance. But there is no hind and no herd, no hewer of wood, and no drawer of water. What of them? you ask. They, I reply, are the rich soil out of which the good corn springs. Let your cook invent a new sauce, your forester become a carver of wooden images, your ploughman a husbandman who can make the waste place flourish, your shepherd a poet, and immediately he steps out of the void of nonentity into the world of reality.

But the Learned Friend, against whom no subterfuge is availing, will discover that I have sometimes put a tale into the mouth of someone to whom it does not rightfully belong. In certain instances this procedure has been forced upon me; in others it has been adopted deliberately for reasons of dramatic expediency.

Finally, I should warn my Learned Friend that he may be shocked by certain opinions voiced by well-known historical personages. In this matter I admit that I have allowed myself a certain latitude, but no more, I think, than might be condoned by the fantastic assumption that such and such a person, from some vantage-point on the other side of death, had kept watch in the succeeding years over the things which interested him while in the world. It was my desire to assemble in one body, as Diodorus Siculus says, a number of men united by spiritual kinship, though separated from each other by Time and Space. Naturally, I have not been consistent, for it is generally conceded that a work of imagination is exempt from the laws which govern a work of erudition. On the other hand, the poetic license has not been abused: I have not conferred the Order of the Garter upon Diomede, nor elevated a skull-splitting Danish viking to the dignity of the doctor's chair.

At the beginning of these remarks I had expected to say very little; probably I have already said too much; certainly it is time to stop, for nobody ever reads prefaces anyway.

J. R. R.

Beaumaris, Anglesey
May, 1938

Contents

THE CARLE OF THE DRAB COAT. *Mac Conglinne*	4
1. HOW BERYN WAS RUINED BY DICE-PLAY. *Adam Scrivener*	14
2. THE SAD END OF PETER THE DICER. *Matteo Bandello*	20
3. HOW THE JONGLEUR OF SENS THREW DICE WITH SAINT PETER. *Jean de Meung*	27
4. THE HEART OF KING ROBERT. *Jean Froissart*	33
5. KING RICHARD ENTERTAINS SARACEN AMBASSADORS AT LUNCH. *Ambroise*	36
6. BROTHER JUNIPER'S HOSPITALITY. *Sordello*	43
7. HOW COLUMCILLE FREED SCANLANN FROM SALT BACON AND BEER. *Geoffrey Keating*	46
8. KING HENRY'S GUEST. *Dick O the Cow*	48
9. THE MAN-EATING MAIDEN OF DUNDEE. *Hector Boëce*	5˜
10. THE FRIARS OF BERWICK. *William Dunbar*	55
11. THE FIGHT FOR THE MARROWBONE. *Eices ind Righ*	62
12. HOW BÖDVAR IMPROVED TABLE-MANNERS AT THE COURT OF KING HROLF. *Einar Rattlescale*	65
13. THE FIGHT ON THE INCH OF PERTH. *Blind Harry*	68
14. THE WERWOLVES OF MEATH. *Giraldus Cambrensis*	71
15. THE LADY OF LANGO. *Jean d'Outremeuse*	73
16. THE WEDDING OF SIR GAWAIN AND DAME RAGNELL. *Adam Scrivener*	75
17. EYJOLF'S LAST FIGHT. *Sturla the Lawman*	86

CONTENTS

18. PAYN PEVEREL'S ENCOUNTER WITH GOGMAGOG. *Fulk Fitzwarin*   89

19. THE BLOOD-LUST OF ALBINA AND WHAT CAME OF IT. *Gogmagog*   90

20. THE GHOST OF FAWDOUN. *Blind Harry*   94

21. HOW AMADAS FOUGHT WITH THE FIEND AT THE TOMB OF YDOINE. *Jehan Madot*   96

22. HOW ELEDUS SLEW HIS HOST. *Raoul Lefèvre*   105

23. CONALL GULBAN AND THE AMHUISH. *Mac Conglinne*   109

24. JEFFREY'S FIGHT WITH THE GIANT MEZEL. *Gaucelm Faidit*   115

25. HOW JEFFREY LONGED TO SLEEP AT CASTLE MONBRUN. *Gaucelm Faidit*   121

26. HOW LANCELOT FOUGHT WITH THE DEMON CATS. *Master Jehan*   130

27. RICHARD SANS PEUR AND THE UNQUIET CORPSE. *Master Wace*   134

28. THE PRIORESS AND HER THREE SUITORS. *John Skelton*   135

29. SENCHAN TORPEIST AND THE KING OF THE CATS. *Cuan O Lochan*   142

30. PANGUR BAN. *Cucuimne*   147

31. THE FLY WITH THE WOODEN LEG. *Paul the Deacon*   150

32. COLUMCILLE'S GARRON. *Adamnan*   151

33. THE INITIATION OF A KING. *Giraldus Cambrensis*   152

34. THE EMPRESS OF ROME AND HER MAIDS WHO WERE MEN. *Blaise the Hermit*   154

35. THE ELEVATION OF PIERRE DE LA BROSSE. *Guillaume de Nangis*   159

CONTENTS xiii

36. THE HANGING OF MARCOLF. *Monk Eustace* 162

37. THE WENCH OF SANTO DOMINGO. *Andrew Boorde* 166

38. GIANNI SCHICCHI AND THE MULE. *Fra Cipolla* 167

39. BERYN AT THE BAR. *Beryn* 169

40. MURDER IN THE JEWISH QUARTER. *Richard of Devizes* 174

41. THE HARD JUDGE. *Robert Mannyng* 178

42. THE FOUNTAIN OF YOUTH AND THE ISLAND OF BIMINI. *Ponce de Leon* 183

43. THE TURKISH DOCTOR. *William Dunbar* 187

44. THE MAD LOVER. *Jehan Madot* 189

45. HOW DUKE ASTOLFO OF ENGLAND FOUND ORLANDO'S WITS ON THE MOON. *Sir John Harington* 198

46. FULK FITZWARIN'S SEAFARING. *John Leland* 212

47. THE MONSTER OF MALE GAUDINE. *Master Jehan* 219

48. ASMUND'S SEPULCHRAL ADVENTURE. *Saxo Grammaticus* 226

49. THE RETURN OF VIGA HRAPP. *Hallfred Vandraethaskald* 229

50. DIVORCE BY DEATH. *Chrétien de Troyes* 231

51. ANASTASIUS BURIED ALIVE. *Guillaume de Nangis* 239

52. THE TRAGIC DEATH OF THE YOUNG COUNT OF FOIX. *Espaign du Lion* 241

53. THE ADVENTURES OF SAINT BRANDAN IN THE WESTERN SEA. *Adamnan* 246

54. GREGORY'S PETRINE PENANCE. *Robert Mannyng* 261

55. QUEEN LANGUORETH'S RING. *Sir David Lindsay* 273

56. THE HERMIT AND THE OUTLAW. *William of Wykeham* 276

xiv CONTENTS

57. THE OUTLAWING OF THORKEL DRYFROST. *Sigmund Brestison* — 281

58. THE DEVILS' CONCLAVE. *Dick O the Cow* — 285

59. THE WHITE SHIP. *Master Wace* — 287

60. HOW OLAF HARALDSON GATHERED SCAT IN THE FAROËS. *Sighvat Skald* — 292

61. EINDRIDI BROADSOLE SHOOTS AT A MARK. *Snorri Sturlason* — 295

62. HOW EUSTACE SOLD POTS. *Monk Eustace* — 300

63. KING FERNANDO AND THE WIFE OF LORENZO D'ACUNHA. *Lorenzo Fongasso* — 307

64. FLORINDA. *Pedro Lopez de Ayala* — 310

65. BUONDELMONTE DE' BUONDELMONTI FALLS INTO A TRAP. *Matteo Bandello* — 314

66. KING EDWARD III RECKONS WITHOUT HIS HOSTESS. *Jean Froissart* — 318

67. THE TOURNAMENT OF TOTENHAM. *Walter Haliday* — 322

68. THE SECOND PRIEST'S TALE OF PEBLIS. *Master Archebald* — 331

69. THE BOY IGNORANT OF WOMEN. *Giovanni Boccaccio* — 337

70. HOW TO KEEP A HUSBAND. *The Goodman of Paris* — 340

71. THE MAID OF ASTOLAT. *Huchown of the Awle Ryale* — 342

72. MARION DE LA BRUÈRE. *John Leland* — 347

73. THE PARDONER AND THE BARMAID. *John the Reeve* — 352

74. EARL RICHARD. *Roaring Dick* — 358

75. THE MIRACLE. *Étienne de Bourbon* — 363

CONTENTS

76. MALGHERITA SPOLATINA AND HER PARAMOUR. *The Clerk of Oxenford*   369

77. CLIDNA'S WAVE. *Cormac of Cashel*   373

78. THE COBBLER OF CONSTANTINOPLE. *Walter Map*   376

79. KINMONT WILLIE. *Lochmaben Harper*   379

80. SAGAMONI BORCAN, THE VIRTUOUS PRINCE. *Marco Polo*   384

81. DWYNWEN VERCH BRYCHAN AND MAELON DAFODRILL. *Dafydd ab Gwilym*   386

82. THE YOUNG MAN MARRIED TO A STATUE. *Roger of Wendover*   387

83. THREE MERCHANTS AND THEIR INOBEDIENT WIVES. *Knight of La Tour Landry*   389

84. BYCORNE AND CHICHEVACHE. *The Goodman of Bath*   392

85. THE TWO MARRIED WOMEN AND THE WIDOW. *William Dunbar*   395

86. THE PROVIDENT MATRON. *Curtal Friar*   404

87. SIR NORBERT LOSES A CORPSE AND REFUSES A WIFE. *Colin Clout*   406

88. ROBERT GUISCARD'S VENOMOUS WIFE. *Roger of Hoveden*   408

89. BELFAGOR'S BARGAIN. *Niccolò Machiavelli*   410

90. ERIC BLOODAXE TAKES A WIFE. *Snorri Sturlason*   420

91. MERLIN AND VIVIAN. *Blaise the Hermit*   422

92. HARALD HARFAGR AND GYDA. *Thormod Kolbrunarskald*   427

93. CAIER'S WIFE AND NEPHEW. *Cormac of Cashel*   429

CONTENTS

94. THE DEATH OF MAELFOTHARTAIG MAC RONAN. *Cuan O Lochan* 430

95. THE BASE AMOUR OF BERENGAR'S WIFE WILLA. *Sordello* 434

96. HOW ASTOLFO, KING OF THE LOMBARDS, LEARNED ABOUT WOMEN. *Sir John Harington* 436

97. MARGARET, COUNTESS OF HENNEBERGE AND HER THREE HUNDRED AND SIXTY-FIVE CHILDREN. *Fynes Moryson* 450

98. THE MIDNIGHT RIDER. *John Mirk* 451

99. THE INORDINATE LUST OF ROMILDA, DUCHESS OF FRIULI. *Paul the Deacon* 452

100. TWO LOYAL LOVERS OF FLORENCE. *Fynes Moryson* 454

101. DIGNA OF AQUILEIA. *Andrea Dandolo* 456

102. WALLACE AND THE MAID OF LANARK. *Blind Harry* 458

103. THE RAVISHED WIFE. *The Goodman of Paris* 464

104. HAMLET IN SCOTLAND. *Saxo Grammaticus* 465

105. THE BASTARS' WIFE OF BUILLON. *Adam Usk* 471

106. THE WEDDED LIFE OF INJURIOSUS. *Jacques de Vitry* 478

107. THE FAIRY LADY OF ELDON HILL. *Huchown of the Awle Ryale* 481

108. THE TATAR PRINCE AND THE KING OF KINGS. *Joinville* 489

109. TAROLFO'S UNSEASONABLE GARDEN. *Giovanni Boccaccio* 490

110. THE NECROMANCER AND THE DEAN. *The Bachelor of Salamanca* 498

111. THE DOG VIGI. *Hallarstein* 501

CONTENTS

112. SHEEP INTO DOG. *Roaring Dick*   505

113. THE NUT-CRACKING THIEF AND THE CRIPPLE. *Ordericus Vitalis*   508

114. THE THIEVES WHO WENT IN SEARCH OF DEATH. *Fra Cipolla*   509

115. THE SECRET OF LOWRY LORC'S EARS. *Henry Castide*   511

116. THE KNIGHT AND THE LION. *John Mirk*   513

117. THE EYES OF LOVE. *Eices ind Righ*   514

118. HOW KING RICHARD WON THE HEART OF MARGERY OF ALMAIN. *Ambroise*   517

119. HOW BLONDEL FOUND KING RICHARD IN GERMANY. *The Minstrel of Reims*   522

120. TWO LUSTY LADIES OF AUVERGNE AND THEIR CAT. *Guilhem IX*   525

121. THE FREEBOOTERS OF AUVERGNE. *Jean Froissart*   527

122. THE WIDOW WHO WORE HORSESHOES. *Hector Boëce*   534

123. THE CRAFTY FARMER. *The Curtal Friar*   536

124. THE STORY OF A SELF-MADE MAN. *Unibos*   539

125. TOMASONE GRASSO, USURER OF MILAN, DOES A SHREWD STROKE OF BUSINESS. *Matteo Bandello*   543

126. PIERS THE TOLLER. *Robert Mannyng*   547

127. THE CHURL AND THE BIRD. *The Clerk of Oxenford*   551

128. QUEEN ELEANOR AND SALAH AD-DÎN. *The Minstrel of Reims*   556

129. QUEEN ELEANOR'S CONFESSION. *John de Rampaigne*   559

130. THE DEATH OF CELTCHAR MAC UTHECHAIR. *Ossian*   562

CONTENTS

131. THE LADY IN THE WALL. *Fynes Moryson*   564
132. THE POISON CUP. *Richard Sheale*   566
133. THE UNTIMELY DEATH OF SAMHER THE LAP-DOG. *Cuan O Lochan*   572
134. SAMSON'S ADVENTURES AT THE COURT OF KING HILDEBERT. *Iolo Goch*   573
135. A SATIRICAL DESCRIPTION OF HIS LADY. *John Skelton*   576
136. HOW MAC CREICHE SLEW THE YELLOW PEST. *Mac Conglinne*   582
137. ORTHON, FAMILIAR SPIRIT OF THE LORD DE CORASSE. *Jean Froissart*   585
138. THE LOVE, IMPRISONMENT AND TREACHEROUS SLAYING OF SANCHO DIAZ, AND WHAT BERNARDO DEL CARPIO DID ABOUT IT *The Bachelor of Salamanca*   589
139. FUN WITH A CORPSE. *Dick O the Cow*   594
140. HOW OLAF TRYGGVISON PAID A DEBT. *Sighvat Skald*   598
141. JARNSKEGGI'S DAUGHTER. *Einar Rattlescale*   600
142. QUEEN MEAVE'S LAST BATH. *Mac Conglinne*   602
143. SVANHILD AND RANDVER. *Thormod Kolbrunarskald*   603
144. ROSMUNDA'S REVENGE. *Paul the Deacon*   607
145. HOW SIR JOHN DE CAROUGES AVENGED THE HONOUR OF HIS WIFE. *Jean Froissart*   609
146. THE BARNS OF AYR. *Blind Harry*   613
147. GWENDOLEN OF CORNWALL. *Master Wace*   619
148. TURGESIUS KEEPS A TRYST. *Geoffrey Keating*   622

CONTENTS

149. THE VESPERS OF MONREALE. *Giovanni Villani*	626
150. THE RAIN OF FOLLY. *Peire Cardenal*	639
ACKNOWLEDGMENTS	643
BIBLIOGRAPHY	645
INDEX OF PERSONS AND TITLES	653

MEDIAEVAL PAGEANT

*G*OOD MORNING, SIR, 'tis a lovely day."
A sharp wind with a hint of rain in it was blowing off the Rock of Cashel. To the southeast, between a layer of leaden sheep-shearings and the purple black of the Commeragh mountains, an edge of saffron light betrayed the presence of a discouraged sun. But I would not be outdone in courtesy by an Irishman in his own land, so I said:

"It is, indeed, God bless you."

"God and Mary bless you," replied Mac Conglinne, for it was none other than that famous scholar of abundant knowledge. "Are you for the Rock?"

"I am so," I answered.

Together we mounted the gentle acclivity that leads to the quondam chapel and stronghold of Munster's king and archbishop. There my companion kindly related to me many things concerning the history of the Rock and its buildings. In the time of Corc son of Lughaidh its name had been Fairy Ridge or Woody Ridge. Two swineherds, Ciolarn and Duirdre, used to pasture their hogs in the woods of the ridge. One day they beheld a figure as bright as the sun, which blessed the hill and the place in a voice sweeter than any music: It was the angel Victorius foretelling that Patrick should come to the Rock. When tidings of this vision reached Corc, he at once went to Woody Ridge and built a fortress there; and when he had become king of Munster, it was on this rock that he used to receive his royal rent. Thereafter the place was called Cashel from the *caiseal,* or enclosing rampart of Corc's fort.

He told me, too, how Cormac mac Cuilennan had met his death in the battle of Ballymoon, how his head had been cut off by some over-zealous warrior, and how Flann Sinna, though the enemy of Cormac, was horrified at such a deed.

"And the stone whereon the holy bishop's head was cut still stands," said Mac Conglinne, "on the site of the battle, two Irish miles north of Carlow."

Thereafter he explained to me the significance of the design on the stone coffin of King Cormac mac Carthy: The endless chain of intertwined serpents and wolf-hounds, he said, indicated Time passing from nowhere to nowhere.

With this and other talk the morning passed, and it was noon. I invited Mac Conglinne to lunch, for he himself had nothing in his satchel but a couple of black bannocks and a strip of old bacon. We made out very well with roast beef and mealies.

After lunch Mac Conglinne and I set off on a first-class road for Caher, where the scholar showed me the original foundations of the circular stone *cathair* whereon the Norman castle was later built. Thence we took a second-class road which brought us to Fermoy, where Mac Conglinne told me the legend of St Finnchua's mother. The king of Fermoy was pursuing her to kill her, but a cloak of darkness miraculously fell between her and the king, and she escaped.

From Fermoy we took a third-class road, bearing ever south. The going was rough, but my companion seemed not to mind it, for he had on an excellent pair of shoes.

"Those are fine shoes you have there," I said.

"They are so," he replied; "I made them myself. Have you ever heard the tale, now, how the fox ate St Ciaran's shoe-strings?"

I said that I had not, so he told it to me. In return I related to him how the camel, a wise person and an excellent legist, had given King Noble the benefit of his learning in the law during Renard's trial for seducing the wife of Isengrim.

The Illustrious Scholar thanked me for my tale, and we walked on in silence. But neither my feet nor my shoes were as good as Mac Conglinne's, and the road was worse than both, so I asked him if he would stop for a few moments' rest.

"I will, indeed," said my companion readily. "And while we ease our legs and wet our throats, it may cheer your mind if I tell you about THE CARLE OF THE DRAB COAT . . ."

It was a day of gathering and of conference appointed by Finn son of Cumall son of Art son of Trenmor grandson of Baeiscne, with the seven battalions of the reserve and seven of the regular Fianna, at the Hill of Edar son of Edgaeth; and as they threw an eye over the sea and great main they saw a roomy and a gallant ship that upon the waters bore right down for them, from the eastward and under a press of sail. She was fitted out as though for war and contention; and they had not long to wait before they marked a tall, bellicose, impetuously valiant *óglaech* rise by means of his javelins' staves, or of his spears' shafts, and so attain both his soles' width of the white-sanded beach. A polished and most comely lorica he had on; an armature that was solid and infrangible surrounded him; his handsome red shield surmounted his shoulder, and on his head was a hard helmet; at his left side a sword, wide-grooved, straight in the blade; in his two fists he held a pair of thick-shafted spears, unburnished but sharp; a becoming mantle of scarlet hung on his shoulders, with a brooch of the burnt gold on his broad chest.

Thus equipped, then, and in this fashion, he came into the presence of Finn and of the Fianna; and Finn spoke to him, saying: "Of the whole world's bloods, noble or ignoble, who art thou, warrior; or out of which airt of the four art come to us?" "Cael an Iarainn is my name, the king of Thessaly's son; and in all that time which I have perambulated the globe, I have not left either isle or island but I have brought under tribute of my sword and under my own hand. What now I desire therefore is to carry off the universal tribute and capital power of Ireland."

Conan said: "We have never seen such *laech* nor heard of warrior but a man to turn him would be found in Ireland."

"Conan," answered Cael, "in thine utterance find I naught else than that of a fool or gaby; for were all they who during these seven years past are dead of the Fianna added now to those who yet live of them, I would in one single day treat them all to the grievousness of death and of life curtailed. But I will do a thing which ye will esteem a condition easier than that: If among the whole of you ye find one only *laech* who in running, or in single fight, or in wrestling shall get the better of me, no more worry or trouble will I inflict on you, but will get me gone back to my own land again."

"Why, now," said Finn, "the runner whom we have, Caeilte mac Ronan to wit, he at this moment is not at home; and were he here he would have a run with thee; but if, warrior, thou be a one who will tarry with the Fianna, and with them make friendship and observe the same while I go to Tara of the Kings to fetch Caeilte— whom if I find not there I shall to a certainty get in Keshcorann of the Fianna—then do so."

"So be it done," Cael assented.

Then Finn started on the road and he had not gone far when he happened on an intricate gloomy wood, the diameter of which a deeply scooped out hollow way traversed throughout. Into this forest he had not penetrated any distance before he met a diabolical-looking being of evil aspect, an irrational wild monster of a yellow-complexioned thick-boned giant having on him a long drab coat down to the calves of his two legs, either of which under him as they carried the great fellow's ill-assorted body was like the mast of some ship of largest rate; like the side of a wide-wombed boat was each brogue of the two that garnished his knobbed feet armed with curved nails; the drab coat that invested him had to it a pewter platter's width of a skirt trimming consisting in a yellow stucco of mud, and this at every step that he took would flap against the calf of one leg so as to knock out of it a report that could be heard half a mile of country away; while every time that he lifted his foot there used half a barrel of mire to squirt upwards to his buttocks and even over his entire yellow-tinted person.

Finn fell to consider the great man for a length of time, for never before had he seen his like, and walked still on his way till the other spoke, saying: "What is this course of trudging or wandering that is befallen thee to make, Finn son of Cumall, all alone and solitary without a man of Ireland's Fianna by thee?"

"Such," replied Finn, "is the measure of my perplexity and trouble that I cannot frame to tell thee that, nor, though I could, would it do me any good whatsoever."

"Unless to me thou do explain the matter, thou wilt for ever suffer the damage and detriment of thy reticence."

"Well, then," Finn began, "if I must tell it thee, know it to be the king of Thessaly's son, Cael an Iarainn, who yesterday at noon came in at Ben-Edar looking to acquire for himself the rent and rule of all Ireland unless only that some one *laech* I may find who in running, in single combat or at wrestling shall overcome him."

"And what would ye do?" the big one inquired, "for I know him well, and there is not a single thing asserted by him but he is able to fulfil; upon the Fianna universally he would inflict slaughter of men and virile *óglaechs*."

Finn went on: "I would proceed to Tara of the Kings to fetch Caeilte, whom if I find not there I shall undoubtedly get in Keshcorann of the Fianna, in order that of yon warrior he may win a running match."

"Verily, then," said the big fellow, "thou art but a kingdomless man if Caeilte son of Ronan be thy grand resource with which to scare away the other."

"Then indeed I know not what I shall do," said Finn.

"But I do," quoth the great man. "Wouldst thou but put up with me, of that hero I would upon my oath win a running wager."

Finn rejoined: "I esteem that in carrying thy coat and huge brogues for a single half-mile of country thou hast thine utmost endeavour to perform, and not to embark in a running bet with that *laech*."

"By all that's positive, unless I win it of him, not a man of all Ireland will bring it off."

"So be it done," consented Finn. "But what is thy name?" And he made answer:

"My name is Bodach an Chóta Lachtna, the Carle of the Drab Coat."

Then Finn and the carle returned back again, nor concerning their travel and wayfaring is anything told us until they reached Ben-Edar. There Ireland's Fianna in their numbers gathered about the big man, for never before had they seen his like. Cael an Iarainn, too, came upon the ground and inquired whether Finn had brought a man to run with him. Finn answered that he had, and exhibited his man. But when Cael had seen the carle he objected to all eternity that he would not run with any such greasy *bodach*.

At this hearing the latter emitted a coarse burst of horse-laughter, saying: "In respect of me thou art deceived, warrior. Acquaint me, therefore, with the length of course that thou wouldst run, the which if I run not with thee, and more too, if such be thy pleasure, thine it shall be to take the stakes."

"I care not," rejoined Cael, "to have in front of me a course of less than three score miles."

" 'Tis well as it happens," said the carle; "three score miles exactly they are from Ben-Edar to Slieve Luachra of Munster."

"So be it done," Cael assented.

"Well, then," suggested the *bodach,* "the right thing for us to do is to proceed westwards to Slieve Luachra to begin with, and there to put up tonight, so that tomorrow we may be ready for our start and our walk."

Those two good *laechs,* Cael an Iarainn, namely, and the Carle of the Drab Coat, set out accordingly, and of their journey there is not any record until, as the sun went under, they reached Slieve Luachra of Munster.

"Cael," said the other then, "it behoves us to knock up some kind of dwelling, whether house or hut, to have over our heads."

But Cael retorted: "By all that's certain, I never will set about building a house on Slieve Luachra for the sake of passing one night there, considering that I have no desire at all ever during the whole course of my life to return thither."

"So be it," quoth the *bodach,* "but if I can manage to put up the like, 'tis far enough away outside of it will be any who shall not have given his help to make it."

The carle entered then into the nearest darkling and intricate wood, where he never stayed nor rested till he had tied up four and twenty couples of gross timber; and these, along with their complement of rafters from the same wood, and of fresh rushes of the mountain, he brought in that one load, and so erected a house long and wide, all thatched and warm. Of the forest's sticks both green and dry he on that lodging's floor made up a vast bonfire, and a second time addressed Cael:

"If thou be a man to come with me and in these woods seek some game or other . . ."

"I understand nothing about it," answered Cael; "and if I did, 'tis not to second the like of thee I would go."

Again the *bodach* sought the nearest wood's recesses, into which he was not permeated far when he roused a drove of wild swine. The stoutest boar that he saw he cut off from the rest and, along every track, through every covert, followed until by strenuousness of running and of painful effort he vanquished and struck him to the earth. Neatly and expeditiously he made him ready, and before that same great fire put him down to roast, with a turning contrivance to the spits that should keep them going of themselves. Then the carle started nor ever halted before he attained to the baron of Inchiquin's house—which was a score and ten miles from Slieve Luachra —and brought away two barrels of wine, two pewter dishes, all as much bread as there was ready in the house, a table and a chair, the whole of which he carried in the one load, and so regained Slieve Luachra. Here he found his meat roasted before him. Half of the boar, a moiety of the bread and a barrel of wine he set aside to provide for the morning. The other half of each he served to himself upon the table, and comfortably, luxuriously, sat down. He ate his full quantum of meat, after which he ingurgitated into his person a barrel of wine. Upon the floor of the caravanserai he shook out a copious layer of rushes, and was wrapped in sleep and lasting slumber until on the morrow's day both the all-brilliant sun rose, and Cael an Iarainn—who during the night had been on the mountain's side without meat or drink—came and roused him from his snooze, saying:

"Rise, *bodach,* it is now time for us to set about our journey and our wayfaring."

With that the carle woke up, rubbed his eyes with his palms, and said: "There is an hour's time of my sleep that I have not worked out yet, but since thou art in a hurry, I yield thee my consent that thou be off, and undoubtedly I will be after thee."

Accordingly Cael went ahead upon the way, not without great misgiving by reason of the small account which he saw the *bodach* make of him. When now the latter had slept his stint he rose to a sitting posture, washed his face and hands, served himself up meat on the table; then at his perfect ease sat down to it, ate up the remaining half of boar and bread, and finally swigged off the second barrel of wine. At this point the carle got up, in his drab coat's skirt he carefully stowed away the pig's bones, and away with him at the speed of a swallow or of a roe, or as it had been a blast of the searing March wind careering over the summit of some hill or rugged-headed rock, until he overhauled Cael an Iarainn and across the way in front of him pitched the porker's bones, saying:

"Try, Cael, whether upon those bones thou mayest find any little pick at all, for sure it is that after passing last night in fasting condition on Slieve Luachra thou art full of hunger."

"Thou shouldst be hanged, carle," he answered, "ere I would go look for meat upon the bones which with thy glutton-tusks thou hast gnawed!"

"Well, then," said the *bodach,* "it were none too much for thee to put on a gait of going better than thou hast done as yet." Then he pushed on as though he were turned to be a madman, and in that one heat went thirty miles. Then he fell to eating of blackberries from the brambles that were on either side of the way till such time as Cael came up to him and said:

"Bodach, thirty miles back from here is the spot in which I saw one skirt of thy drab coat twisted round the neck of a bush, and the second tangled in another bush ten miles behind that again."

"Is it the skirts of my coat?" asked the carle, looking himself all down.

" 'Tis they, just," Cael said.

"In that case," replied the *bodach,* "that which it were the right thing for thee to do would be to delay here eating of blackberries, in order for me to return and bring back the skirts of my coat."

"It is very certain that I will do no such thing," answered Cael.

"So be it," said the *bodach.*

Cael went his road, while the carle returned till he found the skirts of his coat as the other had said. He sat down, pulled out his needle and thread, and so stitched them on in their own place again. This done, he retraced his steps, and Cael was not gone far when the carle caught up with him and said:

"Cael, thou must put on a gait of going better than thou hast yet done if, as thou hast already expressed, thou wouldst carry off all Ireland's tribute, for I will do no more turning back now."

Then with the speed of a swallow or of a roe, or as it had been a blast of the searing March wind the *bodach* set off as though converted into a madman, and such the impetuous rush of pedestrianism which carried him along that soon he surmounted the crown of a certain hill within five miles of Ben-Edar, where he devoted himself to eating of blackberries from the brambles till he had made of himself a juice-filled sack. He then put off his drab coat, again produced his needle and thread, and sewed up the garment so as to make of it a long and wide bag, very deep. This he stuffed to the muzzle with blackberries, and on his skin rubbed a quantity of the same so that he was as black as any smith's coal; said load he hoisted upon his shoulder and, stoutly, nimble-footedly set out, making for Ben-Edar.

The position of Finn and of the general Fianna was that they were filled with great apprehension of Cael an Iarainn's being in front, for without knowing in the world who he was they had pitched all their hope in the carle. Now abroad on a tulach's top Finn had a certain emissary to spy which of the two who raced held the lead; and he, as soon as he caught sight of the carle, went in and told Finn that Cael came along in the road, and the *bodach* dead upon his shoulder. "A suit of arms and of armour," cried Finn, "to him who shall bring us tidings better than these!" And a second messenger, when he was gone out, recognized it to be the *bodach* who was there. Around him the Fianna of all Ireland flocked together joyously, and sought news.

"I have good news for you," said the carle; "but for the magnitude of my hunger it is not possible for me to publish it before I eat my sufficiency of parched corn-meal and blackberries mixed; my share of these I have brought with me, and let you now provide me my fill of such meal."

On Ben-Edar now a great cloth was opened out on which to serve the carle, with a heap of meal in its very centre. In among the meal he shot his sack of blackberries and with a will turned to at eating them.

But soon they saw Cael along the road, with his hand at his sword's hilt, his two eyes blazing red in his head, and he ready to charge in among the Fianna to hew them and to bone-split. When the *bodach* saw him in this array, he picked up his great paw's fill of the meal and blackberries, and upon Cael discharged the mess to such purpose that he banished his head to the distance of a fair scope of ground from his body; then, where the head was, thither he ran, and with it a second time let fly at the trunk of the body in such a way that he fastened it on as solid as ever it had been. The manner of him now, however, was with his face to his back, his poll upon his chest. Thereupon the *bodach* ran at him, dashed his whole carcass violently to earth, lashed him up hard and fast and inextricably, and said:

"Cael, was it not a mistaken thing for thee to say that on this occasion the chief rent and sovereign power of Ireland, though there were none but thyself alone to strive for it, would be suffered to go with thee? Nevertheless, none shall ever have it to say to Ireland's Fianna that to a solitary warrior, he having none but himself to take his part, they would administer grievousness of death and of short life. If, therefore, thou be one to swear by sun and moon in guarantee of thy transmitting the rent of Thessaly yearly during thy life long to Finn and the Fianna, thou shalt have thy life in the guise which thou now wearest."

By sun and moon Cael swore yearly to fulfil that all his life.

Then the *bodach* takes him by the tips of his fingers, leads him to his ship and puts him in sitting posture into her. To the vessel's after part he gave a kick, and with that same sent her seven leagues out to sea.

There you have the fashion in which the expedition of the king of Thessaly's son, Cael an Iarainn, turned out with him: to be dismissed home under the conditions of a fool or a simpleton, without power ever again so long as he should live to strike a blow in battle or in tough single encounter.

The *bodach* came back to Finn and the Fianna and told them that he was the fairy chief of Rath Cruachan who had come to loose them out of the fetters in which they had been. For the fairy chief Finn then made a feast and a banquet of a year and a day.

And thus, shortening the way with tales and stories, we walked through Watergrass Hill without noticing it, topped the rise beyond Blackpool, and descended finally to the River Lee—

> The pleasant Lee that like an island fayre
> Encloseth Cork in his divided flood.

"There should be a guest-house hereabouts," said Mac Conglinne, "and time it is that we found it, for the sun has this long while gone west over the sea."

Therewith he turned west himself till, about a mile and a quarter farther on we came upon the monastery. The door of the guest-house was open, and we went in. The wind had come in, too, and had blown all manner of litter over and under the beds, benches and other furniture. Blankets there were, to be sure, but if they had not been shaken in the morning, nor sunned during the day, neither had they been folded at night, and they were alive with lice and fleas. A bath-tub there was, indeed, with the water of the night before standing in it. No one was there to wash our feet, so Mac Conglinne took off his shoes and himself washed his feet in the bath-tub, and afterwards rinsed his shoes therein; then he offered to wash my feet and would not take "no" for an answer.

Somewhat refreshed by these ablutions we now courageously surrendered ourselves to the blankets. But truly, as numerous as the stars of heaven or the leaves of autumn were the lice and fleas sucking at our legs! And no one came to see how we fared.

"Musha!" cried Mac Conglinne, "it is in Connaught I should have stayed to claim the hospitality of Guaire Aidne Mac Colman rather than be detained thus without food, without drink and without washing after every man in Cork has gone to bed. My curse and Patrick's on these currish, inhospitable monks of Cork!"

Then, since he could not sleep, he brought out his psalter and began to sing his psalms.

"Should we not go to Kildare?" asked a voice from a dark corner.

"And who is that, now?" asked my friend.

"Jehan is my name, Master of Arts, *et quibusdam aliis*. I have come here searching for material wherewith to make a book about Lancelot and Gawain. Thank God my researches are finished, for during the past six months I have enjoyed no better hospitality than you experience tonight. And I have heard that at Kildare is all manner of ease—that devilled larks fly right into your mouth, and roast pigs roam about the streets with a knife stuck in their hams ready for you to cut a slice."

"Let us go to Kildare," said I.

"We will wait a bit," said Mac Conglinne. "It is an early rising when a man cannot see his five fingers against the sky."

By the time we reached Grey Abbey at Kildare the sun was high, but there was little virtue in it. We found Cucuimne in the very middle of the cloister, where the sun shone most fairly, composing a poem on book-skin. Several other scribes had followed his example in bringing their parchment and colours down from the scriptorium.

"O Cucuimne," said Mac Conglinne,

> "Cucuimne read knowledge half through;
> The other half he abandoned for hags."

"Well for him," replied Cucuimne,

> "When it chanced that he became wise,
> He abandoned hags,
> And reads again while he lives."

It is a lovely day," he added, and Mac Conglinne said that it was so.

"What do you want here?" asked the scribe.

"We have come to dinner," replied the scholar.

"It is a long time till sext," answered Cucuimne, and went on with his work.

So Mac Conglinne and Master Jehan loitered about the place, peering over the shoulders of the various scribes. Soon they were joined by Jehan Madot, late of Arras. And as they wandered and watched and listened they learned how books are made in Ireland.

Murchad Riabach: 'Tis a devilish chill there is in the scriptorium today.

Cairbre Corrach: And bad candles too.

Torna Og: And worse materials. O Mary, aid the ink!

Maelmuire: A curse on this pen!

Domnall O Duinnin: And on this defective vellum! Owing to the badness of the ink and the extreme badness of the vellum, I can write scarcely a letter today.

Cithruad Mac Findgaill: Faith, what can one do without chalk, without pumice and with bad implements?

Murchad Riabach: May Mary and Patrick help my hand!

Rugraide Buide: My curse and God's into the bargain I bestow on the woman who muddled together all that I possess of ink, of colours and of books!

Cithruad: There's an end to that, and my seven curses go with it!

Cucuimne: Alas, O hand! How much white vellum hast thou written! Thou wilt make famous the vellum, while thou thyself wilt be the bare top of a faggot of bones.

Giolla Padraic: Sad is the place where I am today, not knowing how I may bear it. The phlegm is upon me like a mighty river, and my breathing is weak. God help my difficulty!

"Bah!" exclaimed Jehan Madot. "You at least have warm clothing, whether by night or day. Now when I was transcribing the *Roman de Troie* at Arras, I had a much more disagreeable time. And would you know why? One night I went out to the tavern for a little relaxation and refreshment. There I met some jolly minstrels and jongleurs who were throwing dice, and who very courteously invited me to join them. Fool that I was, with fingers stiff from copying, it wasn't long before I lost both coat and surcoat. The next morning I was in no circumstances to enjoy the spring weather, you may be sure. Has any of you ever experienced a Flemish—or perhaps I should say an Artesian—fog? The *roman* had to be finished before Pentecost. There was additional reason now for hurrying the work, for my lord hadn't paid me a stiver on it. Moreover, a man-at-arms, with a pike which he seemed to know how to handle, was at my back all the time. And there was I, without coat or surcoat, beside a northeast window for two whole weeks! I have taken good care of my clothes ever since."

"It served you right," observed John of Salisbury. "Not only is dicing the mother of lies and perjury, the father of swearing and strife, the preceptor of homicide, and a waster of goods and substance —it is a childish and undignified pastime!"

"Reverend sir," said Beryn, "I agree with you heartily. But, like Jehan Madot, I had first to learn a bitter lesson."

"Let us hear," said Madot.

"Adam Scrivener has written it out," answered Beryn. "Let him tell it, for I am ashamed."

"As you wish," said Adam.

While Sir Thomas Elyot, Matteo Bandello, John of Salisbury, John Capgrave and others found seats on the flight of steps leading to the nave of the church, Adam took his stand before the armarium near by in the east wall and proceeded to tell

1. HOW BERYN WAS RUINED BY DICE-PLAY

Adam Scrivener

In the time of the emperor Augustine there lived in the suburbs of Rome a senator by the name of Faunus, a worthy man, of high lineage and very rich. He married a lady named Agea, his equal in rank and breeding, and who was wise and beautiful to boot.

For fifteen years Faunus and Agea lived together without having a child, in spite of their prayers, fasting and almsdeed. Finally God heard their prayer and Agea bore a son, whom they named Beryn. Faunus was overjoyed and took extreme care in the rearing of the boy, hardly letting him out of his sight, as is the way with fathers to whom children are born late in life. But Beryn's overmuch cherishing turned out ill for him in the end. Whatever he cried for was immediately given him, for no man said him nay. It would have been much better to have devoted some time to teaching him good manners.

As Beryn grew older he played with other children of the household; but if he did not like the play, he would break the other boy's head, or even hurt him nearly to death with a knife. Then too, there was no knight or squire in his father's household at whom he would not rage spitefully if the man did any little thing which displeased him.

Now Faunus and Agea were right well pleased by these actions of their son, for it seemed to them that such manners betokened a sturdy spirit; but there were those who thought they did not act wisely in failing to correct him. Though many a poor man was sadly vexed and injured by Beryn's behaviour, none dared lodge a complaint, for Faunus was very powerful.

In this wise, as Beryn grew up, he retained all his old bad habits and acquired some new ones. Above all things . . .

"Alas!" interrupted Sir Thomas Elyot, "when will we realize that the children of today are the men of tomorrow, in whose hands lies not only their own fate, but that of their children and their fathers? If evil custom and the pestiferous dew of vice are allowed to infect the hearts and brains of small children, the fruit will grow wild, and by its mortal poison destroy the realm. If you would save the nation, you must begin with the child. Everyday do we hear and see, to our great heaviness, children swearing great oaths and speaking lascivious and unclean words by the example of those whom they hear, and indulging in fits of savage petulance and temper unrestrained by nurse or parent. And if in the beginning ignorant parents of such children rejoice at what they are pleased to call evidences of alertness and sturdiness, in the end they shall smart with torment for their neglect."

"Sir Thomas," agreed Robert Mannyng of Brunne, "what you say is indeed true. Clerks tell us that when the child swore, Diogenes struck the father. The sin of the vicious child is great, but that of his neglectful and indulgent parents is greater. They shall have punishment, as you say, nor wait for the next world for it either."

"How different from yours, O Beryn, was the childhood education of Cuchulain, of Finn, or even of Ossian here," said Cormac of Cashel. "Their boyish sport and play trained them in manliness and virtue. There was no soil available in the Irish state for human weeds."

"Even in my day," put in Jean Froissart, "there were not wanting examples of well-trained youth. Consider the boyhood exercises of Bertrand du Guesclin. He was somewhat violent, it is true, but it was that exuberance of spirit which, under discipline, finally made him Constable of France."

"Obviously," said Beryn, "I was born in a decadent period. But to prove to you that I was not rotten to the core, I will ask Adam to continue with his story. The eating of a mouse includes its tail."

"Well," said Adam . . .

Beryn loved dicing and hazardry and other games of chance, even though he always lost. He spent his nights in dice-play, and many a time he came home quite naked, having staked and lost his clothes. But he cared little for this, for he knew that his mother would give him new clothes.

In this manner Beryn lived till his eighteenth year, and during this period his father was obliged to settle many serious complaints against him. And this was just, for it was his father's fault that he was so wild. A thing that is learned in youth is hard to put away, and true is the proverb which says that you can't teach a trotting horse to amble. But a man who reckons without Fortune is a fool, and now, right at high noon, Fortune turned a spoke backwards for Beryn.

It happened that Agea fell sick, and before dying she wished to convey her last wishes to Faunus. She besought him, for the sake of Beryn, never to marry again, saying that if the situation were reversed, nothing could induce *her* to take another husband. Faunus, who grieved exceedingly at the passing of his wife, readily promised not to give Beryn a stepmother. The priest performed his offices and her relatives bade her farewell. Agea looked about to kiss Beryn; but he was out of the house playing at hazard, as was his wont, for as soon as he had gulped down a meal, out he would run. When Agea missed him, her heart burst for grief.

A little earlier a maidservant had been sent to town where Beryn was playing. It happened that he had staked his gown, and as the maid came in, he was swearing like mad, as is proper to that game, for he was on the point of losing it. The maid said:

"Sir, you must come home. Your mother is dying, and you will have to hurry if you want to speak to her alive."

"Ha! you scurvy wench!" said Beryn, "who bade you give me such a message?"

"Your father," said she.

"Go home, ugly mug," he replied, "and a curse go with you. May the devil of hell tear you to pieces! Have you nothing else to do but interfere with my game? By God in heaven, by Peter and by James, were you not my father's messenger, you should never eat bread again! I would rather you and my mother also were dead than that I should lose this game."

Therewith he gave the maid a clout under the ear so that the blood gushed out, and returned to his game. He made his cast and lost his stake. At this he was so enraged that he stood up and batted the winner on the crown, and would have struck others if they had not slipped away. His gaming companions had no lust to fight with him, but only to win his goods.

Many folk mourned Agea's death, but not Beryn. He sought out another fellowship and played with them, returning home late at night as usual.

Faunus made a splendid funeral for his wife, and during four weeks she lay in lead in the house. But in all that time Beryn came not where she lay, nor repeated a single paternoster for her soul. His father could do nothing with him, for he had passed the age of correction. It is truly said that a man who has passed youth and remains without lore is like a rootless tree, or one that will neither bend nor bear fruit. So Faunus was no longer able to control

HOW BERYN WAS RUINED BY DICE-PLAY

Beryn. The boy slept at home; then, dining unwashed, would rush off to his companions to play. This, except fighting, was his sole occupation.

So Agea was buried, and Faunus lived a widower for three years. Finally it came to the ears of the emperor that Faunus was wifeless and seldom jocund, and that he lived like a hermit, sorrowing for Agea. This displeased the emperor, and he took counsel with the senators and the Seven Sages about the case. Their opinion was that the only remedy for vexation was consolation. So the emperor determined that since Faunus was grieving for the loss of a wife, he should be consoled by the abundant gentleness of some lady of pulchritude. Now before the emperor had married he had had a mistress who outshone all other women in fairness and beauty. Her name was Rame, and her he bestowed upon Faunus as his new wife. The Seven Sages were right, for Faunus soon became so besotted on Rame that he was never out of her presence, and spent his time gazing at her resplendent beauty. Thus Agea was forgotten.

Now Rame saw well how Faunus doted on her, and, such is the nature of women, the more he sought to please her, the more distant she bore herself, and sulked. And, still working against nature, it was her purpose to arouse strife between Faunus and his son.

In the meantime Beryn continued in his old habits, and Rame made him good cheer—as no woman might more—providing him with gold and clothing to replace his losses. And though she spoke him fair, she would much rather have eaten his heart without salt or bread.

One night when Faunus and his new wife were abed he took her in his arms and caressed her, as one should to one's mate, and he said: "My earthly joy, my heart's desire, my weal, my paradise, my life's sustenance, why are you not merry? Why are you so dull? Come now, my love, my own heart, if anything grieves you I will mend it, if it be in my power."

With a heavy sigh Rame untied the bag of treachery and complained that when she had married him her wheel had gone amiss, but that she would bear it as well as she could. She blubbered and sighed and wrung her hands, and always the refrain was: "Alas that I married you!" Thus with bitter words she struck through Faunus' heart, and his skull too. The sum of her complaint was that she might have a child, and that any child would be better dead than grow up to be like Beryn. In the last month she had given him fifteen new suits; he would waste half their property if he went on thus.

Faunus said he would call Beryn to account. The next morning when Beryn asked for some new clothes his father exhorted him to give up his evil ways and choose good men for his companions, for from now on Beryn would have to stand on his own feet. If he would reform, he should have his patrimony; otherwise he should have nothing.

At these words Beryn scowled. "Is this a sermon or a lecture?" asked he. "You are certainly acting out of your rôle. Send for some new clothes, for my friends are waiting for me and I'm in a hurry to be off. I will give up neither my dicing nor my friends. Enjoy your property as you please while you are alive; when it falls to me, I'll do with it as I please. I say, now, who put you up to this? I swear it must have been Rame, the false whore! You dote on her, don't you? At least that is what everyone says. Alas, that ever a man high in counsel should temper his wisdom according to his wife's tales! You love her so much you have lost your wit. Curse the day you married her! Most stepmothers are shrews and fickle flap-tails, and she is no exception. If I lose at dice, you have lost more —your good name, people's respect and your sense of decency."

When Beryn had finished Faunus gave the chair a kick and dashed out of the room, swearing that Beryn should repent of what he had said. The youth paid no attention, but hunted about for a new shirt. But this time he found none, so he put on such rags as came to his hand. Then he took a look at himself to see what manner of man he was. And if he was wroth, he had good reason, for his belly was bare and his buttocks too. In a rage he started after his father.

"Look at my clothes!" he shouted, "and don't laugh, for my shame is yours also."

Faunus let him clatter and went out without a word. At this Beryn began to think it was not all a joke—what his father had said. "Alas!" he cried, "now I know well that my mother is indeed dead."

Master Beryn will now have a chance to learn something of the world, for true it is that a man is never beaten so sore as with his own staff. He went to his mother's grave and wept so that he fell into a swoon. When he came to himself he stamped and tore his hair, scratched his face like a madman, and cursed the times he had been unkind to his mother. He asked God to pardon him.

But let us return to Rame. When she saw how matters had turned out she thought she would be blamed, and she said to Faunus: "Sir, what have you done? Though I spoke a merry word in jest, it was not my intention that you should send your son to town in rags. What will people say? Certainly they will say that I, his stepmother, am the cause of all this anger and wrath and gall that is between you and your son. Wherefore, I pray you, bring him home again."

"Now by my troth," answered Faunus, "he shall not come yet, so far as I am concerned. Since he recks so little of my words, as little shall I alter his estate. Who cares if he goes naked? His dicing will be blamed, not you."

But Rame pressed him, and at last Faunus consented to take his son back. "But," said he, "it is only for your sake; for all of me, grass should grow on the pavement first."

Vainly did Faunus seek Beryn in all his old haunts. Finally he found him weeping at his mother's tomb and they were reconciled. Faunus said he would get the emperor to knight him.

"Gramercy," said Beryn, "but I will not have it so. You love your wife tenderly; if you have children, she will seek to make them your heirs, and if you spend your goods on me, she will whet her tusks and smite you with her tongue, and glower continually under her hood. Thus she would shorten your life, and I do not desire that. Wherefor, to please everybody, I have determined to relinquish my inheritance and become a merchant. If you want to do something for me, do this: Fit me out with five ships of merchandise and let me go."

Faunus objected that that was a hazardous undertaking, and he might not only lose his goods, but his life also. But Beryn was obdurate, so father and son rode home together. When Faunus told Rame how matters stood, she made him much better cheer than heretofore: she coddled and petted him, threw her arms about his neck and made herself small and meek.

Finally the business was settled. Faunus provided his son with goods and ships. Beryn on his part signed a release on his inheritance in the emperor's presence, and the bond was placed in the hands of a third party till the ships were ready. Rame danced for joy, for now she had gained the thing she wanted most in life.

Beryn intended to sail for Alexandria, if he might. So, on a day when the wind was good he hoisted sail. For three days and three nights they had calm weather, but after that there arose such a mist that no man could see his fellow, and he who had his mother's blessing thought himself fortunate. For three days the darkness hung upon them so that no ship could sight another; master and crew were in despair.

On the fourth day the weather began to clear, but such a wind arose that all the ships were blown clean off their course, and separated one from the other. Beryn and all his men now began to shrive themselves, each man to his mate, while thunder and lightning, wind and rain raged all night long. Who was sorry now but Beryn that he had not given up this venture as his father had advised?

"In the opinion of some," said Sir Thomas Elyot, "it was Lucifer who invented dice-playing. However that may be, true it is that hazardry constitutes a veritable devil's treasury. And verily, the name of this treasury, whereof the door is left wide open to dice-players, is Idleness. And if in approaching it men happen to bring with them learning, virtuous business, liberality, patience, charity, temperance, good diet or shamefastness, they must leave them without the gates, for Evil Custom, who is the porter, will not allow them to enter."

"With those observations, Sir Thomas, I thoroughly agree," said Bandello. "To me it seems that the rascalities and foul deeds whereof we are daily witnesses arise largely from games of hazard, though it is a question whether the greatest evils are caused by dice or cards. Now whereas there are a thousand examples of the way in which Fortune displays her malice through games of chance, it was dice-playing that was at the root of the circumstances of a strange, pitiful and cruel case which happened not long since in Venice."

2. THE SAD END OF PETER THE DICER

Matteo Bandello

In the said city of Venice there lived not long ago a certain Peter, youngest son of that doctor-apothecary whose device is a golden apple. From his earliest childhood Peter had practised hazardry, and as he grew older the inordinate appetite for play so increased that he dedicated himself to it entirely, abandoning everything else; never was he without three dice in his hand.

Thus things went so that while he was still a boy he got into a quarrel about his point with a fellow dice-player, and stabbed him in the breast so that he died. Peter fled, and being summoned by the law, and failing to appear, he was outlawed with simple banns for contumacy and disobedience. But he had not been exiled long when he bought commutation from another bandit, as our law allows, and returned to Venice.

However, this affair in no wise hindered him from returning to his old habits, and he took up hazardry again more eagerly than ever, to such an extent that no household goods that he could lay hands upon were safe from him, and often he filched things from the shop itself.

Peter's father was exceedingly grieved by his son's passion for play, and thought he would marry him off, to see whether the obligations of wedded life would cure him of his folly; but this measure was vain, for Peter continued his customary dicing. Wherefor, seeing that no good came from scolding, reproof and exhortation, Peter's father decided to evict him from the paternal house. So he assigned to him his portion of his patrimony and turned him loose, hoping that the necessity of providing for the needs of his wife and household as well as himself would bring him to his senses. But it seems true, as I have heard, that an inveterate vice cannot be eradicated except with the greatest difficulty. The truth is that from that day forward Peter went from bad to worse, throwing dice more assiduously than ever, selling first one article and then another from the household property, to the tune of his wife's constant expostulation and reproach.

Now Peter had an aunt, the sister of his mother, whose husband, at his death, had left her in easy circumstances, so that she always had some ready money at hand. She was very fond of Peter and had often come to his assistance with twenty or thirty ducats. But when she learned of the miserable circumstances in which he maintained his wife, and that he gambled away whatever property came to his hand, she was very ill pleased, and determined to give him no more money. When Peter approached her she bitterly reproved him and admonished him sharply, saying that he might not expect another stiver from her till he had changed his habits of life. But Peter, before he took leave of her, so played upon her affection for him, promising not to gamble any more, that the good woman gave him ten ducats. As soon as he had the money he got into a dice game, and like so many other good ducats, these also went to Persia.

When his aunt learned this she made up her mind, and gave him to understand in no uncertain terms that he would never get another sou from her. Nevertheless, Peter continued to visit her, feigning a thousand needs at home, in the hope that he might be able to extract some cash. But he sang to the deaf and sowed in the sand.

Peter finally saw that he had nothing to hope for from his aunt, and having no other means of obtaining money, was reduced to despair, for it seemed to him that life without dicing was much worse than death. And since he knew of no way whereby he might put money in his pocket, blinded by his excessive and perverse lust for gaming, he finally formed the plan of killing his aunt in order that he might steal her money, and whatever other silver and gold he could lay hands on. And not only did he intend to murder the good woman, but everybody else in the household.

Such a plan, however, seemed to him to be too complicated to carry out alone, so he discovered his intentions to a certain Giovan Nasone, one of those vicious men who are ready to murder and steal for even the slightest gain. It was not difficult to persuade Nasone, especially as Peter promised him a hundred ducats for his part in the affair. When they had concerted their plans, Peter had two great daggers made and sharpened till they cut like razors. One of these he kept for himself and the other he gave to his accomplice.

Peter was very much at home in the house of his aunt, and even though he could get no more money from her, he often went to visit her or take a meal with her. Now it happened that at this time the festivities which mark the election of a new doge—Pietro Lando, as it happened—were being celebrated in the Piazza San Marco. Peter knew that his aunt, on account of a slight indisposition, did not intend to be present at the celebration, wherefor he determined to put his plan into execution on the day of the festival. Accordingly he notified Nasone to be in the Campo San Maurizio, where his aunt's house stood, about the first hour of night; he himself would be inside the house and would give him a signal when to enter. So, early in the evening, Peter went to visit his relation, who was alone in the house with her little daughter, aged about thirteen, her small son, about six years old, and the housekeeper. There was also a certain shoe-maker who had his shop on the ground floor. It had snowed heavily all day, and the housekeeper went down to sweep away the snow, where she stood talking for a while to the shoe-maker.

Peter decided he would not wait for Nasone, slipped downstairs and locked the door behind the maid, who was still gossiping with the cobbler. Then he rushed back to the first floor, and drawing his knife, killed his aunt with a single blow, and passing on into the adjoining room where the two children were at play, without the slightest human compassion or pity, more like a monster or savage than a Venetian, he killed those two innocents with the same bloody knife. Now descending to the first floor he unlocked the street door and hid behind it, waiting for the housekeeper to come in. She had now finished her sweeping, and with a last word to the cobbler, came through the doorway, where, as she entered, Peter stabbed her terribly in the head so that she died. After this Peter closed the door and returned to the living quarters. He found the keys to his aunt's money-box at her girdle, and at his leisure rifled it of a thousand ducats, together with a number of jewels. Filling his sleeves with the loot, he once more descended to the street, locked the door and found Nasone, who was waiting for the signal agreed upon.

"Let us go," said Peter, "for I have finished the whole affair." He told Nasone what he had done, and counted out a hundred ducats for him, urging him strongly to keep his mouth shut, and to get out of Venice as soon as he could. Then each went his own way.

Now the shoe-maker, who lived hard by, used to perform small services for the good woman, Peter's aunt, and as chance would have it, he was to bring her some candles this very evening. He knocked loudly at the door several times, but getting no reply concluded that she had gone with Peter to dine with the family, for it was the Venetians' custom to dine late in winter.

The next morning the cobbler again knocked at the good woman's door and again obtained no reply. In the evening he returned once more, and getting no answer to his knock, made inquiries among the neighbours, whether they knew the widow's whereabouts. They, of course, knew nothing, so the cobbler went to some of her close relatives, none of whom could imagine what might have happened to the widow and her children. Hereupon the shoe-maker, accompanied by the relatives—of whom Peter was one—laid the matter before the police. The Signori di notte, as they are called, sent sergeants, who broke down the door of the widow's house, and found lying behind it in her own blood the poor housekeeper, with her head split in two parts to the teeth. Shocked by this terrible sight they none the less proceeded to the next floor, where they found the good woman prone before the fire-place in one room, and the two children in the adjoining room, drenched in their own blood. It was a sight to arouse pity even in the hearts of Hyrcanian tigers.

Now began a diligent inquest to discover the perpetrator of these crimes. The relatives lent their assistance, and of these none was more diligent than Peter. He, indeed, showed more grief than any, prostrating himself upon the body of his aunt, lamenting in such a way that it seemed he could never be placated, and swearing to leave no stone unturned to find the malefactor.

The cobbler volunteered the information that he had left Peter with his aunt. The young man admitted as much, but said that he had gone out again almost immediately. The officers informed him that he must present himself before the Signori de la notte. Peter was in no wise dismayed, and readily entered the captain's barque. With him went a cousin of his, a son of the dead woman's sister. Into his cousin's hand Peter slipped a note-book wherein he had entered the amount of money stolen from his aunt, the jewels and silver, and even the hundred ducats which he had paid over to Nasone. "Cousin," he said, "for God's sake, burn this book; then look up Nasone and tell him to leave town as quickly as possible. I trust you to do this for me. The thing is done and there's no help for it now."

Peter was imprisoned, and his cousin went home shocked and bewildered. Finally, for some reason, whether for fear of the law, or because horrified by such a fearful and bloody manslaughter, he was impelled to take the note-book to the police, and to them also he repeated what Peter had told him.

Nasone was immediately apprehended, and without waiting for torture, at once confessed the whole matter. The book was shown to Peter, but he denied everything his cousin had said, and when confronted with the brigand Nasone, said he didn't know what he was talking about. Nor was it ever possible, either by the presentation of evidence, or by any manner of torture, to win a confession from him. While talking with Nasone Peter had thrown his knife into the canal. This was now recovered and identified. The ruffian also knew the smith who had made the dagger; and when he was examined he deposed that he had made two knives at Peter's instance.

With an unmoved countenance Peter denied everything, asserted his innocence, and said that Nasone and the smith were either drunk or had dreamed it. When asked to account for the numerous spots of blood on his clothes, he replied that he had passed by a butcher's shop and must have bloodied his clothes there; or perhaps it had happened when he threw himself in his grief upon his aunt's corpse.

The judges were greatly perplexed by Peter's firm denials; but weighing all the evidence, especially the note-book, which it was proved was written in Peter's hand, they condemned him to be torn with red-hot pincers, along with Nasone, and then quartered.

When sentence had been passed Peter's father and mother, wife and brother, went to the prison to comfort him. On the preceding day Peter had asked his brother to prepare a strong poison that would kill immediately, so that the people of Venice might not see him die so shameful a death. This he did, hiding the vial of poison in the heel of his slipper. When no one was looking the two brothers exchanged slippers.

Peter stoutly maintained that he had been unjustly condemned, and refused to make confession. But his parents besought Bernardino Occhino of Siena to visit their son. This the good man did; but he had hardly spoken fifty words to the prisoner when the poison, which Peter had swallowed a few moments before, began to work in him. His eyes bulged and his face swelled up so that he looked like anything else but a man. Matter ran from his eyes and nose, and from his mouth came a vari-coloured froth that stank abominably. Doctors were sent for in all haste, but it was too late, for the poison had reached the heart and other vital organs.

Now observe to what extent Peter was the prey of the devil himself! Having perpetrated so many foul crimes, and being on the point of death, he ought at least to have saved his soul by confession to a priest. But the wretch preferred to die as a pre-eminent felon rather than as a converted Christian. Not only would he not confess or repent, but having committed so many crimes against God, his fellow-man and himself, he still had no other thought than to persevere in his evil ways to the very end.

Since the poison had by this time deprived him of speech, by gestures and signs he conveyed the idea that the poison had been given him by one of his guards. The man was put to torture, but confessed nothing. What could an innocent man have to confess? Afterwards the brother's slippers were discovered, and the hole wherein the poison had been secreted. The judges sent to arrest him, but he had already fled Venice. The 'prentices of the drug-shop were questioned, and one of them deposed that he had seen Peter's brother mixing poisons, though he knew not for what purpose. Wherefor Peter's brother was banned, and the poor guard was liberated.

In the meantime Peter had died; and just as he was, he and Nasone were paraded through Venice on a barque, and both their bodies fearfully lacerated with hot pincers. Then, as they deserved, they were quartered, and their severed members hung up on gibbets in the salt lagoons to be food for crows and other carnivorous birds.

Such, then, was the end of the unhappy gambler Peter. One of his vices, however, I have forgotten to mention: It was said that he was the most fearful swearer and calumniator of God and the saints in those parts. However, there is no wonder that he was a blasphemer, for that foul vice is as proper to gambling as heat is to fire or light to the sun.

"Sirs," said John Bromyard to Beryn and Bandello, "your tales are instructive, and have a moral tone which should induce even John Wiclif to concede that secular literature may sometimes serve a good purpose."

"Hugh Latimer," said Sir Thomas Elyot, "used often to preach on the theme: 'All things that are written are for our behoof.'"

"'Old things are passed away, and all things are become new,'" answered Wiclif.

"For my part," spoke up John the Reeve, "I have never been able to understand the awe in which scribblers are commonly held. The hand that guides the plough or wields the sword does some useful labour, and by the sweat of his brow that man really earns his bread. But what valuable end is served by putting colours on good white sheepskin? It is a mere idle pastime."

"Well for you that you cannot write—or read—Master Reeve," rejoined Adam Scrivener, "for that opinion, if circulated abroad on book-skin or paper, would not enhance your reputation as an intelligent man. Though you may not know it, this company knows that the Romans were aided more by the pen than by the sword. Scribblers, as you call them, are far from idle. The purely physical labour of writing is back-wrenching, hand-cramping, and sometimes ruinous to the eyesight. Perhaps you remember how the Merchant Adventurer of Bruges took great pains to point out, with abundant reference to authority, that it was to save himself from idleness that he undertook to make one book out of three books of the lives of the saints, and that the task was so arduous that he was half desperate to accomplish it."

"I have heard of that," answered the Reeve; "but I also remember that it was not the fear that idleness would corrupt his soul which gave him strength to finish it, but rather the promise of a buck in summer and a doe in winter."

"At best," remarked Sir William atte Pole, "a writer is nothing more than a paid hack. The really important people of the world are those whose labour is directed towards the acquisition of goods and money, honours and titles."

"Honours and titles they may acquire," conceded Polydore Vergil; "but persons of your class usually lose both their honours and their heads on the scaffold, as did your grandson in 1450."

"Or in a cellar," said Snorri Sturlason gloomily.

"Hacks they are not," stated Master Wace somewhat violently. "And paid they are not; or at least," he added bitterly, "if they are paid they are more fortunate than I have ever been."

"Various crafts are necessary for the commonweal," said John Major, "and every craft is equally honourable."

"Of writers and of writings I know little," remarked Sir John Hawkins, "but no one will be surprised, I think, if I give it as my opinion that among crafts and professions those which give a man an active and moving part on the world's stage are superior to others."

"And yet," said Camden, "you chose to write about the part you played."

"Men," said the Clerk of Oxenford, "pass away; books remain. A wise man, himself a man of action as well as a writer, once said—or rather wrote—that books serve as so many aids and assistances to our memory and experience by recapitulating the deeds of old time. Wherefor a man has greater insight into affairs by reading one single book in three months' time than can be observed or understood by the age or experience of twenty men living successively one after the other."

"You are right, of course," said Robert Mannyng, "yet it often happens that ignorant people know not how to extract the good from writings and tales, and being of light mind, are corrupted."

"Books are not for people of light mind," rejoined the Clerk. "And if any, even of sober mind, is offended and unable to withstand the shock of the message which the writing conveys, let him turn over the leaf and choose another tale."

"I agree," said the Knight of La Tour Landry, "that the flesh is weak, and that some minds are still weaker. But I believe, as Pliny was wont to say—if I can believe my clerk—that there is no book and no story so bad but that some good may be found in it. I except, of course, some of the fabliaux, which are merely koprolitic."

"You might also except books which are merely stupid," said the Clerk. "The fact that such and such a book, poem or tale exists does not constitute proof that it has a right to exist. Books do and should shelter all life within their covers except two things—pure filth and pure stupidity."

"Well," answered the Knight, "within the limits you set it seems to me that even vice may sometimes be turned to good account, and the devil himself made to serve virtue."

"Sir," said Jean de Meung, "that has always been my opinion too, though the Chancellor of the Sorbonne hadn't the wit to see it. Jehan Madot's misfortune puts me in mind of a story which, I think, will illustrate what you say."

3. HOW THE JONGLEUR OF SENS THREW DICE WITH SAINT PETER

Jean de Meung

Once there was a jongleur of Sens—I do not know his name—who was indeed in evil case. Very seldom had he whole clothes, for it frequently happened that he peeled himself at dice. Many a time he lost his fiddle, his coat and his hose so that he went about exposed to the wind in his shirt. I do not lie when I say that he was frequently without shoes. The tavern was his resort, and from the tavern he went to the brothel. Indeed, he was the bell-wether for these two institutions. If I make my meaning clear, he spent everything he could get on dicing, drinking and wenching. He was ill content unless he could be gaming, drinking or whoring. He went about with a green chaplet on his head and wished every day were Sunday or a feast day. Now hear what happened to him.

When the jongleur had lived all his life in sin the day finally came for him to die. The devil, who never ceases from deceiving and taking advantage of mankind, came to his corpse and seized the soul. This particular imp had been wandering about outside hell for a whole month without catching a single soul; so, when he saw the jongleur die, he rushed at once to seize him, for he had died in sin, and no one contested his right; straightway he threw him over his shoulder and dashed off to hell. His companions, ranging through the country, had snatched many souls: One brought champions, another priests, a third thieves, monks, bishops, abbots or knights in great plenty to their master Lucifer in hell.

When Lucifer saw them coming so laden down: "My word," said he, "you are welcome, for it is evident that you have not been wasting your time. These souls will have an evil hostel from now on. But it seems to me that you are not all present."

"Lord," said the imps, "we are all here save one—a wretch who does not understand how to dupe the people or win souls."

But at that moment they saw their companion coming in at his leisure. He had the jongleur slung over his shoulder, and a sorry state was he in, for he made his entry into hell quite naked except for his shirt. The imp threw the jongleur down and Lucifer said:

"Vassal," said he, "tell me now, were you a rogue, a traitor or a thief in the world?"

"Not at all; I was a jongleur, and though I was a good one, I bear with me here everything which the body was wont to have up above. Many times my body suffered cold there, and I endured many a hard word; but now that I have reached this warm hostel I will sing, if you wish."

"Singing doesn't interest us," answered Lucifer. "You will have to follow some other trade here. Since I see you so scantily dressed, you shall tend the fire under the boiler."

"Just as you say," replied the jongleur, "by St Peter, for I certainly have great need to warm myself a little."

So he sat down beside the hearth and mended the fire quickly, and with good will.

One time it happened that the devils all assembled to go out searching for souls in the world. The chief came to the jongleur, who had tended the fire night and day and said: "Jongleur, now pay close attention. I put you in charge of all my people. Guard these souls well, by your eyes, or I will tear them out, both of them. If you lose a single one of these souls I will hang you up by the throat."

"Lord," said he, "have no fear. I will guard them loyally as well as I am able, and return you an account for every one of them."

"I'll take your word for it," replied Lucifer. "But remember this: If a single one escapes, you shall be eaten alive. But if you perform your task well, when we come back I will reward you handsomely

HOW THE JONGLEUR OF SENS THREW DICE

with a fat monk grilled to a turn, with usurer-sauce, or perhaps whoremonger-sauce."

Then the devils took their departure, and the jongleur remained, tending the fire faithfully.

Now I must tell you what happened to the jongleur left in charge of hell, and of St Peter's machinations. St Peter came right down to hell, all alone. He was dressed very handsomely, and wore a black beard and curly moustaches. With him he brought a gaming-board and three dice. He sat down by the jongleur and said softly: "My friend, would you like to play a game or two? Take a look at this fine gambling-table. Moreover, I have three full-sized dice. Probably you could win good pounds sterling from me without much difficulty." And he showed the jongleur a purse full of silver.

"Sir," said the jongleur, "I swear to God that I possess nothing at all but my shirt. For God's sake, go away. I haven't a spot of money."

"Well," said St Peter, "you could put up five or six of these souls."

"Sir," answered the jongleur, "I should not dare, for if I were to lose a single one of them my master would eat me alive."

"Who will tell him?" asked St Peter. "Certainly, you could lose as many as twenty souls without the loss being apparent. Look at this beautiful money here. You have a good chance to win these fine, newly minted pieces from me. Come, I'll lay you twenty sous and you put up their worth in souls."

When the jongleur saw so many silver pieces he coveted them mightily. He took the dice and handled them for a while, and then he said to St Peter: "All right, let's play; one soul a throw and only one."

"No, two," said St Peter; "that's too niggardly; and whoever wins shall stake one more, whether white or brown, it makes no difference to me."

"Very well," said the jongleur.

"You begin," said St Peter.

"The devil!" exclaimed the jongleur; "before we begin, put the money on the table."

"Willingly, in God's name," replied the saint, and put down the pieces.

There they sat by the furnace, the saint and the jongleur, and played *tremerel,* in which the winner's pot is always increased by three.

"You throw for us both," said St Peter, "for you have skilful hands."

The jongleur threw. "My word!" cried St Peter, "it seems to me

I have eight. If you throw 'hasart' [a losing cast] I shall win three souls."

The jongleur threw again, this time for himself, and rolled a trey, a deuce and an ace. Said St Peter: "You have lost."

"By St Denis!" replied the jongleur, "you are right; they read only six."

Now St Peter threw for both of them and the dice read twelve. "Ha!" said he gleefully, "you owe me nine. Three was the stake and you owe me the double of it in addition."

"Right you are," replied the other; "but if I risk more, will you agree?"

"Of course, by my faith."

"Those nine, then, which I already owe you, and twelve more, whoever wins."

"Curse him who refuses," answered the saint.

"Your dice," said the jongleur.

"Very well; now watch. Ah! I see 'hasart,' it seems to me, and you owe me three and ten and eight."

"Look here, now!" said the jongleur. "By the head of God! that never happened before in any game I have played. Are you using four dice? Or perhaps your dice are numbered wrong? I'll change the game now and play for the highest number of points."

"My friend," answered St Peter, "just as you wish. Shall it be on one throw or two?"

"On one throw; the twenty I already owe you and twenty to boot."

"God help me," said St Peter. He threw seventeen and boasted that he would make them worth forty.

"All right," said the jongleur; "now it's my dice."

"That cast isn't worth a herring," said St Peter; "you've lost, for the dice read only five each. This is my lucky day. You now owe me forty-three."

"By the heart of God!" exclaimed the jongleur. "I never saw a game like this! By all the saints of Rome, I wouldn't believe you or any man who said you haven't juggled the dice."

"You are crazy," said St Peter. "Come, it's your throw."

"I'll wager you were a strong thief," replied the jongleur, "since you are still such a trickster in changing and interfering with the cast."

St Peter did not like this speech and replied angrily: "So may God save me! you are a liar. But it is always the rascal's way to complain that the dice have been changed on him when they do not fall to his advantage. If anyone changed the dice, a curse on him, and a curse on you for saying so. You are a filthy rogue to call me a thief. By St Marcel, I've a good mind to anoint your mug for you!"

"A thief you certainly are, sir oldster," replied the jongleur, burning with wrath, "spoiling my play in this manner. But you won't get away with a denier, by my word. Come and get 'em if you think you can!"

Therewith he jumped up to snatch the money, but St Peter seized him by the loose flesh under the ribs so that he dropped the coins with a shriek. He for his part seized St Peter by the beard and pulled, but the saint ripped his shirt down to his middle. Never was the jongleur so wroth as when he saw himself naked to the waist. Back and forth they pulled and beat and punched. But finally the jongleur saw that he could do nothing, for he was neither so big nor so strong as St Peter, and he realized that if he kept up the struggle his dress would be in such condition that he would never more have joy of it.

"Sir," said he, "peace. We have tried each other's strength enough. Let's start again in a friendly way, if you will."

"I take it much to heart," replied St Peter, "that you criticized my play and called me a thief."

"Sir, I spoke folly, and I assure you that I repent of it. You have done much worse to me by tearing my clothes in such fashion that I shall suffer from it from now on. Let's be quits now."

"Very well," said St Peter, and they exchanged kisses.

"My friend," said the saint, "let us understand each other: you owe me forty-three souls."

"Right," replied the jongleur. "I began the game too hastily. Let's throw again now for triple or nothing."

"By God, that suits me. But will you really pay me?"

"Of course, and well, too, whether it be knights, canons, ladies, thieves, champions, freemen, priests or chaplains that you wish."

"All right," answered the saint, "now make your cast."

At that throw the saint got only five and four and a single trey. "I see only twelve," said the jongleur.

"Alas!" cried St Peter. "Alas! unless Christ has mercy on me this last throw has ruined me." And he made his cast violently and threw only fives and one deuce. "By God!" exclaimed St Peter, "this tie will turn out well for me in the end. Twenty-two, now, win or lose."

"All right," said the jongleur.

"I'll throw now, by St Julian," said the saint, and he rolled two sixes and a single ace. "I threw well," said the saint; "I passed you by a point."

"Look, now," said the other, "how he has done for me in passing me by a single point! I never did have any luck! All my life I've been a miserable, unfortunate wretch, both here and in the world."

When the souls in the fire heard that St Peter had won, they cried out to him from all sides: "Sir, in the name of God, we place our faith entirely in you." "You and I both," said St Peter. "In order to get you out of this torment I am risking all my money. If I had lost everything you would have no chance at all. But you shall be in my company before night, please God."

Now the jongleur was speechless for a moment. Then he said: "Sir," said he, "either I shall acquit myself fully, or else I shall lose everything, both souls and my shirt; there is no other alternative."

There is not much more to tell. St Peter held the jongleur in play so long that finally he had won all the souls; in great gangs he led them out of hell into Paradise. But the jongleur remained below, fearful, sorrowful and wroth.

And now behold the devils have returned. When the master came in and looked about and up and down he saw not a single soul, fore nor aft, neither in the furnace nor in the cauldron. He called the jongleur. "Come, now," he said, "where are all the souls which I left in your charge?"

"Sir," said the other, "I'll tell you, but for God's sake have mercy on me. Not long ago an old gentleman came in bringing a great deal of money with him. I thought I could get it all, so we played dice together—to my great vexation. He used loaded dice, the false, disloyal traitor! I swear to you I never had a single lucky throw; and in that way I lost all your people, for the souls were my stake."

When the master had heard him to the end he almost pitched him into the fire. "Bastard whoreson!" said he. "You rogue! Your jugglery costs me too dear. Cursed be he who brought you in! By my head, he shall pay for it!"

Hereupon all the devils gathered round him who had brought the jongleur to hell, and beat and thwacked and thumped him, and so maltreated him that he was glad to promise never to bring in another soul of either roisterer, pander, jongleur, or anyone else addicted to dice-throwing. Then said the master devil:

"Now, my good friend, get out of my hotel. A curse be on your jugglery that has cost me my meiny! Get out of my house, I say, for I have no wish for servants like you. Never again will I look for a jongleur or any of his kidney. Let them go their ways. God, who loves jollity, may have them all. Take yourself off to heaven; scat!"

You may be sure the jongleur lost no time, and the devils assisted his departure. He went straight off in the direction of Paradise. When

St Peter saw him coming he ran to open the door for him and had him handsomely put up.

Now let jongleurs make merry to their heart's content; never shall they be tormented in hell, for he who lost the devil's souls in a game of dice redeemed them all in advance.

"You illustrate your opinion very cleverly," said the Curtal Friar; "and we see too from your tale that there is apparently justice somewhere, if not in the world. But I must arise and go now," he said, heaving himself to his feet, "and pluck a few beans for dinner."

"Beans, is it?" asked Mac Conglinne. "What do you mean by 'beans'? We came here expecting to find all sorts of dainties in plenty. Is not this the Land of Cockayne?"

"Ha!" snickered the Curtal Friar. "You have been dreaming—or reading a book. We live mostly on beans and pease here."

"Beans!" expostulated John the Reeve. "In my country I would provide"—with a covert glance at King Richard—"a venison pasty and a cask of old claret which a friend of mine brought me at great risk and expense from Bordeaux."

"That would be eminently suitable for the occasion," said King Richard. It seems to me I have been hungry ever since the king of Almain kept me on short rations."

"But he gave you royal meat, my liege, a lion's heart," said Ambroise.

"Gentlemen," remarked Jean Froissart, "the subject of hearts may be a delicate one in this company."

"Well," said Robert the Bruce, "it is true that I once felt some bitterness on that score. As some of you know from John Barbour's book, I entrusted James Douglas with an important mission in regard to my heart, but instead of proceeding to Jerusalem, as he promised, he dallied in Spain and lost it."

"I lost my life, too," said Sir James bitterly, "in attempting to execute that bit of Quixotism."

"How was that?" asked Peter Bell.

"If King Robert permit, I will tell you," answered Froissart.

"Tell on," replied Robert; "there is little feeling left in it now."

4. THE HEART OF KING ROBERT

Jean Froissart

King Robert the Bruce, when sickness and old age was hurrying him on towards his death, called together his chiefs and barons, exhorting them to preserve the kingdom intact for his son David. Then he summoned my lord James Douglas and said: "As you know, it is not long since that I made a vow to the effect that if God gave me peace at home I would go to the Holy Land to fight the enemies of the Christian faith. But I have had so much domestic trouble in my lifetime that I could never get away. And now, since sickness prevents my body from accomplishing the desire of my heart, I will send my heart instead of my body to fulfil my vow. And as I do not know any knight so gallant or enterprising, nor any who is better formed to complete my intentions than yourself, I entreat you, my dear and special friend, that you will have the goodness to undertake this expedition for the love of me, and acquit my soul to Our Lord; for I have that opinion of your nobleness and loyalty that if you undertake it, it cannot fail of success, and I shall die contented. As soon as I am dead, you must take the heart from my body and have it well embalmed. You will also take as much money from my treasury as seems to you necessary to perform the journey for yourself and your companions. At Jerusalem you will deposit your charge at the Holy Sepulchre of Our Lord. Do not be sparing of expense, but provide yourself with such a company and with such things as may be suitable to your rank. And wherever you pass, let it be known that you bear the heart of King Robert of Scotland to the Holy Land beyond seas."

At these words all the lords present began to weep and wail bitterly. When at last Lord James was able to speak he said: "Gallant and noble king, I give you a hundred thousand thanks for the high honour you do me, and for the dear and valuable treasure which you entrust to me. I will most willingly do all you command in so far as lies in my power." Then said the king: "Thanks be to God, for now I can die in peace, since I know that the most valiant and accomplished knight of my kingdom will perform for me that which I cannot do for myself."

Soon after this the valiant Robert Bruce departed this life on the seventh of November, 1337. His body was buried in the monastery of Dumferline, and his heart embalmed. Early in the spring Lord Douglas made provision of everything that was proper for his expedition. He placed the heart in a silver enamel casket, and this he hung from his neck by a chain. Then he embarked from the port of Montrose, or from Berwick, as others say, and sailed directly for Sluys, where he expected to take ship for Jerusalem. There he stayed twelve days and would not set foot on shore, but remained the whole time on board, keeping a magnificent table, with music of trumpets and drums, as though he had been the king of Scotland. His company consisted of one knight banneret, and seven others of the most valiant knights of Scotland, with their men-at-arms. His plate was of gold and silver—pots, cups, basins, porringers and other such things. He had likewise twenty-six tall and gallant esquires of the best families of Scotland to wait on him; and all who came to visit him—that is, all of a certain rank—were handsomely served with two sorts of wine and two sorts of spices.

Now when my lord Douglas had rested twelve days at Sluys he heard that Alfonso, king of Spain, was waging war against the Saracen king of Granada. He considered that if he should go thither he would be employing his time in accordance with the late king's wishes, and that when he had finished there he would go on to complete the task with which he was charged. So he made sail and landed at Valencia—though Barbour says it was at Seville; this must be wrong, for Seville is not a seaport—whence he proceeded to join the king of Spain, who was lying with his army very near the king of Granada's frontiers.

The two opposing monarchs ranged their armies for battle, while Lord James drew off to one side to watch proceedings. When he thought the armies were on the point of going into action, wishing ever to be among the first on such occasions, he and all his company struck spurs to their horses and galloped into the midst of the Saracens. He expected that he would be supported by the Spaniards, but in this he was mistaken, for not one of them moved that day. Sir James and his knights performed prodigies of valour, but to no end: they were all killed.

"I grant you," said John Barbour, "that Seville is not a seaport; neither is Athens. But I should like to correct you on a matter of graver import: Robert the Bruce did not die in the year 1337, but on June 7, 1329."

"Indeed?" said Froissart; "I will make a note of it."

"Well," said the Sacrilegious Caroller, "since there seems to be an objection to hearts, I will bear in hand the boar's head."

"We must have oatmeal cakes," said the Lochmaben Harper.

"Why must we?" inquired Henry Knighton.

"Because oatmeal bread is good bread," answered John Major. "The main strength of the Scottish and English armies is in men who have been tillers of the soil—a proof that oaten bread is not to be laughed at. Just eat this bread once and you will find it far from bad."

"I will furnish the savoury," said Iolo Goch—"causs boby."

"You'll eat it yourself," said Andrew Boorde.

"With pleasure," answered Iolo, "if I can keep any of it from Gerald de Barry and Adam Usk."

"Beans! Oats!" cried King Richard; "this cereal diet nauseates me."

"Pardon me, my liege," said Gerald de Barry, who liked to be known as Giraldus Cambrensis, "beans is not . . ."

"Are not," interrupted the Clerk of Oxenford.

"Beans is not a cereal," went on Gerald. "Whereas oats and corn are farinaceous seeds produced as the fruit of certain grasses, beans is . . ."

"Are," said the Clerk.

"Beans is a vegetable of the vine, as faba phaseolus, faba dolichos and faba faba."

"Who cares?" asked the Curtal Friar.

"As I was saying," continued Richard, "beans either as a cereal or as a vegetable nauseates—nauseate—me. Let us have food for men! I see no horses here."

"But some asses?" inquired the Clerk of Oxenford.

"Perhaps you would prefer a Saracen's head?" suggested the Minstrel of Reims.

"I have heard of various kinds of heads," said Peter Bell, "returning heads, such as that of the Green Knight, heads carried in the hand by their owner like a lantern, as is related of Dionysius and Bertrand de Born, heads hung at saddle-bows or at stirrups as trophies—one such bit Earl Sigurd in the leg and caused his death—and of various speaking heads, such as those of Mímir, Albertus Magnus and Gerbert. Was a Saracen's head like any of these?"

"No," said Richard.

"The wild Irish," offered Gerald, "heaped the heads of their slain enemies in cairns as tallies of victory."

"That seems to be true," agreed Fynes Moryson. "When I was travelling in the island of Egg I saw a sepulchral urn full of human bones, but there was no skull among them. When I asked the guide what had become of the heads he replied that they had been cut off with a two-handed sword and borne away by the victors in battle. Perhaps you used Saracens' heads similarly."

"Not at all," replied Richard. "We were on short rations at Acre . . . but Ambroise can tell the story better than I."

"Very well, my liege," said Ambroise, "I will tell it."

5. KING RICHARD ENTERTAINS SARACEN AMBASSADORS AT LUNCH

Ambroise

When King Richard landed at Acre he lost no time in setting up his pavilion by the hospital of St Thomas; and he also set up his movable tower Mate Griffon, which had served him so well at Messina. And with his perrières and mangonels he threw a thousand beehives over the walls of Acre into the city. While the Saracens fled to cellars and drains to escape the bees' stings, Richard set his miners and sappers to work at the Accursed Tower, and before noon he had accomplished more than had been done by anyone else in seven years.

But this sudden and furious activity had its evil effects: the travail on sea, the sudden change from cold to fierce heat, the corrupt air of the country, the change of food and drink, brought Richard to his bed with a tertian fever. The Christian host was stricken with grief at the prostration of their leader, and as one man they offered up prayers for his recovery. Their supplications were heard. Richard turned off his ague, indeed, but had no desire for food, nor for wine nor water; only one thing did he crave with overwhelming passion, and that was pork meat.

Servants were sent here and there in search of pork, but in that country they could find none for gold, silver or other money, though they should be hanged. The cook was at his wits' end till an old knight drew him to one side and said: "Take a fat young Saracen, kill him, flay him and open him; then boil him quickly with powder and spices and good saffron. When the king has eaten his fill thereof and supped the brewit, and then slept and sweat a little, by God's grace and my counsel, he shall be fresh and hale."

Not to make a long story of it, a heathen shrew was slain and sodden, and brought before the king as he lay in bed. "Here," said the stewards, "is the pork which you craved." A knight carved for the king, but he ate faster than the man could carve, and gnawed the bones clean, while his people turned aside and laughed for joy. When he had drunk, he drew in his arm, and the chamberlain wrapped him up warm. After he had slept and sweat a little, he arose whole and sound and called for his armour. You may be sure that the host was rejoiced to see the king walking abroad again.

In the meantime Saladin was attempting to storm the Christians' position in order to rescue the Saracens within the city. But now Richard rode into the heathen army: One he slit down to the saddle, another he cut in two at the saddle-bows; all whom he smote fell to earth. In such wise did Richard give a good account of himself that day till the infidels were utterly put to flight.

Richard returned to his tent, sorely fatigued. His squire unlaced his armour and the chamberlain brought him a sop in wine. But that was slight refreshment after the doughty dints he had dealt all day. "Bring me," said he, "the head of that swine whose flesh I ate lately, for I am feeble and fordone. I fear my illness will return on me unless I have that head for my supper."

At these words the cook shook from top to toe. "Sire," said he, "I have not that head at hand." "By God," cried Richard, "unless I see the head of that swine, you shall lose yours." The cook saw that evasion was impossible, so he brought the head and fell on his knees before the king, crying him mercy.

When Richard saw the swart visage and the black beard, the white teeth and the grinning mouth—"What the devil is this?" he cried, and laughed as though he were mad. "Is Saracens' flesh really so good? That is certainly news to me. By God's death and His resurrection! we shall never die for lack of food in this campaign so long as we can slay Saracens, and boil or roast, or else bake them, and gnaw their flesh to the bones. Now that I have once tasted such flesh, I and my folk shall eat more, rather than be woe for hunger."

On the morrow the battle was renewed with such vigour by the Christians that finally the city capitulated, and the Saracens therein were held to ransom. Richard himself had taken prisoner knights of great importance—chief lords, princes, dukes' sons, admirals and sultans of Heathennesse. From their prison they sent word to Saladin, begging him to rescue them. Accordingly Saladin sent off ten earls, all old men, relatives of the prisoners, to treat with Richard for their release. And with them he sent a mule bearing as much gold as twenty men could lift.

Richard replied to the ambassadors: "Share the gold among yourselves, for I have no need of it; in my ships I brought more gold and silver than is possessed by Saladin or three like him. But for my love I bid you stay now and have lunch with me, and after I have sought counsel, I will give you an answer to bear back to your lord."

Then Richard called his marshal and said to him privately: "Go to the prison and choose out those infidels who are of most renown and most nobly born; smite off their heads and write each man's name on a scroll of parchment; take the heads to the kitchen and have the cook boil them, first removing the hair from head, lip and chin. When we are at table, serve them in this manner: Put each head on a platter in such wise that the grinning teeth are uppermost, and see to it that each head is identified by the scroll bearing its owner's name. Then bring a good hot head and place it before me." The steward did as he was bidden.

Now when it was noon and the attendants blew for hand-washing, Richard said to the envoys: "Friends, you are welcome." When they were seated at table, salt was set on, but no bread, nor water nor wine, neither white nor red. "Alas, what curious service is this?" said the ambassadors one to the other. Richard was seated on a dais with dukes and earls in splendid array. The first course came from the kitchen to the sound of pipes and trumpets and tabours, and the steward took right good care to bring Richard a Saracen's head all hot, lest he have an evil hap after lunch. And the ambassadors were similarly served, with a Saracen's head between each two, with the name of its owner written on the forehead. When they saw those grisly heads they were sore adread, and the tears ran out of their eyes; and when they had read the identification scrolls, they feared to meet a similar fate themselves.

King Richard watched his guests closely and saw how they changed colour. Well might they forbear to laugh and jest, for these heads belonged to their near kin. None of them would approach his portion nor eat a bit thereof.

Now the knight whose duty it was to serve the king began to carve with a sharp knife, and when Richard began to eat with a right good heart, the Saracens thought he must be mad. They nudged each other and said: "This man who slays our folk and eats them is the devil's brother." But King Richard looked about him sharply, with stern eyes and wrathful countenance, and he said to the ambassadors: "Now for my love, make good cheer and take your ease. Why do you not carve your portion and eat readily, as I do? Tell me, why do you lower so?"

The Saracens sat still and shook in their boots, for they dared neither speak nor look, and would have crept under the earth had they been able. King Richard said to the steward: "Bear this away and set some other meat before my guests." Then the servants brought bread and venison and cranes and good roast, piment, clarée and other good drinks. "Come, now, my friends," said Richard, "do not be squeamish. This is the manner of my house, God wot, to be served first with Saracens' heads all hot. Forgive me if I did not know your manners of etiquette. But as I am a Christian king, I give you my word that you shall have safe conduct hence. For nothing in the world would I have it said that I had such bad manners as to mistreat envoys. Go home," said he to an old Saracen, "and tell your lord that you came too late; the meat was already dressed before you arrived. And say, too, that though he prevent victuals from coming to us, we shall not starve as long as we can kill Saracens and roast their flesh. I can feed nine or ten of my men with one heathen; and, indeed, there is no flesh so nourishing to an Englishman, whether it be partridge, plover, heron, swan, cow, ox, sheep or swine, as is the head of a Saracen. Every day we shall eat as many as we can get. Indeed, we will not return to England till they be all eaten."

It is said that when the messengers returned to the sultan, Saladin almost went mad with rage and sorrow on hearing their report.

"Speaking of hot dishes," said John Barbour, "would the company like a nice hot Scotch haggis?"

"It would not!" shouted Mac Conglinne and Senchan Torpeist together. "Rather a Saracen's head!"

"Well," said Bartholomew Anglicus, "if the learned scholar and the eminent poet object to haggis, perhaps they will provide something more succulent to the tooth?"

"I was always abstemious," Senchan excused himself. "But I believe there is still half a boiled egg remaining from the light reflection which Guaire Aidne Mac Colman was able to arrange in my honour."

"And you?" asked Bartholomew, turning to Mac Conglinne.

The scholar made an impatient gesture. "Musha! All I have is a piece of dirty bacon in my book-satchel, and that is somewhat the worse for wear. I brought nothing else with me from Cork, for those dunghill monks gave me only a little whey and water."

"Half an egg! Dirty bacon! Whey and water!" exclaimed Bartholomew. "You shall both eat Barbour's haggis, and like it."

"A truce to this brawling!" roared Guilhem IX. "As to the Friar's beans, I can use them, and I guarantee that none of this fastidious company shall have cause to object to them when they appear in a cassoulet—a dish for which my country is justly famous. After Senher Faba has been subjected to the fires of hell for fifteen hours in a tight earthen pot, in the company of a succulent sausage and a bit of garlic, he is as coy as a maid. You, Richard, shame your ancestry. Run along, Friar, and pluck your beans."

"Gentlemen," spoke up Earl Marshal, "I have a better idea: You shall all be my guests, and Bartholomew shall arrange the entertainment."

"Excellent," said King Henry II; "I have long wished to visit Pembroke castle."

"My lord," said Bartholomew, "I am deeply honoured by the confidence you repose in me; but have I a free hand?"

"Just what does that entail?" asked the earl cautiously.

"Various things," replied Bartholomew, "are necessary for the honour and dignity of a supper. The first is proper time, for it is desirable that supper be made in due time, and neither too early nor too late. The second is proper place, large, pleasant and sure. The third is the heartiness and glad cheer of him who makes the feast: the supper is not worthy of praise if the lord of the house be of heavy cheer. The fourth requisite is a variety of dishes, so that he who does not like one may taste another. The fifth is divers wines and drinks. The sixth is the mannerliness and decency of the servants. The seventh is the pleasant friendship and company of those who sit at supper. The eighth thing is the mirth of song and musical instruments, for noble men do not ordinarily make suppers without harp or symphony. The ninth is plenty of light from candles, prichettes or torches, for it is a shame to sup in darkness, and hazardous also, on account of the flies and other filth. The tenth item is the delicious savour of all that is set on the board, for at supper it is not customary to serve coarse and common meat as at dinner, but light and delicate foods, particularly in lords' courts. The eleventh is the long duration of the supper, for it is usual for men to sit long at supper after the full end of work and travail, since food hastily eaten is prejudicial to the strength; consequently one should eat with leisure and not hastily at supper. The twelfth is sureness, by which I mean that everyone may accept an invitation to supper without fear of harm or damage. . . . These things are, of course, in addition to proper provision for the preparation and service of the food."

"Well," said the earl with a smile when Bartholomew had finished, "I am sure that Pembroke will be able to provide all you require. For a moment you made me uneasy, but I see it is a mere trifle."

"There is one thing more," added Bartholomew; "I must have the assistance of Bonvesin da Riva and the Goodman of Paris."

"That you shall have with good will," said the Italian courteously.

At Pembroke castle Bartholomew and his coadjutors inspected the larder and made an inventory of the stock. They found—

14 oxen lying in salt	3 bushels apples
2 fresh oxen	11 thousand eggs
6 score heads of sheep, fresh	50 swans
6 score carcasses of sheep, fresh	210 geese
12 boars	5 herons
14 calves	5 dozen pullets for gelée
140 pigs	12 dozen pullets for roasting
3 tuns of salt venison	100 dozen pigeons
3 does of fresh venison	12 dozen partridges
12 gallons cream	8 dozen rabbits
11 gallons curds	10 dozen curlews

                12 cranes   8 dozen other capons
                   wild fowl enough   60 dozen hens
                   lard enough   200 pairs of connies
                6 score gallons milk   4 pheasants
                50 extra-fat capons   6 kids

To this, with the assistance of the earl's seneschal and butler, they added what seemed necessary, and succeeded in preparing some really fine menus. Thanks to the knowledge, the skill and the understanding of Bartholomew, the munificent generosity of Earl Marshal and the housewifely competence of his lady, it would be no exaggeration to say that the boards set out in the Great Hall fairly groaned with meat and drink. As a tribute to both Bartholomew and the earl, the fourth course is subjoined herewith.

BALLOCK BROTH   CAUDLE FERRY

LAMPREYS EN GALENTINE   OYSTERS IN CIVEY   EELS IN SORRÉ

BAKED TROUT

BRAWN WITH MUSTARD   NUMBLES OF A HART   PIGS Y-FARSED

COCKYNTRYCE

GOOSE IN HOGEPOTTE   VENISON EN FRUMENTY   HENS IN BREWET

SQUIRRELS ROASTED

HAGGIS OF SHEEP   PUDDING DE CAPON-NECK   GARBAGE

TRYPE DE MOUTON   BLAUNDESORYE

CABOGES   BUTTERED WORTS

APPLE MUSE   GINGERBREAD   TART DE FRUIT

QUINCES IN COMFIT

ESSEX CHEESE   STILTON CHEESE

CAUSS BOBY

ALE, OLD	PORT	CLARET	METHEGLYN
ALE, NEW	CLARÉE	HOCK	PERREYE
MEAD	SACK	BEER	HIPPOCRAS

UISCE BETHA

In deference to the number of continental guests present the Goodman of Paris was asked, and readily agreed, to prepare a special menu for them. Among its more succulent dishes were found pimpernel pasties, black puddings, tench with sops, rissoles, mallard à la dodine, bourreys with hot sauce, neffles, sugared flawns and cookies.

During the intermissions between courses, while the Sacrilegious Caroller and his band were providing soothing or merry music under the watchful eye of Walter Haliday, there could be heard many a complimentary remark on both the steward and the host.

"The leek soup was excellent," said Geoffrey of Monmouth.
"I never drank better mead," conceded Seithenyn ab Seithyn Saidi, "even out of the Hirlas Horn."
"Owen Glyndwr never provided such hospitality as this," admitted Iolo Goch.
"I have travelled far," remarked Fynes Moryson, "and often fared worse."
"So have I," said Sordello.
"It is myself who could tell a tale on that score," said Mac Conglinne. "Sixty miles we walked from Cashel to Cork, and went to bed supperless."
"So did I," said Sordello.
"How was that?" asked Walter Map.

6. BROTHER JUNIPER'S HOSPITALITY

Sordello

It was towards the end of February in the year 12—. I was sitting at Scamorza's trattoria in the Borgo Ognissanti one evening, enjoying a glass of wine as much as the prospect of the incessant rain outside would permit, and thinking of nothing in particular, when who should stamp in but Ferrari da Ferrara, Nicoletto da Torino, and Simon Doria. We had hardly exchanged greetings, ordered fresh bottles and cursed the weather when we were joined by Alberto Malaspini.

In such company you can well imagine that the conversation turned mainly on love and literature. Simon asked me if I had anything new, and I was forced to confess that I had just completed a canso in the Provençal tongue. The companions very courteously begged me to sing it, and with equal courtesy I did so.

"Gentlemen," said a new voice when I had finished, "with your permission I will introduce myself. I am Raimbaut de Vaqueiras, late of Les Baux and Montferrat, now travelling for my health. I should not be guilty of such gross bad manners as to thrust myself upon you in this way were it not that, being a Provençal and a composer of cansos myself, I should like to extend my hearty congratulations to the poet who has just sung so well."

I rose and bowed. Alberto rose and clapped the stranger on the back. "Sir," said he, "I know you this long time by reputation, and now I thank the devils who stirred up this brutto temporale since it has blown you into our trattoria in person. Will you not join us?"
"Nay," answered Raimbaut, "I cannot leave my companions," and he nodded toward a corner table. "By Bacchus!" said Alberto, "they are welcome too, if they are friends of yours."

It was thus we made the acquaintance of Gaucelm Faidit—who, I see, is with us tonight—Guilhem de la Tor, and Uc de Saint Circ. Glasses were filled, and I can't say which flowed the faster, wine or talk, till of a sudden Alberto rapped on the table with the pommel of his poniard. "Gentlemen," he said, "our friend Gaucelmo has disputed my opinion on a delicate point. The question is: Which are the greater, the pleasures or the ills of love? I have challenged him to a tenzone, and you gentlemen shall be the judges."

Well, not to drag it out, there being five Italians and two Frenchmen, Alberto was judged to have won the contest. At this decision Guilhem de la Tor muttered something under his breath.

"It is hard words you give us, Senher," said Simon Doria, who was sitting next to him.

"Then I will give you something soft," replied Guilhem, pushing a handful of cream cheese into his face.

"He can't take it!" gurgled Gaucelm Faidit.

"Can you?" asked Nicoletto, emptying a dish of tripe down the fat troubadour's jerkin.

In the meantime Guilhem had snatched up Alberto's dagger from the table, and Simon Doria had seized a flask of Chianti by the neck. Of what happened next I have no clear recollection. When I again came to my senses wine was dripping from my hair and ears, and I was alone in the trattoria with a dead man in the middle of the floor. Do I bore you? Well, I suppose they thought I was dead too, and I had no wish to make a fact of that hypothesis by falling into the hands of the sbirri. Florence suddenly seemed very unhealthy to me, and I had about decided to move anyway, for my rent was long overdue. Taking advantage of what darkness still lingered in the nooks and corners, I managed to saddle my landlord's horse without rousing anyone, and by sunrise I had reached Pontassieve.

Passing by Arezzo and Perugia I was able to reach Todi on the Tiber before the week was out, but in a state of almost complete exhaustion. I must, indeed, have presented a sorry spectacle as I sat there on the church steps, with my head between my hands and my elbows between my knees. Certainly, I was in no condition to be tapped on the shoulder. But it was only Brother Anselm, a religious from the neighbouring house of monastics. Without being impertinent, he inquired into my case. It was enough for him that I was cold and hungry and weary, and for my part I needed no second bidding to accompany him to the friary. "There will be a warm fire," he said, "and warm food. Before coming away this morning we left Brother Juniper in charge of the kitchen with instructions to prepare our evening meal. And if the beds are not what you have been used to, you will at least have a roof over your head."

At the gate we were greeted by the porter. "We shall have good cheer tonight," he said. "I have just looked into the kitchen. Brother Juniper has a great fire going, and he is dashing about from pot to pot; you would think he was preparing a marriage feast."

It was not long now till we heard the bell, and the brothers filed in to the refectory. Soon Brother Juniper came in, flushed and red from the fire and from his exertions. Said he: "Fall to and eat heartily, and then let us hasten to prayer. No one will have to think about cooking again for a long while, for today I have cooked enough to last us for a fortnight or more."

Therewith Brother Juniper set his stew on the table. But seeing the brothers hang back, he urged us on, saying: "Come, now, eat your food. These hens are strengthening to the brain, and this stew will be a restorative to the body, so good is it."

But the brothers held their noses and turned away.

What was the matter with the food? you ask. I will tell you, as I found out later. When the brothers went forth in the morning, delegating Brother Juniper to cook their evening meal, he said to himself: "Now this is all nonsense and a lot of useless trouble. The duties of the kitchen always keep one brother away from prayer; but I will remedy that. Since I am to be cook this time, I will cook up enough in one batch to last for a week or two." So he went into the country and begged meat and eggs and firewood and the like. And when he had got everything home, do you know what he did? He put everything into the pots together—the eggs in their shells, the fowls with their feathers, the fish with their scales, and the hares in their skins! Believe me when I say there was not a hog in all the land from Messina to Aquileia so famished as to have touched the least part of that mess. That night I went to bed without any supper.

"Well," said the Goodman of Paris when Sordello had finished, "you can repair that lack now. Help yourself to this cochon farci, and do try these reversed eels; both are prepared according to my own recipe."

"Thank you," said the poet, "I will."

"You Italians," said Geoffrey Keating, "are too dainty about your food. I wonder what you would have done had you been in Scanlann's boots?"

"Who was Scanlann?" asked Bonvesin da Riva, and what did he do?"

"I will tell you," answered the historian . . .

7. HOW COLUMCILLE FREED SCANLANN FROM SALT BACON AND BEER

Geoffrey Keating

When Columcille had been thirty years in Scotland, anxiety seized the men of Ériu to see him and speak with him before he died. So they sent messengers to him that he might come to commune with them at the great convention which King Aed son of Ainmire was about to hold at Druim Ceta. And the reason why Columcille came from the east was this: That he might act as a peacemaker between King Aed on the one hand, and the poets and the men of Scotland and Scanlann on the other. Scanlann, now, was the son of Cennfaelad, son of the great king of Ossory. His father had given him as a hostage into the hand of Aed son of Ainmire, and Columcille went surety that he would be released at a year's end. But he was not released, and no hostage was accepted in his stead. Around Scanlann was constructed a wicker building having no passage out of it save a way whereby a little salt bacon and a small supply of ale used to be given to him. And fifty warriors were wont to be around the building outside, guarding him, and nine chains upon him in the building. And when he would see anyone going past what he would say was: "A drink!" says he. And this was reported to Columcille at Hy, and he wept greatly at what he heard, and this it was that brought him quickly from the east.

Now when Columcille came from the east he went to visit Aed.

"Release Scanlann," said Columcille.

"I will not do that," replied Aed, "till he dies in the hut wherein he is."

"We will not pursue the subject," said Columcille. "But if it be pleasing to God, let it be Scanlann who shall take off my sandals tonight at matins in whatsoever place I may be."

Then Columcille went out of the assembly till he came to Dubhregles in Derry. It was not long after his departure until a thunderbolt came into the convention, and all turned their faces to the ground. Afterwards a bright cloud came to Scanlann to the place in which he was, and a voice in the cloud said to him: "Rise, O Scanlann, and leave thy chains and thy prison, and come forth and put thy hand in mine." Scanlann came out, with the angel before him. The guards heard the noise of something passing by them and they said: "Who is this going past us?" "It is Scanlann," answered the angel. "Don't be silly," said the guards.

Thereafter Scanlann and the angel went to Derry. And when

HOW COLUMCILLE FREED SCANLANN

Columcille at matins was going through the chancel screen, it was Scanlann who assisted in removing his sandals. And Columcille said:
"Who is this?"
"It is Scanlann."
"Have you any news?" asked Columcille.
"A drink!" answered Scanlann.
"Have you brought us a blessing?"
"A drink!" said Scanlann.
"Tell how you came here," said Columcille.
"A drink!" answered Scanlann.
"May delay in answering attend your posterity," said Columcille.
"Say not so," replied Scanlann; "you shall always have their rents, their tributes and their tolls," said he.
"May bishops and kings be of your race forever," said Columcille. "Here is one drink for you," he said, "even a vat of ale containing enough for three."
Then Scanlann lifted the vessel between his two hands and drank its contents in one draught. Afterwards he ate his meal, to wit, seven joints of old bacon and ten wheaten cakes. Thereafter he lay down and was three days and three nights in one sleep.

"That was a long drink," said Seithenyn ab Seithyn Saidi.
"And enough bacon to last me for three half years," added Mac Conglinne.
"Ah!" sighed Ossian. "In the old days the Irish never stinted themselves in the matter of meat and drink. But Patrick changed all that, and I have been hungry ever since."
"It is true," remarked Cuan O Lochan, "that the enjoyment of food and drink came to the Irish honestly from ancient times. Our historians and poets relate that during the hostilities between the Fomorians and the Tuatha De Danann, Lug sent the Dagda to the Fomorian camp to arrange a truce till the men of Ireland could assemble. Now it was well known to the Fomorians that the Dagda loved stew, so in order to preserve their reputation for hospitality they prepared a magnificent pottage for the envoy. Into a cauldron they put eighty gallons of fresh milk and an equal amount of meal and fat; to this they added a number of goats, sheep and swine, and boiled all together. When the mess was cooked, they dug a hole in the ground and poured the stew into it. 'Here is a slight refection for you,' said they to the Dadga, 'and you shall have death if you leave any of it uneaten.' Then they gathered round to see what the Dagda would do. And what he did was this: He took his spoon, wherein a man and a woman might lie comfortably, and tasted the pottage.

'This is delicious,' said the Dagda. He ate it up to the last drop and morsel, and then ran his finger round the rim of the pit to wipe up the grease. Then he took a nap."

"I once heard of a lady," said Dick O the Cow, "who also had an appetite more keen than fastidious. But hers was not an inborn greediness, as the Dagda's seems to have been. The story of her prowess has been preserved in a ballet, which goes like this . . ."

8. KING HENRY'S GUEST

Dick O the Cow

> Let never a man a-wooing wend
> That lacketh thingis thrie:
> A rowth o' gold, an open heart
> And fu' o' courtesy.
>
> And this was seen o' King Henrie,
> For he lay burd alane;
> And he has ta'en him to a haunted hunt's ha',
> Was seven miles frae toun.
>
> He's chaced the dun deer thro' the wood,
> And the roe doun by the den
> Till the fattest buck in a' the herd,
> King Henrie he has slain.
>
> He's ta'en him to his hunting ha',
> For to make burly cheir,
> When loud the wind was heard to sound,
> And an earthquake rocked the floor,
>
> And darkness covered a' the hall
> Where they sat at their meat;
> The grey dogs, youling, left their food
> And crept to Henrie's feet.
>
> And louder houled the rising wind,
> And burst the fast'ned door,
> And in there came a griesly ghost,
> Stood stamping on the floor.
>
> Her head touch'd the roof-tree of the house,
> Her middle ye weel mot span.
> Each frighted huntsman fled the ha',
> And left the king alone.

KING HENRY'S GUEST

Her teeth was a' like tether stakes,
Her nose like club or mell,
And I ken naething she appeared to be,
But the fiend that wons in hell.

"Sum meat, sum meat, ye King Henrie!
Sum meat ye gie to me!"
"And what meat's in this house, ladye,
That ye're na wellcum tee?"
"O ye'se gae kill your berry-brown steed,
And serve him up to me."

O when he killed his berry-brown steed,
Wow gin his heart was sair!
She eat him a' up skin and bane,
Left naething but hide and hair.

"Mair meat, mair meat, ye King Henrie!
Mair meat ye gie to me!"
"And what meat's i' this house, ladye,
That ye're na wellcum tee?"
"O ye do slay your gude grey houndes,
And bring them a' to me."

O when he slew his gude grey houndes,
Wow but his heart was sair!
She's ate them a' up, ane by ane,
Left naething but hide and hair.

"Mair meat, mair meat, ye King Henrie!
Mair meat ye gie to me!"
"And what meat's i' this house, ladye,
That I hae left to gie?"
"O ye do fell your gay goss-hawks,
And bring them a' to me."

O when he felled his gay goss-hawks,
Wow but his heart was sair!
She's ate them a' up, bane by bane,
Left naething but feathers bare.

"Some drink, some drink, ye King Henrie!
Sum drink ye gie to me!"
"And what drink's i' this house, ladye,
That ye're na wellcum tee?"

"O ye sew up your horse's hide,
And bring in a drink to me."

O he has sewed up the bluidy hide,
And put in a pipe of wine:
She drank it a' up at ae draught,
Left na a drap therein.

"A bed, a bed, ye King Henrie!
A bed ye make to me!"
"And what's the bed i' this house, ladye,
That ye're na wellcum tee?"
"O ye maun pu' the green heather,
And mak a bed to me."

O pu'd has he the heather green,
And made to her a bed,
And up he's ta'en his gay mantle,
And o'er it he has spread.

"Now swear, now swear, ye King Henrie,
To take me for your bride!"
"O God forbid," King Henrie said,
"That e'er the like betide,
That e'er the fiend that wons in hell
Should streak down by my side!"

When day was come and night was gane,
And the sun shone through the ha',
The fairest ladye that e'er was seen
Lay atween him and the wa'.

"O weel is me," King Henrie said,
"How lang will this last wi' me?"
And out and spake that ladye fair:
"E'en till the day ye die,

"For I was witched to a ghastly shape,
All by my stepdame's skill,
Till I should meet wi' a courteous knight
Wad gie me a' my will."

"That was a spirited ballet," said William Cecil, "and you shall have a new coat for it."

"Thank you, my lord," replied Dick; "it will come in handy."

"Your heroine was indeed a valiant lady," said Snorri Sturlason, "and she might have entered the contest with Loki, if not with Logi."

"What was that?" asked Dick.

"According to our ancient histories," answered Snorri, "Loki and Logi once entered into competition to see which could eat the more quickly. A wooden kneading-trough was placed in the middle of the floor and filled with meat. Loki took his place at one end and Logi at the other. Each ate as fast as he could till they met at the middle of the trough. Loki, it was found, had indeed eaten all the meat from the bones; but Logi had eaten not only the meat, but the bones and the trough as well."

"The French have always been good trenchermen, too," remarked Guillaume de Nangis, "though of course they cannot compare with gods or demons. The great Charles, though he thought little of bread, and drank only thrice during a meal, was a great lover of flesh. At one sitting he was wont to eat a goose or a peacock, or a couple of hens, or a swine's shoulder or a quarter of a wether."

"And did he not die of apoplexy?" inquired the Curtal Friar.

"No, indeed, for abundance of food and drink prolong life rather than shorten it."

"With that view I cannot concur," answered the Friar. "And I will tell you why. The stomach, as you know, is right in the middle of a man's body, and everything a man eats or drinks goes there first of all. Now the stomach may be likened to a cauldron on the fire wherein one cooks one's food. Everyone knows that when the cooking pot is filled too full it cannot be tended properly, for the food either runs over the rim and puts out the fire, and so remains uncooked; or if the fire is not put out, what remains in the pot is scorched, and so also remains uncooked. But when the kettle is properly filled and the food is properly sodden, and is clean and good and wholesome, then all the household partake of it with pleasure. But if the food is spoiled, then the family remain unsatisfied and unnourished, and their joy and strength are abated. Now all this may be applied to man's stomach. The stomach lies close to the liver, which is its fire for cooking whatever a man eats or drinks. And when the stomach is properly filled with food, then the food is well digested. And if the stomach is adequately nourished, so also are all the members which depend on it stronger and healthier. But when there is too little in the stomach, the members are underfed and lose their strength and health, though it is better to have too little than too much. And when the stomach is crammed to overflowing, no matter how hot the liver may be, some of the food remains undigested and the stomach must cast it out, or else it spoils there. And if the superfluity overflows into the various members, then their balance and well-being are upset, and grievous ills arise in those members, so that a man may lose his sight, or his hearing, or go lame. . . ."

The Friar would have continued, but was stopped by Bonvesin da Riva's upraised hand. "We will gladly hear your sermon on another occasion," he said, "but while we are at supper we will hinder neither the stomach nor the liver in their functions by talk of a lugubrious nature."

"Very well," answered the Friar. "But you see that I am healthy, and I live mostly on beans and cress and sour milk. I have a wealth of experience which I should be glad to put at the disposal of this company."

"What would you say to nettle soup?" asked Henry Castide.

"I wouldn't mention it at all," replied the Friar shortly.

"What is nettle soup?" asked the Goodman of Paris in astonishment.

"When I was living in Ireland," said Castide, "there was a story current that Columcille existed during the last years of his life on such a pottage."

"How extraordinary!" exclaimed the Goodman.

"But true," said John Colgan. "One day the saint happened to be wandering over the rocks and crags, the fields and moors, the heaths and brakes of Hy when he came upon a miserable old woman cutting nettles. 'What is the meaning of what you do?' asked the saint. 'This is the meaning on it,' answered the woman. 'I am cutting these nettles to make pottage.' 'Indeed?' said Columcille. 'It is so,' answered the woman, 'that I have only the one cow, and she with calf, and nettle pottage is what serves me this long time while I wait for her to come fresh.' That seemed good to Columcille. 'Since it is only for expectation of the one cow that the woman is in this great hunger,' said he to himself, 'how much more fitting is this food for us, though sore were the hunger in which we should be, since it is the eternal kingdom which we expect?' So he said to his servant: 'Pottage of nettles from thee every night, and bring not the milk with it.' 'It shall be done,' said the cook. So Columcille was served with nettle soup and died of hunger."

"The story goes," remarked Blind Harry, "that the Gyre Carling of the Tinto Hills considered green and raw hides a great delicacy; and yet some people object to Scotch haggis."

"'Each man to his own taste' is, I suppose, a venerable precept," said Hector Boëce, "yet Columcille's soup appeals to me as little as the diet preferred by a lass of my home town."

"What about her?" asked Christine de Pisan.

" 'Tis a sad story," answered the historian. "Will anyone offer me a drink?"

Dunbar pushed his flask of usquebaugh nearer to his countryman, and after Hector had wet his throat he began the story of . . .

9. THE MAN-EATING MAIDEN OF DUNDEE
Hector Boëce

It is said that in the tyme of King James II thair was many marvellis that prognosticat the kingis death. The night befoir his deceas thair appeared an cleir comet. In the yeir preceiding thair was one borne quhilk had the memberis both of male and female, called in oure language ane scratch, in whom manes nature did prevail, bot becaus his dispositioun and proportioun of bodie represented ane voman, he being in ane manes hous in Linlithgow, and so associating in bedding with the guidman of the hous his dochter, maid hir to conceave with chyld; quhilk being devulgit throw the countrie, and the matrones vnderstanding this damosell deceived in this manner, being offendit that this monster tratour should sett him forth as ane voman, being ane verrie man, they gatt him accused in judgment, to be brunt quick for his schamfull behaviour.

"Sir," interrupted Bartholomew, "stop there. Your language is obscure to some of this company. I daresay it is the fault of your native fogs and mists, and that constant indulgence in usquebaugh has finished the ruin begun by the climate. If you must speak a foreign language, choose Latin or French, which everyone can understand."

"Nay," replied Hector, "do not asperse the drink. I will not speak in French, and if the Scots tongue displeases you, then you must be content with such English as I can command."

Then taking another drink the historian continued.

About this time there was taken a brigand, along with his whole family, who haunted a place in Angus. This mischievous man had an execrable fashion of taking all young men and childer which he could steal or bear away quietly without anyone's knowledge, and eating them; and the younger they were, the more tender and delicious did he esteem them. For the which cause and damnable abuse, he, with his wife and bairns, were all burnt, with the exception of one young wench a year old. She was saved and brought to Dundee, where she was brought up and fostered, until she also came to be burned for the same crime of which her father had been convicted.

It is said that when she was coming to the place of execution, there gathered a great multitude of people, especially of women, cursing her for being so unnatural as to commit such damnable deeds. She turned about upon these women, saying with an ireful countenance: "Why do you chide me, as though I had committed an unworthy act? Give me credence and believe me when I say that if you had had experience in eating the flesh of men and women you would think it so delicious that you would never forbear it again." Thus, without any sign of repentance, this unhappy creature died in the sight of the assembled multitude.

"I am sorry," apologized Hector, "that I am unable to give you the best version of this affair. Robert Lindsay has a better account of it, but his manuscript is under lock and key."

"A pity," said the Clerk of Oxenford. "I wonder why Lindsay wrote, if it was not with the hope that his message might reach as many people as possible?"

"You need make no excuses," said John Major. "Probably you have said enough. It is a distasteful subject."

"And yet," remarked John Stow, "following Andrew of Wyntoun and Walter Bower, you yourself record the perverted taste of Crysty of the Klek, who set traps for women and children in the vicinity of Perth, and ate all he could catch."

"The circumstance is not peculiar to Scotland," said John Mirk. "I have read that when Titus besieged Jerusalem the citizens were so reduced that they ate their boots and shoes for hunger. Among the other starving people was a well-born woman who had a small boy. To him she said: 'Dear son, I have suffered a great deal more pain for you than you for me; wherefor it seems proper that I should appease my hunger with your body rather than that I should die and you too.' Then she slew her child and roasted half of him, laying up the other half raw. As the flesh was roasting the odour of it penetrated to the street and attracted some passers-by. The woman would have hidden the meat from them, but they insisted on sharing with her. So she said: 'What I am roasting here is half of my son. Since you will not leave me, here is the other half raw, which I was saving for tomorrow.'"

"Romance!" exclaimed Polydore Vergil. "Fantasy!"

"Nay!" protested Higden. "When the Tatars ravaged Pannonia in 1239 so great was the dearth of food that people there too were driven to eat their own children."

"The historian is right," said Raoul Lefèvre. "When I was in my early thirties war had spread famine and pestilence over all France.

It was pitiful to see the multitudes of poor who died daily from sheer want, lying in heaps on the dunghills. At a village near Abbeville a woman was arrested on the charge of having murdered several children, which she kept hidden in her house pickled in brine. The crime was discovered by some foragers who discovered parts of the bodies of these children in her house. She confessed herself guilty and was publicly burned at Abbeville according to the sentence of the law."

"Gentlemen," protested Bonvesin da Riva, "this conversation is in the worst possible taste."

"Well," offered Dunbar, "if anthropophagy distresses your stomach I will give you a tale which will comfort it, I hope."

"Pray do so," said the Goodman of Paris.

10. THE FRIARS OF BERWICK
William Dunbar

At Tweed's mouth there stands a noble town called Berwick, walled about with stone. Therein dwell many lords of great renown, many fair ladies, and many a lusty gallant. There, too, is the great church and the Maison Dieu; and the four orders—Jacobins, Carmelites, Austin Friars and Friars Minor are not far to seek, for they all dwell in this town.

Now it happened one day that two of the ablest and most cunning of the Jacobins, Friar Allan and Friar Robert, were sent on a visit to their upland brethren, as was the custom. These friars knew well how to talk flatteringly with women; wonderfully well did they please all wives, telling them tales of the holy saints' lives until such time as they were ready to return home. But Friar Allan was very tired and wet and could not travel well; also, he had a touch of the gravel. Friar Robert was young and hot-blooded, and on the trip he carried the clothes and all the gear, for he was strong and sturdy.

Now night was coming on as they drew near Berwick, when Allan said: "Dear brother, it is late; I fear the gates be closed; we are tired and ill prepared to lodge outside the walls, except we find some good house wherein we may be harboured this night."

It happened that they knew an excellent hosteler by the name of Simon Lawrear dwelling not far outside the town. As fair and blithe a wife he had as might be found anywhere, except that she was somewhat cool and aloof. When the friars came to the hostel they greeted her courteously, and she answered them in like manner. Friar Robert asked after the goodman, and she replied that he had been in the country since Wednesday buying up corn and hay and other necessities. Robert wished him god-speed and asked dame Alison for a stoup of ale, "for," said he, "we are wondrous dry." The goodwife brought bread and cheese and ale, and for a little they sat there at their ease. Then said Brother Allan: "Come hither, dame; sit down by me and fill the cup at least once." "You shall be well paid," added Brother Robert.

Thus both friars were cheerful and told merry tales until suddenly they heard the prayer-bell of their abbey. Thereat they were somewhat disturbed, for they knew that now the gates were closed indeed and that they could certainly not get in. Then they prayed the goodwife for charity's sake to grant them lodging for the night. But she answered sharply: "The goodman is from home, as I told you. If I were to harbour friars in the house with me, what would Simon say, indeed, but that I abused his place in his absence? Lady Mary forbid," said she, "and keep me from peril and shame."

Then said old Friar Allan: "Nay, fair dame, listen to me. The gates of our abbey are closed now and we cannot get in. The road is bad and I am tired and wet. We should be dead before day if we went abroad now. It would be a great sin if you were to cause us both to perish thus. Therefore, of very necessity, we must abide, and you may do with us what you please."

For a moment the goodwife looked at the friars in silence. "By God who redeemed us," she said, "you shall not stay here unless you are willing to lie up in yonder loft at the end of the hall. There is straw there, and I will provide some bedclothes. If this does not please you, wend your ways, for under no other conditions will I harbour you."

The friars followed the goodwife and the maid up the ladder to the hay and corn loft at the end of the hall. She made their bed and then passed down and closed the trap-door. Allan bedded himself down as best he might, but Robert said he would look if he might see some sport or other.

Now as to Alison—she was right blithe to have the friars shut up in the loft, for she had made a tryst to prepare supper for her lover, Friar John, that very night, and she was not anxious for other company since he was to lie with her. John was a Grey friar of great fame, from Berwick, where he had the abbey in his governance, with plenty of silver and gold at his command. He had a privy postern of his own which he could use when he wished his goings and comings to remain unknown.

The goodwife now beat up the fire, thrust fat capons on the spits, laid plump rabbits to roast, and bade the servant-girl tend all zealously. Then she went to her chamber . . . clothed herself in a fine red kirtle of silk adorned with silver, and on her head she put a fair white kerchief. Her other garments shone with red gold; on every finger she wore two rings and was as proud as a parrot. Afterwards she spread the table with a cloth of costly weave, and her napery was of the finest. When these preparations were completed, she went to see if anyone were coming, for she thought it a long time till she met her lover John.

Shortly now Friar John knocked. Alison knew his manner and let him in, welcoming him with every courtesy. John thanked her and said: "My own dear love, I have brought you these two leather bottles, each holding a gallon of Gascon wine; take this brace of newly killed partridges also, as well as this basket of finest white bread, and make good cheer. Since Simon is from home, I will be homely with you, my own dear love." "You know," replied Alison, smiling brightly, "that you are welcome here any time you wish to come." Therewith Friar John pressed her hand tenderly, and they talked to each other amorously for a while.

I will now leave the goodwife and the friar to their sport and say something about those two simple friars who were locked up in the straw-loft. Friar Allan lay quietly, but Robert was curious, and with his bodkin he made a little hole through which he was able to see everything that passed in the room below, and hear everything that was said. He beheld the goodwife proud and fresh and gay, and heard how she called the friar "sweetheart," "leman," "lover." You can imagine that Friar John's courage rose when she whispered privately in his ear.

After a while, when Alison saw that the supper was ready, she set the table and put on the two bottles of wine. But she had hardly set them down when they heard the goodman cry out as he knocked sturdily at the gate outside. Both were aghast. John started up and would have run away, but alas! there was no way out. Said Alison: "That is Simon making all that noise. I thought he was well away. If I live another half year you may be sure I shall be quits with him for disturbing us in this manner; we can't bide together now." "What shall I do?" asked John. "Hide in yonder big kneading-trough in the corner," she replied, "until he goes to bed"; and she helped him creep under it, urging him to lie quietly. To the servant-maid she said: "Take the meats from the fire and then slake it; strip the table and lock everything up in the aumry, meat, ale and wine; and sweep the floor clean so that there may be no appearance of a feast." Afterwards she quickly put off her gala attire and went to bed, suffering Simon to knock his fill the while.

Now when Simon was tired knocking he went to the other side of the house and cried out for Alison. At last she answered crabbedly: "Who is it who knows my name so well? Go away, for Simon is not at home, and I will harbour no guests, by my faith." Said Simon: "Fair dame, do you not know me? I am your Simon, and husband of this place." "Are you Simon?" she asked; "alas! who would have expected you home so late?" Then she rose, got a light and opened the gate. She relieved him of all his gear and gave him a most hearty welcome.

Simon bade the maid kindle the fire and prepare him some supper, and that hastily. Said Alison shortly: "There is no food here fit for you." "How so, fair dame? Get me some cheese and bread and fill the stoup; and don't argue with me, for I am very tired, wet and cold." Alison dared not disobey, but covered the board and quickly set on a soused neat's foot, a sheep's head, some cold meat and a stoup of ale. When the goodman sat down to this he was blithe enough. "By Allhallows," he said, "I should have no complaint to make if I had a fellow to eat with me. Dame, do you eat and drink with me, if you please." "Devil a bit can I taste," answered she; "and as for you, you ought rather to be in bed than sitting here wishing for company."

Brother Robert, who had seen and heard all this from the loft, now whispered to Allan: "Dear brother, I wish the goodman knew we were here—he might fare somewhat better. Indeed, my heart will be sore if Simon cleans up yon sheep's head when there is such muckle good cheer in the aumry." And with that word he coughed.

"Who is yon?" asked the goodman. "It is only two friars," said his wife. "What friars?" asked Simon. "Friar Robert and old Friar Allan," said Alison. "I gave them shelter after hours." "They are heartily welcome," said Simon. "Go call them down so that we may drink together." "If you take my advice," replied the dame, "you will let them be; they had liefer sleep than sit in company." Said Simon to the servant-maid: "Go call the friars and ask them to come down to me." And she did as she was bidden.

The two friars greeted Simon, and he welcomed them heartily. "Come, my dear brothers, sit down beside me and bear me company, for, as you see, I am alone. Take your part of such cheer as we have." Said Friar Allan: "I pray God save you, for here is enough of God's good." "Nay," replied Simon, "I'd give a crown for some really worthy food and drink for the three of us." "What food and drink would you have?" asked Brother Robert, "for I have various and sundry arts which I learned beyond sea in Paris, and I would gladly put them to the test for your sake, and for the sake of your dame who gave us shelter. If you will keep the matter a secret, I guarantee to produce the best food in this country, and Gascon wine, too; if there be any within a hundred miles, it will be here shortly now." The goodman was amazed. "My heart will never be whole," he said, "if you do not put that art into practice before you leave."

Thereupon Robert took his book and walked about for a while turning the leaves. First he faced east, then he turned west and read a passage from his book. But he glanced frequently, too, at the aumry and at the trough where Friar John was lying. Afterwards he sat down, cast back his hood and grinned and grimaced as though he were mad. One while he would sit studying, another while he would read from his book, another while he would clap his hands and glower and gape. Then he turned thrice about to the south, and when he came by the aumry he louted low.

Alison beheld all this with great perturbation, for she suspected that Robert knew how she had arranged matters. She observed how he fixed his attention on the aumry and said to herself: "Alas! he knows all! What shall I do? Woe the day I was born, for if Simon catches on, it will be dear doing."

By now the friar had left his studying. He stood up and said: "Thanks to my art the matter is now finished. We shall have plenty of the best bread and wine in the country. Go quickly to yon aumry, fair dame, and open it, and bring us a couple of bottles of Gascon wine—they must hold a gallon and more, I think; and bring us the basket of fine bread, and the pair of fat rabbits, piping hot; the capons, too, you shall bring us, and the two brace of partridges, and two plovers. That is all, I believe."

The goodwife perceived that the friar knew all her secret and that it was useless to make denial, so she opened the cupboard and found everything he had named. She started back as though in amazement, and crossed herself. "Ha! God's mercy! What may this be? Who ever saw such a marvel before? Indeed, the holy friar spoke the truth." So she brought out all the food and set it on the table, both wine and other things, as you have heard. Robert watched her closely to see that there was nothing missing.

When Simon beheld all this he was amazed and swore by the moon that Robert had done his task well. "He who brought us all this so quickly through his great subtlety and knowledge of philosophy may be called a great man of science," he said; "in a good hour came he hither. Now fill the cup and let us drink together and make good cheer after this wearisome day, for I have ridden a wonder toilsome road." So Simon and his guests pledged each other with

Gascon wine, and made merry with loud song, and thus drove away the long night.

Once Simon called to Alison: "Come hither, dame; sit by me and partake of our good cheer. And I pray you thank this friar for his great skill and art in having provided us so abundantly." But all their sport and merriment brought little joy to Alison, for something else was in her mind. Her heart was a-flutter with dread lest the friar betray her. So she sat still and drank with feigned cheer.

Finally, after the wine had worked in them and they were right blithe and merry, Simon said: "I marvel indeed how you were able to bring us so many dainties with such speed." "There is nothing to marvel at," replied Robert. "I have a privy page who comes to me without anyone's knowledge and brings me whatever I wish. If you want more, I will get it for you. But I pray you, keep it a secret, and let no man know that I can do such a thing."

Simon swore by heaven that so far as he was concerned the affair should be well concealed. "But, dear brother," he said, "I should like to see your servant so that we may drink together." "Nay," said Robert, "you must not have sight of him, for I give you to understand that if you were to see him in his own form and figure you would straightway go out of your mind, so foul and ugly is he. I dare not take the responsibility of bringing him hither, particularly now, so late at night, except as it were translated and disguised from his own shape into another." Said Simon: "I will not urge you; whatever pleases you, pleases me; but I would fain see him." "Well," said Robert, "in what likeness shall I make him appear?" "In the shape of a friar," answered Simon, "the white kind, like yourself, for white will harm no one." Robert said that could not be, for it would be a great despite to his order. "But you shall see him in the likeness of a grey friar," he said. "Now pay heed; be still, and whatever you see or hear, speak no word and stir not till I have finished my business. You, Simon, stand up beside me with a staff in your hand; but fear not, I will protect you." Said Simon: "So be it," and he got up and seized a cudgel, somewhat apprehensive, but stout of heart. "What shall I do?" he asked. "Nothing," replied Robert. "Stand still by the door and give close attention to me. When I bid you strike, lay on stoutly. See to it that you hit him right on the neck." "I will," said Simon, "with all my might."

Hereupon Robert took his book and turned the leaves busily for a long while. Then he approached the kneading-trough and said thus: "Ha! How! Hurlybas! Now I conjure you that you rise up before me in the likeness of a grey friar; get up out of this trough where you lie, and make no din or outcry. Do no harm to anyone here;

withdraw your hands into your sleeves and pull your hood down over your face. You may thank God you get so much grace. Go back to your own dwelling without delay. Make speed over the stair and harm no one in your going. And see to it that you come here no more unless I command you."

At this Friar John, who thought he had been in the trough a long time, scrambled out and rushed to the door with heavy cheer, for never ere had such a chance befallen him. When Robert saw him going he called to Simon: "Lay on! Strike hardily, for now is the time." With that Simon let fly a felon flap with his staff, and hit Sir John on the neck, but the blow was so violent that with the impetus of it he fell over a sack and broke his head against a stone mortar. In the meantime Friar John went down the stair in such wise that he missed the steps, and fell into a puddle of mire forty foot wide at the bottom of it. He got up with clothes all bespattered, drearily made his way through the slop, and climbed quickly over the stone wall. He was glad enough to escape, and will be loath to come again, I trow.

Now Friar Robert looked and saw where the goodman lay wondrous low on the floor with a bloody head. He thought he was dead, and quickly carried him to the door; but when the fresh wind had blown twice in his face, Simon came to his senses. "What ails you," asked Robert, "to be afraid?" "It was yon friar," answered Simon. "Never mind," said Robert; "the worst is away; make merry and mourn no more. You knocked him clean down stairs so that he fell into the mire. Let him go, for he was a graceless ghost. And as for you, you had best make ready for bed."

Thus Simon's head was broken on a stone, Friar John has leaped into the mire, besmutted from top to toe, and Alison in no wise got her will. Of this story there is no more.

"It was good right down to the end," said Sir John Harington. "Your characters seem really to live as human beings. But what I admire most is the way you stick to the point and pass from one point to another without wandering into discussions of Providence, Free Will or the nature of dreams."

"The art of story-telling," said Mac Conglinne, "is not new among the Celts."

"When I was in Kilkenny . . ." began Fynes Moryson. But what had happened to the assiduous traveller in Ireland the company were fated never to know, for they were suddenly startled by a series of sharp brittle noises. Ossian had gnawed the last shred of meat from a haunch of venison and was now snapping the bone between his thumb and forefinger to get at the marrow. Bonvesin da Riva looked on with astonishment as the Fenian gouged a bit of recalcitrant marrow from the knuckle with his little finger. "What manners!" he murmured.

Ossian directed a mild blue eye toward him, but said nothing.

"What abominable taste in food!" added Peter Bell.

"You are right to be shocked," said Gerald de Barry. "The Irish are like no other people in the world. For instance, when a child is born in Ireland . . ."

"We will keep the conversation clean," interrupted Bartholomew sternly.

"What about Irish taste and Irish manners?" inquired Geoffrey Keating. "Would you have the Irish eat like Germans or drink like Flemings? Have they no right to manners or tastes of their own?"

"Gentlemen," said William Camden, "you must overlook the Fenian poet's peccadilloes; he is of the meere Irish of a ruder day. In his time—or not long after it—marrowbones were considered a delicacy."

"True for you," agreed Ossian. "A marrowbone was the cause of considerable disturbance one time at the banquet of Dun na nGedh."

"Will you tell us about it?" asked Colin Clout.

But Ossian was ranging about, looking for something to eat.

"I will tell the story," said Eices ind Righ.

11. THE FIGHT FOR THE MARROWBONE

Eices ind Righ

It was in the time when Congal Claen made a journey to the kings of Alba and of Britain to seek aid against Domhnall son of Aedh, king of Erin. When he had finished his business in Alba, Congal went to Britain, where the king of Britain and the king's men received him gladly and asked his news. Afterwards an assembly was convened by them round Congal and the rest of the Ultonians to hold a consultation on the project of armed assistance for him.

While they were assembled at the meeting they saw a single great hero approaching them—fairest of the heroes of the world, larger and taller than any man, bluer than ice his eye, redder than the fresh rowan berries his lips, whiter than showers of pearls his teeth, fairer than the snow of one night his skin. A protecting shield with a golden border was upon him, two battle lances in his hand, a sword with knobs of ivory and ornamented with gold was at his side. He had no other accoutrements of a hero besides these. He had golden hair on his head, and a fair ruddy countenance he had.

When the hero arrived at the border of the assembly he stopped not till he came to the place where he saw the countenance of the king, and he sat at his right hand, between him and the king of Ulster.

"Why hast thou sat thus?" said all.

"I was not ordered to remain anywhere else," said he, "and because it was I myself who selected the place; if there had been a better place, it is there I would sit."

The king smiled and said: "He is right in what he has done." Then they asked him his news, and he told them all the news in the present world, for there was not, they thought, a story under heaven which he had not. And they loved him very much, both men and women, for the goodness of his countenance and for his eloquence.

Then the hosts repaired into the palace and left him alone outside on the hill whereon the meeting had been held. I was sojourning in Britain at that time and I drew near to him and asked him his news, and he told me everything save his name and the name of his tribe. "Who art thou thyself?" he asked, "for I perceive by thy dress that thou art a poet." "I am Eices the royal poet," I answered, "and it is to the king's palace I am now repairing."

A heavy shower fell then, consisting of rain intermingled with snow, and the hero put his shield between me and the shower, leaving his own arms and battle dress exposed to the snow. "What is this for?" I asked. "I say unto thee," he replied, "that if I could show thee a greater token of veneration than this, thou shouldst receive it for thy learning; but as I cannot, I can only say that I am more fit to bear rain than one who has learning." "If thou thinkest proper to come with me this night to my house," I said, "I will procure food and a night's entertainment for thee." "I think well of it," replied the hero. So we went home and got a sufficiency of meat and drink there.

Then it was that the king's messenger came for me, but I said that I would not go unless it were the wish of the unknown youth who was my guest. The hero replied that it was meet for me to go to the assembly, for there were three places at which a poet obtained the greatest request, namely, at a meeting, at a wedding and at a banquet. "And I will not be the cause," said he, "that the host of Britain should be assembled together in one place and go away without thy getting anything from them."

So we went to the palace, and I was seated in the presence of the king, and the youth was seated elsewhere. Food was distributed and we got our fill of meat and drink. Now before entering the palace I had told the stranger youth that if a bone should be brought on a dish in his presence, he should not attempt breaking it, for there was a young man of the king's household to whom every marrowbone was due, and that if one should be broken against his will, its weight in red gold must be given him, or else battle in single combat, and that he was the fighter of a hundred. "That is good," said the hero. "When that will be given, I will do my duty." He stopped not till a bone was brought on a dish to him, and he put a hand on each end of it and broke it between his two fingers, and afterwards ate its marrow and flesh.

All beheld this and wondered at it. The hero to whom the marrow was due was told of this, and he rose in great anger, and his heroic fury was stirred up to be avenged on the person who had violated his privilege, and who had eaten what was due to him.

When the unknown hero perceived this, he flung the bone at him, and it passed through his forehead and pierced his brain, even to the centre of his head. Now the king's people and his household rose to slay him in revenge for this deed. But the hero attacked them as the hawk attacks a flock of small birds, and made a great slaughter of them, so that their dead were more numerous than their living, and the living among them fled. Then he came and sat by my shoulder, and the king and queen were seized with awe of him when they had seen his warlike feats and his heroic rage and champion fury roused. But he told them that they had no cause to fear him unless the household should again return to the house. The king said that they should not return.

Now then, the hero took his golden helmet off his head, and fair was his visage and countenance after his blood had been excited by the fury of battle. And there we sat for a time while the queen conversed with him, and he told her his news.

"If the eating of marrow seems to me bad taste," said Bonvesin da Riva, "spilling men's blood for the sake thereof impresses me as being still more reprehensible."

"Indeed?" said Keating. "I should be curious to know what judgment you would pass on the manners and habits of the Dubhgall, otherwise known as Vikings? St Elphege, I understand, thought them atrocious, and you must admit that he had good opportunity to judge."

"Your words are obscure to me, sir," said the Italian.

"I think I know to what the learned doctor refers," said William of Malmesbury. "Svein Forkbeard, in revenge for the murder of his sister, was ravaging King Ethelred's realm up and down. A party of his marauders captured Aelfheah, or Elphege, Archbishop of Canterbury, and held him for ransom; but he could not or would not comply with their exorbitant demands. So, as a means of softening his stubbornness, every day at dinner they brought him into the hall, set him in a corner, and as fast as they had gnawed the meat from a knuckle of beef, they would hurl the bone at him. Thus he died."

"It is true," said Matthew Paris, "that St Elphege's effigy adorns the façade of Salisbury cathedral, and he holding the instruments of his martyrdom in a fold of his gown. But they seem to me to be stones, and not beef-bones. You yourself, in your History, said he was stoned to death."

"Yes," said William, "but you, who are also an historian, know very well that some things cannot always be written just as they happen."

"I had better taste and omitted the matter entirely," said Snorri Sturlason.

"The custom of throwing beef-bones at dinner guests is of hoary antiquity," remarked Camden. "Did not Ctesippus fling an ox-hoof at Odysseus in his own hall? Perhaps that branch of the Nordic race which migrated northward preserved the custom."

"There are illustrations of it in our records, to be sure," said Einar Rattlescale.

"Will you give us one?" asked Matthew Paris.

"If you like," answered the skald, "I will tell . . ."

12. HOW BÖDVAR IMPROVED TABLE-MANNERS AT THE COURT OF KING HROLF

Einar Rattlescale

There was a prince called Björn. He loved a maid called Bera. He met a violent end. Soon after Björn's death Bera bore three sons at a birth. The youngest of these was Bödvar, and him his mother loved dearly.

Now after the death of Björn's father, King Hring, Bödvar took over his grandfather's kingdom and ruled quietly for a time. Then one day he called his men together and announced that he intended to ride forth on adventures. So he went away alone, with neither gold nor silver nor other property on him, though he was well provided as to clothes.

One day it rained heavily and Bödvar was wet through. The road was heavy with mud and the going difficult for the horse. By nightfall he had the good fortune to light upon a peasant's hut, where he asked for admittance and shelter. Here Bödvar was well received and his wants satisfied. In the evening he asked his host a great many questions about King Hrolf and his heroes' mighty deeds, and if it were far to his hall. "Not far," said the old man; "are you bound thither?" "That is my intention," answered Bödvar. "That may be very well for you," said the old fellow, "for I see that you are a large and well-built man; and the king's men, too, seem to be sturdy and capable fellows."

At these words the old wife began to weep and wail. "What is the matter with you, old woman?" asked Bödvar. "My husband and I have a son," she answered, "named Höttr. One day he went to the king's burg to amuse himself. The king's men played their tricks on him, and when he did not take it in good part, they seized him and put him among the sweepings and bones in a corner of the hall. With them it is the custom, at meal-time, as soon as they have gnawed a bone clean, to hurl it at Höttr. It often happens that he gets great harm when one of the bones hits him. I do not know whether or not he is still alive. But if you find him living, I ask no other payment for my hospitality except that you throw only little bones at him."

"I will do as you ask," said Bödvar; "and I must say that it seems to me ill beseeming to heroes to throw bones at people, or mistreat children or weak folk."

"Do as you have said," replied the carlin, "for you have a strong hand, and I know for sure that he will not survive it unless you spare him."

The next morning Bödvar took his way to Hleidargard, King Hrolf's hall. Without asking permission he put up his horse in the stable beside the best horses of the king, then he entered the hall, where he found only a few men present. He sat down on one of the lower benches, but he had not been there long when he heard a knocking in the corner. As he looked, he saw a black and grimy hand emerge from a heap of bones lying there. Bödvar went to the corner and asked who was hiding in the bone-heap, whereupon a very small voice replied: "I am Höttr, dear chap." "Why are you here, and what are you doing?" asked Bödvar. "I am making a shield-burg for myself, dear chap," replied Höttr. "What a miserable fellow you are with your shield-burg," replied the prince, and pulled him bodily out of the bone-heap.

Thereupon Höttr shrieked and said: "Now you're going to kill me! Please don't! I had just fortified myself so nicely, and now you have demolished my shield-burg! I had just built it up high enough around me so that I was protected from all your shots—for none has hit me for a while now—but I had not yet completed it to my satisfaction."

"You will not have to build shield-burgs from now on," said

Bödvar. "Are you going to kill me?" whined Höttr. "Don't yell so loud," answered the prince.

Then Bödvar took the wretch out to a fountain and washed him from top to toe. Afterwards he returned to his place in the hall and sat down, with Höttr beside him. The latter, though he seemed to understand that this man intended to help him, was so frightened that he trembled all over.

As evening came on people began to come into the hall, and Hrolf's champions saw that Höttr was sitting on a bench. They thought he must be a brave man who had dared to place him there. Höttr had a bad moment when he saw his friends, for his life was dear to him; he had had nothing but evil from them, and would have fled again to his bone-heap, but Bödvar held him fast.

Now the king's men resumed their old game and began to throw bones, at first little ones, across the hall at Bödvar and Höttr. The prince paid no attention, but Höttr was so frightened that he could touch neither food nor drink, and it seemed to him very certain that he should now be knocked to death. Said he to Bödvar: "Dear chap, they are aiming a big bone at you now, and it is certainly meant to be our death." Bödvar told him to shut up. Then he raised his hand, cup-wise, and so seized in mid air the marrowbone with a whole shank still attached to it. This he sent back at the fellow who had thrown it, and with such good aim and power that he killed him on the spot.

At this Hrolf's warriors were frozen with fear. News fled to the king and his body-guard that a very imposing hero had entered the hall and killed one of his men, and that his retainers now wished to kill the stranger. Hrolf asked whether the slain man had been guiltless or not. "Practically guiltless," said the messengers. But the king got the truth out of them, and said that the newcomer should certainly not be slain. "For you have assumed," he said, "a nasty practice of flinging meat bones at innocent strangers; that redounds to my dishonour and your shame. I have often spoken about this matter before, and you have paid no heed. I think the man whom you have vexed must be a person of importance. Call him to me that I may find out who he is."

Bödvar came to King Hrolf and greeted him courteously. "What is your name?" asked the king. "Your people call me 'Höttr's champion,'" he replied, "but my name is Bödvar." "What compensation will you give me for my man?" asked Hrolf. "He got what he gave," answered Bödvar. "Will you become my man and take the place of the slain one?" asked Hrolf. "I will not refuse that," replied the prince, "but only on condition that Höttr and I remain together, and that we both sit nearer to you than the other did. Otherwise we shall go our ways." "I see no great honour for me in Höttr," said the king, "but I will not deny him food and drink."

Thereupon Bödvar chose a seat that pleased him: he pulled three men out of it and sat down there with Höttr; and that was nearer the king than the place that had been indicated. Hrolf's people considered Bödvar to be a very irritable man, and were very much incensed against him. But Bödvar kept his seat.

"A moment ago," said Blind Harry, "Messer Bonvesin remarked that it was vile to fight for marrowbones and such. I am perhaps inclined to agree with him—when my belly is full. But would the gentleman think it proper to fight for honour, and to obtain peace?"

"Honour is always worth fighting for," said Bernardo del Carpio, "to the death."

"Peace we must have," asserted Marsiglio of Padua, "even if we have to fight for it. When the clash of two seemingly irreconcilable opinions disturbs the peace of all, there remains no choice but to pit one opinion against the other till one of them disappears, either by defeat or change, and equilibrium is restored."

"I have in mind a tale," answered Blind Harry, "which illustrates what you say exactly. It was like this. . . ."

13. THE FIGHT ON THE INCH OF PERTH

Blind Harry

In the year 1396, during the reign of Robert III, a great part of northern Scotland beyond the mountains was disturbed by two pestiferous caterans and their followers. Christie Johnston led the Clan Quhele, and Strabrek the Clan Kay.

These clans lived at continual strife with one another. They would not abide by the terms of any pact or treaty, and no art of the king or his lieutenants was able to reduce them to order. In their mutual raids they burned and slew, sparing neither man nor woman. For many a day Thomas Dunbar, Earl of Murray, and David Lindesay, who afterwards became Earl of Crawford, had striven to make peace between them, but they could effect nothing. Each clan violently asserted its own superiority. The only terms either side would accept were that the other side should acknowledge itself inferior and become its dependents.

Now the Earl of Dunbar was a wise man, and he made a proposal, the same one to each clan, namely, that thirty men from one should fight in the lists with thirty men from the other, with swords and axes only, and with no other body armour but their doublets. The side which won should be the master of the other clan after that.

Both leaders accepted this wise lord's suggestion. The day of combat was accordingly set for the Monday before the feast of St Michael, and the place was to be the north Inch of Perth on the river Tay.

When it came time to advance into the field it was found that there was a man wanting on one side. The twenty-nine would not engage the thirty, and the thirty would not withdraw a man. Thereupon a big bold busteous churl who was standing among the spectators offered to fill the missing fighter's place for pay. The king and the magnates agreed to this.

Then the heralds cried: "Let them go! Let them go! God show the right!" Now the battle axes swung, and swords were flourished in such wise that on both sides men fell like slaughtered cattle. Up and down, back and forth they fought till all were slain save eight —or as some say, eleven—on one side, and a single man on the other. When the lone warrior saw that all his companions were down, he thought it would be no child's play to remain, so he leaped the barriers and swam over the Tay.

After that there was peace in those parts for a while.

"Your story," said Jorge Ferreira de Vasconcellos, "reminds me of a tourney which took place in England between twelve English and twelve Portuguese knights. The English courtiers, for some reason, dispraised the beauty, and questioned the honour of the ladies of the court. The truth or falseness of their assertions was to be decided by a tourney; and since no English knight could be found to enter the contest on their behalf, the Duke of Lancaster found them champions in Portugal. That was no difficult matter, for the Portuguese knights—at least in the time of King João—bore the palm for chivalry and courtesy. Need I say more? The honour of the English ladies was abundantly vindicated and their names cleared by the twelve Portuguese gentlemen in the presence of the king himself."

"I remember that affair," said Henry Knighton, "and I have never been able to understand it, for the reproach brought by the English lords against the ladies of the court was certainly well founded. Many of them used to ride to tournaments themselves, travestied in men's clothes, and making use of the occasion to indulge in all sorts of folly and wantonness."

"What you say is only one of many proofs," remarked Robert

Mannyng, "that tournaments are the well-spring of all the seven deadly sins."

"It seems to me," spoke up Jean Froissart, "that the purpose which inspired thirty Breton knights to engage thirty English knights—or rather, twenty English, six Germans and four Brabançons—was far nobler. Your Clan Kay and your Clan Quhele fought for nothing but physical supremacy, inspired by that stiff-necked pride and baseborn envy which cannot endure a fellow. They remind me of nothing so much as a pack of savage dogs snarling over a bone. The knights of Brittany, however, fought in defence of their peasantry, as they were bound to do according to the conventions of feudalism. Their hard-won victory was a brilliant proof that right must prevail over injustice."

"The encounters which you and Hector describe," said Francesco Guicciardini, "are not without a parallel in the annals of my country. I remember two dogs—as you say—snapping over a bone. They were Louis XII of France and Ferdinand V of Aragón, and the bone was the Capitanata, a province north of Naples. The war was led by Louis d'Armagnac, Duc de Nemours, on the one side, and by Gonçalvo de Cordoba on the other. The French, with the aid of two thousand Swiss mercenaries, made some slight territorial gains. This initial success led a swaggering Frenchman by the name of Charles de Torgues, who had come to Barletta to negotiate an exchange of prisoners, to asseverate that Gonçalvo might as well give up the struggle at once, that he could never win the field with the soldiers at his command, for the Italians were an effeminate and pusillanimous people. This opinion was pronounced while Torgues was a guest at supper in the house of Don Enrico de Mendoza. Indico Lopez, one of Gonçalvo's captains, who was also present, took issue with the French officer, praising the courage and fidelity of the soldiers under his command. The upshot of the discussion was an agreement that thirteen Italians should encounter thirteen Frenchmen on a field between Andre and Correto. The victors were to receive not only the arms and horses of the vanquished, but each was to have one hundred gold crowns to boot from his beaten opponent. On the appointed day the combatants met as arranged. Great skill and courage were displayed on both sides, but the affray ended with unconditional victory for the Italians. And since the French, in their great pride, had not provided themselves with the necessary hundred crowns' ransom, they were hailed off captive to Barletta, where the generous Gonçalvo paid their fines out of his own pocket. Would you approve of such an engagement in defence of honour, Sir Jean?"

"By all means," answered the chronicler.

"No contest of the sort can possibly be condoned," stated Caesar of Heisterbach categorically, "for the souls of those slain in jousts and tournaments go to hell."

"It is true," observed Roger of Hoveden, "that Pope Alexander III forbade tournaments, and yet it is only by practice in such sham wars that knights are able to keep in trim for the actual wars in which they may at any moment be called upon to engage. You must allow, I think, the desirability of having well-trained fighting men to put into the field."

"We do not disallow it," said John Wiclif, "but we reprobate the useless and senseless, nay, criminal shedding of blood."

"I regret that too," said John Major; "but I regret also that the king of Scotland and his nobles were unequal to the task of taming those factions. In my opinion the matter was badly handled. I realize that it is customary for the king to allow two fractious litigants to settle their differences by single combat; but it is a custom whereof I do not wholly approve in the case of two men, and certainly not in the case of sixty."

"I was interested," said Matthew Paris, "in the circumstances which the skald related a moment ago. When I visited the North I heard something about Björn and Bera and their three unusual sons. Was there not some tragedy connected with their lives?"

"There was, indeed," replied Einar. "Björn's stepmother, when he repulsed her amorous advances, magically transformed him into the shape of a bear, and as such he was hunted down and slain by his father's men. But when Bödvar had reached young manhood, he took due revenge for that deed: he drew a sack over the queen's head and beat her to death—the witch."

"It sometimes happens," remarked Giraldus Cambrensis, "that occult power is fearfully and even unjustly misused. I heard of an extraordinary incident during my travels in Ireland which is to the point."

"What was that?" asked Henry Castide.

14. THE WERWOLVES OF MEATH

Giraldus Cambrensis

About three years before the arrival of Earl John in Ireland it chanced that a priest, who was journeying from Ulster towards Meath, was benighted in a certain wood on the borders of that province. While, in company of only a young lad, he was watching by a fire which he had kindled under the branches of a spreading tree, lo! a wolf came up to them and immediately addressed them to this effect: "Rest secure and be not afraid, for there is no reason why you should fear where no fear is." The travellers, being struck with astonishment and alarm, the wolf added some orthodox words referring to God. Then the priest implored him and adjured him by almighty God and faith in the Trinity not to hurt them, but to inform them what creature it was that in the shape of a beast uttered human words. The wolf, after giving catholic replies to all questions, added at last: "There are two of us, a man and a woman, natives of Ossory, who, through the curse of one Natalis, saint and abbot, are compelled every seven years to put off the human form and depart from the dwellings of men. Quitting the human shape entirely, we assume that of wolves. If at the end of seven years this luckless man and woman chance to survive, two others being substituted in their places, they return to their country and former condition. And now she who is my partner in this visitation lies dangerously sick not far from here; and, as she is at the point of death, I beseech you, inspired by divine charity, to give her the consolations of your priestly office."

At these words the priest followed the wolf trembling as he led the way to a tree at no great distance, in the hollow of which he beheld a she-wolf, who, under that shape, was pouring forth sighs and groans. On seeing the priest, having saluted him with human courtesy, she gave thanks to God who in this extremity had vouchsafed to visit her with such consolation. She then received from the priest all the rites of the church duly performed as far as the last communion. This she importunately demanded, earnestly supplicating him to complete his good offices by giving her the viaticum. The priest stoutly asserted that he was not provided with it, whereupon the wolf, who had withdrawn to a short distance, came back and pointed out a small missal-book containing some consecrated wafers which the priest carried suspended from his neck on his journey. He then entreated him not to deny them the gift of God and the aid destined for them by divine providence. And to remove all doubt, using his paw as a hand, he tore off the skin of the she-wolf from the head down to the navel, folding it back. Thus she immediately presented the form of an old woman.

When the priest saw this, compelled by fear more than by reason, he gave the communion, whereof the recipient partook devoutly. Immediately afterward the he-wolf rolled back the skin and fitted it to its original form.

These rites having been duly rather than rightly performed, the he-wolf gave the travellers his company during the whole night at their little fire, behaving more like a man than a beast. When morning came, he led them out of the wood, and leaving the priest to pursue his journey, pointed out to him the direct road for a long distance. At his departure he also gave him many thanks for the benefit he had conferred, promising him still greater returns of gratitude if the Lord should call him back from his present exile, two parts of which he had already completed.

"I recall that story," said Henry Castide, "though the circumstances took place out of my district."

"Somewhere," said Étienne de Bourbon, "I have read that a similar curse was visited upon the inhabitants of Kent by St Austin. When they refused to listen to his teaching, and drove him out of town by flinging fish-tails at him, the saint prayed that God might send them a shameful token; and thereafter the children of that region were born with tails. Surely Gregory was right when he warned Austin through Mellitus—*duris mentibus simul omnia abscidere impossibile esse*. And that is a saying which applies also to other times and other places."

"Some people, particularly the Gauls," said John Major, "tell that story with great unction. But if it ever happened that the citizens of Rochester were born with tails, it must surely have been for a time only, as a warning not to contemn the teachers of divine things."

"I have travelled in various parts of the world, too," spoke up Jean d'Outremeuse, "nor did I fail to note down the legends connected with the various places which I visited. Your werwolves were condemned to only seven years' transformation. But what would you say to the case of a lady transformed to dragon shape, and bereft finally of all hope of release?"

"We could answer that question better if we knew the story," said Colin Clout.

"Then I will tell it," said the notary of Liège.

15. THE LADY OF LANGO

Jean d'Outremeuse

When I was in the east I spent some time at Patera, where St Nicholas was born. From Patera the way lies past the island of Crete, which the emperor gave to the Genoese. Thence one passes to the isles of Colchos and Lango, and of these islands Hippocrates was once lord. It is said that Hippocrates' daughter, in the likeness of a great dragon, still dwells in the island of Lango. Some say she is a hundred fathoms long: I do not know, for I never saw her. They of the isles call her the lady of the land. She lies in a cave in an old castle and makes her appearance but twice or thrice a year, and does no harm to any man unless he harms her. She was thus changed and transformed from a fair damsel by a goddess called Diana. And it is said that she shall endure in that form till there come a knight who is so hardy that he dares to kiss her mouth; then she shall return to her own nature and be a woman again, but shall not live long thereafter.

Not long since, indeed, a knight of the Hospital of Rhodes, hardy and doughty in arms, said he would kiss her. He mounted his horse, rode up to the castle and entered the cave. But when the dragon lifted up her head towards him, and he saw her in such a hideous and horrible form, he fled away. But the dragon caught him and carried him to a high rock in spite of himself, and from that cliff she cast him into the sea, so that both horse and man were lost.

According to another legend, a young man who knew nothing of the dragon, disembarked at Lango and went through the island till he came to the castle and the cave. On exploring it he found a chamber, wherein he saw a damsel looking in a mirror and combing her hair. There was much treasure lying about her, so he thought she was a common woman who received men there to do folly. At length the damsel saw his shadow in the mirror and asked him what he wanted. He replied that he would be her paramour. She inquired if he were a knight, and he said that he was not. Under those circumstances, she said, he could not be her leman; he must return to his companions, have himself knighted, and come to her on the morrow. She would come out of the cave to him and he should kiss her on the mouth. She said also that he should have no fear, for though he saw her in the likeness of a dragon, she would in no wise harm him. "Though you see me hideous and horrible to look upon," she said, "know that I am so made by enchantment. You may rest assured that I am really a woman as you see me now, so fear nothing. And if you kiss me, you shall have all this treasure and be my lord, and lord of the island also."

The youth returned to his fellows on board ship and had himself dubbed. On the morrow he came back to kiss the damsel, but when he saw her come out of the cave in the form of a hideous and ugly dragon, he was so terrified that he fled back to the ship. She followed him, but when she saw that he would not turn back, she began to cry like a thing that had much sorrow, and returned to her cave. Thereafter the knight died, and every knight who saw her since that time died.

"Your heroine, as you suggest, was a truly unfortunate lady," said Adam Scrivener, "and my heart, though not gentle, is moved with pity for her. I recall a similar situation in one of the odds and ends of manuscripts which my master Chaucer—or perhaps it was Gower —turned over to me for analysis so that he might work it into a story. You know what Chaucer did to it—or perhaps it was Gower. But now I will give you the true version as it came to me in my manuscript."

16. THE WEDDING OF SIR GAWAIN AND DAME RAGNELL

Adam Scrivener

The events of the story I am about to relate took place in the time of Arthur, and that courteous and noble king himself played a large part therein. Arthur was the flower of all kings, and whithersoever he went, he bore away the honour of all knighthood. In his country was naught but chivalry; knights were loved by that doughty king and cowards evermore shent.

Now listen to my tale for a while and I will tell you about King Arthur and what befell him once upon a time. He went with his bold good knights to hunt in Ingleswood. The king was set at his trestle-tree to bring down the wild deer with his bow, and his lords were gathered round him. As the king stood, he caught sight of a large and fair stag, and set forth after him quickly. The hart was in a fern-bracken; he heard the hounds and stood quietly concealed, as the king saw. "Hold still, every man," he said; "I will go myself, if perchance I can stalk him." The king took a bow in his hand, and in woodman-like fashion he stooped low to stalk that deer. When he came close, the stag leaped forth into a briar, and the king followed. Arthur pursued his quarry for about half a mile in this wise, I think, and no man was with him. At last he let fly at the stag and hit him sore and surely, such was his luck. The deer tumbled down into a great brake of fern, and the king brittled him.

Now as the king was alone there with the stag, up came a handsome fellow well armed at all points. A strong and powerful knight he was. Grimly he spoke to the king and said:

"Well met, King Arthur! You have done me wrong many a year, and now I shall pay you back here in kind. I should judge that your life days were about done. Wrongfully did you give my lands to Sir Gawain. What have you to say to that, sir king, now that you are here alone?"

"Sir knight, what is your name, if you can tell it with honour?"

"Sir Gromersomer Joure," he said.

"Ah, Sir Gromersomer, now take thought; you would get no honour by slaying me here. Remember that you are a knight. If you kill me now in this case, all knights will refuse your company everywhere so that shame shall never be apart from you. Forget your intention and be sensible, and whatever is amiss, I will amend it before I go."

"Nay," said Sir Gromersomer, "by the king of heaven! I tell no lie when I say that you shall not escape so. I have you at my advantage now, and if I were to let you go thus with mockery, another time you would certainly defy me."

Said the king: "So help me God! except my life, ask whatever you wish, and I will grant it. You will win only shame by slaying me in venery, you armed, and I clothed only in green."

"All this will certainly not help you," said Sir Gromersomer, "for as a matter of fact, I wish neither land nor gold, but only that you shall meet me on a certain day, which I will set, and in the same clothing."

"Very well," said the king; "here is my hand on it."

"Yea, but wait, O King, and hear me a little: First you shall swear upon my brown sword that when you come again you will show me what it is that women love best in country and town; and you shall meet me here without fail this day twelvemonth; and you shall swear upon my good sword that, by the Rood, none of your knights shall come with you, either known or unknown. And if you do not bring an answer, you shall certainly lose your head for your trouble. What say you, O King? Come, now, have done."

"Sir," replied Arthur, "though I am loath, I agree to your conditions. I promise that as I am a true king I will come again at this twelvemonth's end and bring your answer. Now let me go."

"Go your way, then, King Arthur. Your life is in my hand, I am sure. You do not know what grief is in store for you. But take care, King Arthur, and think not to beguile me. Keep this matter close, for if I thought you intended to betray me, by Mary mild, you should lose your life first!"

"Nay," replied Arthur; "that cannot be; you shall never find me an untrue knight; I had rather die first. If I am alive, I will come on the appointed day, even though I should not escape death. Farewell, sir knight, ill met!"

The king blew his bugle; all the knights heard it and recognized its note and rushed to him. They found the king and the deer. But their lord's cheer was heavy; no lust had he to laugh. "Let us go home to Carlisle, now," said King Arthur, "I am not well pleased with this hunt."

To Carlisle came the king, and his heart was wondrous heavy, but no man knew the cause of his melancholy. Therein he abode so long that many knights marvelled. At last Sir Gawain said to the king:

"Sire, I wonder very much what grieves you so sorely."

"Gentle Sir Gawain," said Arthur, "I will tell you. As you know, I was hunting in Ingleswood and I brought down a hart all alone, by myself. There I met an armed knight who told me his name was Sir Gromersomer Joure. It is on his account that I make moan, for he threatened me direly and would have slain me violently; but I spoke him fair, for I had no weapons about me. Alas! On that account my worship is now gone."

"On what account?" asked Gawain.

"What is the use of words? I do not lie when I say he would have slain me without mercy, and that pleased me ill. He made me swear that at the twelvemonth's end I would meet him again, and thereto I plighted my troth. Also, on that day, I should be prepared to tell him what it is that women desire most; otherwise I should lose my life. I gave my oath on this, and swore also that I would tell the matter to nobody, for I had no choice. If I fail to bring an answer, I know I shall be killed straightway, for part of the condition was that I should come back in no different accoutrement than I then bore. This is the cause of my dread and fear, so blame me not if I am a woeful man."

"Yea, Sire," said Gawain, "be of good cheer. Have your horse made ready to ride into strange countries; and wherever you meet a man or a woman, ask what they say in answer to your question. And I will ride another way and make inquiry of every man and woman, and write their answers down in a book."

"By the Holy Rood," said the king, "this is well advised, O Gawain the good."

Soon both Gawain and the king were ready. Arthur rode one way, Gawain another. Each continually inquired of man and woman what it was that women held most dear. Some said they loved to be well dressed; some said they loved solicitous attention; some said they loved a lusty man to hold them in their arms and kiss them. Some said one thing, some another. In this wise Gawain got many an answer, and by the time he returned to court he had a great book full. The king also returned with his book, and each examined the other's record.

"This can hardly fail," said Gawain.

"By God," said the king, "I am sore adread. I will search a little more in Ingleswood. I have but a month to my appointed day, and I may hit upon some good tiding."

"Do as you please," answered Gawain; "whatever you do is agreeable to me; it is well to be inquiring. But have no fear, my lord, but that you shall speed well. Some of your saws will meet your need, otherwise it were fearful bad luck."

The next day King Arthur rode into Ingleswood. There he met a lady: she was far and away the most ungoodly creature that man ever saw, and King Arthur was vastly amazed by the sight of her. Her face was red, and her nose snotted all over. Her mouth was wide, her teeth yellow and protruding over her lips; her cheeks were as broad as a woman's hips, and her bleary eyes were larger than balls. On her back it seemed she bore a lute. Her neck was long and thick; her hair was cluttered in a tangle; a yard wide she was in the shoulders, with hanging paps that would have been a load for any horse; and her figure was like that of a barrel. Indeed, there is no tongue able to rehearse the foulness of that lady, for she had enough and to spare of loathsomeness. But the palfrey on which she sat was richly caparisoned, adorned with gold and many a precious stone. That was an unseemly sight—so extraordinarily foul a creature to ride so gaily; there was neither reason nor right in it. She rode up to Arthur and said:

"God speed you, O king! I am well pleased to meet you. If you will take my advice, you will speak with me now before you ride farther. I warn you that your life is in my hand."

"Why, lady, what would you with me?"

"Sir, I should like to speak with you and tell you true tidings, for none of the answers that you are able to rehearse will help you at all. That is the truth, by the Rood. You think I do not know your secret; but I warn you that I know every bit of it. Unless I help you, you are no better than dead. Sir king, grant me but one thing and I will guarantee to save your life; otherwise you shall lose your head."

"Lady, what do you mean? Tell me quickly, for your words vex me. Tell me why my life is in your hand and I will grant you anything you ask."

"The truth is," answered the lady, "that I am not really a foul thing. You must grant me a knight in marriage: his name is Gawain. For my part I will make covenant with you to the effect that if your life is not saved through my answer, I will relinquish my desire; and if my answer saves your life, you must grant me Gawain as my husband. Choose now, sir king, or else you are but a dead man."

"Mary!" said Arthur. "I cannot guarantee that Gawain will marry you. The decision rests with him alone. But I will do my best in order to save my life. I will put the matter to him."

"Well, go home now and speak Sir Gawain fair. Though I be foul in appearance, nevertheless I am really a lady gay. Through me he can either save your life or assure your death."

"Alas!" cried the king, "woe is me that I should cause Gawain to marry you, for he will be loath to refuse me. So foul a lady as you are I never in my life saw walk on ground. I know not what to do."

"My foulness is beside the point," answered the lady. "Even an owl has a right to choose his mate. You will get no more from me. When you come back with your answer I'll meet you here. If you bring a refusal you are lost."

"Farewell, lady," said the king.

"Yea," she answered, "there is a bird called the owl, and yet a lady I am."

"What is your name, pray?"

"I am called Dame Ragnell, and never yet have I beguiled a man."

"Good day, now, Dame Ragnell."

"God speed you on your way, sir king. I will meet you here to have your answer."

Thus they parted fair and well, and the king rode into Carlisle with a heavy heart. The first man he met was Gawain, who asked him how he had sped. "Forsooth," replied the king, "never so ill. Alas! I am on the point of killing myself, for it seems that I must die at all hazards."

"Nay," said Sir Gawain; "I had rather be dead myself. These are indeed ill tidings."

"Gawain," said Arthur, "today I met the foulest lady I ever saw, truly. She said she would save my life, but first she must have you for her husband. Therefore am I woebegone, therefore do I make my moan."

"Is that all?" asked Gawain. "I will marry her and marry her again, though she were the fiend. If she be as foul as Beelzebub I will marry her, by the Rood, or else I am no friend of yours. You are my liege lord and have supported me honourably in many a stour, and I will not be hanging back now. Now it is my duty to save your life, my lord; otherwise I should prove to be a great and false coward; and my honour will be enhanced thereby. What about the lady?"

"Indeed, Gawain, I met her in Ingleswood. She said her name was Dame Ragnell. She told me that unless I used the answer she would furnish me all my labour would prove to be in vain; and if her answer did not help me in my need, then she would withdraw her demand. But if her answer helped me, then she would have you at all odds. That is the sum of it."

"As regards that," said Gawain, "there will be no difficulty. I will marry her at whatever time you set. And I pray you, take no more thought about the matter, for if she were the foulest wight that ever a man might behold, for your love I would not hesitate."

"Gramercy, Gawain," said King Arthur. "Of all knights whom I have ever known, you are the flower. You save my life and my honour forever, wherefor my love shall never part from you as long as I am king of this land."

Within five or six days Arthur must needs go his ways to render his report; Sir Gawain accompanied him out of town. When they had reached the forest: "Farewell, Sir Gawain," said the king; "I must go west and you shall ride no farther." "God speed you on your journey," answered the knight. The king had ridden hardly more than a mile when he met Dame Ragnell.

"Ah, sir king," said she, "I think you must be riding to give the answer that will avail you nothing."

"Since it cannot be otherwise," said Arthur, "tell me the right answer now and save my life. Gawain has promised to marry you, for my sake, and you shall have your desire in bower and bed. Tell me quickly now, for the time has come, and I dare not tarry."

"Sir, you shall know what women desire most, whether they be of high or low degree, and I assure you that what I say is true. Some say we desire to be fair, or that we wish to be courted by a variety of different men, or that we like to take our pleasure in bed, or that we desire to marry often. But you men know nothing about it. We desire to be considered fresh and young and not old, to be sure, and you men can always win us by flattery and guile and sly tricks, and so get whatever you want; I will not deny that you act cleverly. But the thing wherein rests our entire fancy is something else still; and now you shall know what it is. Above all things, I tell you truly, we desire to have the mastery over men, whether of high or low degree. For though a knight be never so fierce and gain the victory in battle, where we have the sovereignty, all is ours. Such is our craft and our deceit that we would have the control over the manliest of men. So, sir king, wend your ways and reply to the knight as I have said—that what women desire most is lordship. He will be wroth and vexed, and will curse bitterly her who taught you this answer, for his labour will be lost. Go forth, sir king, and keep your promise, for your life is now quite safe, I assure you."

THE WEDDING OF GAWAIN AND RAGNELL 81

Arthur rode forth a great way as fast as he could, through mire, moor and fen to the place of assignation, and there he met Sir Gromersomer, who addressed him sternly.

"Come, now, sir king, let us see what your answer will be, for I am all ready."

The king pulled out two books. "Sir, there is my answer. I daresay one or the other will prove the right one."

Sir Gromersomer read every one of the answers in the two books. "Nay, nay, sir king, you are a dead man and shall bleed now, at once."

"Wait a bit," said Arthur, "I have one other answer which will certainly serve."

"Let me have it then," said Sir Gromersomer, "or else, so help me God, you shall get your death."

"It seems to me," said Arthur, "that I can see very little gentility in you. By God who is ever merciful, here is our answer once and for all: Women desire sovereignty above all things, for that is their pleasure and their wish. If they can rule the manliest of men, then they are happy. Thus did they teach me to rule you, Sir Gromersomer."

"And she who told you, Sir Arthur, I pray to God that I may see her burning in a fire, for she was my sister, Dame Ragnell, the foul scutt, may God give her shame! If it had not been for her, I would have tamed you fully, but now I have lost much labour. Go where you will, King Arthur, for you need have no fear of me from now on. Alas that ever I saw this day! Now I know well that you will be my enemy and that I shall never get you at such an advantage again. Well may my song be: Well-away!"

"You are right," said the king. "I assure you that the next time we meet I shall have some harness wherewith to defend myself. I vow to God you shall never again find me in such a plight. If you do, you may bind and beat me to your heart's content."

"Good day," said Sir Gromersomer.

"Farewell," said King Arthur.

Now Arthur turned his horse toward the plain, and there he soon met Dame Ragnell again in the place where he had left her.

"Sir king," said she, "I am glad that you have been successful. I told you how it would be. Now keep your promise. Since it was I and none other who saved your life, Gawain, the true gentle knight must marry me."

"Nay, lady, I shall not fail to keep my word. You shall have your will, but if you will take my advice, you will marry Gawain secretly."

"Nay, sir king; that I will not do. Before we part you must agree that we be married openly, otherwise you will be shamed. Ride on ahead and I will follow to your court. Do not argue with me; just remember how I saved your life and rest assured that I desire no man's shame."

The king was very much embarrassed by her, but he rode forth for all of that till they came to Carlisle. The lady rode beside him into the court, avoiding no man, and the king liked it ill. All the people wondered hugely whence that foul unsweet thing might come; never had they seen such an ugly creature.

Into the hall rode the lady. "King Arthur," said she, "send quickly for Sir Gawain. Plight our troths for weal or woe in the sight of all your chivalry so that I may be assured. Come now, have done. Bring forth my love Sir Gawain straightway, for I have no desire for further tarrying."

Then Sir Gawain stepped forth. "Sir," he said, "I am ready to keep my promise to you and fulfil all agreements."

"God's mercy!" said Dame Ragnell then; "since you are of such good will, I wish, for your sake, that I were a fair woman."

Thereupon Sir Gawain plighted his troth for weal or woe, as he was a true knight, and Dame Ragnell was happy.

"Alas!" cried Dame Guenevere; and so said all the ladies in her bower, and they wept for Gawain. "Alas!" said both king and knight, "that he should ever wed such a creature." So foul was she, I will not hide it, that on each side of her mouth she had two teeth like boar's tusks, a large handful in length. One tusk went up, the other down. Her mouth was wide, and foully ingrown with many a grey hair. Her lips lay bunched on her chin; and as to neck, forsooth, none was seen on her. She was a loathly one!

Now Dame Ragnell would in no wise consent to be married unless the banns were cried throughout the shire in town and borough; and she summoned all the ladies of the land to come and assist at the bridal.

The day on which Sir Gawain was to be married to that foul lady came at last. All the ladies of the court had great ruth thereof. The queen prayed Dame Ragnell to be married early in the morning as privily as possible. "Nay," said she, "I will not consent to that for anything you can say, by the king of heaven. I will be married openly, for such was the covenant I made with the king, be sure of that. I will not go to church till high mass, and I will dine in the hall in the midst of all the company."

"Very well," said Guenevere, "though the course you have chosen is one which gives you most honour and worship."

"Yea, as for that, lady, God save you. I tell you without boasting that I will have my worship this day."

Finally Dame Ragnell made ready to go to church, and with all possible pomp. She was arrayed in the richest fashion, even more freshly than Dame Guenevere. Her apparel was worth three thousand marks of good red nobles, so richly was she dressed. But in spite of her attire, she bore the bell for foulness above any of whom I have ever heard tell. No man ever saw such a filthy sow. But to conclude: When she was married, all went home and sat at meat, and this ugly lady had the place of honour at the high dais. All said, and it was true, that she was filthy and unmannerly. When the service came to her, she ate as much as six others there, so that many a man marvelled. Her nails were three inches long, and therewith she broke her meat in an ungoodly fashion. Three capons she devoured, and three curlews; and she swallowed down great baked meats, pardee, so that all men were astonished. No dish came before her but she ate it up to the last morsel—that pretty foul damsel! Everyone who beheld her, both knight and squire, bade the devil gnaw her bones. So she ate till dinner was done, the cloths removed and hands washed, as the custom is.

Many would tell of the divers dishes served at the feast, but you may take it for granted that there was enough of both tame and wild. In King Arthur's court there was no lack of anything that might be obtained by the hand of man, whether in forest or field. There were, too, minstrels of divers countries, who probably did their best to enliven that sad feast. I cannot say for sure, for at this point in the narrative there was a leaf missing in my manuscript. But as the proverb says, "Be the day never so long, at last it ringeth to evensong," and finally it came time for the newly wedded pair to retire. When they were alone in their chamber and the lights had been extinguished: "Ah," said Dame Ragnell, "since I have married you, now show me your courtesy in bed; it cannot be rightly denied. Indeed, my lord, if I were fair you would act differently than you do. You pay no heed to the rights and obligations of wedlock, yet, for Arthur's sake, kiss me at least. Grant me this request and let us see how you speed."

"Before God," answered Gawain, "I will do more than kiss you." Then he turned towards her, and what he saw was far and away the fairest creature he had ever beheld. "What is your will?" asked Dame Ragnell. "Ah, Jesus," cried Gawain, "who are you?" "Sir," she answered, "I am your wife. Why do you act so strangely?" "Ah, lady, my fair one, I am at fault and I cry you mercy. It was not my intention to be rude, but I see you now a fair lady whereas earlier today you were the foulest wight that ever I set eyes upon. Happy am I, lady, to have you thus."

Therewith Gawain clasped her in his arms and kissed her and made great joy, I assure you.

Said Dame Ragnell: "You shall choose one of two things, so God save me, for my beauty will not last: Will you have me fair by night and foul to all men's sight by day, or will you have me fair by day, and as ugly as possible at night? Choose one or the other, for one or the other you must needs have. Choose, sir knight, which you would rather have to save your worship."

"Alas!" answered Gawain, "the choice is hard. To have you fair only by night would grieve me sorely and cause me to lose my worship. And if I choose to have you fair by day, then I should have rude fare at night. I would willingly choose the best, but I know not what in the world to say. But you, my fair lady, do as pleases you. I put the decision in your hand. I leave the matter entirely to you so that you can loose me whenever you please, for I am bound whichever way I turn. Body, heart, goods, all are yours to buy and sell as you please, I swear to God."

"Gramercy, courteous knight," replied the lady. "Blessed may you be above all earthly knights, for now I am treated with honour. Consequently, you shall have me fair both night and day, and bright and fresh as long as I live; so be not any longer grieved. My stepdame—God have mercy on her!—transformed me by witchcraft and necromancy, and it was my fate to retain that deformed shape until the best knight of England had married me and given me authority over himself and his goods. And you, sir knight, courteous Gawain, have given sovereignty to one who will not vex you early or late. Kiss me, sir knight, right now and here. Pray be glad and make good cheer, for all has now turned out well for me."

Then the two of them made more joy than can be told, as was reasonable and natural. The lady thanked God and Mary that she had been rescued from her foul form, and so did Gawain. He made good cheer and thanked the Lord, I tell you truly.

Thus they passed the night with joy and mirth till daybreak, when that fair lady made ready to rise. "You shall not get up yet," said Gawain, "but lie and sleep till prime, and then let the king call us to meat." "Very well," said she. And thus the day wore on till noon.

"My lords," said the king, "let us go and find out if Gawain is still alive. I am very much afraid lest the fiend have slain him." When they had come to the chamber: "Arise," said the king; "why are you lying abed so long?" "Marry, sir king," replied Gawain, "I should take it as a favour if you would leave me alone, for I am well at ease. But wait a little and I will unfasten the door; then I think you will see that things have turned out well for me and understand why I am loath to rise."

Sir Gawain rose and took his fair lady by the hand, went to the door and opened it wide. There she stood in her smock by her lord, her hair, as red as gold, falling down to her knees. "Behold," said Gawain to Arthur, "this is my solace, my wife, Dame Ragnell, who once saved your life."

"Sir Gawain," said the queen, "thank God. I thought she would have ruined you, and was sore aggrieved in my heart; but now I see it is otherwise."

Then there was game and revel and sport, and everyone said to the other: "She is a fair wight." Afterwards the king told them all how Dame Ragnell had helped him at his need. And he related to the queen how he had been bestead in Ingleswood by Sir Gromersomer Joure, and what the knight had made him swear. Then Gawain told the king and the company how Dame Ragnell had been misshaped by her stepmother until such time as a knight came to her aid. And for her part she told the king what choice she had offered Gawain, and how he had resigned decision to her. "May God reward him for his courtesy," she said, "for he has saved me from ill hap and villainy, and a state that was foul and grim. Wherefor, courteous knight and gentle Gawain, I shall surely never do anything to vex you, I promise you that here and now. As long as I live I shall be obedient—I swear it by God above—and never strive nor quarrel with you."

"Gramercy, lady," replied Gawain. "I am right happy with you, and trust to continue so. Since you have been so kind to me, you shall have my love nor never need to ask for it."

Said the queen and all the ladies: "She is the fairest in all the hall, by St John!" And Guenevere added: "Lady, you shall always have my love for saving my lord Arthur, I swear as I am a gentlewoman."

To Gawain Dame Ragnell bore a son whom they called Gyngolyn, a knight of good strength and blood, who became a member of the Round Table. When that lady was present at any great feast, she always bore away the prize for fairness and beauty wherever she went.

Gawain loved Dame Ragnell as he had never loved any other in all his life, I tell you truly. Indeed, he lay by her day and night like a coward, no longer frequenting jousts and tournaments as he should have done. Thereat the king was greatly astonished. She, for her part, besought Arthur, of his courtesy, to be a good lord to

Sir Gromersomer as regards the matter wherein he had offended. "Very well, lady, for your sake," said the king, "for I know that he is unable to make adequate amends for the discourtesy he did me."

Now I will make a short conclusion of this gentle lady's story. She lived with Gawain only five years, and that was a grief to Gawain all his life. In all her days she never vexed or annoyed him, wherefor no woman was dearer to him. When she was alive she was the fairest lady in all England—so said the king.

Thus ends the adventure of King Arthur who in his life was often sorely grieved, and the Wedding of Sir Gawain. Many times was Gawain married, but he never loved any other woman so dearly, as I have heard tell.

"We will all bow, I think, to the courtesy and breeding of Gawain," said King Hákon.

"We will concede further that he was a strong man of his hands in battle," said Sturla the Lawman. "But everyone knows, too, that there always hung about him an afflatus of divinity, or if you will, of the supernatural. The dog may indeed break his chain, but always he drags behind him a few links as he flees. So with Gawain and his pristine divinity. We of the North also had those demigods, but we saw in the end that men, as men, were far worthier of our admiration.—Now since some strictures have been passed on jousts and tourneys, and the quality of heroism therein displayed has been questioned, I would call to your attention what seems to me an example of very high spiritual as well as physical courage."

"Tell on!" cried Guilhem IX and his great-grandson Richard.

"I will," said Sturla, "the more willingly because I am glad to render tribute to a brave man, even though he was an enemy of my family."

17. EYJOLF'S LAST FIGHT
Sturla the Lawman

When Bishop Gudmund, through the vicissitudes of his struggle with the Sturlungs, was driven to take refuge on the island of Grimsey, there were few men who stood by him save the kinsmen Eyjolf and Aron. Sighvat Sturlason and his son Sturla fell upon him there. The bishop's followers fought manfully, but were outnumbered, and Aron was sorely wounded. Eyjolf found him sitting in the place where he had fought with Sturla, his weapons by him, and all about him lay dead men and wounded. Eyjolf asked his kinsman whether he felt able to get away or not. Aron said he was able, and stood up. Then the two of them went along the shore till they came to a hidden creek, where they saw a boat ready afloat, with five or six men at the oars, and the prow from land. This was Eyjolf's provision in case it proved necessary to get away quickly. Eyjolf told his cousin that the boat was intended for both of them, for he saw no hope of doing more for the bishop at that time. "But," said he, "I have no doubt that better days are in store for us." "This seems strange business to me," said Aron, "for it was my thought that we should never abandon Bishop Gudmund in his trouble. I have a suspicion that there is something behind this, and I will not go on board the boat unless you go first." "Kinsman," said Eyjolf, "I will not do that, for the water is very shallow here, and I will not have any of the rowers leave his oars in order to shove off; moreover, it is farther than you can walk with wounds like yours; so you will have to go out to the boat." "Well," said Aron, "I will believe you if you will lay your weapons in the craft."

Eyjolf did as Aron asked him, and the wounded man got aboard. Eyjolf waded after the boat, for the shallows extended considerable distance. Then, when he thought he had gone far enough, he snatched up a heavy battle-axe out of the stern and gave the boat a shove with all his might. "Farewell, Aron," said Eyjolf; "we shall meet again when God pleases." And since Aron had many and severe wounds, and was growing weak with loss of blood, it had to be as Eyjolf wished. Aron thought this a grievous parting, for he never saw his kinsman again. Eyjolf called to the boatmen and told them to row hard, and not to let Aron come back again that day, nor for many a day if they could prevent it.

Now Aron went his ways, but Eyjolf returned to the land, to a boat-house wherein there was a large scow belonging to Gnup the bonder. At the same moment he saw the Sturlung band come rushing down from the settlement after their ill work there. He retired quickly to Gnup's boat-house and took his stand there, resolving to defend it as long as he was able. There were double doors to the boat-house, and these he buttressed with heavy stones.

There was a man named Brand, a famous warrior, one of Sighvat's followers. He caught sight of a man moving, and said he thought he recognized Eyjolf Karsson there, and that they ought to make for him. Without Sturla, who was absent, there were nine or ten men altogether. They came up to the boat-house where Eyjolf was, and Brand asked who was there. Eyjolf named himself. "Then you will please come out," says Brand, "and come before Sturla." "Will you promise me safe conduct?" asks Eyjolf. "There will be scant amount of that," answers Brand. "Then it is for you to come to me," says Eyjolf, "and for me to be on guard. And it seems to me the shares of this business are unfairly divided."

Eyjolf was wearing a coat of mail and had a great axe, and that was all the arms he possessed. Now the men set upon him, and he defended himself well and valiantly. He cut their spear-shafts through. There were many stout blows on both sides. In that onset Eyjolf broke his axe-haft; but he seized an oar and defended himself therewith, and then he took another; but both broke with the violence of his blows. Then Eyjolf got a thrust under his arm and it went through. Some say he broke the shaft from the spear-point and let it stay in the wound. He saw that now his defence was at an end, so he made a dash out, and that succeeded before his assailants were aware of it. And though they were surprised, they were not long at a loss: A man named Mar hewed at his ankle so that his foot hung by a shred, and therewith Eyjolf limped down to the beach, where the sea was at high tide. In such plight Eyjolf made shift to swim, and reached a skerry lying twelve fathoms from shore. He knelt down there, and afterwards fell at his length upon the earth, where he stretched out his hands and turned to the east as if to pray.

Now the Sturlungs launched a boat to search for Eyjolf. When they came to the skerry a man drove a spear into him, and then another; but no blood flowed from either wound. So they left him and went back to land to find Sturla and give him a faithful account of all their doings. When Sturla heard their news he agreed with the other men that this had been a glorious defence.

The company were silent for a while when Sturla had finished, and only the crackling of the logs in the great fire-place could be heard, while the flames cast shifting shadows from end to end of the long hall. Finally Fulk Fitzwarin spoke:

"That was a brave man; I never heard of a braver. Yet I beg leave to tell of one of my countrymen, who may also be considered to have been a man of courage, for he fought with the fiend himself. His adventure took place not far from here in the early years of King William's occupation of this island."

18. PAYN PEVEREL'S ENCOUNTER WITH GOGMAGOG

Fulk Fitzwarin

As William the Bastard was making his progress through Wales, he observed a very large town, now burned and ruined, but which had once been enclosed by high walls. He had his pavilions set up in the plain below the town, and camped there that night. Thereafter the king inquired of a native Briton the name of the town and the reason of its ruin.

"Sire," said the Briton, "I will tell you. Formerly the castle was called Castle Bran, but now it is called La Vele Marche. In olden days Brutus, a very valiant knight, came into this country, and with him Corineus, from whom Cornwall is named, with many others of Trojan lineage. At that time these parts were uninhabited save by a very ugly people, great giants, whose king was called Gogmagog. These giants learned of Brutus' arrival, and marched to oppose him. In the end all the giants were killed except Gogmagog, who was marvellously big. The valiant knight Corineus said that he would like to wrestle with Gogmagog to try his strength. At the first encounter the giant hugged Corineus so straitly that he broke three of his ribs. This annoyed Corineus, and he gave Gogmagog such a kick that he sent him flying from a high rock into the sea, and there he was drowned. But afterwards a demoniac spirit entered the body of Gogmagog and haunted these parts, and so lorded it over the country for a long time that no Briton dared live there. Many years afterwards Bran, the son of Donwal, rebuilt the city, raised the walls, cleaned out the ditches, set up a fort and a great market-place. But when all this had been done, the devil came by night and bore away everything within the city, and no one has dared live there from that out."

The king was greatly astonished at this tale. Payn Peverel, a proud and hardy knight, cousin to the king, who had heard everything, said that that very night he would test the truth of that marvel. Accordingly he armed himself richly and took his shield shining with gold whereon there was a cross "azure endentee," and with fifteen knights and their sergeants proceeded to the highest palace, and took up his stand there.

When night had fallen the weather became so ugly, black and thick, with a tempest of thunder and lightning, that all the party became so frightened they could move neither hand nor foot, but lay flat on the earth as though dead. The sturdy Payn was also much frightened, but he trusted in God and in the sign of the cross which he bore, for he saw that he should have no aid save from God alone. He knelt and devoutly prayed God and Mary to help him that night against the power of the devil.

Hardly had Payn finished his prayer when the devil, in the guise of Gogmagog, made his appearance, bearing a great mace in his hand, and casting such fire and smoke from his mouth that the whole town was illuminated. Payn made the sign of the cross and attacked the demon valiantly. The sprite raised his mace to strike Payn, but the knight avoided the blow and put forward his shield. Thereupon the devil, by virtue of the cross, was frightened and lost his strength, for demons cannot endure that sign. Payn now advanced upon his foe and struck him such a blow with his sword that he fell flat to the ground. He surrendered and said: "Knight, you have conquered me, not by your own strength, but by virtue of the cross which you bear." "Tell me, foul creature that you are," said Payn, "who you are, and what your business is in this town. I conjure you in the name of God and the holy cross." Then the demon began to tell, word for word, the story already related earlier by the Briton.

At the close of Fulk's narrative there was an uneasy stirring among the shadows, and one shadow seemed to grow darker and thicker and higher as it detached itself from the rest, and finally assumed the shape of a man taller by three times than the tallest man in the hall.

The man, or the shadow, spoke and said: "I had thought, and hoped, to rest in peace, but the good knight yonder has stirred the bones of memory; and since he has told the last chapter of an eventful history, it is only right that you should know how it began."

No one said him nay.

19. THE BLOOD-LUST OF ALBINA AND WHAT CAME OF IT

Gogmagog

Thirty-nine hundred and seventy years after the beginning of the world there lived in Greece a puissant king, valiant, noble and proud, for he was over-king above all other potentates. A beautiful and noble wife he had, who bore him thirty daughters, very beautiful, all of them. I do not know their names, except that the eldest daughter, a very handsome wench, was called Albina.

When the girls were the proper age their father and mother gave them in marriage to kings and princes of noble line, and each one thus became a queen. But by reason of their excessive pride they thought up a fearful outrage, which in the end turned out ill for them. They secretly took counsel together and determined that none should be such a silly fool as to suffer the mastery of lord or neighbour, brother, cousin or husband; they were the daughters of a very powerful king, who was subject to none, nor would they consent to be subject to any; rather, said they, they would be mistresses over their husbands and whatever they possessed.

When they had reached this conclusion the women took oaths that each on one and the same day would kill her husband as he lay in her arms expecting nothing but solace; and they set the day. All agreed, as you have heard, except the youngest, for she loved her husband, and was in no wise inclined to commit so grievous a sin against him. However, in council she said nothing, for she dared not oppose her sisters: they would have killed her without mercy or hesitation had they found her to be at variance with them.

On reaching home the youngest sister was so ill able to conceal her distress that her husband noticed it and inquired into its cause. She threw herself at his feet and cried for mercy for the great treachery which had been plotted, revealing how her sisters had forced her to swear his death. The young man took her in his arms, and kissed and comforted her. "Lady," said he, "be quiet now and let this pass."

The next day the young prince made ready to go to the king his father-in-law, and bade his wife come with him. When the two young people had told him in detail what his daughters had plotted, the king was much astonished, and caused their consorts to be summoned. On their arrival he roundly rated his daughters for the fearful treachery which they had intended against their husbands, pointing out the great shame and dishonour which it reflected on both them and him. The women were greatly dismayed to find that their purpose had been discovered, and each defended herself as well as she could. But their words were in vain, for the king was so wroth that he would have put them all to death. He questioned each one very shrewdly so that in the end each stood accused of outrageous malice except the youngest. Thereupon all the king's daughters, except the youngest, were seized and cast into prison, where they suffered great penance, awaiting the day of judgment.

Now the judges were wise, and on account of their noble and honourable lineage, as well as for the honour of their husbands, it was their decision that the prisoners should not suffer a shameful death; but they unanimously agreed, and so it was doomed, that they should be exiled from their native land for all time without reprieve. This doom they must needs abide, willy-nilly. Accordingly the women were led to the seaport and put aboard a great ship unprovided with tackle, and without food. They cried out miserably, but no one had any pity on them because of their great sin.

The boat was shoved off, the waves dashed it here and there until they were upon the open sea. Now these women, who had once been rich queens, might well wonder whether they would escape with their lives or not. The boat tossed at the mercy of the wind and sea; huge waves threatened them; but nothing caused them so much distress as the hunger which increased day by day. At other times they were so frightened by the peril of the sea that they forgot their hunger. The wind and the waves dashed and shook them, now up, now down, so that finally they fell into a swoon for three days and three nights, and lay prone here and there in the boat.

At last the fierce storm carried them near to a shore of land. The weather cleared and the ship flew along by the west till it grounded on the land which today is called England, though at that time it had no name, for no man inhabited it. Then the flood of the sea retreated, leaving the ship high and dry on the shore. The ladies now came to their senses, and rejoiced greatly at having made land at last. Albina, the eldest, leaped ashore before her sisters, and standing upon the ground took seisin thereof. After her came the others, considerably weakened by the rigours of the sea and their long fast.

Now their great hunger came upon them again as they sat weak and dejected upon the strand. They had no thought for anything except food, and for want of anything else, they ate the raw fruits and herbs which they found in abundance; there were plenty of acorns, haws, chestnuts, sorbs, pears and apples; other meat they found none.

The sisters wondered greatly where they might be, what was the name of the country, and whether it was at war or peace. As they recovered somewhat from their harrowing experience, they wandered farther inland to find out what manner of people lived there. On this errand they roamed all over the land without encountering a human being in wood or plain, mountain or valley, nor did they see any evidence that man or woman had been there before them; which astonished the sisters hugely. Wild beasts, however, they found in great numbers, and land birds, and rivers full of fish.

Finally, when they had made certain that they had come to an uninhabited country and that there was no means of returning to their own land, Albina said: "It is sure that we are exiled from home, and it is our destiny never to return to it. But Fortune has granted us this land, and thereof I should be the chief ruler, for it is I who took seisin of it on issuing from the sea. If anyone wishes to dispute this matter, let her show reason why it should not be as I say." All readily agreed that she should be their chief. Then said the lady Albina: "Here we shall stay, for the land lacks nothing."

By this time the ladies were growing hungry for meat, for they saw great numbers of wild animals and flocks of birds which tempted their appetite. For a long time they considered ways and means whereby they might catch bird or beast. They were well skilled in hunting, both in the wood and along the river, it is true, but in the present circumstances they had neither bow nor arrows, neither falcon nor dog wherewith they might take any prey fit for food. However, they were cunning and ingenious, and with withes and branches they constructed more than a hundred devices for taking deer and wildfowl; and so cleverly did they make their traps that they took as many beasts and birds as they could wish. They made fire by striking flints, and when the venison was dressed, they seethed the flesh in the hides, or else roasted it over the coals; and for drink they had water of the spring.

Thus these sisters led their life till health and strength were restored and they began to build up blood and flesh. Thereupon natural heat aroused in them an overwhelming libidinous desire and yearning for human company. Now the demons who are called *incubi*— that is, spirits who have the power of assuming human form—perceived how these women were tormented by the desire of the flesh, and so lay with them, and afterwards disappeared. Each lady had a demon for herself. Never did they see their paramours, but only felt them, as a woman should in such cases.

In this wise were engendered the children who became giants and afterwards held sway over the land. And later, when the children had arrived at maturity, they lay with their mothers and aunts, with their brothers and sisters, and got male and female children who likewise grew up into tall strong giants. You know this to be true by reason of the great bones which have been found in many places in the island; numerous great teeth, rib and leg bones, and thigh-bones four feet long have been discovered, and shoulder-blades as large as shields have been seen, too.

This demoniacal people increased so greatly in number that they finally spread over all the land. They made caves in the earth and surrounded them with walls and dikes. The remnants of their great walls are still visible in many places, though they have been largely cast down by time and the forces of nature. Some of the giants, too, took up their dwellings in the mountains, where they thought to find greater security.

Now these giants held the land till the Britons came, and that was in the year 1136 before Christ. And from the time when the women gave the name Albion to the island until Brut took away that name and called it Britain, was 260 years, according to your chroniclers. In this period the giants multiplied to such an extent and became so haughty and overbearing that each wished to be lord over all the others. Strife broke out among them for this reason, and so fiercely did they fight among themselves that at last only twenty-four of them were left when Brut arrived in the land. The Britons conquered all the giants save one, who was their chief. Brut spared his life, for he marvelled at his bigness—twenty feet long he was. Brut inquired of him his lineage, and how his ancestors had come to the island. The giant related all that I have just told you; his name was Gogmagog, and I am he.

The cavernous voice ceased, and the thick patch of gloom that had seemed a man or a giant disintegrated in the light of the dancing flames as the Curtal Friar stirred the logs.

John Major looked about shrewdly to see how many of his companions had been impressed by this story. His glance met that of William Camden, who smiled slightly, whereupon he shrugged and forbore to speak.

A brand cracked and flew out of the fire-place, blazing at the feet of Blind Harry. "I am reminded," said the minstrel, as he threw it back into the fire, "of an adventure that befell William Wallace in the early years of his struggles against the southern enemy. It was something to try the nerves of even so wicht a man as he."

20. THE GHOST OF FAWDOUN

Blind Harry

One time the English of Perth thought to take Wallace as he lay with his mistress in her house. But she confessed to him how they had threatened to burn her and had so forced her to connive at his betrayal. Wallace kissed her and forgave her. Then, disguising himself in one of her dresses, he stole out through the pickets and joined his band of forty men.

When Sir John Butler found that his prey had escaped him, he set out in pursuit with a detachment of three hundred. Wallace fought his way through to Tay-side, but half his men could not swim, so he turned about to make for Gask Wood, fighting Butler's men as he went. He escaped, indeed, but with only sixteen followers.

As Wallace pressed on toward Gask Wood one of his men, Fawdoun, grew weary and said he could go no farther. This seemed strange, for Fawdoun was a sturdy man and had suffered but little fatigue. But he was known to be of brittle temper. If Wallace left him behind and he proved false, he would go over to the English; if he were a true man, the Southrons would slay him. So Wallace drew his sword and took the head off him.

With thirteen men Wallace entered Gask Hall and took lodging there. They soon had a fire going, but food they had none till they took two sheep from a near-by fold. While the men were hurriedly preparing something to eat they heard a loud and raucous blast of horns, and Wallace sent out two men to find out what might be forward. They were gone for a long time, but no tidings did he get, and the harsh noise of the fiercely blowing horns continued. Then Wallace sent two other men into the wood, but they did not come back, and the horns continued to blow. Angrily Wallace sent out others; and when he was finally left alone, the awful blast grew louder and louder. Sir William thought the English must have discovered his retreat, so he drew his sword and went in the direction of the noise. But just beyond the threshold it seemed to Wallace that he was met by Fawdoun carrying his own head in his hand. As Fawdoun suddenly hurled the head at him, Wallace caught it by the hair and flung it back. Sir William was greatly terrified, for he thought that this was no human sprite, but rather some demon playing sad jokes. It occurred to him that there was little advantage in remaining longer where he was, so he ran up through the hall to a stair leading to the close. As he ran the planks broke in two, so that he made a fifteen-foot leap out of that inn.

Sir William took his way hastily up stream, and as he looked back it seemed to him that the ugly Fawdoun had set the whole hall on fire, and stood in the midst of it with a great flaming rafter in his hand.

Wallace would tarry no longer. He marvelled greatly that his men could have become lost through this fearful fantasy. By reason of such demoniacal mischief they might have been slain by the English, or drowned. Glad enough was he to escape from that cruel peril, whatever was the cause of it. Sir William took his way thence, mourning for his men, and trying in his own mind to find some reason why, if he had pleased God, He should put him to such tests. And as he walked he took thought how he might have amends from the English.

"Speaking of ghosts and demons," said Jehan Madot, "I recall part of a romance which I was one time copying at Arras. The hero was named Amadas, and the heroine Ydoine. Amadas loved the lady madly—and that is no figure of speech, as I will show you on another occasion—and after suffering terrible vicissitudes of fortune, it seemed that the course of true love was about to run smoothly for him again, when it was interrupted by a demon. Ydoine, on her way from Nevers to Rome to obtain spiritual advice, found her lover at Lucca. While she pursued her journey to the holy city, Amadas attended a tournament in the neighbourhood."

21. HOW AMADAS FOUGHT WITH THE FIEND AT THE TOMB OF YDOINE

Jehan Madot

On the day of his return to Lucca after his glorious exploits at the tournament Amadas received the very welcome news that Ydoine and her escort had been observed approaching the city. He rode out to meet her and himself conduct her into Lucca.

Ydoine's man, Garinet, and the baggage had already arrived at the hotel, and she was following along behind at her leisure, her palfrey being led by a trusted old knight, as the custom was. As they were traversing a small bridge over a low ravine just outside the city, a big handsome knight on horseback started up from the bridge-head at the right, seized Ydoine, placed her on the saddle in front of himself, and dashed away at a gallop. The few men-at-arms who followed her were not too amazed to set off in pursuit, and those who had gone on ahead now returned and blocked the stranger knight's way at the head of the pass. When he saw that his purpose had failed, the stranger set Ydoine down, and vanished suddenly and mysteriously. At this moment Amadas rode up with a great crowd of people and conducted her joyfully into town.

But alas! the world is unstable, and evil fortune still pursued these two lovers. When the company had sat down to dinner and the seneschal was serving the first course, Ydoine was seized with such cruel and grievous illness that she became black and blue and green, and lost her strength. From time to time she fainted and lost her power of speech. In torment like this she endured for a long time— nearly five hundred lines.—Finally, about vespers, Countess Ydoine passed away with the setting of the sun.

On the outskirts of the city of Lucca was an antique place, broad, level and cleanly, and enclosed by a wall. All the noble men and women of the land were buried there. There too they buried Ydoine in a tomb of black marble, and commending her body and soul to

God they returned to the city. There was nothing else to do, for, as my author laconically observed: The living to life and the dead to death. That is the way of the world and will be always.

Ydoine's men made their preparations to continue their journey home to Nevers. They asked Amadas if he would accompany them, but he declined their invitation, saying that he had business in Lucca which would keep him there for a time.

That night, when all the city slept, Amadas rose quietly and dressed; and since he did not know what might happen, he put on his armour. Then he mounted horse, and taking lance and shield, rode away from the hostel till he came to the place of antiquity outside the city. There he dismounted and tied his horse securely to a branchy pine. His shining shield and his lance he set up against the wall, for he thought that he should be safe enough. Thereupon he went to Ydoine's tomb, and with bowed head made his bitter lament. Tears dropped from his eyes upon the cold marble, and such was his anguish that it is a wonder his heart did not break. He knelt and rose, and then he knelt again. He embraced the tomb and kissed the cold marble a hundred times, sighing and sorrowing. There he made his moan— for about a hundred lines—after which, for very anguish and weakness he had to sit down by the tomb, bedewing the black marble with his tears. Never would he part from it, he thought.

But as Amadas was sitting there within the enclosure, hearken to the marvel and the adventure that befell him. All of a sudden, about midnight, he was aware of a noise that at first seemed to come from far off, from a valley to the right; and then it seemed to fill the whole enclosure and the whole cemetery. On all sides he heard a great clamour—men talking, horses neighing and stamping so that the very ground trembled.

Amadas was not exactly frightened, but he shuddered somewhat, for he thought the fiends were coming to carry away the body, as he had heard it said they would. But then, gentle knight that he was, he determined that if all the demons of hell were to assemble there, they should not, rightly or wrongly, bear away the body of his lady without killing him first.

In the midst of such reflections the youth looked up and saw approaching in a mass more than a thousand men, as it seemed; they came up in two companies, covering all the field and plain. Many kinds of men were in those companies: nobles, richly accoutred, clerks, knights, ladies, damsels, squires, maids. The clerks' company went straight to the cemetery, bearing with them a bier with a corpse thereon, covered with a pallium rich with gold. Amadas saw them stop just beside the wall and place the bier on the ground, and then stand quietly. On the other side of the enclosure he saw that the company of great people had stopped beside the wall. With them they led a palfrey as white as a flower, richly caparisoned, with bridle rein adorned with gold and rich stones. No dame or damsel ever possessed a palfrey with such splendid housings, for the little bells which hung from the reins, the poitral and the stirrups rendered strange music, filling the whole cloister with sweet sound. The gentlemen in this company dismounted, gathered by the wall and remained there in silence.

Now an armed knight started forth upon a swift destrier. He was large and handsome and well formed. His accoutrement was rich and became him well, for it was excellently made in every respect. Completely equipped as he was, he directed his armed charger to the wall and applied the spurs. In the sight of all the horse joined his four feet and leaped more than a fathom over the wall without touching or grazing it.

The stranger knight went boldly up to the tomb. When he saw Amadas there he cried out in fierce pride: "Ha! now, what are you doing there beside the tomb where lies my lady for whom I grieve? Your heart must be overflowing with pride and folly and presumption. You are not at all prudent to have undertaken such foolishness; indeed, you must be the greatest madman in the world."

Amadas replied calmly: "He who has folly round his own neck thinks himself wise, and all others fools; but often enough the event has proved him wrong. You inquire haughtily who I am. Well, I am a knight."

"What are you doing here? What do you seek?"

"I am guarding this tomb."

"You speak folly, false knave. Be on your way!"

"Why so? I like it here. I will certainly not go away."

"Why not, pray?"

"Because I do not fear you nor anything you can do."

"You are talking nonsense. Get away from here, for I shall have no mercy on you."

"Why should I leave when I am comfortable here, and something which I love lies here also?"

"What! You will not budge at my request?"

"No, indeed, nor for your threat, either."

"Now I know that you are mad, if you love this black marble. Tell me, by the God in whom you believe, why are you on watch here at this hour? Why do you lament for the body here interred?"

When Amadas heard the stranger speak of God, he was reassured and replied: "My friend, I do not know who you are who inquire so closely about my affairs, but since you ask, I will tell you the truth: In this marble tomb lies she whom I loved most in all the world, and on whose account I shall have sorrow from now on all my life."

The other laughed and said: "Know for sure, sir knight, that you are not the first to be deceived and duped by a woman, and I will tell you why. According to your tale the lady in this tomb loved you with whole heart above all others. But I deny it, for she had another lover whom she loved more. And I will give you the proof if you will agree to resign her to that one on recognition of the testimony."

"Who is he?" asked Amadas.

"I am he," said the other, "and was, and shall be. And I will show you the proof of which I spoke, whether you like it or not." Therewith he showed Amadas the ring which he had once had made for Ydoine and said: "This is the ring which you gave your lady one day. In return she gave you her ring and therewith seised you delightfully with herself and her love; and she said that never would the ring part from her as long as that love lasted. She spoke truly, for she soon forgot the matter: she gave me both the ring and her love, and accepted me as her lover. Now you can see very well that when she gave as a love-token to a strange knight that gift of yours which she cherished most, she was not a loyal lover. I am he whom she loved, wherefor you must yield her to me. And I want her right now, to bear her body away; nor will I relinquish her for any mortal man."

When Amadas saw the evidence of the ring he was filled with anguish and ire. He was in doubt whether or not to believe the stranger's words. Never in his life had he expected to hear such a charge brought against Ydoine. Rather would he have been dead than misbelieve her. So deep and bitter was his grief that he almost fell in a swoon at the feet of his rival. Indeed, he began to lament his case, cursing all lovers who had loved loyally, such as Tristan, Paris, Achilles, Ulysses, Floire, Roland, Eneas, Alexander, Solomon and Samson. But then he remembered that some women had loved loyally also, such as Dido, Lucretia, Julia and Thisbe, though probably they committed some folly, too, if it were only known. At any rate, the treachery of Ydoine was enough to prove that all women were false deceivers. And yet, of all women, Ydoine was surely the least disloyal and tricky.

At this point in his reflections Amadas looked at the tomb and remembered many sweet intimacies which had passed between him and his lady; and as he remembered them he cursed himself for ever doubting her.

Now the strange knight broke in upon his melancholy reverie. "Vassal," he said, "you are certainly an ignorant, blown-out fool for not quitting this tomb. If you don't take to your heels straightway, I'll stretch you out cold and stiff with a gaping gullet. Your death is waiting for you here in the butt of my lance."

On hearing this menace Amadas' heart caught fire, and he decided that whatever his own fate might be, he would abase the outrageous pride of the stranger knight without delay. "Vassal," said he, "you have a lot of words, and they are all silly. The wise man says in his proverb: 'Of a fool the words are foolish,' and that fits your case. You boast of hardihood and prowess, but it seems like nonsense to me when you say that you will thrust that lance of yours through my body. If it were not for those outside there, whom I see in great number, you would not have jangled so much, nor shown yourself so bold. And nevertheless, in spite of them, I will not refrain from telling you that you are overflowing with too great pride and presumption when you say that you will strike me with the butt of your lance. I assure you that you will have plenty to do with the iron part of it before you leave me, for I am provided with a fine hauberk and a well-ground sword, with a steel helm, a strong shield, and a lance whose iron tip is first-rate for cutting veins and sinews; certainly it is worth your truncheon. Your presumptuous defamation of my lady will be repaid you with interest. I think you are a liar, and if my strength serves me, I will prove it to you. Your threat should never be voiced in any place except on good grounds; and I tell you that, rightly or wrongly, you shall never bear away the body of Ydoine unless you kill me first."

"Are you brave enough to defend her against me?" asked the stranger.

"Assuredly," replied Amadas; "for four days ago I loved her more than my life, and he who respects loyalty and honour does not forget perfect love in so short a time."

Said the knight courteously: "Now by the Lord God! if you are so hardy as to undertake battle against me, body to body, you need pay no heed to the others, but only to me." Then he turned to his company and commanded that whatever they might see happen, none was to move, on pain of death.

Amadas quickly prepared himself for the battle; he laced his helm and his ventail, mounted his horse, and with shield and lance took his stand in the middle of the place before the tomb. The other knight withdrew for about the distance of an arpent. Each now enarmed his shield and placed lance in rest. In the first rush the shield of each was pierced, and their lances shattered; with such violence did they shock together that all four of them, horse and man, fell to the ground in a heap. But they leaped to their feet and battered each other with their truncheons. Then they drew swords, and, with shields held high over their heads, began the struggle again alongside the tomb. So fiercely did they lay on that fire flashed from their helms, and the rivets of their hauberks were undone; and each gave the other grievous wounds.

So long and stubbornly did the combat endure that each knight finally had to pause from very weakness. They drew back to rest a little. Amadas kept his place before the tomb, leaning upon his hacked and battered shield; opposite him was the stranger knight, who supported himself by his buckler, naked sword in hand.

"Vassal," said he, "you are indeed a fool not to fear my blows more, and I will tell you why: There is so much hardihood in me that you cannot defend yourself against me a great while. I would have killed you long ago if I had really put my heart into it; but I had pity for your courage and valour in defending the body of one who never loved you. Now, my friend, I advise you to leave the stour while you are well and healthy."

"That I will not," replied Amadas. "From now on let each one do the best he can, and let the worse be beaten."

Again they took up their shields and their sharp swords. No one ever saw such an affray as that which followed, nor heard of such in song or fable. Blue fire sprang from their arms and hauberks like flashes from the anvil, and all the grass round about was withered by the sparks. So fiercely did they batter each other that the soundest of the two was so sorely wounded that the ground became slippery with blood. Amadas was so closely pressed that he knew not what to do. The stranger knight gave him such a blow with his sword that he cut the shield right down to the bosse, and shore away a hundred links from the hauberk; and then he gave him seven blows all together such that he could do nothing but attend to warding them off. The stranger knight forced him away from the tomb in spite of himself.

"Vassal," said he, "now you see well enough who is in the wrong." And therewith he gave Amadas a stroke that almost brought him to earth. "It is obvious," he continued, "that you cannot defend yourself against me; so, if you will acknowledge yourself beaten, I, in my great courtesy, will let you go with no more ill than you have received. But first you will have to swallow the evil words you have said; otherwise you shall not escape."

When Amadas heard this the burden of his grief was so increased that he could not speak; no man would be able to describe the anguish in his heart. And from that wrath and anguish were kindled new force and vigour, hardihood and courage. He glanced toward his lady's tomb and saw that by a brand of steel and the body of a single knight he had become separated from it against his will. He had thought that never in his life would the body of just one knight cause him to give such an exhibition of cowardice. He gripped his sword and put up what was left of his shield, and fiercely sought out him who had battered him so much. He gave back his seven blows to the stranger knight with such weight that he dazed him. Then he pressed him relentlessly all over the plot, dislodging him from one place after another, so that by very fury he made the knight leave the tomb where he had taken his stand. Finally Amadas laid such a blow on the stranger's golden helm that he cut off more than a quarter of it, a hundred links from his hauberk, together with a palm's breadth of flesh and hide from the head itself; the blow continued downwards and reached the shield, cutting off a foot and a half of it; then it came to the right arm and made there such a rent in the mail that the sword, with the hand still grasping it, flew wide into the field.

Now the stranger knight saw well that the battle was over for him. "Grace, fair sir," he said, "and peace, for my strength is gone. God! what great joy awaits you. No man will experience a greater after you, I think, for by your valour you have rescued the body of Ydoine, because of which, before daybreak, you will be one of the happiest men in the world."

Amadas drew back a little, leaning upon his shield, to hear more. The stranger, now much weakened, continued. "Sir, you are an excellent knight of arms, and in loyalty you have this night excelled all the lovers of the world. Inasmuch as you have conquered me, I think there is nowhere on earth your equal for prowess and valour. Since you are so courteous and so noble, and since you have suffered so deeply for true love, and because of your chivalry, I will tell you some news which ought to please you more than any you ever heard."

Then the stranger knight told Amadas that Ydoine was not really dead, but only seemingly so, for it was he who had borne her off at the bridge-head as she was approaching Lucca; and before setting her down he had put on her finger an enchanted and invisible ring that had caused her to die a false death. If Amadas would remove the ring, taking care to leave it in the tomb, Ydoine would revive and would be as well and beautiful as ever.

"And now," he concluded, "I must tell you that I cannot be killed

HOW AMADAS FOUGHT WITH THE FIEND 103

by arms: my nature will not suffer it. I cannot tarry longer now, for day approaches. I commend you to God."

Therewith he turned away and mounted his destrier. The horse joined his four feet and leaped briskly over the wall. His company gathered about him and led him off with great lamentation.

Amadas hastened to the tomb, and just as day was breaking, prized off the cover. There he found his gentle lady and took her in his arms, and kissed and caressed her. And when he had removed the ring, Ydoine awoke as though from a long sleep. Who was a happy man now but Amadas?

"What kind of man is that?" asked James Yonge.

Madot stared at his questioner.

"He means," explained Sir Thomas Elyot, "who is the happy man, or what makes a man happy?"

Madot shrank away and said nothing.

"Come," said the Clerk of Oxenford, "was he like any man here?"

"My lords," said Madot finally, "is this the way you reward me for my tale—by plaguing me with riddles?"

"I suppose you are right," said the Clerk. "Let us ask someone else." He ran his eye over the company, passing by Richard and his father, Snorri Sturlason and Caesar of Heisterbach, Joinville and Ossian, Pia de' Tolomei and Christine de Pisan, Ponce de Leon and Bernardo del Carpio, Blind Harry and Conrad of Montferrat, Cormac, Leland and the Lochmaben Harper, until it rested as by chance on the rubicund countenance of Walter Map.

"Do not ask me," said Map. "I was always too busy to think about the matter."

"There is no happiness where there is no safety," ventured Iolo Goch; "and there is no safety but has its care."

Adam Usk: You say well. What cares have not gnawed at my heart! Too few have been the pleasures of my life—two, to be exact —while my troubles have been as countless as the grains of sand on the shore.

Peire Cardenal: I would say that he is happy whom nothing makes less strong than he is. He is the happy man who has beaten out a path for himself and stays in it, depending on none but himself, for he who leans on any prop whatsoever is likely to fall.

Saxo Grammaticus: I cannot agree. Evil to the lonely man and burdensome to the single man remains every dwelling in the world.

Blaise the Hermit: Nay, long ago Timon discovered that there is no way to be happy except by avoiding the society of other men.

Geoffrey Keating: On the contrary, the happy man is he who knows the world, yet cares not for it.

Andrew Boorde: But we live in the world, and as world dwellers are susceptible to mundane stimuli. If the mind cannot be contented, the heart cannot be pleased. If the heart and mind be not pleased, Nature doth abhor. And if Nature do abhor, mortification of the vital and animal and spiritual powers doth consequently follow.

"I have read somewhere in the chronicles preserved in my country," said Pedro Lopez de Ayala, "some testimony offered by Abd er-Rahman III on this head. 'I have reigned,' he is reported as saying, 'above fifty years in victory or peace, beloved by my subjects, dreaded by my enemies, and respected by my allies. Riches and honours, power and pleasure have waited on my call, nor does any earthly blessing appear to have been wanting to my felicity. In this situation I have diligently numbered the days of pure and genuine happiness which have fallen to my lot: they amount to fourteen.'"

"I, too, recall an ancient authority," said William Camden. "It is related of Solon the Athenian that he one time visited King Croesus at Sardis. The king, who, like Sir William atte Pole here, thought that happiness lay in wealth, determined to seek confirmation from so eminent a philosopher. But his expectations were disappointed, for after several vain attempts to elicit a flattering answer from his guest, Croesus lost patience and asked: 'Am I not, then, to be reckoned happy?' 'O king,' replied Solon, 'while a man lives he may in greater or less degree partake of the goods of Fortune; but as no human being is in all respects self-sufficient, so he cannot possess all Fortune's advantages. It is therefore impossible to say who is happy while he still lives. But he who has constantly enjoyed the most of Fortune's goods while he lived, and then ends his life tranquilly, may, in my judgment, O king, deserve the name of happy.' Thereupon Croesus dismissed Solon without conferring any favour upon him, for he considered him a very ignorant man."

"Pliny put the matter in a slightly different way," remarked Polydore Vergil, "when he said that no mortal is happy, and that at best a man can but say that he is not unhappy if Fortune has dealt indulgently with him."

"The mistake of those who run after happiness," said Machiavelli, "lies in thinking that they can find it by so doing. Job complained that man is born to trouble as the sparks fly upward. That may, indeed, be the normal lot of human beings. But once that fact is accepted, is there no crevice, crack nor cranny left in life unoccupied by trouble into which some happiness may not be thrust? Probably both Job and Pliny were right; and yet to my mind it seems that we may deem those mortals happy who from the experiences of life have learned to bear its ills without being overcome by them."

"Someone has said," spoke up Sir John Harington, "that happiness is above all things the calm glad certainty of ignorance. We may assume that Scanlann was happy after he had been freed from a restricted diet; but his was perhaps too esoteric an experience to be universally applicable. But take Seithenyn ab Seithyn Saidi, now, who cannot distinguish morning from afternoon . . . ? Still, perhaps he is not altogether happy either, for Doctor Boorde tells me that he has worms."

At these words John of Gaddesden regarded the slumbering monarch with deeper interest. He would have spoken, but was prevented by Raoul Lefèvre.

"Sir," said Lefèvre, turning to Blind Harry, "your flaming rafters at Gask Hall remind me of an incident which I once read in some romance. As the final act of a quarrel originating in a game of chess the young knight Eledus had slain the seneschal of the king of Tubie. He regretted this deed, not so much because the seneschal—an overweening boor—had not deserved killing, as because it deprived him of any further opportunity for displaying his prowess. And since he was most violently in love with the king's daughter Serene, he needed nothing so much, pending his lady's grace, as occasions for the display of chivalric virility. At one coup he had rashly disposed of his only foil. He cudgelled his brains to think of some exploit whereby he might keep his fame alive in the king's mind, and supply yet another proof of his love for Serene. Seeing him in despair his squire Sapyn suggested, more or less facetiously, that he could probably win as much honour and renown as would last him for the rest of his life if he were to slay the powerful felon knight Cuizelot. 'That is the very thing,' said Eledus when the nature and deeds of Cuizelot had been explained to him. So next day he set out with Sapyn to find the lord of Montipatre."

22. HOW ELEDUS SLEW HIS HOST

Raoul Lefèvre

At the city harbour Eledus and Sapyn came upon two shipmen who set them over water for five sous. On landing they saddled their horses and rode all day till, by nightfall, they had reached a meadow blooming with flowers, and a pine tree with a fountain springing under it. "Here," said Eledus, "we shall rest until tomorrow." The night was soft and clear, and to the music of bird-song Eledus fell asleep and dreamed of Serene.

On the following morning Eledus ranged through the wood in search of game. Before long he started a buck and wounded it, and when he would have gone up to kill it, lo! a lion jumped out at him. The manner of the lion was this: He wore a gleaming crown set with rich flashing jewels of twelve sorts, the best of their kind in the world. "If I could win that crown," thought the knight to himself, "I would give it to the king." He descended from his horse, drew his sword and made a stroke at the lion that almost knocked him down, giving him a great wound on the shoulder. This made the lion angry, and he returned the knight's blow, striking him so violently on the helm that he broke the visor, and also the shield that hung at his neck. Now Eledus dropped his shield and laid on with his sword. For his part the lion seized the knight's hauberk with his paw and ripped away a great piece of it, almost dashing its owner to the ground. Eledus was now so furious that blood gushed from his nostrils. He gave the lion such a blow on the neck that it cut through all the hide, and the crowned head flew a fathom into the field. "Now," said Eledus, "if I can find Cuizelot and am permitted to return home again, the king shall be crowned with this."

Eledus put up his sword and proceeded to follow the wounded stag. For a league he pursued him, and finally brought him down at the foot of a high hill. On the crest of the hill he saw a strong castle, well built with stone, and well fortified. As he stood there looking at it, an armed knight rode up on a dappled horse, lance in hand.

"Who are you," shouted the knight, "who go about doing deeds of violence in this forest?"

"And who the devil are you, who do not properly salute strangers?" asked Eledus. "No matter; perhaps you can tell me where I can find Cuizelot?"

"What do you want of him?" countered the other.

"By God!" said Eledus, "I want to fight with him."

"Indeed?" said the stranger. "You are a twenty-four carat fool, for I am Cuizelot. In an evil hour did you seek me out, for you have found your death. You are going to lose your head for killing my stag there."

"By that same head," replied Eledus, "you are a liar. It is you who shall die, and your head will come off before mine, if it please holy Mary. You shall pay dearly for your pride and folly, and for the outrage and shame you have visited on this honourable land in burning and spoiling it, and for treacherously slaying its lord and inhabitants."

"Ha!" said Cuizelot, "I had good right to do so, for the seigneur killed my father. And anyone who dares come this way buys his passage dearly, for none has respite; and you also shall lose your life."

"Faugh!" answered Eledus. "If he killed your father, he got what he deserved, for he slew his liegeman, the Count of Lere, and did not make his peace for the homicide."

"You know too much about my business," replied Cuizelot, "and by the faith I owe my sire, you shall die for it. But tell me your name, so that I may know the identity of the handsome, well-spoken knight whom I shall have killed."

"That I will not tell you," said Eledus, "because you are such a low churl. Take your distance and let us see who knows best how to give blows."

At these words Cuizelot became wroth and took his distance, expecting to kill the youth at the first blow. I will spare you the details of the ensuing battle—you can find such encounters described on almost every page of any good *chanson de geste*. Suffice it to say, they astounded each other with their dints. Finally Eledus cut off the head of Cuizelot's horse, and he, in reprisal, cut in two the neck of Eledus' charger. Hereafter they fought for a while on foot till Cuizelot broke his sword on Eledus' helm and asked for a truce till he could obtain a new one. "By St John, you shall have none," said Eledus; and throwing away his own sword started to wrestle with his opponent. Then they wrestled on the ground, and punched and kicked each other with hands and feet until both fainted from exhaustion.

At last Cuizelot suggested that they become brothers-in-arms. "It would be a shame if two knights of such outstanding valour and prowess should kill each other," said he. "By God!" said Eledus, "I do not trust you, for you pledged your faith to your liege lord also, and then slew him treacherously." So they fell to wrestling again till they once more swooned away with weakness. "My friend," said Cuizelot finally, "I conjure you by the lady whom you love that you give over and become my companion."

When Eledus heard the knight speak thus, his heart was softened because of Serene, whom he loved so tenderly. He made peace with Cuizelot and they took oaths to be loyal to each other.

"Now," said Cuizelot, "let us go up to the castle and break our fast, for dinner must be nearly ready."

Up to the castle they went and entered the hall. Eledus thought it somewhat strange that no man came to meet or greet them. Cuizelot took off his armour himself and helped Eledus to disarm. "My friend," said he, "sit down now while I go to the kitchen to see if the food is on the way." So Eledus, all unarmed, sat down by the fireplace and began to think of Serene. Suddenly he looked up, and whom should he see but Cuizelot coming into the hall with a long sword in his hand. Now he knew indeed that he had been betrayed, and was so wroth that he nearly went out of his head.

"Ha! false companion that you are, have you led me into a trap?"

"Not at all," answered Cuizelot. "I merely wish to make sure that you never offer similar combat to me or any other knight." With that he stuck the point of his sword into a crack in the floor, and leaning on the hilts grinned crookedly at the young knight sitting on the stool.

As I have said, Eledus was dressed in nothing but hose and kirtle; his arms lay at the other end of the hall, and Cuizelot stood between. Now you know that in the old days young men were instructed in the game of chess not as an idle pastime, but as a definite part of their military education. Like Tristan, Eledus was a good chess-player; so in this emergency he was not at a loss. In less time than it takes to tell, Eledus did two things simultaneously: He grasped his stool with one hand and therewith knocked Cuizelot's supporting sword from under him; with the other hand he seized a length of fir sapling that was blazing in the fire; and while Cuizelot staggered in regaining his balance, Eledus assisted him with a smart blow under the chin with the blazing brand. Finally Cuizelot got a good grip on his two-handed sword and raised himself on his toes to give weight to his blow. But Eledus swerved aside quickly, and gave the renegade such a stroke on the right arm with his flaming faggot that he paralysed it, and made the sword drop to the floor. Quickly the young knight snatched it up and landed a blow on Cuizelot's head such that he split it quite in two. As the felon knight lay weltering in his blood Eledus said: "God forgive me for killing the man to whom I lately pledged my word of honour."

Eledus now went on a tour of investigation, keeping the dead knight's sword in a handy position. But he found no one till he came to the soller, where a lady sat weeping. When Eledus had heard her sad story he lost no time in coming to her aid. With the key from Cuizelot's pouch he opened the prison where the false knight had confined her lord and his twenty companions. In sorry state they were, barely clad and barely shod, loaded with irons, gyves, manacles, fetters and chains. In the stable they found thirty good horses. Each of the company chose his mount and the remaining seven horses were laden with harness, gold, silver and other loot of the castle, not forgetting, on the way, the lion's crown.

Soon the company overtook Sapyn, who by this time believed his master dead. All that night they rode in order to reach Tubie on the morrow, for Eledus was in great heat to see Serene, and would neither eat nor drink till he was with her again.

"Good, now," said Mac Conglinne, "Cuizelot was only a man of flesh and blood after all; and though Amadas may have fought at the tomb with a fiend or a demon, it was a fiend who lacked, in my opinion, any distinctive character, and betrayed very little originality. In Ireland, now, we have—or had—something really different from the common run of demons. . . ."

"One would expect that, in Ireland," interrupted Giraldus.

"And with your leave I will repeat to you a tale which was told me by Guaire Aidne Mac Colman's cook."

23. CONALL GULBAN AND THE AMHUISH
Mac Conglinne

When the king of Erin went away to give military assistance to the king of Iubhar, he left his son Conall Gulban behind to keep the wives and sons of Ireland till he should come back. There was not a man left in the realm of Erin, and there was not left a man in the realm of Leinster but the daughter of the king of Leinster and five hundred soldiers to guard her.

Then sorrow struck Conall, and melancholy, that he should stay in the realm of Erin by himself; that he himself was better than the people altogether, though they had gone away. He thought there was nothing that would take his care and his sorrow from off him better than to go to the side of Ben Eidin to the green mound. He went, and he reached the green mound; he laid his face downwards on the hillock, and he thought that there was no one thing that would suit himself better than that he should find his match of a woman. Such a woman was not to be found but the one that the king of Leinster had left within his castle, and it would not be easy to get to her on account of all the soldiers that her father left to keep her; but he thought that he could reach her.

Conall took his burden upon him, and he went on board of a skiff, and he rowed till he came on shore on the land of the king of Leinster. He was on a great hillock that was there, and below him he saw the very finest castle that ever was seen from the beginning of the universe to the end of eternity. The dun was guarded by nine ranks of soldiers, and nine warriors behind every rank, and six heroes and three heroes behind every warrior, and a great man behind these three who was as mighty as the whole of the people that were there altogether.

Conall looked at the men who were guarding the dun; he went a sweep round about with ears that were sharp to hear, and eyes rolling to see. A glance that he gave aloft to the dun, he saw an open window, and Breast-of-Light, the king's daughter, on the inner side of the window combing her hair. Conall stood a little while gazing at her, but at last he put his palm on the point of his spear, he gave his rounded spring, and he was in at the window beside Breast-of-Light.

"Who is this youth who has sprung so roundly in at the window to see me?" said she.

"It is one who has come to take you away," answered Conall.

Breast-of-Light gave a laugh and she said: "Did you see the soldiers guarding the dun?"

"I saw them," said he; "they let me in and they will let me out."

She gave another laugh and said: "Many a one has tried to take me out of this, but none has done it yet, and they lost their luck at the end. My counsel to you is that you do not try it."

Conall put his hand about her waist; he raised her in his oxter; he took her out to the rank of soldiers; he put his palm on the point of his spear, and he leaped over their heads. He ran so swiftly that they could not see that it was Breast-of-Light he had with him, and when he was out of sight of the dun he set her on the ground.

Breast-of-Light heaved a heavy sigh from her breast. "What is the meaning of your sigh?" asked Conall. "It is," said she, "that there came many a one to seek me, and who suffered death for my sake, yet it is a coward of the great world who has taken me away. I little thought that the coward of Erin should take me out, and that my father should leave five hundred warriors to watch me without one drop of blood being taken from one of them."

"Stay here," said Conall, "and I will go and break the news to them."

Conall turned back to the dun, and nothing in the world in the way of arms did he fall in with but one horse's jaw which he found in the road. And when he arrived he asked the soldiers what they would do to a man who should take away Breast-of-Light. "It is this," said they, "to drive off his head and set it on a spike."

Conall looked under them, over them, through and before them. He drew his sword and began on them; and he killed the ranks of warriors and the six heroes and the three full heroes till he had but the big man left. Conall struck him a slap and drove his eye out on his cheek, and told him to carry his news to the king of Leinster.

Conall returned, and he reached the woman after he had finished the hosts. "Come, now," said he to Breast-of-Light, "and walk with me; and if you had not given me the spiteful talk you gave, the company would be alive for your father; and since you gave it, you shall now walk. Let your foot be even with mine."

She rose, well pleased, and went away with him. They reached the narrows, they put out the ferry-boat and they crossed the strait, and they came to land at the lower side of Ben Eidin in Erin. When they reached the green mound at the foot of Ben Eidin Conall told Breast-of-Light that he had a failing: Every time that he did any deed of valour he must sleep before he could do brave deeds again. "There now," he said, "I will lay my head in your lap."

"You shall not," said Breast-of-Light, "lest you fall asleep."

"And if I do, will you not waken me?"

"What is your manner of waking?"

"You shall cast me greatly hither and thither, and if that will not rouse me you must take a piece of flesh and hide from the top of my head. If that will not wake me, seize yonder great slab of stone and strike me between the mouth and the nose. If I do not stir for that, you shall cut off the joint of my little finger; and if that does not rouse me you may let me be." He laid his head in her lap and in a little instant he fell asleep.

Conall had not been long asleep when Breast-of-Light saw a great vessel sailing in the ocean, and the road was level for her till she came to the green mound at the side of Ben Eidin. There was in the ship but one great man, and he came on shore at the shoulder of the mound. He came where Breast-of-Light was, and Conall asleep with his head on her knee.

"What side is before you for choice?" asked Breast-of-Light as he gazed at her.

"Well," said the big man, "they were telling me that Breast-of-Light, daughter of the king of Leinster, was the finest woman in the world, and I was going to seek her for myself; but whether you be she or no, past you I will not go."

"I am not she," said Breast-of-Light, "but a farmer's daughter, and this is my brother."

"Be that as it will," said the big man, "there is a mirror in my ship that will not rise up for any woman in the world but Breast-of-Light, daughter of the king of Leinster. If the mirror rises for you, I will take you; and if it does not, I will leave you here."

He went to the mirror, and fear would not let her cut Conall's little finger, and she could not waken him. The man looked in the mirror and the mirror rose up for her. "But I will be surer of my matter before I go," said the big one. He plucked Conall's blade from the sheath and it was full of blood. "Ha!" said he. "I am right enough in my guess. Waken your champion and we will try with swift wrestling, might of hands and hardness of blades which of us has the best right to you."

"Who are you?" asked Breast-of-Light.

"I am Mac-a-Moir Mac Righ Sorcha," said the big one, "and it is in pursuit of you that I have come."

"Will you not waken my champion?" asked she.

He went and felt him from the points of the thumbs of his feet till he went out at the top of his head. "I cannot rouse the man myself. I like him as well asleep as awake."

Breast-of-Light got up and began to rock Conall hither and thither, but he would not take waking. "Unless you wake him," said Mac-a-Moir, "you must leave him in his sleep and go with me."

"Give me," said she, "your three royal words that you will not seek me as a wife or a sweetheart till the end of a day and a year after this, to give Conall time to come in my pursuit." He gave his three royal words. Then Breast-of-Light took Conall's sword from the scabbard and wrote on the sword how it had fallen out. She took the ring from Conall's finger and put her own ring in its stead. Then she went away with Mac-a-Moir and they left Conall in his sleep.

When Conall woke on the green mound he had but himself, a shorn one and bare alone except for the herdsmen of the king of Erin and the king of Leinster. Said one of the herds: "I saw the one who was with you putting a ring on your finger." Conall looked, and it was the ring of Breast-of-Light that was on his finger. "I saw her writing something on your sword," said the herd, "and putting it back into the scabbard." Conall drew his sword and read: "There came Mac-a-Moir, the king of Sorcha, and took me away. I am free for a year and a day in his house waiting for you if you have so much courage as to come in pursuit of me."

Conall returned the sword to its sheath. "I lay it on myself as spells and crosses," he said, "that stopping by night and staying by day is not for me till I find the woman. Where I take my supper, there I will not take my dinner, and that there is no place into which I go that I will not leave the fruit of my hand there to boot, and the son that is unborn he shall hear of it, and the son that is unbegotten he shall hear tell of it."

"There came a ship to the port down there," said the herd; "the shipmen have gone, and if you are able, you may be away with the ship before they come back."

Conall went on board the ship. He gave her prow to the sea and her stern to the shore, and he went till he reached the realm of Lochlann, but he did not himself know where he was. He was going on when he saw a little man come laughing toward him. "What is the meaning of your laughing at me?" said Conall.

"It is that I am in a cheery mood at seeing a man of my country," said the little man.

"Who are you," asked Conall, "to be a countryman of mine?"

"I," said the little man, "am Duanach Mac Draodh, the son of a prophet from Erin. Will you take me as a servant-lad?"

"I will not take you," said Conall; "I have no way of keeping myself here, to say nothing of a gillie. What realm is this in which I am here?"

"You are in the realm of Lochlann," answered Duanach.

They went on and Duanach pointed out the great town of the king of Lochlann and his house. They saw another house and Conall asked what it was. Duanach said it was the house of the amhuish, the best warriors in the realm of Lochlann. "I have heard my grandfather speak about the amhuish," said Conall, "but I have never seen them. I will go to see them." "That would not be my counsel," said Duanach.

Conall went on to the palace of the king of Lochlann, and he clashed his shield, battle or else combat to be sent to him, or else Breast-of-Light, the daughter of the king of Leinster.

That was the thing he should get, battle and combat, and not Breast-of-Light, for she was not there to give him. Nor would he get any fighting at that time of night, but he should get lodging in the house of the amhuish, where there were eighteen hundred amhuish and eighteen score. He would get battle in the morrow's morning when the first of the day should come.

'Twas no run for the lad, but a spring; and he would take no better than the place he was to get. He went, and he went in, and there was none of the amhuish within who did not grin. When he saw that they had made a grin, he himself made two.

"What is the meaning of your grinning at us?" asked the amhuish.

"What was the meaning of your grinning at me?" asked Conall.

"Our grinning," said they, "meant that your fresh royal blood will be ours to quench our thirst, and your fresh royal flesh to polish our teeth."

"And," said Conall, "the meaning of my grinning is that I will look out for the one with the biggest knob and the slenderest shanks, and knock out the brains of the rest with that one, and his brains with the knobs of the rest."

Then every one of the amhuish rose and put a stake of wood against the door. He himself rose and put two stakes against it so tightly that the others fell.

"What is the reason you do that?" asked they.

"What is the reason you did it?" countered Conall. "It were a sorry matter for me though I should put two there when you yourselves put one there each of you."

"Well," said they, "we will tell you the reason: We have never seen coming here anyone a gulp of whose blood or a morsel of whose flesh could reach us except yourself and except one other man, and he fled from us; and now everyone is doubting the other lest you should flee also."

"That was the thing which made me do it myself likewise, since I have got yourselves so close as you are. I feared I should have to be chasing you from hole to hole and from hill to hill, so I did that."

Then he went and began upon them. He gazed at them, from one to two, and he seized on the one with the slenderest shanks and the fattest head. Upon the rest he drove, sliochd! slachd! till he killed every one of them; and he had not a jot of the one with whom he was working at them but what was in his hands of the shanks. He killed every man of them, and though he was such a youth as he was, he got his fill of that work. Then he began redding up the dwelling that was there, to clean it for himself that night. And he put the amhuish out in a heap all together, and he let himself drop on one of the beds that was within and went to sleep, for, as I have said, that was a failing of his.

"I can well imagine," said Gaucelm Faidit, "that Conall might wish to sleep after such exertion. The exercise of heroism has always seemed exhausting to me. That is one reason why I never took it up," he added, after a pull at his tankard. "But I remember a tale which was current in my country—Limousin—later put into rhyme by a poet whose name I have unfortunately forgotten, the hero of which also longed to sleep after performing great deeds of arms. Shall I tell you the story?"

"Pray do so," said Hákon Hákonson.

"Very well," said Faidit. "First I will give a brief introduction to the incidents which I had in mind. It happened that King Arthur was one day holding court when an overbearing and outrageous knight named Taulat de Rogimen rode into the hall, insulted the queen and rode out again. There was present a young knight named

Jeffrey. Some critics have alleged that Duke Guilhem yonder was in some way related to him; but I wouldn't know about that. This Jeffrey, now, undertook to ride after the intruder and chastise him for his insolence. Sir Kay urged him on with suitable words. All afternoon Jeffrey rode after Taulat. He got no rest that night by reason of fighting with a certain Estout, whom he conquered and sent to Arthur's court. On the second day he killed the Defender of the White Lance; and sleep was postponed for that night also by his encounter with the Knight of the Spits. . . ."

24. JEFFREY'S FIGHT WITH THE GIANT MEZEL

Gaucelm Faidit

In spite of heat, fatigue and lack of sleep, Jeffrey valiantly continued his pursuit on the third day without pausing for delay. But now as he rode along there came towards him a leper holding a child in his arms; a woman crying, weeping and tearing her hair came after him. When she had come even with Jeffrey, "Sir," she said, "for God's sake have mercy and lend me your aid in restoring my child, which the leper yonder carried away right from before my door." "Lady," said he, "why did the leper steal the child?" "Sir, by my faith, for no reason except that it pleased him to do so." "Was there no other reason?" asked Jeffrey. "Sir, by the faith I owe to God, there was not." "Then," said Jeffrey, "I will get the child back for you at once, if I can, alive or dead, for the leper is in the wrong."

Jeffrey put spurs to his horse and quickly overtook the leper or mezel, and the woman followed after. Jeffrey cried out: "Mad mezel, foul churl, put down the child, for you will not get any farther." The mezel's only reply to this summons was to make the sign of the fig at Jeffrey, not only once but three times. "Have that in your throat," said he.

"By my head, you stinking leper," said Jeffrey, "you shall pay for that. Your manners are too loose by far. If I can, I'll take your life for that insult."

By this time the mezel had reached his hostel and went into it. Jeffrey descended at the gate. The woman, too, had come up, weeping and wailing. Jeffrey ordered her to hold his lance and take care of his horse till he came back. Then, shield on arm and sword in hand, he entered the house.

The hall was fair and large. On a bed lay another hideous giant mezel, and he was holding to him a damsel whose equal for beauty was not in the world, I think, for her colour was fresher than the new-blown rose. He had torn her gown down to the waist, exposing a breast whiter than any flower. The girl was making great dole, and her eyes were swollen with weeping.

On the knight's entrance the mezel stopped what he was doing and seized a great mace. When Jeffrey got a good look at him he was horrified, so foul-looking was he: He was as long as a lance, two spans broad in the shoulders; great arms he had, ending in bulging fists, the fingers covered with gouty lumps. His face was patched with fearsome whelks, his brows were hairless, swollen and hard, his eyes dark, cloudy, striated and reddened round about; his jaws were bared and blue and swollen. Long were his teeth, wormy and stinking, and flaming red like a glowing coal. His nose was flat and flaring at the corners. His breathing was hard and stertorous so that he could hardly speak.

The mezel approached Jeffrey and asked: "What are you doing here? Have you come to give yourself up?"

"No," said Jeffrey.

"Then what is the occasion of your intrusion? What do you seek?"

"I am looking for a leper who entered here just now with a child. The child was stolen and its mother has implored me to recover it for her."

"Whatever you find, you will certainly find someone who will prevent you from doing that, you fool, you bumptious churl. In an evil hour did you follow up that adventure, for your life will be short."

So saying the mezel let fly on Jeffrey's shield with his mace so that he battered it down with the first blow; and he would have let fly another, but Jeffrey saw it coming, and agilely avoided it. Well for him that he did so, for the stroke made all the house tremble. Now the knight rushed boldly at the mezel and gave him such a stroke with his sword that he cut off a hand's-breadth of his white gown, a quarter of his shirt and pants, together with the knob of his shank, for that was as high on him as he could reach; and with that blow the sword went into the floor a palm's breadth.

When the mezel saw himself wounded and felt his blood flowing, he raged after the knight with raised mace. Jeffrey dodged behind a pillar, and the mezel hit it such a whack that he dislodged it, and it almost fell; all the house quivered with the force of that stroke. Before the mezel had time to recover from the vehemence of his blow, Jeffrey leaped forward and cut off his arm with his sword.

Now when the leper saw his arm lying on the floor, he was quite enraged, and shrieked with sorrow. He sprang at Jeffrey; the knight avoided him, but not so completely but that the blow grazed his head and brought him to his knees with the blood issuing from nose and mouth; and the leper's mace struck so on the floor that it broke in two. Now with his sword Jeffrey hit the mezel below the knee so that he severed skin, flesh and bone, and cut it off. In falling the big man made a noise like the crashing of a great tree. Sword in hand Jeffrey ran up to him.

"Now," said the knight, "on my faith, peace will be made between you and me." And with his word he gave him such a stroke on the head that he clove his skull right down to the teeth. In his dying struggle the fellow kicked out and dashed Jeffrey against the wall with such violence that he lost his senses, nor could he talk any more than a mute; he measured his length on the floor and moved no more than a tree-stump.

During this time the damsel had been busy praying for the knight and herself, and when she saw Jeffrey so served she thought he was dead. She unlaced his ventail and helm, got water and splashed it in his face. Jeffrey sighed and got to his feet with an effort. Still in a daze, he mistook the damsel for the leper and gave her such a push that he stretched her out on the floor: if his hand had held a sword, she would have been cut in two. Then he ran here and there like one out of his mind. But the maid came to her senses and spoke gently, pointing out that their enemy was dead.

At these words Jeffrey approached the mezel, all stretched out, lacking an arm and a leg, with head so villainously split open that the brains were running out; then he sat down on the bench to gather his wits. When he had rested a little while he went searching through the house for the child which the other leper had brought in; but he found him not, to his sorrow and wrath.

"By God!" said Jeffrey, "where has that mezel gone with the child? Damsel," he asked, "did you see him go out, perhaps?"

"Sir, I know nothing at all of the matter. I had so much trouble of my own with the giant leper there that one might have stabbed me and I should not have known who had done it."

"Well," said the youth, "I'll find him, either inside or out; and I value myself less than a denier if I don't restore the child to his mother and sell him dear the insult he gave me. Since he isn't here, I'll look for him outside."

So saying he went to the door, intending to go out—but that he could not do. Whatever he did or said, he was unable to pass through, and this astonished him greatly.

"By God!" cried Jeffrey, "am I enchanted that I can't get out of here?" Therewith he attempted to leap out, but was unable to lift a foot from the floor. When he saw his efforts were vain, he turned back and sat down, melancholy and vexed, sighing and snorting with ire. Afterwards he went as far away from the door as possible and took a running jump. But it was quite useless: he might have kept on for a month or two years, or three, without getting out.

While the knight was lamenting his deplorable circumstances he heard a child's voice loudly crying for help. He started to his feet and ran through the long hall till he came to a smaller one, the door of which was barred and locked inside. "Open up!" he shouted. But nobody said a word, so he shook the door down and sprang in, sword in hand. Inside he found the first leper with a great knife in his fist: he had just killed seven children, and between twenty-five and thirty others, large and small, all weeping bitterly, were waiting their turn. Jeffrey gave the mezel a kick that stretched him out on the floor. In fear the fellow cried out for his master.

"By God!" said Jeffrey, "you swollen swine, scabby runt that you are, you'll never see your master again, for he is quite dead. And right now you are going to lose your hand—the one with which you gave me the figs. You shall never make that sign to anyone again."

Thereupon Jeffrey struck off the leper's hand. The wretch threw himself at the knight's feet and cried him mercy, protesting that he had been forced against his will to kill the seven children so that his master might cure his leprosy by bathing in their blood.

"If you wish to continue in this life," said Jeffrey, "tell me truly whether or not you can get me out of this place."

"Yes, my lord," answered the mezel, "so help me God. If you grant me my life, you shall be freed from here at once, but if you kill me, you shall remain in ignorance of the mighty enchantments of the place."

"Well, hurry up, for my business presses and I am in haste to be on my way."

"It is like this," replied the man: "Standing in the window in the wall there is the image of a boy's head; break the head and straightway all the enchantment will disappear. However, you will be sorely wounded in doing so, for the whole house will collapse when the enchantment is undone."

"Is that so?" asked Jeffrey.

"Yes, indeed," replied the other.

Therewith Jeffrey tied the mezel's arms and gave him into the custody of the maiden. "Damsel," said he, "guard me this mezel well; if he is lying to me, I'll make him die an evil death." Then he sent them both out together with the children, he alone remaining.

Now the young knight put on his helm and went to the window. He found the head and gave it such a blow that he cut it right in two. Hereupon the head rose and cried out and shrieked and carried on so that it seemed heaven and earth and all the elements were battling with each other. Every stone fought with a stone, every beam strove with another beam, at the same time giving Jeffrey such a beating that it was a wonder he survived it. After that it grew dark with thunder and rain. As storm and lightning broke over him, the knight protected his head with his shield. There was neither beam nor rafter, tile, block nor building-stone that failed to give him a blow or a punch. The storm in the sky swept everything before it and would have borne Jeffrey away too, except for the grace of God. Of the house there remained nothing, as though it had never been; and Jeffrey was so broken up with wounds and dints that he hardly knew what to do. He went and lay down, for he was indeed played out.

Now the woman whose child Jeffrey had saved, the damsel and the menial mezel ran up to him where he lay. "Noble knight," said the girl, smiling, "how do you do?" "I have no mortal wounds, I think," replied the hero, "but I have withstood a great deal of battering, and I should like to rest here a while." Then the maiden went up to him and kissed his eyes, his mouth and his face.

Said Jeffrey to the mother of the child: "Woman, have you got back your offspring?" "Oh, yes, my lord, thanks to you," she replied. "Well, then," said Jeffrey, "go along with this beautiful damsel here who has such charming manners, take the child and mezel with you, and don't stop till you come to the castle of Carduel where Arthur is. Greet everyone from me, and tell your adventure to all whom you meet."

Then he called for his horse and his lance, and as he was preparing to mount, the damsel, dissolved in tears, came forward. "Noble and valiant knight, will you not go with us a piece of the way?" she asked. "That would delay me too much," replied Jeffrey; "rather must I follow him whom I cannot find, for I shall have neither joy nor rest till I have caught up with him." "Whom do you seek so eagerly?" asked the girl. "Damsel," said Jeffrey, "his name is Taulat, and a day or so ago he violently and wrongfully killed a knight sitting in the hall beside Queen Guenevere. I go seeking him until I shall find him and avenge that shame or double my own." So saying Jeffrey rode on his way.

Now when our hero had killed the giant leper and extricated the damsel from her embarrassing predicament; when he had humbled the small leper and restored the stolen child to its mother; and when he had abated the enchantments of the wicked house, he felt so weary, feeble, fatigued, wounded, battered and utterly undone that he could hardly keep his seat in the saddle. For three days he had been without food, and for two nights he had had no sleep. So hungry and sleepy was he that he drowsed on horseback, wobbled to and fro, and almost fell off. And in this manner he continued till evening, not knowing whither he went.

Gaucelm paused for breath and a drink.

"What happened to the other children in the house who had not been slain?" inquired Peter Bell.

"The story doesn't say," replied Gaucelm briefly.

"A curious conceit," mused Thomas Linacre; "I mean about curing leprosy by bathing the patient in children's blood."

Alexander Neckam: It has Pliny's authority.

Hartmann von Aue: And that of Salerno. A Salernian doctor prescribed that remedy for one of my relatives.

Caesar of Heisterbach: But I believe he did not make use of it, preferring that the maiden whose blood was to be spilt should sacrifice herself to him not by death, but as his wife.

John Mirk: Well, there is the case of the emperor Constantine, who assembled three hundred—some say three thousand—boys in order to bathe in their blood.

Mac Conglinne: But Constantine did not kill the children. Peter and Paul persuaded him to accept baptism instead—or so I have read.

Lanfranc of Milan: At all events, leprosy, as Pliny says, was little known in Italy.

Walter Map: Still, the bath of blood was actually employed by Amelius—or was it Amicus?—who cut off the heads of his two children to heal his friend.

Andrew Boorde: A monkish fable!

Joinville: King Louis once asked me which I would rather—commit a mortal sin or be a leper.

Sir John Harington: And what did you say?

Joinville: I said I would rather commit thirty mortal sins than be a single leper.

"What is the cause of leprosy?" asked Peter Bell.

"Lepra, or mezelry," answered Bartholomew, "is a universal corruption of members and of humours. But Constantinus says that every elephantiasis or leprosy is caused by melancholic humour being corrupted."

"In my time," said Andrew Boorde with a wink at Linacre, "it was caused by an exclusive diet of fish, and sometimes by drinking pig's milk. These are also the causes of gout, fevers and the king's evil."

"Can it be cured?" asked Peter Bell.

"Michael Scot recommends a bath composed of hot water mixed with the blood of a dog," answered Boorde.

"Rather," spoke up John of Gaddesden, "you should take the fat of a horse, mix with salt, and smear with that. Then prepare a bath of hot water into which has been put ash rind, quickbeam rind, holly rind, black alder rind, spindle tree, sedge, ploughman's spikenard, hayrife and marrubium. Then make a salve of marrubium in butter, with meal of earthworms, viper's bugloss and hayrife. Take half this salve and mix it with triturated helenium, and smear the patient with it till he gets better; then smear with the other half."

"Thank you," said Peter Bell with a shudder.

"Have you any remedy for weak eyesight, now?" inquired Ossian. "For the past three or four hundred years my eyes have not been so strong as they once were."

"Yes, indeed," answered Gaddesden. "Take a crab and put his eyes out; then put him alive again into water, and put the eyes on the neck of the man who has need, and he will soon be well."

"I never thought of that," said Ossian.

"No, no!" protested Gilbertus Anglicus. "Weak eyesight is due to lethargy, and to cure it one must first begin with that. For lethargy take the heart of a robin and the heart of an owl. . . ."

"Good master," interrupted Sir John Harington, "we will gladly hear you on another occasion—when we are flat on our backs and cannot help ourselves. For the present we have had enough of materia medica. If the excellent troubadour has recovered his breath and inspiration, we should be pleased to listen to the remainder of his tale. And if his hero does not discover a remedy for lethargy, then we will hear yours."

"Very well," said Gaucelm.

25. HOW JEFFREY LONGED TO SLEEP AT CASTLE MONBRUN
Gaucelm Faidit

The night was clear and calm when Jeffrey came at last to a park all enclosed by a marble wall. I think there was no kind of beautiful tree in the world whereof there was not a specimen or two therein, nor fine plant nor beautiful flower. There too was a fragrance so fine and sweet-smelling that it seemed like Paradise.

All the birds of the countryside, for a day's journey round about, used to come at nightfall to sing in those trees, and so softly and sweetly that no instrument could produce such beautiful music; and thus they did till dawn.

This park belonged to a damsel named Brunesent the Belle. She was mistress of Monbrun castle, the chief of her many holdings. The lady had neither father nor mother, husband nor brother. Seven porters had the castle, each of whom had a thousand knights under him to guard the seven gates. Night and day five hundred maids waited upon Brunesent, who exceeded them all in beauty. For if one were to search all the world for especially beautiful women, one would not find a lady so handsome and so gently formed as Brunesent; just her eyes alone, and her face, caused all the other girls to be forgotten, for she was more lovely, fresher and whiter than snow new fallen on the branch, or than a rose or fleur-de-lis. So well made was she that no fault could be found, for she was neither too large nor too small. Her mouth was so beautifully formed that it seemed always to be saying: "Come kiss me!" And she would have been twice as beautiful had it not been for the dolour under which she had suffered nigh unto seven years: Four times a day, and three times at night, she and all her people had to surrender themselves to lamentation and grief. When these intervals had passed, it was Brunesent's custom to listen to the birds in the park, and rest and sleep a little.

Now let us return to Jeffrey. He dismounted and entered the park by a large and handsome gate, and unbridling his horse, let him roam to crop the fresh grass at his will. As for himself, he put his shield under his head, for he intended to get some sleep at all hazards; and it was indeed not long before he was sleeping soundly.

At this time, between the hour of supper and of retirement, Brunesent was amusing herself with the knights and ladies of her court, and when the company made their adieux, Brunesent entered her chamber apart. She thought she would listen to the birds' song, as she did every night when she went to rest. On this occasion, however, she did not hear them, and was greatly vexed. It seemed to her probable that some animal, or perhaps a stranger knight, had entered the park and frightened the birds; so, through a maid, she summoned her seneschal.

"I am badly served," said Brunesent, "for someone has entered the park and disturbed the birds so that they will not sing. Go, see who it is, and if it is a man, let him be taken or killed."

"Lady," said the seneschal, "I am at your service." And he went away quickly with two squires, each of whom bore a great torch. In the park they found Jeffrey sleeping with his head on his shield. The seneschal very haughtily summoned him to get up, but Jeffrey neither heard nor understood. Thereupon the officer prodded and shook him roughly.

"Get up quickly," said the seneschal, "or you are a dead man."

Hereupon Jeffrey rose to a sitting posture and replied courteously: "Noble chevalier, give me a sample of your good breeding and gentility, and let me have my fill of sleep."

"You shall sleep no more," replied Brunesent's man, "but you shall come with me before my lady, whether you like it or not. You will not be so indifferent when she has taken vengeance on you for entering her park and frightening the birds."

"As God is my protector," answered Jeffrey, "not without battle will you carry me off till I have had my fill of sleep."

When the seneschal understood that Jeffrey wanted to fight, he sent one of the squires for his arms, and in the meanwhile Jeffrey dozed off again. "Get up," cried the seneschal, "for you have found your opponent." But Jeffrey never said a word and kept on sleeping. The seneschal shook and poked him till he came awake.

"Chevalier," said Jeffrey, "it is really too bad of you not to let me sleep, for I am so drowsy I can hardly bear it. But since I see you want to fight, I will first make terms: If I unhorse you, will you let me sleep in peace?"

"I will, indeed," answered the seneschal, "by God!"

Jeffrey mounted his horse and the two knights rode at each other with great fury. Our hero never budged with the shock, but the seneschal got such a blow that he was felled to the ground.

"From now on," said Jeffrey, "I hope you will let me sleep."

"By my faith," replied the officer, "you may die here for all of me." And he rode away ashamed and wroth.

When the seneschal came back to the palace: "What did you find in the park?" asked Brunesent.

"An armed knight," replied the man; "and I hope I shall never meet a better one. He was sleeping so soundly I could hardly waken him."

"Well, why didn't you bring him to me?" asked Brunesent. "By God! I shall not eat till I see him hanged."

"By my faith," replied the officer, "he wouldn't come for me, nor could I tear him from his sleep."

"Is that so?" replied the lady. "Go call up the watch for me."

In a short time five hundred knights of the watch assembled in the hall. In a vexed and evil humour Brunesent said to them: "Sirs, a proud and overweening knight has entered my park and frightened the birds, to my great annoy. So haughty is he that he refuses to come to me at my seneschal's bidding. Unless I have his head, or cause him to die an evil death, I will never hold fief more."

Then spoke up Simon le Ros, a big knight, handsome and haughty. "Lady, I will bring him to you alive or dead."

"Do so," said Brunesent.

"By my head," said the seneschal, "don't think this is child's play; the stranger understands well enough how to defend himself; he will be a valiant knight who can win against him."

Simon entered the park, where he found Jeffrey sleeping. "Come, now," he cried, "get up out of here." But Jeffrey kept on sleeping, for he heard never a word. Then Simon gave him a rap on the ribs with the truncheon of his lance, and Jeffrey started up. "Knight," said he, "it is very wrong for you to strike me and wake me up after promising that you would not. Your word doesn't last long. Your behaviour is that of a churl. Let me sleep, for Christ's sake, for you see that I am so drowsy that I can hardly stand on my feet." "You shall not sleep here any longer," replied Simon, "and if you don't come along willingly to speak to my lady, I will make you do so in spite of yourself." "First," said Jeffrey, "we shall see which of us is the stronger and doughtier." Therewith he mounted his horse.

Simon came at him with such vigour that he broke his lance on Jeffrey's shield, and Jeffrey struck him out of the saddle with such force that he just failed of breaking his neck; and he would have finished him, but Simon cried: "Mercy, sir knight! I yield to you." "If I spare your life," said Jeffrey, "will you let me sleep?" "As much as you wish," answered Simon, "so far as I am concerned."

So Jeffrey returned to the place where he had been lying and went to sleep again. But Simon turned away, head bowed, abashed, ashamed and all befouled with dirt; and he entered the palace without half the noise he had made on going out. The seneschal saw him coming and smiled a little. "Lady," he said to Brunesent, "here comes your champion, and he is not bringing the knight with him. It seems to me he must have made terms." "By God!" said Brunesent, "I'll unmake those terms before I eat or sleep."

Now up spoke one of the seven porters, who thought himself a good knight. "Lady, by my faith, if you give me leave, I will bring the fellow to you however hardy he may be, in spite of all he can do—unless he flees."

"Sir," said Simon, "he will not flee, he'll wait for you, for if he had wanted to be off, he would not have gone to sleep again. Do him neither harm nor injury, for that would be shameful, so valiant and well-mannered a knight is he."

Said the seneschal: "I hope God may defend me from evil as well as that knight will defend himself against you. And you are not in such a hurry to go as you will be to come back."

However, the knight rushed off to the park, where he found Jeffrey sleeping. "Sir knight," said he, "get up out of here or die, or else come before my lady." Jeffrey said nothing. "You'll go in spite of yourself, by my faith," continued the porter. "Whatever terms Simon or the seneschal may have made with you have no validity with me." So saying he gave Jeffrey such a blow that he made him jump.

When our hero felt that knock he got to his feet in a daze. "By God!" said he, "I am mocked. I hardly let this fellow go when he comes back and whacks me and wakes me up. Twice he has broken his word and jested with me; but this time he will not escape death."

The porter now bawled out: "Up now, vile churl, scurvy presumptuous boor! In an evil hour did you enter here, for my lady is so annoyed that she intends to have you torn limb from limb."

Said Jeffrey: "That she will not; and as for you, speak more courteously, for whoso speaks villainously does so to his own harm and not to his gain. The courtesy I showed you earlier has been ill repaid. Twice I let you go, but it will not happen so a third time, so help me God!"

Thereupon the two knights encountered. The opposing chevalier broke his lance. Jeffrey struck through his shield, past his arm, through his hauberk, right into the body, so that the lance came out more than a hand's breadth behind. Jeffrey saw that he was so severely wounded that it would be hard to heal him. "Now," said he, "perhaps you'll let me sleep." And he went and lay down again.

Two squires, who saw their master wounded, carried him into the palace. When Brunesent saw him she said: "My lords, if you do not take vengeance for this deed, you are no longer men of mine. If this fellow escapes, the insult which he has put upon me will be thrown in my face forever."

"There is no question of vengeance," said the seneschal. "The stranger is so powerful and hardy that no single knight will ever take him, by my faith. He forced both Simon and myself to let him sleep, and you see what happened to this knight. The same fate lies in wait for any single knight of Monbrun."

Said Brunesent: "I am served by a poor lot. Let fifty, or a hundred, or more go, if necessary. Whoever wishes to be a man of mine, or remain at my court, let him go forthwith."

Hereupon many knights descended into the park, where they found Jeffrey sleeping. They said nothing, but one took him by the legs, another by the arms, another by the hands, another by the shoulders, and one by the head.

Jeffrey was not at all amused when he woke up to find himself thus seized. "God!" said he, "what people is this? Mary to my aid! Lords," he cried, "hold a little and tell me what people you are, whither you are taking me, and what it is you wish. Are you demons? I think you must be, or revenants, since you come at this hour. For Christ's sake and His mother's, go about your business and let me sleep!"

"On the contrary," replied one of the knights; "you shall come before my lady; you shall dearly abide your trespass and the vexation you have caused her. You shall not get off alive."

Thus they bore him, completely armed as he was, into the hall before Brunesent; and Jeffrey, handsome in his glittering armour, stood on his feet before her. The lady looked at him closely and said: "Are you he who has caused me so much ill and vexation tonight?"

"Lady," said Jeffrey, "that is not so. I was never in any position to cause you any grief whatsoever. On the contrary, if anyone has done so, I will take your side with all my might."

"That is not true," answered Brunesent. "Did you not enter my park, and have you not wounded one of my men almost to death?"

"Lady," he replied, "that is so. But he was in the wrong, for he disturbed my sleep: Three times he came and knocked on my ribs with his lance. Moreover, he had twice sworn to me on his faith that he would not molest me or do me any ill. But if I had known he was your man, and if he had been twice as vexatious and uncivil, I would never have wounded him."

"By all the saints in heaven!" cried Brunesent, "you shall never cause me any trouble in the future, for, so help me God! I'll have you hanged, or blinded, or make you an expert with crutches before tomorrow!"

When he heard her speak like that Jeffrey thought she must be angry. "Lady," said he, "do with me as you please, for you in your chemise, with no other accoutrements whatsoever—you would have conquered me more quickly than ten fully armed knights. If I have occasioned you any displeasure, take your vengeance for the same, for I will touch neither sword nor shield nor lance to defend myself."

Brunesent was somewhat appeased by this gallant speech, nor was the handsome bearing of the young knight without effect upon her;

but, for appearance's sake she dared not immediately show any diminution of sternness.

"Lady," continued Jeffrey, "I ask of you but one boon: Let me sleep my fill, then do with me as you please, for against you I have no power of resistance."

"There is no harm in what he says," observed the seneschal. "Let him sleep, at least until we find out who he is and whence he comes. Nowadays many who are rich men and of great estate go through the world seeking adventures."

"Very well," conceded Brunesent. "But take care that you turn him over to me tomorrow morning."

"That I will," replied the seneschal, "for I have no desire to lose your favour."

"And put a strong guard over him," insisted Brunesent.

"God is my witness," said Jeffrey, "that you alone have so much power over me that you could hold me with a piece of string better than a thousand others."

Brunesent sighed and cast a love-laden glance at him. The knight was not so sleepy that his heart did not leap at that. And he sweat, too, and not from heat, but from the love which enflamed him.

Now the seneschal had a fine large bed set up in the hall, with all that pertained thereto, and set a hundred knights to guard the stranger. He turned courteously to Jeffrey and asked his name, his country and his adventure.

"I am from Arthur's court," replied our hero. "But for God's sake ask me no more now—let me sleep." So, dressed, shod and armed as he was, he threw himself on the bed and was soon unconscious.

After this it was not long till the watch of the tower cried out that it was again time to indulge in lamentation and wailing—as they did four times a day and three times at night. Brunesent and her maids of course participated in these expressions of grief, and altogether there was such a hideous clamour that Jeffrey woke with a start, and in no good humour. "God!" said he, "I never saw such people. Sirs, what is the reason for all this uproar?"

At these words his guards turned upon him, calling him evil names, beating him with dagger, sword, lance or mace. Not one of the hundred failed to give him a blow, or two or three. No kettle-smith ever laid on more vigorously than they with their weapons. But Jeffrey's hauberk was good, and he wrapped himself up so in the bed-clothes that he got no wound. Finally the noise died down. The guards thought they had killed their prisoner. "Now we can go to sleep ourselves," said they, "for there is no fear that he will flee."

Jeffrey, however, was now wide awake and heard everything. He remained quiet and prayed earnestly to God, for he thought truly that he was in hell. And when he recalled the exceeding beauty of Brunesent his wonder increased that such a lovely creature should be found among such evil people. And while he was plunged in sweet thought as to the possibility of winning the love of that delightful lady, the watch yelled again, once more waking all the people to their lamentable duty. Neither I nor anyone else could describe the hideous din they made. This time Jeffrey lay quietly, for he was utterly astounded. Said he to himself: "By my head, this is certainly an unpleasant and evil hostel! I'll risk ten lances through my body rather than remain longer in the custody of these folk, for they are very evil company. It is not possible that they should be of flesh and blood—rather, so help me God, are they devils of hell—raising such a clamour as they do when all decent people want to sleep. If God is my aid, they will not find me here tomorrow."

The howling died away and Jeffrey's guards threw themselves down by his bed again. When he saw that they had dozed off, he rose, took his lance and shield from the rack, went out cautiously, and found his horse where he had left him. When he had got safely away: "Thank God," said Jeffrey, "I never expected to escape so easily. But it is too bad about the lovely lady. I never saw one so beautiful or one who pleased me more. However, the company she maintains is too villainous for words, and it is impossible to put up with them." And thus he rode away from Monbrun in the grey dawn.

"Sir," said Doctor Boorde, "I commend your hero's desire to sleep. When a man has exercised himself in the day-time, he ought to sleep soundly and surely at night, whatsoever chance may befall. But moderate sleep is most praiseworthy, for it aids digestion, nourishes the blood and qualifies the heat of the liver; it sharpens, quickens and refreshes the memory; it restores nature and quiets a man's humours and pulses; in a word, it animates and comforts all the natural, animal and spiritual powers of a man. And contrarily, immoderate sleep and sluggishness doth humecte and make light the brain; it engenders rheum and imposthumes; it is evil for the palsy, whether it be universal or particular; it is evil for the falling sickness called epilentia, analentia, cathalentia, apoplexy, soda and all other infirmities of the head, for it induces and causes obliviousness in that it doth obfusque and obnebulate the memory and the quickness of wit; and specially it doth instigate and lead a man to sin, and it doth induce and infer brevity of life. Sleep should be measured according to man's natural complexion, in respect to his strength or weakness, youth or age, health or sickness. If men of certain complexions go too long without sleep, it may prove highly disastrous for them, as I will show by a familiar example.—There were two men who sat at dice together a day and a night and longer. The weak man said to the other: 'I can play no more.' 'Fie,' said the strong man. 'Fie on thee, bench-whistler, wilt thou break away now?' So the weak man, in order to content his companion's mind, desire and appetite, continued to play, and thereby killed himself.—Night-time is best for sleep, but if a man find himself compelled to sleep at any other time, let him stand and lean and sleep against a cupboard, or else let him sit upright in a chair and sleep. Sleeping after a full stomach—*pace* Bartholomew—doth breed diverse infirmities: it hurts the spleen, it relaxes the sinews, it engenders dropsy and gout, and makes a man look evil-coloured, as you may see for yourselves by looking at Seithenyn ab Seithyn Saidi yonder."

"Doctor," said Sir John Harington, "we thank you for your advice, especially as it is gratuitous; and since you have discoursed at such length on the subject, I will remain silent."

"Now that the matter of sleep has been disposed of so neatly," said the Minstrel of Reims, "I should like to inquire what happened to Breast-of-Light?"

"Oh, after many heroic adventures Conall rescued her from Mac-a-Moir," answered Mac Conglinne, "and they lived happily ever afterwards, save that at times she had a cut slicing tongue, like most women. Shall I continue the story?"

"No need," said John Gower; "that part of it is purely banal."

"Gentlemen," said Master Jehan, who had not spoken since we had left Cork, "this distinguished company may not know it, but it is nevertheless true that Sir Lancelot, here present, performed a deed of daring and courage which may be favourably compared with the exploits of Amadas, Eledus, Conall or Jeffrey. Not one lion or cat did he kill, but forty or more, and a live corpse as well. But it was not weariness which interfered with his sleep so much as hunger. That incident took place in Ireland. . . ."

"That seems very likely," interrupted Giraldus Cambrensis.

"As he was riding on his way," continued Jehan, "to abate the marvels of Rigomer. I have just come from collecting the facts of those extraordinary adventures, and if my lords will listen, they shall hear . . ."

26. HOW LANCELOT FOUGHT WITH THE DEMON CATS

Master Jehan

Late in April Lancelot took ship at Anglesey and landed at Baile Atha Cliath. Many of whom he asked information had indeed heard of Rigomer, but it was a long time before he found any who could give him sure directions how to reach that dreadful place, and in the course of a fortnight he had wandered as far as Brefny. All one morning he had ridden through a forest of beech trees, tall and old. Overhead were the shiny new leaves, not yet fully green, but so dense that the sun's rays hardly penetrated, though it must have been near noon. Underfoot in a carpet were the dead leaves from many a preceding season, so thick that it seemed no living foot had troubled them for a long time. And between the old and the new rose the slender stems, greyish blue in the dim light. No sound broke the silence save the occasional snapping of a twig or the creaking of a leather strap.

Thus rode Lancelot alone in the beech wood with whatever thoughts he had, when Morel, his good horse, suddenly shied, and with good reason. Directly before him there appeared a strange figure which seemed to be a man. The figure was absolutely naked save for the covering afforded by the hair which spread over his shoulders, sides and back, mingling with the long beard which reached to his waist; hair grew from his ears, too, matted together with that of his scalp so that his two rheumy eyes were almost hidden. Here and there a sharp bone protruded from the hairy covering, betraying a fearful state of emaciation; without any movement at all the man's frame seemed to rattle. Even Lancelot was startled, but with his customary courtesy and sangfroid he saluted the old man, and he, after several raucous attempts, returned the knight's greeting.

"Are you acquainted hereabouts?" inquired Lancelot.

"I am that," replied the old man. "It is above a hundred years that this forest has been my home, and I was in and out of a hundred when I came into it."

"I do not doubt your word," answered Lancelot. "If you live here perhaps you have some shelter which you will allow me to share with you this night?"

"Shelter I have none," said the man. "For my sins I lie upon the earth under the open sky."

"Is there then," asked Lancelot, "a castle or an abbey anywhere near at which I might find hospitality? Last night and the night

HOW LANCELOT FOUGHT WITH THE CATS

before I spent in these woods, and for two days past neither horse nor man has touched food or drink."

"An abbey there is half a day's journey ahead of you—or was, fifty years ago. I cannot vouch for the hospitality dispensed there nowadays, for the world has grown evil since my time. But since you have not broken your fast for so long, you would honour me by sharing my poor fare. Our meeting at this moment is most providential. I have a few crusts of barley bread which I have been saving for a feast day—and tonight is St John's Eve. I can make some leek soup; and only last Saturday some hunters, in their charity, made me a present of the lights and numbles of a buck; they are not very wormy yet, considering that the season is somewhat advanced. I pray you heartily, sir, stay and partake of my frugal meal. Let it never be said," he added somewhat wistfully, "that a king of Ireland was deficient in hospitality."

"Nay, thank you kindly, good father. My business presses and I am even now long overdue. I will go forward. God be with you."

The old man took several tottering steps as though he would still have urged the knight to stay. But in a few moments, when Lancelot glanced warily over his shoulder, his ancient figure had become hardly distinguishable in the bluish gloom.

All the remainder of that day Lancelot rode until, by evening, he had reached the border of the wood—which marked the end of Brefny and the beginning of Connaught—yet never could he find the abbey indicated by the hermit, nor any other suitable hospice. Such a situation was not new to Lancelot. As on other occasions, he now dismounted under a tree to rest himself and his horse for a while. Soon, as the dusk grew deeper, he perceived at a short distance a light, and curling smoke as from a hearth-fire. On investigation he found, not an abbey, but a large, handsome and well-appointed house, which he lost no time in entering. In the fire-place was a cheerful blaze. At one side of the room was a bed with a handsome quilt spread over it. On the other side he distinguished a bier upon two trestles—a sight which gave him a premonition of evil. Four massive candles were burning at head, foot and both sides, and round about the bier was gathered a company of wild cats, as large as leopards, sitting on their haunches. There must have been forty of them. Lancelot glanced at the cats angrily, and they seemed just as ill pleased at his presence. Certainly, they had no fear of him, and began to miaul hideously. At their cries more cats made their appearance—so many that the whole house was filled with them.

To Lancelot it seemed that the cats made the room too crowded for his comfort, and that something would have to be done about the matter if he were to pass the night there peaceably. Accordingly he seized a burning brand from the fire and with it gave the biggest cat such a blow that he knocked it senseless to the floor. Hereupon the others, as though at a signal, attacked him *en masse*. They jumped upon his shoulders and stuck their claws through the meshes of his hauberk so that the blood flowed. For his part, Lancelot dealt out doughty blows on flanks and necks with his burning brand. The cats blooded him and lacerated his back, but could do him no further harm. The knight continued to lay about him stoutly with his flaming club on heads and rumps to such good effect that he finally beat the snarling mass of felines out of the house. Then he slipped inside quickly and carefully closed the door.

Lancelot stood for a moment, wiping the sweat and blood from his eyes, and then turned back toward the fire. But as he approached the fire-place the bier standing beside it slowly rose to meet him. What new nonsense is this? thought Lancelot. Dropping the brand, which was now only a smouldering stump, he seized his sword, and as the bier came on steadily, he cut it in two with a double-handed stroke. What was his astonishment to find that there was no one in it! "By God!" said he, crossing himself, "this is either enchantment or the work of the devil." Therewith he threw the whole affair into the fire and stirred it about till it was entirely consumed.

Lancelot's fight with the cats in the heated room brought on new pangs of hunger and thirst, and he now thought longingly of the hermit's invitation to lunch. There was no help for it, however, so, fully armed as he was, he threw himself on the bed and fell into a troubled sleep.

The next morning Lancelot left Brefny, and for two weeks pursued his way through Connaught without much adventure till he came to a handsome manor house. The lord thereof was a rich burgess who administered field and forest for a day's journey round about. With him he took shelter for the night and found good entertainment.

After supper, while the company was shortening the night with story-telling, there came a knock at the door. A varlet opened it, revealing a knight with his head tied up in a bandage. The stranger saluted the company, and they returned his greeting, inviting him to make himself at home. Little desire had he for sport or jollity, however, for the bandage concealed a grievous wound: he had lost an eye. The company were shocked by the news of this misfortune and courteously asked to be informed who had served him thus. The knight replied that he had lost his eye at Rigomer, which cursed land he had just left. "But I did not lose my eye entirely," he added, "only provisionally. I still have it with me, carefully wrapped up in a piece of cendal."

"Indeed?" said the host; "and what is the reason for that?"

"I will tell you," replied the knight. "The damsel who gave me the piece of cendal told me that a man would come who should abate the marvels of Rigomer, and after that my severed eye would be restored. That is why I carry it about with me."

"A wise precaution," agreed the burgess.

All the company were astounded at this tale, and asked the knight for other particulars concerning Rigomer; and he attempted to satisfy their curiosity from what he had heard and from what he had himself experienced.

Lancelot, you may be sure, was glad to learn that he was now within six days' journey of his destination. The following morning he thanked his genial host, and about undern entered Thomond—a land abounding in reivers and savage beasts.

"But that is another story," added Master Jehan, "and my throat is dry."

"Sir," said Giraldus Cambrensis, "I have seen some strange things myself, and heard of others. I am, I believe, no more incredulous than most men, and I will accept your self-moving bier or corpse, but I must object to a falsification of known facts."

"What do you mean?" asked Master Jehan.

"There are," answered Giraldus, "no beech trees in Ireland."

"What is your authority for that statement?" asked Peter Bell.

"My book, *Distinctio tres, capitulo* . . ."

"In that case you had better be silent," remarked William of Newburgh. "Your reputation for veracity is no better than that of Geoffrey of Monmouth. You can hardly impose on *us* as you did on the burghers of Oxford."

"I thought they were beech trees," said Lancelot.

"And you were right," said Sir John Harington. "Anyone who has actually been in Ireland has seen plenty of them there."

"Amen," said Fynes Moryson.

"Now that that point has been settled," remarked Wace, "I should like to express my approval of Lancelot's courage and address; but I think I can match his exploit, at least in part, from the chronicles of the dukes of Normandy."

"What have you in mind?" queried Ordericus Vitalis.

"It is," answered Wace, "the story of . . ."

27. RICHARD SANS PEUR AND THE UNQUIET CORPSE

Master Wace

Richard sans Peur, son of Guillaume Longue Espée and third duke of Normandy, well deserved his eponym. Not only did he love knights and chivalry, but also clerks and the clergy.

Now it was a habit of Richard's to walk abroad much at nighttime, so restless was his eager spirit, and on these occasions, it is said, he saw as well in the dark as in the daylight. During such rambles he disturbed many an ugly ghost, and dislodged many a fantasm lurking in nooks and corners; but he was never afraid of anything, whatever he might see, whether by night or day.

When Richard roved about at night it was his custom to enter any church that might lie in his way, and if the church were closed, he would offer up a prayer in the porch. One night as he was riding along, his men being scattered before and behind him at some distance, he came to a church and wished to make his orisons as usual. He tied his horse outside and entered without let or hindrance. Just inside the door-way he found a corpse lying on a bier. He crossed himself and passed by, throwing his gloves upon a lectern, and knelt down before the altar. But he had not been there long when behind him in the nave he heard the bier creak as though the corpse were moving about; indeed, when Richard looked over his shoulder, he saw that the corpse had risen on one elbow and was gazing at him intently. "You, there," said Richard, "whether you be of good or of evil, be quiet in this holy place and do not be moving about; lie down and take your rest, as you ought." Then he continued with his prayer. When he had finished he crossed himself and repeated the lines—

> Per hoc signum Sancte Crucis
> Libera me de malignis
> Domine Deus salutis

and commending his soul to God, took his sword and turned away from the altar.

But the devil rose up and stood beside the door with arms extended as though he would lay hold on the duke in passing. Richard seized his brand, and with one blow cut the corpse in two just below the arm-pits, and it fell onto the bier again in two parts. Richard now passed out, found his horse, and had already made his way out of the cemetery when he remembered that he had left his gloves behind on the lectern. He did not want to lose them, so he returned to the chancel and took them up again. Not many men would have passed the dreadful bier twice again for the sake of a pair of gloves.

"I admit," said Wace when he had told his tale, "that my story lacks the detail of the cats."

"Och! Cats!" shuddered Senchan Torpeist.

"Except for cats," said John Skelton, "your anecdote reminds me somewhat of the prioress and her suitors."

"How was that?" asked several voices.

"I found the poem among the papers of my predecessor at Diss," answered Skelton, "if you can call it a poem. It goes like this—though I should warn you that the first fourteen lines contain very little matter apprehensible to the senses."

28. THE PRIORESS AND HER THREE SUITORS
John Skelton

O glorious God our governor, gladden all this guesting,
And give them joy that will hear what I shall say or sing.
Me were loath to be undernom of them that be not   [*reproved*
      cunning:
Many manner of men there be that will meddle of everything,
     For reasons ten or twelve.
     Divers men faults will feel
     That know no more than doth my heel,
     That they think nothing is well
     But it do move of themself.

But it do move of themself, forsooth, they think it right naught;
Many men are so used—their terme is soon taught;   [*reached*
Simple is their conceit when it is forth brought.
To move you of a matter, forsooth I am bethought,
     To declare you of a case.
     Make you merry, all and some,
     And I shall tell you of a nun,
     The fairest creature under the sun,
     Was prioress of a place.

The lady that was lovely, a lord's daughter she was,
Full pure and ful precious proved in every place;
Lords and laymen and spiritual gave her chase;
For her fair beauty great temptation she has.

  Her love for to win
  Great gifts to her they brought;
  Many her love, none she sought.
  To guard herself from being caught
  She wist not how to begin.

There wooed a young knight, a fresh lord and fair,
And a parson of a parish, apparelled without pair,   [*peer*
And a burgess of a borough. List and ye shall hear
How they laid their love upon the lady dear,
  And none of other wist.
  They go and come,
  Desired of her love soon;
  They swore by sun and moon
  Of her to have their lust.

The young knight for the lady's love narrow turned [*carefully*
  and went;
Many bucks and does to the lady he sent.
The parson presents her privily, his matters to amend;
Beds, brooches and bottles of wine to the lady sent
  The burgess, to her brought.
  Thus they troubled through tene.
  She wist not how herself to demean
  For to keep her soul clean,
  Till she her bethought.

The knight bethought him marvellously with the lady to [*speak*
  melle:
He flattered her with many a fable—fast his tongue gan telle;
Leasings leaped out among as the peals of a bell: [*as numerous*
"Madam, but I have my lust of you, I shall myself quelle; [*kill*
  Your love unto me grant;
  In battle bolde there abide,
  To make the Jews their heads hide,
  With great strokes and bloody side,
  And slay many a great giant.

"All is for your love, madame, my life would I venter, [*risk*
So that ye will grant me, I have desired many a winter,
Underneath your comely cowl to have mine intent."
"Sir," she said, "ye be our lord, our patron and our president;
  Your will must needs be done,
  So that ye will go this tide

THE PRIORESS AND HER THREE SUITORS

  Down to the chapel under the wood-side,
  And be ruled as I will ye guide."
  "All ready," said he then.

"Down in the wood there is a chapel, right as I you hight; [*inform*
Therein must ye lie all night, my love and ye will get;
Lie there like a dead body sewed in a shett,   [*sheet*
Then shall ye have my love, mine own honey swett,   [*sweet*
  Unto morrow that it be light."
  "Madame," he said, "for your love
  It shall be done, by God above!
  Who saith 'Nay,' here is my glove
  In that quarrel to fight."

The knight kissed the lady gent, the bargain was made;
Of no bargain since he was born was he never half so glad.
He went to the chapel, as the lady him bade;
He sewed himself in a sheet, he was nothing adread,
  He thought upon no sorrow.
  When he came there, he lay upright,
  With two tapers burning bright;
  There he thought to lie all night,
  To kiss the lady on the morrow.

As soon as the knight was gone, she sent for Sir John;
Well I wot he was not long, he came to her anon.
"Madame," he said, "what shall I do?" She answered him then,
She said: "I shall tell you my counsel soon,
  Blown it is so broad:
  I have a cousin of my blood,
  Lieth dead in the chapel wood;
  For owing of a sum of good
  His burying is forbode.

"We are not able to pay the good that men do crave,
Therefor we send for you our worship for to save.
Say his dirge and mass, and lay him in his grave;
Within a while after my love you shall have,
  And truly keep counsel."
  His heart hoped his will to work;
  To do all this he undertook,
  To say his service upon a book
  He swore by heaven and hell.

"Do thy devoir," the lady said, "as farforth as thóu may;
Then shalt thou have thy will of me." And certain to thee I say
Sir John was as glad of this as ever was fowl of day.
With a mattock and a shovel to the chapel he takes the way
    Where he lay in his shett.   [*sheet*
    When he came there he made his pett,   [*pit*
    And said his dirge at his fett.   [*feet*
    The knight lieth still and dreamed it
    That his love was his swett.   [*sweet*

As soon as the priest was gone the young knight for to bury,
She sent after the merchant. To her he came full merry.
"Down in the wood there is a chapel, stands fair under a
    peré;   [*pear-tree*
Therein lieth a dead corpse, thereto must ye steer ye,
    To help us in our right.
    He oweth us a sum of gold—
    To forbid his burying I am bold.
    A priest is thither, it is me told,
    To bury him this night.

"If the corpse buried be and our money not paid,
It were a foul shame for us so for to be betrayed;
And if ye will do after me, the priest shall be afraid:
In a devil's garment ye shall be arrayed,
    And stalk ye thither full still.
    When ye see the priest stir
    To bury him that lieth on bier,
    Leap in at the choir door
    Like a fiend of hell."

"Madame, for your love, soon shall I be attired,
So that ye will grant me that I have oft desired."
"Sir," she said, "ye shall it have, but first I'll be assured
That our counsel ye will keep that it be not discovered.
    Till tomorrow that it be day,
    If thou flinch or else flee,
    For ever thou losest the love of me."
    "I grant, madame," saith he,
    And on with his array.

He dight him in a devil's garment, forth gan he go.
He came in at the church door, as the dirge was do,

Running, roaring, with his rakles, as devils seemed to do.   [*chains*
The priest brayed up like a buck, his heart was almost go,
    He deemed himself but dead,
    He was afraid he was too slow.
    He rose up, he wist not how,
    And broke out at a window,
    And broke foul his head.

But he that abode all the brunt, how shrewdly was he egged,
For to hear his dirge done and see his pit degged!   [*digged*
"I trow I had my dame's curse; I might have been better bedded,
For now I am but lost, the lighter but I be legged."
    And up he rose then.
    The devil saw the body rise;
    Then his heart began to grise: [*feel horror*
    "I trow we be not all wise"—
    And he began to run.

His rags and his rattles clean he had forget—
So had the young knight that sewed was in the sheet;
The priest deemed them devils both, with them he would not meet;
He spared neither hill nor holt, bush, trap nor grit—
    Lord! he was foul scrapéd!
    The other twain were ill afeared,
    They spared not the stile nor sherd,
    They had liefer than middle erd
    Either from other have scapéd.

The priest took a by-path, with them he would not meet:
His head was foul broken, the blood ran down to his feet.
He ran in a furred gown, he cast off all his clothes, all his body reeked,
    To the bare breek
    Because he would go light.
    He thought he heard the devil loush;   [*follow madly*
    He started into a briar bush
    That all his skin gan roush
    Off his body quite.

The knight ran into a wood as fast as he might wend;
He fell upon a stake, and foul his leg did rend;
Thereof he took no care—he was afraid of the fiend;
He thought it was a long way to the path's end,
    But then came all his care:
    In at a gap as he glent,   [*darted*

>   By the middle he was hent,
>   Into a tree top he went
>   In a buck's snare.

The merchant ran into a dale, there where grow no thorns;
He fell upon a bull's back, he caught him upon his horns.
"Out! Alas!" he said, "that ever I was born,
For now I go to the devil because I did him scorn,
>   Unto the pit of hell."
>   The bull ran into a mire:
>   There he tossed our fair sir—
>   For all the world he durst not stir
>   Till that he heard a bell.

On the morrow he was glad that he was so scapéd;
So was the priest also, though he was body naked.
The knight was in the tree top, for dread fear he quakéd:
The best jewel that he had he would have forsakéd
>   For to come down.
>   He caught the tree by the top—
>   Yea, and eke the caltrop;   [*snare*
>   He fell and broke his fore top
>   Upon the bare ground.

Thus they went from the game, beguiled and beglued;
Neither of other wist, home they went beshrewed.
The parson told the lady on the morrow what mischief there
    was shewed,
How that he had run for her love, his mirth was but lewd,
>   He was so sore dread of death.
>   "When I should have buried the corpse,
>   The devil came in, the body rose:
>   To see all this my heart grose;   [*felt horror*
>   Alive I 'scaped unneath."   [*hardly*

"Remember," the lady saith, "what mischief hereon goeth:
Had I never lover yet that ever died good death."
"By that Lord," said the priest, "who made both ale and meat,
Thou shalt never be wooed by me while I have speech or breath,
>   While I may see or hear."
>   Thus those two made their boast;
>   Forth he went without the corpse.
>   Then came the knight for his purpose,
>   And told her of his fare.

"Now I hope to have your love, I have deserved it sore,
For never bought I love so dear since I was man i-bore."
"Hold thy peace!" the lady said, "thereof speak thou no more,
For by the new bargain, my love thou hast forlore
    All these hundred winters."
    She answered him, he went his way.
    The merchant came the same day,
    He told her of his great affray,
    And of his high adventure.

"Till the corpse should be buried, the bargain I abode;
When the dead body rose, a grimly ghost aglow,
Then was time I should stir, many a leaf I bestrode;
There was no hedge for me too high, nor no water too broad,
    Of you to have my will."
    The lady said: "Peace," full blithe.
    "Never," she said, "while thou art man on life,
    For I will show it to thy wife,
    And all the country it tell,

"And proclaim it in the market town, thy care to increase."
Therewith he gave her twenty marks that she should hold her peace.
Then the burgess of the borough, after his decease,
He endowed unto the place with deeds of good release
    In fee for ever more.
    Thus did the lady free:
    She keepeth her virginity,
    And endowed the place with fee,
    And salved them of their sore.

"Such," concluded Skelton with a sigh, "is the tale to which many refer, but which none brings forward. Some of you may think it would have shown better taste if I too had allowed it to rest quietly under the detritus of Time. But I thought it might be interesting to see how an Englishman handled the theme of *Decameron* IX, the first tale. And in spite of the corrupt text and the doggerel, the narrative seems to me to have certain virtues—though it has no cats."

"Cats! Cats!" shrieked Senchan Torpeist. "Why must you always be talking about the filthy creatures?"

"Why not?" asked Skelton innocently.

"Perhaps," said Cuan O Lochan, "the great ollave's harrowing experience is unknown to you and others of this company. With his permission I will relate it."

Senchan shuddered, closed his eyes, and sank his white beard lower upon his breast as though he would also close his ears. "You will tell it anyway," he sighed.

29. SENCHAN TORPEIST AND THE KING OF THE CATS

Cuan O Lochan

In the time of Diarmait son of Fergus Cerrbheoil, the chief professor of the poets of Ireland was Dallan Forguil. When he died, the associate professors assembled and elected Senchan Torpeist to be his successor and their chief. On such occasions it was customary to make an inaugural procession round Ireland, and the Great Bardic Company now debated what province they should go to first on their professional visit.

"It would be proper," said Senchan peremptorily, cutting short their wrangling, "to visit that person who has never been satirized or reproached about his liberality or abundance of property or goods."

"Who is that?" they asked.

"He is," said Senchan, "Guaire son of Colman."

Then the entire of the Great Bardic Association said it would be proper to go to Guaire first, since Senchan had said so, and messengers were dispatched to Guaire Aidne mac Colman, king of Connaught.

Now you should know that in my day the professors of Ireland were not a cringing lot of pusillanimous Laodiceans: they were able and respected men, and in the satire they possessed a powerful weapon against evil-doers. A satire pronounced by one of the Bardic Company against a man would cause blisters blue and red to break out on his face; boils would appear on his neck and back, and between his toes and fingers; an internal burning would rage in his vitals, and he would waste away to be utterly consumed.

But the satire was a two-edged weapon, and it was sometimes evilly employed by pontifical and overweening poets. To Senchan, newly elected to the chairmanship of his caste, and yearning to display his power, it was like a new toy to a fractious child. If he could succeed in satirizing Guaire, a blameless person, he would by that act not only silence the murmurers in his own ranks, but establish his position forever, and remain superior to kings themselves.

Said Senchan: "Though the name of Guaire be excellent for hospitality, I will on this occasion take but a few of my household with me." So he took in his suite only thrice fifty professors of the first class, thrice fifty professors of the second class, thrice fifty hounds, thrice fifty male attendants, thrice fifty female relatives, and thrice nine of each class of artificers. And that number arrived at Durlus, Guaire's royal abode.

Guaire went forth to meet them, and he bestowed kisses on their chiefs, and gave welcome to their learned men. They were led into a large mansion, and viands were laid out before them. And Guaire said that whatever they might desire, they should ask for it and they should have it.

It was very difficult to procure some of the things which the Bardic Company demanded, but with the aid of his brother Marvan Guaire succeeded in maintaining his reputation as a perfect host for the better part of a year; and in all this time Senchan had found no cause for which he might satirize the king. The situation was very annoying to him, and he fasted for three days so that his wits might be sufficiently sharpened to know what to do about it.

On the third night of Senchan's fast a woman named Brigit desired her maid, Beaidgil, to give Senchan some of her spare food. "What leavings hast thou?" inquired Senchan. "A hen egg," replied Brigit. "It is almost enough for me," answered Senchan, "and it will suffice for the present."

For a long time Beaidgil searched for the remnant of the food and did not find it. "I believe it is thyself that art eating the leavings," said Senchan. "Not I, O chief bard," replied the maid, "but the nimble race it is who have eaten it, namely, the mice." "That is not proper for them," said Senchan. "There is not a king nor a chief, be he ever so great, but that these mice would wish to leave traces of their own teeth in his food; and in this they are at fault, for food should not be used by any person after the prints of their teeth; and I will satirize them."

And Senchan began to satirize them, and said:

> *Senchan:* The mice, though sharp their snouts,
> Are not powerful in the battles of warriors.
> Venomous death will I deal out to the tribe
> In avengement of Brigit's leavings.
>
> *Mouse:* Small were the leavings you left—
> It was not abundance you retired from.
> Receive payment and compensation from us,
> And do not satirize us, O learned bard.
>
> *Senchan:* Thou mouse in the hole there,
> Whose utterance is opposition,
> It was thou, whose claws are not short,
> That ate my leavings in thy rambling.

Mouse: Bianan, my own son of the white breast,
Thou non-observer of ordinances,
Now thy contumacy is known to the
Mighty Bardic Company, thou doomed wretch.
Senchan: Clear ye out of your spacious abodes,
For we are prepared to convict you.
Come out of the hole, now,
And lie down here, O ye mice!

Then, when ten mice fell dead in the presence of Senchan, he said to them: "It is not you whom I ought to have satirized, but rather the party whose duty it is to suppress you, namely, the tribe of cats. And now I will satirize them effectively, and also their chief lord and brehon, namely, Hirusan son of Arusan, where he is in his cave of Cnogda. And I will satirize his spouse, Fiery-mouth daughter of Sharp-pointed-teeth, and his daughter, Pointed-tooth, and her brothers, Purrer and Rough-claws. And I will satirize Hirusan himself, for he is their chief and lord responsible for them." And he said:

"Hirusan of the over-sized claws, remnant of the otter's food, with beau-ish tail like that of a cow, similar to a horse watching another horse—a monster is Hirusan. Now I will explain this: Hirusan of the monstrous claws, that is to say, when a mouse gets into the hole he misses him and only darts his claws at the hole. Refuse of the otter's food he is for the reason that the ancestor of the cats formerly lay asleep on the margin of a lake, and the otter came up to him and bit off the tops of his two ears, so that every cat since has been jagged-eared and defective. Of the hanging-down cow tail is he, for no quicker does a cow's tail drop down than does his tail when a mouse escapes him. A horse watching a horse, for the cat and the mouse are similar to two horses yoked together, for there is close attention between them, the ear of one listening to the other, and the ear of the other is listening to him. And those are the satires."

Now the influence of these satires reached Hirusan in the cave of Cnogda, and he said: "Senchan has satirized me," he said, "and I will be avenged on him for it." His daughter, Reang of the sharp teeth, said: "We would rather that you brought Senchan to us here so that we might ourselves take vengeance on him for the satires." "I will bring him in due time," said Hirusan; and he made ready to go, telling his daughter to send her brothers after him.

It was told to Senchan that Hirusan was on his way, coming to kill him. The professor then requested Guaire to come with the nobility of Connaught to protect him against the cat. They all gathered about him, and they had not been there long when they heard a vibrating, impetuous and impressive sound similar to that produced by a tremendously raging fiery furnace in full blaze; and it appeared to them that there was not in Connaught a plough-ox larger than Hirusan. His appearance was as follows: blunt-snouted, rapacious, panting, determined, jagged-eared, broad-breasted, sharp- and smooth-clawed, sharp- and rough-toothed, nimble, powerful, deep-flanked, angry, terror-striking, vindictive, quick, purring, glare-eyed; and in that similitude he came toward them. He passed through them and beyond them, above them and below them, and he did not stop till he came to the place where Senchan was. He took hold of the bard by one arm, jerked him onto his back, and went by the way he had come, for he had no other object than to come for Senchan.

Now, however, the poet had recourse to flattery of Hirusan, praising his leap, his progress in running, his power, strength and activity, and he said: "Hirusan son of Arusan, of the race of the Faigli Fithise, I invoke God between you and me, and I implore Him to deliver me." Nevertheless, Senchan was not let down till they reached Clonmacnois of St Kieran.

As they were passing the door of the saint's forge where Kieran happened to be, he perceived Hirusan with Senchan on his back, and he said: "It is a great pity that Guaire's hospitality should be tarnished, and there goes the chief bard of Erin on the back of the cat."

There was at the time a flaming bar of iron held by the pincers, and Kieran made a fortunate brave throw at the cat, and hit him on the flank with the bar of iron, and it passed out on the other side and left him lifeless.

Then Senchan dismounted from Hirusan and he uttered a vindictive expression: "My curse on the hand that gave that throw," said he. "Why so?" asked Kieran. "Because," said the poet, "I am dissatisfied in the highest degree that I have not been let go with Hirusan to be eaten by him, that thereby the Great Bardic Association might be able to satirize Guaire; for I would rather that Guaire should be satirized than that I should live and he not satirized," he said.

Then he proceeded back to Durlus, where the nobility of Connaught desired to welcome him. But Senchan would not have a kiss or welcome from any of them; and though the Great Bardic Institution passed away the time with abundance of the best of viands and in feasting, Senchan was bitter and brooded in silence, apart.

"And never after," concluded Cuan O Lochan, "even when he had recovered the story of *The Cattle Raid of Cooley* did he regain his spirits, as you can see for yourselves. And thus you now understand the great ollave's aversion for cats."

"Right he was, too," said the Curtal Friar, "and other people would do well to dislike them also. All the world should beware of the cat. She goes and licks a toad, where she finds it, under a stone or elsewhere, so that the toad bleeds. Thereupon, by reason of the poison in the toad, the cat becomes thirsty; and when she comes to water which people use for drinking or preparing their food, she drinks thereof and pollutes it, and so infects humans that some of them come to grief therethrough, lying sick for half a year, or perhaps a whole year, or even a lifetime; or else death seizes them suddenly. Often the cat drinks so fast that a drop from her eye falls into the water, or else she sneezes therein. Whoever eats or drinks what she has sneezed upon must endure fearful death. You should drive the cat from you, for the breath that comes out of her throat is exceedingly noisome and perilous. Let her be driven from the kitchen, or wherever you may be, for she is mortally unclean."

"I can't imagine where you got those bits of unnatural history," said Bartholomew Anglicus; "they are not in Pliny nor in Aristotle. The cat is called *muriligus* and *musio* and also *catus;* and he has the name *muriligus* because he is an enemy to mice and rats; but he is commonly called *catus,* and he has that name on account of ravening, for he ravishes mice and rats. The name *catus* comes from the Greek, and by it is to be understood 'sly' and 'witty,' as Isidore says, *libro* xii°. The cat is most like the leopard, for he has a great mouth with sharp saw-teeth, and a long, pliant, thin and subtile tongue; and he laps therewith when he drinks, as do other beasts that have the nether lip shorter than the over. For because of the unevenness of lips such beasts suck not in drinking, but lap and lick, as Aristotle says, and Pliny also. When young the cat is swift, pliant and merry, and leaps and jumps at everything before him, and is led by a straw, and plays therewith. And in time of generation he is, as it were, wild, and prowls about continuously, for he is a right lecherous beast in youth. Among cats there is much hard fighting for wives in time of love, and one scratches and rends the other grievously with biting and with claws; and he makes a ruthful and ghastly noise when he proffers to fight with another. In old age he is a right heavy beast and very sleepy, and lies slyly in wait for mice, and is aware of them more by smell than by sight; and he hunts and seizes upon them in privy places; and when he takes a mouse, he plays therewith and eats him after the play. Sometimes the cat dwells in the woods, where he is a cruel beast, hunting small game such as conies and hares. It is a characteristic of the cat that he alights on his feet when he falls out of a high place, and is hardly hurt at all when he is thrown down from a height. When the cat has a fair skin, he is, as it were, proud thereof, and walks about in a stately manner; but when his skin is burnt, then he abides at home. And often, for his fair skin, he is taken by the skinner and slain and flayed."

"Well, well," said Cucuimne, "that is indeed a learned discourse. But there is one quality of cats which you have not mentioned, and that is their companionability. All cats are not like Hirusan—whose retaliation the candid mind must confess was richly deserved by Senchan. They are frequently splendid company for lonely people, whether lay or religious. For my part, I love the active, eager, smooth, intelligent creatures. Here is a poem which I made about my white Pangur."

30. PANGUR BAN
Cucuimne

White Pangur, my cat and I, each of us has a separate art. His mind is fixed on hunting, and mine is engaged with my specialty.

I myself love quietude better than any renown, industriously labouring at my little book to understand it.

White Pangur wants no part of my delight, for he is satisfied with his own sprightly play.

Thus, as we two live together, each of us has unlimited opportunity for employing the keenness of his wit;

At times, through a nimble hero-feat, a mouse sticks fast in the net of his claws,

While into my net there may fall the comprehension of a law with a difficult meaning.

Pangur directs his bright eye to the wall, and joyous is he in his swift spring if a mouse emerge;

My unclear eye I direct toward the sharpness of knowledge, and I too am happy when I understand a dear difficult problem.

In this way neither of us hinders his companion, and to each one his own art is pleasing and profitable.

"If St Helenus kept a crocodile, I don't see why we should begrudge you a cat," said Sir Thomas Elyot. "Still, cats, in contrast to horses, have little stability of character. You recall the story of the cat that fell in love with a handsome young man and implored Aphrodite to transform her into a woman. The young man saw her, fell in love in his turn, and took her home. But as they lay in the nuptial chamber, Aphrodite thought she would determine whether or not the cat, in changing the form of her body, had also changed her character; so she sent a mouse scurrying across the floor of the room. Thereupon the metamorphosed cat, forgetting her new status, leaped out of bed after the mouse to eat it. This action so vexed the goddess that she changed her back into her feline form."

"I agree with you," said John Bromyard. "Cats, as the learned doctor says, may indeed free our houses of vermin, but as you have shown, they are untrustworthy. I once heard of a silly fellow who found that the mice were eating up the cheese which he kept in a wooden chest; so he put his cat into the chest to protect the cheese. But what did the cat do? He ate not only the mice, but the cheese also."

"You are probably right," said Ralph Higden. "It is frequently a mistake to trust cats too implicitly. Their intelligence may sometimes be little more than malice, or at least employed towards no good end. When I was a young man I heard of a certain scribbler named John who kept a cat which he said was his familiar. By suggestion of some sort from the beast he was induced to proclaim publicly at Oxford that he was the real heir to the English throne. He was tried by the king and his court at Northampton, convicted of lying—or rather of treason—and drawn and hanged."

"I remember a similar, though less tragic, case," said Caesar of Heisterbach. "At Hemmenrode there was a certain lay-brother who was much given to the sin of sloth in church, for he was almost always asleep there. Another lay-brother, who was shocked by his behaviour, regarded him closely and observed that on his head there sat a cat; as soon as it placed its paws on the brother's eyes, he began to sink into somnolence. Now when the offending brother was informed of this circumstance, he determined that he would not continue to be deceived by the devil; wherefor he arranged his stall in such a fashion that if he were to begin to fall asleep the seat would slip and cast him out of it. Thus the demon of sluggardry was outwitted, and the brother rendered more assiduous in the service of God."

"The argument," said William Langland, "seems to me to be leaving the substance of cats and embarking upon what may or may not be purely accidents. Bartholomew has pointed out a real service which felines render man, and the Irish poet has indicated another. You all know that Richard Poore allowed anchoresses to keep cats for one or other of these reasons. Now in the fair field by Malvern Hill I saw, among other things, a rout of rats and small mice, more than a thousand. They had come to take counsel for their common profit, for it seemed that there was a cat, who came when he liked and pounced upon them, and took them whenever he wished, and played with them perilously, and pushed them about. Indeed, he worried them so that they were loath of life. 'If we could withstand him in some way,' said they, 'then we might be able to live free from dread.' Then spoke up a rat of renown most ready of tongue. 'In London,' said he, 'I have seen certain persons wearing neck-rings and ornamented collars about their necks, and they went wheresoever it pleased them without restraint. Now if there were a bell attached to such collars, it seems to me that one might know when they approached, and so could run away. Wherefor,' said the rat, 'it is my suggestion that we get a brass bell, or perhaps a silver one, attach it to a collar, and hang the collar on the cat's neck—for our common behoof. Then we shall be able to hear when he rambles or rests or runs to play. And if he wishes merely to play, then we may appear in his presence and abide him while he is in a good mood; but if he is in a bad temper, then we can beware and shun his path.'

"All the rout of rats approved this proposal. The bell was bought and attached to the collar. But then there could not be found in the whole throng of them one rat that had sufficient courage to hang it on the cat's neck though he should have been rewarded with the realm of France or England. So they were very despondent, considering that their labour and their long study had been lost.

"Then there came forward boldly and stood before them a mouse who, it seemed to me, had a great deal of good sense, and to the rats he said: 'If we killed this cat there would come another to scratch us, even though we hid under benches. Therefore it is my counsel that we leave the cat alone, nor be so bold as even to show him the bell. You know that we mice would spoil many a man's malt, and you rats would chew up men's clothes, were it not for the cat that can overleap us all. Moreover, while the cat is catching conies he covets not our persons, and even though we miss a shrew from among our ranks from time to time, better is a little loss than a long sorrow.'

"And the moral of this tale is, gentlemen, that the cat, if he is properly trained, and his activities properly directed, is a force for good in the community."

"I," spoke up Mochua, "am inclined to agree with Higden. Cats may be intelligent, if you wish, even without malice; but on everybody's showing they are predatory. Now in my familia there was a fly which, I think, was much superior to Cucuimne's cat, for he was a learned clerk.—During my time of retirement from the world," continued Mochua, "the only worldly wealth I had were a cock, a mouse and a fly. The use of the cock was to get me to rise betimes for matins at midnight. The use of the mouse was to prevent me from sleeping more than five hours from daylight until night; and if I desired to take more sleep, wearied out with praying and prostrations, he would come and scratch my ear, and thus waken me. And the fly's service was to walk on every line of the Psalter that I read; and when I ceased from reciting the Psalms, the fly remained on the line where I had stopped until I returned to that line again. Thus we lived together for many years until those three treasures died. . . ."

"Reverend sir," said Paul the Deacon, "may you not also have been deceived by the devil in disguise? I remember that King Cunincpert was given a bad quarter of an hour by the Old Enemy travestied in the form of a fly."

"How was that?" asked the Monk of Heisterbach.

31. THE FLY WITH THE WOODEN LEG
Paul the Deacon

We read in the Chronicles of the Lombards that King Cunincpert had been dispossessed of his realm for a time principally through the machinations of Aldo and Grauso, citizens of Brescia. He slew the usurper Alahis in the battle of Kornate, and though Aldo and Grauso escaped him for the moment, he did not by any means dismiss them from his mind. Indeed, as soon as he had returned to his palace at Ticino he summoned his field marshal and began to discuss with him plans for suitably punishing the traitors. While they were talking about this matter they were alone in the room save for a very large fly, which kept buzzing about their ears and faces, to the king's great annoyance. Finally it came to rest on the sill of the window before which they were standing; Cunincpert, in great irritation, made a cast at it with his knife, and though he failed to kill it, cut off one of its feet.

Now Aldo and Grauso, who were ignorant of the king's intention toward them, were making their way toward the palace at Ticino. On the road they were met by a lame man who lacked one foot, who told them that Cunincpert intended to kill them if he could lay hands on them. At this news Aldo and Grauso took sanctuary in the church of the holy martyr Romanus.

When Cunincpert learned that the traitors had thus escaped him, he was very wroth, and bitterly accused his field marshal of betraying his plans. But the man stoutly denied the accusation on his oath. "You know," he said, "that we were alone in the room when we conferred about this and that, and you know that I have been in your presence ever since. How, then, could I have told anyone what you intended?" Cunincpert was forced to admit the truth of this, so he sent to Aldo and Grauso in the church of Romanus, asking how they had come to take refuge there. "My lord," they replied, "we learned that you wished to kill us." "How did you find that out?" asked the king. "My lord," said they, "as we were on the way to the palace we were met by a lame man who had a wooden leg as far as the knee; it was he who told us of the punishment which you planned for us."

On receiving this reply the king understood that the fly whose foot he had cut off by a blow of his knife was an evil spirit, and that it was he who had betrayed his secret thoughts. Forthwith he pardoned Aldo and Grauso and accepted them as members of his bodyguard.

"My fly," protested Mochua indignantly, "was not of that calibre. Not only was he a learned clerk—he was a good Christian."

"If it is a good Christian for which you are searching among the dumber animals," said Columcille, "I would call your attention to a servant of mine. Adamnan, my faithful biographer, had preserved the account of his attachment to me."

"O law giver of women," said Sir John Fortescue, "let us hear that story."

"Willingly," replied the abbot of Hy.

32. COLUMCILLE'S GARRON

Adamnan

In the year 597 while the Dove of the Church was celebrating the offices of the mass on the Lord's day it was suddenly made manifest to him that the fatigues and labours of his life in the flesh would come to an end on that day week.

Now on the following Saturday he and his faithful servant Diarmait went to bless the monastery's barn, which was near by, and the corn that was in it. After this the saint left the barn, intending to return to the monastery; halfway he rested at a place where a cross has since been erected by the road-side. As the saint, bowed down with age, but joyful nevertheless at his imminent release, sat there to rest a little, behold, an old white drudge-horse, that was a willing servant to carry the milk vessels from the dairy to the monastery, came up to the saint and laid its head on his bosom. The horse, knowing that its master was soon to leave it, and that it would see him no more, began to utter plaintive cries, like a human being, and to shed copious tears on the saint's bosom, wailing greatly.

On seeing this Diarmait would have driven the weeping mourner away, but the saint forbade him, saying: "Let the beast alone, since it loves me so greatly; let it pour out its bitter grief into my bosom. Behold, you are a man and have a rational soul, and yet you can know nothing of my departure save what I have told you; but to this brute beast, devoid of reason, the Creator has vouchsafed the intelligence that its master is about to leave it forever."

And so saying, the saint blessed the work-horse and turned away from it in sadness.

"A truly remarkable story," observed Alexander Neckam.

"An edifying one," added Mochua.

"It is a matter of common knowledge," said Sir Thomas Elyot, "that the horse is one of the noblest of domesticated animals, for he shines with the virtue of gratitude. I am interested in that poor old drudge-horse, Adamnan. Columcille's fate was sealed, but what of his garron?"

"The point is well taken," said Raoul Lefèvre. "He should have had some reward. My friend Commines once told me that after the battle of Montlhéry he was riding back on a tired old horse; the beast accidentally thrust its head into a pail of wine and soon finished it. 'Afterwards,' said Commines, 'I found him much refreshed.'"

"I can cite a case of equal consideration," said Andrew Boorde. "There was a man of Gotham who rode to market with two bushels of wheat, and in order that his horse might not bear heavy, he carried the corn upon his own neck as he rode upon his horse."

"You need be under no apprehension as to the treatment received by horses in Ireland," said Giraldus Cambrensis. "The Irish, in contrast to the highly civilized Welsh, have always considered horses as their brothers. Such, at least, is the construction which many put upon the horrible circumstances which I am about to relate."

33. THE INITIATION OF A KING

Giraldus Cambrensis

There are some things, indeed, which one should be ashamed to tell, for a filthy story seems to cast a stain upon the narrator, though it may display his cleverness. However, history and truth are severe taskmasters, and do not allow us to flinch or affect modesty. What may be shameful in itself may yet be related by pure lips in decent words.

Know, then, that in the northern and most remote part of Ulster, namely, at Cinel Conaill, there is a race which practises a most barbarous and abominable rite in creating their king. When the whole people of that district have assembled into one place, a white mare is led into their midst, and he who is to be inaugurated, not as a prince, indeed, but as a brute, not as a king, but as an outlaw, comes

THE INITIATION OF A KING 153

crawling before the people on all fours, confessing himself a beast with no less impudence than imprudence. The mare is then immediately killed, cut in pieces and boiled, and a bath is prepared for the candidate from the broth. Sitting in this bath of broth, he eats the pieces of horse-flesh which are brought him, and the people standing round partake of it also. After this he is required to drink the broth in which he is sitting, not with any cup or vessel, but by throwing it into his mouth with his hand. These unrighteous rites being duly accomplished, the man's royal authority and dominion are thereby ratified.

"That," cried Geoffrey Keating, "is a base and scurrilous calumny."

"To be sure it is," agreed William of Newburgh calmly. "But why pay it any heed? For it has long been known that Giraldus, in spite of his protestations, has none of the qualifications of an historian, and that most of what he wrote about Ireland was manufactured by himself."

"I would have you know, sir," answered Giraldus, "that the reverend university of Oxford was awed by the brilliance of both my *Topography* and *Conquest*."

"I observe," rejoined William, "that you say nothing about the truth of either. Besides, it takes very little to overawe a horse-boy or a cook's scullion, who, I understand, were the only people who actually attended your reading; and they came for the sake of the food and drink."

"Sit down, all three of you," commanded Bonvesin da Riva. "There shall be no brawling at the supper."

"Have you ever observed," said Camden, turning to Sir John Harington, "that these witty meere Irish have no pleasure in the wit of others?"

"It is my experience," broke in Fynes Moryson, "that the only way to get on with an Irishman is to put a good idea into his head and make him think it originated there—to asseverate what you do not believe, for he may be counted upon to defend the contrary."

This undiplomatic speech was not calculated to smooth the ruffled feelings of any Irishman present, and the atmosphere might have become still more electric had not a diversion been caused by the rumbling tones of Blaise the Hermit.

"Gentlemen," said Blaise, "I beg leave to change the subject. With your permission I will tell you about one of Merlin's adventures as it was related to me by Merlin himself."

"That ald corrupit vaticinar," muttered John Major.

"Pray do so," invited Chrétien de Troyes.

34. THE EMPRESS OF ROME AND HER MAIDS WHO WERE MEN
Blaise the Hermit

In the time of Julius Caesar Merlin made a journey to Rome. On the night before the prophet's arrival the emperor lay in his chamber with the empress, and during his sleep he had a vision. He thought he saw a sow in the courtyard before his palace, and never had he seen one so large; the bristles on her back were so long that they trailed on the ground; and upon her head she had a circlet of fine gold. When the emperor reflected, it seemed to him somehow that he had seen her before, and that he had bred her up. But he was doubtful, and as he pondered, twelve lion whelps came out of his chamber and one after another lay by the sow in the court, as he thought. On the morrow the emperor rose and attended devotions, and afterwards, as he sat at meat, he fell into such a great study that no one dared to disturb him.

Now while the emperor sat thus pensive among his barons, Merlin entered Rome and worked a marvellous enchantment, for he turned himself into a stag, the largest and most wondrous that had ever been seen, with five-branched antlers and one white forefoot. Thus he ran through Rome as fast as though all the world were chasing him; and indeed, high and low ran after him with staves, axes and other weapons. They chased him through the town till he came to the principal gate of the palace, where the emperor was sitting at meat. There he violently drove in the gate and ran among the tables, tumbling meat and drink to the floor, with a fine muddle of pots and dishes. Finally he came before the emperor, kneeled and said: "Julius Caesar, emperor of Rome, why are you so pensive? Leave your study, for it is useless. Never will you have the explanation of your vision till it is certified to you by a wild man, so think no more of it." Therewith he rose, and seeing the gate of the palace closed, he worked his enchantment to the end that all the doors and gates of the palace opened so rudely that they flew to pieces. He escaped and fled through the town, and when he reached the open fields he vanished so that no man knew what had become of him.

When the emperor learned that the hart had escaped, he was wroth, and issued a proclamation to the effect that he would give half his realm and his fair daughter to wife to the man who should bring him either the hart or the wild man; and if he were of gentle birth he should have all his realm after him.

Hereupon Grisandolus, the emperor's steward, searched backward and forward throughout the forest for a week without success. Then one day, as he was praying under an oak, the hart came to him. The stag instructed him to bring food, cook it and dress it on a table, and then retire with his company; then, no doubt, the wild man would make his appearance.

Grisandolus did as the stag had bidden. Then came Merlin in the guise of a wild man, smiting great strokes from oak to oak with a heavy staff. He was black and rough and tousled, with a long beard, barefoot, and clothed in a rough pilch. He approached the fire and ate the food; and when he had had enough, he lay down thereby to sleep.

Hereupon Grisandolus and his men came and bound the wild man about the middle with a great chain of iron, placed him on horseback and secured him to the saddle, with a man riding behind to hold him. Grisandolus rode along beside him, and when the wild man looked at the steward, he laughed. Grisandolus asked him why he laughed, and he replied: "Creature formed by nature, changed into another form, from henceforth beguiling all, venomous serpent, hold your peace, for I will tell you naught till I come before the emperor."

As the party rode on they came to an abbey, where many poor people had gathered before the gates, waiting for alms. Here the wild man laughed right loud. When Grisandolus courteously prayed him to explain his behaviour, he said he would do so when they came before the emperor. So they rode forth.

On the morrow they came to a chapel where a priest was celebrating mass, and a knight and a squire were attending the service. Grisandolus and his company alighted also, and as they were performing their devotions, the knight's squire came forth from his corner, gave his lord such a flap that all the chapel could hear it, and then returned to his place. But no sooner had he reached his corner when he returned and gave his lord another rap, to the great astonishment of the knight and all the others present. And yet a third time he came and gave his lord a sore stroke, and then returned to his corner. On all three occasions the wild man laughed, each time louder than before. When the service was finished the knight asked his squire why he had struck him. The youth replied that he did not know, but that he had been moved to do so. Grisandolus asked the wild man why he had laughed, and he answered that he would tell when he came before the emperor.

After this Grisandolus and the wild man, the knight and his squire, rode forth toward Rome. When they had come into the presence of the emperor Grisandolus said: "Sir, here is the wild man, and I herewith turn him over to you to keep henceforth, for I have had much trouble with him." The emperor sent for a smith to bind him in chains and fetters; but the wild man, that is, Merlin, told him that was unnecessary, and assured him by his Christianity that he would not leave court without the emperor's permission. Then Grisandolus related how the wild man had laughed and would not tell why. "Why did you laugh on those occasions?" asked the emperor. "I will tell you in due time," replied the wild man; "but first send for your barons."

On the fourth day the lords and barons were assembled in the chief palace where the wild man sat beside the emperor. Caesar explained to the company that he had called them together so that they might hear the wild man expound a dream of his. Now the wild man said he would tell nothing till the empress and her twelve maidens had come. The empress came at once, with glad semblance, as though she feared nothing that might befall. At her entrance the barons rose out of respect, but when Merlin saw her he turned his head aside and laughed scornfully. After a while he looked intently at the emperor, and then at Grisandolus, and then at the empress, and finally at the twelve maidens who accompanied her. Then he turned towards the barons and laughed again, as though in despite. At the emperor's invitation the wild man stood up and said aloud so that all might hear:

"Sir, if you will promise here before your barons that no harm shall come to me, and that I may have leave to go when I have expounded your vision, then I will tell you its true signification." The emperor acceded to this request. "But first," he said to the wild man, "relate the substance of the dream, for I have made it known to no man, so that I may be the better able to credit your explanation."

Merlin related the circumstances of the dream, as you have heard, and the emperor said that he had spoken truly, and the barons expressed their willingness to hear his explanation. "Know then," said the wild man, "that the sow which you saw signifies my lady the empress; that the long hair on her back betokens the long robes wherein she is clothed; that the circlet shining upon her head means the crown of gold wherewith you made her to be crowned. If it be your pleasure, I will say no more at this time." "You must tell all there is, if you are to be quit of your promise," answered the emperor. "Very well," said the wild man. "The twelve lion whelps which you saw come out of the chamber betoken those twelve maidens there with the empress. And know it to be the very truth that they are not women, but men. Cause them to be undressed and you will see the truth for yourself. As often as you leave the city the empress causes them to serve in her chamber and in her bed. Now you have heard your dream and its meaning, and you may make trial whether or not I have said sooth."

When the emperor understood his wife's unfaithfulness he was so abashed that he said no word for a long while. Then he called Grisandolus and said: "Undress those damsels, for I wish the barons here to know the truth." Forthwith the steward and others came forward and despoiled the maids before the emperor and the barons; and they were found to be men. Then the emperor was so wroth that he knew not what to do. But he took oath that he would have justice done as soon as judgment was awarded. The barons judged that the empress should be burned, and the adulterers hanged, though some suggested that they be flayed alive. When the emperor knew what sentence had been passed, he had the malefactors bound hand and foot and cast into a fire. The pyre was huge, and they were all burned up in a short time. Thus did the emperor take vengeance on his wife; and when the people heard of it his renown was greatly increased.

After this matter had been attended to the emperor and his barons prayed the wild man to explain the cause of his various cachinnations. "Sir," said the wild man, "at the abbey I laughed because before its gate there is buried in the earth a treasure which far exceeds in value the abbey and all that the monks possess; and yet poor people stood thereon asking alms. In the chapel I laughed at the buffets which the squire gave his master, not for rudeness, but because of their significance. The first buffet denotes that the rich have become so proud by reason of wealth that they fear neither God nor the future of their own souls—no more than the squire feared to smite his lord. The second buffet denotes the rich usurer who delights in his treasure and scorns his poor neighbours when, in their need, they come to borrow anything from him. The usurer lies in wait intending to ruin his neighbour, and little by little he makes loans to the needy one till he has such a great load that in spite of himself he has to sell his land to him who has long coveted it. The third buffet betokens false pleaders, men of law who sell and ruin their fellow men behind their backs by reason of covetousness and envy because they see them prosper, and because they are not subservient to them; for when these lawyers see that their neighbours do them neither reverence nor service, they think out ways and means to complain against them and make them lose what they have. And I laughed at Grisandolus because a woman by her guile had taken me as no man could have done, for you must know that Grisandolus is the best and truest maiden in your realm. And I laughed because she calls herself Grisandolus, though her real name is Avenable, and she is the daughter of Duke Matan, who was driven from his heritage by Duke Frolle. Moreover, I laughed because she had assumed the guise of a man and taken another habit than the one proper to her. And all the ambiguous words I spoke to her are true, for many an honest man is deceived by a woman. So I called her deceiving, for by women many cities are destroyed and burned, many a rich land wasted and despoiled, and many people slain. But I say not this by reason of any evil in *her:* You yourself may readily perceive that a man may be vexed and shamed by a woman whom he has long loved. But reck not of your wife, who has well deserved what she has got, and do not on her account mistrust other women—though there is possibly not one of them who has not done amiss by her lord in some degree. As long as the world endures it becomes only worse. All that women do is only by reason of the great sin of lechery wherewith they burn; for such is the nature of woman that when she has the worthiest man in the world as her lord, she thinks she has the worst. And this is by virtue of their great frailty, and their foul thought and foul desire to accomplish their will where they may best do so. But be not vexed, for there are true women in the world, and if you have been deceived by your wife once, you shall have another wife, who is well worthy to be empress. Now you have heard the reasons why I laughed; and if it please you, I would take my leave."

The emperor sent for Grisandolus, or Avenable, and she was indeed found to be one of the fairest maidens in the land that anyone could find anywhere. The emperor was quite amazed that Grisandolus, who had been his steward, was now Avenable, and a woman. On the advice of Merlin and the barons he made her his empress.

"On behalf of the company I thank you," said Robert Mannyng. "That was a pleasing tale."

"But why all the hocus-pocus?" inquired Peter Bell.

"What do you mean, 'hocus-pocus'?" asked Blaise.

"Why, getting himself up as a stag and running through the city, and then the masquerade as a wild man. Why couldn't he have said simply: 'Julius, I am Merlin; I will expound your dream'?"

"And who would have believed him?" countered Blaise. "It is clear that you understand little about the nature of either warlocks or literary criticism. Merlin was unknown in Rome. First of all he had to arouse interest and arrest attention. When he had shown everyone what an extraordinary individual he was, then he had prepared the public mind to receive with credit the extraordinary revelations he had to make."

"I never thought of that," admitted Peter Bell.

"Your story has a familiar ring," said Pedro Lopez de Ayala. "I recall having read something of the sort concerning Maria de Aragón.

But she had only one young man dressed up as a maid; and though the emperor Otto III forgave her on that occasion, he burned the man. She was not so lucky when Otto discovered her attempted intrigue with the Count of Modena."

"What happened to her?" asked Christine de Pisan.

"She was burned, and the Count of Modena's name was cleared. It developed that it was the empress, and not the count, who had made improper advances. Godfrey of Viterbo could tell you the whole story."

"Well, since Godfrey is not here," said Benvenuto da Imola, "perhaps the company would accept a substitution in a tale about Pierre de la Brosse and Marie de Brabant which is in some ways similar. I see Guillaume de Nangis on the other side of the table; perhaps he will favour us."

"Willingly," said Guillaume.

35. THE ELEVATION OF PIERRE DE LA BROSSE
Guillaume de Nangis

In the household of King Philippe III of France there was a knight who was his counsellor, and privy to him in all things, for he had much more confidence in that man than in any other. This knight was called Pierre de la Brosse, and in spite of the fact that he had come of low stock, was a good speaker, and had charming manners. Formerly, as a poor man, he had followed the profession of surgeon or barber, and when King Louis IX was suffering from a diseased leg, he had cured him. When Saint Louis died, his son Philippe made him his high chamberlain, and showed him affection by giving him many towns and castles. The king so showered gifts on him, indeed, that at last he had two thousand livres of land, and more than a hundred thousand livres of other property. I heard that the notary who made an inventory of his possessions after his death was heard to remark: "If the king had had nothing to do subsequent to his return from Tunis but give his attention to bestowing gifts on Pierre, that alone would have kept him busy." Pierre's power at court enabled him to aggrandize his wife's family as well as himself. He caused one of his wife's cousins, Pierre de Benais, to be made bishop of Bayeux; and for his own children he obtained splendid matches. The people, because of the chamberlain's influence over the king, feared him greatly.

Now in the year 1274, when Pierre's ascendancy over Philippe was at its height, Philippe was advised to marry, and he took to wife Marie, daughter of the Duke of Brabant, a very beautiful girl, prudent and virtuous. The king soon loved her madly, to Pierre's great displeasure, for he feared lest the queen should supplant him both in the king's affections and in personal power. Moreover, as events later proved, Pierre knew not how to govern himself according to the fortune God had given him. He and his wife became so unbearably proud that he maintained a greater state than the princes of the king's own family, to the great envy and scandal of the barons of the realm. His wife, for her part, who was in attendance upon Marie, wished to keep up as splendid a court as the queen herself; wherefor the queen held her in despite. And when the queen did not show her as much favour as she did other dames and damsels who served her, Pierre and his wife plotted to arouse discord between her and the king.

It happened soon after Philippe's marriage that his eldest son Louis, by Isabella of Aragón, died. In the midst of the monarch's mourning Pierre suggested to him that Marie de Brabant, wishing to secure the succession of the crown to her own children, was probably not too friendly disposed toward Philippe's children by another wife. At the same time it seems that Pierre set on foot at court the rumour that young Louis had been poisoned by the queen. When this reached the king's ears, his heart was sorely moved, for he loved his children dearly.

Not long after this someone circulated a calumnious report respecting the morals of the king himself. Learning that there was a soothsayer, a holy woman, at Nivelle in Flanders, he determined to send messengers to inquire into the source of the slander, and learn, if possible, the truth about the poisoning as well. Pierre, who was constantly in touch with what happened at court, was forewarned. He recommended that if the king wanted a true and faithful messenger for this business, he could do no better than send Pierre de Benais, Bishop of Bayeux. The king agreed, and sent with him Mathieu, abbot of St Denis.

On his return to court the bishop reported that there was no truth in the slander connected with the person of the king; but the holy woman had told him confidentially that Prince Louis had been poisoned by someone in the queen's suite. When pressed to name the criminal the bishop replied only that he had said enough, and that the king could now easily guess who was the author of his son's death. Other historians give a different version, and say that the bishop only heightened the king's curiosity and suspicion by refusing to divulge what had been told him, as he said, in confession. But true it is that Philippe later sent other messengers to the holy woman—Thibaut, Bishop of Dol, and Arnoul, a knight of the temple. They

THE ELEVATION OF PIERRE DE LA BROSSE 161

brought back the message that Queen Marie was a good woman, pure and faithful to her husband in all ways. Hereupon Philippe began to suspect the integrity of some of his courtiers; but he put a good face on it and gave no hint of his real feelings.

You can well imagine that Marie de Brabant was not the type of woman to endure calmly the affront which had been put upon her. She laid her plans with care, and easily enlisted that part of the nobility that had become alarmed and disgusted by the pride and insolence of Pierre and his wife. Within the next two years she and her adherents found their opportunity in the strained relations existing between Philippe and Alfonso X of Castille. Letters were brought to the king purporting to have been found on the body of a messenger who had died at an abbey near Melun. The letters were examined and were found to be sealed with Pierre de la Brosse's seal. They were read; but what they contained was never made public.

King Philippe was now convinced that Pierre was a traitor, and taking horse for Paris, had his chamberlain arrested. Many barons were summoned to pass judgment upon him according as he deserved. He was surrendered to the hangman whose duty it was to hang common thieves. Early one morning before sunrise the Duc de Bourgogne, the Duc de Brabant, the Comte d'Artois, all friends of the queen, conveyed him to the gibbet. The hangman placed the rope about his neck, and asked if he had anything to say. Pierre said that he had not. So the hangman did his office, and left Pierre hanging among the thieves of Montfaucon on the morning of June 30, 1278.

"The cause of Pierre's death," said Benvenuto when Guillaume had finished, "was explained to me differently. I heard that Marie was so jealous of Pierre's favour with the king that she laid before her husband an utterly false accusation saying that he had written her love letters. Thereupon the credulous Philippe flew into a rage and ordered him hanged. Others allege that the queen was actually Pierre's mistress. But it seems to have been Dante's understanding that the queen invited Pierre to be her lover, and that when he repulsed her, she accused him of the fact to the king, who had him hanged, but unjustly."

"I have heard those stories," replied Guillaume, "but to me it seems more likely that Pierre's overweening arrogance was the real engine of his destruction. The world is full of men and women, each demanding his share of life, and no single individual can usurp for long, or with impunity, what rightfully belongs to another."

"Where and what is Montfaucon?" asked Peter Bell.

"I can tell you that," said William Dunbar, "for I saw it many times when I was at Paris. It is an elevated spot situated between the Faubourg Saint Martin and the Faborg du Temple. On its summit is a solid mass of masonry, about sixteen feet high, forty long and thirty broad. Upon the surface of this mass are sixteen stone pillars, thirty-two feet in height; these serve to support large beams, from which hang iron chains wherein the dead bodies of felons are placed. There are usually fifty or sixty criminals waving in the air. When there is no room for another dead body, that which has been there longest is taken down and pitched into a lower chamber through an opening in the centre of the enclosure."

"Your account is ample," said Peter, "and somewhat malodorous."

"Pierre was a fool," said Unibos. "His upraising from humble state to great place I think did addle his wit or destroy it quite; and so was he double a fool, for wit is the only weapon possessed by the lowly with which they can themselves against the mighty with their castles, their men at arms and their codes of law defend."

"In that connection," said Eustace the Monk, "I recall a story about one of your rank who was condemned by a mighty king to be hanged; but his native wit, uncorrupted by the casuistry of the court, helped him nicely out of that scrape."

"Would you tell us that story?" asked Unibos.

36. THE HANGING OF MARCOLF

Monk Eustace

This noble company doubtless calls to mind the famous Judgment of Solomon—how two women both claimed the same child, how Solomon ordered it to be split in two and half given to each woman, by which sleight he discovered the real mother of the infant. Well, the witty fellow to whom I alluded was present at this scene, and he asked Solomon how he was able to identify the true mother. "By the changing of her colour and by the effusion of tears," replied the king. "You who are so wise," said Marcolf the wit, "ought to know better the craft of women; you might easily be deceived by a few tears. While a woman weeps with her eyes, she laughs with her heart. Women can laugh with one eye and weep with the other, and in their faces they give semblances of things which are not in their thought. Many times they promise what they cannot perform, and they change their countenances as their minds run. The craftiness of women is unfathomable."

This speech, though Master Blaise here would doubtless have approved it, displeased the king, and he undertook to defend women with some heat. Marcolf thought his praise extravagant and largely undeserved. "You have overpraised women," said he; "but I guarantee that you shall dispraise them as much before you sleep tonight." "Go away," answered Solomon, "and see to it that you never speak ill of women in my presence."

Marcolf left the palace and called to the woman whose child had been restored to her by Solomon's judgment. "Do you know," he asked, "what was concluded in the king's council today?" "My child was restored to me alive," said she; "what else I know not." "Well," said Marcolf, "the king has commanded, and is firmly determined, that you shall come before him again tomorrow, and that you shall have one half of the child and your companion the other half." "What a false and untrue sentence is that!" cried the woman. "Ay," said Marcolf; "but I will show you other and weightier matters. The king and his council have ordained that every man shall have seven wives. You had better take thought as to what is best to be done about this. You know that if one man has seven wives there will never be rest or peace in the house, for he will love one and be displeased with the others; she whom he loves best shall be with him most, and the others never or seldom; she shall be well clothed and the others forgotten. His favourite shall have rings and jewels; she shall have the keys of the house; she shall be honoured by all the servants and called mistress; and when the goodman dies, all his goods shall fall to her. The other six may well say that they are neither widows nor wedded, nor yet unwedded. There will always be anger and strife and brawling and envy in the house. If a remedy is not found, great inconvenience will arise from this edict. Since you are a woman, and well acquainted with woman's temperament, make haste to inform all the women of the city, and advise them not to consent in any manner, but to withstand the king and his council with all their might."

Hereupon Marcolf returned to the court and hid himself in a corner. The woman, who thought that he had spoken the truth, ran through the city clapping her hands, crying out with open mouth all she had heard, and more. And every neighbour or gossip communicated the news to another, so that in a short time nearly all the women of the city had assembled. They went to the king's palace to the number of six thousand, broke open the doors and attacked the king and his council with great outcry.

In reply to the king's demand for an explanation of this outrage one woman, more eloquent than the others, spoke for all, and reproached him for the wrong and injustice which had been done the women of the city. "What injustice or wrong have I done?" asked Solomon with great impatience. "As great a wrong as could be imagined," replied the woman, "for you have ordered that every man shall have seven wives. Certainly that may not be, for there is not a prince, a duke nor an earl so rich and puissant but that one woman alone is quite sufficient to fulfil all his will and desire; what, then, should he do with seven wives? It is beyond any man's strength or power. Rather should you have commanded that one woman should have seven husbands."

Solomon laughed and said: "It did not occur to me that the men were fewer in number than the women." Then all the women cried out like folk bereft of reason: "You are an evil king, and your laws are false and unjust. It is now quite evident that what we heard about you is true, namely, that you have spoken evil of us; and now you mock us to our faces. Who was so evil as Saul, who reigned over us first? And yet David was worse; and now this Solomon is the worst of all."

Then the king was wroth and said: "There is no malice like the malice of women, for it were better to dwell with serpents or lions than with a wicked woman. All ills are indifferent compared with the cursedness of a shrewd woman. Woman assumes wickedness like sand falling into the shoes of old people going up hill. An evil wife makes a patient heart." And much more he said to the same purpose.

Finally Nathan the prophet said: "Why do you thus shame and rebuke all the women of Jerusalem?" "Have you not heard," answered Solomon, "how they have said shameful things about me contrary to my deserts?" "He who will live in peace and quiet with his subjects," replied Nathan, "must sometimes be blind, dumb and deaf." "A fool must be answered according to his folly," said Solomon.

Hereupon Marcolf, Unibos' clever ancestor, sprang out of his corner and said to the king: "Now have you spoken as I wished. Once today you praised women out of all measure, and now you have dispraised them as much. That is what I wanted. You always make my words come true." "Foul wight," said Solomon, "do you know anything about this commotion?" "Not I," replied Marcolf. "Nevertheless, you should not believe everything you hear." "Get out of my sight," said Solomon, "and I charge you never to let me see you between the eyes again." And forthwith Marcolf was thrown out of the king's palace.

"Lord," said those who stood about Solomon then, "say something to appease these women so that they may depart." Solomon did so, and praised good women and good wives so highly that they all blessed him and departed.

Now what did Marcolf do when he had been banned from Solomon's court? It happened that it snowed that night. Marcolf took a small sieve in one hand and a bear's paw in the other, and having reversed the shoes on his feet, crawled on all fours into an old bake-oven which stood not far outside the town.

In the morning one of the king's servants found the footprints, and deeming them to be the spoor of some marvellous beast, went in all haste to inform Solomon. Hunters and dogs followed the tracks as far as the oven. Solomon descended from his horse and looked in. There lay Marcolf all crooked, with his back toward the opening. "What are you doing here and why are you lying thus?" asked Solomon. "Well," answered Marcolf, "you commanded me never to let you see me between the eyes again, so now you may see me between the shoulder-blades."

Thereat the king was sorely moved, and commanded his servants to take Marcolf and hang him from a tree. "My lord," said Marcolf, "would it please you to allow me to choose the tree whereon I must hang?" "So be it," replied Solomon; "it is immaterial to me on what kind of a tree you are hanged."

Then the king's servants led Marcolf out of the city and through the Vale of Josaphat, and over Mount Olivet, and thence to Jericho, and could find no tree that Marcolf would choose to be hanged on. Thence they passed over the Jordan and all through Arabia, and thence through all the Great Wilderness as far as the Red Sea. But never was Marcolf able to find a tree on which he would choose to be hanged.

So, by means of his ready wit Marcolf escaped out of Solomon's hands and returned to his own house, where he lived many years in peace and joy.

When Eustace had finished his tale there was considerable laughter from such persons as Martin Scabby and Roaring Dick.

"I wish your hero had fallen into my hands at Messina," said Richard Cœur de Lion. "As it was, I hanged a lot of his descendants, and the world has been the better for it ever since."

"I read somewhere," said Étienne de Bourbon, "about a certain robber who kept the vigils of the Virgin on bread and water, repeating the Ave Maria, and praying fervently that she would not allow him to die in sin. However, one day he was captured by the forces of the law. He was suspended from the gibbet for three days, but could not die, and called out to passers-by, asking them to bring a priest. When the holy man had come the thief related to him that for three days a most beautiful maiden had supported him by the feet so that he did not choke. After he had promised to amend his ways, he was cut down and allowed to go free."

"That reminds me," said Andrew Boorde, "of a story which I heard on one of my travels."

37. THE WENCH OF SANTO DOMINGO
Andrew Boorde

During the time that I was travelling in Navarre I stopped several days at Santo Domingo, which is on the road to Campostella. A youth, on his way to the shrine of St James, also stopped at Santo Domingo, and was hanged there, but unjustly.

It seems that while the young pilgrim and his parents were putting up at the inn the landlord's daughter fell violently in love with him and would have had him meddle with her carnally. But when the youth repulsed her advances as being unseasonable, the girl took offence and resolved to be even with him for the unwonted affront. Unseen by anyone she hid a piece of silver in the young man's skrip. The next morning he and his parents joined other pilgrims on their way to Campostella. They had not been long gone from the inn when the landlord's daughter raised officers to pursue them, who overtook them and found the silver piece in the young man's wallet. For this reason he was brought back to town and condemned to be hanged, and hanged he was on a pair of gallows.

Now overseas it is the custom that whoever is hanged shall not be cut down, but shall continue upon the gibbet. So the young man's father and mother, on their way back from Campostella, stopped at the gallows of Santo Domingo to pray for their son's soul. But when they came there the youth spoke and said: "I am not dead. God and his servant St James have preserved me alive. Go, therefore, to the Justice of the town, and bid him come and let me down."

You may be sure the youth's parents lost no time in carrying out his bidding. They found the Justice at home, just sitting down to a supper of two great chickens, one a hen, the other a cock. When he heard the report of the circumstances the Justice said: "It seems to me that your tale is as likely as that the fowls in the dish before me could stand up and crow." Hardly were the words out of his mouth before the chickens stood up in the platter and crew. Thereupon the Justice, in procession, went and fetched the young man alive from the gallows.

Priests and other credible persons told me that as a memorial of these stupendous happenings a white cock and a hen are still kept in a cage in the church. I did indeed see a cock and a hen in the church. As for my tale—I repeat it as it was told me, not by three or four persons, but by many.

"It's the old story of Herod appropriated to St James," said Walter Haliday. "There are also a number of ballads on the same subject. But I daresay your study is as little on ballads as on the Gospel of Nicodemus."

"Master Blaise," said Fra Cipolla, turning to the hermit, "an element of your tale reminds me of an incident which occasioned considerable scandal in Italy at one time. I refer to Avenable's changing her attire and assuming a character different from her real one. In Florence there was a certain *joculator,* Gianni Schicchi by name, who was famous everywhere for his skill in impersonation. One time his talents were employed in an enterprise no less hazardous than profitable."

"I should be glad to hear about it," said Master Blaise courteously.

38. GIANNI SCHICCHI AND THE MULE

Fra Cipolla

The story runs that a certain Buoso Donati of Florence fell ill of a mortal sickness, and when he knew that his end was certain, it seemed to him only just and proper that he should make a will. Such action did not meet with the approval of his son, Messer Simone, who feared that thereby his father's considerable fortune would be dissipated. So by one means or another he obtained from his father the promise that he would not make a will, and the old man died intestate.

Simone kept his father's death a secret, and immediately took counsel with Gianni Schicchi, who, as I have said, was able to imitate perfectly the voice and manner of all kinds of people, and particularly of Messer Buoso, with whom he had been intimate. Between them they came to an agreement by which both expected to profit.

"Send for the notary," said Gianni, "and let it be known that Buoso wants to make a will. But first I will get into the bed and shove Buoso over against the wall, and put on his night-shirt and night-cap. When the notary has come I will dictate any kind of will you wish. But you may as well make up your mind that I intend to be the gainer thereby." Simone agreed to this.

In Buoso's bed, dressed in Buoso's clothes, Gianni counterfeited the old man so cleverly that it seemed indeed to be he; and when the notary had prepared his parchment and ink, and the witnesses were ready, Gianni began to dictate:

"Twenty soldi," he said, "I leave to Santa Reparata, five lire to the Friars Minor, and five to the Preaching Friars . . ."

And so he continued for a while, leaving small sums to the clergy.—
"And to Gianni Schicchi," he said, "I leave five hundred florins."

"It is not necessary to put that in the will," interrupted Simone. "I will give the florins to Gianni out of what you leave to me."

"Simone," said the false Buoso, "let me dispose of my goods in the manner which seems to me proper; I am leaving you so well off that you ought to be content in any case." So for fear Simone was silent, and Gianni continued: "And to my dear friend Gianni Schicchi I leave my mule, the best mule in all Tuscany."

"Oh, Messer Buoso," cried Simone, "Gianni cares very little about mules, and he will not appreciate this one. Why waste it on him?"

"I," said the false Buoso, "know better what Gianni wants than you do."

By this time Simone was beginning to get hot and nervous, but for fear he again kept silent; and Gianni continued: "And to Gianni Schicchi I leave the hundred florins which my cousin Corso Donati owes me. For the rest I designate Simone as my universal heir on condition that he execute every bequest in this testament within a fortnight; otherwise the estate shall go in its entirety to the Friars Minor of Santa Croce."

Now the will was finished and sealed by the notary, and when both he and the witnesses had departed, Gianni got out of bed, and Buoso was put back in his place. And when Gianni had safely left the house unobserved, Simone broke the sad news that his father Buoso had passed away.

"That was a scurvy trick," said the Clerk of Oxenford.

"And a most reprehensible evasion of the law," added Adam Usk.

"You would have no fault to find had the mule been a horse, I daresay," remarked Iolo Goch.

"Look you, now, I stole no horse, if that it what you are so uncourteously hinting at," replied Adam. "It happened that I defended Walter Jakes in a suit for rape, look you, and got him off; and since he refused to pay me my fee, I took the value thereof in goods. Besides, he had promised me the horse."

"You may be right," said Fra Cipolla to the Clerk; "at least Dante thought so too, for he placed Gianni in hell."

"I have always thought," said Benvenuto da Imola, "that Simone, or Taddeo, as some call him, should have enjoyed the same fate."

"Master Blaise," said Will Langland, addressing the hermit, "your remarks on men of law were very much to the point, as Father Onion's story proves. I also can speak on that subject, and from bitter personal experience. In my famous Vision on Malvern Hills I saw a hundred sergeants of the law dressed in silk hoods, pleading causes for pounds, or even pence; but for the love of God they never opened their lips. You had to show your money before you could get a word out of 'em."

"It is by the law," spoke up John Gower, "that wrongs are redressed and righteousness maintained. Where the law is reasonable, the community is at ease. But what is the use of going to law unless you have just judges? Woe is the people of the land whose judges are swayed by covetousness, for then wrong will be rampant. Whereso law supports right and justice, there the people is glad, but if the law turn amiss, the people is misturned also."

"Gentlemen," said Beryn, "I know something of judges and law-courts from sad experience too. Adam Scrivener has told you how I learned about dicing. If you please, I will tell you how I learned about law-courts in the realm of Blandie."

39. BERYN AT THE BAR

Beryn

On the morning after the storm, of which you have heard, we spied land and soon made port. I went ashore with a page to acquaint myself with the situation. But now hearken to a wonderful thing: In all the wide world there were no people so false or so deceitful as the people who dwelt in that port. It was a cursed custom of theirs that if any foreign ship came to harbour they would hide in their houses, as though they neither knew nor cared anything about merchandise and traffic. It was for this reason that I traversed the whole town to its end without meeting anyone, and all the doors were closed. Finally I came to a manciple's house, where, strangely enough, the doors were open. As I learned later, that citizen was the slipperiest fellow in the whole city; whatever he gained by treachery or guile—as some friars do now—he shared with his false compeers. This goodman was playing chess with one of his neighbours, a fellow as upright and honest as himself. I alighted at this house in order to make inquiries.

As soon as the burgess spied me he knew by my dress that I was a person of importance. He pushed the chess-board aside and seized my hand. "God bless you," he said, "what good wind has blown you hither? Please make yourself at home and excuse the poorness of my provision."

The other burgess, who had also risen, said to the manciple: "You seem to know this stranger." "Indeed I do," replied the manciple. "In his own country he is a right worshipful gentleman. Stay by him for a few moments while I see to his horse; entertain him while I am gone and then I will broach some wine." Accordingly the second burgess sat down and inquired politely about my country and kin. I replied to his questions, and told him also about the five ships riding in the harbour.

When the manciple came back the tables were laid and we ate and drank very well. After dinner my host invited me to play a game of chess. This I was loath to do, for games of any sort now aroused in me only aversion. But he insisted, and so, not wishing to prove as discourteous a guest as he was a host, I complied. After I had won three games from him easily enough, I would have returned to my ships, for I thought my men must be growing anxious about me. But my host the manciple called to his aid the old dodge, saying that since I had won, I ought to give him a chance to get even with me. It seemed to me that three games were enough to prove whatever skill he had, but again I complied with his request. This time the conditions of the game were that the loser was to do whatever the winner demanded or else drink up all the water in the sea. We played, and somehow the manciple mated me in four moves.

My patience was now at an end. I wanted to return to my ships, but do you think I could? I had indeed reckoned without my host, for at his bidding I was immediately surrounded by his sergeants. "Remember the conditions of the game," he said. "You have lost. The loser must do what the winner demands. I demand that you surrender all your possessions to me."

This was quite absurd, and I refused to do it. Thereupon his sergeants hailed me before the seneschal of the town and lodged complaint. The manciple's position was supported not only by the seneschal, but by all his countrymen, and it was only with difficulty that I obtained a remand of three days in which to prepare my defence. My ships I had to surrender as security for my reappearance.

As I was leaving the court Hanibal, the city provost, whispered to me privately that if I would give him my merchandise he would arrange the matter with the seneschal, and I could indemnify myself from the goods in his, the provost's, warehouses. This seemed to me a fair and business-like exchange, and I agreed. But imagine my surprise when, on visiting the warehouses, I found no merchandise in them! I proceeded to lay a complaint with the seneschal, who very graciously permitted the case to go over till the following day.

After this, as I was turning back to my ships, a blind beggar laid hold of me and haled me before the seneschal. Why, do you think? He accused me of stealing his eyes and of refusing to return them.

Again I requested that the case might be delayed till I could get advice.

Hardly had I once more issued from the seneschal's court when a woman with a babe in arms accosted me, shrieking out that I had broken troth-plight and that I was the father of the child she was carrying. She summoned me before the seneschal and there repeated her ridiculous charge, which the official received with the utmost gravity. Again I requested and received a postponement of the suit.

Now as I was casting about here and there for someone to give me advice there came a man who made me a present of a valuable knife. He counselled me that I should give the seneschal ten talents and the knife as a bribe. I was at my wits' end, and since such procedure seemed to conform to the custom of the country, I offered no objection to this proposal. Away we went to the seneschal. And what happened then? My unknown friend immediately claimed that my five ships belonged to him, alleging that they were the property of his father, who had taken them to Rome for repair. He further charged me with the murder of his father, saying that the proof of the homicide was his father's knife, which I had in my pocket. The seneschal nodded gravely and consented to postpone the case till the morrow. You can imagine my state of mind by this time.

I had almost reached my ships when another stranger accosted me. I shook him off, but he hung on. It appeared that he was a Roman like myself, by the name of Geoffrey. He had had to go into voluntary exile because his wit and cleverness had won him the envy and enmity of the Seven Sages of Rome. Seeing a fellow countryman in distress, and having a score or two of his own to settle with the Blandiens, he volunteered to act as my advocate. What could I lose? I accepted his offer.

In due time, when my cases were called, Geoffrey, assuming the character of a fool, received permission to speak in my defence, for what had they to fear from a fool?

Well, to make a long story short, this is what happened. To my host, the manciple, he said: "Beryn will give up nothing. He is quite ready to drink up all the sea-water, but of the river waters that flow into it he will drink nothing. After you have turned aside all the rivers, he will perform his part of the bargain." The manciple said it could not be done. We threatened to take the case to the king, but dropped suit when he agreed to pay a large fine.

Now as regards my case against Hanibal: When we inspected the warehouses we found that they contained nothing but two butterflies; wherefor, since he had promised to load my ships with the contents of his warehouses in return for my cargoes, Geoffrey now demanded that my five vessels be loaded with butterflies. The provost also paid a large fine.

The blind beggar's suit came next. Geoffrey admitted that I had taken his eyes, but had given my own, which were the better pair, as a loan. If, now, the blind man would give me back my eyes, said Geoffrey, I would return his. The blind man preferred to pay a fine.

To the woman who accused me of troth-breach Geoffrey conceded that I might be the father of the child; but since it was the duty of every wife to follow and obey her husband, she must henceforth follow and obey me. This she was unable to do, because she already had a husband, the real father of her brat—who paid her fine.

Geoffrey admitted, too, that Martin's knife had been found on my person. But he explained that one day, seven years ago, I had plucked it out of my own father's heart, and not knowing to whom it belonged, had kept it. Since Martin acknowledged the knife as his property, it must be that Martin had slain my father. After paying heavy damages Martin was dismissed.

Thus did I gain another valuable lesson in the ways of the world, and at the same time doubled my wealth. When Isope, king of Blandie, got news of these matters, he was so pleased that he invited me to dinner. Subsequently he took such a fancy to me that he gave me his daughter Cleopatra to wife.

"I have met people like your Blandiens in more than one city," said Richard of Devizes. "Nor is it necessary to go to Blandie—wherever that is—to find corrupt courts and corrupt judges. Those are phenomena of which we have plenty of examples at home."

"Ay," agreed Sir David Lindsay, "that is so. Once I lent my gossip my mare to fetch home coals, but he drowned her in the Quarrel Holes,

> "And I ran to Consistorie for to plain me,
> And there I found a greedy meiny.
> They gave me first a thing called *citandum;*
> Within eight days I got only *libellandum;*
> After a month I got *ad opponendum;*
> In half a year I got *interloquendum,*
> And afterwards—what is it called?—*ad replicandum,*
> But never a word could I understand 'em.
> Then they made me lay down many placks
> Of coin to pay for twenty acts;

But before they came half way to *concludendum,*
Devil a plack was left for to defend 'em.
Thus they postponed me two years with their train
Until—*hodie ad octo*—they bade me come again,
And then those rooks cawed wondrous fast,
Crying for 'sentence silver' at the last.
Of *pronunciandum* they made me wondrous fain,
But I never got my good grey mare again."

"Neither civil nor ecclesiastical courts were better in my time," said Thomas Gascoigne; "the very stones cried out against their abuses. I daresay that John Gower and Will Langland had ample cause for dissatisfaction with legal forms and usages, and yet, had they lived on into the next century they might have been driven to despair; the growth of litigiousness reached enormous proportions, owing to the increase in the number of felons and criminals. As Master Blaise remarked, 'As the world grows older it grows worse.'"

"Do you not perhaps forget," spoke up Sir John Fortescue, "that the volume of law business was swelled in other ways? In your day, and particularly in mine, far-reaching changes had taken place in all departments of public and private life. Step by step, as the dead hand of feudalism relaxed its grip on society, new elements rose to the surface, and new forces made themselves felt. When the administration of justice was taken out of the hands of the temporal baron and the clerical lord, and made more and more a prerogative of the king, the sovereign had to find other officers of the law to take their places. Also, the serf, who had no rights, disappeared, and was replaced on the social scene by a great number of persons who did have rights, which it became the business of the law to define and protect. Again, the rise of a new class of landowners, and of merchants who traded upon land or sea, necessitated the formulation of laws to determine their obligations and maintain their rights. As interests increase, conflicts increase, and so also the number of those whose function it is to adjust them."

"You argue powerfully," conceded Richard of Devizes; "yet I wonder if you can palliate a vice of the legal profession which seems to be independent of time or change? I will try to make my meaning clear by the following tale. . . ."

40. MURDER IN THE JEWISH QUARTER
Richard of Devizes

During the absence of King Richard in the Holy Land the Jews of Winchester, studious of the honour of their city, procured themselves notoriety by murdering a boy in Winchester. The case was thus.

There was a Christian boy, an apprentice in the art of shoe-making, an orphan and under age, and of abject condition and extreme poverty. France was his native land. Now a certain French Jew, having unfortunately compassioned the boy's great miseries in France, by frequent advice persuaded him that he should go to England, a land flowing with milk and honey. He praised the English as liberal and bountiful, and said that in England no one would continue poor who could be recommended for honesty.

The boy, ready to like whatever you may wish, as is natural with the French, having taken a certain companion of the same age as himself, got ready and set forward on his foreign expedition, having nothing in his hands but a staff, nothing in his wallet but a cobbler's awl.

When he bade farewell to his Jewish friend the latter said: "Go forth like a man. The God of my fathers lead thee as I desire." And after having laid his hands upon the boy's head as though he had been a scapegoat, after certain muttering in the throat and silent imprecations, being now secure of his prey, he continued: "Be of good courage. Forget your own people and your native land, for every land is the home of the brave, as the sea is for fish, and as the whole wide world is for the bird. When you have entered England, if you should come to London, you will pass quickly through it, as that city greatly displeases me. Every race of men out of every nation under heaven resort thither in great numbers. No one lives in it without offence. There is not a single street in it that does not abound in miserable, obscene wretches. There, in proportion as any man has excelled in wickedness, so much is he esteemed. I feel in myself no uneasiness about you unless you should abide with men of corrupt lives, for from our associations our manners are formed. But let that be as it may. You will come to London. Behold! I warn you; whatever of evil or perversity there is in any part of the world whatsoever, you will find it in that city alone. Go not to the dances of panders, nor mix yourself up with the herds of the stews; avoid the talus and the dice, the theatre and the tavern. You will find more braggadocios there than in all France, while the number of flatterers is infinite. Stage-players, buffoons, and those who have no hair on their bodies, Garamantes, pick-thanks, catamites, effeminate sodomites, lewd musical girls, druggists, lustful persons, fortune-tellers, extortioners, strollers by night, magicians, mimics, common beggars, tatterdemalions—this whole crew has filled every house. So if you do not wish to live with the shameful, you will not dwell in London. Nor does my advice go so far as that you should betake yourself to no city. With my counsel you will take up your residence nowhere but in a town, though it remains to say which. Therefore, if you should land near Canterbury, you will have to lose your way, even if you should but pass through it. Everywhere the citizens lie in the open streets for want of bread and employment. Rochester and Chichester are mere villages, and they possess nothing for which they should be called cities except the sees of their bishops. Oxford scarcely—I will not say satisfies, but sustains—its clerks. Exeter supports men and beasts with the same grain. Bath is placed, or rather buried, in the lowest parts of the valleys, in a very dense atmosphere and sulphury vapour, as it were at the gates of hell. Nor yet will you select your habitation in the northern cities, Worcester, Chester, Hereford, on account of the desperate Welshmen. York abounds in Scots, vile and faithless men, or rather rascals. The town of Ely is always putrified by the surrounding marshes. In Durham, Norwich or Lincoln there are very few of your disposition among the powerful—you will never hear anyone speak French. At Bristol there is nobody who is not, or has not been, a soap-maker, and every Frenchman esteems a soap-maker as much as he does a footpad. Moreover, at all times account the Cornish people for such as you know our Flemish are accounted in France. For the rest, the kingdom is generally most favoured with the dew of heaven and the fatness of the earth; and in every place there are some good people, but much fewer in them all than in Winchester alone. In those parts Winchester is the Jerusalem of the Jews, for in it alone they enjoy perpetual peace. It is the school of those who desire to live well and to prosper. There are therein monks of such compassion and gentleness, clergy of such understanding and frankness, citizens of such civility and good faith, ladies of such beauty and modesty, that little hinders but I should go there and become a Christian with the Christians. To that city I direct you, the city of cities, the mother of all. There is but one fault, and that alone, in which they customarily indulge too much: with the exception, I should say, of the learned men and of the Jews, the people of Winchester tell lies like watchmen, for in no place under heaven are so many false rumours fabricated so easily as there. Otherwise they are true in everything. I should still have many things to tell you about your business; but for fear you should not understand or should forget, place this familiar note in the hands of the Jew my friend, and I think you may sometime be rewarded by him." [The short note was in Hebrew.]

Now the boy and his companion came to Winchester, where he delivered the note, as he had been directed. His awl supplied him well in service with the Jew. But he did not reside continually with him at his work, nor was he permitted to complete any large thing all at once, lest his abiding with the Jew's family should apprise him of the fate intended for him. And as he was remunerated better for a little labour there than for a great deal elsewhere, he frequented the wretch's house more freely, allured too by his gifts and wiles. But wherever the two companions worked by day, at night they both slept in the same little bed in the cottage of a certain old woman.

Day after day and month after month went by till the day of the Holy Cross arrived. On that day our hero was working at the Jew's, and by some means was put out of the way. Passover, the Jewish feast, was at hand.

Now that evening the boy's companion was greatly surprised at his absence, for he did not come home to bed; and as he himself lay down to sleep, he was terrified by visions and dreams. When the companion had sought for several days in all the corners of the city without success, he came to the Jew and asked simply if he had sent his friend away anywhere.

The Jew immediately flew into a passion. The youth noted the incoherence of his words and the change of his countenance. Thereupon he also fired up, and having a shrill voice and an admirable readiness of speech, broke out into abuse, and with great clamour accused him of taking his companion away. "Thou son of a stinking harlot," he said, "thou robber, thou traitor, thou devil, thou hast crucified my friend. Woe is me! Why have I not the strength of a man that I might tear thee to pieces with my hands!"

The noise of this quarrelling was heard in the street, and Jews and Christians came running up from all quarters. Deriving courage from the crowd, the boy persisted, and addressing those present alleged his concern for his comrade as his excuse. "O good people," he said, "tell me if there is any sorrow like my sorrow! That Jew is a devil. He has stolen away my heart from my breast. He has butchered my only friend, and I presume that he has eaten him, too. A certain son of the devil, a Jew of French birth, gave my friend letters to that man which proved to be his death warrant. To this city he came. He was often in attendance upon this Jew, and in this house was he last seen."

The lad was not without a witness on some points, for a Christian woman who acted as nurse to the young Jews in the house swore steadfastly that she had seen the cobbler-boy go down into the Jew's store without coming up again. The Jew denied it. The case was referred to the judges. The accusers were found defective, the boy because he was under age, the nurse-woman because she had become ignominious by taking service with Jews. The accused Jew offered to clear his conscience of the evil report. Gold contented the judges, and the controversy ceased.

"Such abuses as you illustrate," said James Yonge, "seem to me to be due in a measure to an imperfect perception of the correct relation of one thing to another. Thus, we may say that the world is like a garden of God surrounded by walls of righteousness. Similarly, the righteous judge is a lord circumscribed by law, and law is a staff wherewith the king rules his realm. The king is a shepherd who is protected by his barons. The barons are like soldiers sustained by money. Money is wealth gathered by subjects. Subjects are servants governed by justice, and justice constitutes and guarantees the subjects' well-being."

"The philosophy of the law is simple enough," broke in Colin Clout. "If you look at it with utter detachment you see that law protects you and law protects me. So long as you and I abide by its provisions it is inactive and invisible; but if I injure my neighbour, or he injures me, such an act automatically rouses law to presence and action; and at this moment contek or conflict also appears, for though man has made law, he assumes that he has made it for other men and not for himself. As soon as law raises its arm to punish him a man exerts all his power and skill to avoid or circumvent it, either by sleight or force. He buys or intimidates the lawyer, the judge and the executor of the sentence. In his *Mirror of Justices* Andrew Horne has given pages of advice how to evade the law. It is not law which is at fault, but men. Though not entirely futile, in actual practice the machinery of the law is little more than an irritating obstacle to men who are determined to be individually superior to the community. We are faced with two alternatives: Either the torts, malfeasances and crimes to which the law applies must disappear from society, or law must be perfected to the point where it will be able to defend itself as well as you and me."

"It is easy enough to say what should be done," remarked Robert Mannyng, "but hard to do it. As Will says, lawyers labour little in the lord's vineyard. I do not suggest that they should give their services and learning for nothing, as I would not expect a cobbler to make me a pair of shoes for love. But I would have them employ discretion and discrimination, not only in passing sentences, but in fixing fees. Justice should be the focal point of both the letter and the spirit, as I will show by the story of . . ."

41. THE HARD JUDGE
Robert Mannyng

I heard once of a judge who lived overseas of whom it was commonly reported that he gave hard doom and oftentimes unjust judgment. Good men often besought him, on behalf of the poor to whom he did wrong, not to be so grim against them, that he should have mercy on them, and despoil them only moderately, so that they might live in peace in his shire.

To such exhortations the judge always answered and said: "I pronounce judgment only in strict accordance with the law." He paid no attention to the fact that many laws are antiquated, and consequently inapplicable unless tempered with mercy. In no wise would he mend his procedure.

Then one time he fell grievously sick; but he was neither chastened nor warned, for he repented not of his evil ways. His illness grew more serious, and it became evident that he could not live long. Indeed, everyone wished that he might die soon.

One day those who sat about his bed were frightened to the point of death because it seemed to them that there were devils in the room. They looked at the sick man and saw that his colour changed often, that he tossed about from side to side so that the bed almost broke in two; and he cried out: "Lord, have mercy on me!" Then a voice spoke out of the air and replied to him: "In your life you never had compassion on any man, nor shall I have pity on you."

Forthwith he died; and his spirit went, I think and hope, to eternal damnation.

"Does anyone feel pity for that hard judge?" asked John Mirk. "For my part, I do not."

"Well," said Jocelin of Brakelond, "perhaps some of you have had unfortunate experiences. On the other hand, we of St Edmundsbury must have been particularly fortunate under Abbot Samson's rule. Though he was a literate man and well skilled in the liberal arts and in theology, he knew little of the secular law at the time he was made abbot. For that reason he associated with himself two learned clerks to aid him in the transaction of the abbey's secular business. The result was that he soon came to be regarded as a very discreet judge, for he always proceeded strictly according to the form of the law in the cases which he tried. Wherefor I overheard one man say: 'Cursed be the court of this abbot wherein neither gold nor silver avails me to confound my enemy!'"

"In my day," sighed Thomas Gascoigne, "those who served the law knew neither law nor justice. Once I heard a bachelor of the law exclaim: 'Would that there were more criminals so that we lawyers could get rich faster!' To such men law was merely a means whereby they might heap up riches for themselves. Indeed, they not infrequently caused a man to be thrown into prison so that they might get ten marks for bailing him out."

"For my part," said Sir John Fortescue, "I would not asseverate that those who criticize law and lawyers have no ground for their complaints, but it seems to me that they lack both insight and hindsight, or, like James Yonge, are impossibly idealistic. The wrongs and abuses of which they carp are in some cases partly due to faulty integration of the various elements of the social fabric. Though it is true that law is based on use and custom as well as on expediency, still, law always lags behind use and custom like the tail of a kite."

"There is probably a great deal of truth in what you say," agreed John Mirk. "And yet your explanation does not cover another aspect of the legist's character. I am inclined to agree with Langland and Gower and Lindsay. Somewhere I have read a story which illustrates what I have in mind.—There was a great advocate who entered the Cistercian order and became a monk. By reason of his former secular profession his abbot appointed him to defend the monastery's suits; but he always lost them. After this had been going on for some time the abbot and the monks waxed wroth and inquired: 'How does it happen that you always lose our suits, whereas, when you were in the world you always won your case?' Said the lawyer: 'When I was secular I was not afraid to lie, and so I overcame my opponents many a time by fraud and perjury. But now, since I dare tell nothing but the truth, the contrary happens to me.' After this he was confined to the cloister and meddled no more with the abbey's business."

"There are mountebanks in all professions," protested Sir John mildly. "Sometimes the man brings honour to his occupation; sometimes it is the profession which confers honour upon the man. So it is with the law. From the time of Moses the dignity of the law has been superior to individuals, and impervious to whatever venality might inhere in its servants."

"Perhaps that is the trouble," ventured Andrew Boorde; "the ideal is so high that few mortals can reach it, or even understand it."

"And yet," returned Fortescue, "our best thinkers have agreed that idealism is a good thing. But whether good or bad, it is a matter about which my colleagues of the medical faculty concern themselves but little. What idealism can there be in a cadaver, what philosophy in a fistula?"

"We claim none," replied Arnaldus de Villanova. "With us the substance of our profession is pure science, and if human beings happen to profit thereby, that is a supererogatory gain for humanity."

"Very little science," said Jocelin of Brakelond, "was displayed in the case of Abbot Hugh of St Edmundsbury. When he fell from his horse and hurt himself so that the knee-cap lodged in the flesh of his leg, the doctors visited him and put him to great pain in many ways, but they healed him not."

"And yet he probably got off cheaply," said Lambert li Tort. "Look at me! I was a straight man before the walls of Acre, but a stone from an infidel slinging machine crushed all my right side, and I was left on the field for dead. By moonlight one of your pure scientists came along looking for experimental material. He hauled me off to his tent. First he gave me lettuce seed and ice water, and when I spewed it out, he knew I was alive. Then he gave me ground pimpernel and mensore, and since it flowed out at my wounds, he knew I should live. But what a life! You see me now with five ribs and a shoulder-blade sacrificed to the cause of science."

"You were indeed unfortunate," said Conrad of Montferrat. "I had a shorter way with the doctors who attempted to poison me at Tyre."

"One can certainly not credit doctors with humanitarianism," said Jean d'Outremeuse. "When I was laid up with the gout a few years back some bungling experimenter by the name of John Mandeville, all alight with scientific curiosity, prescribed a cataplasm of cantharides. He might as well have prescribed the Spanish boot—had that article of foot-gear been made in Germany then—for I had to walk with a cane on most of my travels."

"Did you reach Scotland on any of your excursions?" asked John Barbour.

"It is a land which lies beyond the confines of the seven climates, is it not? But why do you ask?"

"If you had visited it you might have found there a remedy for your ill, as did the good knight Fergus."

"How was that?" asked Lambert li Tort.

"Many here," answered Barbour, "have, like myself, doubtless read the romance of Fergus. You remember that the disappearance of his lady Galiene cast him into pretty woeful dumps, and that he wandered for more than a year trying to find some trace of her. He encountered the usual adventures, but news of his lady he could find none. In all those thirteen or fourteen months he had eaten no bread or cooked food, subsisting solely on the wild game of the forest. He was thin and haggard; his hauberk fell loosely about him; his hair and beard were long and shaggy; his bliaut was torn and tattered; and his horse was in similarly evil condition. One day while he was riding through a thick and leafy wood he came upon a fountain flowing toward the east. It was a virtue of this fountain that if any man drank of its water he would immediately regain his health and happiness. When Fergus saw the water rising and bubbling out, he was seized with a desire to drink a little, so he dismounted and drank his fill from his cupped hand. As soon as he tasted that wonderful water his thought and his spirits, his strength and keenness returned forthwith; his body filled out and bloomed, his mind was relieved of all its brooding, and he seemed to have acquired the eager courage of a lion. He felt and said that if Galiene were dwelling among the shades of hell, for love of her he would go there and suffer with her till the day of doom. Fortunately, he was not put to that test; Galiene was recovered by less exacting demands upon his valour, as you know. If you had found that fountain, sir notary, your ills might have been easily cured."

"Well," replied Jean d'Outremeuse, "perhaps I discovered one equally good, for you see that I carry no staff now. At the foot of the mountain called Polombe in India there is a great and fair well which has the odour of all kinds of spices, and at every hour of the day it changes its odour. Whoever drinks three times fasting of the water of that well is made whole of all manner of sickness which may be upon him. I drank of it three or four times and, as you can see, I fare the better for it. Some people call it the Fountain of Youth inasmuch as those who drink of it seem always youthful and in good health. It is said, too, that the fountain springs from Paradise, and has its peculiar virtue on that account."

"Sir," said Ralph Higden, "the fountain you describe is well known to me by report, but I marvel that you place it at the foot of Mt Polombe, of which I never heard. The Letter of Prester John says distinctly that it is at the base of Mt Olymphas, in his land. At all events, there is a fountain there such that whoever, fasting, drinks thrice of its water, has no sickness upon him for thirty years. And he says further that when such a one has drunk it will seem to him that he has eaten the best food and spices in the world, so fulfilled is it with the grace of God. Moreover, whoever bathes in that fountain, even though he be two hundred or a thousand years old, will return, as it seems, to the age of thirty years. When Prester John wrote this he confessed to being five hundred and sixty-two years old, and affirmed that he had himself bathed in the fountain six times."

"You may be right," rejoined the notary of Liège, "but why quibble? Polombe or Olymphas—it is all one—to me."

"And is it the same as Babylon too?" inquired Sir John Bourchier. "I recall that Huon of Bordeaux found such a fountain in the garden of the Sultan of Babylon."

"Our romantic friends are pulling our legs," said Polydore Vergil. "For my part I do not believe such a fountain exists either at Polombe or Olymphas."

"I can assure you that there is no such fountain in Broceliande," said Master Wace. "I looked."

"It was once related to me," said Étienne de Bourbon, "by one who had lived beyond the seas, that he had heard of an old man, forwearied, who had come upon a certain fountain by accident, and being thirsty, drank of its water, and also bathed in it; whereupon he was straightway transformed. But later he could never find the fountain again. It seems something of a miracle to me."

"Report of a report once reported is not evidence," said Polydore.

"There can be no doubt that the fountain once existed," said Lambert li Tort, "for it was discovered and tested by Alexander the Great, along with the fountain of immortality and the spring which resuscitated the dead."

"Polydore's scientific scepticism does him credit," remarked the Clerk of Oxenford. "Though he says nothing about a fountain of youth, nevertheless we have the authority of Isidore for many kinds of wells and springs which are perhaps no less marvellous. He speaks of a fountain near Rome which healed wounds; the Fons Ciceronis cured lesions of the eyes; the fountain of Zama in Africa gave melodious voices to those who drank of it; a fountain in the island of Chio made one sluggish and dull. In Boeotia, says Isidore, were two fountains, one of which revived the memory, the other brought oblivion. The fountain of Cyzicus bereft one of amorous passion, whereas he who drank of another fountain in Boeotia became inflamed with love. In Thessaly were two streams: if a sheep drank of one, he was turned black; if he drank of the other, he was turned white; if he drank of both, he became spotted. Need I continue?"

"You have proved—from authority—" said Arnaldus de Villanova, "that extraordinary fountains have existed; but, as you say, you have proved nothing about a fountain of youth."

"Well," said Sir John Bourchier, "I followed my authority, too, and he said that as regards the Babylonian fountain of youth, though it existed in Huon's day, it was destroyed ten years afterwards by the Egyptians who invaded the emir's land."

"Alas!" exclaimed Juan Ponce de Leon. "Gentlemen, this discussion fills me with anguish. Was ever a life wasted like mine? If I believe some of you, it appears that I sought for the Fountain of Youth in the wrong place, for I was told that it lay in the Island of Bimini. If Sir John Bourchier is correct, the fountain was destroyed long before my time. If I credit others, such a fountain never existed at all!"

"Where is Bimini?" asked Peter Bell. "Is it at the foot of Mt Polombe?"

"I do not know," answered Ponce de Leon; "I myself never found it."

"Where did you think it was?" inquired Richard de Haldingham.

"I thought it lay north of Hispaniola among the Caycos, about forty leagues east of Bahama. But if you are interested, I will relate to you that tragic chapter of my life."

"Pray do so," invited Sir John Hawkins.

42. THE FOUNTAIN OF YOUTH AND THE ISLAND OF BIMINI
Ponce de Leon

You know that I accompanied the great admiral Don Cristóbal Colón on his second voyage in 1493, and that I became lieutenant-governor to Ovando, administering for him that portion of Hispaniola called Hiquay. During my residence there I learned that the neighbouring island of Boriquen was rich in gold. In the year 1510, after a severe struggle with the natives, I conquered it and was made governor. But in my absence from the court of Castille I, who had won the island, was superseded in the government by two interlopers, court-pets named Juan Cerón and Miguel Díaz. No matter, that is the way of the world. Anyway, I had sufficiently enriched myself with Indian gold, and I now planned to do something to win honour, consolidate my estate and settle down.

For years I had been hearing from the Indians of Cuba and the Indians of Hispaniola that somewhere to the north there lay an island called Bimini, and that therein was a wonderful fountain or stream such that old men bathing in it were restored to the age and condition of youths. The discovery and use of that fountain was worth more to me—and to a certain young lady back home in Léon—than all my wealth. The Cuban Indians were so sure of the existence and virtues of that water that not many years before the appearance of the Castilians in the New World a party of them had sailed north in search of it. They set up a community there, and I am told that their offspring still survive. If the natives were convinced, who was I to doubt? And certainly, at the age of fifty-three I had more need of that fountain than any New World cacique—or so Isabella of Léon thought.

Accordingly, with two caravels and a brigantine well provided with everything necessary, I set out from San German on March 3, 1513, sailing with fair wind to Caycos, and thence to Yaguna, Amaguayo and Maniguá. On the fourteenth of the month we reached Guanahaní, the island discovered by Cristóbal Colón, who called it San Salvador. Thence we sailed northeast, and on March 27, which was Easter, commonly called *de flores,* we raised an island which we did not recognize. We coasted along, east-north-east as far as 30° 8′, seeking port. On Easter Sunday, April 8, we landed. I went ashore and took possession of the island in the name of Castille, and in honour of the day called it La Florida. The Indian name for it was Cautío. Here, after some slight trouble with the Indians, who killed one of my sailors, I turned south, doubled Cabo de Corrientes, which has since been named Cañaveral, and sailed north for a distance. After somewhat more serious fighting with the Indians I decided on June 14 to return to Hispaniola, intending to keep close watch on the way for the island for which I was in search. We reached Las Tortugas and La Vieja, and later other islands lying below the Lucayos and to the westward. On July 25 I left them, always keeping a sharp watch for Bimini, but my course was hindered by shallow water and numerous sand-bars. We were forced to alter our direction, skirting San Juan and an island of the Lucayos called Bahama. Finally we put in at Guatao or Guanimá.

By this time it seemed to me that I had laboured much in vain. And though it was greatly against my will—for I myself wished to be the discoverer of Bimini—I sent out a ship under the command of Juan Pérez de Ortubia and Antón de Alaminos to continue the search for that rich and marvellous island from which treacherous currents and contrary winds had deflected me.

I arrived at San Juan of Puerto Rico on September 21. Not long afterwards came my ship and Captain Pérez with the report that he had found Bimini—but not the fountain—saying that it was a great island fresh with water and trees. Well, this put an end to one doubt at least: Bimini did exist. So I sailed for Spain and obtained authority to colonize the island of Florida and the island of Bimini.

But on returning to Puerto Rico Indian wars delayed me there till 1521. At last I was able to set out with a large number of colonists, and we reached Florida, which I was now convinced was identical with Bimini. There I landed and made preparations to search for gold and the wonderful fountain. But now I must tell you of an extraordinary thing: Our progress was blocked by a party of Indian chiefs and caciques from Cuba and Hispaniola. The report of the existence of the marvellous fountain coupled with news of my former expedition in search of it, had renewed their interest and aroused their curiosity to the highest pitch. While I had been fighting in Puerto Rico, they had been searching Florida from one end to the other in search of the fountain or river which turned old men into young ones. They had bathed in every river, spring, fountain, lake, lagoon and swamp in Florida, with no result save that they were all eight years older than when they had started out. Their resentment at failure was perhaps natural; but I cannot but feel that it was unfair to make me the victim thereof, since it was due to the tales of the natives themselves that I had first started on my search.

"And now," he finished with a sigh, "I find that the Fountain of Youth was never in Bimini at all, but in Prester John's land."

"You should have read my book," said Jean d'Outremeuse.

"To what end?" queried Fynes Moryson. "I have read it, and such a *broddium germanicum* of misinformation I have never encountered even in *my* travels."

"Those voyages of yours," broke in Sir John Hawkins, "may not have been very profitable for your immediate needs or wishes, but they were of immense value to the science of navigation on the one hand, and to the progress of the world in general. If you did not discover the Fountain of Youth, you eternalized yourself more surely by the discovery of Florida."

"Thank you," said Ponce de Leon simply.

"Well," remarked John Arderne, "be it Polombe or Olymphas, Bimini or Babylon, it is only a few who can travel for their health, especially to such remote parts. The mass of mankind must remain at home, and physicians must take care of them. I grant you that pill-doctors should be given frequent large doses of their own medicine, but what of men wounded in battle? The surgeon must come to your aid with both skill and advice. And when he gives advice, it should be followed. Neglect of the physician's counsel may have the most serious results. Take the case of Richard Cœur de Lion.

When he was besieging Chalus he was wounded by an arbalestrier. The leeches searched his wound and told him to take care of his movements and diet. But the king—saving Your Grace—was always proud and headstrong; he said it was a mere scratch and despised the doctor's orders. He indulged at bed and board with his usual vehemence, with the result that the wound mortified, and on the eleventh day Richard was dead."

"I grant you," said Langland, "that surgeons are sometimes necessary for sawing off a gangrenous limb; but as for the common run of ailments—it is my opinion that if people would only eat temperately the doctors would have no choice but to become farmers."

"There is a measure of truth in what you say," agreed Arnaldus of Villanova; "and every intelligent and God-fearing physician does what he can to cure people with proper foods rather than with drugs."

"People should follow the example of St Edmund of Canterbury," put in John Capgrave, "who scorned both medicines and electuaries, and lived to the ripe old age of seventy."

"It is true," said Roger Bacon, "that proper diet is of great efficacy in the treatment of disease, but so are medicines and electuaries. You must not blame the drugs, but rather the ignorance of practitioners. There is hardly any profession so ignorant as that of the doctors. They know not the nature of drugs, nor how to compound them into medicines, nor what medicines to apply to a given disease. And if they do not know how to prescribe, neither do they know how to diagnose. Moreover, doctors are not only ignorant of alchemy and agriculture, but also of biology, botany and mineralogy. Particularly do they neglect astronomy, for they are unaware that earthly and lesser bodies are affected by the changes and movements of the heavenly bodies. The whole system of medical art is affected by the atmospheric changes caused by the heavens and the stars. The physicians of my day, instead of studying languages, so that they might be able to understand authoritative books written on their subject, spent their time in argumentation and debate; and instead of experimenting with the cause and cure of disease, they devoted themselves to hurling corrupt quotations at each other. As to drugs, however, it is true that people who do not use drugs are stronger, better looking, and have a longer life than those who are addicted to the use of medicine. It is better to preserve health than to cure disease; and the rules for this are simple: Joyfulness, singing, the sight of human beauty, the touch of young girls, warm aromatic water, the use of spices and strengthening electuaries, bathing on an empty stomach after getting rid of the superfluities protect and increase health and life."

"The deficiencies which you point out had not disappeared from the medical profession in my day," said Dunbar. "I once knew a cursed impostor or a friar who was as good a leech as he was a doctor, and no worse an apothecary than he was a leech."

43. THE TURKISH DOCTOR
William Dunbar

  As young Aurora raised her veil
  And showed in th' east her visage pale,
  A dream did quickly me assail,
   Of sons of Satan's seed.
  Methought a Turk of Tartary
  Came through the bounds of Barbary,
  And lay as fugitive in Lombardy
   In vagrant wanderer's weed.

  That baptism he might eschew,
  There a religious man he slew,
  And clad him in his habit new,
   For he could write and read.
  When known was his dissimulance
  And all his cursed governance,
  He fled for fear and came to France,
   With mickle Lombard greed.

  To be a leech he feigned him there,
  Which many rewed for e'er and e'er,
  For he left neither sick nor sare
   Unslain ere he went hence.
  Veins in two he cleanly carved:
  When of his stroke so many starved,
  For fear to get what he deserved
   He quickly posted thence.

  To Scotland then the nearest way
  He came, his cunning to assay;
  To some men there it was no play,
   Who experienc'd his sciénce.
  Dispensing drugs he caused great pain,
  He murdered many in medicine—
  That juggler had a cunning gin—
   His forebears were giants.

> In leechcraft he was homicide:
> His fee for one night to abide
> Was a hackney and the hurt man's hide,
>   So fruitful was his wit.
> His irons were as rough as rafters—
> Where *he* let blood there was no laughter;
> Full many an implement of slaughter
>   Was in his cabinet.
>
> His dose for looseness of the wamb
> Would kill a stallion or a ram:
> Whoever tried it, wife or man,
>   Their legs went hither-thither.
> His cures were never put to proof
> Without quick death or great mischief—
> He had a purge would make a thief
>   Turn cold without the halter. . . .

"A likely tale," interrupted Gaddesden. "First you tell us you knew the man, and then you say you dreamed it."

"If you were more familiar with letters," replied Dunbar equably, "you would know that since the time of the *Roman de la Rose* it has been impossible to write poetry without making use of the fiction of the dream. All the best writers do it—and some of the poorest ones."

"Well," said Jean de Meung, "I could never see much difference between a lawyer and a doctor. To me it seems that they are both tarred with the same brush. Both of them charge exorbitant fees for the use of their learning, whereas it is well known, as Arnaldus says, that he who educates himself in his chosen branch for gain rather than science is an abortion. Both lawyers and doctors are so fond of money that the leech wishes he had sixty patients instead of one; and the lawyer, as Gascoigne remarked, is so covetous that he would like to plead two hundred causes in place of a single suit."

"And yet," said William de Harsley quietly, "it was a doctor who cured your Charles VI of wandering wits. I am not so ungrateful as my patients, for I herewith render thanks to Jean Froissart, who made a record of that cure for the information of posterity, to his fame and mine."

"Would that you had lived till my day!" sighed John Leland.

"It was perhaps fortunate that you did not live in mine," said Chrétien de Troyes. "I had to cure Yvain of madness without the aid of a physician, and your therapy would have spoiled a good story."

"I remember something of the sort, too," said Jehan Madot, "in connection with Amadas."

44. THE MAD LOVER

Jehan Madot

As you have heard, Amadas, son of the seneschal of the Duke of Burgundy, was in love with Ydoine, the duke's daughter. Like Sir Cawline he had to lie on a care-bed for two and a half years before he was able to break down her resistance and obtain from her an acknowledgement that she also loved him. You know, too, that at Ydoine's behest he rode abroad seeking *pris et los* in knightly encounters until his renown might have compared favourably with that of Earl Marshal yonder.

During Amadas' absence from the court of Burgundy the lovers used to exchange letters with each other through a privy messenger, and by means of these the fire of love was kept hot and bright.

After three years of hard knocks Amadas decided to return to Dijon to see the lady whom he loved more than anyone alive. One bright spring morning he rode out from a certain city with his men who, also, were eager to see their wives and sweethearts again. At the head of the troop rode Amadas, his arm flung familiarly about the neck of a well-loved companion; and as he rode, he sang a Poitevin love-song, so did his heart overflow with joy at the expectation of seeing his lady soon.

While the companions were listening with pleasure to Amadas' song, they saw a valet running towards them on foot. In his hand he bore a gaily painted messenger's wand, and at his girdle a box of letters. Amadas recognized him at once as Garinet, Ydoine's messenger, for the lad had borne him many a sweet message from her in the past. Now he spurred his palfrey and galloped to meet him, and alighting, took the lad in his arms. "Friend," said he, "how is my lady, my darling, my joy, my life? Is she happy and well? When did you see her last? Tell me quickly."

Garinet was somewhat taken aback at this violence and hesitated to reply, for he had news which he feared to tell. However, after a moment, he said: "My lord, I will give you true tidings. First, your lady sends you, as a lover, as many greetings as have ever been exchanged between lovers. But she also greets you as the most sorrowful lady-love under heaven today, for she has been given in marriage, and the wedding will take place shortly. The Count of Nevers will be her husband on the fourth day from now. But I can tell you privately that it will be in an evil hour that he will take her; he will never have joy of her; as long as she lives with him she will never be free from great suffering. She has loved you, and still loves you so much, and so passionately does she invoke your name that I fear for her life if she be separated from you. I think there is not so dolorous a lady in all the world. However, I bring you her letters, which will explain all these matters."

When Amadas heard this tale of misfortune he was seized with such anguish that he could not say a single word, but remained like one stunned and dazed. After a little he said: "My friend, tell me, is this the truth?" "Yes, indeed," replied Garinet; "it is quite true." "Someone else is going to have her, then," exclaimed Amadas. "What! shall any living man take my sweet lady in his arms and I fail thereof?—I who have loved her so long? Shall she have a lord other than myself?" "That is true, sir," replied the youth. "The Count of Nevers betrothed her the other day at Dijon, whether she would or no; I saw it myself. Whether it be for joy or sorrow, she shall be married in four days, and go away with her lord to Nevers."

On receiving this assurance Amadas' heart became so troubled and inflamed with the heat of folly that his brain was turned with lunacy, and madness seized him. All reason left him in a moment, so that there was not such a madman as far as Aleppo. Straightway he raged and roared. In furious madness he leaped at the messenger, and with his closed fist gave him such a buffet that the blood flowed; then he bit him so in the shoulder that the flesh was torn and the bone laid bare. The lad dashed away in great fright, and Amadas after him. The madman stretched out his hand and seized Garinet's coat, tearing it all away in his wrath. You may be sure that the youth had no liking for that kind of play; he twisted out of the knight's grasp and fled, for he had a great desire to be elsewhere. Amadas followed him in a fury.

When the companions observed this scene, they knew that their lord had lost his wits, and spurred after him as fast as they could. Thereupon Amadas left Garinet to his own devices and fled toward the forest at full speed. Only with great difficulty did his men overtake him at the edge of the forest. After considerable struggle they got hold of him, and were glad enough of that, though grieved at his condition. They spoke gently to him, but to everything they said he replied crabbedly and like a witless person. He rolled his eyes and raved and laughed immoderately, and burst into senseless chatter.

Imagine the grief of his brothers-in-arms at this spectacle! They lamented his great prowess, his noble conduct, his vassalage, his generosity and his frank character. They were at a loss what to do, for they had considerable apprehension and shame in contir..ing to Burgundy. But after taking counsel they determined to conduct Amadas secretly to one of his father's castles in their own country, where his father and mother would guard him well. So, with great difficulty, they bound him, and seated him on a good palfrey in front of a sturdy knight who held him in his arms and wept as he rode. Thus they set out for Burgundy, the saddest company of men in the world.

In due time Amadas' companions arrived at a castle belonging to his father. The seneschal, informed in advance, rode out to meet them, grieving bitterly. Cautiously and secretly, so that the people might know nothing of the matter, they got Amadas into the castle and put him in a privy chamber. At sight of him his mother swooned, and on coming to her senses wept and wrung her hands, and tore her hair, for her whole heart was wrapped up in her son. Certainly, she was one of the most doleful ladies alive.

Amadas was now kept quietly in a secret room. They gave him a number of medicines, but none did him any good, for he remained so mad that he had to be bound continually.

The matter was kept quiet for a long time, but, as the master says, there are some misadventures which cannot be hidden from the people for long. When the circumstances of Amadas' derangement became known in Burgundy everyone was much afflicted—clerks, laymen, knights, youths and squires, rich and poor, gave way to marvellous great dool, and maids and ladies wept when they heard the news. The duke too, who loved no man better, was much grieved. As for Ydoine—she would have killed herself if she had not hit upon a cunning plan whereby she hoped that Amadas might have her in the end. But the scheme which she laid is too complicated to relate at this point. Suffice it to say that the Count of Nevers got no solace of her.

One day Amadas' father sat looking at him, remembering his chivalric exploits and his brilliant promise. His lady sat by, weeping and wringing her hands. "Lady," said the seneschal, "there is no help in that; all rests with God, whether of life or death, and I am content that that should be so. But, by my faith, whatever come of it, good or ill, I will remove the fetters from my son." At that he called his sergeants and they unlocked the fetters.

How good it seemed to Amadas to be outside! Mad as he was, he went here and there, up and down, to the great sorrow of the people. Thus did he roam at large for a long time. But one day it happened that he was left without a guard; that pleased him. Moreover, the gate of the castle was open, and he whose duty it was to look to it was lying on his back under the influence of wine. When Amadas passed that way he leaped out as swiftly as a stag in the wood, for no man contested his passage. As it happened, he met no one in the street. He bounded away cross-lots. All night he fled, passing through many a burg and village.

You can understand that there was small delight in the castle when they discovered how Amadas had evaded them. Knights, sergeants and boys mounted straightway on swift horses to seek him out. There was not a street or path, wood or copse which did not overflow with searchers. But none of them had any luck, for Amadas, mad as he was, had traversed so much ground day and night that it would be a marvel to tell. The searchers returned to the castle, and Amadas went his way, seeking his fortune in many a strange country.

At this time Ydoine was lying at Nevers, pale, weak and discoloured, and very near death with sorrow. One day as she called to mind the love that had been between her and Amadas she came to a decision, and determined to know at least whether he were alive or dead. She summoned her loyal valet, Garinet, and sent him out to seek news.

At the seneschal's castle they told Garinet what had happened, and the information placed him in a quandary. Finally he decided to ride at random to see if he could by that means get any intelligence of the wandering fool. He searched Berry and Burgundy, Auvergne and Gascony, Brittany and all the country as far as the Spanish sea— in vain.

Garinet dared not return to Ydoine without news, so he left Normandy and rode on till he came to Lombardy. There he halted at the city of Lucca, and put up at a very fine hotel in the main street. The host received him courteously, and sending a groom to care for his horse, invited him to join the company at dinner, which was about to be served. At this moment, however, they were disturbed by a fearful noise in the street. Garinet paid no attention, but those who were privy to the affair—it was a daily occurrence—ran to the doors and windows to watch the spectacle. At last Garinet asked the cause of the noise. "Sir," replied the host, "it is an amusing sight. Come and see a foolish lunatic who has been with us in this town for a year now. Every day he is wont to take his turn through this street. He is quite mad."

These words made Garinet thoughtful, for it occurred to him that this might be Amadas. So he ran to the window and looked out. What a sight met his eyes! There was Amadas indeed, utterly bewildered and senseless, with cropped head, wearing not a stitch of clothing, and fearfully dirty. He was coming down the street past the door of the hall with the rabble and riff-raff of the city following at his heels. The noise of the boys and children as they beat him through the street with sticks and staves was deafening. They mistreated him foully: some soaked old rags in the street puddles and slapped him on the back with them, while others beat him on the sides and thighs with long rods so that the blood ran out in many places; and those who could not get close to him did not for that reason refrain from throwing things at him, such as mud and lights from the slaughter-house.

This was surely a sorry sight, and Garinet wept with sorrow and compassion. The host noticed his emotion and led him gently away from the window.

After dinner Ydoine's messenger took the host to one side and confided to him the circumstances which we know, pledging him to secrecy and enlisting his aid. He learned that Amadas had his lair in a dilapidated vault, and that he lay there at night on the bare rock. The host promised that while Garinet returned to Nevers to take counsel with Ydoine, two men should watch the madman day and night, and protect him as much as possible from the public.

At Nevers Garinet found Ydoine suffering more from love than ever Iseult had suffered for Tristan. To her he related the success of his search. Ydoine well deserved her name, for she lost no precious time in repining, but proceeded to action at once. It was her plan to make a journey to Rome for the purpose, she told her husband, of praying to Saint Peter for delivery from her illness. The count agreed to her proposal and aided her in every possible way. With a sufficiency of money and a guard of five knights she set forth on her journey, and by dint of forced marches soon reached Lucca, whither her heart yearned. Garinet went on ahead to apprise the host and to take lodgings for her. She had a fine room with an oriel overlooking the street.

Now once more, as the company were about to wash for dinner, a tumult arose in the highway, for Amadas was making his daily round. Down the street he came, followed by a hundred of the city's ruffians and hoodlums, and everyone rushed to the doors and windows. Ydoine heard the noise and grew faint at heart, for she understood what it meant. The hostess ran to her and said: "Lady, do come and see one of the most amusing fools in forty countries; certainly, you never saw such good sport since leaving your own land. You'll be sorry if you do not catch sight of him as he passes."

Ydoine did not know what to do: she wanted to see Amadas, and yet she shrank from looking at him in that condition. However, she made her way to the window. There, coming down the street, she saw the man whom she loved most in the world shamefully plagued by a crowd of hooligans. The street was full; the crowd pressed about him; one pulled him back, another tripped him up; another tugged, another shoved. Those who were farthest away threw mud and old shoes and rags. Those nearest gave him heavy blows on flank and ribs, shoulders and back. They pricked him with long rods so that his breast was covered with blood. This was a sorry plight in which to see any man, particularly him whom one loved.

Just as Amadas was passing in front of Ydoine's window a great hound leaped out of a house opposite. When he saw a man fleeing before the people, he did as his nature bade him do: he joined his feet and leaped, seizing Amadas high on his withered shoulder with his teeth. The hound furiously threw him down onto the pavement so that all his face and nose were skinned, while blood ran copiously from the wound in his shoulder. But Amadas jumped up quickly and dashed away. At this sight Ydoine lost heart and swooned to the floor of the oriel; but with the assistance of the women she soon regained consciousness and the command of her emotions.

That night, when all was quiet in the city of Lucca, Garinet led Ydoine to the abandoned vault where Amadas lay in troubled sleep. At sight of him Ydoine wept tenderly. She threw off her mantle and knelt beside her lover. Under his head she put her arm, and on his mouth she put her lips, kissing and embracing him sweetly. The kisses wakened the madman. He was frightened and leaped to his feet and would have fled. Ydoine tried to hold him back, but he brushed her aside, and gave her such a blow on the temple with his closed fist that she was quite dazed; but she held on. Still, Amadas would have escaped had not Garinet and two guards held him in spite of his struggles.

Ydoine was frightened. Nevertheless, she talked to the madman in a low sweet voice. "Friend," she said, "I am your lady, daughter of the Duke of Burgundy. Do not be so distraught, for in time, God willing, you shall be well again, and have your lady too. Amadas, dearest Amadas, this is Ydoine, your sweetheart, who beseeches you."

Amadas heard the name of Ydoine, and forthwith his madness was unsettled, and his senses began to clear. Through the name of his lady, Ydoine, the madness which he had suffered so long left him. His heart was flooded with sweet relief, and he sighed, for it seemed to him delightful to hear again the name of her for whom he had suffered so much ill, and he grew calm.

As soon as Ydoine perceived that the sound of her name abated his rage, she put her arms about his neck and repeated it softly time and again, and kissed him, weeping. At last, through the medicine of her name, Amadas returned to his senses and his madness left him completely.

At Ydoine's behest Garinet took the knight to a hostel in a different part of the city. There he was bathed, his hair dressed, and handsome clothes were provided for him. When all his wants had been furnished, Garinet left him to complete his recovery by sleep. Ydoine, for her part, gave thanks to God that so much of her plan had met with success.

"Very pretty," admitted Gilbertus Anglicus, "but hardly scientific, and certainly not orthodox."

At the mention of science Thomas Linacre looked at his colleague curiously, but said nothing.

"I have read," said Alexander Neckam, "that when a man is out of his wits his friends should take petra oleum and make Christ's mark on every limb except the cross on the forehead, and that shall be made with balsam. In the case of a lunatic, one should take the skin of a porpoise and make it into a whip, and swing the man therewith. Soon he will be well."

"When the man is fiend-sick, or the devil possesses him from within with disease," John of Gaddesden hastened to add, "the doctor should prepare a spew-drink as follows: Lupin, bishopswort, henbane, cropleek; pound these all together, add ale for a liquid, let the mixture stand for a night, and then add fifty lib-corns and holy water. Another good drink for a fiend-sick man is made thus, and must be drunk out of a church bell: Githrife, cynoglossum, yarrow, lupin, betony, attorlothe, cassock, flower de luce, fennel, church lichen, Christ's mark, lovage. Work up the drink off clear ale; sing seven masses over the worts, add garlic and holy water; drip the drink into every drink which the fiend-sick man will drink and let him sing the psalm 'Beati immaculati,' and 'Exurgat,' and 'Salvum me fac, Deus,' and then let him drink the drink out of a church bell, and let the mass-priest after the drink sing this over him: 'Domine sancte pater omnipotens.'"

Jehan Madot regarded the doctor with open mouth. "I expect the seneschal of Burgundy never thought of that," he said, "though his good lady did indeed pray often to St Avertine."

"You are beside the point," said Bartholomew Anglicus. "If I understand the story correctly, Amadas was neither an idiot nor possessed of a demon. There are various kinds of mental derangement, such as frenzy and woodness and melancholy and amentia, and each must be treated according to its causes.

"Frenzy, says Constantine, is a hot postume in certain skins and cauls of the brain, and therefrom arise waking and raving. Another cause of frenzy is red choler, heated and made light by fevers, and made turbulent and forced upward through the veins and sinews and pipes till it gathers into a postume, and thus induces a state of frenzy. Or frenzy comes from fumosity and smoke that rises to the brain and disturbs it; then it is called para-frenzy.

"This derangement has dreadful accidents, such as exceeding thirst, dryness, blackness and roughness of the tongue, great griefs and anguish, coughing, and swooning through default of spirits and the changing of the natural into unnatural heat.

"True frenzy is accompanied by afflictions of other members of the body, such as postume of the stomach or the womb; and when these members are brought again into their own good state, then the brain turns again to its own good condition, whereupon this evil is checked and the man is saved. But if the postume is in the substance of the brain, then we have the worst and most grievous kind of frenzy, and most perilous.

"These are the signs of frenzy: Discoloured urine during fever, with madness and continual waking, moving and rolling the eyes, raging and stretching and agitation of the hands, moving and wagging the head, grinding and gnashing of teeth. The patient cannot be kept in bed; now he sings, now laughs, now weeps and eagerly rends and bites his warden and his leech. He is seldom still, and cries much. Such a patient has most perilous sickness, but he does not know that he is sick. At this point he must be speedily helped, both in diet and with medicine, or his sickness will grow worse. His diet must be very frugal, as of bread-crumbs soaked in vinegar. He must be well held, or else bound in a dark place. Divers shapes of faces and semblances of paintings shall not be shown before him lest he be borne down with madness. All those about him must remain still and silent; no one shall reply to his nice words. At the beginning of the medical treatment he shall be let blood from a vein in the forehead as much as will fill an egg-shell. Digestion shall be restored and red choler quenched by medicine. Labour above all things to bring him to sleep with ointments and balming. His head, when it is shaved, shall be plastered with the lungs of a swine, or a wether, or a sheep, or of an ox, as Constantine says in his *Practica*. The forehead must be anointed with the juice of lettuce or of poppy. If the madness continues three days without sleep after these medicines are applied, there is no hope of recovery. But if the urine takes on a good colour, there is hope.

"Amentia and madness are one and the same thing. Madness is infection of the middle cell of the brain, with privation of reason, as

Constantine says in *Libro de Melancholia*. Melancholy is an infection that has dominion over the soul, and arises from dread and sorrow. In the passion called inania, it is principally the imagination that is hurt.

"Amentia, melancholy, inania come sometimes from melancholic foods, and sometimes from drinking strong wine, which burns the humours and turns them to ashes. Sometimes these derangements arise from passions of the soul, as of anxiety and great thoughts, from sorrow, and often from great study and apprehension. At times they are occasioned by the bite of a mad dog, or some other venomous beast, sometimes by corrupt and pestilent air that is infect, sometimes by the virulence of corrupt humour which has the power of breeding such sickness in the body of a man.

"As the causes are diverse, so the tokens and signs are diverse. For some afflicted ones cry and leap and hurt themselves and other men, and darken and hide themselves in privy and secret places. The medicine for this is that the patient be bound so that he hurt not himself and other men. And he shall be refreshed and comforted, and removed from the cause of busy thoughts. And he shall be gladdened by the sound of musical instruments, and be some deal occupied. And finally, if purgations and electuaries suffice not, he shall be helped by the craft of surgery, that is, by letting blood."

"Doctor," said Andrew Boorde, "you have commented admirably on a dark and abstruse subject."

"I wonder," mused Geoffrey of Monmouth, "whether the regimen you suggest would have been availing in the case of Merlin Silvester, from whom God took his reason every other hour."

"That ald corrupit vaticinar," muttered John Major.

"It appears that I wrote better than I knew in curing Yvain by means of an unguent," said Chrétien de Troyes.

"There is something soothing in that, surely," said Jehan Madot. "Nevertheless, I prefer the kiss, coupled with the loved one's name employed by my author."

"I fear," said Lodovico Ariosto, "that neither kiss nor swine's lights, unguent nor potion drunk from a church bell would have had much effect on Orlando; for, as Bartholomew says, the remedy must be suited to the nature and cause of the derangement. Orlando's case was in some ways similar to that of Amadas, Yvain, Tristan and others, for he lost his wits on receiving convincing proof that his lady had jilted him for Medoro. First it had to be determined whither his wits had fled before it was possible to take measures to bring them back."

"And whither had they fled?" inquired Peter Bell.

"I have told the story in *Orlando Furioso*," answered Ariosto, "and I should be glad to give a reading from that book were it not that your countryman, Sir John Harington, has retold it very fairly in English."

"Let us have it, Sir John," said Hákon Hákonson.

"Sir," said the Englishman to Ariosto, "you do me too much honour; but if the company does not object to a tale of some length, and in verse to boot, I will try to deserve your opinion of me."

"Tell on," cried several voices.

45. HOW DUKE ASTOLFO OF ENGLAND FOUND ORLANDO'S WITS ON THE MOON

Sir John Harington

You doubtless recall how Duke Astolfo, after destroying Atlante's palace, mounted the hippogriff, and on his back travelled over France, Spain and Africa till he reached Nubia, the kingdom of Senapus in Abyssinia; how he expelled the harpies from the king's hall and pursued them to the entrance of the Inferno situated at the base of a high mountain, and how he blocked up the entrance thereof with rocks and logs. During this labour the stench and fetor of the infernal cave not only impregnated his clothes, but stained his skin; wherefor, Astolfo, being an Englishman, took a bath. Much refreshed, he again mounted the hippogriff and directed his flight towards the mountain which constituted the next item on his itinerary.

> This hill nigh touch'd the circle of the Moone,
> The top was all a fruitful pleasant field,
> And light at night, as ours is here at noone,
> The sweetest place that ever man beheld:
> (There would I dwell if God gave me my boone)
> The soyle thereof most fragrant flowres did yeeld,
> Like rubies, gold, pearles, saphyrs, topas stones.
> Chrysolites, diamonds, iacints for the nones.
>
> The trees that there did grow were ever green,
> The fruits that thereon grew were never fading;
> The sundry colour'd birds did sit between
> And sing most sweet, the fruitfull boughs them shading;
> The rivers cleare as crystall to be seen,
> The fragrant smell the sense and soule invading,
> With air so temperate and so delightsome,
> As all the place beside was cleare and lightsome.

Amid the plaine a pallace passing faire
There stood above conceit of mortall men,
Built of great height, unto the clearest aire,
And was in circuit twenty mile and ten;
To this faire place the Duke did straight repaire,
And viewing all that goodly country then,
He thought this world, compared with that pallace,
A dunghill vile, or prison void of solace.

But when as nearer to the place he came,
He was amazéd at the wondrous sight:
The wall was all one precious stone, the same,
And then the carbuncle more sanguine bright;
O workman rare, O most stupendious frame,
What Dedalus of this had oversight?
Peace, ye that wont to praise the wonders seav'n:
Those earthly kings made, this the King of Heav'n.

Now while the Duke his eyes with wonders fed,
Behold a faire old man in th' entrie stood,
Whose gown was white, but yet his jacket red,
The tone as snow, the tother look'd as blood,
His beard was long and white, so was his head,
His countnance was so grave, his grace so good,
A man thereby might at first sight suspect,
He was a Saint, and one of Gods elect.

He comming to the Duke with chearfull face,
Who now alighted was for rev'rence sake,
Bold baron (said the Saint) by speciall grace
That suff'red wast this voyage strange to make,
And to arrive at this most bleséd place,
Not knowing why thou didst this journey take,
Yet know that not without the will celestiall,
Thou commest here to Paradise terrestriall.

The cause you came a journey of such length,
Is here of me to learn what must be done,
That Charles and holy Church may now at length
Be freed, that erst were welnigh overrun,
Wherefore impute it not to thine own strength,
Nor to thy courage, nor thy wit, my son,
For neither could thy horn nor wingéd steed
Without Gods help stand thee in any steed.

But at more leisure hereof we will reason,
And more at large I mind with you to speak,
Now with some meat refresh you, as is reason,
Lest fasting long may make your stomach weak;
Our fruits (said he) be never out of season.
The Duke rejoycéd much, and marvel'd eke;
Then chiefe when by his speeches and his coat
He knew 't was he that the fourth Gospell wrote.   [*John*

* * * *

He here assuméd was in happy houre,
Whereas before Enoch the Patriark was,
And where the prophet bides of mighty power,   [*Elijah*
That in the fiery coach did thither passe.
These three in that so happy sacred bowre
In high felicity their dayes did passe,
Where in such sort to stand they are allow'd,
Till Christ return upon the burning cloud.

These saints him welcome to that sacred seat,
And to a stately lodging him they brought,
And for his horse likewise ordainéd meat,
And then the Duke himselfe by them was taught
The dainty fruits of Paradise to eat,
So delicate in tast, as sure he thought
Our first two parents were to be excus'd,
That for such fruit obedience they refus'd.

Now when the Duke had nature satisfi'd
With meat and drink, and with his due repose,
(For there were lodgings faire, and all beside
That needfull for mans use man can suppose)
He gets up early in the morning tide
What time with us alow the Sun arose;
But ere that he from out his lodging mov'd,
Came that Disciple whom our Saviour lov'd,

And by the hand the Duke abroad he led,
And said some things to him I may not name;
But in the end (I think), My son, he sed,
Although that you from France so lately came,
You little know how those in France have sped;
There your Orlando quite is out of frame,

For God his sinne most sharply now rewardeth,
Who most doth punish whom he most regardeth.

Know that the champion your Orlando, whom
God so great strength and so great courage gave,
And so rare grace, that from his mothers wombe,
By force of steel his skin no hurt might have,
To th' end that he might fight for his own home,
And those that hold the Christian faith to save,
As Sampson erst enabled was to stand
Against the Philistins for the Hebrew land,—

This your Orlando hath bin so ungrate
(For so great grace receiv'd) unto his maker,
That when his country was in weakest state,
And needed succour most, he did forsake her
For love (O wofull love that breeds Gods hate)
To woo a pagan wench, with mind to take her,
And to such sin this love did him intice,
He would have kild his kinsman once or twice.

For this same cause doth mighty God permit
Him mad to run, with belly bare and breast,
And so to daze his reason and his wit,
He knows not others, and himselfe knowes least.
So in times past our Lord did deem it fit
To turn the king of Babel to a beast,
In which estate he sev'n whole yeares did passe,
And like an oxe did feed on hay and grasse.

But for the Palladins offence is not
So great as was the king of Babels crime,
The mighty Lord of mercy doth allot
Unto his punishment a shorter time.
Twelve weeks in all he must remaine a sot,
And for this cause you suffer'd were to clime
To this high place, that here you may be taught
How to his wits Orlando may be brought.

Here you shall learn to work the feat I warrant,
But yet before you can be fully sped
Of this your great, but not forethought on arrant,
You must with me a more strange way be led,
Up to the Planet that of all the starres errant

Is nearest us, when she comes over head;
Then will I bring you where the medicine lies
That you must have to make Orlando wise.

Thus all that day they spent in divers talk,
With so great solace as never wanteth there;
But when the sun began this earth to balk,
And pass into the other hemispheare,
Then they prepar'd to fetch a further walk,
And straight the firie charet that did beare
Elias when he up to heav'n was cari'd,
Was ready in a trice, and for them tari'd.

Foure horses fierce, as red as flaming fire,
Th' Apostle doth into the charet set,
Which when he faméd had to his desire,
Astolfo in the carre by him he set;
Then up they went, and still ascending higher,
Above the firie region they did get,
Whose nature so th' Apostle then did turn
That though they went through fire, they did not burn.

I say although the fire were wondrous hot,
Yet in their passage they no heat did feel,
So that it burn'd them nor offends them not.
Thence to the moone he guides the running wheel.
The moone was like a glasse, all void of spot,
Or like a piece of purely burnisht steel,
And look'd, although to us it seem'd so small,
Welnigh as big as earth and sea and all.

Here had Astolfo cause of double wonder:
One, that the region seemeth there so wide,
That unto us that are so farre asunder
Seems but a little circle, and beside,
That to behold the ground that him lay under,
A man had need to have been sharply ey'd,
And bend his browes, and mark ev'n all they might,
It seem'd so small, now chiefly wanting light.

'T were infinite to tell what wondrous things
He saw that passéd ours not few degrees—
What towns, what hils, what rivers and what springs,
What dales, what pallaces, what goodly trees.

HOW ASTOLFO FOUND ORLANDO'S WITS

But to be short, at last his guide him brings
Unto a goodly valley where he sees
A mighty masse of things strangely confus'd,
Things that on earth were lost, or were abus'd.

A store-house strange, that what on earth is lost
By fault, by time, by fortune, there is found,
And like a merchandize is there ingrost
In stranger sort than I can well expound;
Nor speak I sole of wealth, or things of cost
In which blind fortune's power doth most abound,
But ev'n of things quite out of fortune's power,
Which wilfully we wast each day and houre.

The precious time that fooles mis-spend in play,
The vaine attempts that never take effect,
The vowes that sinners make and never pay,
The counsels wise that carelesse men neglect,
The fond desires that lead us oft astray,
The praises that with pride the heart infect,
And all we lose with folly and mis-spending
May there be found unto this place ascending.

Now as Astolfo by those regions past,
He askéd many questions of his guide,
And as he on tone side his eye did cast,
A wondrous hill of bladders he espi'd;
And he was told they had been in time past
The pompous crowns and scepters full of pride
Of monarchs of Assyria and of Greece,
Of which now scantly there is left a peece.

He saw great store of baited hooks with gold,
And those were gifts that foolish men preferd
To give to princes covetous and old,
With fondest hope of future vaine reward;
Then were there ropes all in sweet garlands rold,
And those were all false flatteries, he hard;
And in cicalas, which their lungs had burst,*
Saw fulsome lays by venal poets versed.*

There did he see fond loves that men pursue,
To look like golden gyves with stones all set;

---

* These two lines are from the translation by W. S. Rose.

Then things like eagles' talents he did view—
Those offices that favourites do get;
Then saw he bellowes large that much wind blew—
Large promises that lords make and forget,
Unto their Ganimeds in flowre of youth,
But after, nought but beggery ensu'th.

He saw great cities seated in faire places,
That overthrowne quite topsie turvie stood;
He asked, and learned the cause of their defaces
Was treason, that doth never turne to good.
He saw foul serpents with faire women's faces,
Of coiners and of theeves the curséd brood;
He saw fine glasses all in peeces broken,
Of service lost in court a wofull token.

Of mingled broth he saw a mighty masse
That to no use all spilt on ground did lie;
He asked his teacher and he heard it was
The fruitelesse almes that men give when they die.
Then by a faire green mountain did he passe,
That once smelt sweet, but now it stinks perdye;
This was that gift (be't said without offence)
That Constantine gave Silvester long since.

Of birdlime-rods he saw no little store,
And these, (O ladies faire) your beauties be.
I do omit ten thousand things and more
Like unto these that there the Duke did see,
For all that here is lost, there evermore
Is kept, and thither in a trice doth flee;
Howbeit, more nor lesse there was no folly,
For still that here with us remaineth wholly.

He saw some of his own lost time and deeds,
But yet he knew them not to be his own,—
They seem'd to him disguis'd in so strange weeds—
Till his instructor made them better known.
But last, the thing which no man thinks he needs,
Yet each man needeth most, to him was shown,
By name man's wit, which here we lose so fast
As that one substance all the others past.

It seemed to be a body moist and soft,
And apt to mount by every exhalation;
And when it hither mounted was aloft,
It there was kept in pots of such a fashion
As we call jarrs, where oyle is kept in oft.
The Duke beheld (with no small admiration)
The jarrs of wit, amongst which one had writ
Upon the side thereof: Orlando's wit.

This vessell bigger was than all the rest,
And ev'ry vessell had ingrav'n with art
His name that erst the wit therein possest.
There of his own the Duke did find a part,
And much he mus'd and much himself he blest,
To see some names of men of great desert,
That think they have great store of wit, and boast it,
When here it plaine appear'd they quite had lost it.

Some lose their wit with love, some with ambition,
Some running to the sea great wealth to get;
Some following lords and men of high condition,
And some in faire jewels rich and costly set.
One hath desire to prove a rare magician,
And some with poetrie their wit forget;
Another thinks to be an alcumist,
Till all be spent, and he his number mist.

Astolfo takes his own before he goes,
For so th' Evangelist doth him permit:
He set the vessel's mouth but to his nose,
And to his place he snuft up all his wit.
Long after, wise he liv'd, as Turpin showes,
Untill one fault he after did commit,
By name, the love of one faire northerne lasse,
Sent up his wit into the place it was.

The vessel where Orlando's wit was clos'd
Astolfo took, and thence with him did beare.
It was far heavier than he had suppos'd,
So great a quantity of wit was there.
But yet, ere back their journey they dispos'd.
The holy prophet brought Astolfo where
A pallace (seldome seen by mortall man)
Was plac'd, by which a thick dark river ran.

I need not tarry at this point to tell you that the palace was filled with fleeces of various sorts—wool, lint, silk or cotton; that three old women were spinning, measuring and cutting the threads made thereof, that is to say, the lives of mortals; that to each thread was attached a tag, whether of gold, silver or brass, whereon was written the name of the owner; and that a spry old man called Time carried these labels away in his apron and threw them into a river called Lethe. Suffice it to say that Astolfo returned to the Earthly Paradise, with St John, bearing Orlando's wits in a bottle. He there mounted the hippogriff again, and after certain adventures arrived upon the field of battle before Biserta. There, with Senapus' army at his back, he was joined by friends from France, to wit, Dudo, Brandimarte and Oliviero. These had hardly recognized and embraced each other when their attention was attracted by a disturbance not far distant: a naked man was laying about him furiously with a cudgel.—

> Astolfo eke when as he did behold him,
> And saw how madly he about did range,
> And no man durst him meet, nor none could hold him,
> He wondered greatly at the sight so strange,
> And by the marks that erst St John had told him,
> He knew it was the man; but such a change
> There was in all his shape, from top to toe,
> He rather seemd a beast, more then a man in show.
>
> Astolfo straight did call unto the rest
> And said: My lords, this man that you have view'd
> Orlando is. At this themselves they blest,
> And ev'rie one his wofull pickle rewd.
> Well, said the Duke, to help our friend is best,
> And not to wayle, and therefore, to conclude,
> Come joyne your force to mine, and let us take him,
> And I do hope ere long I'le sober make him.
>
> To this they soone assent, and Brandimart
> With Sansonet and Olivero jolly,
> And Dudon clos'd him round on ev'rie part;
> But he, as full of strength, as foole of folly,
> At Dudon strake, and save the blow in part
> Was broke by Oliver, and fell not wholly
> On Dudon, sure I thinke that staffe accurst
> His shield, his headpeece, head and all had burst.

His shield it brake, and thundered on his scull,
That noble Dudon therewithall fell backe;
But Sansonet strake with his sword so full
That of the staffe three yards he made him lacke.
Now Brandimart thinks backward him to pull,
And leaps behind, a pick pack, on his backe,
And holds his armes; the Duke doth then devise
To hold his legs, and Oliver his thyes.

Orlando shakes himselfe, and with a spring,
Ten paces off the English duke he cast;
But Brandimart from him he could not fling,
That was behind him and did hold him fast;
But yet with Oliver he was to bring,
For with his fist he smote him as he past,
That down he fell, and hardly scapéd killing,
From mouth, nose, eyes the bloud apace distilling.

Of headpeece strong he never had more need,
For sure he could not have escapéd death
Except it had a good one bene indeed.
This while Astolfo now had taken breath,
And Dudon both, who late for want of heed
Were by Orlando tumbled on the heath,
With Sansonet, that par'd his staffe so well—
All these at once upon Orlando fell.

Good Dudon that endevors him to cast,
With Brandimart, about his shoulders hangs;
Astolfo and the rest his arms hold fast;
He seeks to loose himself with sudden pangs.
Whoso hath seene a bull with mastives chast,
That in his eares have fixt their cruell fangs,
How he doth runne and rore, and with him beares
The eager doggs, that still hold fast his eares—

Let him imagine that Orlando now
In such sort drew the warriours on the plaine.
But Oliver, that had the broken brow,
Againe on foote recovered up againe,
Did cast within his mind a reason how
To do with ease that they did seeke with paines;
He doth bethink a way that will not misse
To do the feat, and his device was this:

Full many a halser and full many a cord
With sliding knots all knit he doth provide,
And to the leggs and armes of this mad lord
He made them on a sudden to be tyde;
And then their ends on each side by accord
They all of them amongst themselves devide.
Thus were those princes faine to do unto him
As smiths do to an oxe when they do shoe him.

Then fell they on him when he lay on ground,
And then they bind him sure, both hand and foote.
Orlando, when he felt himself thus bound,
Doth strive in vaine, for driving will not boote.
Astolfo, that doth meane to make him sound,
And saw his skin look blacke as any soote,
Requested them unto the shore to beare him,
Which soone was done, for now they need not feare him.

Then seav'n times was he washéd in the place,
And sev'n times dippéd over eares and hed
To get the scurfe from of his skin and face
Which with his naked going had bene bred.
Then with some herbs the Duke gat in this space,
He made them stop his mouth, for why he sed,
For certaine secret reasons that he knowes,
He must not fetch his breath but at his nose.

Then kneeling downe as if he askt some boone
Of God or some great saint, that pot he brought
Which he had carride from beyond the moone—
The jarre in which Orlando's wit was caught—
And clos'd it to his nostrills; and eftsoone,
He drawing breath, this miracle was wrought:
The jarre was void, and empty'd ev'rie whit,
And he restord unto his perfect wit.

As one that in some dreame or fearfull vision
Hath dreamt of monstrous beasts and ugly fends
Is troubled when he wakes with superstition,
And feareth what such ugly sight intends,
And lying wake, thinks of that apparition,
And long time after in that fancie spends—
So now Orlando lay, not little musing
At this his present state and uncouth husing.

He holds his peace, but lifting up his eyes
He sees his ancient frends, King Brandimart
And Oliver, and him that made him wise—
All whom he knew, and lovéd from his heart.
He thinks, but cannot with himselfe devise
How he should come to play so mad a part.
He wonders he is nak't, and that he feeles
Such store of cords about his hands and heeles.

At last he said, as erst Sileno said
To those that took him napping in the cave:
Solvite me, with countenance so stayd,
And with a cheare so sober and so grave,
That they unlooséd him, as he them prayde,
And sufferd him his liberty to have,
And clothéd him, and comforted his sadnesse
That he conceivéd of his former madnesse.

Thus being to his former wits restord,
He was likewise deliveréd cleane from love;
The lady whom he erst so much adord
And did esteeme all earthly joyes above,
Now he despisde, yea, rather quite abhord.
Now onely he applies his wits to prove
That fame and former glory to recover
Which he had lost the while he was a lover.

When Orlando had recovered his senses he concerted with Astolfo such an attack upon the heathen city of Biserta, near Tunis, as left that burg in flaming ruins. From the deck of the ship which had brought him in flight from France King Agramante beheld its tragic fate and would have killed himself in despair had he not been dissuaded by Sobrino, king of Algocco.

To avoid an approaching storm Agramante anchored his ship off a small island near Sicily. There he and Sobrino found Gradasso, king of Sericana, likewise a fugitive. It was the latter who proposed a duel with Orlando, hoping by his death to destroy the main support of the Christian army. Agramante would not be left out of such an encounter, and Sobrino, too, demanded his share, suggesting that the three of them meet three Christian knights on the deserted island of Lampedusa. Such a challenge was sent to Biserta and was joyfully received by Orlando, who chose Oliviero and Brandimarte as his companions in the affair.

You know how the tripartite duel turned out: Oliviero and Sobrino were soon rendered *hors de combat;* Gradasso killed Brandimarte, in revenge for which deed Orlando killed both him and Agramante. With the aid of Sobrino's squire Orlando bore the wounded Oliviero and the dead Brandimarte to their skiff. When Brandimarte had been buried with due pomp and ceremony in Sicily, Orlando set sail for France. On the way Oliviero was healed of his wound by an island hermit, who also converted Sobrino to the true faith. Taking leave of the hermit with appropriate thanks the companions re-embarked, and soon arrived at Marseilles, where they met Astolfo.

"What happened to the bodies of Gradasso and Agramante?" asked Peter Bell.

"I have no idea," answered Sir John indifferently.

"I can tell you that," offered the Lord of Joinville.—"When Saint Louis had fortified Sidon and Caesarea and Jaffa, the patriarchs and magnates of the country came to him and said that after due deliberation they had been unable to think of any way in which his further sojourn in the Holy Land would prove profitable to them or anyone else, and they advised him to make preparations for returning to France. So, during Lent, the king had his ships put in order, whereof he had thirteen, whether dromons or galleys.

"On the vigil of St Mark after Easter we got a good wind and set out. On St Mark's day the king told me that that was the day on which he had been born, and I replied that he might consider himself born anew inasmuch as he had escaped from so dangerous a country.

"On Saturday we raised the island of Cyprus, where we took on fresh water and other things of which we stood in need. Afterwards we raised an island called Lampedusa, where we took as many conies as we could wish. There we found a hermitage among the rocks, and a garden which the hermits had planted aforetime, abounding with olive trees, fig trees, vines and other fruitfers; and in the centre of the garden was a fine spring of water. The king and his suite walked on to the head of the enclosure where, in the first arch, there was an oratory on whose white-washed roof was painted a red cross. On entering the second vault we found the bodies of two men, shrivelled and stinking; the ribs of their torsos still held together, and their hands were crossed thereon. They were laid toward the east as if for burial.

"These," said Joinville, "were perhaps the bodies of Agramante and Gradasso."

Polydore Vergil shook his head. "Chronology," he murmured; "chronology."

"What did you do then?" asked Peter Bell.

"We returned to our ships. But when we got aboard we found that one of our sailors was missing. The master mariner gave it as his opinion that the man, succumbing to the odour of sanctity which pervaded the place, had remained behind to become a hermit; accordingly the king's sergeant left three sacks of biscuit on the shore for him.

"Continuing our voyage we raised an island called Pantaleone, inhabited by Saracens subject to the king of Sicily and the king of Tunis. The queen besought Louis to send three galleys thither to obtain fruit for the children. The king complied with her request, giving orders that when his ship passed they should rejoin the fleet. The galleys entered port easily enough, but when our ship sailed up, we neither saw nor heard anything of them. The sailors grumbled at waiting for the laggards, pointing out that the Saracens had probably seized both ships and shipmen since they were the subjects of the king of Sicily and the king of Tunis, neither of whom had any reason to bear great love to King Louis. 'Let us continue quickly,' they said, 'and we will soon put you beyond the reach of this peril.' 'Indeed,' replied the king, 'I will never leave my people in the power of Saracens without lifting a hand to rescue them. Turn about and bear down!' 'Alas!' cried the queen, 'this is all my fault.'

"However, as we were putting about we perceived our galleys issuing from the port. When they had come alongside the king demanded an explanation. The sailors said that they had had no choice but to wait on account of the sons of certain burghers of Paris who were busy swallowing down the fruit in the gardens, and refused to come away. Thereupon the king commanded that those men should be towed astern in the barge. On hearing this the bourgeois began to scream, offering indemnity of all their goods rather than be placed in the barge like murderers and thieves. The queen and the rest of us did all we could to induce the king to change his mind, but that was impossible. The men were towed astern till we reached Hyères. And they had an unquiet time of it, I assure you, for in the heavy seas the waves dashed over their heads, and they had to crouch low in order not to be carried away by the wind. And it served them right, for their gluttony caused us a delay of eight days while the king had the ship turn this way and that through a serpentine course.

"We also had another untoward adventure before we reached France. For example . . ."

"Pardon me," interrupted John Leland, struggling to extract a great wad of papers and oddments of manuscript from within his cloak. "Pardon me a moment. I had a note somewhere about Tunis or

Carthage or Bougie. You may think it odd of me, but I'm sure I had a note on some subject or place connected with the Saracens of Africa. Ah, yes, here it is. I find that Fulk Fitzwarin sailed those waters. Not only did he touch at New Carthage, but he stayed some time at Tunis with King Messobryn, and even, in single combat, won a bride for his host."

"That seems curious," said Peter Bell. "I have been accustomed to think that the adventures of that outlaw occurred mainly in mountain and wood and town."

"That is true," rejoined the antiquary. "And yet it is equally true that Fulk increased his experience of life by visiting lands across the sea. If you are interested, I shall be glad to give you an account of some of his marine adventures."

"Pray do so," said several guests.

Thereupon Leland, arranging his notes in front of him with a faltering hand, told the story of . . .

46. FULK FITZWARIN'S SEAFARING

John Leland

You must know that for a time during his outlawry Fulk served Llywelyn, prince of Wales, loyally and well. But when King John perceived that Fulk continued to escape his vengeance, he wrote to Llywelyn, who had married his illegitimate daughter Joan, offering him the restoration of all his lands in return for Fulk's person. Now Joan was Fulk's friend, and she warned him, whereupon the knight and his companions took leave of the prince and made their way to Paris. There, under the assumed name of Amis du Bois, Fulk took service with King Philippe, who held him in high esteem.

But when news of this reached King John in England, he wrote to Philippe, begging him to banish from his court his mortal enemy Fulk Fitzwarin. The French king declared that there was no man by that name in his entourage, and wrote John to that effect. Fulk got wind of the matter, and not wishing to embarrass his host by his continued presence, begged leave to depart.

Now Fulk and his company proceeded to the coast. There he saw ships in plenty riding at anchor, but the weather was clear, and there was no wind for England. Fulk caught sight of a sailor, who seemed a hardy and capable fellow, and called to him.

"Are you the master of yonder ship?" he asked.

"Ay, sir."

"What is your name?"

"Mador, of Mount Russia, where I was born."

"Are you well skilled in this business of transporting people to divers regions over the sea?"

"Indeed, sir, there is no well-known land in Christendom to which I should not be able to bring my ship safely."

"Well, it seems to me that you follow a perilous trade. Tell me now, Mador, how did your father die?"

"He was drowned at sea."

"And your grandfather?"

"He died in the same manner."

"And your great-grandfather?"

"He met the same fate, as have all my kin, so far as I know, to the fourth degree."

"Well, then, if that is so, it seems to me that you are extremely foolish to trust yourself to the sea."

"Sir, how so? Every creature will die the death destined for it. Now, if you please, will you answer some questions of mine?"

"Surely."

"How did your father die?"

"In his bed."

"And your grandfather?"

"In bed also."

"And your great-grandfather?"

"In bed. All my line have died in bed, so far as I know."

"Indeed, sir, since all your ancestors died in bed, I am much astonished that you should have the hardihood to enter one."

After this Fulk talked at length with Mador and found that he understood ships perfectly; so he besought the mariner to construct a ship for him, whereof he would defray the cost. Mador agreed, and in a near-by wood the ship was built according to his instructions, and furnished with the necessary tackle. When it was finished Fulk and his men went aboard and set sail for Britain.

Fulk spent that entire year coasting England, intending no harm to any save King John, and often he took the king's goods, and whatsoever else he could get. Thereafter he sailed for Scotland; but there came a west wind, which drove them before it for three days beyond Scotia. Finally they saw what seemed to them a very fine and pleasant island. They made for it, and found a good port.

Fulk and his four brothers, with Audulf and Baldwin, went ashore to look about and seek provisions. Soon they came upon a young fellow minding sheep, who, when he saw the knights, approached and addressed them in a language they could understand only with difficulty. Fulk asked if there were any provisions for sale on the island. "No, my lord," replied the man; "none at all. This isle is inhabited by only a few people, who live by their beasts; but if you will be pleased to come with me, you shall have such victual as I possess, and willingly."

Fulk thanked the shepherd, and they accompanied him to a very handsome underground cavern, in which their host provided them with seats, and treated them very courteously. "My lord," said he, "there is a serving-man of mine in the mountains; allow me to summon him by a blast on my horn so that we may eat right soon." "By all means," answered Fulk. The shepherd went outside, blew six long notes, and returned.

Now all of a sudden there appeared six tall, sturdy and truculent hinds dressed in coarse and filthy tabards, each bearing a tough, strong club in his hand. Their appearance caused Fulk to suspect foul play. These serving-men went into another chamber and exchanged their foul tabards for clothes of green scarlet and shoes stitched with gold thread; in all respects they were as richly attired as a king could be. Re-entering the hall they saluted Fulk and his companions. They called for chess-boards, and handsome boards with gold and silver chess-men were brought them. Sir William sat down to a game, but quickly lost it. Sir John played a game and lost too. Then Philip, Allan, Baldwin and Audulf each lost their games one after the other. Hereupon the most ill-favoured of the hinds said to Fulk: "Will you play a game?" Now you must remember that Fulk owed his outlawry primarily to an ill-fated game of chess with Prince John when they were boys together. "No, thanks," said Fulk. "By my faith," said the fellow, "you'll play or wrestle, whether you wish or no." "You foul-favoured rascally churl," replied Fulk, "you are a liar. But since I must either play or wrestle, I'll play according to the method I learned." Therewith he jumped up, seized his sword, and dealt the fellow such a stroke that his head flew to the middle of the floor. Then he hit another, and a third. In the end Fulk and his companions killed all those vile poltroons.

After this Fitzwarin entered a chamber where he found an old woman. She was holding a horn in her hands and frequently put it to her lips, but she was unable to wind it. When she saw Fulk, she cried him mercy. The knight asked her what effect the horn would have if she blew it, and she replied that succour would come in plenty. Thereupon Fulk took the horn away from her and passed into another chamber, where he found seven exceedingly beautiful damsels, richly attired, working at a handsome tapestry. On Fulk's appearance they went to their knees and cried him mercy, but he raised them and inquired who they were.

"My lord," said one of the damsels, "I am the daughter of Aunflorry of Orkney. While my lord was sojourning at his castle Bagot in Orkney, which castle is situated beside the sea near a beautiful forest, it happened that I and these ladies, together with four knights and others, entered a boat to amuse ourselves on the sea. During our pastime the seven sons of the old woman yonder, along with their company, sailed up and fell upon us. They killed all our people and carried us hither, where, against our wills, God knows, they shamed our bodies. Wherefor we pray you in the name of God that you deliver us from this captivity, for I see very well by your appearance that you are not one of the inhabitants of this country."

Fulk comforted the ladies and said he would aid them as much as he could. Elsewhere in the cavern he and his companions found great store of food, arms and riches. It was there he found the hauberk which he esteemed so highly in later life that he would never give nor sell it. Fitzwarin stored his vessel richly, set the ladies on board, and ministered to their comfort as far as he was able. When, in accordance with his orders, his men had all armed themselves, he blew a long note on the horn which he had taken from the old woman. At that sound more than two hundred ruffians of the isle came running up through the fields. Fulk and his company fell upon them, and though they defended themselves sturdily, it was in vain. In that passage of arms were killed more than two hundred thieves and robbers, for in all that island there lived only robbers and reivers, whose habitual occupation was slaughter and rapine by sea.

After the battle Fulk asked Mador if he knew the way to Orkney. "Yes, indeed," replied the sailor; "it is only an island, and castle Bagot is near the port." "I should like to visit that castle," said the knight. "Lord," said Mador, "you shall be there before nightfall."

When the vessel had arrived in port Fulk asked the ladies if they recognized the country. "Indeed," said one of them, "it is the kingdom of Aunflorry, my father." So Fitzwarin made his way to the castle and restored his daughter, with her ladies, to the king. Aunflorry received them right honourably, and to Fulk he gave rich presents.

In search of marvels and adventures Fitzwarin continued his seafaring till he had circumnavigated the seven isles of the Ocean—Little Britain, Ireland, Gothland, Norway, Denmark, Orkney and Scandia. In Scandia lives no man, only serpents and other foul beasts. In that land Fulk saw horned serpents whose horns were very sharp; they had four feet and flew like birds. One such serpent attacked Fulk and struck him with its horn so that it pierced right through his shield. The knight was much astonished by the blow; but he noticed that the serpent could not readily withdraw his horn from the shield, so he ran his sword through its heart while it was in that predicament.

"Oh, come, now, Master Leland," interrupted Polydore Vergil. "Whoever saw a horned serpent?"

"They are by no means unknown," asserted Jacques de Vitry. "When I was in the East I was told about various strange and fearful serpents which are found in India. Some were so huge that they could swallow a whole deer. Others, they said, lived on white pepper and had a precious stone in their head. Still other Indian serpents, I was informed, have horns like those of a ram, wherewith they attack and easily overcome any man who comes in their way."

"But you never *saw* such a serpent?" persisted Polydore.

"No," conceded Jacques. "But there is no harm in believing in their existence provided that belief does not interfere with morals or the Christian faith."

Polydore smiled, but forbode to continue the discussion. "Pray go on with your romance," he said to Leland.

In the same land of Scandia Fulk saw also a beast of foul aspect which had the head of a mastiff, beard and feet like a goat's, and hare's ears. Many of the beasts which Patrick drove out of Ireland were confined there through the power of God, who had a high regard for Patrick.

After this Fulk sailed northwards through the Ocean beyond Orkney till he encountered such cold and frost that no man could endure it, nor could the ship make headway by reason of the ice. Mador turned back toward England; but now arose such a frightful tempest that all were in fear of their lives, and cried devoutly to God and St Clement to be delivered from the peril. The storm raged for two weeks; but finally they sighted land, though they knew not what country it might be.

On shore Fulk found a very handsome castle. The gate was open, so he went in; but he found no living man or beast there, nor in all the country-side. This circumstance impressed him as being very strange, and he returned to the ship to tell his fellows about it. "Lord," said Mador, "let us leave a guard on the ship and all the rest go ashore; we shall probably find an explanation easily enough."

On landing the party met a peasant. Mador asked him the name of the country and the reason why it was uninhabited. The man replied that it was the kingdom of Iberia, and that the particular district wherein they stood was called Cartagena or New Carthage. The castle, he said, belonged to the Duke of Carthage, a vassal of the king of Iberia. The duke had a daughter, the most beautiful damsel in the whole realm. One day when the girl had ascended the main tower of the castle, there came flying a dragon, which seized her, bore her to a high mountain in the sea, and there devoured her. Indeed, the dragon had ravaged and destroyed the whole province so that no man dared live there; and so fearsome was the beast that the duke did not dare enter the castle.

Fulk returned to his galley and pursued his voyage till he came to a high mountain in the sea. "My lord," said Mador, "this is the dragon's abode; we are all in extreme peril." "Be silent," said Fulk; "there is nothing untoward to be seen yet. Are you going to die of fright? We have seen many a dragon, and God has always delivered us from danger."

Fulk took with him Sir Audulf de Bracy, and step by step they ascended the high mountain. At the top they saw many hauberks, helms, swords and other arms lying about; and beside the arms they saw nothing but human bones. There was also a beautiful tall tree, under which bubbled a fountain of bright clear water. As the knight looked about him he perceived a cavern which had been hollowed out of the rock. Crossing himself reverently he drew his sword and entered boldly. Inside he found a very beautiful damsel, weeping and making great moan.

"My lord," said the girl in answer to Fulk's question, "I am the daughter of the Duke of Carthage. I have been here seven years, and I have never seen any other Christian here save such as has come against his will. If it lies in your power, for God's sake, get hence; for if the dragon that inhabits this cave were to come, you would never escape alive."

"Well," answered Fulk, "I will not go just yet; I will stay to see and hear more. How does the dragon treat you? He does you no harm, I hope."

"My lord," replied the damsel, "the dragon is fierce and strong, and able to bear to this mountain in his claws any knight fully armed. Many such has he brought here and eaten—you can see their bones outside there—for he is fonder of human flesh than of any other kind. And when his hideous face and beard are all dripping with blood, then he comes to me, and I have to wash his face and beard and breast with clear water. When he wishes to sleep he lies down on his couch of gold; for since gold is cold by nature and he is very hot by nature, he sleeps on gold so that he may cool off. But before he lies down, he takes a great stone and blocks the entry for fear that I will kill him while he sleeps, for he has a man's wit, and stands in great doubt of me. I know that he will kill me in the end."

"By my faith!" exclaimed Fulk; "he will not, if it please God." Thereupon he placed the lady under Audulf's care and they came out of the rock. Hardly had they come forth when they saw the dragon flying toward them, spitting horrid flame and smoke from his hot mouth. A very hideous beast he was, with his great head, square teeth, sharp claws and long tail.

The dragon lost no time, but darted at Fulk, and in passing struck his shield in such a way that he ripped it in two. The knight raised his sword and hit the monster on the head with all his might; but the blow did him no harm, and daunted him not at all, so hard were his hide and scales. Hereupon the dragon took his distance in order to deliver a harder blow. Fulk was unable to meet his attack, and swerved aside behind the tree by the fountain. He understood well enough that he could not harm his adversary in a frontal attack, so he waited till the beast made a turn, and then lodged a blow on the middle of its body such that its tail was cut in two. Now the beast screamed and roared. He leaped at the damsel, as if to bear her away, but Sir Audulf protected her. In spite of the knight's address, however, the dragon seized him so straitly in his claws that he would have crushed him had not Fulk come speedily to the rescue; he cut off the dragon's paw and thus delivered Sir Audulf. This advantage he followed up by plunging his sword into the monster's mouth, and thus, reaching his heart through his gullet, killed him.

This encounter had wearied Fulk considerably, and he now rested for a while. Later he went to the dragon's lair, took whatever gold he found and carried it to the galley. John de Rampaigne, who was as skilled in medicine as in minstrelsy, examined and treated Sir Audulf's wound, and Mador steered for Carthage. When they made port Fulk restored his daughter to the duke, who was overjoyed to see her. The lady gave her father an account of the life she had recently led and related how Fulk had slain the dragon, whereupon the duke fell at Fitzwarin's feet and gave him thanks for his daughter's safe return. Also, he urged the stranger lord to remain in the country and accept Carthage together with his daughter's hand. Fulk thanked the duke graciously for his handsome offer and said that he would gladly marry the lady were it not that his Christian religion forbade him to wed while he had a wife living.

Fitzwarin tarried at Carthage till Audulf's wound was healed, and then took leave of the duke, who was sad to see him go. At parting he gave many a fine jewel, good and swift destriers, and other rich gifts, to Fulk and his companions. Mador set sail for England and at last brought the ship safely to Dover.

It was this same damsel, whose name was Ydoine of Carthage, whose hand Fulk later won in single combat for Messobryn, king of Barbary.

"That wasn't much of a dragon-slaying," commented Mac Conglinne. "Tristan had a much harder time of it in Ireland."

"Irish dragons are notably tough," agreed Master Jehan, "as Lancelot here had good cause to know. Possibly it was his experience with Celtic dragons which enabled him to come off victor in another encounter, of which I will tell you, if you like."

47. THE MONSTER OF MALE GAUDINE
Master Jehan

As Gaucelm Faidit has already indicated, it was a custom of Arthur's customs not to eat, especially on a holy day, till he had received intelligence of some extraordinary adventure. Most of the writers who have related his story and that of his knights have paid due respect to this scruple of his; but in recent years there has sprung up a race of poets too ignorant to understand this circumstance, or too ill-bred to treat it seriously.

Now one Friday when Arthur lay at Estriguel the court had long forgone dinner according to the custom when, towards evening, a weary and travel-stained lady rode up to the perron. Gawain courteously helped her from the saddle and led her before the king and queen. From her bodice the damsel took a letter and gave it to Arthur, who handed it to his chaplain to read. The letter announced that the orphaned daughter of the King of Quintefeuille was being attacked by her cousin, who disputed the right of a woman to succeed to the throne, and who had threatened her people with dire vengeance if any should dare to stand against him. He had, however, grudgingly allowed the matter to be adjudicated by single combat, though stipulating that he would accept no antagonist save Arthur himself. It was to implore Arthur to come to her assistance that she had dispatched her maid on a journey of fifty-one days.

To the entreaty of her mistress' letter the damsel added the eloquence of her own tears, so that Arthur had no choice but to promise help to the beleaguered queen. That night the girl rested in the gracious hospitality of Guenevere and her ladies, and on the following morning rode homeward with her joyful message.

As to Arthur—he was secretly overjoyed that a situation had at last arisen which called for his personal attention. Of late years the well-meant, but none the less rather officious eagerness of his knights to spare him every hardship and danger had begun to irk him, and he welcomed this occasion as a providential opportunity to show the court that he was still the Arthur who had conquered half the world.

The king's best armour was prepared, and his most spirited war-horse led out. Gawain held his stirrup for him, and as he swung into the saddle he laughed aloud. Guenevere, who found the king's departure a matter for public tears, regarded his mirth as untimely, as well as insulting to herself. But Arthur declared that he had good and sufficient reasons for laughing. First, on the eve, or rather on the morning of engaging in a perilous exploit he felt himself a match for any king in the world, whether Christian or heathen; secondly, because he pressed between his knees the best war-horse that had ever borne a knight; and thirdly, because he had had the best knight in the world to hold his stirrup for him.

Guenevere admitted the justness of the first two reasons, but stuck at the third. When urged she unwillingly gave it as her opinion that it might be possible to find, not far away, a knight as good as Gawain. This attitude and answer so enraged Arthur that he swore to have her head off the same day unless she could substantiate her words. Thus was the splendour and good humour of the occasion suddenly obscured, and things might have gone badly with the queen had it not been for Gawain's diplomatic intervention. He persuaded Arthur to respite his consort till his return, and in the meantime make his adieux in a friendly manner. Guenevere was naturally overjoyed at the prospect of postponing acquaintance with the headsman, and taking advantage of Arthur's predicament, asked that she might be allowed to choose his shield-bearer. Arthur granted her request, and she named Lancelot.

On the seventh day of their journey toward Quintefeuille Arthur and Lancelot drew near to a certain castle which certain bandits had made into a robbers' stronghold. Five of the ruffians who watched their approach thought that these men, whom they took to be merchants, would prove easy prey. As one of them made for the king, Arthur gave a shout of joy; but before he could put lance in rest, Lancelot had laid the fellow in the dust with a broken hip. Hereupon another of the robbers spurred forward; but Lancelot got in the way again, and served him like his companion. Now the three remaining bandits rode down upon them all together. By this time Lancelot was warming to his work. The first attacker he laid in the dirt unconscious; the second he bore out of the saddle at the point of his lance with such fury that he flew into the branches of a medlar tree, where he hung choked to death by the thongs of his shield. While Arthur roared with laughter at the fellow's situation, Lancelot knocked the last robber out of the saddle so violently that he broke his arm and collar-bone; a thrust with the sword finished him.

After these brisk encounters Lancelot felt hungry and thirsty—he had never quite outlived his experience in Connaught—so while Arthur still laughed at the man in the tree, they rode to the castle and refreshed themselves with a side of beef.

On the third day from that out Arthur and Lancelot reached the edge of the Male Gaudine, or Evil Forest. This forest was the abode of all sorts of savage beasts; it teemed with apes, bears, lions, serpents, leopards, and certain other animals with great heads and sharp teeth, who had been the death of many a brave man. Dwellers near the wood, who were cognizant of the circumstances, had hung up maces and Danish axes on the branches of the trees whereof travellers might make use in protecting themselves; and the convention was that when they had passed through the forest they should hang up the weapons again at the farther side for the use of others going in the opposite direction. But Arthur and Lancelot knew nothing of this custom, and ignored the weapons.

As the two were on the point of entering the forest they were met by a well-armed knight on his war-horse; blood was running copiously from wounds in every part of his body. Lancelot saluted him and the knight returned his greeting. "I advise you," he said, "not to pass that bridge yonder; if you do, you will find grief in plenty." Lancelot perceived that the man was wounded and inquired: "Sir," said he, "tell me who is responsible for your sad state?" "Sir," replied the other, "you will learn, though no one will tell you." "What kind of a miracle can that be?" asked Lancelot. "Sir," answered the knight, "this wood is full of savage beasts; no one can pass through and return without being killed, or at least wounded as you see me, who am so served that I can hardly make my way. However, help yourself to those sharp axes and maces; they will stand you in good stead, whereas you can put no trust in sword or lance. The beasts are not far away." "What beasts?" asked Lancelot; "can you give me their names?" "Yes," returned the other, "some of them: Bears, lions, boars, leopards are everywhere; then there are apes, and nippers that bite people in the back and in the nape of the neck with poisonous fang; there are immense snapping turtles, cassels and crested serpents; there are vipers and scorpions and snakes, too, from which may God deliver you! But worst of all is the monster called Pante that ranges over all the forest snorting flame and fire from his throat and nostrils. He is a fearsome foul beast, and of little discrimination, for he hesitates at neither king nor count, but gluttonously swallows either, if he can reach him."

While the knights were thus talking four sergeants with bows and arrows, who also wished to pass through the forest, came up on foot. You may be sure they were very pleased to find several knights bound on the same errand. After some discussion they agreed to make trial of the forest together, and passed over the bridge. No sooner had they done so than they saw a marvellous sight: Right through the middle of the wood there came a great rout of small animals—squirrels, conies, hares, ermines and beavers; then came badgers, foxes, wolves and tigers in great numbers; after them followed does, stags, kids, fallow deer, rushing at top speed; then came boars and bears and leopards, and obscene apes in a great throng; and I cannot tell all the kinds of snakes there were. At the last came a legion of lions, as a sort of rear-guard. All these animals were looking backward fearfully, for the monster Pante followed them not more than a league and a half away, spouting marvellous flames from his nose and ears; his mouth was so large that no beast ever had a greater. The animals had felt his breath and were fleeing for that reason: they took no delight in his summons; each feared for his skin, for it was the period of the monster's ravenous hunger. At that moment he would have gulped down any beast in the world, no matter how proud. Head, neck and body he measured fifty feet, and he was thick in the middle. A horse with its armed rider would have been only a single swallow for him. Thus you can understand why the animals were fleeing before him without pausing to do any harm to the knights and men-at-arms.

The animals had almost all passed when Lancelot's attention became fixed on the lions at the rear. "Ha!" said he; "look at all these lions! I'm going to have a try at them; they sha'n't get past me like this." "Sir," said the wounded knight, "for God's sake have some sense. The monster is on his way hither and is not far off now. He is very quick on his feet, and will soon be up with us, I warrant you. And I assure you also that if it had not been for him the beasts would already have killed you. Neither one nor the other of us shall escape his gullet. Let us pray God, and get out of the way where he can't see us."

By this time the lions had run past. Lancelot yelled at them insultingly, but none of them paid him any heed; they were so frightened of the monster, whom they feared more than a thousand ironclad knights, that they forgot all about their honour. And when it finally became clear to Lancelot that there was a monster coming up whose character was such as the wounded knight had reported, he ceased to have any interest in the lions. "Well," said he, "I'm very anxious to make the acquaintance of this monster of yours, and to lodge my lance between his ribs. If the spear is strong enough to penetrate his hide, you'll never see him rambling about here any more, for I'll kill him with my hands."

Said the wounded knight: "That's the least you'll do. You talk nonsense. If you were a thousand of yourself the monster would still ruin you. For my part, I don't mean to wait. I'm going to find shelter somewhere. Good-bye."

Away went the wounded knight, and three of the men-at-arms with him. The fourth archer got behind the biggest oak he could find and swore by St Bride and St Andrew that he would not budge till he saw how Lancelot was going to act. As an act of precaution he placed an arrow on the string. This pleased the knight of the Round Table, not because he thought the man would prove to be of any assistance, but because he admired his courage. As a matter of fact, had it not been for the archer, Lancelot would have come off worse than he did.

Now at last Arthur spoke up. He had paid close attention while the wounded knight was describing the monster, and he saw also that Lancelot's mind was set on fighting with the beast. "Lancelot, my dear fellow," said he, "abandon this rashness. He who faces certain death when he might save himself is a fool. Moreover, our business presses. If there are any monsters around when we come back this way we can have a go at them then."

Said Lancelot: "I'm going to wait for him. I wouldn't leave for the possession of all Mantes and a quarter of your kingdom without seeing the creature and running a course with him. What would they say of us back home if they discovered we had had this splendid opportunity and had neglected it? I'll brew such poison for this Pante that it shall have more than enough! I'll clear this passage; he'll take no more highway toll here, even though he be a maneater who respects neither gold, silver, nor iron arms! He'll find little pastime in eating men from this out, for I am going to deliver travellers from his arrogance. I daresay he is a stupid monster. This good youth here doesn't fear him—why should I? Moreover, I've never seen a Pante before. Get out of my way and watch me."

"I shall indeed watch you," replied Arthur, "for I shall be right here with you. I will not go back to Britain alone. If you perish, so shall I."

On looking about him Lancelot perceived a clump of lindens with thick leafy branches. Do you know what he did? He cut down a certain quantity of foliage and covered helm and hauberk therewith, taking particular care for his face; and he similarly covered his horse from nose to tail as a protection against the monster's fiery blast.

Hardly had the knight finished these preparations when the Pante galloped up. Lancelot faced him; on his right was the king, and on the other side was the archer with drawn bow. I do not see how the monster could get out of such a strait without battle. He, also, was evidently at a loss, for he paused, snorting fire and flame. Lancelot went right up to him at once and gave him a mighty blow on the left nostril so that the blood gushed out. It was a small wound, yet the Pante took it much to heart, and sat whimpering on his haunches: He was not accustomed to receive such resistance.

It would now have been possible for Lancelot to have got away without difficulty had he been so minded. But no: It was his practice to conquer by sheer force everything in the world that opposed him. Never before had he resorted to such a stratagem as hiding behind bushes; but if he had not done so, he would have been burned to a cinder. Again he thrust at the monster, sending the length of his lance down its gullet. This was a more serious wound, and the Pante was very much astonished; he was unable to understand why he felt so badly, for he could not perceive who or what had injured him. He looked straight ahead and would certainly have gulped down any enemy whom he found before him, if he could have seen one; but to his short sight it seemed that there was nothing there but leaves and branches.

Now Arthur in his turn prepared to attack the creature, and sent his lance right through the thick of its body into its liver. The sergeant, for his part, let fly an arrow with such good aim that he hit the Pante in the eye, and the point penetrated to the brain. Then he shot another arrow immediately and hit him in the ear —a stroke which annoyed the monster quite as much as the first one. Again the bowman aimed still a third arrow and struck him fairly.

These three wounds filled the Pante with wonder and vexation, for he could not see the archer behind the broad oak which protected him. That smart and boiling in his brain seemed to him nothing short of marvellous since it came to him, so far as he could judge, from nowhere. He became quite angry, and reared his head to see if he could perceive his enemy. He belched forth wondrous great fire; the leaves were consumed, the branches burned, and the underbrush round about took fire with the tremendous heat which he emitted. Lancelot, who was right in front of him, was taken unawares, and received the full force of this blast. His horse fell dead under him, and he himself was so scorched inside his armour that he did not know what to do with himself. If he had not taken the precaution of covering himself with the leaves and branches he would have been burned to the marrow of his bones.

It seems to me that Lancelot was now scantly provided with ease or comfort, or any other pleasant thing. All three men would certainly have been burned down at once were it not that the Pante was so much annoyed and distracted by the wounds in his eye and ear, to say nothing of the stroke on the nose, the spear in his belly and the lance in his liver. Blood and brain oozed from his head together; he tottered and shook with amazement. All of a sudden he let out a roar and whinny such that all the forest reverberated therewith as though wracked by a tempest; and before one could have run a rod, he tumbled over dead.

Lancelot staggered out of the way and fell down in a faint of exhaustion beside a bramble bush. Arthur ran up to him, and when the knight did not rise, became very much alarmed, for he thought him dead. The archer, too, showed considerable concern. Between them they bore Lancelot on his shield to the place where the other companions had halted on hearing the beast's death roar. They laid him under an oak, and with difficulty removed the hot armour sticking to his clothes and flesh.

Arthur felt the prostrate man's pulse and found it still beating. "By God," said he, "he's not dead after all. Lancelot, my dear fellow, come, wake up. Remember your manners; don't leave me alone here in a strange country. Besides, I don't know where to get another shield-bearer now. Moreover, if I return to Britain without you, they will say I killed you for reasons which everyone knows better than I am supposed to."

The king was indeed much vexed. But, as we all know, Fortune turns low to high in a moment. While Arthur was lamenting, behold, a lady in gleaming white, the most beautiful they had ever seen, rode up to the group swiftly on a white horse. In her hand she held a gold-adorned ivory box containing a healing unguent. This lady, bright as the morning star, alighted in their midst and saluted the king. "May God," she said, "augment the prowess of the knight who lies here." "Fair lady," replied Arthur, "it would be more to the purpose to pray for his soul, for his body, it seems to me, is beyond aid."

By way of reply the lady drew near to Lancelot's prone body. From the box she laid out medicaments and prepared a cloth, for she was well learned in what she had to do. With the sweet-smelling unguent she thoroughly anointed Lancelot's face, head and neck, then his shoulders and arms, and finally the torso, legs and feet. After a moment or two Lancelot was quite healed: The scorched skin fell from his body and limbs, and was replaced by new. The bystanders were awe-stricken, and murmured: "Look! he is healed! This must be Mary Magdalene, who has brought some of the salve whereof she made a present to Christ." "No," said the others, "it is the Blessed Virgin herself; no one else could accomplish a thing like this."

As a matter of fact, it was my lady Lorie, Gawain's friend. She would not divulge her name on this occasion, but the news got round later.

Lorie very graciously made a present of her horse to Lancelot, said good-bye, and disappeared as though she had been a white cloud. They could understand neither whence she had come nor whither she vanished.

However, Lancelot, who had neglected to thank Lorie either for the horse or for other favours, was well again. The king laughed for joy when he saw him resume his now cooled arms with all his former vigour. He and Lancelot had many other splendid adventures before they arrived at Quintefeuille, but I will spare you an account of them.

"Sir," said Saxo the Grammarian, addressing Leland, "in the course of your narrative you twice mentioned an excavation or cavity, one underground and one on the top of a mountain—which seems a strange place for a cave, if I may say so—wherein your hero had some agreeable and some disagreeable experiences—I mean to say a cave wherein Fulk performed deeds of valour. The reference to caves and caverns strikes a chord in my memory, and calls to mind certain things of which I heard, or rather read; and since you seem to be sympathetic to the subject, unless I misjudge you, you may also be interested in . . ."

48. ASMUND'S SEPULCHRAL ADVENTURE

Saxo Grammaticus

Early in the history of Denmark there was a king called Frode, son of Fridleif. At that time Eric the Eloquent reigned in Sweden, and Gothmar in Norway. Now in Norway there were two petty kings, Bjorn of Vík, and Alf of the near-by kingdom of Heathmark. Bjorn had a son named Aswit, and Alf's son was called Asmund.

One time Asmund ranged abroad on the hunt, but had small success. A darkness came down and separated him from his beaters. For a long time he wandered alone, without horse, without proper clothes, and with no food except the roots and mushrooms growing in the forest. Finally he arrived by chance at the hall of King Bjorn, who received him well. There Asmund remained for some time, and became such close friends with Aswit that each swore to the other the oath of inviolable companionship. Each young man took a vow that he who lived the longer should follow his dead companion to the grave.

It was soon after this that Frode and Eric, one by sea and the other by land, attacked Norway. The Norse were unable to withstand the combined power of the two kings and fled to Halogaland.

In the meantime young Aswit died of a fatal sickness, and, according to the custom, was buried with his horse and dog in an earthen barrow. And Asmund, by reason of the oath he had taken to be buried with his sworn brother, went into the cavern with him, taking along a small supply of food.

About this time it happened that King Eric of Sweden was crossing the Uplands in his march across Norway, and came upon Aswit's barrow. His men, thinking that it concealed treasure, broke it open with spades. There they found a hole deeper than they had anticipated, and cast lots to see who should go down to investigate. The lot fell to a bold young man, who was lowered in a basket at the end of a rope. Asmund, at the bottom of the pit, watched the approach of the basket, and when it reached the bottom, threw the man out, got into it himself, and signalled to be drawn up.

The Swedes thought they were hauling up a great lot of treasure; but when they saw an unknown man get out of the basket, it seemed to them the dead had come to life. They let go the rope and fled in all directions. One could readily excuse them, for Asmund looked awful, pale and wan, covered as he was with funereal corruption.

Asmund called out to the fleeing soldiers, assuring them that he was a living man. When he was brought before Eric the king marvelled greatly, for his face was not only stained, but blood was still pouring from gashes in his cheeks here and there. In reply to the king's question Asmund gave an account of himself.

"Do not be aghast," he said, "to see me pale and earth-stained, for you know well that he who dwells among the dead loses his colour like the leaves in autumn. Fate was hard to me, and it should not be a cause for wonder that in the cold pit there under the earth my strength should wane. Night was before my eyes, and my courage sank in my breast. Everywhere was the oppressive stench of the hideous grave and the rotting corpse. My strength was nearly exhausted, and it seemed that I was beginning to decay myself. And yet that was not horror enough, for I had to fight with a dead man! I know not if any god was angry with me and conjured him up from hell, but Aswit, who was buried in that barrow, returned to wrestle with me. First he tore his horse to pieces with his teeth and ate him; madly he seized upon and ate his dog. It turned my stomach. Not satisfied with these, he rushed upon me, attacking me with demoniac strength, tearing my cheek with his nails and wrenching off my ear. But the loathsome revenant did not himself escape unharmed: I gave him a bad one. I managed to seize my sword. I cut off his head and pegged his filthy carcass down with a stake. I was about to dig my way out when your man came down in the basket."

That was Asmund's adventure. I do not know what happened to him after that.

"Among most peoples death puts an end to a man's activities," said Joinville; "but apparently the case is different among you Northerners."

"It is so," answered Saxo, "and I will not venture to explain it."

"The phenomenon described by the Grammarian is not an isolated one," said Hallfred Vandraethaskald, "nor is it restricted to us Northerners. You have already heard of Lancelot's adventure with the live corpse in Brefny, and of the corpse which appeared to Richard sans Peur. I am in no better position to explain the matter than Saxo; yet it would seem that only the spirits of those men return who have unjustly and prematurely been cut off by death, in order that they may finish the performance of some deed, whether of justice or revenge. Some of the guests here recall the fearful disturbances at Frodis-water occasioned by the failure of Thorod to execute exactly and completely the dying behest of Thorgunna. Stir, also, the father-in-law of Snorri the Priest, wrought considerable havoc in the women's bower at Horseholt after his death. Perhaps the most fearful revenant in our histories was Thorolf Baegifot, who died of heart-burnings because he was overmatched by Arnkel and Snorri the Priest, whom he had tried and failed to overmatch. When I was in Iceland I heard, too, about the ghost-walking of Viga Hrapp, whose story may serve as an illustration."

49. THE RETURN OF VIGA HRAPP
Hallfred Vandraethaskald

Hrapp was the name of a man who lived in Salmon-river-dale on the north bank of the river opposite to Hoskuldstead. The place was later called Hrappstead, but is now waste land. Hrapp was the son of Sumarlid and was called Fight-Hrapp. He was Scots on his father's side, and his mother's kin came from Sodor, where he was reared. He was a very big, strong man, and one not willing to yield to another even in the face of some odds; and for the reason that he was most overbearing, and would never make good what he had done amiss, he had to flee from West-over-the-Sea. His wife was named Vigdis, and was Hallstein's daughter.

It is told of Hrapp that he grew most violent in his behaviour, and did his neighbours such harm that they could hardly hold their own against him. As old age came upon him Hrapp's temper remained the same, but his physical powers waned so that he had to lie in bed. He called his wife Vigdis and said: "I have never been of ailing health in life, and it is therefore most likely that this illness of mine will put an end to our life together. Now when I am dead, I wish my grave to be dug in the door-way of my fire-hall, and that I be put thereinto standing up there in the door-way. Thus shall I be able to keep a more careful eye on my dwelling."

After Hrapp died all was done as he had bidden, for Vigdis did not dare gainsay him. And as evil as he had been to deal with in life, just so was he by a great deal more when he was dead, for he walked again frequently after he was buried. People said that he killed most of his servants in his ghostly appearances. He also caused a great deal of trouble to those who lived near by, and Hrappstead eventually became deserted.

After a while Hrappstead was acquired by Olaf Peacock by purchase. He moved his chattels thither and renamed the place Herdholt. One evening the man who looked after the dry cattle came to Olaf and asked him to set some other man to look after the cows, and to give him some other work to do. Olaf replied that he wished the man to go on with the work he was doing. The thrall said that he would sooner go away. "Then you think there is something wrong," said Olaf, "and I will go with you this evening when you put up the cattle. And if I think there is any excuse for you in this, I will say nothing about it; but otherwise you will find that your lot will take some turn for the worse."

That evening Olaf left home with the house-carle, taking with him his gold-set spear, the king's gift. They came to the fold, which **was** open, and Olaf bade the house-carle go in. "I will drive up the cattle," he said, "and you tie them as they come in."

The thrall went to the door of the fold. All unawares Olaf finds him leaping into his open arms. Olaf asked why he had become so terrified. "Hrapp stands in the door-way of the fold," answered the man; "he reached for me, but I have had my fill of wrestling with him."

Thereupon Olaf went to the fold door and thrust at Hrapp with his spear. But Hrapp took the socket of the spear in both hands and wrenched it aside so that forthwith the spear-shaft broke. Olaf was about to run at Hrapp, but he disappeared there where he stood; and there they parted, Olaf having the spear-shaft and Hrapp the spear-head. After that Olaf and the carle tied up the cattle and went home.

The next morning Olaf went to the place where Hrapp was buried and had him dug up. Hrapp was found undecayed, and there Olaf also found his spear-head. Afterwards he had a fire made, and Hrapp burned on it, and his ashes were flung out to sea. Thereafter no one had any more trouble with Hrapp's ghost.

"Your unlaid spirits," said Chrétien de Troyes, "strike me as utterly repulsive, and your buryings alive as senseless and absurd. One could imagine a man and a *woman* entering into such a bond as that between Aswit and Asmund, for love forces mortals to do strange deeds; nor is it inconceivable that one lover, driven by grief, might wish, in the excess of frenzy, to bury himself with the other —as in the case of the widow of Ephesus, whose story has been so charmingly retold by John of Salisbury yonder. But even a southern imagination balks at the suggestion that one *man* would willingly be buried with another man. To sacrifice one's life for one's friend on the high stage of heroic action is understandable, but to go to one's death for no reason of fame or advantage is silly."

"We of the north," said Snorri Sturlason, "have learned that there are worse things than death."

"Considering the natural deficiencies of the country and climate in which you dwell," replied Chrétien, "I daresay that point of view is a natural one. However, when we of the South die, we are very dead; we do not return, either for good or ill; so we like to make the most of life, such as it is. Sometimes, it is true, our fury to win happiness brings us very near death's door, as I will show by the story of Cliges and Fenice which I found in an old book at Beauvais."

50. DIVORCE BY DEATH

Chrétien de Troyes

The father of Cliges was Alexander, prince of Constantinople. On the death of the old emperor he would normally have succeeded to the throne, but he preferred to retain his liberty of movement, and allowed his younger brother Alis to be crowned in his stead. As the price of this concession, however, he stipulated that Alis should not marry, so that, lacking an heir, Cliges should succeed to the throne after his death.

No sooner had Alexander died, however, than Alis broke his promise and married the daughter of the German emperor, carrying her off by force, though she was betrothed to the Duke of Saxony. On the occasion of this abduction Cliges was in his uncle's suite, and the two young people had hardly caught sight of each other when they fell mutually in love.

There was nothing to be done about it for the moment, but Fenice, for that was the bride's name, thought she would help Fate to shape things in such a way as would be agreeable to them both. With the aid of magic she contrived that Alis should be her husband in name only.

Soon after this Cliges, in compliance with his father's wishes, went to Arthur's court, there to make test of his prowess. After performing many gallant deeds, and achieving many splendid victories, he returned to Constantinople with a full measure of fame.

One day, quite a while after he had returned from Arthur's court, Cliges went alone to the chamber of her who was in no wise his enemy, and I assure you that the door was not closed against him. The lovers sat down beside each other and Fenice's maids withdrew. First Fenice inquired about England, questioning him about the culture and breeding of my lord Gawain. Other questions she asked, too, until she came as though by chance to the subject which she hesitated to broach: Had he fallen in love with any maid or lady while in England?

Cliges was not slow in replying. "Lady," he said, "while I was in England I was indeed in love, but not with anybody of that country. I do not know what happened to my heart after I left Germany; perhaps it followed you, so that while my body was in England, my heart must have been here. And that is why I have returned to Greece. But even here my heart does not come back to me, nor can I entice it, nor do I wish to do so. But how has it gone with you since you have been in this country? Do you like the people and the land?"

"A little while ago," replied Fenice, "I was pleased with neither the people nor the country; but now, indeed, a joy has sprung up in me such as I would not exchange for the kingdom of Persia. I, too, am really only a shell, for I also live without a heart. I was never in Britain, it is true, and yet my heart has been engaged in some sort of an affair there without me. It must have been with you."

"Then, lady," said Cliges, "both hearts are here with us now, since you have mine, and yours, you say, resides with me."

"That is true," replied Fenice; "moreover, when my heart went to you it brought with it the body in such wise that no one but yourself shall ever have part therein. I assure you that your uncle has never had any part of me, nor has he known me as Adam knew his wife. It is wrong to call me lady, though those who call me dame do not know that I am a maid. Even your uncle does not know it, for he has drunk a potion which makes him think he is awake when he is really asleep, and causes him to believe that he is taking his pleasure with me just as though I lay in his arms. But I have assuredly locked him out of that. I was so distraught for love of you that I thought I should never recover—no more than the sea can dry up. But though my heart and my body are yours, I make you a promise that you shall never have more solace of me than you have now unless you are able to hit upon some plan whereby I may be removed from your uncle's bed and board, and in such fashion that he may never be able to find me again, nor have grounds for blaming either of us. Give thought to this matter tonight and tell me your scheme tomorrow. I also will think about it, and we will put into execution the plan which we consider best."

The following morning Cliges said: "Lady, it seems to me that we cannot do better than go to Britain. I have thought out a way of taking you there without difficulty. There will be more rejoicing over you and me throughout my uncle's land than ever there was at Troy over Paris and Helen. If this proposal does not please you, tell me your plan, for I am quite ready to do what is most agreeable to you."

"I will never go away with you in that manner," answered Fenice, "for when we had gone there would be evil talk. People would consider me wanton and dissolute, and you a fool. It is a prudent thing to stop evil mouths, and I think I can do so if you will agree to my proposal. It is this: I will counterfeit illness and in due time feign that I am dead. You, for your part, must make proper arrangements for my sepulture; you must make sure that the tomb is so constructed that I do not suffocate and die in very truth. Also, you must see to it that there is no guard near the tomb during the night when you come to fetch me away. Furthermore, it will be necessary to find some retreat where no one but you shall see me. You shall be both my lord and my attendant, and whatever you do will seem good to me. I will never be lady over any empire unless you are its master. A poor place, obscure and vile, would seem to me more splendid than these halls providing you were with me. If I have you and see you, I shall be mistress over all desirable things, and the world will be mine. Now if this business is done with due skill and caution, no ill can be spoken, for it will be thought throughout the empire that I am rotting in my grave. My nurse, Thessala, will aid me loyally; she is very clever, and I have great confidence in her."

"Lady," said Cliges, "if you think this plan is feasible, and that your nurse can succeed in carrying it through, then nothing remains to be done save to set the wheels in motion as quickly as possible."

Thereupon Cliges took his leave to seek out a servant of his. The man's name was Jehan, and he was a skilled carpenter, cabinet-maker, mason and mechanic.

Fenice sent for Thessala, whom she had brought with her from Germany. "Nurse," said she, "I have always found you prudent and faithful, and I love you for your loyalty. The time has come, however, when I must take you more fully into my confidence than ever, and I know that what I am about to say will never be divulged by you. You know what trouble is upon me, and what it is that I desire. I have found my peer; he loves me and I him. Now I will tell you the plan we have agreed upon whereby we may be able to consummate our love."

Thessala assured her mistress that she would aid her in any way she could, and urged her to have no apprehension. She would prepare a potion which would turn her stiff, cold, colourless, speechless and breathless in such wise that everyone would think the soul had really left the body; but in spite of appearances she would be well and alive, though unable to feel ill; nothing would grieve her for the space of a night and a day.

"Nurse," said Fenice, "I place myself unreservedly in your hands. Now tell these people to go away; say that I am ill and that they annoy me."

In the meantime Cliges conferred with Jehan the joiner, whose services he commanded, and whose discretion he bought with a promise of manumission. Jehan agreed to construct a coffin of the proper kind, and as to a place of safe retreat—would Cliges come with him now? Below the city, in a retired spot, Jehan had constructed a tower with great skill and labour in his spare time, and now he led his master through it from room to room. When Cliges thought he had seen everything, he expressed his admiration, for the dwelling was indeed excellently suited to his purpose.

"There is more here than meets the eye," said Jehan, "for there are apartments underground accessible only through a concealed door." Thereupon he operated the mechanism of the door and they went below. The underground apartment proved indeed an admirable place for concealing a lady. The chambers were tastefully decorated, and furnished with everything any woman might need or desire. There were even bath-rooms with running hot water.

Cliges examined everything attentively and then said: "Jehan, this is the very place, and in return for the same I hereby set you free, you and yours forever." "Thank you, my lord," said the man; "but now let us return to the city."

As Cliges and Jehan were making their way back to the palace they overheard the people talking about the sudden illness which had seized the empress, and Cliges hastened his steps. It seemed that the empress had forbidden anyone her chamber while she felt so ill both at head and heart, though if the emperor or his nephew should come they might be allowed to enter. Cliges hurried to Fenice's bed and told her quickly what he had done and found. But Fenice cried: "Go! Go! I am so ill I really cannot have anyone here." So Cliges withdrew with downcast looks, though his heart sang with joy.

After this Fenice carried on in such a manner that the emperor was easily convinced that she was seriously ill. He would have sent for doctors, but the empress would not allow it. "There is only one doctor," said she, "who can restore me to health, if he wishes to do so." Everyone thought she meant God, but it was Cliges whom she had in mind. In this way Fenice took care that no doctor should get access to her; and in order to emphasize her deception, she would neither eat nor drink, and her colour faded.

It was now Thessala's turn, and she hastened to concoct the potion whose ingredients she had long had on hand. Shortly before nones she gave Fenice the drink. As soon as she had drunk it her face became white, as though she had lost blood, and she fell unconscious; she would not have moved hand or foot if she had been flayed. And though she neither stirred nor spoke, she heard well enough the great uproar of lamentation that filled the hall at the announcement of her decease. But I will spare you an account of how the citizens of Constantinople cursed Death for this outrage.

Now it happened that in the midst of this demonstration of grief three physicians from Salerno arrived in the city. They inquired into its cause, and when they had been told they said: "It is evident that God hates this city, for if we had only been here yesterday, Death might have considered himself very clever if he had been able to wrest anything from our hands." "My lords," said a citizen, "there are plenty of good doctors in Constantinople, but our lady would have nothing to do with them, nor allow them to visit her in her illness." "Indeed," said the physicians, "is that so?" Then they recalled that Solomon's wife had so hated him that she deceived him under the guise of death: perhaps this lady had done likewise. But if they might investigate the case they would not conceal any trickery—if any came to light.

The doctors betook themselves to the court, where the noise of lamentation had become uproarious. The master physician, the wisest of the three, went up to the bier. No one said: "Keep your hands off!" and no one pushed him away. He placed his hand on Fenice's breast and felt that there was certainly life in the supposed corpse. To the emperor standing near he said: "Take comfort, for I assure you that this woman is not dead. Give over your grief, for if I do not restore her to you, you may slay or hang me."

At these words there was a hush throughout the palace. The emperor gave the doctor permission to do as he saw fit, promising that if he restored Fenice to life he might name his reward himself, but that if he proved to be a liar, he should be strung up like a thief.

"Very well," said the master physician; "you need have no mercy on me if I do not make her speak to you. Have the hall cleared, for I must pursue my investigations in privacy. Let only these two doctors, my companions, remain."

Cligès, Thessala and Jehan would have opposed these measures, but they might have suffered at the hands of the enraged court had they done so; hence they kept their peace and retired with the others.

Now the three doctors rudely ripped off the winding sheet. "Lady," said they, "do not be afraid, but speak out confidently. We know for a certainty that you are alive. Be prudent and fear not, for if you need advice, be sure that all three of us will aid you to the extent of our power. We will keep faith with you whether in concealing or aiding. And now that we have offered you our skill and assistance, do not keep us talking." Thus they thought to dupe and deceive her; but it was no good, for she had no desire for their services.

When the doctors saw that they could not gain their end either by prayer or flattery, they took Fenice out of the bier and beat and mauled her. But they acted like fools, for they got no word out of her. Then they threatened, saying that if she did not speak she would certainly repent it, for they would make such a wondrous example of her as had never before been made of any woman's body. "We know that you are alive and shamming," they said, "and that you are tricking the emperor. If any one of us has vexed you just now, pass it over and confess your folly before you are further maltreated, for you are acting very foolishly." But all their words were in vain.

Thereupon they attacked her again, beating her with their leather belts till fearful bruises appeared on her soft white flesh. So much and so long did they beat her tender body that blood was splashed about here and there. But this was useless, too, for they could get neither a word nor even a sigh out of her, nor did she stir under their lashings.

At this point the doctors held a consultation, and said they would have to bring fire and lead; they would melt the lead and pour it into the palms of her hands rather than desist from their attempts to make her speak. And as they said, so they did. Thus did the vile ruffians torture and abuse the lady. Boiling from the fire they poured the lead into both her palms, nor were they satisfied when it passed right through from one side of the hand to the other. The pitiless wretches promised that if she did not speak soon they would put her on the grill till she was quite roasted. But Fenice said nothing.

The doctors were indeed on the point of putting Fenice on the grill when about a thousand women of the city, who had assembled before the palace, saw through an aperture of the door the torture which these ruffians were perpetrating on the helpless body of their empress. They broke down the doors with clubs and sledges, and if they had been able to reach the physicians, the doctors of Salerno would have received their fee. Among the women who rushed into the palace was Thessala; she found her mistress lying before the fire, naked, mauled and bloody. She placed her on the bier again and covered her over with the pallium. In the meantime the crowd of women went about looking for the doctors without the aid of emperor or seneschal, so that they might pay them. They found them at last, and hurled them down from the high windows to the court so that all three broke their arms and legs and necks. No women ever did a better job of work than that.

You may be sure that Cliges was very much distraught when he heard tell of the suffering and torture which his lady had undergone for his sake. He almost went mad, for he thought—and with reason—that she must surely be dead or undone by the torment she had undergone. But Thessala brought a very precious unguent wherewith she gently anointed Fenice's wounds. The ladies recomposed the body of their empress on the bier, spreading over it a pallium of white Syrian stuff, leaving the face uncovered. All that night they did not cease to wail, and all through the city rich and poor, high and low, made grievous lamentation.

On the morrow the emperor sent for Jehan and commanded him to do his utmost in providing a handsome sepulture. The artisan replied that he had one ready to hand which he had destined for a holy body when he had begun it. "But," he said, "it is suitable for the empress, for it seems that she must be holy." "You are right," replied Alis; "and she shall be buried in the churchyard of St Peter in accordance with the promise I made her before she died. Set up your tomb in the fairest spot of the cemetery."

Jehan hastened about his work. Because of the tomb's hardness and coldness he placed a bed of down therein, and strewed flowers and leaves round about so that it might smell sweetly. The service for the dead was performed, the bells rung, and the body was removed to the tomb amid the general wailing of the citizens. The grief and inattention of the bystanders gave Jehan ample opportunity for arranging the sepulchre in his own fashion. He closed and sealed it well; and he would have been clever indeed who had been able to open it without doing it violence.

You may be sure that Cliges lamented more bitterly than anyone; indeed, he almost went out of his mind, and it is a wonder that he did not kill himself. Still, he stayed his hand until he should have disinterred his lady and determined whether she were alive or dead.

During the night Fenice's tomb was guarded by thirty knights in the light of ten great candles. But as the night drew on, the guards became weary with sorrow and watching; and when they had partaken of meat and drink, they fell asleep.

Cliges stole away from the palace, and with Jehan hurried anxiously to the churchyard. It happened that the place was enclosed by a high wall, and having locked the gate on the inside the guards considered that all was safe enough against intrusion. For the moment Cliges was at a loss how to effect an entry; but Love spurred him on: being light and agile, he swung over the wall and let himself down on the other side by a tree growing near. The first thing he did was to open the gate for his man; then he extinguished the candles.

Jehan went to the tomb and opened it without leaving any trace of disturbance. Cliges lifted up his lady, limp and feeble; gently he kissed and caressed her, not knowing whether to rejoice or lament, for she made no move. Jehan closed the tomb again, and as fast as they could the two men made their way to the isolated tower with their burden.

In the underground apartment they loosened Fenice's shroud and laid her down gently. Cliges, who knew nothing of the potion which had deprived her of the power to move, thought his lady was dead indeed, and now wept with uncontrollable grief. However, the hour was approaching when the potion should lose its force. Fenice could hear her lover sorrowing, and strove to win back the use of her faculties so that she might comfort him with word or glance. It almost broke her heart to hear him lament.

"What marvellous thing do I behold!" wailed Cliges, "my lady dead while I live on! What a vile thing you are, O Death, to take the good and lovely and respite the mean and wretched."

Now Fenice spoke feebly. "O lover mine," she said, "I am not quite dead, but nearly. I intended a joke and trick, but Death did not appreciate my humour, for as it has turned out, I must complain in very truth. It is really a miracle that I have escaped alive, for the doctors wounded and tore my flesh grievously. However, if skill avails anything now, my nurse would be able to restore me to health completely." "Dearest lady," said Cliges, "if that is true take comfort, for I will bring her to you at once." "Nay," answered Fenice, "let Jehan go for her rather than you."

Jehan brought Thessala with her unguents and electuaries to the tower. Just the sight of her made Fenice think she was already healed, so great was her faith in her old nurse.

"Can you cure her?" asked Cliges anxiously. "Oh, yes, my lord," answered Thessala. "In a fortnight she will be as well as though she had never suffered ill." Thereupon she went about her business to such good purpose that Fenice recovered completely. Cliges was so happy that the possession and lordship of any riches or secular power in the world would have seemed to him mean by comparison.

Now certainly Love did not degrade or debase himself by blessing these two, for when they kiss and caress each other it seems that all the world must be the better for their love. Ask me no more. All I can say is that each lover has found his peer.

"Yours is certainly an artistic and poetic arrangement of rather gruesome details," said Guillaume de Nangis when Chrétien had finished; "and your story is not unmotivated as my colleague Saxo's seems to be. But whereas the Grammarian's tale may be a reflection of vulgar superstition, and yours an equally extravagant flight of your author's imagination, I propose to tell you about a burial alive that was sober historical fact."

51. ANASTASIUS BURIED ALIVE
Guillaume de Nangis

In former times there was a certain bishop of Clermont named Cautinus who, after his succession to the see, behaved himself in such a manner as to arouse the contempt of all. He was excessively given to wine, and was frequently so deep in his cups that four men were hardly sufficient to carry him from the scene of his potations. As a result of such indulgences he later in life became epileptic. In avarice too, his greed reached such a degree that it seemed to him he would die if he failed to get into his own hands some part or all the estates which bordered on his own. If the owner of such lands was a person of rank, it was Cautinus' practice to pick a quarrel with him, and rob him with abuse; if he was a person of lower standing, Cautinus seized the property by force.

Now in these days there was in Clermont a priest named Anastasius, a man of good family, who owned certain property by virtue of a charter granted him by Queen Clotild of glorious memory. On several occasions Cautinus had begged Anastasius to turn the queen's charter over to him and cede him the land. When the priest showed himself reluctant to yield to the bishop's will, Cautinus had recourse first to blandishments and then to threats. Finally he had Anastasius brought to the city, and had him detained there in the most high-handed manner, giving orders that unless he surrendered the documents in question, he should be subjected to corporeal hurts and starved to death. Anastasius still resisted sturdily, and refused to give up the charter, saying that he would rather waste away himself for lack of food than leave his children in misery. So, according to the bishop's orders, he was turned over to the soldiers to be starved to death.

Now under the church of the holy martyr Cassius there was a most ancient and very secret crypt; it contained a large sarcophagus of Parian marble wherein lay the remains of some person long dead. The live priest was thrust into this tomb on top of the dead man, and the stone wherewith it had previously been covered was replaced. Guards were posted at the crypt door; but they, confident that the stone lid would keep their prisoner down, lit a fire and fell asleep under the influence of the wine which they warmed thereat.

Anastasius, like a new Jonah, began, from the confinement of his tomb as from the bowels of hell, to implore the mercy of the Lord. As I have said, the sarcophagus was roomy, and though he was unable to turn himself completely, still, he was able to stretch out his hands somewhat. As he used to tell afterwards, the bones of the dead man beneath him exhaled a fearful stench, such as convulsed not only his external organs of sense, but his very vitals. As long as he could stop his nostrils with his cloak he was not too much incommoded; but when he felt himself on the point of suffocation and removed the cloak a little, the nauseous odour invaded him not only through the mouth and nose, but, one might say, through the ears as well.

However, it seems that the Lord had pity on him, for the next time he stretched out his hand to the edge of the sarcophagus he found an iron crow-bar which had remained between the rim of the tomb and the stone lid when the latter had been lowered into place. Moving this lever a little at a time, God's aid working with him, he felt the stone shift. Soon he was able to put out his head, and then rapidly widened the aperture so that there was room for his whole body to pass.

By this time it was growing dusk, yet there was enough light to enable Anastasius to make his way to another door of the crypt. This he found secured by exceedingly strong locks and bolts, but it was not so well put together but that one could see out between the planks. As Anastasius was peering out he perceived a man, and called to him in a low voice. Fortunately the man heard him, seized his axe and cut through the boards which bore the locks, and so opened a way out for the prisoner. Thus, about nightfall, Anastasius made his escape and took his way homeward.

On arriving home the first thing the priest did was to look for the precious deeds given him by Queen Clotild. When he found them he went to King Lothar, to whom he related how his bishop had attempted to bury him alive. All those in the king's presence who heard this story were amazed, declaring that not even Nero or Herod had ever been guilty of so vile an act as to put a man alive into the tomb. At this moment up came Bishop Cautinus, whether with the intention of lodging a complaint, or on some other business, I do not know. The fact is that he could not stand in the face of Anastasius' accusation, and went away again beaten and confounded. From King Lothar Anastasius received instruments confirming his claim to his property, whereof he remained in possession during his lifetime, and bequeathed to his descendants after his death.

"Sir," said Bonvesin da Riva, "we thank you for your story."

"Fenice," observed Bandello, with a glance at Chrétien, "survived her terrible ordeal like a true heroine; but I cannot recommend the use of potions; not only are they unreliable, but so also are the people who handle them. Romeo and Giulietta had good reason to know that."

"I have heard that tragic story," said King Hákon. "I recall too that an evil potion was the bane of one of the mightiest heroes of the North. It was Grimhild's drugged drink that caused Sigurd to forget Brynhild and marry Gudrun instead. And while the drink was in him his death could be plotted with assurance. But little good came to Gunnar or to Brynhild from his slaying: The score was settled with interest one day later at Atli's court, for Gudrun was a high-minded woman."

"I also," said Jean Froissart, "reprobate the use of potions. Who knows whether the drink be a love-potion, a sleeping-potion or a poison? The poet Lucretius, they say, went mad from drinking a love-potion—as though poets were not mad enough already! Perhaps I was not sufficiently mad, for my verses never made much stir in literary circles; or perhaps life's prose is sweeter than its rhyme, as someone has remarked. At all events, what I meant to say is this: While travelling in the south of France I learned from a good source how the use of poison, administered as a love-charm, had the gravest consequences for a brave and honourable gentleman. My informant is present, and perhaps he will not object to relating those facts again."

"With pleasure," said Espaign du Lion.

52. THE TRAGIC DEATH OF THE YOUNG COUNT OF FOIX
Espaign du Lion

In the arm of the upper head-waters of the Garonne lies the county of Foix, intervening like a wedge between Gascony on the east and Languedoc on the west. Beyond the Pyrenees to the south lie the principality of Catalonia, the kingdom of Aragón and the kingdom of Navarre.

Count Gaston Phoebus de Foix was, as Froissart has said, a gallant and courtly gentleman, and a learned one to boot, for he is the author of a *Traité de la Chasse*. Such being the case, many of us thought it regrettable that he and his lady were not on good terms. The cause of their estrangement was the lady's brother, the king of Navarre.

It happened that the Comte de Foix held in prison the Lord d'Albreth for a sum of fifty thousand francs ransom. The king of Navarre pledged himself for this sum; but the count, knowing him to be crafty and faithless, would not accept him as security. This attitude piqued the countess and raised her indignation. Finally the count said: "At your entreaty, and out of regard for my son, not out of love for you, it shall be done as you wish." Accordingly the king of Navarre acknowledged himself the count's debtor in the sum of fifty thousand francs, and the Lord d'Albreth was set at liberty. He, at his pleasure, paid the fifty thousand francs to the king of Navarre according to his obligation; but the king never paid this money over to the Count of Foix.

Now the count said to his wife: "Lady, you must go to your brother in Navarre and tell him that I am very ill satisfied with him for withholding from me the sum he has received on my account." The countess replied that she would cheerfully go thither, and set out from Orthès with her attendants.

On her arrival at Pampeluna her brother received the countess with much joy, and the lady delivered her message. Then said the king: "Fair sister, the money is yours as the dower owing to you from the count your husband, and since I have got possession of it, it shall never leave the kingdom of Navarre." "My lord," said the lady, "by this action you will create a great hatred between the Count of Foix and myself; and if you persist in this determination, I shall never dare return to him, for he will put me to death for having deceived him." The king, who was unwilling to let such a sum pass out of his hands, replied: "I cannot say how you should act, whether to remain or return; but as I have possession of the money, and as it is my legal right to act as the banker of your settlement, it shall never leave my kingdom."

Unable to obtain any other answer from her brother, the Comtesse de Foix dared not return home, and remained in Navarre. Count Gaston, perceiving the malice of the king, began to hate his wife, though she was in no wise to blame. And thus things remained for a time.

Now young Gaston, the count's son, grew up and became a fine young gentleman, and was betrothed to the daughter of the Comte d'Armagnac. The boy might be about fifteen or sixteen years old; he made a handsome figure and resembled his father exactly.

On a time young Gaston took it into his head to journey into Navarre to visit his mother and his uncle. But this was an unfortunate journey both for him and for his country. He stayed with his mother for some time and was splendidly entertained. On taking leave he tried to persuade her to accompany him back to Foix, but in vain, for the lady knew that her husband was a cruel man when displeased with anyone. She asked him if his father had ordered him to bring her back. Young Gaston replied that no such orders had been given, and so the lady feared to trust herself with him.

THE TRAGIC DEATH OF THE YOUNG COUNT

Hereupon the young man went to Pampeluna to take leave of his uncle. The king entertained him well and kept him upwards of ten days. On his departure he made handsome presents to the young count and his attendants. The last gift which the king gave him was the cause of his death, and I will tell you how it happened.

As the youth was on the point of starting out the king took him privately into his chamber and gave him a bag full of powder, which powder was of such pernicious quality that it would cause the death of anyone who ate of it. "Gaston, my fair nephew," said the king, "will you do what I am about to tell you? You see how unjustly the count hates your mother; and since she is my sister, that enmity displeases me as much as it should displease you. Now if you wish to reconcile your father and mother, you have but to take a small pinch of this powder, and when you see a good opportunity, scatter it over the food destined for your father's table; but take care that no one see you. The instant he shall have tasted it he will be impatient for his wife, your mother, to return to him; and they will love each other henceforward so passionately that they will never again be separated. You ought to be anxious to see this accomplished. But tell no one, for if you do, the powder will lose its effect."

Gaston believed everything his uncle told him and replied that he would cheerfully do as he had directed. On this he departed from Pampeluna and returned to Orthès. His father received him with pleasure and asked him what was the news in Navarre, and what presents and jewels had been given him. "Very handsome ones," replied young Gaston, and showed them all save the bag of powder.

In the hôtel de Foix it was customary for young Gaston and his bastard brother, Evan, to sleep in the same chamber. One day Evan found Gaston's coat lying on the bed; he noticed the bag of powder in the breast of it, and asked what it was. Gaston gave him a short answer and was very thoughtful for the rest of the day. Not long after this Gaston quarrelled with Evan at tennis and gave him a box on the ear. The younger boy ran in tears to the count, who inquired what ailed him. "Gaston has beaten me," replied Evan; "but he deserves beating much more than I do, for he wears at his breast a bag of powder. I do not know what use he intends to make of it, but several times he has said to me that his mother would soon return hither, and be more in your graces than ever she was." "Ho!" said the count. "Hold your tongue, and take care that you repeat to no man living what you have just said to me."

The count continued to think about this matter till dinner time, when he rose and seated himself as usual at his table in the hall. It was young Gaston's duty and custom to place the dishes before him and to taste the food. As soon as the boy had served the first dish in the usual manner, the count looked up and saw the strings of the pouch hanging from his pourpoint. The sight made his blood boil, and he said: "Gaston, come here, I want to whisper something to you." The youth stepped to the table, and the count, undoing his pourpoint, cut away the bag of powder with his knife. The young man was thunder-struck and said no word, but turned pale with fear, and began to tremble exceedingly, for he was now conscious that he had done wrong.

Count Gaston opened the bag, took some of the powder and scattered it on a piece of bread, which he gave to a dog to eat. The instant the dog had eaten a morsel his eyes rolled round in his head and he died. On this the count was very wroth, and with reason. Rising from the table he would have struck his son with his knife, but knights and squires rushed between them, saying: "For God's sake, my lord, do not be too hasty; make further inquiries before you do your son any harm."

For a few moments the count was speechless with wrath, then finally he broke out in Gascon: "Ho, Gaston, thou traitor! For thee, and to increase the inheritance which would have come to thee, have I made war and incurred the hatred of the kings of France, England, Spain, Navarre and Aragón, and have borne myself gallantly against them, and thou wishest to murder me! You must have an infamously bad character, and you shall die with this blow." Then leaping over the table, knife in hand, he would have slain the lad. But the knights and squires again interfered and on their knees said to him: "Alas, my lord! For heaven's sake, do not kill Gaston. You have no other child. Let him be confined, and inquire further into the business. Perhaps he was ignorant of what was in the bag and may therefore be blameless." "Well," replied the count, "let him be confined to the donjon, but so safely guarded that he may be forthcoming." So the youth was confined in the tower.

Count Gaston now arrested many of those who had served his son, and put to death not fewer than fifteen, saying that they must have been acquainted with his son's secrets. They should have told him, he said, that Gaston constantly wore on his breast a bag of such and such a form. This they did not do, and suffered terrible death for it. That was a pity, for there were not in all Gascony such handsome and well-bred squires as these.

This business struck the count to the heart, as he plainly showed, for he assembled at Orthès all the nobles and prelates of Foix and Béarn, and others the principal persons of the country. When they had met he told them how culpable he had found his son, and informed them that he intended putting him to death since, in his opinion, he deserved that penalty. The magnates unanimously opposed this action. "He is your heir," they said, "and you have no other."

When the count heard his subjects declare their sentiments in favour of his son, he hesitated. On second thoughts he considered that the youth might be sufficiently chastised by two or three months' confinement; after that he would send him on his travels for a few years till his evil conduct should be forgotten. So he dissolved the meeting. But the people of Foix would not quit Orthès until the count had assured them that Gaston should not be put to death, so great was their affection for the boy. The count promised, and Gaston remained a prisoner.

Young Gaston's place of confinement was a room in the donjon. During the ten days in which he remained there he scarcely ate or drank anything of the food which was regularly brought him, but threw it aside. The count would not permit anyone to remain in the chamber to comfort or advise him. Wherefor he grew melancholy, for he did not expect such harshness, and cursed the hour he was born, lamenting that he should come to such an end.

One day the servant who attended him said: "Here is food for you, Gaston." He paid no attention to it, and only told the man to put it down. Looking about him the servant saw that all the food which had been brought in the last days remained untouched, and closing the door he went to the count. "My lord," he said, "for God's sake, look to your son, for he is starving himself in prison. I believe he has eaten nothing since his incarceration ten days ago, for I see all that I have carried to him lying to one side untouched."

On hearing this the count flew into a rage and without a word left his apartment and took his way to the donjon. At this moment he happened to have in hand a knife, which he held so closely by the blade that only a thumb's breadth of the point appeared. "Ha! traitor," he said, "why dost thou not eat?" And without saying or doing anything more he left the room. As ill luck would have it, however, as he thrust aside the tapestry which covered the entrance of the chamber, the knife which he had in his hand struck his son in the throat. The point of the knife, small as it was, severed a vein. The boy was weak from fasting, and frightened by the tempestuous arrival of his father, and when he understood the nature of his wound, he turned himself on one side and died.

Hardly had the count reached his apartment again when his son's attendant came in and said: "My lord, Gaston is dead." "Dead!" cried the count. "Yes, God help me, he is indeed," replied the man.

Count Gaston would not believe it, and sent one of his knights to see; but the knight confirmed the attendant's statement. You may be sure that the count was now bitterly moved. "Ha! Gaston," he cried, "what a sorry business this has turned out to be for thee and me! In an evil hour didst thou visit thy mother in Navarre. Never shall I regain the happiness which I once enjoyed."

Then Count Gaston Phoebus de Foix ordered his barber to be summoned, and was shaven quite bare; afterwards he clothed himself and his whole household in black. The body of the youth was borne with tears and lamentations to the church of the Austin friars at Orthès and buried there.

Thus have I related to you the death of Gaston de Foix. His father killed him, it is true, but it was the king of Navarre who was the real cause of this sad event.

"We thank you," said Bartholomew Anglicus, "for your excellent tale."

"Master Leland," said Adamnan, addressing the great librarian, "you have related how Fulk Fitzwarin sailed among the islands of the North, experiencing marvellous adventures here and there. You, Master Jehan, have told us how Lancelot renewed his skin. And you, Sir John, at the instance of the poet of Ferrara, have related how Astolfo reached the Earthly Paradise. It occurs to me," he continued hesitantly, "that this company might care to know more about the Land of Behest. . . ."

"We should, indeed," encouraged Higden.

"And how it was visited by a countryman of mine. His voyage lasted seven years, and in the course of it he found, no fountain of youth, indeed, but he saw many other wonders. And Lancelot may be interested in hearing how another man lost his hide and regained it."

"Pray favour us with your tale," said Ponce de Leon before Lancelot could wipe his moustaches to reply.

"We are all ears," said Sir John Hawkins.

Thus encouraged Adamnan began the tale of . . .

53. THE ADVENTURES OF SAINT BRANDAN IN THE WESTERN SEA

Adamnan

The holy man St Brandan was a monk, born in Ireland of noble parents. There he became abbot of a house wherein were a thousand monks, whom he governed with prudence and discretion, living a strict and holy life in great penance and abstinence.

Never did St Brandan cease to pray God for himself and his familia, for the living and for the dead; but most insistently did he pray God that he might be vouchsafed a sight of that paradise wherein Adam dwelt at the beginning—the heritage from which we have been evicted. He knew that great glory and delight were therein, and that none except those free from the stain of the world were allowed entry to that place. Nevertheless he fervently desired that he might, before he died, know what abode the good were to have, where the evil-doers should dwell, and what reward should be theirs. He likewise yearned to see hell, and behold the pains which shall be endured there by those proud mortals who war so eagerly against God and religion, and among themselves enjoy neither faith nor love.

One time Brandan went to confess himself to a holy ascetic, a servant of God named Barintus, who lived with three hundred of his followers in a near-by wood. From him Brandan learned of the voyage which he had once undertaken in search of his son Mernoc. He had found him, said Barintus, on an island which lay close to the Island of Stones. Thence he and Mernoc had sailed to another island called the Terra Repromissionis Sanctorum which, because of the sweet scent which afterwards pervaded his garments, he took to be the Earthly Paradise. The holy man's words increased Brandan's longing and strengthened his resolution to seek that land himself. Forthwith he set about the preparations necessary for a voyage. From among his monks he chose the best fourteen he could find and divulged to them his intention. They took counsel and declared themselves pleased with the project, praying that he would take them in his company.

Now Brandan and his monks fasted and prayed forty days, and when that time had elapsed the abbot heard the voice of an angel from heaven saying: "Arise, Brandan, for thou shalt receive that which thou hast requested from God, namely, a sight of the Promised Land." And Brandan rejoiced in his heart.

Hereupon the abbot confided his purpose to the remainder of the brothers, placing them in the care of the prior during his absence. Then he kissed each one and went his way. Sadly did they weep because he would allow only fourteen of the fraternity to accompany him.

Brandan took his way down to the sea, to the place where he knew he was destined by God to commit himself to the deep, a place now vulgarly known as St Brandan's Seat. Thither he caused timber to be brought for the building of his vessel. Inside it was all of pine, covered outside with cow-hide; and he caused it to be well greased so that it would sail smoothly over the wave. In the boat he placed whatever furniture was necessary, together with victuals for forty days.

When all was ready, and the saint and his companions had finally entered the ship, behold, three brothers came running up, who cried out: O father, we could not endure your absence, wherefor we have followed you hither. Do not leave us behind, but accept us as companions with you. Brandan consented to receive them, but moved by a spirit of prophecy he warned them of the future. Two of you will suffer eternal torment with Dathan and Abiron, he said, and the third, fearfully urged by temptation, will yet be saved by the grace of God.

After this Brandan raised his hands and prayed God that his followers might be protected from peril on the voyage, and he stretched out his right hand and blessed them. They raised the mast and gave the sail to the wind, and with a fair breeze from the east they sailed westward over the sea. Soon all was lost from sight save wave and sky. Thus they held their course for two weeks till the wind failed—to the brothers' great dismay. But Brandan admonished them to trust in God. "When there is wind, we will sail," he said; "when there is no wind we will row." So the brothers seized the oars and began to row in God's name, but knew not whither to direct their course unless it were westward over the ocean.

For a month did the monks row without wind till food and strength failed them together, and they were sore afraid. Then they saw before them a great high land, and made for it, but they found no harbour where they could moor their boat, for the land was quite surrounded by rocks which none dared to scale. The cliffs rose high in the air and projected far over the water, and at their base the sea rolled back at them from hollows in the rock, endangering them greatly. Three days they spent looking here and there till they finally found a port wide enough for a single boat, hewn out of the grey limestone.

The monks made the ship fast, and all went ashore. A path led them to a large and handsome castle situated in splendid grounds; it might have been the estate of some emperor. They passed beyond the wall, which was all of hard crystal, and inside was a palace built of marble. The gems wherewith the walls were decorated gave out a great light. One thing in particular aroused their wonder: there was no man in the city. Brandan sat down inside the lofty palace, and yet no human being appeared. Said the saint: "Search the kitchens and larders and see if you can find that whereof we stand in need."

The brothers did, indeed, find food and drink in great plenty, and beautiful vessels of gold and silver as well. Said the abbot: "Let us take what food and drink we need to refresh ourselves, but I forbid you to take in excess. Let each man pray God that he be not led into temptation by the fiend." Thus did the abbot warn them, for he knew what was going to happen. The brothers ate what they needed and thanked God.

That night when all were asleep Satan seduced one of their number: He put into the mind of a certain brother the idea that he should secretly take some of the gold which he saw about him in such great abundance. The abbot was awake and saw well how the devil held the brother in his grasp and offered him a goblet of gold. The monk took it and stowed it away secretly, and then returned to bed. The abbot observed all this from his couch, and without candlelight, for when God wished to show him anything it was not necessary to light a taper.

On the fourth day of their stay in the Silent City, as they were preparing to leave the abbot said: "My brothers, I pray you, carry nothing away with you, not a crumb of bread, not a drop of water." And weeping sorely he added: "Behold, here is a thief; pray for him, for he shall die yet today." Hereupon, in the sight of all, the devil issued from the thieving monk's body, crying: "Alas now, Brandan, for what reason do you evict me from my dwelling?" Afterwards the brother was assoiled, and when he had received communion, death took him in the sight of all. This brother was one of the monks whom Brandan had received last into the ship.

Now when they got to the place where their ship was moored, behold, there came to them a messenger from God bearing food and drink, who exhorted them to be of good faith and fear nothing, whatsoever peril they might encounter. The monks raised sail and voyaged over the sea for a great part of the year, suffering great hardships. At last they raised land and rowed for it eagerly, and on going ashore they saw a great number of white sheep as large as stags. "We will remain here for three days," said the abbot. "Today is Maundy Thursday, and we will celebrate the feast of the Last Supper. Draw up the boat and take one of those sheep and prepare it for Easter Day. Since there is nothing else at hand, we will ask God's permission to use this." The brothers did as Brandan commanded them.

While they were on this island there came on Saturday a messenger, who greeted them in the name of God. His hair was long and white, but his eyes were young. He brought them large loaves of white unleavened wheat bread from his place of dwelling, and whatsoever else they required. Brandan courteously asked him about himself and his manner of life, but got little out of him. Then the saint remarked on the size of the sheep on the island, whereupon their host replied: "That is not to be wondered at, for this is the Island of Sheep. Here there is never cold weather, but it is always summer; it is that which causes the sheep to be so large and white, for they eat the best grass and herbage to be found anywere. Now enter your ship and make for yonder island; you shall pass the night there and celebrate your festival there on the morrow."

Brandan did as the hoary old man commanded, and though the designated island lay at considerable distance, they reached it in a short time. They hove to, and all the brothers landed save Brandan. That night and the following morning they celebrated their rites. When they had finished service on board, as in a church, they bore their food to the island to cook it. And when the fire was right hot and the meat nearly cooked, behold, the island began to move. The monks were terrified and fled to the ship, leaving their food and utensils behind them, marvelling greatly at the island's moving. But Brandan comforted them, saying that it was really only a big fish by the name of Jasconius that strove night and day to put its tail in its mouth, but was never able to succeed on account of its size. From their boat the fraternity watched the apparent island moving rapidly away, and for a distance of ten leagues they could distinguish the fire they had kindled there.

Soon after this the voyagers came to a fair island full of flowers and herbs and trees. Beside a fountain there was one tree so filled with birds that hardly any leaf could be seen, and the birds sang so merrily that it was a heavenly noise to hear. One of the feathered creatures flew down to Brandan, and the flickering of his wings made a sound like that of a fithele. In reply to Brandan's question the bird said that he and all the other birds had once been angels in heaven, but that when their master Lucifer fell they, for their offences, fell with him. But since their trespasses had been small, the Lord had set them on the tree, some higher, some lower, according to the nature of the sin of each. The bird also informed Brandan that he and his company should wander six more years, that finally they should come to the Land of Promise, and that they should keep every Easter festival on the back of the whale Jasconius.

On this island Brandan remained eight weeks and repaired his vessel. Thence he sailed again to the Island of Sheep and took on provisions. Afterwards the companions continued their seafaring till they came to the Island of Ailbe, by the abbot of which place and his monks they were well entertained.

After the companions had taken leave of the abbot of Ailbe they sailed for a long time without seeing land. Then the wind failed, and their provisions also, so that they suffered cruelly from hunger and thirst. The rowers could make little headway, for the sea was not only calm, but thick like the muck of a swamp, and they feared for their lives. However, the wind freshened finally, and they were able to perceive land. It was an island, and thereon was a stream of fresh water with fish in it; of these they took a hundred or so. "Do not drink too much of this water," said Brandan. But the monks paid no heed, and drank what they wished. Some drank so much that they seemed stupefied, and lay down, overcome with sleep. Some remained in a coma for a day, some two days, some three. But Brandan prayed for his monks till they were restored to their senses. On awakening they considered themselves to have been great fools. Said Brandan: "Let us flee this place lest you fall again into forgetfulness. It is better to endure honest hunger and thirst than to forget God."

After this they touched again at the Island of Sheep, and on Easter evening came once more to the place where the great fish awaited them. On its back they saw the cauldron which they had left there twelve months earlier. They kept the service of the Resurrection there as they had been bidden.

When Easter services were finished Brandan's ship flew before the wind ever to the west till they struck such a calm that it was difficult to proceed. One day while they were there the devil came in a dreadful and accursed form, and settled on the mast in front of Brandan; but none saw him save Brandan only. The saint asked the fiend why he had come before his proper time, that is, before the great resurrection. "To be tortured in the depths of the dark black sea am I come," replied the devil. Then the abbot asked him: "How so? Where is that infernal place?" "Sad is that," said the devil; "no one can see it and survive." However, the evil one showed Brandan the door of hell, and he saw its pains and misery. His companions asked the holy man to tell them with whom he was conversing, and Brandan told them some portion of the pains which he beheld. Said one of the company: "Let me see some of those pains." On being permitted to see the varied pains of hell he died forthwith, and as he expired he said: "Woe for all those who have come, for those who do come, and for those who shall come into this prison." Thereupon Brandan prayed and restored to life his compaion who had died.

One day as the companions were on the sea there happened something which frightened them more than any hardship they had yet endured. They saw approaching them more swiftly than the wind a serpent as fiery as a furnace. The great hot flame issuing from his mouth threatened them with cruel death. Vast was his size, and he roared like fifteen bulls. As the monster reared himself on high in front of their boat, Brandan prayed to the Lord; and when he had finished his prayer, they saw another similar monster coming from the western quarter to meet the first monster, and it waged war against the first beast. The two of them raised their heads high in the air, and fire leapt from their nostrils. They battered each other with their fins and paws, with their teeth as sharp as swords they wounded each other. The blood which issued from these grievous wounds stained all the sea round about, and the water was lashed to a foam by their struggle. Finally the newcomer vanquished the first beast, and when he had done this they saw the monster which had pursued the boat rising in three pieces to the surface of the sea. Then the monster that had done this deed returned triumphant with victory to the place whence it had come. Not long after this, as they were traversing the dreadful deep, they saw an island of extraordinary beauty, full of roots and fragrant herbs. When they landed they perceived on the strand before them the hinder part of the great beast. Said Brandan: "Dear brothers," said he, "here is the one whose endeavour was to kill and devour you; now do ye devour him and eat your fill of his flesh."

Another day, when Brandan was celebrating the feast of Peter in his boat the sea all round them was so pellucid, bright and clear that they could see all the fish and monsters of the ocean like so many herds of cattle on wide level plains, forming, as it were, walls round about the boat. And when the brothers perceived them, they besought Brandan to say mass in a low voice, so that the monsters might not hear the sound which he made. But Brandan laughed at them for the greatness of the wonder which he felt that they should be afraid, when God had so often delivered them from danger; and he said mass louder than he had ever done before. And when the monsters heard the voice of the holy man, they fled away from the boat so that not a trace of them was seen henceforth.

From this out they rowed for a while over the ocean in a westerly direction till they found a pleasant little island with a number of fishermen on it. On making a circuit of the island they came upon a small stone church, and therein was an aged man, pale and sorrowful, making his prayer; and he had neither flesh nor blood, but merely a thin miserable skin over his hard and yellow bones. When he saw the companions the old man said: "Flee, Brandan, with all speed, for there is here now a sea-cat as big as a young ox or a three-year-old horse, which has thriven on the fish of the sea and of this island; beware of it now."

At this Brandan and his men betook themselves to their boat and rowed over the sea with all their might. And as they were thus, they saw the monstrous sea-cat swimming after them. Each of its two eyes was as big as a cauldron; it had tusks like a boar's, sharp-pointed bristles, the maw of a leopard, the strength of a lion, and the rage of a mad dog. Then each of the brothers began to pray God by reason of the great fear that was on him. Thereupon a great whale rose up between them and the cat-monster, and each of the two beasts set to work to try to drown the other in the depths of the sea, and neither of them ever appeared again. At that Brandan and his company gave thanks to God and turned back to the place where the shrivelled old man awaited them. He wept for the greatness of the joy which possessed him and said: "I am of the men of Erin, and there were twelve of us when we came on our pilgrimage. We brought that bestial sea-cat with us, and were very fond of it. Afterwards it grew enormously, but it never hurt any of us. Of our original company eleven have now died and I am left alone, waiting for thee to give me the body and the blood of Christ that therewith I may go to heaven." He revealed to them also the little country they were seeking, that is, the Land of Promise; and after receiving the body and the blood of Christ the elder went to heaven.

On a time as Brandan and his companions were on the sea they perceived a land clouded over with a thick black fog, a stinking putrid vapour such as might exhale from the foulest carrion. The island was hideous, mountainous, dark, with a rugged summit, without trees or herbs, but full of houses like forges. Brandan and his company would rather have been far from it than near, and they did their best to take another course; but in vain, for the wind drove them irresistibly thither.

"My brothers," said Brandan, "we have been driven to hell. Never before have you had such great need of God's protection." As they drew nearer they saw more evil: Great burning flames shot forth from the deep clefts and fosses; the wind roared with raging fires worse than any thunder; sparks and sheets of fire, burning rocks and flames flew high into the air, obscuring the light of day. As they drew nearer still they beheld an individual whose aspect filled them with horror. In his hand he bore an iron hammer as big as a pillar. He looked about him with eyes flaming with living fire, and saw the companions. Then it seemed to him that he delayed too long in preparing his torments, and he bounded back to his forge, belching flames as he went. Almost immediately he returned with a sparkling and glowing mass, and raising it aloft, sent it hurtling toward the ship more swiftly than a whirlwind, or a shaft from an arbalest, or a missile from a sling. Luckily, the charge went past them, and the sea where it fell burned like brushwood in a clearing for a long time. By the grace of God the wind bore them away. Looking back they saw the isle alight and covered with smoke. Demons they saw by the thousand, and heard the wailing and weeping of the damned. As well as they could they endured the smoke, which spread afar over the sea, till they had passed beyond it.

Then one of the monks began to cry and weep sorely, saying that his end had come and that he might abide no longer. And anon he leapt out of the ship into the sea, whereupon he roared fearfully, cursing the time that he was born, and the father and mother who begot him, because they had seen no better to his correction in his youth. Brandan looked at him and saw a multitude of demons round him, and he burning in their midst. After this the wind swept them away and they drove toward the south.

Another day when Brandan and the companions were on the sea they perceived something jutting above its surface. They thought it might be a rock, and so it proved to be as they drew near. On the rock sat a naked man in exceeding great misery and pain, for the waves of the sea had so beaten his body that all the flesh was gone, and nothing remained but sinews and bones. About his head was tied a rough cloth, like a veil, which beat his body sorely with the blowing of the wind. Desperately he clung to the stone so that the sea might not wash him under, for the waves battered him severely. One wave struck him so that he almost sank, then another dashed him back to the rock again. Danger was before and behind him, to the right and to the left. From time to time could be heard his piteous lament: "Ha! Jesus, Lord of majesty, will my death come neither summer nor winter? Ha! Jesus, whose compassion is boundless, will the day of my release never come?"

Brandan was much moved at the sound of this lamentation, and drew nearer to the rock; at his approach the wind that was buffeting the man died down. "Tell me, O wretch," said the abbot, "who you are and why you suffer these torments." And for weeping the holy man could say no more.

In a hoarse voice the man replied: "I am Judas, who betrayed Our Lord. I am he who sold his master and hanged himself for sorrow. And since I died without confession, I am forever damned. You behold nothing of the pain which I suffer in hell. This here is surcease from the torment upon which I enter every Saturday night. All day Sunday till vespers, the fortnight of Christmas, on festival days of the Blessed Virgin, and at Easter and Pentecost I have respite. Sunday at vespers I leave this place to enter torment again."

"Since this is repose," said Brandan, "tell me, I pray you, what you consider pain and torment. Where do you go when you leave here?"

"The devil's fief," answered Judas, "is not far away; indeed, close by are two hells whose pains are exceedingly grievous. The least of them so punishes its inmates that they think no pain comparable to theirs. But except for myself there is no one who is in a position to judge the relative merits of the two, for I, wretched one that I am, suffer in both. One hell is on a mountain, the other is in a valley, and the salt sea separates them. The mountainous hell is the harder to endure, whereas that in the vale is the more horrible. One reaches into the air, hot and suffocating; the other sinks cold and fetid into the sea. One day and night I am on the mount; an equal time am I in the vale. Thus do I shift from one to the other, not for the alleviation of my pains, but for their augmentation.

"Monday, day and night, I am hooked onto a wheel which revolves as swiftly as the wind can whirl me here and there. Ever I go, back and forth. On Tuesday, quite stupefied, I am hurled over the sea into the vale to the other hell. There I am straightway fettered and mocked by demons, and placed on a bed of spits; then they pile rocks and weights and lead upon me, so that my body becomes pierced as you see it now.

"On Wednesday I am heaved up to a new torment. Part of the day I boil in pitch, so that I become discoloured, as you now see me. Then I am removed from that and set to roast, tied to a post between two fires. The post was placed there for my special benefit. The fire catches in the pitch which adheres to my body, and thus increases my pain. After a while I am dipped in the pitch again in order that I may burn more briskly. There is no marble so hard that it would not melt if subjected to the same treatment. But I, alas, whatever I suffer, am unable to perish.

"Thursday I am placed in the vale to suffer a contrasting torment in a cold place, dark and gloomy. There I endure so much pain by reason of the cold that I long to be back again in the fire which burns so fiercely; and it seems to me there is no torment like unto the cold which congeals me. However, I think the same about all the other torments—that each one is the worst wherein I happen to be.

"Friday I rise. On that day the demons flay my whole body and then stir it about in soot and salt with a red-hot stake. Then the new skin grows again so that the torment may be repeated. Ten times a day they skin me and salt me. Afterwards they force me to drink lead melted with copper. On Saturday they pitch me down to the valley, and I am tumbled, without benefit of a cord, into the filthiest, foulest jail in hell. There I lie in darkness and stench. So great is the fetor that it seems to me my heart must burst at any moment, nor can I relieve myself by vomiting, because of the molten copper which the devils have forced me to drink. Consequently, I swell up, and the skin stretches, and I suffer much anguish because I do not burst.

"Such heat, such cold, such stench, such torments suffers Judas. Yesterday, which was Saturday, I came here between nones and noon for repose. Very shortly I shall have a bad night, for a thousand devils will come, and I shall have no rest when once they lay hold upon me. But you, whom I know to be holy and pious, I beseech you, procure me respite for this night, if you can!"

Brandan said: "You shall not be carried hence till morning. But what is the garment which flaps about your head and beats you under the eyes?" "It is the garment which I gave to a poor man out of the portion of my Lord when I was His chamberlain; but since it was not mine to give, it turns to my loss now, and not to my ease. And this stone which supports me out of the sea is a stone with which I repaired a public road when I was in the world."

When the hour of vespers had come the fraternity saw a huge host of demons approaching them, who said: "Leave this now, O man of God, for you know that we cannot go to our comrade there so long as you are with him; and we dare not look on the face of our lord till we bring this, his special friend, to him. Give us our morsel this night, then." Said Brandan: "It is not I who keep him this night, but Our Lord Jesus Christ has permitted him to remain this night as he is." Then the senior demon cried: "Why do you invoke the name of the Lord on behalf of yonder man who delivered up the Lord to cross and passion?" "I command you," said Brandan, "on the part of Christ, that you inflict no pain or torment on the man this night." Thereupon the demons departed.

Now on the morning, when Brandan was preparing to sail away, the doors of hell were opened, and countless hosts of demons issued forth; they spoke with loud and hideous voices, saying: "O servant of God, accursed be your journey to us, for our master has treated us with contumely because we have not exhibited to him his special servitor. Because you helped him last night, we will torment him doubly during the week." Said Brandan: "You shall inflict no pain on him save such as you have inflicted before." After these words the demons raised Judas high into the air with shouts of ribald laughter.

Now afterwards when the monks numbered their company it was

found that one was missing, and no one knew what had become of him. Said the abbot: "Take no thought about the matter, for God has done with him as He pleased. You may be sure that he has his reward, whether of rest or pain."

Brandan now sailed southwards three days and three nights till, on Friday, the companions saw an island. Brandan sighed and said: "I see the island whereon dwells St Paul the hermit, and he has dwelt there forty years without meat or drink ordained by the hand of man."

When they made a landing St Paul came and welcomed them humbly. The brothers wondered greatly at the garb of the man, for he had no clothing save the hair of his head and beard, and the hair of the rest of his body. And this hair was such that no snow was whiter than it, owing to the great age of the holy man.

Brandan asked Paul how he had come to that island, where he had lived previously, and how long he had endured that life. "Sometime I was a monk of St Patrick's abbey in Ireland," said Paul, "and was warden of the place where men enter St Patrick's Purgatory. One day a man came to me and I asked him who he was. 'I am your abbot, Patrick,' he said, 'and I charge you to depart from this place early tomorrow morning and go down to the sea. There you will find a ship which God has ordained for you; enter it and fulfil His will.' The next day I found the ship and entered it, and by the purveyance of God I was brought to this island the seventh day afterwards. On leaving the ship I walked up and down on the island for a good while when, by the providence of God, there came an otter walking on his hind feet; between his two forefeet he held a flint and iron wherewith to strike a fire, and about his neck he had great plenty of fish, which he cast down before me and went his way. When, on the third day, the supply of fish was exhausted, the otter came again; and thus, through the mercy of God, has he done these thirty years. In the island is a great stone from which God caused a spring of clear and sweet water to issue, wherefrom I drink daily. Thus have I lived sixty years. I was fifty years in my own land, so that to this day the sum of my years is one hundred and forty. And I am still waiting in this human body for the day of my account, and if it pleased the Lord, I would fain be discharged of this wretched life."

Then the old man bade Brandan take some of the water from the spring and carry it to his ship. "It is time," he said, "that you be on your way, for a long journey lies before you, a journey of forty days till Easter eve. You shall keep Easter as you have done the other years; then you shall touch once more at the island of the Paradise of Birds; after that you shall sail to the Land of Promise, where you shall abide forty days. Thereafter God will bring you safe to your native land."

Brandan and his company bade farewell to St Paul and steered their boat south. On Easter eve they came to the Island of Sheep and were welcomed by their host of former occasions. At night they embarked again and their host with them. They found the great whale in its accustomed place, and there they performed their services till morning. When they had finished their masses, the huge animal proceeded on its own business, and they all standing on its back. The whale went straight forward till it reached the shore of the land called the Paradise of Birds, and deposited them and their boat there without loss of any of them. There the fraternity remained till the octave of Pentecost, and when the feast of Pentecost was past the host said: "Embark now in your boat, and I will be with you as a guide, for you cannot find the land you are seeking unless I am with you."

Now the holy man set his course towards the east, without fear of going astray, since he had a guide. Forty days they sailed till, finally, by the providence of God, they drew near to the bank of mist that veils the Paradise of Adam from Adam's heirs. Said the host: "Delay not, but spread the sail." As they approached the cloud parted for the width of a street, and they passed along it. For three days they sailed thus with the cloud on both sides of them. On the fourth day they issued joyfully from the mist, for they could now distinguish Paradise.

First of all they saw a wall which reared itself as high as the heavens. It had neither crenellation, gallery, outwork or tower. None knew whereof it might be made, but it was as white as any snow, and the Sovereign King was its architect. The gems wherewith the wall was set flashed everywhere; there was many a choice chrysolite set in gold clasps. The wall flamed and gleamed with topaz, chrysoprase, jacinth, chalcedony, emerald, sardonyx; jasper and amethyst glowed at the borders. Clear jacinth with crystal and beryl were there, each giving light to the other; he who set them was a skilful workman. Great was the luminosity of colours flashing back and forth.

This smooth, uninterrupted wall, so high as to be superable by none, was set upon a lofty mountain. Below, and far from the wall, the mount was of hard marble, beaten continuously by the dashing of the waves; above, it was all of gold. Entry through the wall was by means of a gate, but Brandan and his companions deemed that it would be difficult to pass, for it was guarded by fiery dragons; and right over the entrance, blade down, hilt up, hung a sword. The sword dangled and whirled so that just the sight of it made one dizzy, and neither iron nor rock nor adamant was proof against its edge. It is no wonder if they were afraid.

At this moment the companions perceived a handsome young man approaching them. He was God's messenger, and bade them disembark. As the brothers landed he called each by name and kissed him. Afterwards he pacified the dragons, making them crouch humbly on the ground, and the sword he caused to be immobilized by an angel who came at his summons. Thus the passage-way remained free, and all went joyfully through the gate of Paradise, the youth preceding the others as their guide.

Within the gate they beheld fine woods and plains, meadows and gardens in full bloom. The odour which rose from the trees and pleasant flowers was like that in the abode of the blessed. No bramble, thistle or nettle was there, and there was no tree nor herb which did not continually exhale sweetness. Flowers and trees were always in bloom, and wasted not by reason of yearly seasons, for in that place was always sweet summer, which brought forth profusion of fruit and flowers. The woods were full of deer and the streams of fish, and certain streams there were which ran with milk. The reeds by the banks exuded honey by virtue of the dew which dropped from heaven. The mountain was of most pure gold and the sand of precious gems. No cloud obscured the brightness of the sun, which always shone clear; no wind or breeze disturbed so much as a hair of the head. He who entered this place would never suffer heat nor cold, sorrow nor hunger, poverty nor any adversity—rather would he enjoy a wealth of delights. Whatever he most desired he should not want, secure in the knowledge that it would be ever ready to his wish.

When Brandan beheld this abundance of delight it seemed to him that he was granted all too short a time in which to see it, for he would have wished to remain there time without end. The guide led them about, expounding this and instructing them in that. As they paused upon a mountain adorned with cypress trees they beheld sights which they could not explain: They saw angels and heard them rejoicing at their coming; they heard the splendid melody, but could not endure it, for their human nature was unable to apprehend or understand such great glory.

At last they came to a fair river, but durst not go over. Said the guide: "Now let us return, for I will not lead you beyond this point; it is not permitted you to proceed, for you would be able to comprehend very little. This water separates the world asunder, and to the region beyond this water may no man come while he is alive. Here, Brandan, you behold that Paradise for a sight of which you so often besought God. Before and beyond you lies glory one hundred thousand times greater than whatsoever you have seen hitherto. At this time you shall learn no more; you must wait till you come again. Though you have come here in the flesh now, soon you shall return in the spirit. Go now, and await that time. As a sign and memorial of Paradise, take with you some of these precious stones." So saying, the young man passed on.

Now Brandan and his monks took leave of the saints of Paradise, Enoch and Elijah, and returned to their ship. They left their host behind them, for this was his proper dwelling: he must have been John. They hoisted sail, and with a fair wind and by the grace of God they reached Ireland in three months.

And soon after this the holy man St Brandan waxed sick and feeble, and had but little joy of this world. In a short time thereafter, being full of virtues, he departed out of this life to life everlasting, and was worshipfully buried in the abbey which he himself had founded.

"Your tale is instructive in many ways, I suppose," said Richard de Haldingham. "As a cartographer I confess that I am most interested in the route pursued by St Brandan to reach the Earthly Paradise. It is situated in the east, is it not?"

"That is true," replied Adamnan.

"And Brandan sailed continually west, and then south and east?"

"Yes."

"He did not, perchance, sail north, and then east and south?"

"Not so far as I know."

"Then it is clear that in the sixth century the world must have been globular in form and not, as some would have it, shaped like an inverted soup-dish or a candle extinguisher."

"I know nothing about that," protested Adamnan, looking helplessly about for Dicuil—but Dicuil had gone to measure the depth of the sea in Milford Haven.

"But," said Alexander Neckam, "if I heard correctly, St Brandan's course was due *east* for the last forty days before he reached Paradise."

Bartholomew Anglicus and Giraldus Cambrensis drew near to hear what explanation the cartographer would give to this circumstance, and as he moved away to demonstrate his opinions on the bald skull of Seithenyn ab Seithyn Saidi, who was snoring in the embrasure of a north window, the group was joined by Ponce de Leon and Sir John Hawkins.

When they had gone Robert Mannyng broke the silence. "The picture of Judas on his half-submerged rock, battered by the waves, with the wind beating about his face, recalls to my mind certain circumstances connected with the life of Gregory the Great. If you like, I will make as straightforward a tale as I can out of the various versions which have come to my notice in old books."

"Anything relating to Gregory should be of interest to Englishmen," said William of Wykeham.

"But not to Welshmen," remarked Dafydd ab Gwilym. "He referred to my ancestors in very unflattering terms."

"The sodden unconsciousness of Seithenyn ab Seithyn Saidi yonder," observed Andrew Boorde, "would seem to corroborate his judgment—and Gildas' too."

"Well, if Seithenyn was and is a fool, Taliesin was bright enough—for his time; and certainly nothing can be urged against Merlin . . ."

"Except that he was a Scot," interposed Sir Thomas Gray.

"And if Gerald, Walter and Geoffrey have not vindicated the Welsh," went on Dafydd, paying no heed to the interruption, "there is myself."

"Robert," said Camden, "if you do not quickly tell us about Gregory we shall be forced to listen to some Welsh poetry in a moment."

"Very well," answered Mannyng; "but I cannot tell the story quickly."

54. GREGORY'S PETRINE PENANCE
Robert Mannyng

Once there was an earl of Aquitaine of whom many men stood in awe. His wife was called Edayne. They had two children, a boy and later a girl; Edayne died in giving her birth.

After some years it came time for the earl to die also. As he lay on his sick-bed he thought of his daughter, and what fate should be hers. Summoning his children he said to his son in the presence of his barons: "My son, do not weep at my passing from you, for I shall leave enough land and rent to support your state. But when I am in my grave and you are master of the fief, take care that you do no harm to your sister in any way. It is a matter of great regret to me that during my lifetime I did not marry her fittingly." Therewith he took the girl's hand and placed it in that of his son.

"Father," said the boy, weeping, "we are of one blood, and nothing shall ever come between us nor destroy our love for one another. Have no further concern on her account, for I will take care to marry her richly."

Now the earl could tarry no longer, for Death was jumping at him by leaps and bounds. He was houseled and shriven, and so died and was buried.

The story says that the brother took loving care of the sister, as their father had bidden. They had the same education, they dressed in similar fashion, they went everywhere together, they drank from one cup and ate from one trencher. Indeed, they even lay in the same chamber in beds near each other, for they were loath to be separated. It was this circumstance which gave the fiend his opportunity to tempt them.

One night, as the young earl was lying in his bed unable to sleep, the devil put it into his head to go to his sister's bed. The girl suspected no harm when her brother joined her, and so she said and did nothing to repulse him. The more he looked at her and the more he kissed her, the more violent became his perturbation. The devil continued so to spur and urge him that he raised the coverlet and lay by her. When the girl felt his embrace she became so frightened that she broke into a sweat. She would have jumped up and raised the alarm, but her brother calmed her with kisses and caresses. The young woman was much abashed and distraught, for if she consented to the sin, they were both damned, and if she cried out, her brother would be shamed and disgraced. So she remained quiet, and that was the worst thing she could have done. She was too weak to guard her body from him, and let him, perforce, do all his will. Thus was Gregory begotten.

Now the fiend rejoiced, for this was the end at which he had been aiming, and it seemed to him that he had snared and ruined them both forever. Time and again he urged them to repeat their sin.

As the days and weeks passed the maiden lost her mirthfulness and began to complain. "Alas," she said, "that I was ever born, for all my joy is turned to sorrow and my soul is lost!" Her brother heard her and said: "Sister mine, weep no more, for you fill my heart with grief." "Brother," she replied, "I may well weep now and ever, for we have done a sorry deed whereby you are lost and I also. It will not be long now till the fruit of our sin will be visible to all men, unless we conceal it. But do not imagine that I will allow the babe in my body to be mishandled." "That was not in my thought," answered the young man; "moreover, I hope to find a better way out of this trouble. I know a faithful knight who will be able to give us advice and assistance." "Send for him quickly and secretly then," said she, "for my time is near. If this matter comes to light I think I shall die." "Do not harbour such thoughts," said the youth, "for thereby you only increase my suffering. I will send for the knight, and by God's grace, his counsel shall turn our woe to weal."

When the knight had been informed of the trouble which lay upon the brother and sister he said: "It seems to me best that you, sir, should go on a pilgrimage to Rome. Give the lady into my care in the meantime so that she may be delivered at my court. But before you go, take measures to make your sister's state secure from injury or injustice."

The young earl approved this advice, and summoning his barons, with their consent he seised his sister with the fief, and then left her in the charge of the loyal and discreet knight. The vassal took her to his castle and lodged her secretly in the tower. To his wife he said: "Dame, the lady who has just arrived is no other than the old earl's daughter, and she is with child by her brother. Keep the matter close." "Sir," she replied, "may the sweet Lady of Heaven be her aid. No one shall know of this through me."

When the time came the countess was easily delivered of a knave child, and she besought God to instruct her how to act, for she dared not keep the child with her. At last she said to the knight: "Cause a good strong cask to be made; set the child therein in his cradle; place the cask in a boat, and about midnight let men row out and set the cask adrift. If Christ is pleased with the birth and begetting of this child, He will know what to do; if his begetting and birth were against His will and He lets the child perish in the sea, no man shall be the wiser." "Madame," said the knight, "it shall be done as you command."

Then said the countess: "Alas, woe is me! I am fated never to see my first-born again, and my soul shall be lost therefor. Sweet Jesus, be Thou my succour!" Then she gave the child suck till it was satisfied, and made the sign of the cross over it to protect it from the demon. At the head of the cradle she placed a sum of gold and silver so that if anyone discovered the child he might pay himself for rescuing it. In the cradle, too, she placed a pair of ivory tablets whereon she had written an account of the babe's begetting and birth, with a prayer that if it were borne to land anywhere alive it might be christened for the love of Him who wrought all things. "O son," she said, "if you live and see these tablets, read them attentively, and bear in mind her who is left sorrowing for you." Thereupon she bade the cask be taken to the sea, and so it was done. Sorrowful was the mother at that parting, and dreary her mood.

Now as to her brother the earl, who had set out for Rome—many a time he sighed sorely for sorrow. At last he lay down sick, and never rose after that. You may be sure that the news of his death was most unwelcome to the countess. "Alas!" she cried, "I have caused my brother's death. O God! my grief will drive me mad!" And when she came into the hall where her brother's corpse lay she swooned thrice for excess of woe. People feared for her life, and she had to be borne away from the bier.

After the death of the young earl the countess assumed charge of her heritage, as she ought, and no one disputed her claim to the earldom. When the news spread abroad that she had inherited Aquitaine, kings, princes and counts sought her hand in marriage, greedy for the land. People of every rank and degree reckoned her a clean maid. But she dismissed all her suitors, vowing that she would take no lord. And thus she lived for a number of years, attending to her affairs in the world, but giving, in contrition for her sin, much of her goods to the poor and needy.

Among the countess' suitors was a powerful duke who had made up his mind that he would wed that fair lady so rich in land, and he sent knights and sergeants to learn if she would entertain his proposal. But the countess replied to him as to the others, saying that she would not take him nor any man. On receiving this answer the duke assembled a great army and made war upon her: if he could not win the lady, he thought that he would at least ruin her land. In this emergency the countess said to herself: "Only by force shall the duke have my body, before such time as my son—who was set adrift in a cask—shall come of age. If, by the grace of God, he has survived, he may be able to bring this war to naught." So the great lords of the land came to her aid and gave the duke his fill of fighting for a time.

Let us leave the countess now and return to her son. When the child was set adrift the wind drove him out to sea. It happened that two brothers, fishermen, took their hooks and nets that very night to procure fish for a certain abbey. About daybreak they perceived the cask wallowing in the trough of the waves. They thought it must contain goods, and that its owners had been lost at sea, so they took it up into their boat. But the rough sea gave them so much to do that they had no chance to examine their find before reaching shore. The abbot came to meet them, for God willed that the child should be saved. "Whence came the cask in your boat?" asked the abbot, "and what is in it?" "Lord," said they, "it is some of our gear, and of no importance." At that moment the child began to scream. Abbot and fishermen were much astonished, and the men then told a true story.

When the cask was opened the child lying beneath the silken

coverlet in the cradle smiled up at the abbot with grey eyes. "Blessed be thy sending, O Lord," said he. Then he found the ivory tablets and read what was written thereon. Now it happened that one of the two fishermen was poor and had a large family, but the other was well-to-do, and had no children save a daughter who was living away from home. To the former the abbot gave ten marks of money, and to the latter the child, instructing him to say that it was his daughter's; and upon both he laid a command of strict secrecy. He himself took charge of the silken pall, the ivory tablets and the four marks of gold.

The abbot of whom I speak was named Gregory, and so the foundling was baptized with his name. When young Gregory was five years old the abbot put him to book, and he learned so quickly that at the age of twelve he had become adept in both law and arts. Moreover, he was so sweet-tempered that everyone loved and praised him.

One day when Gregory was fifteen years old he and other boys were running at the bar, and Gregory beat his companion. The other lad took his defeat much to heart, and ran home and told his mother how Gregory had beaten him. Now a woman is a wonderful thing, for she cannot restrain her emotions nor her words. Said the boy's mother to Gregory: "Why, O waif and foundling, have you shamed my son? It is unfitting for you, for I think there is no man alive who knows the identity of your father and mother." Thus she said, for the wife of the poor fisherman had wormed out of her husband an explanation of the ten marks of money which they had come by so mysteriously.

On hearing this reproach Gregory stood as still as a stone for a moment, then, with heavy heart, took his way to the abbot. "Who has offended you?" asked the abbot. "The fisherman's wife," answered Gregory. "She says I am a waif and stray, and that no one knows my kin. O Lord! of thy grace, send me to the place where I was born so that I may die there." "Be still," said the abbot, "and avoid such thought and words. You can read well and sing clearly, so I will accept you into this house; and I will so influence the monks that after my death you shall be chosen abbot in my place." "Nay," replied Gregory, "that is far from my thought. If you wish to do anything for me, let me take arms and be a knight, for I am drawn to the profession of bearing shield and hauberk. I will take no other orders while I am thus young and agile."

So the abbot procured harness for Gregory and knighted him. But even then he would have retained the youth whom he had nourished and loved. "Stay," he said, "and I will find you a fief, and make a good marriage for you." To this proposal Gregory replied: "I shall never be blithe till I learn the identity of my father and mother. I will flee this shame, though I drown in the salt sea."

Seeing that he could say nothing to dissuade the boy from his purpose the abbot brought out the silk coverlet, delivered to him the ivory tablets and bade him read what he found there. Afterwards he told Gregory the circumstances which we know. "Sir," said Gregory, "I will go to another land where my shame may be concealed; and I will seek my kin from this out."

The abbot found a ship for Gregory and provided him with all that was needful for a voyage. The wind was fair, and drove him, as it chanced, to the shore of that land which was his mother's fief. On disembarking he made a brave showing with helm, hauberk and shield as he bestrode his horse. He certainly seemed to be a good knight, and the port-reeve gave him lodging, for he esteemed Gregory to be a man of importance.

One day Gregory asked his host if there were any war afoot, or if he knew any lord who would employ an unknown stranger knight. The host replied that there was indeed such a war in progress that neither city, burg nor vill, save only the present impregnable fortress, had escaped its ravages. "Why doesn't your count do something about it?" asked Gregory. "There is no count," replied the host, "only a young woman, gracious and beautiful; and it is because of her that this war is going on." "How can I gain speech with her?" asked Gregory. "You can see her at mass tomorrow," replied the man, "and for my part I will say a good word for you to her seneschal."

On the morrow the fair and handsome Gregory, well clothed in silk, went to church and greeted the lady. The countess did not recognize him, of course, though her heart was strangely moved at the sight of him. She thought she knew the silk he was wearing, but then, she reflected, one piece of silk was very much like another, and dismissed the matter from her mind.

The countess' seneschal received Gregory courteously and gladly accepted his offer of service. Not long after this the mighty duke of Rome sat down before the castle with his army, set up his tents far and wide, and planted his banners and gonfanons.

Gregory was a man not only fairly formed, but wise and judicious. Said he: "It is shameful to be lamenting in security here inside the castle; whoever has a hauberk and a coat of mail, let him put them on, and we will give this bellicose duke his fill of battle."

The knights were much encouraged by these words and went to arm themselves. Gregory himself issued from the postern with sword and spear. Thunderously he rode up before the duke's army and felled many a man to the ground with lance and sword. Thereupon the castle knights came up and were met by the duke's men. Before sunset many a head got a knock, and many a knight was run through the body so that blood ran in streams. During the engagement Gregory distinguished the Duke of Rome and rode through the host after him, shouting that he was going to present him with a lance. The proud duke was wroth and awaited the levelled spear: but he was borne over his horse's crupper with such violence that he grunted like a bear. When he did not rise, Gregory seized him by the nasal of his helm and carried him to the countess in the castle. The countess had hated him since she was a child; she bade that he be closely guarded, and took oath that he should never get his release till he had made amends for all the shame he had done her and her people. The duke offered ransom for his body and swore to give indemnity for the destruction he had caused. As the duke rode away she said: "I give you a gift—you shall never take me to wife." After these terms were concluded the countess was able to live in peace.

Gregory, though an excellent knight, was exceedingly poor; so now that this war was finished, he desired to seek other lands where he might find opportunity to win pence. Often he sighed when he thought of his hard fate—his begetting. When he announced to the countess his intention of seeking deeds of arms elsewhere she was much perturbed and said: "Sir, you shall not go." And to her seneschal: "What can we say to him, or give him, that he go not away thus bare? for you know he avenged us on our foe." The seneschal replied: "There is no other knight like him in all the land. If you let him go away I think you will be acting to your own harm. He is true, steadfast and strong. If you are willing to take a lord, you might do well in choosing such a knight. The people think so too."

The countess summoned her barons and laid this matter before them, and in council it was decided that Gregory should marry her. The lords of the land led her to church, and there the priest read from his book how a man shall receive his wife at hand, at bed and board. Thus did Gregory become earl and lord of Aquitaine; and since he had married his mother, the devil's industry was again crowned with success.

The people of Aquitaine held their new lord in great esteem, for he loved right and not wrong. Knight and swain swore him manrede, that is, to be buxom to his will, and fealty. However, the rich earl could not forget his old sorrow, written on the tablets which had been put into the cradle with him. Often he went to them in secret, reading them again and again. He took thought how he might hide the tablets, and at last concealed them under a stone in a dark and unused chamber. Access to that chamber was forbidden to all, and thither he often repaired to indulge his sorrow.

But there is no deed so well concealed that it shall not some time be disclosed. A woman observed Gregory's privy goings to that chamber, and his mournful cheer when he emerged. One day when the earl had gone to hunt the woman reported the matter to the countess. Together they went to the chamber, and the countess sought here and there till she found the tablets. When she recognized them as the very tablets which she had written herself, her fair fresh colour turned to yellow.

The seneschal sent a messenger for Gregory, saying that something was amiss with the countess. The earl came and knelt beside her bed, and kissed her tenderly. "Lady," said he, "tell me the cause of your sorrow and distress." After a little, when the countess was able to master her tears: "Tell me," she said, "where were you born, and who were your father and mother?" At this question Gregory's heart grew troubled, and he remained silent. "Why do you not answer?" asked the countess. "Be still," said Gregory, "and do not concern yourself about such matters; you have yourself chosen me for your love, and that is sufficient." Thereupon the countess brought forth the tablets. "Whose story is written here?" she asked. Then the earl's heart grew cold as ice; he sat in thought for a while, then said: "I am he who was cast adrift on the wave, for I was begotten in sin. That is known only to God, to you and to me." "Alas!" cried the countess, "the whole weight of my sorrow now falls upon me. Nowhere is there so sinful a woman as I, for I am now wedded to my own son, who was begotten by my brother. O God, who sittest above, now in your love and mercy succour us sinful wretches."

"Now," said Gregory, "I find what I have long sought; I finally know my kin, and certainly I am not pleased. But he who was before shall be behind, namely the devil, who brought us to this; and he shall be as sorrowful in the end as he was joyful in the beginning." "Sir," said the countess, "I lament for both our sakes; but what is your rede?" "Mother," replied the earl, "we shall now part, and never be seen together again till we meet before God on Judgment Day. He has summoned us from sin to make our prisoned souls free. Better is late than never." Then the earl bade his mother spend her life in doing almsdeed in penance for her sin so that she might win heaven therethrough. "And each of us," he said, "will pray for the other."

After this Gregory put off his rich robes and dressed himself humbly in poor clothes; of his spear he made a palmer's spiked staff;

and before the light of a new day dawned he abandoned his earldom, and fared abroad in the guise of a penitent.

On the third night Gregory had reached the sea, but he could find no lodging save the house of a churlish fisherman, whom he asked for food and shelter for one night. The fisher asked who he was, and Gregory replied that he was a penitent wandering at large for his sins. Said the man: "Your body is white, your flesh is tender, and it is not long ago that your feet wore shoes. By God in heaven! you shall not lie in my house! If you did, I should not be able to sleep for anxiety, for it seems to me very likely that you are a spy in the pay of merchants."

Gregory knew not how to reply to such language, and would have gone on his way, barefoot, to mend his sins; indeed, he was somewhat pleased that the man should revile him. But when the fisher's wife saw the wanderer, she wept bitter tears of compassion, so that the fisherman was constrained to call him back. That night, though he was brought in out of the wind and rain, he dared not approach the fire, but crouched in the corner where a bed of straw was laid down for him.

When it was time to sup, the board was set, the cloth laid and the fire mended, for the wind blew cold outside. The goodwife was eager that the guest should sit down to supper; but her lord was a hard man and harsh, and showed Gregory grudging cheer. The penitent said nothing, but washed his hands and sat down by the fire. A napkin was spread, drink was set before him in a brown mazer, and white wheaten bread. Said Gregory to the woman: "I ask no such food as this; barley bread and clean water would be good enough for me." At this the fisherman flared up: "You thieves' companion! You provoke one to speech. If you were alone by yourself I daresay you would eat this great fish here, both body and head, and gnaw the bones. No good food would be too rich for you, and you would drink wine aplenty." Answered Gregory: "You have put it mildly; I am much worse than you allege." "Husband," said the goodwife, "you are too quarrelsome; try not to insult a man while he is under your roof. If he doesn't want to eat fish, what do you care? And if he prefers water to wine, what business is it of yours? Since it costs you nothing, don't make such a fuss about it."

To this the fisherman replied: "Is it credible that this gallowsbird here would wish to sink himself with water? You should have been a friar, or even a hermit in a wood or by the water's edge." "I have had that in mind," said Gregory, "but a proper place has not yet been found. I should be very glad if such a stead were pointed out to me so that I might lead my life there in peace."

"Ha!" said the fisherman; "I know the very place—a great rock in the sea where I go fishing. I don't think anyone has visited it for a hundred years, and I myself have seen it only from the surface of the water. If you want a solitary hermitage you couldn't find a better place, for the rock is hollowed out like a house. You would be hairy enough before you were discovered." "Then for the love of Him who died on the Rood," said Gregory, "bring me to that rock." "By St John," replied the fisher, "I will take you there at daybreak. And I will do something else for you, too. I have some iron fetters, and if you like, I will put them on your legs for you." "Sir," said Gregory, "that would please me very well, and I thank you for the suggestion." At this reply the host held his peace.

On the morrow the fisher was in such haste to conduct his guest to the rock that Gregory forgot to take his tablets with him—an oversight for which he later felt very sorry. When he had mounted the rock, the fetters were locked fast on his legs and the key cast into the sea. Then the fisher went his ways and forgot about him. But Gregory prayed that the key might never be recovered till his soul had been lightened of the sin which had abased it.

On that island in the sea Gregory dwelt with penance and fasting, making his moan to God, for seventeen years. He had no proper food or drink except what water collected in a crevice of the rock beside him when it rained. His clothes rotted away from him, leaving his nakedness exposed to sun and storm. Such, says the true story, was his life.

Now let us leave Gregory for a while. At Rome it happened that the pope died and quickly went to heaven. The cardinals convened and prayed God to instruct them in the choice of a new pope to guide Christendom. During their deliberations an angel came down to them from heaven and said: "The selection has already been made. The King of heaven has chosen your pope and bids you seek him quickly, for there is no one in the world so worthy of the office as he. The man dwells on a rock out in the sea, and his name is Gregory."

On hearing this the cardinals returned thanks. Seven messengers were chosen to search for Gregory, and the Lord showed them the right way to the land where he was dwelling. By the help of Mary they arrived at the fisher's house where the penitent had taken shelter years before. They asked the man for lodging, and I think the fisher was glad to give it, for the clerks brought plenty of spending money with them.

It happened that at this time the fisherman had been on the sea all day and had taken many fish. If his guests would select one, he said, he would clean and prepare it for them. The clerks chose the best and largest fish and bade him boil it in two waters. The fisherman set about his work, and while he was cleaning the fish's belly he found a key. This circumstance reminded him of Gregory, whom he had considered doomed to death, and as he turned the matter over in his mind it seemed to him that he had been guilty of great sin in leaving the penitent on the rock as he had.

After the strangers had supped and refreshed themselves their host asked them whither they were bound. "We are on a long journey," they answered, "searching for a penitent who dwells on a rock in the sea, we don't know where. The pope has died at Rome, and the grace had fallen on this man. We are sent to fetch him if we can find him." "By St John!" cried the fisher, "I can certainly instruct you how to find that man, for I myself put him on that rock. However, I think he must be dead by this time. When I rowed him out to the rock, I bound him fast in fetters there, as he allowed me to do, and threw the key thereto into the sea. But just now a marvellous thing has come to pass, for I found that very key in the belly of the fish which I cleaned for your dinner." Therewith he showed the key to the messengers, and they rejoiced. "After I had locked the fetters on his feet," continued the fisher, "I left him there. That is seventeen winters ago. I never gave him a thought afterwards, and in that I have done amiss."

"Fisher," said one of the clerks, "may you be blessed for your tidings. We will reward you well if you will lead us to the rock of which you speak." "Come with me tomorrow," answered the fisher, "and if he is alive, you shall see him."

On the morrow the fisher rowed the messengers out to the rock in his boat, and there they did indeed find a man. Someone called out to determine if he were alive. "Here I am," answered Gregory. When they heard his voice, I assure you they were blithe. They mounted the rock and found Gregory to be nothing but skin and bones, and covered with hair. After they had announced their errand Gregory said: "Sirs, for God's sake, why do you mock me thus? Let me be; it does not beseem you to play tricks on such a one as I am." Then one of the company explained the matter more fully, whereupon Gregory said: "I will not budge from here till I see the key to the fetters which was cast into the water." Then they told him how the key had been recovered, and Gregory knew forsooth that God had unbound him from his sins, and gave thanks to the Lord.

Gregory was now willing to leave the rock, but he was so feeble that he could not walk, so the clerks bore him away in their arms. A bath was prepared for him at the fisher's house, and he was given every attention till he was strong enough to stand on his feet.

But now he remembered his ivory tablets, and would not go away without them. The messengers were much vexed, and asked their host if he knew anything about any ivory tablets. "I never heard of them," replied the fisher. But finally, when a search had been made and the compost cleared away, the tablets were found, fair and white, in the place where Gregory had left them.

After this Gregory took the way to Rome, and many were glad of his coming. When he beheld the great city he went to his knees and offered up a prayer. "O Lord," he said, "grant me a boon—that when the last day comes and both the sinner and the righteous man stands before you, I may have so lived as to deserve your grace."

No clerk could tell the whole tale of the miracles which took place at Gregory's coming to Rome, but among others—the bells rang out at his approach independently of the touch of any man, and they who were sick became whole. He was led to the mother church and set in his see by the emperor, as was proper, and therein he served God with all his might while he lived.

Before we end this story we must not neglect to tell how a lady came to Rome to pray for the remission of her sins. As she confessed herself at the pope's feet, Gregory knew that she was his mother, and he thanked God that both he and she had been saved by grace. He had a convent built for her in the city; it still stands, and the nuns thereof wear black habits.

By this example you may see that God forgets not those who turn to him with contrition in their hearts. God grant us all that we may end our life as well as that man did.

Peter Bell drew a sigh of relief. "I'm glad that's finished," he said.

"I am not squeamish," said Sir John Harington, "but I think I should have preferred the Welsh poetry."

"Or even a Welsh song," added Andrew Boorde.

"What is the matter with Welsh music?" asked Iolo Goch.

"It has twenty-four times as much opportunity to be worse than any other kind of music," answered Walter Haliday.

"And takes advantage of all of them," added the Sacrilegious Caroller.

"His song and his voice and his harp do agree," said Andrew Boorde, "much like the buzzing of a humble-bee."

"I am not precisely fastidious, either," said Sir Thomas Gray, "but I have a somewhat literal mind; and granting, for the sake of argument, that any fish would be fool enough to swallow a great iron key, I find it somewhat difficult to believe that he would—or could—have harboured it within him for seventeen years. It must have proved an exceedingly embarrassing burden, not only to his movements, but to the digestion of more regular articles of diet."

"The incident seems to have been of fairly common occurrence," said the Clerk of Oxenford. "Bishop Egwin of Worcester threw the key to *his* fetters into the river Avon, where it was swallowed by a fish; but his men caught that very fish, and recovered the key, at Rome."

"I suppose you have read your Herodotus," said Camden, "and if so, you recall how Polycrates' ring was swallowed by a fish, and restored to him five or six days later by a lucky fisherman?"

"Ay," returned Sir Thomas, "it is not to five or six days that I object, but to seventeen years! Just imagine the mutually deleterious effect the key and the fish would have on each other in that length of time!"

"A similar fate happened to Queen Languoreth's ring under rather romantic circumstances," said Sir David Lindsay.

"What was that?" asked Chrétien de Troyes.

55. QUEEN LANGUORETH'S RING
Sir David Lindsay

In the days of St Kentigern there ruled over Scotland a king named Rhyderch or Roderick. His queen was named Languoreth. She, living in plenty and surrounded by all delights, was not faithful to the marital bed, as she ought to have been; the heap of her treasures, the exuberance of her means of sensuality, and the elevation of power were wont to provide incentives and fuel to the desire of the flesh. She cast her eyes on a certain youth, a soldier, who seemed to her, judging by the perishing beauty of this perishable flesh, to be beautiful and fair of aspect beyond many who were with him at court. And he, who was ready enough for such service as this without external temptation, was easily induced to sin with her.

As time passed the forbidden pleasures, frequently repeated, became more and more delightful to both of them, for, as Solomon says, bread eaten in secret is pleasant. So, from a rash act they proceeded to a blind attachment, as a seal of which Languoreth very impudently and imprudently gave the young man a royal ring of gold set with a precious gem which her lawful husband had bestowed upon her as a mark of his conjugal love; and the young man, still more impudently and imprudently placing it upon his finger, opened the door of suspicion to all who knew how the queen had come by it.

The ring was observed by one of the king's faithful servants, and he lost no time in communicating to the king the secret of the queen and her soldier. Roderick lent an unwilling ear to this tale, for true is the old proverb which says that a cuckold is loath to credit him who reveals the failings of a beloved wife: the odium is more likely to fall on the informer than on the accused. But the faithful servant who had detected the adultery was a man whose opinion was difficult to change, and in support of his statement he pointed out to the king the ring on the soldier's finger.

Roderick veiled his wrath against Languoreth and the soldier under a calm demeanour, and appeared, if anything, more than usually kind and cheerful. But when there came a bright and sunny day, he went out hunting and ordered the young soldier to be his companion. When the dogs had been unleashed and the beaters stationed at different posts, Roderick and the soldier came down to the banks of the river Clud. They found a shady place on the green turf there, and thought it would be pleasant to sleep for a while. The soldier suspected no danger, and lay down, one arm under his head and the other hanging loosely at his side. But the jealous king only simulated slumber. The sight of the ring on the soldier's finger roused his wrath, and it was only with difficulty that he restrained his hand from his sword. However, instead of shedding blood, he drew the ring from the young man's finger and threw it into the river; then in a little while he wakened him and ordered him to go home with his companions. The soldier obeyed, and never discovered the loss of the ring till he had entered his own house.

On Roderick's return from the hunt the queen came forth and saluted him in her usual manner; but to her greeting he replied nothing save a continuous stream of threat, contempt and reproach. With flashing eyes and menacing countenance he demanded the ring which had been entrusted to her keeping. Languoreth said she had it laid up in a casket, whereupon, in the presence of the courtiers, Roderick commanded her to bring it to him with all haste. Much perturbed, the queen now sent a messenger to the soldier, telling him what had happened, and begging him to return the ring at once. The youth sent back word that he had lost the ring, he knew not where, and made haste to leave the court in fear of the king's vengeance.

When Languoreth still delayed, making show of seeking here and there, the king's fury escaped all bounds. He kept on calling her an adulteress, and broke into curses, saying: "God do to me, and more also, if I do not judge you according to the law of adulterers and condemn you to a most disgraceful death. You have neglected the king your lawful spouse, and have clung to a young wanton in secret. But I will act openly, so that your shame and ignominy may be manifest under the sun."

When the king had said this, and much more in a like strain, the courtiers prayed for some delay, but only with difficulty could they persuade him to grant a respite of three days. You can imagine how Languoreth's guilty conscience was tormenting her by this time. Through the inspiration of the Lord she hit upon a wise expedient: She sent a most faithful messenger to St Kentigern, revealing the whole matter, and urgently praying him to deliver her from her strait. She begged that he would intercede with the king on her behalf, since there was nothing so weighty that the king could or ought to deny him.

The saintly bishop, instructed by virtue from on high, knew the whole story from point to point before Languoreth's messenger arrived. So, when he came, the holy man ordered him to take a hook and go to the banks of the river Clud, cast the hook into the stream, and bring back straightway the first fish that was caught and taken out of the water.

As the man was bidden, so he did. To St Kentigern he brought back a large fish of the variety commonly known as salmon. The saint ordered it to be gutted in his presence, and when that had been done, he found in the fish's belly the ring in question. This he at once sent to the queen by her messenger.

When Languoreth saw the ring, I assure you that her heart was filled with joy and her mouth with thanksgiving; her grief was turned to happiness, and the expectation of death into a dance of exultation. She rushed into the hall, and in the sight of all his court, returned to Roderick the ring which he had demanded.

At this turn of events the king and his court were sorry for the injuries which the queen had suffered, and Roderick, on his knees, humbly besought her pardon, swearing that he would inflict severe punishment, or even death or exile, on her slanderers, if she wished it. But Languoreth, wisely considering the rôle she had to play, asked only that he show mercy to her accuser, and put away resentment against herself. So the king and queen were restored to peace and mutual love.

As soon after this as she could get away, Languoreth betook herself to the man of God, and confessing her guilt, made satisfaction therefor according to his advice. She carefully corrected her life, and kept her feet from similar falls in the future.

Languoreth never revealed the truth of these matters to anyone so long as the king lived, but after his death she told the story to anyone who wished to know it.

"I am sorry," said Mannyng, "if my tale of Gregory has in any way given offence. But I should think this cosmopolitan company would be as charitable of heart as was the abbot who nourished up the foundling in spite of what he read in the ivory tablets. I daresay, however, that you gentlemen have allowed your attention to rest too heavily on the story's purely secular elements."

"That is a fault of judgment which it is very easy to make," said William of Wykeham, "and is made, not only by laymen, but also by those of supposedly holy and religious life. I could illustrate from my own personal experience, but I prefer to tell you about a hermit who was of considerably different kidney from either St Paul on the Rock or St Gregory on the Rock."

56. THE HERMIT AND THE OUTLAW

William of Wykeham

I will tell you of two brothers who lived in times past and what happened to them, according to common report. One of the brothers was an arrant thief, a wild outlaw who took delight in robbing and reiving. The other was a good hermit, dressed in grey, who lived in the wild wood shaw and went barefoot; and, for the love of God, he wore a hair shirt to bite and irritate his skin. Never would he come to town to hold converse with man or woman and thus perchance be led to sin, as do hermits nowadays. These latter-day ascetics reck not what they say, nor in what manner they enter upon sin. The world is full of examples of the manners of men and women who do not avoid evil-doing.

As regards the outlaw, who lay in wait in the wood to slay men: One Good Friday he observed a great crowd of folk passing barefoot by the way, and their unshod condition aroused his curiosity. Among them he saw a woman, barefoot like the rest as a sign of contrition for her sins. "Stop," he said, "I will kill you at once unless you stand still." "Sir," said she, "for God's sake do me no shame or evil. I have been a sinful woman for thirty-three winters and more, for I was the commonest wench in the land."

"Tell me," said the outlaw, "I command you, why you and the other passers-by are going barefoot." "Sir," said the woman, "I will tell you. It was on this day that the Jews killed Christ so that you and I might be saved. He who forsakes his folly and beseeches Christ for mercy shall attain heaven's bliss."

"Woman, your courteous words persuade me to wend to church with you to find out what men do there, for by Him who made the world, I have not heard God's service in the last twenty years. I never had any desire to hear mass or learn any goodness, but have been living continuously in the forest. Even though I might be seized and hanged, I will go to church with you and hear God's service."

As the outlaw stood in the church he looked about him as though amazed, for he thought it wonderful. He went to the altar and leaned on his bow, and while he stood there he had a religious experience.

The vicar approached and showed him by means of an example that if he would abandon his evil way of life and do penance, he also might be saved.

"Sir vicar," said the outlaw, "tell me what the penance shall be. But impose nothing severe, for if you do, I warn you I will not perform it. It has always been my principle to lead an easy-going life."

"Ah, my son, you must go barefoot and wool-clothed for seven years."

"Nay," said the outlaw, "that I will never do if I never get to heaven."

"God forbid. Can you fast on bread and water?"

"No, indeed, I never could; death would be more welcome to me than to hear any more about that."

"Then you must say a paternoster and an ave every day for remission of your sins."

"By St John! I know neither paternoster nor avemaria; I have no idea how to begin."

"Can you endure no distress? Some penance you must needs perform if you will win heaven. Since you are still a young man, go on a pilgrimage, either the greater or a lesser."

"I cannot make a pilgrimage, for I have no money, and I know not how to beg. I would rather smite off my head than go begging my bread of any man or woman."

The vicar turned toward the cross and so earnestly did he pray that the tears ran from his eyes: "Lord," said he, "Lord who hast gained all this world, what is your advice in this matter? Suffer not this man to be lost!"

"Sir vicar," said the outlaw, "good-bye. I see very well that nothing can help me. You have wasted your time, for there is no penance I can do though I should be damned."

"Son, listen to me: you may yet be saved by God's grace. Tell me truly, what thing do you most hate to do?"

"Sir, as I hope for health, the truth of the matter is that drinking water is the thing most distasteful to me. Ever since I was a suckling my body would never endure water under any circumstances."

"Son, whatever may befall, for remission of your sins, drink no water today and I will freely assoil you. If you abide by this article I will demand no other penance."

"Sir, I will faithfully perform the penance you have imposed. I will drink no water today even to save myself from shame or death."

"Good-bye, my son, turn your thoughts to God and implore his mercy. Go in Christ's name."

"Farewell; God knows when we shall meet again."

Now give ear to a wonderful thing: soon after the outlaw left the church he was put to the test. He had gone hardly a mile when he was seized by such a thirst that he thought he was burning up. He would lever have drunk a draught than owned all the goods in the world, so keen was his craving.

Now as he walked along the street he met a wench who seemed to him a proper girl. She bore a jar on her head, and the clear fresh water was running over the brim. "Girl," said the outlaw, "I am sore athirst. If that is water you are carrying, set down your pot right here." "Sir," said the girl pleasantly, "you may drink as much as you like."

The outlaw took the pot and would have drunk, but then he remembered his penance and shrank back. "Lord," said he, "whence comes this craving of mine? Young or old, I have never liked water, and now I would rather have a draught than all the gold in the world. Still, though I die, I will drink no drop."

Then he left the girl standing there with her pot. In reality it was the devil who had sought to tempt him. By God's grace he was prevented from drinking. Down the street went the penitent, and there another wench met him. She had a pot in her hand and also a good cup. "Girl," said the outlaw, "whither go you?" "Sir," she said, "why do you ask? If it is a drink of water you want, here it is, and there is none finer anywhere." She filled a cup and handed it to him. But the outlaw remembered the vicar and refused it. Thus did the devil tempt him a second time. "O good Lord!" cried the outlaw, "how is this? I have such a thirst it seems to me my heart will break. However, though it do, I will drink no water."

So he fared on for something less than a furlong in bitter distress. On the way he came to a fountain at which a girl was filling a pot with clear water. By this time he was so weak and faint that he could hardly stand. The thirst had so mastered him that he could barely speak, and he thought his heart would break. He dragged himself to the edge of the well and looked at the water. He saw the maid filling her can and cried out for a drink. The girl filled a dish and bade him drink deep. That old shrew the devil was a cunning one, was he not? Then, right at the edge of the well, the outlaw thought of the knife hanging at his side. He undid a sleeve and slashed a vein of his arm so that the warm blood gushed out. There he drank his own blood, and it seemed to him that it did him much good.

But the outlaw's wound was deep and wide, and he bled copiously. He was not able to staunch the blood. So sorely did he bleed that it was finally clear to him that he must die. So he fell on his knees and cried: "Jesus mercy! Grace, O Lord whom Mary bore! Do not suffer my soul to be lost, if it please Thee." Thus he prayed till he fell to the ground dead. Hereupon, out of the bliss of heaven came more angels that I can tell with tongue. Blithely and joyfully they took up the outlaw's soul, leaving his body lying at the brink of the well.

In their flight the angels passed by his brother's hermitage, and he, when he heard the angels' song and saw his brother among them, fell to his knees and cried: "O Lord, what is the meaning of this joy and honour which is now enjoyed by that brother of mine who never did anything good in all his life, but only woe and sin? In my opinion I live too long; or else God does me injustice in allowing him to win heaven, whereas I suffer pain and distress, going barefoot, and fasting on bread and water. It seems to me a great wonder that he can get to heaven before I do, for all his life he was a bad one, defouling maid and wife without ceasing his livelong day. I will stop being a hermit and be an outlaw. I will throw away my grey habit and hair shirt. I will rob and slay and get to heaven as my brother does. That is the best course for me."

Thus did the hermit repine against God. Whereupon straightway came an angel to him and said: "Sir hermit, I assure you that your brother suffered more today than you have suffered in all your life. Today he abandoned his sinful ways, and was shriven clean by the vicar who imposed penance on him. In order that he might keep his word to the vicar and duly observe his penance, he killed himself. His body, with knife in hand, lies beside such and such a well. Take good care, O hermit, that you do not prevent him from being given Christian burial, for he is a martyr. As for you, continue your life as you began it; be a forthright and good man; do not be astonished at God's might, for His mercy is ever ready for those who pray to Him." Then the angel departed.

The hermit left his cell and went to the vicar. "Sir," said he, "for charity's sake, give me leave to tell you privately of a wonderful happening. I had a brother, a bold outlaw, but just now an angel told me that his body lies dead beside such and such a well, and that his soul has gone to heaven."

"Such a man came to me today," replied the vicar. "I remember him. Let us go together to seek his mortal remains."

Then the hermit and the vicar sought up hill and down dale till they found the outlaw's corpse lying under a linden tree by the brink of the fountain. They perceived the knife in his hand, and saw that his mouth was all bloody, wherefor the vicar understood that he had drunk his own blood.

"He must have killed himself to abide by the conditions of his shrift," said the vicar. "Let us thank God and Mary."

Afterwards they brought the body to church and sang masses, for the outlaw was worthy thereof.

Thus did the outlaw win heaven. And from that out the hermit was a good man, as the angel had bidden him be, and after some years, when he made his end, angels bore his soul to heaven's eternal bliss.

God grant us in our life grace to shrive ourselves of our sins and perform our penance equally devoutly.

"Why didn't he drink wine or ale?" inquired Peter Bell.

Wykeham looked at his questioner glumly: "I suppose he had no imagination," he replied; "nor were English outlaws trained in schools of casuistry, as a rule."

"I must say," spoke up Sturla the Lawman, "that you seem to have a very peculiar idea of what constitutes an outlaw. Among us of the North the man you describe would be considered not an outlaw but a professional reiver and murderer. With us there was the greater and the lesser outlawry. The latter, called *fjörbaugsgarþr*, was a punishment of three years' exile for torts, minor felonies and misdemeanours, or an avowed man-slaying; the former, called *skóggángr*, was a punishment of twenty years' banishment for undeclared manslaughter, that is, murder, during which time the outlawed man wore the wolf's head and might be killed, like a wolf, by any member of the social group with impunity. If he outlived his twenty years' exile, it was considered that he had expiated his crime, and was received again into society. I should say that your outlaw belongs to neither of these classes, for society could lay hands on him at any time, and he mingled freely with the folk. In our annals I recall only the case of Hörth, who, with his brother Geir, became the leader of a band of lawless men somewhat like your Robin Hood or Gamelyn. But among Icelanders the outlawry of Grettir and Gisli more nearly illustrates the temper of our law. Somewhat similar, though with romantic aspects, was an outlawing that took place in Norway during the reign of Earl Hákon Sigurdsson."

"I think I recall those circumstances," said Sigmund Brestison, "if it is the case of my father-in-law which you have in mind."

"That is it," answered Sturla.

"Once upon a time," said Iolo Goch, "I knew a gallant prince and honourable gentleman upon whom the sentence of outlawry was unjustly passed so that he had to become an outlaw in fact. For nearly fifteen years he struggled in vain to make Wales independent of Henry Bolingbroke. All Wales could not have provided a more splendid monument to the great patriot than was Mt Snowdon, where he died, nor any more fitting epitaph than the memory of him which all Welshmen bear in their hearts. He was my friend. I should listen gladly to any account of other brave men in similar heroic and distressed circumstances."

"Such matters touch me very near also," said Eustace the Monk. "May we hear your story?"

"It is more romantic than heroic," answered Sigmund, "but I will tell it as it was told to me."

57. THE OUTLAWING OF THORKEL DRYFROST

Sigmund Brestison

The circumstances whereby my cousin Thori and I came to Norway need not be told here, for they are connected with the story of Thrond of Gate as recorded in the Flatey Book. It is enough to say that about the time our fathers were slain at Dimun in the Faroës, Harald Grayfell, the king of Norway, was dethroned, and the realm was taken by Earl Hákon Sigurdson. Now since our money had come to an end, and since our fathers had served the earl in their time, we thought it might be to our behoof to seek Hákon out in the north.

We left the Vík, where Rafn had harboured us two winters. I was twelve and Thori was fourteen years old. First we went to the Uplands, then across Heidmark, and north to Dofrafell. It was winter when we got there, and we were ignorant of the way, yet we determined to go forward, for there was no advantage in stopping or in going back. We fared badly and went astray, and at last both our food and our strength were exhausted. I was the stronger, and carried Thori on my back for a time. Finally, one evening, we came upon a little house in a dale, and went into it. In the room were two women, one of mature age, the other a young girl, and both were very fair. They received us kindly, gave us dry clothes and food, and found a place for us to sleep. When the goodman, Ulf, came home, he grumbled somewhat. But next morning he was in a better humour, and said we might stay if we liked.

So we took up our lodging with Ulf, his wife Ragnhild, and his daughter Thurid. We could not have been better treated by our own fathers and mothers. And I stayed all the more gladly for Thurid's sake.

When I was eighteen years old and Thori twenty, we decided that it was time for us to go away, for my father had often said that a man's life is a poor thing unless he has experience of the ways of other men. Our foster-father said that it should be as we wished. He had new clothes made for us, and fitted us out with other things necessary for our journey. The two women took the parting much to heart, especially the younger one.

Ulf accompanied us on our way over Dofrafell until we came in sight of Orkadale. Here we sat down to rest, and Ulf said he would like to know whom he had fostered, of what kin we were, and what had happened to us before he took us in. We told him how our fathers had been slain, and what part Thrond of Gate had had therein, and Ulf was very sorry. "Now, foster-father," said I, "let us hear the tale of your life and what has happened in it."

"My story," replied Ulf, "is of little consequence, but I will do as you ask.—In Heidmark in the Uplands there dwelt a bonder whose name was Thoralf. He was a man of great worth, and steward to the Upland king. His wife's name was Idun, and their daughter Ragnhild was reckoned among the fairest of women. Not far away there lived a man called Steingrim, a good bonder and well-to-do. His wife was called Thora, and their son Thorkel.

"Steingrim's son Thorkel was a hopeful lad, and well grown. In his boyhood his father had schooled him in athletic exercises, and so well had he taught him to shoot that he became an excellent marksman. Every winter when the frost took, and ice lay on the water, Thorkel would lie out in the woods with certain of his companions to hunt wild beasts. Since Thorkel occupied himself thus during the season of frost, he was given the surname Dryfrost.

"Now one day Thorkel came to talk with his father, and said that he wished to marry, if Steingrim could arrange the match for him with Thoralf's daughter Ragnhild. Steingrim said he was aiming high. Nevertheless, father and son went to see Thoralf and asked for Ragnhild in marriage. The steward replied that he expected to bestow his daughter on a man of more worship than Thorkel. So the parley came to naught, and father and son fared home again.

"Not long after this Thorkel learned that the steward was away from home on business connected with his office. Taking one of his companions he went by night where Ragnhild was sleeping, took her up, and bore her away home with him. Steingrim was not well pleased by this deed. He said that Thorkel had got a stone that was too heavy for him, and that he would not have him there unless he took the girl back home. When Thorkel was unwilling to do that, Steingrim bade him go his ways. So the young man took Ragnhild and eleven of his men, and lodged out in the wood.

"Now when Thoralf came home and was aware of these tidings, he gathered men till there were a hundred. He went to Steingrim's and bade him yield up his son and restore Ragnhild into his hands. Steingrim said the young people were not there, whereupon Thoralf ransacked every building in the homestead, but found not what he sought. Afterward he and his men proceeded to the wood and searched there, dividing the task between all the men so that there were thirty men in Thoralf's party.

"It happened one day that Thoralf saw twelve men in the wood and a woman with them, and made for them. Thorkel saw him coming and prepared to defend himself. Thoralf attacked at once, but Thorkel and his fellows fought manfully, and the upshot of the contest was that Thoralf lost twelve men and Thorkel seven. The steward got his death wound in that encounter, and was borne home by his men. Ragnhild went with them. Thorkel and his four companions went home to Steingrim, who kept them hidden till they had recovered from their wounds. But Thoralf died of his wound at his homestead.

"After these happenings the Upland folk summoned a Thing, and made Thorkel Dryfrost an outlaw, for it was said that it was he who had slain Thoralf. The other four men were allowed to pay wergild. It was, of course, impossible for Steingrim to harbour a wolf's head; but he told Thorkel about a cave in the cliffs by the river, known to him alone. So Thorkel took food and hid there while the search for him was at its height. But that kind of life seemed dull to the young man after a while. One night he left the cave, made his way to Thoralf's homestead, and carried away Ragnhild a second time, making for the woods and fells.

"And here," concluded Ulf, "I made my dwelling, and here I have been ever since with Ragnhild my wife; it has been eighteen winters, and that is the age of my daughter Thurid. Thus have I told you the story of my life, for Thorkel is my right name."

I thanked my foster-father for his story, and confessed, too, that his fosterage had been worse repaid than he deserved, since Thurid had confided to me that she was with child. Then I asked him not to give her in marriage to any other man, for I meant to have her for my wife, or no other woman. "I have long known that there was love between you and the girl," answered Thorkel, "but I would not forbid it. My daughter could not marry a better man. But this I will ask of you, Sigmund: if you ever find favour with any chief, that you bring me to a reconciliation with my countrymen, for I have become very tired of this wilderness." I said that I would surely do so. And I kept my word, for when I reached Earl Hákon, and laid my case before him, and had spent two winters in expeditions of one sort or another, I became so intimate with him as to be chosen member of his body-guard. Then at the All-Thing in the spring the earl, at my request, caused the sentence of outlawry to be lifted from Thorkel Dryfrost, and had him removed from the fell, for the twenty years provided by law had now expired. Thorkel stayed with the earl the following winter, having with him his wife Ragnhild, his daughter Thurid, and Thurid's child Thora. Later I took Thurid and Thora with me to the Faroës.

"I think," said Hallfred Vandraethaskald, "that Earl Hákon deserves praises for many things, especially for the crushing of the Jomsberg vikings, but dispraise for others. Not only was he a masterful man, often meddling with the bonders' wives, but also, he did not profess the true faith. During his reign the trolls and the imps had an easy time of it in Norway. But all that was changed when Olaf Tryggvison came.—I remember that once King Olaf came to Naumudale, and laid up his ships there while waiting for a favourable wind south. One evening some of his men wandered out of camp on business of their own. In the course of their walk they spied a party of fiends sitting round a fire in a cavern, and overheard them lamenting the evils occasioned by the rising tide of Christianity. One fiend, so he said, while attempting to injure King Olaf's men in wrestling, had been squeezed nearly to extinction by King Olaf himself. Another, who had visited the king's bedchamber in the guise of a woman, had had his skull fractured by a heavy book which Olaf threw at him."

"Ha!" exclaimed William atte Pole, "I now see some justification for books, even bad ones, such as the *Topography of Ireland*, or the *Miroir des Histories*."

"St Brandan would have loved the man who threw the book," said Adamnan. "You remember that the devils complained bitterly of him when he warded off their torture from Judas on the rock, and that their complaints and remonstrances were unavailing."

"You may be interested," said Dick O the Cow, "in knowing what happened to my brother, a poor farmer living near Sempringham."
"Is your tale of mirth or of wit?" asked Wykeham.
"You shall judge," answered Dick.

58. THE DEVILS' CONCLAVE

Dick O the Cow

There was a poor husbandman whose cow grazed abroad in the fields all day and used to come home to the byre without fail every night. But a mischance happened to her, for Friar Rush fell upon her and slew her where she stood in the field.

When the poor man saw that his cow did not come home at her usual time nor long afterwards, he thought that all might not be well with the beast, so he went out in search of her. He wandered through one field after another till finally he found half his cow. The other half was clean gone, and she had been so exactly divided into two parts that it seemed to him the operation could not have been performed but by the hand of man, for if any wild beasts had done it, they would have spoiled the flesh. So he turned sadly homeward. But before he had gone half the distance, the night had become so dark that he could not see his way, and he wandered at a loss, for he could see no house. At last he came to a hollow tree, and there he sat down, thinking to take his rest there for the remainder of the night.

It seemed to him that he had scarcely settled himself in the tree when he was wakened by a fearful uproar and outcry; peering out he saw something that made him tremble with fright, for round about the tree was an assembly of many fiends, who were sitting and arguing one with the other. And as he looked, he saw sitting in a chair one who impressed him as being fouler in face and bearing than the others. This personage bade all the other demons give a reckoning of the deeds in which they had been engaged.

"You, fellow," he said, "what have you been doing?" "I," said the fiend, "was at a wedding, where I did a foul deed, for by my strength of hand I slew both the wife and the husband; and in addition to that I caused all the guests to quarrel so that they set about killing one another."

The master fiend looked at him askance and set his tale at naught. "How long did it take you to do that?" he asked. "Only a twelvemonth," replied the other. "For that evil deed you shall have evil thanks and a beating to boot," said the master fiend.

Then he called another, and with flashing eyes asked him violently: "Where have *you* been?" "I have been on the sea," replied the other demon, "where I have caused much sorrow to men. I have ruined ships without number in storm and tempest—twenty thousand at least." "I daresay," said the devil. "How long were you at it?" "Seven winters all together," replied the fiend.

This answer put the master fiend into such a bad humour that he ordered the ship-wrecking imp to be flogged.

Now a third demon was brought before the master as he sat there, and Satan asked him where he had been and what he had done. He said that he had been in the desert, labouring to stir a hermit to sin, but that the holy man had always been so steadfast and virtuous that it had given him the greatest difficulty to induce him to commit fornication just a few nights ago.

"How long were you engaged in so beguiling him?" asked the master. "Forty winters," replied the imp. On hearing this the devil was mightily pleased; he rose from his chair and kissed his minion, and set a crown on his head. "Come and sit beside me," he said, "for you are worthy of that honour, and have won my love."

After this, other fiends made their reports, and it was well for them, for the master devil was now in such a good humour that he found little to cavil at.

"What have you done for us?" he asked one called Beelzebub. "Sir," said Beelzebub, "I have caused strife and debate to fall between brother and brother in so much that one has slain the other." "That is well done," said Satan, "and you shall be well rewarded for your labour." Then he called another named Incubus and inquired what he had done. "Sir," said Incubus, "I have caused great debate and strife to fall between two lords, through which they have had great wars, and many men have been slain." "You are a true servant to us," said the master devil, "and shall be well rewarded for your trouble. Noirpeil," said he to another fiend, "what have you done for us?" "Sir," replied Noirpeil, "I have been among the players at dice and cards, and I have caused them to swear many great oaths, and one to slay the other." "That was well done," said the master, "and you shall be well guerdoned for your toil." Now another imp came forward and said: "Sir, I have caused two old women to fight so sorely together, and so to beat one another about the head that their eyes flew out." "That was well done," said Satan, "and you shall have great thanks for your labour."

So it went till near cock-crow. At the faintest hint of day the demons broke up their assembly to scatter abroad in the world to finish and make an end of the enterprises they had in hand. When the poor farmer sitting in the tree saw that they had gone, he rejoiced in his heart, for he had shivered all night in fear and dread lest they perceive him. At the first streak of dawn he clambered down as well as he was able for fright and cold, and made his way home.

"I recall those circumstances," said Robert Mannyng. "I related the affair in my Manual under the authority of Saint Gregory."

"You say," said Sir John Hawkins, addressing Hallfred the Troublesome Poet, "that King Olaf lay becalmed for a time at Naumudale. I have been much astonished that Fulk Fitzwarin never had any trouble to speak of on his various voyages, and I have been particularly amazed that St Brandan, though he once put in for repairs, was never broken up during the seven years he was on the sea. Certainly such luck was remarkable."

"God was with him," said Adamnan.

"If Fulk ever suffered shipwreck, the history fails to mention it," said Leland.

"I had a good ship-master," said Fulk.

"Sir John is right," interposed Master Wace. "Seafaring is seldom without hazard, nor has the length of the voyage anything to do with its good or bad fortune. I will illustrate, not from a saint's life nor from a romance, if you will hear me."

"Tell on," said Ponce de Leon.

59. THE WHITE SHIP

Master Wace

King Henry I, by Matilda, had a son named William. With the fondest hope and surpassing care he was educated and destined to the succession. To him, when scarcely twelve years of age, all the free men of England and Normandy, of every rank and condition, and under fealty to whatsoever lord, were obliged to submit themselves by homage and by oath. While still a boy, too, he was betrothed to and received in wedlock Matilda, the daughter of Fulco, Earl of Anjou, who was herself scarcely nubile. As her dower his father-in-law bestowed upon him the county of Maine. Moreover, Fulco, when he set out for Jerusalem, committed his earldom to King Henry on the understanding that it should be restored to him if he returned, and if not, it should go to his son-in-law. By the exertions of his father-in-law, also, and of other relatives, King Louis of France was induced to concede to him, on his doing homage, the legal possession of Normandy. Thus many provinces looked forward to the governance of this boy, for it was supposed that the prediction of King Edward would be verified in him, and it was said that now it might be expected that the hopes of England, like the tree cut down, would through this youth again blossom and bring forth fruit, and thus put an end to her sufferings. So, through the indulgence of his father, the young prince, now about seventeen years old, possessed everything but the name of king.

In discussing and peaceably settling these matters King Henry spent four years in Normandy, and when affairs had been satisfactorily concluded, he decided to return to England. Accordingly, a large fleet was fitted out in the harbour of Barfleur, and the gallant company who were to sail with the king having assembled, Henry and his attendants embarked in the first watch of the night, with the south wind blowing. They hoisted sail and put out to sea, and in the morning those to whom God permitted it embraced the shore of England.

Now I must tell you that before the king sailed he was approached by a certain mariner named Thomas, who said: "Sire, my father was Stephen, the son of Airard, and during his whole life he served your father as a mariner. It was he who, in his own ship, conveyed your father, William the Conqueror, to England when he crossed the sea to make war on Harold. In services of this description he was employed by your father as long as he lived, and gave him such satisfaction that he honoured him with liberal rewards. Now, my lord king, I ask you to employ me in the same service, for I have a vessel, called the White Ship, fitted out in the best manner, and perfectly adapted to receive a royal retinue."

To this the king replied: "I grant your request, but I have already selected a ship that suits me, and I shall not change. However, I entrust to you my sons, William and Richard, whom I love as myself, with many of the nobility of my realm."

When Thomas made known this decision the mariners were in great glee. They approached the prince, and with fair words asked him to give them something to drink. William gave orders that they should have three muids. No sooner was the wine delivered to them than they held a great drinking-bout, and pledging their comrades in full cups, indulged too much and became intoxicated.

By King Henry's command many barons with their sons waited to embark with William in the White Ship—about three hundred souls in all. The crew consisted of fifty experienced rowers, besides an armed marine force. These latter were very disorderly, for as soon as they got aboard they insolently took possession of the rowers' benches; and being very drunk, forgot their station and scarcely paid respect to anyone.

Now, though it was night, these imprudent youths, overwhelmed with liquor, launched the vessel from the shore, driving away with contempt and shouts of laughter the priests who came to bless them. Besides the king's treasure and some casks of wine, there was no cargo on board, but only passengers. They urged Thomas to use his utmost endeavour to overtake the royal fleet. He, in his drunken folly, confiding in his seamanship and in the skill of his crew, boasted that he would soon leave behind him all the ships that had started earlier. He gave the signal: some seized the oars without delay, while others joyously handled the ropes and sails; and they made the ship rush through the water at a great rate. Swifter than the winged arrow flew the White Ship, sweeping the rippling surface of the deep.

Not far from Barfleur there was a great rock, left dry every day when the tide was out, but covered over at high water. Now as the drunken rowers exerted themselves to the utmost in pulling the oars, the luckless pilot steered at random and got the ship out of its due course. The starboard bow of the White Ship struck violently on that huge rock.

In the greatest consternation the sailors immediately ran on deck, and with loud outcry got ready their boat-hooks, endeavouring for a considerable time to force the vessel off; but Fortune resisted and frustrated their every effort. Several planks had been shattered by the collision, and the prow hung immovably fixed. Some of the crew were washed overboard, others were drowned by the water which poured into the cracked vessel. A few, however, succeeded in launching a small boat, and the prince was received into it. He might certainly have reached shore and been saved had not his sister, the Countess of Perche, now struggling with death in the larger craft, implored her brother's assistance, shrieking out that he should not abandon her so barbarously. Touched with pity, the prince ordered the boat to return so that he might rescue his sister; thereupon the skiff, overcharged by the multitudes that leaped into her, sank and buried all indiscriminately in the deep. Thus did the unhappy youth meet his death through excess of affection.

Roger, Bishop of Coutances, whose son was aboard the White Ship, lingered on shore with some companions watching its departure. They, as well as the king and his suite—though they were a long way off at sea—heard the fearful cries of distress raised by the shipwrecked crew and passengers; but they did not learn what caused the shrieks till the next day.

Now there were two passengers of that ill-fated ship who seized hold of the yard-arm from which the sail was set. They hung on to it during the greater part of the night in the hope that they would receive aid in some form or other. One of these men was a butcher of Rouen; the other was a young man of gentle birth named Geoffrey, the son of Gilbert de l'Aigle.

Thomas, master of the vessel, after his first plunge into the sea, gained fresh energy, and recovering his senses as his head rose above water, perceived the two men clinging to the yard-arm. "What has become of the king's son?" he cried. The sailors replied that the prince and all who were with him had perished. "Then," said Thomas, "it is misery for me to live any longer." And so saying, in utter despair, he abandoned himself to his fate, preferring to meet it at once rather than face the rage of the king in his wrath and sorrow for the loss of his children, or drag out his existence and expiate his crime in a dungeon.

Meanwhile Berold the butcher and Geoffrey, hanging by the yard-arm, called upon God to save them, and heartening one another waited in fearful anxiety for the end to which it should please Him to bring their misery. The night was bitterly cold and frosty, so that the young Geoffrey, after fearful suffering from the severity of the weather, lost his power of endurance, and commending his companion to God, sank into the sea and disappeared. Berold, however, the poorest man of all the company, was wearing a sheepskin dress, and was the only one among so many who survived till the dawn of another day. In the morning three fishermen took him into their skiff, and so he reached land. When he had revived a little, he related the particulars of the sad event to a crowd of anxious inquirers. He himself lived in good health for twenty years longer.

The melancholy news of the shipwreck was soon spread by the common people along both shores, and finally came to the ears of Theobald, Count of Blois, and other lords of Henry's court; but for that day no one ventured to make the circumstances known to the king, who was in a state of great anxiety, and was making constant inquiries. The nobles shed many tears in private, and were inconsolable for the loss of their friends and relatives; but in the king's presence, hard as it was to do so, they concealed their grief, lest its cause should be discovered.

On the next day following, by a well-devised plan of Count Theobald, a boy came and threw himself at the king's feet, weeping bitterly. When he was questioned as to the cause of his sorrow, the king learned from him about the wreck of the White Ship. So sudden was the shock, and so severe the king's anguish, that he instantly fell to the ground; only when he had been conducted to his chamber did he give full vent to his feelings.

When the grief of their sovereign became evident, the servants of the crown no longer strove to conceal their own sorrow, and their lamentations continued for many days. The people, also, mourned for William the Aethling, whom they considered the lawful heir to the throne of England, and who had thus suddenly perished with the flower of the highest nobility. On him was fastened not only his father's love, but the people's hopes.

No shipwreck ever occasioned so much sorrow to England; none was ever so widely celebrated throughout the world. Together with the prince perished his half-brother Richard, whom a woman of rank had borne to the king; his sister, the Countess of Perche, as I have said; and the king's niece, the Countess of Chester. Indeed, in that disaster there perished almost every person of consequence about the court, whether knight or chaplain, or young nobleman training up to arms. And it is said that among those who were lost were no fewer than eighteen females who were either daughters, sisters, nieces or wives of kings and earls. For all the nobility eagerly hastened from all quarters, expecting no small addition to their reputation if they could either amuse or show their devotion to the young prince.

The calamity was augmented by the difficulty of recovering the bodies. Various persons sought them along the shore, but in vain; delicate as they were, they became food for the monsters of the sea. Only the bodies of Earl Richard, and several others—identified by those who recognized their clothes—were found some days after the wreck, cast ashore far from the spot where the vessel had broken up.

This disaster took place on the 25th of November in the year 1120.

"I remember that tragedy," said Henry of Huntingdon. "I used to see Prince William habited in robes of silk interwoven with gold, surrounded by troops of attendants and guards, and with almost celestial splendour. But when I observed the excessive state in which he lived, and especially his own headstrong pride, I had misgivings of future calamity. This pampered prince, said I to myself, is destined for hell-fire. He, in his proud eminence, gloried in the thought of his future earthly kingdom. But God said: Not so, unrighteous man, not so. The people of England sympathized, indeed, with the king in his sorrow; but you have exaggerated, I think, their grief for the prince himself, just as you have drawn a kindly veil over his more loathsome vices."

"What you say is probably true," said John Stow, "for I have read somewhere that Prince William used to boast openly how he would treat the English if he ever came to rule over them: He said he would make them pull at the plough like oxen. No people has cause to love such a prince in his lifetime, nor to lament overmuch at his death."

"There were no oxen at Runnimede on June 15, 1215," stated Wiclif.

"If," asked Peter Bell, "Roger of Coutances was standing on the shore and heard the cries of the sinking passengers, why did he not send out a boat, or boats, to investigate?"

"You remind me," said William of Newburgh, "of the parishioner who asked St Augustine what God did when he had finished making the world."

"And what did He do?"

"He created hell for people who ask foolish questions."

"It seems to me that Peter's question is not so foolish," said Sigmund Brestison; "but if it is accounts of disaster through wind and wave that you want, I think the people of my race are as well qualified as any to speak. Olaf Peacock the Icelander narrowly escaped, off the coast of Ireland, the fate which actually overtook your Harold Godwinson on the coast of Ponthieu; and Olaf's son-in-law, Giermund Roar, sailed one night onto some hidden rocks near Stade, and he and all his crew perished. On one occasion I myself made two attempts to set out from the Faroës with scat and dues for King Olaf, and twice my ship was beaten back and wrecked. But occurrences like these were so usual among us that we never paid them much heed, nor gave them special prominence in our records."

"Your remark about bearing scat to the king from the Faroës," said Sighvat Skald, calls to mind the difficulty experienced by Olaf Haraldson in that business long after the incident to which you refer."

60. HOW OLAF HARALDSON GATHERED SCAT IN THE FAROËS
Sighvat Skald

About ten years after Olaf Haraldson had been king over Norway there came out of the Faroës at his invitation Gille the Lawman, Leif Ossurson and Thoralf of Dimun, together with many other bonders' sons. When the Faroëse arrived in Norway the king called them to him in a conference and explained the purpose of the journey which he had made them take, namely, that he would have scat from the Faroës, and also that the people there should be subject to the laws which the king would give them.

At that meeting it appeared from the king's words that he would make the men who had come out answerable, and would bind them by oath to put his wishes into effect. He also offered to take into his service the men whom he considered most able, and bestow honour and friendship upon them. At all events the Faroë men understood the king's words so, namely, that they must dread the turn which the matter might take if they did not submit to all that the king desired. They held several meetings about the business, the upshot of which was that the king's wish prevailed. Leif and Gille and Thoralf went into the king's service and became his court-men. Thereafter the Faroëse prepared to return home.

Now the king ordered a ship to be rigged, and manned it, and sent men to the Faroë Islands to receive the scat which the inhabitants were to pay him. It was late in the season before they were ready, but at last they set out. And of their journey all that is to be told is that they did not come back, and no scat either.

When summer came, and no ship and no scat, King Olaf fitted out another vessel, manned it and sent it to the Faroës for the dues. They got under weigh and proceeded to sea. But as little was ever heard of this ship as of the former one, and many conjectures were made about what had become of them.

In the summer of 1026 a ship sailed from Norway for the Faroës with messengers bearing a verbal message from King Olaf that one of his court-men, Leif Ossurson or Lawman Gille or Thoralf of Dimun should come over to him from the islands. When this message was delivered to the men whom it concerned, they met together to determine what might lie under it, and they came to the conclusion that the king wanted to inquire into the real state of the event which some said had taken place upon the islands, namely, the failure and disappearance of the king's earlier messengers, and the loss of two ships. It was decided that Thoralf of Dimun should go to Norway in reply to the king's summons.

Not many hours after Thoralf had sailed it happened that Thrond of Gate went to the house of his brother Thorlak. There he found his two nephews, Thord the Low and Sigurd, lounging at their ease. "Well, well," said Thrond, "how times have changed! When I was a young man it was rare to find an able fellow sitting or lying at his ease, and even now it seems incredible that Thoralf of Dimun should appear more active and enterprising than the sons of Thorlak. I suppose the vessel I have in the boat-house will go to rot under its tar. And it seems too bad, I must say, that the storehouses should be full of wool which is neither used nor sold. Young men give themselves great airs; but when there is anything difficult or important to do, it is still the old men who have to do it. Unfortunately, I am too old."

Sigurd sprang to his feet, saying that he would not endure Thrond's ill language. He called to Thord and Gaut the Red, a relative of theirs, and with the servants they launched the vessel, loaded the cargo, and put to sea. All this was done so quickly that they overhauled Thoralf's ship and kept her in sight most of the course to Norway. Both vessels came to land off the Hennöe Islands one evening and cast anchor not far from each other.

That night Thoralf of Dimun and a companion went ashore for a certain purpose. When they were preparing to return to the ship, this is what happened: A cloth was cast over the companion's head and he was thrown into the sea; when he had disentangled himself and won back to shore, he found Thoralf with his head cloven down to his shoulders.

Tidings of this matter were brought to King Olaf, whereupon he summoned the Faroë people of both vessels to a Thing. "I think," he said, "that the motive for this deed must have been to prevent Thoralf from telling about the murder of my scat-gatherers." Sigurd offered to clear himself by the ordeal of the hot iron, and this was agreed to.

That night Sigurd remarked to his ship's people that there was a stiff breeze blowing, and hoisted sail. "Let Thrond bring his wool to market himself," said he, "for I do not think I shall ever be coming to Norway again."

"To my mind," said Will Langland, "Olaf was well served. Let us be ruled, indeed, but by the hand of Justice, not of Tyranny."

"By what right," exclaimed Marsiglio of Padua, "did Olaf stretch forth his arm to the islands of the sea and say to their free peoples: 'You and you shall pay me dues and tolls?' Not by law, for the Faroëse had made no law whereby money should be transferred from their pockets to Olaf's. Any constraint otherwise placed upon them was illegal."

"The strong king makes his own law," growled Richard the Lionheart.

"You should have lived on to June 15, 1215," answered Langland, "so that you might have been present at Runnimede, between Windsor and Staines."

"I," said Fulk Fitzwarin, "did live to see that day."

"So did I," said Earl Marshal. "I had lived through many vicissitudes of war and peace and tangled statecraft without particularly feeling the hand of Time, though I was sixty-nine years old; but the burdensome difficulties of the rôle I was forced to play as King John's intermediary in those negotiations left me an old man."

"John learned indeed," said Matthew Paris, "that no man, though a king, is stronger than Right. But that is a lesson which is soon forgotten, and requires to be taught over and over again. For one of the principles of Tyranny is that it is just for one to have more than all."

"Affairs might have turned out differently for the Faroëse," said Snorri Sturlason, "had the islands been nearer at hand. It was by reason of our isolation that we Icelanders were once able to set King Harald Gormson of Denmark at defiance. But beware of the mailed fist when it is able to reach you! Eindridi Broadsole could tell you something about tyrants!"

"We should be very glad if you would tell us," said Eustace the Monk.

"Very well," agreed the historian.

61. EINDRIDI BROADSOLE SHOOTS AT A MARK

Snorri Sturlason

Towards the close of the spring that Leif Ericson went to Greenland, King Olaf Tryggvison was engaged in fitting out his ships off Nidaros. When the work had got well under way, the king gave an entertainment for the men of his levy. There was considerable drinking, so that in the end both the king and his men were in the merriest of moods.

There was, of course, a great deal of talk about this and that, till finally the conversation turned to the subject of Christianity in Norway. Someone asked whether the whole land was now Christian, and all the people baptized. At this Olaf's standard-bearer, Ulf the Red, spoke up. "I think that can hardly be the case," he said; "and I should not be surprised if there were some unbaptized people not far from us." "Do you know what you are talking about?" asked the king. "I have heard tales," answered Ulf. "Don't be vague," said Olaf. "Well," replied Ulf, "up in Thrandheim there is a man called Eindridi, nicknamed Broadsole. He is young, handsome, free-handed, and very popular. I have been told that he is not baptized." "In that case," said the king, "there is only one course to pursue: take men with you, and ask him to pay me a visit."

Ulf did as he was bidden, and was well received by Eindridi. When he had delivered his message his host replied: "I have decided to remain at home, but I will not avoid the king if he should wish to seek me out. You may also say to him that I am willing to be his friend if he will be mine."

Ulf reported these words to Olaf. Then the king asked what conclusion he had come to regarding Eindridi's religion, and if he had seen much evidence of sacrificing. Ulf answered that he had seen nothing to make him think that Eindridi worshipped idols. "Since he will not come to me," said the king, "it will not be long till I visit him unawares in his own house."

On hearing the king express such an intention, Ulf sent his servant secretly to Eindridi to warn him.

During the night the king sailed up the firth with three hundred men, and arrived at Eindridi's farm-stead in the morning. Eindridi welcomed him, and invited him with all his men to partake of the entertainment which had been prepared. As they walked together towards the homestead he said: "It is said that our religions differ, and if for that reason you do not care to associate with us, you may have one room, and I and my men will occupy another." "As a rule," replied the king, "I do not care to mix with heathen men, but on this occasion I should like you to sit with me so that I may talk to you."

A stool was brought for Eindridi, and he took his place in front of the king's table; on his knees he held a boy of four or five years, a very pretty child. "You are a stout and handsome man," said Olaf, "and if your deeds accord with your looks, there are probably few in the land who can equal you. Are you a married man?" "No," answered Eindridi. "Even so, is that pretty boy sitting on your knees yours?" "I have no child," said Eindridi; "this boy is my sister's son, but I could not love him more if he were my own."

After that the king inquired into Eindridi's religion, and found that since he had not been better instructed, he preferred to follow the belief which had been that of his father and kinsmen.

"Have you not heard," inquired the king, "how I have punished those who would not listen to my words when I bade them accept Christianity?" "I have heard," said Eindridi, "but I have no fear that you will punish me. Indeed, I will pay homage to no chief; rather will I suffer death than any man's oppression. And though you may have caused others to stand in fear, I tell you that our community here is so well manned that I have no apprehension of coming under anybody's thumb. But if you deal fairly with me, I will deal fairly with you."

"Your words," answered the king, "show me that you are bold of speech and have a sense of right and wrong. However, we will speak no more of the matter for the moment. Now I have heard tell that you are very skilful in bodily exercises: what feats have you which you deem out of the common?" "Sir," said Eindridi, "that is soon answered. I am not skilled in any feats. I am little more than a youth, and during the period since my father's death I have devoted my energies principally to the administration of the estate and to the maintenance of my men." "Don't be afraid to speak out," said the king; "I shall not begrudge you whatever skill you possess, and what you say may perhaps be to your advantage." "Since you harp on the matter," answered Eindridi, "I may say that though I do not consider swimming among my accomplishments, nevertheless, I do look on when boys are disporting themselves in the water." "You do well to avoid self-praise and boasting," replied Olaf; "it is true that a man may be a spectator at sports without necessarily being skilled in them himself. What else have you to mention?" "I see that I shall not escape your importunity unless I make some answer or other," said Eindridi. "Well, when other boys shot at marks, I also took the bow; but I understand little about archery." "It may be," replied the king, "that you do not shoot straight at first. But now name your third feat." "Sir, you pounce greedily upon my words, and I find it difficult to sail between the reef and the swell. It would not be courteous for me to remain silent with you, and yet when I speak, you deliberately give my words a meaning which I did not intend them to have. However, when I was a boy, I used to play awkwardly at daggers, nor do I at present reckon myself proficient in that sport." "Perhaps you need exercise," said Olaf. "Well, you have entertained us very nicely, and you may now be at liberty for the rest of the day."

On the morrow, after he had drunk a while, the king summoned Eindridi and said: "Will you let yourself be baptized and take the true course without resistance?" "I am not so silly," answered Eindridi, "as to be of one mind yesterday, and of another today." "In that case," said Olaf, "I have thought out an agreement which I will make with you. I will find a man among my people to compete with you in feats of athletic skill. If you are overcome, you shall believe in Jesus Christ; if you prove to be the better man, you shall be free from my importunity, and hold what faith you please." "I have not spoken of any skill in feats," replied Eindridi, "for I have none; but a lord's word is master. Who is the man whom you choose to compete with me?" "It seems to me very likely that I shall go against you myself," replied Olaf, "for in that case I can more readily judge what you are; and whichever of us two proves himself the better man, there shall be no shame in it for you."

Eindridi objected that it would be unfair to expect him to match his skill against King Olaf's, even were he the most accomplished athlete. The king said that it would indeed be best for Eindridi not to engage with him, but that in that case he must acknowledge himself beaten already. "I can still make that choice after I have seen your prowess as a swimmer," answered Eindridi.

The two men undressed and went into the water. There they contended with one another for a long time, but the upshot of the struggle was that the king forced Eindridi down twice, and he was obliged to admit himself beaten.

On the next day the king said they would test their ability in archery. "It seems to me," said Eindridi, "that you have interpreted my words unfairly; there is no need for me to compete with you in shooting, for I know even less about that than about the art of swimming." "That would please me well," answered Olaf, "if it were true; if you like, you may refuse and admit yourself beaten." "That choice will not be made for a long time," replied Eindridi.

Thereupon they went to the wood which lay a short distance from the farm-stead. Here the king put up a target at the butt, intending to shoot at long range. At his first shot the arrow struck the outer border of the target and stuck there. Eindridi's arrow hit farther in, but not in the centre. When the king had shot again it was found that the arrow had hit the very centre of the target, and everyone acclaimed it a famous shot. Eindridi also praised the king's good marksmanhip and said that there was now no further need for him to shoot. Then Olaf said he might leave the contest if he wished, and acknowledge himself outmatched in archery. Eindridi replied that he would still have time to make such a confession after he had tried his luck again. He shot, and his arrow struck the notch of the arrow which the king had just shot, and there they both stuck.

"That shot has made you famous," said Olaf; "nevertheless, we must make further trial of your skill. We will take the fair boy whom you love so greatly, as you said, and set him up as a target."

The boy was placed in the way the king directed, and a chess-man was balanced on his head. "Now," said Olaf, "we will shoot the piece off the boy's head without injuring him." "You can, of course, do as you will," said Eindridi, "but if the lad suffers any scathe, you may be sure that I will avenge it."

A long kerchief was tied about the boy's head, and two men held the ends of it so that he could not make the slightest movement on hearing the whirr of the arrow. The king took his position, and signed himself and the point of the arrow with the sign of the cross, while Eindridi stood by, flushing darkly. The king's arrow flew, and passed under the chess-man, leaving it behind on the child's head.

But so near did the shaft come to the lad's skull that blood seemed almost to be oozing out of it.

Now the king bade Eindridi take his position and shoot after him if he would. But on the other side up came Eindridi's mother and sister, and with bitter sobbing begged him not to go. "Well," said Eindridi, "though I have no fear that I should injure my boy if I shot, I will not shoot this time." "It seems to me," said Olaf, "that you are overcome." "Let that be as seems good to you," replied Eindridi. "Doubtless your judgment is as much at fault this time as it has been on the other occasions." "Of course I have judged unfairly," answered the king; "but if I have, it turns out to be to your behoof."

Then they all returned home to the hall, and the king was in a most cheerful mood.

"Well," said Eustace, "Eindridi was obviously a gentleman, and Olaf was a churl."

This remark brought Hallfred Vandraethaskald to his feet, but Eustace never moved a muscle as the Northerner towered over him. "Will you defend that statement on a field of battle?" asked the skald.

"I see no occasion for fighting," replied Eustace; "moreover, I abandoned the use of arms long ago."

"Sit down," commanded Hákon Hákonson; "you know the monk is right."

"William Rufus was in a good humour, too," said Walter Map, "when he had rooted out thirty-six mother churches from the New Forest, driven away the people, and given it over to wild beasts and the sport of dogs. But it happened that the instigator of his sin became also the instrument of his punishment. As the king was one day coursing the deer in New Forest, Walter Tyrel, his companion, let fly an arrow which passed right through the quarry, and lodged in the breast of the beast despised by God. The death of this basest of kings relieved the world of a sore burden."

"Do you suggest," asked Hallfred wrathfully, "that Olaf Tryggvison was a tyrant who should have served as a mark for one of Eindridi's arrows?"

"My words are plain and unequivocal," answered Map coolly, "and I cannot be held accountable for your interpretation of them."

"Sir," said Bonvesin da Riva, "we will have no quarrels or disturbances at this supper. If you have differences with Walter and Eustace, you must settle them at another time and place."

"The combination of new wine and old bottles was never a fortunate one—for the bottles," said Sturla the Lawman. "The world moves and institutions change; some men change with them, some do not; but always the laggards are kicked into line. It was as inevitable that Christianity should come to the North as that feudalism should finally reach it. Of Christianity Olaf, in his time, had but the vaguest idea; but he was very sure of his royal rights, for feudalism had had time, since Harald Harfagr's day, to work and settle. It was not more unfortunate for Eindridi than it was for the North as a whole, that he attempted to impose the new religion with the feudal fist. In the end, even feudalism became christianized, and kings were believed to rule by divine right. It was this idea which later—rather than the mailed fist—taking root in the broken soil of civil dissension in my country, overcame the old Icelandic independence, to which my uncle Snorri has referred, and added the island to King Hákon's crown."

"What you say is, of course, historically true," said John Major. "However, it seems to me equally true that everywhere, from the beginning of the world, a free people, as Marsiglio has suggested, confers power on the first king, whose authority is derived from the whole community. But in the turmoil of circumstances over a period of centuries certain truths become obscured, covered over, as it were, by a kind of social and political slough. Thus, feudalism, in attempting to correct some errors, bred others. Feudalism rescued the man who had fallen into a pit, to be sure, but scratched and battered him considerably itself in the process."

"Just now," said Eustace to Sturla, "your eminent uncle said something about eluding the mailed fist at home. If the company please, I will tell you how I eluded it for many years, and at the same time wrought revenge for a miscarriage of justice."

"Tell on," said Langland.

62. HOW EUSTACE SOLD POTS

Monk Eustace

You must know that my father, Baldwin Busket, was treacherously killed by Hainfroid de Hersinguehans as the result of a quarrel over a lawsuit. In the trial by combat which followed my indictment of Hainfroid my champion, Manessier, was killed. That would seem to have proved that Hainfroid was innocent, but I declared to the count of Boulogne that I was unsatisfied with the verdict, and that I would myself avenge my father's death. But how could a simple monk hope to prevail against the codes of law and swords of steel? Well, I had wit on my side, and Nicholas Trivet and Thomas Walsingham could testify, if they would, that I gave the count sufficient reason to be sorry for not having done me justice for my father's murder. What I am about to tell you is only an incident in a long series of bad quarter hours which I gave the count of Boulogne.

One day the count was riding out to hunt when one of his spies informed him that I had been seen in the forest. That was good news to the count, for he desired nothing so much as to lay hands on me. Straightway he changed his clothes and led his company into the wood, where they laid ambush in a fosse. One of my men discovered them and informed me. Thereupon I sought out a charcoal-burner whose place of business was near by. I put on his soiled and rough clothes, smeared my face, neck and hands with charcoal dust so that I was well disguised. The burner's ass was ready laden for the market, and in the rôle of his master I drove him off toward Boulogne. I went quite openly past the count, who paid no more attention to me than to a clove of garlic, and did not even deign to pass the time of day. "My lords," said I, "what are you doing here?" "What business is it of yours?" asked the count. "By St Omer," I replied, "I will tell you my business: I am going to the count of Boulogne to lodge a complaint that Eustace's men treat me shamefully. I did not dare use my nag to carry these coals today for fear Eustace would seize it. Indeed, right now he is lying at his ease by a good fire, with plenty of roast venison to keep him company. He set fire to all my charcoal—which has cost me no end of trouble and labour."

At this the count pricked up his ears. "Is he near by?" he asked. "He is not far away," I answered. "If you wish to speak with him, follow this path here." Therewith I whacked up Roamer, and the count and his men went on into the wood. They found the charcoal-burner dressed in my clothes, and mistaking him for me, gave him a fearful beating. "Lords," cried the man, "mercy, for God's sake! Take these clothes, if you wish, for I have no other goods. As a matter of fact, even these clothes belong to Eustace, who is on his way to Boulogne this moment with my ass and charcoal, and wearing my hood."

"Sirs," said the count, "do you hear? By the teeth of God! By the living devil! He has duped me again. He was the burner who was just speaking to us. Quick, now, after him!"

The count and his men leaped to their horses and were off after me pell-mell. In the meantime I had washed my face and made myself somewhat more tidy. Coming in my direction was a potter crying his wares. I knew I should soon be followed, so I made a deal with the potter: For my ass and charcoal I exchanged jugs, pots and jars. I became a potter, and the potter became a charcoal-burner, the more fool he.

Now as I went along crying "Pots for sale!" the count came rushing out of the wood. "Have you seen anything of a charcoal-burner?" he asked me. "Lord," I answered, "I saw one with a laden ass on his way toward Boulogne." So the count and his men spurred on their horses, and soon overtook the quondam potter with his ass. They beat him shamefully, and gave him a hard drubbing. Then they tied his hands and feet and mounted him on a nag with his face toward the tail. The churl roared and howled: "My lords," said he, "for God's sake, have mercy on me! Why have you seized me? If I have harmed you in any way, I will do all I can to make amends."

"Ha! master rascal," screamed the count. "Ha! You think to escape by fair words, but you are vastly mistaken. It will not be long now till I hang you up by the neck."

But one of the count's knights looked more closely at the prisoner, and knew him well. "What the devil turned you into a charcoal-burner?" he asked. "You used to be a potter. No man can prosper who takes up so many trades."

"Sir," answered the fellow, "I cry you mercy. I traded my pots to a burner for his ass and a load of coals, may God curse him. It is his fault that I have got into these straits. I think he probably stole those wares. Even now he is going toward the woods crying 'Pots for sale! Pots!'"

Said the knight to the count: "Eustace knows plenty of tricks. A moment ago he was a charcoal-burner and now he is a potter." "So!" snarled the count. "By liver and lights! After him full speed! Bring me everybody you can find today and tomorrow." So they set the potter at liberty and hurried away into the forest.

Now I threw my pots into a bog, for I was heartily sick of carrying them, and climbed a tree to a kite's nest. When the count rode by I imitated the cry of a bird: "A-keel, a-keel, a-keel," I called.

"I'll kill him right enough, by St Richier," said the count, "if I can lay hands on him."

"Yoo-weel, yoo-weel," I shrilled.

"By God!" said the count, "I will indeed, if I can find him."

"A-dai, a-dai, a-dai," I piped.

"Right you are," said the count; "it is today I will kill him with my own hands, if I can lay hold on him."

After this the count went on with his hunt, firmly believing that the bird's cries had been a favourable omen for him.

During the day's search four monks were arrested and locked up; afterwards, four mercers and a broker, three poulterers and two ass-drivers were imprisoned, sixteen fishermen along with their fish; and these were joined later by four clerks and a parish priest. There were more than forty companions in the count's prison in the end.

Now when the count came to Neufchatel you may be sure there began a very curious process of law. I watched his movements closely and entered the city after him. For this occasion I was dressed as a woman, and I flatter myself that I made a very good-looking one. My hair was concealed by a caul, and over that was a delicate veil with gold threads in it. My gown was of stiff silk, falling to the feet and tightly gathered at the waist with a handsome girdle, while on my feet were a pair of embroidered velvet shoes. The distaff which I carried helped the impersonation.

The lawsuit interested me not so much as finding some opportunity for vexing the count. Soon I spied the sergeant who was taking care of his lord's horse. "Let me have a ride on him," I said to the sergeant, "and I'll do business with you later." "Right willingly," replied the man. "You may certainly have a ride on this fine ambling palfrey, my girl, and four sous to boot, if you will do business with me." "Certainly," I replied. "And I know something about horsemanship myself, and will teach you how to have a good seat right now." Therewith I swung up my leg with gusty exuberance such as has seldom been equalled. "Ha! my girl," said the squire, "you seem to be troubled with flatulence." "That's right, dear friend," I answered; "but pay it no heed; it is on account of this saddle."

Now the young man also mounted horse, and we trotted off side by side to the forest. Said he: "Let us not go farther now; I am riding my lord's horse, and you have his best palfrey. I shall get into trouble unless we hasten. Let's get to work now." "My lad," said I, "you are in too much of a hurry. All in good time will I teach you how to have a firm seat. Let us go a little farther so that no one may spy on us." "Sweet maid," answered the youth, "I hope you intend no trickery, for if you deceive me, by the bowels of St Mary! I'll have your life." "Dear friend," said I, "be not so suspicious. My dwelling is only a little way ahead." So, in his folly, he rode after me.

When I got to my people in the wood I seized the varlet by the neck, and then it dawned on him what a fool he had been. True is the proverb which says: "The goat scratches till he makes himself a poor bed."

"Get off the good horse now," I said; "you'll never attend him more. The palfrey is a good piece of horse-flesh, too, and the count will never ride him again." So, amid the laughter of my fellows, we dismounted. "Men," said I, "this varlet here must do his business, for I promised him he should." Therewith I led him off to a bog not far away. "Fellow," I said, "do not stand on ceremony now; off with your clothes, all of them, for I know you are keen to get to work." When the clothes were off, the youth went into the bog, for he had no other choice. "Now for the riding lesson," I said, "and take your time. Ride at full length, for if you do not, you shall be so beaten that you shall not be able to walk, either. You thought you could chaffer with me! Anyone who thinks he can have to do with a black monk ought to be ashamed of himself!"

Said the sergeant: "Sir, for God's sake, have mercy! Don't do me such shame. By Our Lady, I thought you were a girl. I assure you, I have never followed heretical practices in such matters as riding."

"Come out now," I said, "and be off with you; and tell the count from me how I have served you." "I will indeed, and forthwith," answered the lad. He hurried away, it is true, but dared not return to the count to deliver my message. For fear of what might happen to him at the count's hands he fled away into a strange district.

Such are several incidents in my long war against the count of Boulogne. As to the forty prisoners at Neufchatel—they were no worse for a few days' free lodging. Indeed, no one suffered save the count, and he almost burst a blood-vessel when he found that I was not among the catch in his net.

"The abuse of power is doubtless one of society's growing pains," reflected Sir Thomas Elyot.

"Decent and peace-loving men will endure a great deal of wrong from an evil overlord," said Thormod Kolbrunarskald, "in so far as his excesses do not touch their personal honour. When the lord begins to meddle with his subjects' wives and daughters, we may look for the end; for if Nature has imposed the tyrant on society, she also takes care to remove him."

"Again I concur," said John Major. "Just as the people first possessed the right to appoint the ruler, so the people may depose him for his offences. That should be done to kings which is most for the good of the commonwealth."

"Long ago," remarked John of Salisbury, "I pointed out that the king shall defend his people, not despoil them. The monarch has a sword for his people's enemies, and he who turns it upon his subjects is as much a fool as though he were to cut off his own hand or foot. Not only is it permitted to slay tyrants—it is a duty to put them out of the way as public enemies."

"Your salutary injunctions seem never to have come under the eye of King John," said Henry Knighton; "or if they did, he disregarded them. As you know, John was crowned at Westminster by

Hubert, archbishop of Canterbury, in the year 1199. In pride, egotism and prepotence there have been, indeed, kings who could equal him, but in the matter of luxury he left all others behind. The sight of a lovely lady, whether matron or maid, produced in him an effect resembling the symptoms of hectic fever, and he could get no rest until he had satisfied his lust. And if the deed was bad, John made it worse by sneering at the man he had wronged. Such injuries were the seed whence later sprang war and sedition.

"Now among the king's table companions was a brave knight and noble baron by the name of Eustace de Vescy, who was married to a very beautiful woman, chaste and modest. The king hungered for her beyond measure, but by reason of some hindrance or other, was never able to obtain his desire.

"One day when John and Eustace were sitting at table the king's glance rested on the knight's ring. He asked the loan of it, saying that he had a similar stone which he wished to have set in a similar style. Eustace readily gratified the king's seemingly innocent desire. Immediately John summoned a page, and despatched him to Eustace's wife with a message, ostensibly from her husband, to the effect that she should hurry to London if she wished to see him alive; the ring served as his credentials. When Eustace's lady saw the ring, she thought the message true, and made all haste to London. Arrived in the city it happened that while she was hurrying to her lord's house, she encountered him in the street. Eustace, greatly astonished, asked her what she was doing in London, whereupon the lady told him the whole story. 'Ha!' cried Eustace, 'you have been summoned to serve the king's pleasure. However, get some bawd or harlot, dress her up in your clothes, and let her go in to the king in your place.' As Eustace bade, so the lady did.

"One day later, when John and Eustace were talking together, the king could not forbear to boast of his evil deed. 'Your wife, O Eustace,' said he, 'is not only lovely by day, but particularly attractive in the silence of the night.' 'How do you know that, O king?' asked Eustace. 'Through personal experience,' answered John. 'It was not as you think,' replied the knight; 'it was not my wife with whom you lay, but with a filthy prostitute dressed up in her clothes.'

"On receiving this intelligence King John almost burst with rage, and he swore to have Eustace's head. But the knight escaped to the north country, where he was joined by other magnates whose honour King John had violated. That was the beginning of the internecine warfare which divided the kingdom against itself, and laid waste and desolate a once flourishing realm."

"A few moments ago," said Thormod Kolbrunarskald, "Hallfred

could find little to blame in the character of Earl Hákon Sigurdson save that he was an unbeliever. Perhaps the skald intentionally glossed over the earl's uxoriousness, for he himself was never conspicuously tender of husbands' feelings. But Hákon paid the price for his evil behaviour. There was one man, Brynjolf of Gaulardale, whom he could not overawe; and when Hákon forcibly wrested from him his beautiful and highly accomplished wife, Brynjolf roused the country-side against him, and he was hunted down like a wild dog. In the end Earl Hákon was stabbed in the neck by his thrall Kark, as they both lay hiding in a hole dug under the floor of a pigsty."

"Again I am bound to observe," said James Yonge, "that maladjustment frequently arises from an imperfect perception of values. The king or lord should realize that his subjects are his treasure whereby his realm is confirmed. Or they are like a garden of various trees, not a waste land bearing thorns without fruit. As long as the subjects live in content and prosperity, so long shall endure the defence of the kingdom and the regal power. Obviously, then, it behooves a king to govern well, and protect his people from wrongs, and help them in their need, rather than exploit them for his own selfish ends."

"Well," remarked Guicciardini, "your Earl Hákon and King John had an imperial model. It is related that in the time of the emperor Avitus there lived in the city of Trèves a certain man of senatorial rank named Lucius. He headed a political faction of his co-citizens, and was blessed with a very beautiful wife. Now Avitus, during a visit to the city, caught sight of her, and being lustful by nature, thought of a scheme whereby he might gratify his desire. He feigned himself sick, took to his bed, and commanded that all the senators' wives should come to see him. When Lucius' wife came to pay her respects, he forced her. The next morning, when Avitus met Lucius on the street he said: 'You have fine hot baths here [for Trèves has always been noted for its natural baths], and yet *you* wash with cold water.' The point of this taunt was not lost upon Lucius, and it so enraged him that he roused his party, and persuaded them to surrender the city to Avitus' enemies, the Franks."

"I remember," said Lorenzo Fongasso, "a similar case of prepotence. I doubt if King Fernando of Portugal ever heard of Avitus, but at all events, he had no need of that monarch's example."

63. KING FERNANDO AND THE WIFE OF LORENZO D'ACUNHA
Lorenzo Fongasso

After the departure of the Earl of Cambridge from Portugal there was great trouble in that kingdom, but thanks to God, things turned out well in the end. But if the Lord had not interfered, matters must have ended badly, and all from the fault of Don Fernando, our last king.

King Fernando fell desperately in love with the wife of one of his knights, called Lorenzo d'Acunha, and was so much enamoured that he would have her by force. The lady made the best defence she could, but at length he succeeded, and told her he would make her queen of Portugal. He had not given rein to his passion in order to lower, he said, but to exalt and marry her. "Ah, my lord," replied the lady, with tears and on her knees, "I beg Your Grace's pardon: I can never have the honour of being queen of Portugal, for you know, as well as all the world, that I have a husband to whom I have been married these five years." "Leonora," replied the king, "that shall not stand in the way. Since I have enjoyed you I will not have any other woman to wife, but I will have you divorced from your husband before I make you my bride."

The lady could not obtain any other answer from her royal lover, and related all that had passed to her husband. The knight, on hearing her story, became very melancholy, and bethought himself what was to be done. At first he resolved never to quit his wife; but later, suspecting that the king had evil designs on his person, he set out from Portugal towards Castile. In that kingdom he was well received by King Enrique, who gave him an appointment in his household.

King Fernando, to gratify his foolish passion, sent for the lady and her husband—but the knight had gone. Then he summoned the bishop of Coimbra, who was chancellor of the kingdom and of his council, and told him his intention of marrying Leonora d'Acunha. At first the bishop was silent, through fear, knowing the violence of the king's haughty temper; but at last he allowed himself to be persuaded by Fernando Audère, the king's bosom friend. The bishop united them and they lived together. Leonora was crowned queen of Portugal with as much pomp and magnificence as ever any queen of Portugal had been. And the king begot on her the Lady Beatrice, who became queen of Spain.

When Beatrice was only five years old Fernando summoned all the nobles, prelates and principal citizens of Lisbon and made them all swear obedience to her, and pledge themselves that they would acknowledge her as heiress of the kingdom after his decease. Many were reluctant to take his oath, for they knew that Beatrice was a bastard, born in adultery, and that the husband of her mother, Don Lorenzo, was alive and residing in Castile. Later, as you know, Beatrice was married to Juan, son of the king of Castile.

When King Fernando died in 1383, the people of Lisbon, in conjunction with the citizens of Coimbra, Oporto and Ourique sent for Don João, the illegitimate half-brother of Fernando, and said to him: "Master of Avis, we will make you our king. Although you be a bastard, we think the Lady Beatrice, your niece and queen of Castile, is more of a bastard than you, for the husband of the Lady Leonora is now living. Since the crown is fallen between two bastards, we will choose the one who will be to our greatest advantage. We had rather give up all to you, that you may defend us, than have the Castilians as our masters."

Don João first assured himself that the nobles of the country were of a like mind with the citizens; then he acceded to this request, and immediately took steps to interfere with any plans which Fernando Audère might have for placing Beatrice and Juan of Castile on the throne of Portugal. Audère was sought and found in the palace of the queen, and there slain. Queen Leonora now retired from Lisbon and joined her daughter Beatrice in Castile, informing the Spanish court how matters stood in Portugal. King Juan I at once made preparations to contest the right of Don João and enforce his own by arms.

Lorenzo d'Acunha, hearing that his wife had arrived in Castile, waited on some of the king's council—by whom he was beloved—and asked their advice. "My lords," said he, "have I any means of obtaining possession of my wife, who is now in Seville? I know that King Fernando took her by force and against her inclinations. Now that he is dead, I ought, in justice, to have her back. Tell me, then, how should I act?" "Lorenzo," replied the lords, "there is not any chance of your ever having her again, for you would risk too much and debase the honour of the lady, as well as that of her daughter, now queen of Castile, and publish her bastardy. Take care not to muddle more by your claims what is already muddled enough, for you will be put to death if you persevere." "What had I best do, then?" asked Lorenzo. "The best way for you to act is to set out instantly for your estate in Portugal," they answered, "and leave the Lady Leonora with her daughter. We see no other means of safety for you."

After this conversation Lorenzo packed up his things and rode off to Portugal. Arrived there, he offered his services to King João. The king was rejoiced at this, restored to him all his property, and made him governor of Lisbon.

Now Juan I of Castile sat down with his army before Lisbon, swearing that he would take the city by fair means or foul. And if he made prisoners of any of the Portuguese in the skirmishes that took place from day to day, he had their eyes torn out, their arms, legs, or other members cut off, and in such maimed state sent them back to the city. But in the course of the year God sent to his camp a pestilence of such virulence that men died while they were talking one to the other, and King Juan was forced to raise the siege and retreat.

And what happened to Lorenzo? His fate constituted one of the sadder aspects of the siege. One day he sallied forth beyond the barriers, accompanied by many gallant friends who, with him, performed many excellent deeds of arms. But in the course of the fray Lorenzo was struck with a dart that passed through his plates, his coat of mail and jacket, though it was padded with silk, and his whole body, so that he was felled to the ground. The skirmish ceased on account of his death.

And thus the Lady Leonora, in one year, was made a widow of both her husbands.

There was silence for a moment or two when the knight had finished his tale. Bernardo del Carpio shifted uneasily in his seat. Finally—"When the world was younger," he said, "it was cleaner, or at least more virile. I hardly know how to express my amazement at the conduct of both Leonora and her husband. What kind of men and women did you breed in the fourteenth century? Had they no blood in their veins? Was failure of nerve a widely spread debility in your age? It was otherwise in the days of Count Julian."

"It was indeed," agreed the Bachelor of Salamanca with a melancholy sigh.

"What was different?" inquired Peter Bell.

"The conception of honour and the courage to protect it," answered Bernardo. "I would tell you about Count Julian and his daughter, but I am neither poet nor historian; yonder sits a countryman of mine who is both."

"I will tell the story," said Pedro Lopez de Ayala.

64. FLORINDA

Pedro Lopez de Ayala

The circumstances of the tragic story which Bernardo has called to mind took place in the reign of Don Roderic, son of Theodofred, son of King Chindaswinth. On the death of King Witiza in 710 the magnates of Spain raised Roderic to the throne. He was a warlike and courageous man, and able in the discharge of his regal duties, yet harsh, and in his morals and manner of life not dissimilar to Witiza, the worst of the Gothic kings.

At this time there dwelt across the strait—later named Gibraltar—a nobleman called Count Julian by the Spaniards, and Ilyán by the Arabs. He was governor of Tangier and Ceuta in territory which marched with that of the Moslems on the east. And though his sympathies lay rather with Eba and Sifebut, the exiled sons of Witiza—for he had married Frandina, Witiza's sister—nevertheless, he loyally performed the duties which he owed to the grandson of Chindaswinth.

According to the Arabian chronicler Abú Ja'far Ibn Abdi-l-hakk Al-Khazraji Al-Kortobi, it was the custom of the Spanish nobles to visit the court of their sovereign at Toledo once a year in the month of August, bringing him such gifts as their domains afforded. Julian, or Ilyán, brought to Roderic, as he had brought to Witiza, hounds and horses, and particularly hunting falcons, whereof the new king was passionately fond.

It was also the custom, as Al-Khozeyní says, for the princes of royal blood, the great noblemen of the kingdom, and the governors of provinces, to send to the high court at Toledo such among their sons as they chose to be promoted and advanced, and at the same time distinguished by the favour of their sovereign, under whose eye they were trained to all military exercises, and were afterwards appointed to commands in the army. In like manner their daughters were sent to the king's palace, and educated with his daughters; and when grown up, the king would marry them to the young noblemen at his court, according to their fathers' dignity, and bestow upon them marriage portions.

It happened that Ilyán, the lord of Ceuta and Tangier, had a young and beautiful daughter named Florinda, and in observation of the aforesaid custom he crossed the strait and took her to the king's court at Toledo. Ilyán's daughter being extremely handsome, the eye of Roderic—or as the Arabs called him, Ludherik—rested on her, and he became deeply enamoured. In such situations to feel was to act; but on this occasion, failing in persuasion, he obtained by force the gratification of his desire. Afterwards he ordered that the act should be kept a secret, and that the girl should be hindered from speaking to anyone lest she communicate with her father and acquaint him with what had transpired. But notwithstanding these precautions, Florinda contrived to inform her father of her situation: She sent him a splendid present, including among the articles composing it a rotten egg.

No sooner did Ilyán see this token than he understood its purport. It is said that he fell into a most violent rage, exclaiming: "By the faith of the Messiah! I will undermine the throne of this king, and disturb his dominions until the whole kingdom is overthrown and annihilated!"

Ilyán crossed over to Spain at once and repaired to Toledo, though out of the time fixed for his presence there, for it was the month of January. When Roderic saw the count come so unexpectedly he said: "O Ilyán, what ails you to come at this season of the year, in the depth of winter?" "My lord," answered Ilyán, "I come to fetch my daughter, for her mother is very ill, and I fear her death; and my wife has expressed a strong desire to see our daughter that she may console her in her last moments." He then asked Roderic to issue orders that his daughter should be delivered to him, and all her baggage prepared for immediate departure. The king granted his request, though not without having previously made Florinda promise that she would not betray their intercourse to her father.

They say, on the authority of Ilyán himself, that when about to take leave of the king the latter addressed him thus: "O Ilyán, I hope that I shall soon hear from you, and that you will endeavour to procure for me some of those very swift *shadhankah* [hawks] which are a source of such pleasure and amusement to me." To this Ilyán answered: "Doubt not, O king, but that I shall soon be back, and by the faith of the Messiah! I shall never feel satisfied until I bring you such *shadhankah* as you have never seen in your life." By this he meant the Arabs, whom he already thought of bringing against his country. But Roderic did not understand the significance of his words.

Thereupon Count Julian took his daughter and returned without loss of time to the seat of his government. No sooner had he arrived there than he repaired to Eastern Africa and entered Kairwan, where the Amir Musa Ibn Nosseyr was residing at the time. To this Musa Julian or Ilyán came to offer his services. He told him what had happened to his daughter, and anxious to avenge the outrage on his enemy, proposed to him to make the conquest of Spain, an undertaking which he represented to Musa as being of very easy execution. He described Spain—or Andalúsia, as it was then called—as an extensive kingdom filled with treasures of all kinds, whose inhabitants would make very handsome slaves, a country abounding in springs, gardens, rivers, and a land yielding every description of fruit and plants.

Musa, who was endowed with much penetration and wit, and who had great experience in all the affairs of war, said to the count: "We do not doubt that you are telling the truth, but we fear for the Moslems on account of the dangers they may encounter. You wish them to invade a country with which they are not in the least acquainted, and from which they are separated by an intervening sea. You, however, are of the Christian faith, and on easy terms with the people. Return, therefore, to your government, call together your vassals and partisans, cross the strait and in person make an incursion into the territory of that king. When you have done this, and have begun hostilities, then it will be time to follow in your steps, if it please Allah."

Ilyán agreed to these conditions. Returning to his government he assembled his men and crossed the water in two vessels. He landed at Jeziratu-l-Khadhra, whence he made forays into the land, burning the houses and the fields, killing, taking captives and collecting considerable spoil; after which he and his companions returned safe to Africa, their hands filled with booty.

The news of this success soon spread over every district of North Africa, with the result that about three thousand Berbers, under the command of Abu Zar'ah Tarif Ibn Malik Al-Mu'awi crossed the sea and landed on an island ever since called the island of Tarif from the name of their general. Like their predecessors, the Berbers under Tarif spread over the neighbouring country, reiving, killing and taking prisoners. They also returned safe to their land.

Now Ilyán went a second time to Musa, acquainting him with the success of both enterprises, and urging him to make the conquest of Andalusia. This time Musa sent for his freedman Tarik Ibn Zeyad and gave him the command of twelve thousand men, Arabs and Berbers. He ordered Tarik to cross the strait and invade Andalusia, bidding Ilyán accompany the expedition with his own troops.

Tarik left Africa in merchant vessels which Ilyán procured for him, and cast anchor close to a mountain, which received his name, and has ever since been called Jebal-Tarik, the Mountain of Tarik. Thereupon he set fire to the vessels which had conveyed him to Spain, saying to his men: "You must either fight or die." He then pressed inland and ravaged the country as far as Cordova. This was in the beginning of October in the year 711.

When the news of Tarik's invasion reached King Roderic, that monarch issued forth to meet him at the head of one hundred thousand cavalry, bringing his treasures as well as his wardrobe in wagons. He himself entered the field in a litter borne by three white mules; a vaulted canopy sprinkled with pearls, rubies and the richest jewels was spread over him to screen him from the rays of the sun; he was dressed in a robe made of strings of pearls interwoven with silk. Following him were long trains of mules whose only burden was ropes to pinion the arms of the captives, for he doubted not that every Arab would soon be his prisoner.

King Roderic marched his army to Cordova with the intention of attacking Tarik. On his approach he chose from among the men of his host a soldier of tried courage, and experienced in the stratagems of war. Him he commanded to go, under some pretext, to Tarik's camp, and observe all the movements of the Arabs so that he might report to him on their numbers, appearance and general circumstances. The man did as he had been ordered. But Tarik, informed of his presence, put into practice the following stratagem to overawe his enemies. He ordered the flesh of those fallen in battle to be cut into small pieces and dressed as though it were to be served for the soldiers' mess. Accordingly the corpses of the slain were cut up and cooked in large cauldrons. When Roderic's messenger saw these preparations he doubted not but that the Moslems fed upon dead human bodies. However, Tarik caused the human flesh to be secretly removed and buried during the night, and beef and mutton dressed in its stead; and when, in the morning, the soldiers were summoned to partake of their repast, Roderic's messenger was also invited to share it, and he ate along with them. On returning to his master he said: "Your kingdom has been invaded by a nation of people who feed upon the flesh of the slain. They have set fire to their vessels and seem determined to conquer or to perish."

This news filled Roderic and his men with utter consternation. However, the contest had now become inevitable, and both armies came to an engagement on a Sunday. The Moslems sustained the fight with great courage in spite of the overwhelming numerical superiority of their opponents. They charged desperately and immediately upon the Christians, whom God was pleased to put to flight. As their first ranks gave way they were closely pursued by the Arabs, who dealt death among their scattered bands and made prisoners in great numbers. Roderic's camp, too, was completely plundered, and the Moslems spread right and left over the country. Everywhere they gained considerable spoils, one fifth of which Tarik religiously set aside for the royal coffers.

What became of Roderic nobody knows. Some say that while fleeing from his pursuers he contrived to hide himself among the bushes on the banks of the river Guadayra, but that later, seeking to push on, he fell into a marsh and was drowned.

"In my turn," spoke up William Cecil, "I must express astonishment that Count Julian should sacrifice his country to his sense of personal wrong, and that you, sir, should seem to take pride in relating a tale of treason."

"I should, as you suggest, be ashamed," answered Pedro Lopez, "were there nothing more in the affair than that. But in the perspective of Time we are allowed to see that while the Goths lost their country, they acquired civility, and in the end a *Spanish* people regained a land more valuable than that from which they had been evicted."

"I am surprised, too," said Camden, "that you should put any faith in what the best historians condemn as a mere fable."

"It would doubtless be presumptuous in me," said the Bachelor of Salamanca, "to enter the lists with historians good or bad, yet I am perfectly willing that the Moslems themselves should do so.—On the wall of a palace of Hamra in Syria is a painting. In the foreground to the right may be seen the naked figure of a woman emerging from the hammam; to the left is portrayed the figure of a prince, and underneath, in Greek letters—for the Moslems referred to all foreigners as Griegos—is the legend: Roderikos. The painting is doubtless intended to represent the occasion of Roderic's first sight of the fair Florinda."

"For my part," said Bandello, "I should like to repudiate Bernardo's suggestion that something other than red blood runs in the veins of men who have lived subsequent to the ninth century, and that moderns are incapable of avenging an affront to the honour of themselves or their women."

65. BUONDELMONTE DE' BUONDELMONTI FALLS INTO A TRAP

Matteo Bandello

Among the noble and powerful families of the city of Florence there were two most powerful by virtue of their wealth and the number of their adherents, and of great esteem among the people, to wit, the Uberti and the Buondelmonti. In second place flourished the Amidei and the Donati.

Now there was a gentlewoman of the Donati family, a rich widow, who had a daughter of marriageable age. Her mother, observing that she was handsome, and having educated her with care, began to take thought about finding her a husband. She brought to mind the persons of many noble and rich young men who pleased her, but Messer Buondelmonte de' Buondelmonti, a splendid and honoured gentleman, rich and young, and head of the Buondelmonte family, pleased her more than any. So she made up her mind to bestow her daughter on him. But either because she thought she had plenty of time, since both the gentleman and the girl were still young, or through negligence, or for some other reason, she deferred the matter from day to day.

Now while the widow delayed, thinking that there was no need for haste, behold, a gentleman of the Amidei family entered into an agreement to give Messer Buondelmonte his daughter to wife. The business was exploited on one side and the other in such wise that the Amidei girl, the dowry being satisfactory, was betrothed to Messer Buondelmonte.

The news of this noble marriage was soon bruited from one end of the city to the other, and the father of the betrothed girl set about making arrangements for the nuptials. But when the Donati widow heard the news, seeing that her design had come to naught, she was much vexed and chagrined. She considered whether there might not still be some means of interrupting the Buondelmonte-Amidei alliance. And when she had cudgelled her brain for a while and could think of nothing else, she decided to try whether or not her daughter's beauty—for the girl was one of the handsomest in Florence—might ensnare the youth. She had observed that Messer Buondelmonte, with no other company than his servants, was accustomed to pass through the street wherein her house was situated. So, one day, she came down to the first floor, her daughter following her, and stood in the doorway. As the young man was passing near her she approached him with smiling countenance and said: "Messer Buondelmonte, I rejoice with you in your approaching happiness, and I congratulate you on your betrothal; may God give you every joy. Nevertheless, it is true that I was keeping this only daughter of mine for you alone." And so saying she drew the girl forward by the hand so that the young man got a look look at her. When he had beheld the rare beauty and the graceful bearing of the young girl, he immediately fell in love with her. Forgetting the faith he had pledged to the Amidei, and the contract already legally executed, nor considering the fearful insult it would be to break off the alliance, nor the discords which might arise by repudiating his affianced bride—vanquished by his desire, and the appetite he had to enjoy this new beauty, no less inferior by blood or wealth to the other, he stammered out a reply to the widow: "Madonna, since you say you have been reserving your daughter for me, I should be the worst of ingrates to refuse her, inasmuch as there is still time to do your pleasure. I will return tomorrow after dinner, when we will talk about this at our convenience."

The good widow was most happy at this turn of the matter. Buondelmonte, taking leave of her and her daughter, went about his business; but that night the cavalier thought so much about the beautiful girl he had seen that every hour seemed to him a year till he could possess her. He determined to waste no time, but to celebrate the nuptials on the morrow. And even though reason urged him that this was most ill done, and unworthy of so honourable a gentleman as he was supposed to be, yet was he so poisoned by a brief glance from the girl's beautiful eyes, and so inflamed and consumed by the subtile fire of love for her that on the morning he went straightway to the widow's house, and that very day celebrated that inauspicious union.

When news of this untimely and hurried marriage was circulated through the city it was the opinion of most that Buondelmonte had acted like a fool, and everyone censured him. But above all, and much more than any were the Amidei bitterly outraged; and the Uberti, allied to them by family ties, were also fearfully incensed. They convened, with other friends and relatives of theirs who were similarly aroused to ire against Buondelmonte, and they decided that that injury and manifest shame was not to be endured in any manner whatsoever, and that such an infamous blot could not be washed away save by the blood itself of him who had despised their kinship. Some there were who, reflecting upon the evils which might arise, were not willing to proceed at such a headlong pace, and counselled that the circumstances be maturely considered. But among those present was Mosca Lamberti, a man exceedingly bold and ready of his hand. He said that those who advised this means and that ended only in adopting none, adding the common proverb: "Cosa fatta capo ha." In a word, the upshot of the family council was that vengeance could not be had without bloodshed, and the task of assassinating Messer Buondelmonte was assigned to Mosca, Stiatta Uberti, Lambertuccio degli Amidei, and Uderigo Fifanti, valorous and spirited youths of most noble parentage.

These young men took what measures were necessary to put such a homicide into effect, and began to spy upon the comings and goings of the cavalier in order to determine whether or not they might fall upon him at unawares, so that he should not escape them. By the time they had as much information as they needed it was Holy Week, and not wishing to delay the deed longer, they decided that they would consecrate Easter Sunday with the blood of the traitor.

On the night preceding Easter the conspirators lay in ambush in one of the Amidei houses situated between the Ponte Vecchio and Santo Stefano, and stood in readiness on Easter morning for Messer Buondelmonte to pass that way, as was his custom. He, thinking perhaps that it was an easy thing to forget such an injury as breaking off an important contract, and considering that the Amidei had no reason to take umbrage at the offence, rode out early on Easter morning on a beautiful white palfrey. He passed by the house I mentioned, intending to cross the river. There the conspirators fell upon him and cast him down from his horse at the foot of the bridge under a statue of Mars, dead from numerous fearful wounds.

At the beginning of Bandello's narrative Niccolò Machiavelli had interrupted his conversation with Polydore Vergil and John Leland to listen attentively. Now he said:

"Ser Matteo, you have told a better story than I, though it must be confessed that my mind was on other matters at that particular point of my *Florentine Histories*. Perhaps I may at this time be allowed to add that the homicide of which you have given an account was the source whence sprang the Guelf and Ghibelline factions and the warfare between them. In the end that strife caused the ruin of many splendid palaces, and the downfall, through exile and bloodshed, of many noble families.—But I have given up history this long while, and will not bore you either with details of the struggle, nor with moralizings upon it. Besides, the subject may be disagreeable to some of the guests present, such as Doctor Lanfranc."

"I am not equally forbearing," said Sir John Fortescue, "for, with reference to the tale told a moment ago, I am bound to say that in my opinion Lorenzo d'Acunha and his wife were the victims of that feudal system upon which the eminent Scots historian has already commented. Among other ills which it fostered was the *droit du seigneur*. Only on such a road could King Fernando have walked so confidently and so boldly into another man's home and life."

"I think," said Froissart, "that you perhaps exaggerate. Crime depends upon character as well as opportunity, whether under the feudal or the monarchical system. Your own Edward III tried a similar démarche, but got little forward—if you will listen to my tale."

66. KING EDWARD III RECKONS WITHOUT HIS HOSTESS

Jean Froissart

When King David of Scotland had sacked and burned Durham he was advised to beat a retreat, for he had gained so much booty that the horses could hardly go with the burden of it. On his return he camped not far from Wark Castle, and next morning continued on his way; but Sir William Montacute, its châtelain, fell upon his rear-guard, plundered the pack-train, and killed upwards of two hundred men. This so enraged him that he turned back and laid siege to Wark.

The castle belonged to the Earl of Salisbury. At this time he was not present, for he had been taken prisoner near Lisle, and now lay in the Châtelet at Paris. For his many deeds of valour and for the many services which he had received from him, King Edward gave him this castle as a wedding gift. Catherine, Countess of Salisbury, was considered one of the most beautiful and virtuous women in England.

King David attacked the castle so stoutly that the defenders deemed it advisable to hasten the assistance of King Edward. Sir William Montacute got out under cover of rain and darkness and found the king at Chertsey. When David learned that the English king was approaching in force, he yielded to the advice of his chieftains, raised the siege and marched for Jedworth Forest. On the very same day Edward and his whole army arrived before Wark about noon, and took up his position on the ground which the Scots had occupied. Learning that they had returned home, he was much enraged, for he had come there with so much speed that both his soldiers and their horses were sadly fatigued. However, he ordered his men to take up their quarters where they were, for he wished to go to the castle to visit the noble dame within, whom he had not seen since her marriage.

As soon as he was disarmed, taking ten or twelve knights with him, King Edward proceeded to the castle to salute the Countess of Salisbury, to examine what damage the attacks of the Scots had done, and note the manner in which those within had defended themselves. The moment the countess heard of the king's approach, she ordered all the gates to be thrown open and herself went out to meet him, so richly attired that no one could look at her but with wonder and admiration at her noble deportment, great beauty and gracious behaviour. Drawing near the king, she made her reverence to the ground and gave him her thanks for coming to her assistance; then she conducted him to the castle to entertain and honour him, as she was very well able to do. Everyone was delighted with the countess. As for the king, he could not take his eyes off her, for he thought that he had never before seen so beautiful and spirited a lady, and it seemed to him that nowhere in the whole world was there any other lady so worthy of being loved.

Thus they entered the castle hand in hand. The countess led him first into the hall, and then to a richly furnished chamber set apart for his use. But during all this time the king kept his eyes so continuously upon her that the gentle dame was quite abashed.

After Edward had sufficiently examined his apartment he retired to a window, and leaning upon it, fell into a profound reverie. The countess went to entertain the other knights and squires, ordered dinner to be made ready, the tables to be set, and the hall adorned and dressed out. When she had given all the necessary orders, she returned with a cheerful countenance to the king, whom she found still musing, and said to him: "Dear sir, what are you thinking about so seriously? So much meditation does not beseem you, saving Your Grace. You ought rather to be in high spirits for having driven your enemies before you, and should leave the trouble of thinking to others." "Dear lady," answered the king, "you must know that since entering this castle there has come to me such an extraordinary idea that it behoves me to reflect upon it. I do not know what the conclusion may be, so I have to give it my whole attention." "Dear sir," replied the countess, "you should be of good cheer, and feast with your friends, to increase their pleasure by your presence, and leave off thinking and meditating, for God has been very bountiful to you in all your undertakings, and has shown you so much favour that you are the most feared and renowned prince in Christendom. If it is about the Scots that you are thinking, reflect that you can make yourself amends for the damage they have done you at your pleasure, as you have done before. Therefore, if it please you, come into the hall to your knights, for dinner will soon be ready." "Dear Lady," replied Edward, "other things than what you think of touch my heart and lie there. I tell you truly that the perfections and beauties of your person have taken me by surprise, and have so impressed my heart that my happiness depends on receiving from you a return to my flame, which no denial can ever extinguish." "Sweet sir," said the countess, "you ought not to amuse yourself by laughing at or tempting me, for I cannot believe you mean what you have just said; it is quite unthinkable that so noble and gallant a prince as you are would ever intend dishonour to me or my husband, who is so valiant a knight, who has served you so faithfully, and who now, in your quarrel, lies in prison. Certainly, sir, such intention would not add to your glory, nor would success be of any advantage to you. So far as I am concerned, no such thought has ever entered my mind, and I trust in God it never will, for any man living. And if I were to prove complaisant in this matter, it is you who ought to blame me, and, in strict justice, have my body punished."

The virtuous lady then quitted the king, who was quite astonished, and went to the hall to hasten dinner. Afterwards, attended by the knights, she returned to the king and said: "Sir, come into the hall; your knights are waiting for you that they may wash their hands, for they, as well as yourself, have fasted too long." After washing, the king and his knights and their hostess seated themselves at the board. But Edward ate very little, remaining pensive the whole time, and glancing, whenever he had the opportunity, at the countess. His uneasy behaviour surprised his companions, for they had never seen the king like this before. They imagined that it was by reason of the Scots having escaped him.

During the whole day Edward remained at the castle without knowing what to do with himself. Sometimes he remonstrated with himself that honour and loyalty forbade him to admit such treason into his heart as to wish to shame so virtuous a lady and so gallant a knight as was her husband. At other moments his passion was so strong that considerations of honour and loyalty were driven from his thought. In this wise did he pass that day, and a sleepless night to boot, in debating the matter in his mind.

At daybreak, however, Edward rose, assembled his army, decamped and went in pursuit of the Scots, to drive them out of his kingdom. Upon taking leave of the countess he said: "Dear lady, God preserve you until I return; and I entreat that you will think well of what I have said, and have the goodness to give me a different answer." "Dear sir," replied Catherine, "may God, of His infinite goodness, preserve you and drive such churlish thoughts from your heart, for I am, and always shall be, ready to serve you consistently with my own honour and yours." The king left her quite abashed, and went with his army after the Scots, whom he proceeded to harry furiously near Jedworth Forest.

However, when Edward, after three days' skirmishing, was unable to draw the Scots into a definite engagement, he retired, and discreet men on both sides arranged a truce of two years between the two kings. One of the conditions of the truce was that in return for the Earl of Moray, whom the English had captured, the Scots king should effect the release of the Earl of Salisbury from French prison; and this was done.

Now Edward, though he was at war in Picardy, Normandy, Gascony, Poitou and Brittany, was unable to forget Countess Catherine. Love reminded him of her day and night, representing her beauties and lively behaviour in such bewitching lights that he could think of nothing else. Out of affection for the lady and his desire to see her the king ordered a great feast and tournament to be proclaimed, to be held in London the middle of August. He sent his proclamation to Hainault, Flanders, Brabant and France, promising passports to all knights and squires, from whatever country they might come, for their arrival and return. He commanded that all barons, lords, knights and squires of his own realm should be there without fail, if they had any love for him; and he expressly ordered the Earl of Salisbury to bring his wife, with as many young ladies as he could collect to attend her.

The earl very cheerfully complied with the king's request, for he thought nothing evil, and the good lady dared not say nay. She came, though unwillingly, for she guessed the reason which made the king so eager for her attendance, though she was afraid to discover it to her husband, imagining that by her conduct and conversation she might be able to divert the king's mind. The ladies and damsels were most superbly dressed and adorned, according to their different degrees, except the Countess of Salisbury, who came in attire as plain as might be. She did not intend that the king should spend too much time in admiring her, for she had neither wish nor inclination to obey him in anything evil that might be for her own or her husband's dishonour.

At this feast, which was very noble and magnificent, there were present great numbers of barons and knights of noble birth. The dancing and banqueting continued for fifteen days. Unfortunately, Lord John, eldest son of the baron Beaumont, was killed in the tournament.

"Regarding the further progress of King Edward's love affair," added Froissart, "I have no precise information. Scarcely had the entertainment broken up when the king received tidings that the Scots were keeping their truce but indifferently, and from France came news that, as the truce of Arras was near expiry, the French were making great preparations for war. Urgent state business may have caused him to relinquish his suit and pursuit. On the other hand, it is not impossible that the beauty of the lady's character, as well as the sensibility of his obligations to her husband, had aroused some feeble stirrings of decency in the king's heart. Whereas, in approaching Catherine—or any other beautiful lady—as he did, he acted only in conformity with the accepted conventions of his age, it must be remembered that the cultured prelate Richard of Bury, afterwards bishop of Durham, had been Edward's tutor as a prince; perhaps all his lessons had not fallen on fallow ground, for the third Edward had little of his father's character. In the founder of the Order of the Garter, too, we might expect to find a soil receptive to those seeds of gentlemanliness which Geoffrey Chaucer later discovered with amazement in Italy, and with which he was so delighted that he referred to them thereafter in and out of season. At all events, so far as I know, Catherine lived in peace from this time forward."

"The Countess of Salisbury," said John Major, "was doubtless sensible of the honour which King Edward wished to show her by a display of chivalric prowess; but I wonder if she was pleased by the death of the young Lord Beaumont? For the most part, I abhor this dangerous game of jousting with the spear merely for the sake of making a show; for anything is hateful which risks the lives of men without necessity. On the other hand, I say that those who thus come into conflict in the course of a war which is just, are not to blame; but if it be in time of peace, and merely for show, they are sorely to blame. And as to confession made before such encounters, that has something vulpine in it, for the intention is immediately thereafter to commit an unlawful deed. I do not, however, deny the right to joust with blunted spears for the sake of exercising the skill of the combatants, with all precaution taken against a mortal wound."

"Perhaps you would have approved," said Walter Haliday, "a tournament which I once witnessed in Middlesex; you might even have been amused by it. I preserved a record of the engagement so that my fame with posterity might be secure. It was like this...."

67. THE TOURNAMENT OF TOTENHAM

Walter Haliday

Of alle these kene conqueroures to carpe is oure kynde;
   Off fel feghtyng folke ferly we fynde,
The turnament of Totenham have I in mynde:
Hit were harme sich hardynesse were holdyn behynde,
     In story as we rede
       Off Hawkyn, of Harry,

THE TOURNAMENT OF TOTENHAM

  Off Tymkyn, of Tyrry,
  Off theym that were dughty
   And hardy in dede.

Hit befel in Totenham on a dere day,
  Ther was made a shurtyng be the hye way:
Thider come alle the men of that contray,
Off Hisselton, of Hygate, and of Hakenay.
  And alle the sweete swynkers:
   Ther hoppyd Hawkyn,
   Ther dawnsid Dawkyn,
   Ther trumpyd Tymkyn,
  And all were true drynkers.

Tille the day was gon and evesong paste,
  That thai shulde reckyn thaire skot and thaire counts caste:
Perkyn the potter in to the prees paste,
And seid: Rondill the refe, a doghter thou haste,
   Tibbe thi dere;
  Therefor fayne wete wolde I,
  Whether these felows or I,
  Or which of alle this bachelery,
Were the best worthy to wed her to his fere.

Upsterte the gadlyngs with thaire lang staves,
  And seid, Rondyll the refe, lo, this lad raves:
How prudly among us thy doghter he craves,
And we ar richer men then he, and more gode haves,
   Off catell and of corne:
  Then seid Perkyn: To Tibbe I have hyght
  That I will be alle wey redy in my right
  With a fleyle for to fyght this day seven nyght,
   And though hit were to morne.

Then seid Rondill the refe: Ever be he waryd,
  That aboute this carpyng lenger wolde be taryd;
I wolde not my doghter that she were myskaryd,
But at hir moost worship I wolde she were maryd:
   Therfor the turnament shalle begynne
  This day seven nyght,
  With a flayle for to fyght:
  And he that is moste of myght
   Shalle brok hir with wynne.

He that berys hym best in the turnament,
    He shal be grauntid the gre be the comyn assent,
Ffor to wynne my doghter with dughtynesse of dent,
And Coppull my brode hen that was broght out of Kent,
        And my donned cow;
      Ffor no spence will I spare,
      Ffor no catell wille I care,
      He shalle have my grey mare,
        And my spottyd sowe.

Ther was mony a bolde lad theire bodys to bede:
    Than thei toke theire leve, and hamwarde thei ghede:
And alle the weke afterward thei graythed her wede,
Tille hit come to the day that thei shulde do thaire dede.
      Thei armyd theym in mattes;
      Thei sett on theire nollys
      Gode blake bollys,
      Ffor to kepe theire pollis,
        From batteryng of battes.

Thei sewed hem in schepe skynnes, for thei shuld not brest:
    And ever ilkon of hem toke a blac hatte in stidde of a crest:
A baskett or a panyer before on thaire brest,
And a flayle in theire honde: for to fyght prest,
      Forth con thei fare:
      Ther was kid mycull fors,
      Who shulde best fend his cors:
      He that hade no gode hors,
        Borowyd hym a mare.

Sich a nother gadryng have I not sene ofte
    When alle the gret cumpany come ridand to the crofte:
Tibbe on a grey mare was sett upon lofte
Upon a secke full of fedyrs for she shuld sitt softe,
      And ledde tille the gappe:
      Fforther wold she not than
      For the luf of no man,
      Till Coppull hir brode hen
        Were broght into hir lappe.

A gay gyrdull Tibbe hade borowed for the nones,
    And a garland on hir hed full of ruell bones,
And a broch on hir brest full of saphre stones,

The holy rode tokynyng was writon for the nones:
    For no spendyng wolde they spare,
    When joly Jeynkyn wist hir thare,
    He gurde so fast his grey mare,
    That she lete a fowkyn fare
        At the rerewarde.

I make a vow, quod Tibbe, Coppull is comyn of kynde.
    I shalle falle fyve in the felde, and I my flayle fynde.
I make a vow, quod Hudde, I shalle not leve behynde,
May I mete with Lyarde or Bayarde the blynde,
    I wot I schalle theym greve.
    I make a vow, quod Haukyn.
    May I mete with Daukyn,
    Ffor alle his rich kyn,
        His flayle I shalle hym reve.

I make a vow, quod Gregge, Tib, thu shal se
    Which of alle the bachelery grauntid is the gre:
I shalle skomfet hem alle, for the luf of the:
In what place that I come thei shall have dout of me,
    Ffor I am armyd at the fole:
    In myn armys I ber well
    A dogh trogh, and a pele,
    A sadull with owt panele,
        With a flece of wole.

Now go down, quod Dudman, and here me het abowte,
    I make a vow thei shall abye that I fynde owte,
Have I twyse or thrise riden thrugh the rowte,
In what place that I come of me thei shal ha doute,
    Myn armys bene so clere,
    I bar a ridell and a rake,
    Poudurt with the brenyng drake,
    And thre cantels of a cake
        In ilke cornere.

I make a vow, quod Tirry, and swere be my crede,
    Saw thu never yong boy forther his body bede,
Ffor when thei fyght fastest and most er in drede,
I shalle take Tib be the hond, and away hir lede:
    Then byn myn armys best,
    I ber a pilch of ermyn,

   Poudert with a catt skyn,
   The chefe is of pechmyn,
    That stondis on the creste.

I make a vow, quod Dudman, and swere be the stra,
  Whil I am most mery thu gets hir not swa;
For she is wel shapyn, as light as a ra,
There is no capull in this myle before her wil ga:
    She wil me not begyle:
   I dare sothely say,
   She wil bere me a Monday
   Ffro Hissiltoun to Haknay,
    Noght other halfe myle.

I make a vow, quod Perkyn, thu carpis of cold rost,
  I wil wyrke wiselier with out any boost:
Ffyve of the best capuls that ar in this host,
I wil hem lede away be another coost.
    And then lowght Tibbe:
   We loo, boyes, here is he,
   That will fyght and not fle,
   Ffor I am in my iolyte—
    Loo forth Tibbe.

When thai had thaire othes made, forth can thei te,
  With flayles and harnys and trumpis made of tre:
Ther wer all the bachilers of that contre,
Thei were dight in aray as thaim self wolde be:
    Theire baner was ful bryght
   Off an olde raton fell,
   The chefe was of a ploo mell,
   And the schadow of a bell,
    Quartered with the mone light.

I wot it was no childer gamme when thei to geder mett,
  When ilke a freke in the felde on his felow bette,
And leid on stifly, for no thyng wold thei lett,
And foght ferly fast, til theyre hors swett,
    And few wordis were spokyn;
   Ther were flayles al to flaterde,
   Ther were scheldis al to claterde,
   Bolles and disshis al to baterde,
    And mony hedis ther were brokyn.

THE TOURNAMENT OF TOTENHAM

Ther was clenkyng of cart sadils and clateryng of cannes:
    Off fel frekis in the feeld brokyn were thaire fannes:
Off sum were the hedis brokyn, of sum the brayn pannes,
And evel were they besene er they went thannes:
        With swippyng of swipylles,
    The laddis were so wery forfoght,
    That thai myght fyght no more on loft,
    But creppid aboute in the crofte,
        As thei were crokid crypils.

Perkyn was so wery that he began to lowte:
    Helpe, Hudde, I am ded in this ilke rowte:
An hors for .xl. penys, a gode and a stoute,
That I may lightly cum of myn owe owte,
        Ffor no cost wil I spare,
    He stert up as a snayle,
    And hent a capull be the tayle,
    And raught of Daukyn his flayle,
        And wan hym a mare.

Perkyn wan fyve, and Hudde wan twa:
    Glad and blith thai were that thei had don sa:
Thai wolde have thaim to Tibbe, and present hir with tha:
The capuls were so wery that thei myght not ga,
        But stille can thei stonde.
    Alas, quod Hud, my ioye I lese;
    Me had lever then a ston of chese,
    That dere Tibbe had alle these,
        And wist hit were my sonde.

Perkyn turnyd him aboute in that ilke throng,
    He fought fresshly for he had rest hym long:
He was war of Tirry take Tib be the hond,
And wold haue lad hir away with a luf song:
        And Perkyn after ran
    And of his capull he hym drowe,
    And gaf hym of his flayle inowe:
    Then te he, quod Tib, and lowe,
        Ghe are a dughty man.

Thus thai tuggut and thei ruggut til hit was ny nyght:
    Alle the wyves of Tottenham come to se that sight,
To fech home thaire husbondis, that were thaym trouthe plight,
With wispys and kixes, that was a rich sight,

>   Her husbondis home to fech:
>   And sum they had in armys
>   That were febull wreches,
>   And sum on whelebarowes,
>   And sum on criches.

> They gedurt Perkyn aboute on every side,
>   And graunt hym ther the gre, the more was his pride:
> Tib and he with gret myrth hamward can ride,
> And were alnyght togedur til the morrow tide,
>   And to chirch they went:
>   So wel his nedis he hase spedde,
>   That dere Tibbe he shall wedde:
>   The chefe men that hir thider ledde
>   Were of the Turnament.

> To that rich fest come mony for the nonys:
>   Sum come hiphalt, and sum trippande thither on the stonys:
> Sum with a staffe in his honde, and sum too at onys:
> Of sum were the hedis brokyn, of sum the schulder bonys:
>   With sorow come they thidur.
>   Woo was Hawkyn, woo was Harry,
>   Woo was Tomkyn, woo was Terry,
>   And so was al the company,
>   But ghet thei come togeder.

> At that fest were thei servyd in a rich aray,
>   Every fyve and fyve had a cokeney,
> And so they sate in white al the long daye:
> Tibbe at nyght I trow hade a sympull aray:
>   Micull myrth was thaym among.
>   In euery corner of the howse
>   Was melodye deliciouse,
>   Ffor to here preciouse
>   Off six mennys song.

"After a tournament or a joust it was the custom, as you know, to hold a banquet, and my heroes were as punctilious in this matter as in their observance of the requirements of chivalry. Since you have heard the chronicle of the one, you must listen to the tale of the other."—

THE FEEST

Now of this feest telle I can,
I trow as wel as any man,
    Be est or be west,
Ffor over alle in ilke a schire
I am send for as a sire
    To ilke a gret fest.

Ffor in feith ther was on
Sich on saw I never non
    In Inglond ne in Fraunce:
Ffor ther hade I the maistry
Of alle maner of cucry,   [*cookery*
    Sith then was myschaunce.

Thar was meyts wel dight,
Wel sesoned to the right,
    Off rost and of sew:
Ther was meyts be heven
That were a maistre al to neven,   [*name*
    But sum I con yow.

Ther was pestels in poyra,
And laduls in rore,
    Ffor potage;
And somm saduls sewys,
And mashefatts in mortrewys,
    Ffor the leese off age.

Ther was plente of alle
To theym that were in halle,
    To lesse and to more,
There was gryndulstones in gravy,
And mylstones in mawmany,   [*hash*
    And al this was thore.

But ghet let thei for no costs,
Ffor in cum mylere posts
    iij in a disshe,
And bell clapurs in blawndisare, [*sauce of wine*
With a nobull cury,   *and spice*
    Ffor tho that ete no fish.

Ther come in jordans in jussall,   [*natural juice*
Als red as any russall,
   Come ther among:
And blobsterdis in white sorre   [*saffron*
Was of a nobull curry,
   With spicery strong.

Ther come chese crustis in charlett   [*flesh with*
As red as any scarlette,   *milk*
   With ruban in rise:
Certes of alle the festis
That ever I saw in gestis,
   This may ber the prise.

Ther was castrell in cambys,
And capulls in cullys,
   With blandamets indorde;   [*glazed with*
The nedur lippe of a larke   *egg yolks*
Was broght in a muk cart
   And set befor the lorde.

Then come in stedis of Spayne,
With the brute of Almayne,
   With palfrayes in paste:
And dongesteks in doralle   [*glazed with*
Was forsed wele with charcoll,   *almond milk*
   But certes that was waste.

Then come in the fruture,
With a nobul savoure,
   With feterloks fried:
And alle the cart wheles of Kent,
With stonys of the payment,
   Fful wel were thei tried.

Then come in a horse hed
In the stid of French brede,
   With alle the riche hide:
Now hade I not this seen,
Sum of ghow wold wene
   Fful lowde that I lyed.

Ther come in the kydde
Dressyd in a horse syde,

THE SECOND PRIEST'S TALE OF PEBLIS 331

>   That abyl was to lese:
> iij yron harows,
> And many whele barowes,
>   In the stid of new chese.
>
> When they had drawen the borde,
> Then seid Perkyn a worde
>   Hymself to avawnce:
> Syn we have made good chere,
> I red ilke man in fere
>   Goo dresse hym to a dawnce.
>
> Ther ghe myght se a mery sight,
> When thei were sammen knytte,
>   With-out any fayle;
> Thei did but run . . . ward,
> And ilke a man went bakward
>   Toppe over tayle.
>
>   *   *   *
>
> Off this fest can I no more,
> But certes thei made ham mery thore,
>   Whil the day wold last,
> Ghet myght thei not alle in fere
> Have eton the meytis I reckend here,
>   But theire bodys had brast.

"Your account," said Robert Mannyng, "proves abundantly the truth of my contention that tournaments are the forcing-bed of all vices."

"Not of all," spoke up Master Archebald. "James III, king of Scotland, who lived after your time, had several vices which owed nothing to jousts or tourneys. One was that, like Rehoboam, he followed the advice of young men, though he did not, like Solomon's son, lose the kingdom. Another vice of his will appear if you will listen to my tale."

68. THE SECOND PRIEST'S TALE OF PEBLIS

Master Archebald

Once upon a time there was a king, and also a queen, as many had been in the land before them. The king was fair of person, lusty and strong, a handsome man on foot, and no less handsome on horseback. However, his character was tainted with several faults:

He was fond of young counsel, and liked to have young men near him; indeed, young men were to him both clerk and priest. He favoured none who were mature, and still less those of age, nor those whose advice was wise and sober. He was always ready for sport and play.

It fell out now that a clerk of great learning arrived in Scotland from over sea, who took great pains to gain a position in the king's household. He perceived very clearly that no man could keep a place with the king unless he laid aside all seriousness; so, with wand and bells, particoloured coat and a pair of ass's ears he feigned himself a fool, and called himself Fictus. He could speak French, Dutch, Italian and false Latin.

This clerk went until he found the king at church. There he greeted him in French and other nonsensical language. "Come, now, sir king," said he, "either you with me or I with you." "By St Katherine," said the king, "this fool has many a wild flighty word. Come home with me, then; you shall have plenty to drink." "Grand mercy," said the fool with a laugh. "Now we shall be able to keep us from dulness and care," said the king, "as long as we have this fool with us."

Thus did the clerk feign himself a fool in word and deed: the wiser the man, the better he can jest. At last he was called the fool of fools, and he remained in close association with the king till he had become quite familiar with his habits and manners, and copied them to perfection.

Not long after this it happened that the king was to ride to a certain town for pleasure. The fool took his bauble and went on ahead, and with him were two or three runners. By the road-side they found a wounded man so sorely hurt that he could not move. When the fool asked the cause of his plight he said: "Reivers and thieves have done me mischief." Now the man's wounds were as full of flies as a nest is with bees. One of the runners, moved to pity, would have brushed the flies away, but the fool said to him: "Man, let them be, for now they are full and only sit; if you frighten them away, hungry ones will come in their place and suck his blood. The oftener the flies are disturbed, the oftener will others come." On this the wounded man said that he was not such a fool as he appeared to be.

Soon afterwards the king came up with mirth and song. In his hand he held a birch branch wherewith to keep the flies and midges away from his face, for it was the season when many were flying about. He too saw the wounded man by the road-side and rode up to him. "What makes you groan thus?" asked the monarch. Said the other: "I have been hurt by both thief and robber; and though all the pain is mine, the fault, sir king, is yours, for if you were in the habit of heeding good counsel, then you would root out reivers and thieves from your kingdom. But you are surrounded only by those who are good dancers and good singers, and you take no thought of your realm's misgovernance." At that moment the king waved his birch branch to drive away the flies. "Alas, sir king," said the man, "do not do that or you will kill me." "You astonish me," said his majesty; "what do you mean? You would soon be hale if the flies were driven away." Said the wounded man: "Your fool has more wit than you have; I could see well by his face that he has more sense than all your company. But my tongue is heavy and my body weak; ask your fool for an explanation, for I am at the point of death and can speak no more. Farewell."

The king moved on in a thoughtful mood, thinking how the country was mismanaged because of his vain and childish pastimes, and because of his predilection for green counsel. And while he was reflecting he wondered what kind of a man his fool might be, what the wounded man could see in him, and why he was wiser than all his suite.

When the king had arrived at his destination he sent for Fictus and gave him a cloth and trencher near his own table where he could observe him. He asked about the wounded man and why he had forbidden the flies to be driven away. Fictus replied as he had done to the runner on the other occasion. He also took this opportunity to point out that the king, with his continual succession of new servants and officers of court, was like the wounded man and the flies, with the result that the realm was sucked dry and the poor put under. "Listen to our fool," said the king. "It seems to me he must have been at school. I'll take my oath, you are not so foolish as you would have us believe." You may be sure that this was a disturbing speech for the king's courtiers who were sitting round about.

One time it happened that a gentleman slew another by accident. Through the intercession of a friend at court he was pardoned; whereupon he went home and killed another man. Again he paid his courtly friend very handsomely, and was again pardoned by the king. Six months later he slew a third man. When the king heard of this homicide he became very wroth, and swore that he would not pardon the murderer for all the gold in India, and if he did, he hoped God would put him out of His mind. The criminal fell to his knees and asked grace, but the king denied him. Then said

Fictus the fool, who was sitting near by: "If you do not hang or behead this man on account of his slayings it will be a great miscarriage of justice. It was he, indeed, who killed the first man, but it is you, Sire, who slew the other two. If you had punished him as he deserved at the beginning, the other two gentlemen would now be alive. You, as king, should be a bulwark and protection to your people, and at the day of doom you shall be held accountable for the manslaughters which have been perpetrated under your rule, just as bishops must answer for the soul that is lost through the fault of priest or preaching."

Said the king: "Woe is me! for I see that I am the fool of fools when I can be instructed by a fool. I will call a parliament of the three estates to consider the truth of Fictus' words." The parliament debated the matter and gave it as their opinion that Fictus' words were true and that he was a wise man. Thereafter the king made a law regarding homicide that was of great behoof for his subjects. From that time, too, he abandoned his light ways and comported himself more soberly.

But there was one folly which he did not forgo, and which had been subject-matter for evil tongues for a long time. There was a strangeness between him and the queen, so that he slept with her but seldom, and lay preferably in lemanry.

A little before Yule feast the king was stopping at the inn of a burgess in a certain town, the fool and five others in his company. The burgess had a daughter whom he loved as the apple of his eye, and indeed she was a bonny wench. The king frequently looked at her with lustful glances, and would fain have shared her bed. Now he knew there was no one in his suite as subtle as Fictus, so he called him privately and said: "Fictus, I am so smitten with love for this burgess maid that I would have her with me tonight at all costs, whether for gold, goods, wage or pledge." Said the fool: "I understand, and I will arrange the matter for you."

Later in the evening, when the company were engaged in their revels, Fictus approached the pretty girl and gave her a lecture on chastity, citing the examples of St Margaret and St Katherine. The girl replied that he was wasting his time, for she had no intention of living any other kind of life than a decent one. The king, however, thought that Fictus had been busy on his errand, and said: "What my fool says is no lie." "Sire," replied the maid, "his words were sufficient, and as he says, so will I do, if God permit."

The king's steward now called him to supper, but before he sat down he said to Fictus: "You see, she has consented; but one thing

I insist upon — no one shall come near her but myself, for she is young, and fears to get a bad name."

After supper Fictus took his way to the queen and said: "Madame, if you will do as I advise there will be neither shame nor harm in it." Then he told her about the king's expectations in connection with the burgess' daughter, adding that it was not his intention to help the king to sin. "But," said Fictus, "the king has given orders to admit us privily to his room when I come with the girl, and then I am to conduct her forth again before daybreak. Now, Madame, my counsel is this: Instead of the girl I will take you into the king with your head and face muffled up for greater precaution. If the deception be discovered, though he hang me, he will do you no harm. So be of good courage." "Sir," said the queen, "I agree to do as you suggest."

So, in the manner you have heard, the queen was stealthily introduced to the king's bed, and there she lay all night in his arms. The king thought no night had ever been so short, such great delight had he in that night's entertainment. A little before dawn the fool returned and took the lady away. In this fashion did the king pass three highly agreeable nights with his own queen, thinking always that his companion was the burgess' daughter. It was no wonder that the king was pleased, for the queen was fair and young. His majesty rewarded Fictus generously, and made him sit beside him on the same settle.

Now when Fictus saw how joyful the king was he said to him privily: "I would fain know, if I may, why it is you take such pleasure in lying with women of low degree, thus putting shame on your queen, who is both fair and good, and able to stand comparison with any other beauty whatsoever. Why have you this spite against her? What solace have you had these last three nights which you could not find with your own consort?" Replied the king: "I really cannot tell; I simply follow my whim. When my fancy falls on some woman or other, many courtiers come and tell me that I do well, reporting evil tales of the queen. The false chatterers put me out of tune, and since I am light-minded by nature, I lose any appetite I may have for the queen."

"Will you admit," answered Fictus, "that you have been well pleased these last three nights?" "Yea, that I grant," replied the sovereign. "Would to God that lady had been the queen!" "What will you give me," asked Fictus, "if I make her legally your wife within three days? If I cannot do so, my head shall be forfeit." "If you do that," answered the king, "you may have gold, lordships or land;

or if you choose to put off your fool's motley and be wise, you may have a bishopric. Here is my hand on it." "Raise your hand," said the fool, "and swear to this without reservation." The king swore to abide by his covenant. "Now," said Fictus, "it does not beseem a king to break his bond, and what I promised you is already done: she whose society you enjoyed these last nights is in very truth your own queen."

"By God! sir fool, I think you will have some trouble in making that good."

"My liege," answered Fictus, "be not wroth, especially after swearing such a binding oath. If the lady pleased you three nights, why should she not continue to do so? A moment ago you wished that person were your wife, and now you quarrel with me when I say that she is so."

"By Him who was borne in Yule!" cried the king, "you are an old scholar at the book. I wonder where you have found such a sophism as to be able to bind me with my own bond! However, I am well content, and heartily accept my own queen. And I swear by heaven that I will never do anything to displease her for odd or even, providing she can prove that she really was the lady who bore me company."

Without more ado the king betook himself to the queen's apartment. There he tested her by various sure tokens, and found that Fictus had told the truth. Then was he joyful indeed. He knelt down and asked forgiveness for his former wantonness and light behaviour. The queen forthwith forgave him whatever he had done in levity, for she understood that his folly had not been intentional.

Now both the king and queen gave thanks to God for the amendment of their fortune, and especially they thanked the fool who had brought about this concord between them. They pulled off his motley coat and put on him a flowing clerkly gown; when so dressed he did indeed seem to be a cunning clerk. Soon afterward a bishop's see fell vacant, and Fictus was appointed thereto. He remained very dear to the royal pair, and was always chief in their councils. Would to God that this example were followed by every king who does not love his queen!

When Master Archebald had finished his story the brief silence was broken by the suave tones of a gentleman sitting with Guicciardini and Marco Polo. "The argument," said Giovanni Boccaccio, "if there is any argument, seems to me to go astray. It is infinitely desirable for married men to keep within their own preserves, I grant you;

but in some cases marriage is but a *pis aller,* as St Paul says, and there are forces of Nature which are susceptible of no factitious control. I will illustrate by a story. Those of you who have been on crusades will doubtless recognize its elements, for it is well known that all stories were brought to Europe from India through the channel of the crusades. Who brought them to India I do not know, unless it was Alexander the Great, or Apollonius of Tyana. However . . ."

69. THE BOY IGNORANT OF WOMEN
Giovanni Boccaccio

In our city of Florence, a good while back, there lived a man, Filippo Balducci by name, a person of rather mean social station, but rich, and sufficiently adroit in such matters as pertained to his rank. He was married to a woman whom he loved exceedingly, and she him, so that they lived comfortably together, each giving heed only to those ways wherein one might please the other. But it happened to them as it happens to all, that the good lady passed from this life, leaving to Filippo no other memento of herself than a son, begotten by him, who at this time was two years old.

The death of his lady left Filippo as disconsolate as any man might be for the loss of a loved one, and perceiving that, deprived of that companionship which he loved so much, he was now left alone, he resolved to be no longer of this world, but to dedicate himself to God's service, and do the like with his little son. Then, bestowing his goods for the love of God, he betook himself without delay to Monte Asinaio, and with his son established his abode there in a little cell. There, living upon alms, he devoted himself to fasting and prayer. He took the most scrupulous care not to speak of any temporal matter in the boy's presence, nor let him see worldly things lest such lure him from ascetic service; rather did he talk with him on all occasions about God, the glory of eternal life, and the saints, teaching him nothing but pious prayers.

Thus Filippo kept his son for many years, never permitting him to leave the cell, nor showing him anyone but himself. But sometimes the good man would go to Florence, and being there provided with his needs by the friends of God, would return again to his hut. One day when the boy was about eighteen years old and Filippo was well on in years, it chanced that the youth asked him whither he went. Filippo told him, and the lad answered: "Father mine, you have grown old, and are ill able to endure fatigue; why do you not take me to Florence and acquaint me with your friends and the devotees of God so that afterwards I, who am young, may go to Florence for our needs, while you remain here?"

The good man, considering that his son was now grown up, and so habituated to God's service that worldly things would hardly be able to lure him away, said to himself: "This is sound advice." Wherefor, on the next occasion, he took his son with him to the city.

In Florence the youth, on seeing the palaces, the dwellings, the churches and all else wherewith the city abounds, marvelled greatly, and in his astonishment asked his father many questions as to how these things were named. Filippo told him, and when the youth was satisfied with one reply, he asked another question.

Thus, the boy questioning and the father replying, they came by chance upon a company of pretty and well-dressed young women who were returning from a couple of weddings. As soon as the young man saw them he asked what they were. "My son," replied his father, "lower your eyes and regard them not, for they are an ill thing." "Well," said the youth, "how are they called?" Filippo, in order not to waken any casual carnal desire in his son's mind, would not call them by their proper name, that is, "women," but said: "They are called geese." Whereupon, marvellous to relate, he who had never seen a woman showed no interest whatsoever in palaces, oxen, horses, asses, money or anything else he had seen, and now he said: "O father mine, I pray you, get me one of those geese." "Alas! my son," answered Filippo, "be still; they are an evil thing." "Are bad things made so?" asked the lad. "Yes," said Filippo. Then said his son: "I do not understand what you say, nor why those objects are bad; but so far as I am concerned, I have not yet seen anything which has seemed to me so beautiful or pleasing as these geese. They are far more beautiful than the painted angels which you have so often pointed out to me. Alas! if you have any regard for your son, contrive that we carry one of these geese back home with us, and I will give it something to eat." "That I will not," replied Filippo. "Little do you know what they feed upon!"

So he said, but he repented of having brought his son to Florence, for now he realized that Nature was stronger than all his wit.

"I am not sure," said the Goodman of Paris, "that I should subscribe to your thesis. Gentilesse, for those who have acquired it, imposes certain laws, or at least operates certain restraints of shame and remorse that may well serve to check all but the most violent and headstrong natures."

"In practice the Goodman is right," said Machiavelli. "The history of civilization might be written from a consideration of the tabus which society has from time to time thought fit to impose on its members. A moral, religious or political Solon, like a magician, plucks a *nescio quid* out of the void, labels it a misdemeanour and sternly says: 'That is a sin—you must not do that!' Viewed under one light he is a baneful nuisance in imposing burden after useless burden upon mankind; viewed under another, he is a benefactor to the race, since by making a man sinful he gives him an opportunity to cleanse himself by confession and repentance. But it is really rather a grotesque comedy."

"Sir," said John Capgrave, "you go too fast for me."

"I will illustrate," answered the historian. "Here is Gaucelm Faidit, clear-eyed, rosy-cheeked, *en bon point,* with unfurrowed brow betraying a mind at rest—in other words, a normal healthy animal. Along comes a physician, say, John of Gaddesden—unless we must adhere strictly to the truth. He sees Gaucelm in passing; he turns back and looks at him sharply and shakes his head in a mournful manner, so that Gaucelm, whose attention is attracted by this mummery, inquiries his business. 'Ah, my friend,' says Gaddesden with a sigh, 'it is lucky you met me.' 'How so?' asks Gaucelm. 'Because I am going to do you a great service and cure you.' 'Cure me! Cure me of what?' 'Is it possible you don't know you are a sick man?' asks Gaddesden. 'Nonsense; I never felt better than at this moment.' 'Nevertheless, your eye is bright with fever, and you have a hectic flush. Is not your spittle sometimes thick, sometimes thin?' 'I never noticed,' replies Gaucelm. 'Do you never feel pains in the back of your legs?' 'Never,' says Gaucelm. 'But you belch after meals, do you not?' 'Of course,' answers the victim, who is a hearty eater and has always considered belching quite normal. At this Gaddesden gravely shakes his head, and finding he is on the right track, pursues it. 'And I daresay you have frequent rumblings of the wamb?' 'That is true,' says the poet, who is fond of cassoulet and black puddings.—And so it goes till the doctor has convinced him that he is a very sick man, and that nothing can save him from almost immediate dissolution save treatment by himself, which treatment will earn the doctor not only a pretty penny, but Gaucelm's undying gratitude. And so it is with the Solons I just mentioned. In order to cure a man, they first make him sick. Also, if there were no rules, there would be no breaking of rules."

During this speech Gaddesden had been fidgeting about on his bench and now he would have said something, but William of Wykeham was too quick for him.

"Sir," said the prelate, "you astound me. Whatever has put such ideas into your head?"

"Oh, various things," returned the Florentine, "but principally watching my farmer break up the ground at my villa with a team of oxen: The straining, sweating, goaded, bellowing ox with the fearful, heavy, wooden yoke upon his neck seems to me to resemble nothing so much as civilized man."

"Discipline and restraint," said Sir John Fortescue, "are necessary to man; such is his nature that we cannot get along without rules."

"I daresay you are right," answered Machiavelli; "and yet, was it not you who just a moment ago cavilled at the restraints of feudalism?"

"You must be mad," said Lord Burleigh; "with one hand you brush away the entire political system . . ."

"And with the other the Church," added Wykeham.

"And with both feet he kicks over the dignity and sanctity of the home and family," objected the Goodman of Paris. "Nay, we will have our ills, and our doctors to cure them."

"When all the world is blind," said Peire Cardenal with a wink at the Florentine, "the one-eyed man is—a fool."

"Nor is the picture so black as you have painted it," continued the Goodman, "as I am going to show by a true story."

70. HOW TO KEEP A HUSBAND

The Goodman of Paris

I used to hear my father say that there was once living in Paris a bourgeoise by the name of Jehanne la Quentine, the wife of Thomas Quentin. She knew that the said Thomas her husband, in a light and foolish manner, frequented and sometimes lay with a poor girl, a wool-spinner. For a long time, without giving sign by word or deed, Dame Jehanne suffered this patiently. Finally, however, she found out where the girl lived and went to visit her. She found the wench quite unprovided with household necessities, whether of wood, bacon, candles, oil or anything else. All she possessed was a bed with a single coverlet, her spinning-wheel, and very little other furniture.

Dame Jehanne said to her: "My friend, I am responsible that no blame fall upon my husband, and since I know that he takes pleasure in you, and comes here to visit you, I pray you, speak as little as possible about him in company, so that he and I and our children may not be shamed. If you, for your part, will hide this affair, I swear to you that I also will hide it; for since he loves you, it is my intention to love you also, and to assist you in whatever you have to do, as you shall see presently. Now since my husband comes of good family, and since he has been accustomed to every attention—well fed, well warmed, well bedded and covered, in so far as I have been able—and since I see that you possess very little wherewith to minister to his comfort, I am more anxious that you and I together should keep him in health than that I alone should take care of a sick man. So I pray that you love and guard and serve him in such wise that he may be prevented from gadding about and falling into divers dangers elsewhere. To that end I will send you, without his knowledge, a big basin, so that you may often wash his feet, a supply of wood for the fire, a good down bed, drapes and coverlets befitting his station, kerchiefs, pillows, hose and clean linen. I will send you clean supplies, and you shall send them back to me when they are soiled. And let him know nothing of the arrangements between you and me so that he may not be ashamed. For God's sake! act discreetly so that he do not discover our secret."

Thus was it promised and sworn. Jehanne took her departure and did as she had said.

Now when Thomas visited the dwelling of the young woman at vespers, she washed his feet; and later he was very well bedded in a down bed, and better provided with covers than was his wont. The next morning he had fresh linen, clean hose and fresh shoes. Thomas was much astonished at this novelty, and gave it considerable thought as he went to mass. When he returned to the girl's house he suggested that these things had come from an evil source, and bitterly reproached her for loose practices, to the end that in her own defence she might be forced to tell how she had come by them. He knew very well that two or three days earlier he had left her poor, and that she could not have grown so rich in so short a time.

The accused girl saw that she would have to reply in her own interest, and she understood Thomas' temperament well enough to know that he would believe what she told him. So she confessed to him all the truth, as you have heard.

After this Thomas returned in shame to his own house in an extremely pensive mood. He said no word to Jehanne, nor she to him, but she served him gladly; and that night they slept together very sweetly, but without exchanging a word. On the morrow Thomas went alone to hear mass, and confessed his sins. Then he went to the girl and made her a present of all the property of his which she had received. And he took an oath to live continently and abstain from all women except his wife as long as he should live.

Thus did Thomas' wife rescue him by her cunning, and heartily and humbly she loved him afterwards. Thus should good women counsel and reclaim their husbands by humility, not by violence and overbearing. But bad women do not know how to do this, nor can their hearts endure to act thus, wherefor their affairs frequently go from bad to worse.

"I wonder," said Huchown, who, as he spoke, looked round for Lancelot—but the blond knight was in a far corner drinking beer with John Gower—"I wonder what lay at the bottom of Lancelot's behaviour in certain circumstances I wot of—headstrong and untutored Nature, or something else? Certainly, it was neither courtoisie nor gentilesse. The Table Rounder may have been a fearless queller of cats and disperser of corpses, but when it came to facing the facts of life, he was as recreant as any dastard of song or story. I much prefer the frank animalism of over-sexed husbands to lovers who kiss and run away. With Master Jehan's permission I will tell you what I have in mind.—You doubtless recall that Queen Guenevere was one time accused of poisoning a Scots knight, and that she was condemned to be burned unless she could find a champion to get her off. The circumstance caused Arthur considerable worry. One morning he called Gawain, his nephew, friend and adviser, and with him retired to the tower of the castle to consider ways and means."

71. THE MAID OF ASTOLAT
Huchown of the Awle Ryale

And as they in their talkynge stode
To ordeyne how it beste myght be,
A feyre ryver undyr the toure yode,
And sone there-in gonne they see
A lytelle bote of shappe fulle goode
To theyme-ward wyth the streme gon te;
There myght none feyrer sayle on flode,
Nor better forgid as of tree.

Whan Kynge Arthure saw that sighte,
He wondrid of the riche apparrayle
That was aboute the bote i-dighte;
So richely was it coveryd, sanz fayle,
In maner of a voute wyth clothis i-dighte,
Alle shynand as gold as yt ganne sayle.

THE MAID OF ASTOLAT

Than sayd Syr Gawayne, the good knight:
This bote is of a ryche entayle.

For sothe, sir, sayd the kynge tho,
Such one sawgh I nevyr are;
Thedir I rede now that we go,
Som aventures shalle we se thare;
And yif it be wyth-in dight so
As with-oute, or gayer mare,
I darre savely say therto,
Bygynne wille auntres or aught yare.

Oute of the toure adowne they wente,
The kynge Arthur and Syr Gawayne;
To the bote they yede wyth-oute stynte,
They two allone, for sothe to sayne;
And whan they come there as it lente,
They byhelde it faste, is not to layne;
A clothe that over the bote was bente
Sir Gawayne lyfte up, and went in bayne.

Whan they were in, wyth-outen lese,
Fulle richely arayed they it founde,
And in the myddis a feyre bedde was
For any kynge of Cristene londe.
Than as swithe, or they wold sese,
The koverlet lyfte they up wyth hande:
A dede woman they sighe ther was,
The fayrest mayde that myght be founde.

To Sir Gawayne than sayd the kynge:
For sothe, Dethe was to un-hende
Whan he wold thus fayre a thinge,
Thus yonge, oute of the world do wende;
For hyr biauté, wyth-oute lesynge,
I wold fayne wete of hyr kynde,
What she was, this sweet derelynge,
And in hyr lyff where she gonne lende.

Sir Gawayne his eyen than on hyr caste,
And byheld hyr fast wyth herte fre,
So that he knew welle at the laste
That the mayde of Ascalote was she,
Whiche he som tyme had wowyd faste

His owne leman for to be;
But she aunsweryd hym ay in haste,
To none bot Launcelot wold she te.

To the kinge than sayd Sir Gawayne tho,
Thinke ye not on this endris day
Whan my lady the quene and we two
Stode togedir in youre play,
Off a mayde I told you tho
That Launcelot lovyd paramoure ay.
Gawayne, for sothe, the kynge sayd tho,
Whan thou it saydiste, wele thinke I may.

For sothe, syr, than sayd Sir Gawayne,
This is the mayd that I of spake:
Most in this world, is not to layne,
She lovid Launcelot du Lake.
For sothe, the kynge than gon to sayne,
Me rewith the deth of hyr for his sake;
The inchesoun wold I wete fulle fayne,
For sorow I trow Deth gon hyre take.

Than Sir Gawayne, the good knight,
Sought aboute hyr wythoute stynte,
And found a purs fulle riche a-righte,
Wyth gold and perlis that was i-bente;
Alle empty semyd it noght to sight.
That purs fulle sone in honde he hente,
A letter there-of than oute he twight:
Than wete they wold fayne what it mente,

What there was wreten, wete they wolde.
And Sir Gawayn it toke the kynge,
And bad hym open it that he sholde.
So dyde he sone wythoute lesynge.
Than found he whan it was unfolde,
Bothe the ende and the bygynnynge;
Thus was it wreten, as men me tolde,
Of that fayre mayden's deynge:

"To Kynge Arthur and alle his knightis
That longe to the Rounde Table,
That corteyse bene, and most of myghtis,
Doughty and noble, trew and stable,

And most worshipfulle in all fyghtis,
To the nedefulle helpinge and profitable,
The mayde of Ascalot, to rightis,
Sendith gretinge, wythouten fable—

"To you alle my playnte I make
Off the wronge that me is wroghte,
But noght in maner to undirtake
That any of you sholde mend it ought;
Bot onely I say, for this sake,
That thoughe this world were throw sought,
Men shold nowhere fynd your make,
Alle noblisse to fynd that myght be sought.

"Therefore to you to undirstand
That for I trewly many a day
Have lovid lelyest in londe,
Dethe hathe me fette of this world away;
To wete for whome yif ye wille founde,
That I so longe for in langoure lay,
To say the sothe wille I noght wounde,
For gaynes it not for to say nay.

"To say you the sothe tale,
For whome I have suffred this woo—
I say Deth hathe me take wyth bale
For the noblest knight that may go:
Is none so doughty dyntis to dale,
So ryalle, ne so fayre thereto,
But so churlysshe of maners in feld ne hale
Ne know I none, of frende ne fo.

"Off foo ne frend, the sothe to say,
So unhend of thewis is there none;
His gentilnesse was alle away,
Alle churlysshe maners he had in wone;
For, for no thinge that I coude pray,
Knelynge ne wepinge, wyth rewfulle mone,
To be my leman he sayd evyr nay,
And sayd shortely he wold have none.

"Fo-thy, lordis, for his sake
I toke to herte grete sorow and care;
So, at the laste, Deth gonne me take,

So that I might lyve na mare.
For trew lovynge had I suche wrake,
And was of blysse i-browghte alle bare:
Alle was for Launcelot du Lake,
To wete wisely for whom it ware."

When that Arthure, the noble kyng,
Had redde the letter and kene the name,
He said to Gawayne, withoute lesynge,
That Launcelot was gretly to blame,
And had hym wonne a reproovyng
For evyr, and a wikked fame,
Sythe she deide for gre lovyng:
That he her refusyde, it may hym shame.

To the kyng than sayd Syr Gawayne:
I gabbyd on hym thys gender day
That he longede, whan I gon sayne,
Wyth lady other wyth som othyr maye;
But sothe than sayde ye, is not to layne,
That he nolde nought hys love laye
In so low a place in vayne
But on a pryse lady, and a gaye.

Syr Gawayne, sayd the kyng thoo,
What is now thy best rede?
How mow we wyth thys maydyn do?
Syr Gawayne sayd: So God me spede,
Iff that ye wille assent therto,
Worshippfully we shulle hyr lede
Into the palys, and bury her so
As fallys a dukys doughter in dede.

Therto the kyng assentid sone.
Syr Gawayne dyd men sone be gare,
And worshippfully, as felle to done,
Into the palyse they her bare.
The kyng than tolde wythout lone
To alle hys barons, lesse and mare,
How Launcelot nolde noughte graunte hyr bone,
Therfore she dyed for sorow and care.

"You suggest," said John Leland, "that Lancelot was a poltroon. Perhaps he was. But I query: Did your heroine face the facts of life more courageously than he? Love, I am told, is a fearful as well as a wonderful thing. There are those present who know more about it than I. But it often happens, I daresay, that among lovers there are some women and some men who bestow their love unwisely. So it was at least with Marion de la Bruère. And I am inclined to think that she was made of sterner stuff than your maid of Astolat."

72. MARION DE LA BRUÈRE

John Leland

You have heard how Fulk Fitzwarin sailed the seas and did many memorable deeds. The tale which I am now about to relate took place in the time of his ancestor, Fulk le Brun.

When this Fulk was a lad his father sent him to be educated by Joce, a powerful and also learned knight, whose seat was the castle of Dinan, or as it was later called, Ludlow. There Fulk was fostered from the age of seven to eighteen.

During this period Joce de Dinan was continually at odds with the Mortimers and the De Lacys. One day Joce succeeded in capturing Hugh de Mortimer. He placed him in a high western tower in the third bailey, and there the turbulent baron had ample leisure in which to meditate upon his sins—and since he had been captured, was he not a great sinner?—to such good purpose that Joce was the gainer by three thousand marks of ransom money and a gage of peace.

But among Joce's enemies the De Lacys were still active, and because their quarrel originated in a dispute about the ownership of land, an amicable settlement between the two barons was hardly to be expected. Years passed in the attempt of one or the other to make good his title by force of arms.

One summer morning Sir Joce rose early and mounted a high tower of the castle to survey the surrounding country. As he looked toward the hill which is called Whitecliff, he saw the terrain covered with knights and men-at-arms, and in the midst of them floated the banner of Sir Walter de Lacy. Sir Joce was not slow in making provision for defence; indeed, he rode out and attacked his enemy to such good purpose that De Lacy's troops were worsted, and Sir Walter himself forced to take flight. Joce pursued him for some distance and would have taken him had not Godard de Bruz, André de Preez and Ernalt de Lys come to the rescue. All four knights then attacked Sir Joce, and he would have fallen. But at that moment Fulk rode up: first he cut Godard de Bruz in two with his axe and remounted his lord; then he gave Sir André de Preez a taste of his axe, cleaving his head down to the teeth. Hereupon Sir Walter and Sir Ernalt, who were both badly wounded, yielded, and were conducted back to the castle of Dinan. They were imprisoned in Pendover tower, a leech was sent to dress their wounds, and they were otherwise very honourably treated. Sir Joce's lady, together with her daughters and maids, visited the prisoners daily, and brought them what solace they could.

Sir Ernalt was a handsome young bachelor, and fell violently in love with one of the maids, a well-born damsel named Marion de la Bruère, who was chief lady-in-waiting to the châtelaine. Sir Ernalt and the girl often talked together when she came to Pendover tower with her mistress. It fell out that the young man, when he saw his time, spoke earnestly to Marion, saying that he loved her above everything in the world, and that he could have no rest, night or day, unless she returned his love. And he took oath that if she would succour him in his distress, he would never love any other woman; and when he was freed he would marry her.

Marion gave ear to this fine promise, and consented that he do his will in all things, taking surety that he would keep his word. Then the girl agreed to aid the two prisoners secretly in whatever way she could so that they might escape from prison. To this end she carried towels and sheets to the tower, fixed them together, and by that means Sir Walter and Sir Ernalt descended from their prison. Marion earnestly besought the two knights to keep faith with her, and hold to their covenant. They replied that they would keep it loyally, and commended her to God. After this Sir Walter and Sir Ernalt went off on foot, and by dawn they had reached Ewyas, one of Sir Walter's castles, to the great rejoicing of his people.

That same morning Sir Joce, after hearing mass in his chapel, sent for his prisoner, for he honoured him to such an extent that he would not sit down to table without him. Of course the prisoners could not be found, but Sir Joce gave no sign that he was much disturbed at their evasion.

After his escape Walter De Lacy took thought how he might be revenged upon Sir Joce, and he assembled fighting men in Ireland, where his father Hugh was a man of great power. But the barons of England, considering the damage and mortality which had resulted from the enmity of these two, succeeded in arranging a loveday, whereat their grievances were redressed, and they parted as friends.

When this matter had been concluded Sir Joce invited Fulk's father, Guarin, and his mother, Melette, to Castle Dinan. On this occasion he offered the hand of his younger daughter Hawyse to Fulk, and half his lands therewith. Guarin accepted this offer on behalf of his son. The bishop of Hereford was summoned, and the nuptials were celebrated. The festivities lasted a fortnight.

Now Sir Joce and Sir Guarin, with their suites, went to pay a visit at Hartland in Devonshire. Marion de la Bruère feigned herself ill and took to her bed, saying that she was so sick that she could not travel without pain. So she remained behind in Castle Dinan. Joce left a guard for her, for he still had some doubt of the De Lacys and other folk. He subsidized thirty knights and seventy men-at-arms, and committed the castle to their care until such time as he should return.

The day after Sir Joce had gone, Marion sent a message to Sir Ernalt de Lys, praying him in the name of their love not to forget the covenant between them. She asked him further to come quickly to Dinan to speak with her, for now the lord and his lady, with most of their people, had gone to Hartland. He should come to her at the very place where he had made his escape from prison.

Sir Ernalt sent the messenger back begging Marion to let him know the distance between the ground and the window through which he had formerly escaped, how many and what sort of people her lord had left behind. Marion, who suspected no guile, measured the distance between window and ground with a silk thread and sent it to Sir Ernalt, together with the desired information about the state of the castle. The young man now replied that on the fourth day, before midnight, he would be at the window, and that she should meet him there.

In the interval Sir Ernalt made a leather ladder of the same length as the silk thread which his lady had sent him. Then he went to his lord, Sir Walter, saying that after Fulk's marriage to Hawyse he and Sir Joce had gone away to Hartland to gather an army; that when they had assembled their host they would come to Castle Ewyas and devastate his lands; that if they could capture him they would cut him to small bits, and so disseisin him and his forever. "And this information," he added, "comes to me from her whom you know well, for she has remained behind and knows their plans."

On hearing this Sir Walter turned pale with emotion. "Indeed," said he, "I can hardly believe that Sir Joce would practise such deceit on me inasmuch as we have been reconciled. I should be very loath to hear our peers say that the peace had been broken by me, and Sir Joce, on the contrary, held to be a loyal knight."

"Sir," replied Ernalt, "you are my lord; I warn you of the danger in which you stand, for I know the truth from her who has learned their intentions. Do not reproach me at some future time with knowing your peril and failing to warn you, nor say that I have failed in my loyalty toward you."

Sir Walter did not know what to do. Finally he asked. "What do you advise?" "Sir," replied the other, "take my counsel and you will do well. I will go with my men-at-arms and take the castle by a stratagem. When Sir Joce has lost his stronghold he will be the less able to harm you, and will abandon the quarrel, and you will be revenged on him for the shame you have often suffered at his hands. You know very well that, rightly or wrongly, a man should be revenged on his enemy." Sir Walter accepted Ernalt's advice, believing that he had spoken the truth.

Accordingly Sir Ernalt put more than a thousand men under arms and came to Castle Dinan by night. Part of his force he stationed in the wood near Whitecliff; another part he ambushed in the shrubbery at the foot of the castle wall. The night was very dark, and the men were not perceived by the watch or anyone else. Accompanied by a squire bearing the leather ladder, Sir Ernalt made his way to the window where Marion was waiting for him. On catching sight of her lover Marion was happy indeed, and let down a cord with which she drew up the ladder and fastened it to a crenel of the wall. Ernalt mounted quickly, and took his lady in his arms and kissed her. They were both very happy at this meeting and went away to a chamber, where they supped, and then went to bed, leaving the ladder hanging.

Now the squire went to the men in ambush and led them to the ladder. A hundred well-armed knights went up to the top of the wall, then descending from the Pendover tower, went along by the wall behind the chapel of St Mary Magdalene, where they found the watch drowsing and unsuspicious of impending death. They would have thrown him down from his tower into the moat, but he cried them mercy. And while he was begging for quarter, the greater number of the garrison, knights and men-at-arms, were cut to pieces. In their beds they screamed and cried for pity, but Sir Ernalt's men had no pity: whomsoever they found in the castle they killed, reddening many a sheet that had been white that evening. Finally they threw the watch into the ditch and broke his back.

Marion de la Bruère lay beside her lover ignorant of the treason whereof he was guilty. When she heard the uproar in the castle, she rose and looked down. There she saw the armed knights with their gleaming helms and hauberks, and heard the screams of the wounded. In a flash she realized that Sir Ernalt had deceived and betrayed her. She wept piteously. "Alas!" she cried, "why was I ever born? for through my misdeed my lord Sir Joce, who brought me up tenderly, has lost his castle and his good men. If it had not been for me nothing would have been lost. Alas! that ever I put faith in this knight, for by his flatteries he has deceived not only me, but my lord, and that is a harder sorrow to bear." Sobbing, Marion drew Sir Ernalt's sword from its scabbard and cried: "Sir knight, wake up, for I must tell you that you have brought a strange company to my lord's castle without leave. Though you, sir, and your squire, were lodged here by me, the others who are within by your instrumentality are not here by my invitation. And since you have tricked me, you cannot reasonably blame me if I reward your service according to its merit. Never shall you boast to any mistress you may have that by cozening me you won the castle of Dinan and its demesne."

At this the knight rose to a sitting posture. Marion, who held the naked sword in her hand, thrust him through the body in such fashion that he died at once. And she realized that if she were taken she would be delivered up to an evil death. For a moment she did not know what course to take; but then, going to a window in the highest part of the castle on the Linney side, she threw herself out and broke her neck.

"Life seems to have become very complicated in polite circles," said John the Reeve. "The higher you gentles climb the rarer seems to be the atmosphere, and the more difficult the breathing. Much of this conversation, and the tales which illustrate it, are above my simple wit."

"You could doubtless bring both low enough," said the Clerk of Oxenford.

"Well," returned the Reeve, "to me a hog is a hog and not a 'tame domestic mammal,' as any one of you giddy star-gazers would know if you had ever cleaned out a byre."

"Well put," answered the Clerk, "and yet were it not for us star-gazers, as you phrase it, most of the rest of you would still be walking on all fours with your hogs."

"Let the man speak," said William Langland.

"He shall clean out no byres here," cautioned Bartholomew.

"I only meant," said the Reeve, "that with us rude folk life is lived much more directly, if harshly. I never heard of a woman in my rank of life who committed suicide for love. On the contrary I could tell you of a maid—ahem—who, it seems to me, had the right manner with lovers."

73. THE PARDONER AND THE BARMAID

John the Reeve

When the goodly fellowship of Canterbury pilgrims had taken their lodging at the "Cheker of the Hope," Harry Bailey ordered their dinner of such food as the town provided. In the meanwhile the Pardoner, who was ranging about, soon spied the barmaid, and took his staff to the tap-room.

"Welcome, my own brother," said she with a friendly look, all ready for a kiss. And he, as a man skilled in such matters, took her by the middle and made her such good cheer as though he had known her for a long time. She led him into the tap-room, where her bed was made. "Here," said she, "I lie naked all night, with no man's company since the death of my lover, Jenkin the Harper. Perhaps you knew him? There was never a lustier fellow for leaping and dancing." Therewith she wept and sniffed and sighed, wiping away the great tears with her apron.

"Benedicite," said the Pardoner, putting his arm about her neck. "You carry on as though you were at death's door." "Small wonder," replied she, and sneezed. "Aha! all whole," said the Pardoner. "Thank God for amendment of sorrow"; and he chucked her under the chin. "Alas!" he continued, "that love is sin! Such a true lover are you, it seems to me, that he could certainly count himself fortunate who could win your love."

"Excuse me," said the barmaid, "for keeping you waiting. Sit down and have a drink." "Nay, my heart's root," said he; "I have not yet broken my fast." "Fasting, are you?" asked she. "I know a good remedy for that." Therewith she fetched a good hot pie and set it before him. "Your name is Jenkin, isn't it?" asked the woman. "It is indeed, sister dear; at least so I am informed by those who fostered me. And what is yours?" "My dame calls me Kit," she replied. "God's blessing on you," returned the Pardoner; "I hope you will deserve your name." Therewith he began to look at her amorously, sighing loudly, and began to hum a song: "Now love, do right by me."

"Eat and cheer up," said Kit. "Why do you not break your fast? It would be silly to wait for more company. Why are you so dull? Are you thinking of your love at home, perchance?" "Nay, sweetheart, it is only of you I am thinking." "Of me? Fie! I'm not worth it." "Nevertheless, it is true," he rejoined. "Well, eat and drink now, and we will speak of that afterwards. They say a burnt cat fears the fire, and I have never loved yet but I got harm from it, for it has always been my way to love too much." "Christ's blessings on all such," said the Pardoner. "See how the heavens bring it about that everyone meets his mate, for to tell the truth, that is my way too, and has been these many years. I can't help myself; nature will run its course, whatever a man swears to the contrary." Thereupon he rose and laid down a groat. "What is this for?" asked Kit. "Nay, I would not have you pay a penny and go away so quickly." The Pardoner swore his great oath that he would pay no less. "It is too much," said Kit; "but since it is your will, I will put it in my purse lest you take it as an offence to refuse your courtesy." And she bowed. "One cannot help admiring your manners," said the Pardoner, "for if you had made a strict reckoning I might have thought you harsh and untrue of heart, and likely to forget me. But we shall meet often." "Indeed," said Kit, "you have a ready tongue. Would that you could as readily explain a dream I had last night."

Kit told the Pardoner her dream, and when he had interpreted it to her satisfaction he took his leave.

When the pilgrims had visited the martyr's shrine they returned to the inn and sat down to dinner. Afterwards Harry Bailey granted them leave to amuse themselves as they chose. Some went here and some there, but the Pardoner went off to the tap-room to find Kit and make arrangements about lodging with her that night. Into the tap-room he stepped confidently and found Kit lounging; she saw him well enough, but feigned to be asleep. Laying his hand on her breast—"Wake up," he cried. "Ah, sir," said Kit, "who would have expected you here? Heavens! I might have been taken prisoner, all alone as I am." "Well, since you are my prisoner," answered the Pardoner, "yield yourself to me." "I suppose I must," replied Kit, "for I can't flee, nor am I strong, and I am young of age, too. But it is no great proof of skill to catch a mouse which is already in a cage so closed in that it can't get out. I might observe that you should have coughed before you came in. Where did you learn manners? Indeed, I must chide you, for women have certain private matters to attend to when they are alone. You should not break in so suddenly."

"Excuse me, my dear; I will not do so again. Hereafter I shall do as you say; but as you know, lovers are often rash and ill-advised. But tell me, how have you fared since I saw you last? That is my real concern, for if there were aught amiss with you, it would change my cheer and trouble my blood."

"I have fared the worse because of you," said Kit. "You have bewitched me with your necromancy. I have nothing but my body, and if it were shamed, I should be undone. You clerks are so cunning in books that you can win a woman at the first look."

Thought the Pardoner: "This goes well," and made somewhat better cheer. "Now tell me," he said, "who shall lie here this night?" "Fine need there is to tell you," replied Kit. "Don't make it so subtle, even though you are a clerk; you know well enough by look and word and deed." "Shall I come, then, Kit, and drive the cat away?" "Shall you come, Jenkin? Now what kind of a question is that? Take my advice and come somewhat late, but do not fail. The door will be ajar; open it softly and take good care not to waken those aloft." "Have no fear," answered Jenkin; "I'm skilful in such matters; no one shall be wakened by my stirring about."

So they drank to the agreement which it seemed Kit had made by her words and by her manner. Pretending that she loved him well, she put her arms about his neck, as though she had learned from some old friar to curry Fauvel. Now the Pardoner took out his purse and gave her money with which to provide a late supper. "Get a caudle with sweet wine and sugar," he said; "I have no desire to eat except in your company, so does my heart long for you." Then he took his leave, as though nothing were forward, and joined the other pilgrims. He said nothing, but thought merrily: "I'm well lodged for the night, and though it has cost me something, I'll do my best to pick her purse and win back my outlay."

After supper the respectable men went to bed. The Miller and the Cook sat up drinking, while the Summoner, the Yeoman, and the Reeve, the Manciple and the Pardoner struck up a song. The Host and the Merchant, busy at their accounts, were vexed by the uproar, and prayed them to go to bed. And so they did, except the Pardoner, who drew off to one side, waiting for the candle to be put out. In the meanwhile the barmaid, her paramour and the hostler, sat together privily and ate the best goose offered for sale in the town. They drank but little, but they ate the caudle that had been made for the Pardoner, according to his directions, with sugar and sweet wine. He who paid for all had not a bit thereof himself. But where is the man whom a woman—I mean lewd wenches like the barmaid, not decent ladies—can't fool if she puts her mind to it?

Now when Kit and her guests had eaten and drunk, she explained how matters stood—how the Pardoner had wooed her, what money he had advanced, and how he expected to lie with her that night. "But he is as like to do so as wear God's cope," said she, kissing her lover. "You and I shall sleep together side by side as usual, and if he come and make a noise, I pray you, dub him knight." "Yea," said her lover, "I will do. You say this is his own staff? He shall have a taste of it." "If he comes my way," said the hostler, "he shall, for love of you, drink without either cup or pot. And if he be so hardy as to waken any guest, I vow to the peacock, he shall pay for it." It was a shrewd partnership; many a one had they served so.

Said Kit to her lover: "You must stay awake for a while. I am sure the Pardoner will be coming within the hour to assuage his heat. Take care you pay him readily and cool his courage. So, my love, do not take off your shoes till the trick be played out." It was nearly nine o'clock now, so Kit went to bed and blew out the light.

When all was still the Pardoner stole forth, as glad as any finch to hear no man talking, and drew near Kit's door to listen. He expected to find the door on the latch, but the fastening and the lock kept him out. Still, he suspected no guile, but went close and scratched at the door like a dog, and whined. "Away, dog, and a foul death to you," said he who was inside, getting ready to unpin the door.

"Ha!" said the Pardoner then, "I think I've been tricked. The barmaid has a lover, and they have been enjoying the caudle which I had made for myself, I guess. Devil take her and her likes. She said I had bewitched her! May Our Lady bring her sorrow! I would to God she might lie in the stocks till I went surety for her! She is the falsest wench I ever knew, though she made fair enough semblance to get the money out of my purse."

Therewith he caught a heartburn and a cold sweat. Whoever is tormented by love-longing and hot courage has many a pleasant thought of anticipation. But now the Pardoner was in evil plight because his plan had failed. Suddenly he got into a furious rage and frenzy through anger and jealousy, for when he heard the man within, he almost went mad. And since he had paid the expenses, it is no wonder if he meditated vengeance.

The Pardoner scratched again, for he would have heard more of what was going on inside. "What dog is that?" asked the lover. "Kit, do you know?" "By my troth," said she, "it must be the Pardoner." "Curse the Pardoner," said her paramour, "and God give him evil." "It is that very rascal himself," said Kit. "You're a liar," shouted the Pardoner, who couldn't hold out any longer, "false wench that you are! May the devil tear you in pieces, for I never found your equal for duplicity." And then he called her more than one name which it would not be decent to repeat among men of rank and worship. But when he was tired of chiding, he asked for his staff, savagely and with harsh words.

"Go to bed," said he who was within; "don't be making so much noise. Your staff will be ready tomorrow, I guarantee." "Truly," said the Pardoner, "I will not budge from the door till I have my staff." "Then here it is," said he who was within, and laid it on his back, right where chapmen bear their packs, and after that twice again by guess; and several other times too, the staff banged him on the brow.

The hostler lay abed and heard this fray. He leapt up quickly and thought he would have a part of it; so he took a stick in hand and joined his friends. "What is the matter?" asked the hostler. "Hist!" replied the paramour. "Jack, you must be wary; there is a thief in the hall door." "A thief?" asked Jack. "Good for you that you discovered him; perhaps we can catch him." "We might indeed, if we had a light," returned the paramour. "May the devil of hell break this thief's bones," said Jack. "The dame has the kitchen key with her in the chamber above, and if she is wakened out of her sleep, she gets into such a rage that no one can please her for a week afterwards. But two of my guests had a little fire as they supped in the hall this evening. Go, look if you can find a brand in the ashes, and I will keep the door so he can't get out." "Nay, by God," returned the lover, "I will not, lest I catch a clout. You know your way about the house better than I; go yourself." "Nay," answered Jack, "it would be wrong to fall upon a man with whom one has no quarrel. Since you have already beaten him with your staff I see no reason why I should get paid for it. He might see my head by the light of the coal and give me my death-stroke." "Let us both look for him then, and whoever meets him first, give it to him on the snout." "I thought I heard him among the pans just now. Take the other side and mind the water-cans."

"Ha!" thought the Pardoner, "are there pans hereabouts?" And he went to that side, thinking of a trick. He found a pan and set it on his head; and as it happened, he had great need thereof. He groped about for something to serve as a weapon, and seized a great ladle. As he rushed between his two enemies, he minded the paramour, who had worked him woe, and gave him a great clout on the gristle of his nose so that all the week thereafter both his eyes and his nose ran both early and late. But little cared she who was the cause thereof. As the Pardoner dashed away, he bumped into the hostler and the pan fell from his head. Jack ran after him as quickly as he could, and the edge of the pan met with his shin so that vein and sinew were cut. He swore by St Amyas that somebody should pay dearly for this, if he could find him. The Pardoner made no move, for he thought he had had blows enough, as arms, back and brow could bear witness.

"Jack," said the paramour, "where has this thief got to?" "I don't know," said Jack; "he passed me just now, and Christ's curse go with him, for I've got a bad hurt." "So have I," returned the lover, "but he doesn't go quits either. If we could only find him he wouldn't be able to walk tomorrow. However, now that the moon is down and there is no light, we had better go back to bed. But fasten the gates so he can't escape. He bears a mark from his own staff by means of which you can recognize him in a crowd tomorrow if you watch carefully when the company is preparing to depart. Do I say well?" "Your wit is clear," answered Jack. So he fastened the gates and went back to bed.

The Pardoner stood aside. His cheeks ran with blood, and he was right ill at ease in his head all night; but he was more hurt at having been duped by a woman—having paid for wine and caudle and had no part of it. He prayed St Julian that the devil might speed her on land and water for so deceiving a travelling man. All he could do to assuage his anger was to curse. Moreover, after his heat he caught such a cold because of the night air that he well-nigh foundered. Then, as he sought his lodging, he happened upon a hound that lay under the stair—a great Welsh dog that had a wooden clog about his neck because of his savage temper and readiness to bite. The Pardoner would have lodged there, but as he lay down the ill-tempered dog was wakened and caught him by the thigh, biting him savagely. Thus he defended his bed so that the Pardoner couldn't get near him. There was nothing else for him to do but lie down in the dog's litter. He wished he had some bread to cajole the beast so that he might get nearer and lie more comfortably. But Fortune said him nay. The dog lay growling, ready to snap, so the Pardoner lay still. Truly, it was a dismal day for him.

On the morrow when the company prepared to get under way, none of the fellowship was ready half so quickly as the Pardoner, for he was ready dressed all night long, and all he had to do was shake his ears a little, tighten his belt and go. However, before he joined the others, he washed away the blood and bound up the cracks on his head with the tippet of his hood. Then he put on a pleasant demeanour so that no one should suspect the state he was in nor the cause of it.

As regards the hostler, however much he pried and sought, he was unable to recognize the Pardoner among the company on the morrow, for he kept to the midst of the company, and to complete the deception, was always singing as long as the inn was in sight. So, for the nonce, he escaped further harm and avoided shame by keeping his injuries concealed. But as they left the "Cheker of the Hope" farther behind, his notes, because of his headache, became lower and lower, and finally he rode along in gloomy silence, meditating on the folly of putting one's trust in common barmaids.

"When you say that you never heard of a woman in your walk of life dying for love, you surprise me," said Lord Burleigh. "Have you never heard the ballet of 'Andrew Lammie' or 'Sweet William's Ghost' or the 'Suffolk Miracle'? Or have you no minstrels in your country?"

"'Evil communications corrupt good manners,'" rejoined the Reeve.

"Your Pardoner," observed Roaring Dick, "came off with nothing worse than a cracked head, and only the barmaid was false. But if you will listen to my ballet, I'll show you what happened to two lovers, each of whom was false to the other."

74. EARL RICHARD

Roaring Dick

"O lady, rock never your young son young
One hour langer for me,
For I have a sweetheart in Garlioch Wells
I love far better than thee.

"The very sole o' that lady's foot
Than thy face is far mair white."
"But nevertheless, now, Erl Richard,
Ye will bide in my bower a' night?"

She birled him with the ale and wine,
As they sat down to sup.
A living man he laid him down,
But I wot he ne'er rose up.

Then up and spake the popinjay
That flew aboun her head:
"Lady, keep weel your green cleiding
Frae gude Erl Richard's bleid."

"O better I'll keep my green cleiding
Frae gude Erl Richard's bleid,
Than thou canst keep thy clattering toung,
That trattles in thy head."

She has call'd upon her bower maidens,
She has call'd them ane by ane:
"There lies a dead man in my bour—
I wish that he were gane!"

EARL RICHARD

They hae booted him, and spurred him,
As he was wont to ride;
A hunting horn tied round his waist,
A sharp sword by his side;
And they hae had him to the wan water,
For a' men called it Clyde.

Then up and spoke the popinjay
That sat upon the tree:
"What hae ye done wi' Erl Richard?
Ye were his gay ladye."

"Come down, come down, my bonny bird,
And sit upon my hand,
And thou shall hae a cage o' gowd,
Where thou hast but the wand."

"Awa! awa! ye ill woman;
Nae cage o' gowd for me.
As ye hae dune to Erl Richard,
Sae wad ye do to me."

She hadna cross'd a rigg o' land,
A rigg, but barely ane,
When she met wi' his auld father,
Came riding all alane.

"Where hae ye been, now, ladye fair,
Where hae ye been sae late?"
"We hae been seeking Erl Richard,
But him we cannot get."

"Erl Richard kens a' the fords in Clyde,
He'll ride them ane by ane,
And though the night was ne'er sae mirk,
Erl Richard will be hame."

O it fell anes, upon a day,
The king was boun to ride,
And he has mist him, Erl Richard,
Should hae ridden on his right side.

The ladye turn'd her round about
Wi' meikle mournfu' din—

"It fears me sair o' Clyde water,
That he is drown'd therein."

"Gar douk, gar douk," the king he cried,
"Gar douk for gold and fee.
O wha will douk for Erl Richard's sake,
Or wha will douk for me?"

They doukéd in at ae weil-head,
And out ay at the other.
"We can douk nae mair for Erl Richard,
Although he were our brother."

It fell that, in that ladye's castle
The king was boun to bed;
And up and spake the popinjay
That flew abune his head:

"Leave off your douking on the day,
And douk upon the night;
And where that sackless knight lies slain
The candles will burn bright."

They left the douking on the day
And doukéd upon the night;
And where that sackless knight lay slain
The candles burnéd bright.

The deepest pot in a' the linn,
They fand Erl Richard in,
A green turf tyed across his breast
To keep that gude lord down.

Then up and spake the king himsell,
When he saw the deadly wound:
"O wha has slain my right-hand man,
That held my hawk and hound?"

Then up and spake the popinjay,
Says: "What needs a' this din?
It was his light leman took his life,
And hided him in the linn."

She swore her by the grass sae grene,
Sae did she by the corn,

She had na' seen him, Erl Richard,
Since Moninday at morn.

"Put na the wite on me," she said,
"It was my may, Catherine."
Then they hae cut baith fern and thorn
To burn that maiden in.

It wadna take upon her cheik,
Nor yet upon her chin,
Nor yet upon her yellow hair,
To cleanse the deadly sin.

The maiden touch'd the clay-cauld corpse—
A drap it never bled.
The ladye laid her hand on him,
And soon the ground was red.

Out they hae ta'en her, may Catherine,
And put her mistress in.
The flame tuik fast upon her cheik,
Tuik fast upon her chin,
Tuik fast upon her faire bodye—
She burn'd like hollins green.

"Love, as Master Leland remarked, is a fearful and wonderful thing," said Andrew the Chaplain. "I have given the subject a lifetime of study, yet I fail to see in what way love entered into the circumstances related by either John the Reeve or Roaring Dick."

"I wouldn't know about that," answered the Reeve.

"Well," said Edmund Spenser, "what is love? I once wrote a hymn on the subject, but I should be glad to hear other opinions."

"Jerome has told us that love is the oblivion of the reason, that it destroys counsel, and shatters the high and noble spirit of man," said John of Salisbury, "and that it is next door to madness."

"His was a purely eclectic opinion," objected Andrew.

"Well, you can't say the same for the experience of Amadas, Orlando and Yvain," remarked Ariosto.

"*Amor deorum infernalium insania est,*" pronounced Arnaldus de Villanova.

"Ah, doctor, you are too sharp," expostulated Boccaccio; "rather is love a sweet evil—venom and honeycomb, as Marbodius said."

"That is merely begging the question," said Andrew.

"Perhaps you will tell us what love is," suggested the Clerk of Oxenford.

"I cannot tell you what it is," answered Andrew, "for it is different for every man and woman; but I can tell you what is necessary to its existence. Love means admiration and respect, confidence and sacrifice, service and selflessness, joy and passion and suffering. Love enters through the eye and permeates the heart and brain and backbone, but is conditioned by what it finds there, so that it lives, or dies, or is transformed into something grotesque and ugly, or remains true love. Above all, love means giving, not getting. Any lover who is intent only upon getting, upsets the equilibrium of forces necessary to perfect love; and two would-be lovers who strive to outdo each other in the game of getting, kill love at the very outset. Knowledge of these things is called Gai Saber, as Peire Vidal and Peire Cardenal yonder know. Love once had a chance in Provence and Limousin, but Folquet of Marseilles, a bad lover, crushed it out, I am told."

"John of Salisbury and Arnaldus lay too much stress on the fleshly aspects of love, it seems to me," said the Knight of La Tour Landry. "A man—or a woman—should have greater regard for less evanescent virtues, such as health, good spirits, good manners, prudence . . ."

"And a good dowry," interposed the Goodman of Paris.

"For these things last and ensure quiet in the house."

"Like Messer Boccaccio and his Marbodius, you also go to extremes," answered Andrew. Fairness of face and form in a woman is as important a bio-psychological element in a man's love as are the broad shoulders, beetling brows, slim waist and hairy arms of a man in a woman's. But these things are not *more* important than intelligence disciplined by breeding. Physical beauty—or attraction—is for youth—Romeo and Juliet; spiritual beauty is for age—Philemon and Baucis. When the two are combined in one pair you have love. He or she who responds only to the one and not to both, might as well bestow his affections on a statue, as did Pygmalion, or the besotted youth who proposed to marry the effigy of Venus in the island of Cnidus."

"Alas!" exclaimed Gower, "if what you say is true, my youth was indeed wasted, for, though you might not believe it, I also made love ditties in my green age. You must be right, for I had great difficulty in getting a second wife."

"Your argument," said Étienne de Bourbon, "seems to me fantastic. In my view love is mostly from the devil, as I will show in a very moral tale."

75. THE MIRACLE

Étienne de Bourbon

Once upon a time there was a convent of nuns who spent their time in the service of God and His mother—not a harsh life was that. I shall not extol their house further than to say that they kept well the vows they had sworn to God, for He was their only protector.

In the convent of which I speak there was a lady very zealous in performing her religious devotions, excelling in humility, abstinence and obedience. She stood firm against all sins and was quite beyond their touch.

This lady was the sacristan of the convent. Now it was a noble custom of hers that on entering the church to ring for matins she would perform a service such as tames and subdues the Old Enemy: before proceeding with her duties she would kneel before the altar of Our Lady and salute her reverently. Never once did she omit to voice the greeting whereby all of us expect to obtain salvation, though she passed the altar a hundred times. Thus for seven years Margerie, for that was her name, never failed to pray before the image, whether at prime, tierce, midday, nones, matins, vespers or compline.

But the Old Enemy, who constantly contrives our hurt, sought a means whereby he might destroy her; envious of good, he wanted to ruin her holy life. Accordingly the felon began to tempt her, and put evil in her heart to such a degree that she suffered great torment and perturbation of spirit. The devil in her spoke something as follows: "Fool, what are you doing locked up here in this way? It will not be long till you begin to sicken with the confinement. Rather should you go out into the world and seek your pleasure there. The wretched, the lazy and the pusillanimous enter religious houses when they fear a scarcity of victuals, it is true, but why should you act like them? Come out into the woods and meadows and listen to the song of birds. Return to the world and amuse yourself. Later, if you come back to the door of your convent, you will find it open for you. Now your face is handsome and fresh, and you can live in the world a long time; but when your skin is blotched, and you are an old woman with wrinkles, then it will be time enough to return to your house."

Thus did the devil incite the nun, and so did the Enemy inflame her mind that she fell in love with a false clerk. The devil, who wanted to ruin them, inspired both one and the other with love. So eager was the clerk that he wished to have possession of Margerie whether by means of gold, stratagem or force; and since he did not have convenient access to the convent, he sent an old woman to fetch Margerie—one of those old women who deceive both man and maid and cause them to fall into mortal sin.

Now when Margerie felt herself in the toils of the Enemy, she was much dismayed. "Alas, holy Mary," she said, "what can a weak creature like myself do against the devil who tempts and spurs me on? Mercy, O Lord, for I have become too negligent in your service! How loath am I to part from you! but the devil has quite overcome me and plunged me into such turmoil that I must go, though it be to wander about the country from this out as a common prostitute." Thus we see that the idea of sin was attractive to Margerie but that she had not the courage to face it.

The next morning when she went to the church at matins, she was like one out of her mind. She had to pass before the altar, and in so doing she pronounced the salutation to Our Lady as she was accustomed to do, though hurriedly. The Old Enemy urged her to hasten to the false clerk who was waiting for her, thinking of nothing but sin. So she hurried on to the door of the church; but there she saw standing the sweet mother of Christ, who said softly: "Where are you going, my friend? You shall not pass here. Not this time shall you go away, for I forbid it."

Her passage thus blocked, the frightened nun retreated and waited till the next night. The following morning when she rose for matins, she passed as usual before the image of Our Lady, adoring her with her whole heart. She greeted her, wringing her hands and tearing her hair. "Lady," she said, "it breaks my heart, but I must leave you." And then she saluted her. Our Lady did not reject her greeting, but went to the door and prevented her from passing. The nun would have gone out, but Our Lady was the stronger. She said: "You shall not go, for this passage is sealed up. Would you leave me here within, and yourself go outside to ruin yourself in sin? I see well that you cast me off." Margerie was ashamed at this reproach and stood in great fear of Our Lady. But the devil in her allowed her to say no word of apology. She rang for matins and then, weeping and sighing, retired to the dorter, where she got no rest.

Now the false clerk was very much vexed that the nun did not come, and wondered what had happened. "Indeed," said he, "I am tricked and deceived, anyone who believes a woman, wise or foolish, is a dolt and a numbskull. A woman is of so many minds that whatever a man says, she will agree and disagree, grant and contradict, approve and deny ten times over. First she loves, then she hates; first she sings, then she weeps; first she's up, then she's down. She is lighter than the thistle-down and more variable than the magpie." So the clerk sent the foul old deceiver—God damn her and her like—who knew the way well, and she gave Margerie the clerk's message. "You are not acting right," she said, "to make us cool our heels out there, and waste our time. It has been a great vexation waiting for you these two nights. The clerk is almost out of his wits. You are a jade to have lied to us twice."

"Good sister," replied Margerie, "by my faith, it was impossible for me to go out, for Our Lady barred the door and kept me within by force." When the cunning old trot heard this she sneered. "How? Does Our Lady regard you so highly? I suppose you greeted her on your way out?" "Alas! What else should I do? Never have I failed to salute her in passing her image." "Well," said the old witch, "I want you to promise me that you will break your habit, and come forth tomorrow without greeting her. If you do as I say, you will not be hindered."

Margerie heard this advice with dismay. "O St Mary, sweet mother! what shall I do? Sorrowful indeed is it that I should undo our companionship. Alas, wretch that I am! the devil has certainly beaten me down if I must stoop to such deeds." But the Old Enemy gave her no respite, and pushed her on so that she promised the old woman to do as she had bidden.

The next day the nun rose betimes to ring for matins. She thought of the image of Our Lady, but turned her back and took another way, for the devil, who was leading her astray, had his noose about her neck so fast that he did not even let her look at the image. She found the door unbarred and there was no door-keeper, so she went out, leaving the door open behind her. Thus, while it was still night, Margerie joined her fool clerk, and he carried her out of the country without delay.

Now did the salutations which the nun was wont to render to the Mother of God in the church stand her in good stead, for the sweet Virgin Mary performed a great marvel for her friend: she served in her office. The Blessed Virgin took Margerie's place both as regards face and form and habit, and performed her services in the church in every particular. She mingled with the other nuns in fasting and waking, in singing and chanting, in the church, the refectory and the dorter so that it was never perceived that the nun had left her post. Thus did she serve for more than ten years, as I heard.

When the years had passed and the lovers, who had been together too much, had become tired of sin and each other, they repented and resolved to part. They made a division of their property; the clerk went his way, and Margerie, who now inclined towards piety, went hers. She took her way back to the convent. In her heart rose a fountain so great that it issued from her eyes; her sighs were not short, but so profound were they that her heart almost broke; and weeping and sobbing she wandered through the fields. Gone were her laughter and her song; only repentance and lamentation and weeping remained. "O Christ," said she, "Thou who dost pardon sin and reward good deeds, to Thee I bring my repentant heart that Thou mayst conduct it to a good refuge. Sweet Lady, holy Mary, comfort thou this sorrowful one. I would rather be beaten every day than denied the privilege of serving thee with all my might."

At last, one evening, Margerie arrived at the village. She was not recognized, for she had become sadly changed. She took lodging near the convent, and that night asked many questions concerning the abbess and the nuns, and what sacristan there was there now. The hostess told her everything she knew, saying that the convent was very holy, and the nuns of exemplary life; that the sacristan was good and sweet and clean and charitable above all others in the world, and had been these thirty years. "You are mocking me," said Margerie. "Someone told me that she went away with a clerk, and is now dead." At these words the hostess flared up with ire and vexation. "Are you mad to invent such a lie about the best lady alive? But *you* shall die, wretch that you are, denying her who performs nothing but good; never in word or deed was there any folly in her. You talk foolishly. Do not repeat such a slander or you'll get a good slap; somebody might hear you."

For once Margerie dared not contradict. She was as confused and embarrassed as a beast in a cage, and trembled like a leaf on a branch. All night she remained so frozen with terror that she could eat nothing; nor did she enter her bed, but remained all night on her knees beside it. Bewildered and dismayed she invoked holy Mary in her thought, imploring her that she would send her succour speedily.

At matins, when she heard the first stroke of the bell, Margerie went as fast as she could to the convent. She was almost drunk with repentance and remorse; no woman ever entered a church with better reason. Quickly she ran to the church and shook the door-ring desperately. Our Lady came at once and opened the door and greeted her. Margerie bowed mutely, for her heart was melting with tears of contrition. She looked at the image and saw it in the place where she had been accustomed to pray. She approached to render thanks for her welcome, but she could not have uttered a word for all the world, so did the hot unquenchable tears of repentance well up in her heart.

Now hearken to the great miracle which Our Lady performed that night for her nun. Our Lady refashioned that one who had been undone by sin. Confession, true love, hope, fear and repentance created her anew. There where she was kneeling Our Lady put off the habit she had worn and clothed the nun therewith, and restored to her the form in which she had been on the day she went away. Then she said: "My dear friend, now you have had your folly while I have served here in your room. For ten years I have earned your bread. I am the mother of Our Lord, and for my sake He has reinstated you. The devotion which you rendered me has not been amiss. Now be as you were before, and serve God from now on, for He has guerdoned you with a rich gift—the remission of your sins. Be not faint of heart, but serve God hardily, for your misdeeds are so hidden that they will never be revealed."

The nun prostrated herself on the ground. "Lady," said she, "who hast kept me from perdition by thy service, it is good and proper that I should serve thee, and henceforth I will serve thee well, to deserve thy love."

Our Lady raised her, blessed her and departed. The sacristan resumed her old position and even became parson of the church, performing her duties devoutly. No one perceived the deception that had been practised; well had she tricked the Old Enemy and arrived at a good port. Thereafter her life was so exemplary that she was considered a holy woman by all about her.

But now you must learn how this miracle was made known, for it was a matter so well concealed that it would never have been divulged save through her who had had the experience. One time when the abbess and the nuns were assembled in chapter, she whose heart was stuffed with her secret, laid bare everything to them, point by point, begging forgiveness. They, however, rendered thanks to God and made every effort to show her honour, and loved her more than before.

Thus was the miracle made public, and the abbess had it written down by a certain man. You who have listened to it, pray God for him who made it.

"The view which you espouse," said Andrew the Chaplain when Étienne had finished, "was responsible for the ruin of Abelard and Héloise, and will ruin many another so long as it prevails."

"Sir," said the Clerk of Oxenford, "several times in the course of your narrative you referred to the 'false clerk' or the 'fool clerk.' I daresay you intended no opprobrium, for of course, in order to whiten your heroine you had to blacken her lover; so we will not arraign you on the charge of slander. However, if my information is correct, it was not a clerk at all with whom your nun eloped into the world."

"The story is well known," growled Caesarius of Heisterbach.

"It is equally well known that she ran away with a knight," returned the Clerk, "and since you seem somewhat illiberal, I would point out also that the convent to which she belonged was far from being the model of religious severity that Étienne portrays. The truth is that the abbess thereof was a lady of high rank who boarded and lodged a score of her indigent relatives, ladies and knights, with their maids and squires."

"That is true," said Gautier de Coinci.

"And it was a nephew of this abbess," went on the Clerk, "who was the hero of the piece. He was a smart young man, well born and of good appearance and manners. Daily association with the beautiful sacristan so inflamed his mind with love that he did not know what to do with himself. Night and day he besought her with prayers and promises till even a woman of stone would have yielded. The abbess was much to blame, for you cannot drop fire on tow without precipitating a conflagration. But when Margerie gave her consent, it was not with the expectation of leading a life of extra-marital fornication, for she exacted from the young man a solemn promise that he would marry her, and so he did. When they left the convent together the youth took her home to his own country and married her in due form. In all the country-side there was no lady so beautiful, so adorned with all graces. And her lord loved her so well that they had many fine children. Moreover, the lovers did not grow tired of love or of each other, as Étienne alleges; they separated for other reasons. One night, after nearly thirty years of married life, Our Lady appeared to Margerie and said: 'Get up. You have lain too long. Your lamp is extinguished, for it lacks oil. Get up and take your veil again, and render me the service which you owe me, or I will close the doors of heaven against you.' Who would have disobeyed an exhortation couched in such terms and coming from such a person? When Margerie told her husband of this vision, he did not cast her off, as has been suggested. On the contrary, he said: 'Lady, sweet friend, I should not wish your soul to be damned on my account. Since Our Lady requires your service, I am well pleased that it should be so, and will do whatever I can to assist you. And whereas you intend to remain no more in the world, neither will I. I will take a monk's habit and retire to a monastery. Whatever land or possessions I hold are not worth to me so much as a rotten egg without your sweet company, my dear lady.'

And as he said, so he did. You can hardly find a better example, I think, of a man and a woman who served *both* worlds as well as these two."

"There may be something in what you say," conceded Étienne, "but I only told the tale as I heard it."

"In that case," said the Clerk, with a glance at Caesar, "perhaps I may be allowed to tell a story which I heard. In my youth I attended the universities of Bologna and Padua where I listened to lectures on civil and canon law. The English nation, then as now, was on friendly terms with the native Italian students, and sometimes, at the inn, over a glass of wine, the conversation turned to other than legal matters. Among our companions was a student from Dalmatia who, one day, when the talk happened to be about tragic themes, related to us the tale of . . ."

76. MALGHERITA SPOLATINA AND HER PARAMOUR
The Clerk of Oxenford

Ragusa, as you know, is a celebrated city of Dalmatia, situated on the coast. Not far distant is a small island which goes by the name of the Middle Island. Thereon is a strong and well-built castle, with its adjacent town. Between Ragusa and the said island is a reef or high rock whereon there is nothing but a little chapel and a miserable little hut. On account of its barrenness and the bad air, no one lived on this rock save a hermit by the name of Teodoro, who devoutly served in the chapel for the remission of his sins. Having no means of supporting life other than the alms of the pious, Teodoro betook himself now to Ragusa, now to the Middle Island to beg his bread.

One day when Teodoro was soliciting alms in the Middle Island according to his wont, he found something that he had never expected to find in all his life, and that was a lovely and graceful young woman by the name of Malgherita. This maiden, who had observed Teodoro's handsome and seemly person on more than one occasion, thought to herself that here was a man more fitted to partake in love and human pleasures than bury himself in eternal solitude; wherefor, she fell so passionately in love with him that she could think of no one else night and day. For his part, the hermit perceived nothing of the effect he had created in the girl's mind, and continued his customary begging for alms, in the course of which he often visited Malgherita's house.

Malgherita did not immediately discover her passion to the youth, but Love, who is the shield and buckler of all who march under his banner, and who never fails to point out the means of arriving at the desired end, gave her courage. On a certain day she detained Teodoro, and in a low and faltering voice said: "O Teodoro, brother and only refuge of my soul, the passion which afflicts me is so violent that unless you take pity on me, you shall soon see me bereft of that life which I endure only for your sake. I am terribly in love with you, and can no longer offer any resistance to the cruel flames which consume me." Her sobs and tears prevented her from saying more for the moment.

The hermit, who had never suspected that the maiden was in love with him, was astounded. But collecting his wits somewhat, he began to comfort her; and their talk was such that at last they abandoned the discussion of heavenly things to consider amorous ones. Finally they came to such an understanding that nothing was left to do but arrange the means whereby they might fulfil their eager desires. The young woman, who was very shrewd, said: "Lover mine, take no thought for these matters, for I will show you what measures we must take, to wit: At four o'clock tonight, place a light in the window of your hut and leave the rest to me, for when I see it, I will come over to you at once." "Alas, my love," replied Teodoro, "how can you manage to cross the sea? You know that neither of us possesses a boat of his own, and to place ourselves in others' hands would imperil the lives and honour of us both." "Have no fear," replied Malgherita, "but leave the affair to me, and I will find a way of coming to you without danger to honour or life. When I see the light I will swim over, and no one shall know anything of our privity." "But you may perish in the sea," answered Teodoro, "for you are young and not very strong; it is a long way, and you might become exhausted and drown." "I do not doubt that I shall be able to keep afloat," said the girl, "for I can swim like a fish."

The hermit, seeing that her mind was made up, agreed to her plan, and when it was fully dark he placed a light as directed, and in great happiness sat down to wait for the coming of his mistress.

When Malgherita saw the light she rejoiced. She took off her dress and stockings and walked to the strand in her shift; there she took off her chemise, and tying it about her head, launched into the water. To such good purpose did she bestir arms and legs that in a quarter of an hour she reached the hut where the hermit was waiting for her. Teodoro led her into his wretched cottage, and taking a clean white towel tenderly dried every part of her body. Then he led her to his little cell, and placing her upon his cot, lay down beside her; and there the lovers enjoyed the ultimate fruits of love.

Before daybreak on the morrow Malgherita, highly satisfied and content, made arrangements with Teodoro for return visits, and then took her leave. Thereafter the young woman became so addicted to the sweet entertainment which the hermit provided for her that she waited impatiently for the signal light. But impious and blind Fortune, enemy of human felicity, would not suffer her to enjoy her dear lover any great length of time; like one envious of another's well-being, she interposed, and destroyed their whole scheme.

One time when the air was filled with dark and shifting clouds Malgherita swam out in answer to the signal, and as it happened, was perceived by some fishermen. They thought the swimming creature was a fish, and gave close attention; but finally they discerned that it was a woman who, on coming to land, entered the hermit's hut. This circumstance aroused their curiosity, so they rowed up to the hut and kept watch until Malgherita came out again and swam off in the direction of Middle Island. Unfortunately, the girl took no care to hide herself, and was recognized. After they had watched this procedure several times the fishermen debated among themselves whether or not to divulge it. Taking into account the scandal which might attach to a decent family, and the risk of death which the girl ran every time she ventured into the sea, they finally decided to disclose the matter to Malgherita's brothers.

When the brothers heard this bitter news, they were unable to believe it except by the evidence of their own eyes. Obtaining ocular proof they decided to kill their sister, and having made a plan, they put it into execution.

At dusk the youngest brother got into his boat and went quietly and alone to the hermit's cottage, begging him for shelter during the night, since such and such a thing had happened whereby he stood in great peril of being seized and condemned to death. Teodoro recognized him as Malgherita's brother, received him kindly, and gave him his company all through the night, entertaining him with talk about worldly miseries and the grave sins which corrupt the soul to the service of the devil.

In the meantime the other brothers took a torch and a long pole, and rowed toward the hermit's dwelling. When they had come quite near, they erected the pole with the torch fixed to it, and waited for what might happen. No sooner did Malgherita see the light than she swam out toward it, as was her custom; and as soon as the brothers heard the sound of her movements in the water, they seized the oars and rowed silently away from the rock. They went so quietly that Malgherita did not hear them, nor, on account of the darkness of the night, did she distinguish them either. On and on she went in the direction of the light. The brothers finally got far away from land, whereupon they took down the pole and extinguished the torch. The wretched girl, seeing the light no longer, not knowing where she was, and already wearied by her long swim, took fright. Then, when it became clear to her that she was beyond human aid, she let herself go completely, and like a broken ship, was swallowed up by the sea.

When the brothers saw that there was now very little likelihood of her escape, they left their miserable sister in the middle of the sea and returned home. At daybreak the youngest brother gave the hermit due thanks for his shelter and entertainment, and also went his way.

Soon the sad news spread through the town that Malgherita Spolatina could not be found. The brothers publicly gave every evidence of grief, but in their hearts they rejoiced exceedingly. The third day had hardly dawned when the dead body of the most unhappy girl was washed up at the hermit's shore by the waves. When Teodoro saw and recognized her, he almost took his life. However, he drew her out of the water and carried her to his hut, and throwing himself upon her dead body, wept uncontrollably, bedewing the white bosom with abundant tears, and often calling out her name. But when his first grief had been somewhat washed away with tears, he took thought about giving Malgherita decent burial, and aiding her soul with prayers and fasting. With his garden spade he dug a grave in his little church. Weeping bitterly he closed her eyes and mouth and placed a garland of roses and violets on her head; then he kissed her and gave her a last benediction, put her into the grave, covered her with earth, and the earth with flowers.

In this wise was preserved the honour of the brothers and the lady; and not until the last brother was labouring on his death-bed was it learned what had become of Malgherita Spolatina.

"Thank you for your story," said Peter Bell; "I have often been curious to know what kind of life a hermit leads."

"You must not take Teodoro as a representative example," cautioned Blaise.

"If you would like to enter upon that kind of life," suggested John Colgan, "I can instruct you further from the lives of many Irish saints and ascetics. I can recommend, too, some islands off the coast of Ériu eminently adapted for the purpose. Take Inis Túiscert, now, or Great Skellig. Then there are the Skerries, or Rathlin."

"He would never make it," interposed Adamnan, "without the aid of Columcille, for Brecan's Cauldron, vulgarly called Corrie Vrekan, lies between, and would swallow him down as it did Brecan the son of Maine the son of Niall of the Nine Hostages."

"Coire Brecain has shifted its location since your day," said Camden; "it now lies between Scarba and Jura off the Scottish coast; John of Fordun put it there."

"But it is none the less treacherous and violent for being Scotch," said Sir Thomas Gray.

"You might do worse than choose a Scotch island," said Hector Boëce; "there are plenty from which to make a selection."

"I visited forty myself," said Fynes Moryson.

"And none of them are very attractive," added Fulk Fitzwarin.

"Well, then," continued Hector, "north of the Scots islands are the Faroës, not all of which are inhabited, and so are splendidly adapted for eremitical purposes."

"The seas in that quarter are just as heavy," put in Sigmund Brestison, "as I have good reason to know, and afford an excellent test of swimming skill. I recommend particularly the passage between Scufey and Southrey."

"I think," said Richard de Haldingham judicially, "that the best place for him would be Hy Brasil. He could take Unibos, Martin Scabby, Jean d'Outremeuse and Giraldus Cambrensis with him."

"'Tis not to any Irish island that the detractor of Ireland shall go," cried Keating with heat.

"But I don't want to go to any island," objected Peter Bell plaintively; "nor do I want to be a hermit."

"I admire a man who knows his own mind," said Richard of Devizes.

"I remember Coire Brecain," said Cormac of Cashel musingly. "The waters of the land and of the sea have played no inconsiderable rôle in the legends of my country. Very early in the history of Ireland we read how Rudraige, Partholon's son, was overwhelmed by the rising of Loch Rury. The waters were also the cause of Tuag's death at the mouth of the Bann, Tuag, on whom Manannan mac Lir had set his love. Ruad, too, the taper-fingered maiden, perished at the mouth of the river Erne while on her way to seek her lover Aed. Not less tragic was the fate of Clidna in the Bay of Glandore. I will tell you the story, if you like."

77. CLIDNA'S WAVE

Cormac of Cashel

With Finn of the Fianna there was an *óglaech* of trust, Ciabhan, son of Eochaid Imdherg, king of Ulidia in the north. The youth was so that, as the moon in her twelve provinces exceeds in brilliance all stars of heaven, even such was the measure in which for form and feature Ciabhan outshone all kings' sons in the world. With him the Fianna grew to be discontented, however, the cause of their discontent being this: among them was no woman, mated or unmated, who was not in love with him. Finn renounced him therefore, yet he was loath to have him go, only that for the greatness of their jealousy he feared the Fianna of all Ireland.

Ciabhan accordingly went his way until he came to Tragh an Chairn in the province of Ulidia, between Dunseverick in Antrim, and the sea, and his men with him. There he saw a high-prowed currach having a narrow stern of copper, and in it two young men, each one of whom wore a robe wrapping him to his shoulders. Ciabhan saluted them, and they returned his greeting. "Whence are ye, O youths?" he asked them. "I am Lodan, the king of India's son," replied one of them; "and yonder other is Eolus, son of the king of Greece. The sea has drifted and the wind driven us, nor do we know what land or what race of the world at large is that in and among which we are." "He who should fancy to sail the sea with you," said Ciabhan, "would ye give him a berth in the currach?" "Wert thou all alone, we would do so," they answered. Then Ciabhan stepped into the currach and bade farewell to his men, who were gloomy and discouraged, for to part from him they felt to be divorcing soul and body. Then Ciabhan ratified amity and friendship with the two young men in the boat.

Now rose at them white and bellowing waves, insomuch that each huge billow of them equalled a mountain; and that the beautiful variegated salmon wont to hug bottom sand and shingle touched the currach's very sides; in presence of which phenomena horror and fear affected them, and Ciabhan said: "By our word and verily, were it but on land we were, we could, whether on battle-field or in single combat, make a good fight for ourselves." In this great extremity they continued till they saw bear down on them an *óglaech* having under him a dark grey horse reined with a golden bridle; for the space of nine waves he would be submerged in the sea, but would rise on the crest of the tenth, and that without his chest or breast wetted. He inquired of them: "What fee would ye give him who should rescue you out of this great strait?" "Is there in our hand the price that is demanded of us?" they answered. "There is so," said the warrior; "namely, that yourselves be by conditions of service and of fealty bound to him who should so succour you." They consented, and struck their hands into the *óglaech's*.

This done the warrior drew all three to him out of the currach onto the horse, abreast and alongside of which the boat swam on its beam ends till they came into port and took the beach in Tír Tarrngaire, that is, the Land of Promise. There they dismounted and went on to Manannan mac Lir's stone fort, wherein an end was just made of ordering a banqueting-hall before them. All four of them were served then: their horns, their cuachs, their cups were raised; comely dark-browed gillas went round with smooth-polished horns; sweet-stringed timpans were played by them, and most melodious dulcet-chorded harps, until the whole house was flooded with music.

Now in the Land of Promise Manannan possessed an arch-ollave who had three daughters, Aeife, Edaein and Clidna Fair-hair. Three treasures of womanhood were they. The daughters of thrice fifty kings used to come to tend the tresses of Clidna's hair. Now upon our three warriors these at one instant cast their affections and appointed to elope with them the next day. At the landing place Aeife and Edaein got into one currach with Lodan and Eolus. Ciabhan and Clidna entered another. They hoisted sail in their frail craft; the wind roared, and the surge of the sea bore them to Trágh Téite in the south of Ireland.

Ciabhan landed on the shore, and while he passed in under the forest's tangled tresses in search of game, he left Clidna afloat there. After he had gone, the outer swell rolled in on Clidna, whereby she was drowned. Not a lucky sound had that wave for Ciabhan.

To the north on this shore is the grave of Téite; to the south lies Clidna's tomb, close beside the *sídh* of Dorn Buidhe. Even today Dornbuie's locks are drenched by the rollers of the mighty deluge which overwhelmed Clidna Cendfind, Genann's daughter.

"As for Coire Brecain," added Cashel's king and bishop, "I am not aware that it was responsible for the death of any lovers, though the death of Cred, beloved of Cano mac Gartnain occurred at a spot not far distant."

"What is this Coire Brecain?" inquired Peter Bell.

"It is a whirlpool or maelstrom between Rathlin and Antrim," said Giraldus Cambrensis before Cormac could answer, "towards which there is a set current of waves from all quarters until, pouring themselves into Nature's secret recesses, they are swallowed up, as it were, in the abyss. Should a vessel chance to pass in that direction, it is caught and drawn along by the force of the waves, and sucked in by the vortex without chance of escape. But Ireland is not the only country which can boast of such a whirlpool," he added, somewhat sourly. "There are three others."

"Where are they?" asked Alexander Neckam.

"One is in Norway, between Wero and Loffoden; another is between Scylla and Charybdis, and . . ."

"The fourth," interposed Roger of Hoveden, as Giraldus hesitated, "is in the Gulf of Adalia, which Chaucer called Satalye."

"Would you tell us about it?" asked Bartholomew.

"Willingly," replied Roger; "but you had better have it from my friend Walter Map, who has embroidered the account of its origin with details more attractive to the romantic taste."

"Well," said Map, "I did not suppose that anyone would ever praise or even remember my trifles; but since I am not busy just now, there seems to be no reasonable excuse for refusing."

78. THE COBBLER OF CONSTANTINOPLE

Walter Map

As Philippe of France, surnamed the Auguste, was sailing home from Acre, he touched, among other places, at the islands of Yse. In former times there lived in one of them a maid called Yse, from whom the islands got their name. The inhabitants say that this lady was loved by a certain young man, but that she rejected his suit while she lived. This she did with good reason, for she was of high degree and he was nothing but a shoe-maker.

This young man, whose name I do not know, plied his trade in Constantinople. He was not only a master craftsman, but had a genuine artistic feeling for his work. He required no more than the mere sight of a foot, whether large or small, fair or foul, to enable him to fit it easily and neatly, and that in the briefest space of time. The fame of his art and skill spread so wide that it became the fashion to be shod by him, and at last he had so much work that he found no time to attend to any but the noble and wealthy.

Now the fame of the cobbler of Constantinople had also reached the lovely Yse in her island home, and one day when she was on a shopping tour in the city she paused beside the shoe-maker's booth, and stretching forth her bare foot, ordered him to make her the best pair of shoes he knew how. The young cobbler gaped for a while in astonishment, for in all his experience he had never beheld a woman's foot so small, so white, so well shaped, so altogether lovely. With such inspiration it may be said that he produced his *chef-d'œuvre*.

That was the end of the matter so far as Yse was concerned, but it was far otherwise with the poor young shoe-maker. The girl entered his life and his heart foot first, and he felt, as had Anacreon before him, that it would be happiness to be walked on by such a foot. But it is one thing to be in love, and quite another to be able to win your lady. Disparity in rank, though a high, is not an insuperable obstacle, and the cobbler determined to surmount it. He sold his business and his patrimony, and entered the military profession, hoping by valiant deeds to raise himself to a position where he might command the lady's favourable notice. Fortune smiled on him for a while, and when his exploits had brought him the desired renown, he went to the islands and sued for the lady's hand. But Yse's father was nowise disposed to bestow his daughter upon a low-born and impecunious churl. The refusal was bitter to the shoemaker-knight, the more so since Yse, who witnessed it, favoured his presumption with a smile of contempt.

Like many another lover in similar circumstances, our hero resolved to return to the island with sufficient men-at-arms to enable him to carry the lady away by force. But again Fortune gave a twist to her wheel: before he could put his design into effect, sure news reached him that Yse had died. Jealous of her in death as in life, the cobbler proceeded by night to her grave and broke it open.— Now over this scene I must draw a veil, or else speak in Latin, which is always decent. Perhaps it will suffice to say that he found the lady more yielding in death than in life—quod cum viva facere non potuit, cum mortua perfecit. After nine months the devil appeared to him and said: Here is your son; cut off his head and keep it by you; and whenever you wish to overcome your enemies or waste their lands, uncover the face of the severed head, and your enemy and his country will forthwith perish on beholding it. When you cover the face again the trouble will cease.

As the voice bade, thus the soldier did, to the terror and despair of many peoples. Some declared him to be a wizard, others a god. But true it is that no one dared refuse him aught.

Now it happened that in the course of time the shoemaker-soldier married—some say the daughter of the emperor of Constantinople. Howbeit, his wife, after the way of women, was curious, and many times she asked him by what art or skill he was able to destroy his enemies. The soldier refused to explain, and told her angrily to hold her tongue. That, of course, has never been a good way to handle women, and you can readily imagine what happened. One day when her lord was absent the lady went to his chest, expecting to find therein the explanation of her husband's secret; and in the chest she did indeed find the detestable head, and rushing from the house she hurled it into the gulf of Adalia.

Sailors say that when the head rises to the surface, as though the bowels of the sea refused to harbour so loathsome an object, the gulf is so agitated that no ship can venture upon it; but when the head sinks again, the sea becomes calm enough for navigation. Others say that the lady had the shoe-maker thrown into the sea with the head, and that the constant effort of the sea to eject these two abominations caused a whirlpool of sucking waters which ever since has swallowed up both man and ship. Credat hoc Judaeus Apella, as Horace says, non ego.

"Cobblers," said Marco Polo, "are notoriously libidinous. When I was in the East I heard of a certain shoe-maker of Baghdad who had been similarly tempted by a fair customer; but since his eye had offended the law, he took an awl and put it out. Subsequently he moved a mountain, to the great awe and consternation of the Calif of the Saracens."

"As a love story your tale leaves a great deal to be desired," said Sir Thomas Elyot; "so does Cormac's, if I may say so. It has been abundantly shown how Tragedy dogs the steps of lovers. Sometimes it turns their very affection against them when no other means will serve. Unlike the Reeve, I do not scoff at death from love. Such occurrences are no doubt the result of a pathological state. A still deeper-lying cause of tragic love is probably the fact that, except in moments of passion, man and woman are really alien to one another. More admirable, in my opinion, are the examples of enduring affection between man and man, wherein circumstances are not complicated by the intrusion of sex. Ancient writers frequently allude to friends whose devotion to each other was noble and often heroic. When men are really friends, there is between them neither mistrust nor suspicion, nor can any surmise of evil report withdraw them from their affection."

"That is true," said Walter Map, "as I pointed out in my story of Sadius and Galo."

"Your position is also well illustrated by the late romance of Sir Eger and Sir Grime," said Sir John Bourchier.

"If the company will listen," said the Lochmaben Harper, "I will give an account of masculine loyalty on a still broader stage."

79. KINMONT WILLIE

Lochmaben Harper

O have ye na heard o' the fause Sakelde?
. O have ye na heard o' the keen Lord Scroop?
How they hae ta'en bauld Kinmont Willie,
    On Hairibee to hang him up?

Had Willie had but twenty men,
    But twenty men as stout as he,
Fause Sakelde had never the Kinmont ta'en,
    Wi' eight score in his cumpanie.

They band his legs beneath the steed,
    They tied his hands behind his back;
They guarded him, fivesome on each side,
    And they brought him ower the Liddel-rack.

They led him thro' the Liddel-rack,
    And also thro' the Carlisle sands;
They brought him to Carlisle castell,
    To be at my Lord Scroop's commands.

"My hands are tied, by my tongue is free,
    And whae will dare this deed avow?
Or answer by the border law?
    Or answer to the bauld Buccleuch?"

"Now haud thy tongue, thou rank reiver!
    There's never a Scot shall set ye free;
Before ye cross my castle yate,
    I trow ye shall take farewell o' me."

"Fear na ye that, my lord," quo Willie;
    "By the faith o my bodie, Lord Scroop," he said,
"I never yet lodged in a hostelrie
    But I paid my lawing before I gaed."

Now word is gane to the bauld Keeper,
    In Branksome Ha' where that he lay,
That Lord Scroop has ta'en the Kinmont Willie,
    Between the hours of night and day.

He has ta'en the table wi' his hand,
    He garr'd the red wine spring on hie:

"Now Christ's curse on my head," he said,
   "But avengéd of Lord Scroop I'll be!

"O is my basnet a widow's church?
   Or my lance a wand of the willow-tree?
Or my arm a ladye's lilye hand?
   That an English lord should lightly me?

"And have they ta'en Kinmont Willie,
   Against the truce of border tide,
And forgotten that the bauld Buccleuch
   Is keeper here on the Scottish side?

"And have they e'en ta'en him, Kinmont Willie,
   Withouten either dread or fear,
And forgotten that the bauld Buccleuch
   Can back a steed, or shake a spear?

"O were there war between the lands,
   As well I wot that there is none,
I would slight Carlisle castell high,
   Tho' it were builded of marble-stone.

"I would set that castell in a low,
   And sloken it with English blood;
There's nevir a man in Cumberland
   Should ken where Carlisle castell stood.

"But since nae war's between the lands,
   And there is peace, and peace should be,
I'll neither harm English lad or lass,
   And yet the Kinmont freed shall be!"

He has call'd him forty marchmen bauld,
   I trow they were of his ain name,
Except Sir Gilbert Elliot call'd,
   The laird of Stobs, I mean the same.

He has call'd him forty marchmen bauld,
   Were kinsmen to the bauld Buccleuch;
With spur on heel, and splent on spauld,
   And gleuves of green, and feathers blue.

There were five and five before them a',
   Wi' hunting-horns and bugles bright;

And five and five came wi' Buccleuch,
  Like warden's men, arrayed for fight.

And five and five, like a mason-gang,
  That carried the ladders lang and hie;
And five and five, like broken men:
  And so they reached the Woodhouselee.

And as we cross'd the Bateable Land,
  When to the English side we held,
The first o' men that we met wi',
  Whae sould it be but fause Sakelde?

"Where be ye gaun, ye hunters keen?"
  Quo' fause Sakelde; "come tell to me!"
"We go to hunt an English stag,
  Has trespassd on the Scots countrie."

"Where be ye gaun, ye marshal-men?"
  Quo' fause Sakelde; "Come tell me true!"
"We go to catch a rank reiver,
  Has broken faith wi' the bauld Buccleuch."

"Where are ye gaun, ye mason-lads,
  Wi' a' your ladders lang and hie?"
"We gang to herry a corbie's nest,
  That wons not far frae Woodhouselee."

"Where be ye gaun, ye broken men?"
  Quo' fause Sakelde; "come tell to me."
Now Dickie of Dryhope led that band,
  And the never a word o' lear had he.

"Why trespass ye on the English side?
  Row-footed outlaws, stand!" quo he.
Then never a word had Dickie to say,
  Sae he thrust the lance thro his fause bodie.

Then on we held for Carlisle toun,
  And at Staneshaw-bank the Eden we cross'd;
The water was great, and meikle of spait,
  But the nevir a horse nor man we lost.

And when we reachd the Staneshaw-bank,
  The wind was rising loud and hie;

And there the laird garr'd leave our steeds,
  For fear that they should stamp and nie.

And when we left the Staneshaw-bank,
  The wind began full loud to blaw;
But 'twas wind and weet, and fire and sleet,
  When we came beneath the castel-wa'.

We crept on knees, and held our breath,
  Till we placed the ladders against the wa';
And sae ready was Buccleuch himsell
  To mount the first before us a'.

He has ta'en the watchman by the throat,
  He flung him down upon the lead:
"Had there not been peace between our lands,
  Upon the other side thou hadst gaed!

"Now sound out, trumpets!" quo' Buccleuch;
  "Let's waken Lord Scroop right merrilie!"
Then loud the warden's trumpets blew
  "O whae dare meddle wi' me?"

Then speedilie to work we gaed,
  And raised the slogan ane and a',
And cut a hole thro' a sheet of lead,
  And so we wan to the castel-ha'.

They thought King James and a' his men
  Had won the house wi' bow and spear:
It was but twenty Scots and ten
  That put a thousand in sic a stear.

Wi' coulters and wi' fore-hammers,
  We garr'd the bars bang merrilie,
Untill we came to the inner prison,
  Where Willie o' Kinmont he did lie.

And when we cam to the lower prison,
  Where Willie o' Kinmont he did lie—
"O sleep ye, wake ye, Kinmont Willie,
  Upon the morn that thou's to die?"

"O I sleep saft, and I wake aft;
  It's lang since sleeping was fleyd frae me;

KINMONT WILLIE

Gie my service back to my wife and bairns,
   And a' gude fellows that speir for me."

Then Red Rowan has hente him up,
   The starkest men in Teviotdale:
"Abide, abide now, Red Rowan,
   Till of my Lord Scroop I take farewell.

"Farewell, farewell, my gude Lord Scroop!
   My gude Lord Scroop, farewell!" he cried;
"I'll pay you for my lodging-maill
   When first we meet on the borderside."

Then shoulder high, with shout and cry,
   We bore him down the ladder lang;
At every stride Red Rowan made,
   I wot the Kinmont's airns playd clang.

"O mony a time," quo' Kinmont Willie,
   "I have ridden horse baith wild and wood;
But a rougher beast than Red Rowan
   I ween my legs have ne'er bestrode.

"And mony a time," quo' Kinmont Willie,
   "I've pricked a horse out oure the furs;
But since the day I backed a steed
   I never wore sic cumbrous spurs."

We scarce had won the Staneshaw-bank,
   When a' the Carlisle bells were rung,
And a thousand men, in horse and foot,
   Cam wi' the keen Lord Scroop along.

Buccleuch has turned to Eden Water,
   Even where it flod frae bank to brim,
And he has plunged in wi' a' his band,
   And safely swam them thro' the stream.

He turned him on the other side,
   And at Lord Scroop his glove flung he:
"If ye like na my visit in merry England,
   In fair Scotland come visit me!"

All sore astonished stood Lord Scroop,
   He stood as still as rocke of stane;

>He scarcely dared to trew his eyes
>   When thro' the water they had gane.
>
>"He is either himsell a devil frae hell,
>   Or else his mother a witch maun be;
>I wad na have ridden that wan water
>   For a' the gowd in Christentie."

"That was a splendid ballet," said Sir James Douglas, "and you shall have a coat and hood for it."

"Thank you, my lord," said the harper, "it is a long time since I had either, for since the spread of a new invention called printing, minstrels have decayed, and gentlemen with them."

"Sir Thomas," said Marco Polo, "the thesis which you support is an interesting one. I take no sides, yet I should like to set before the company some evidence of a slightly different nature. It concerns a man who was the friend not of one man, or of a few, but of all mankind."

80. SAGAMONI BORCAN, THE VIRTUOUS PRINCE
Marco Polo

Ceylon, as you know, is an island, and in the midst thereof rises a lofty mountain, which is so steep and precipitous that it cannot be ascended save by means of the iron chains which men have fixed to the rock. The Saracens say that the tomb of our first parent Adam is on this mountain, but the idolators deny this, asserting that it is the tomb of Sergamo Borgani or Sagamoni Borcan, or Sakyamuni Burkhan, as he is variously called. Him they consider to have been a saint, and the best man who ever lived, and it was only after his time that idols were made among them.

The story goes that this Borcan was the son of a very wealthy and powerful king. From his earliest age his mind was turned wholly away from worldly things; he would not listen to any talk about them, and what was worse, he refused to have any part in the administration of the kingdom. This attitude of Borcan's inspired his father with mingled feelings of rage and grief. He tried all the wiles at his command in the effort to interest his son in his worldly obligations, even offering to abdicate and allow him to be crowned at once in his place. All was of no avail, and the good king was almost at his wits' end with wrath and despair, especially as Borcan was his only son, and there was no one else to whom he might leave the kingdom at his death.

After meditating on his problem for considerable time the old king resolved to try one more expedient. He caused a large and handsome palace to be built for his son's exclusive use. Therein he placed all manner of delights, but took particular care to choose three hundred of the most beautiful maidens that could anywhere be found as the sole servitors and entertainers of Borcan's leisure. To them he gave categorical orders that they were to amuse themselves with the prince night and day—that they should dance before him, sing and recite verses, or use any other means of their own invention whereby they might draw his heart to worldly enjoyments. But all was in vain, for Borcan looked on with bored or apathetic eye at those rare times when he was not, as it seemed, contemplating the vistas of some private world. One by one the girls, with chagrin and amazement, were forced to admit to the old king their failure to arouse the least inclination toward wantonness in the young man's breast.

Towards the end of the year Borcan began to feel the need of fresh air and exercise, and went for a ride. Not far from the palace he saw a corpse lying by the roadside. Now he had never seen a dead man before, and inquired what that object might be. "That," said his master, "is a dead man; he seems to have starved to death." "What!" exclaimed the prince; "do men die, then?" "Oh, yes," said his master; "all men in their time." Borcan said nothing, and they rode farther. After a while they came up to an old fellow sitting beside the road; he was so aged that he could no longer walk, and he had not a tooth in his mouth nor a hair on his head. "What is the meaning of this?" asked the prince. Then the master explained that the man was suffering from extreme old age. "What!" cried the young man, "do all men lose their hair and teeth?" "Oh, yes," answered his master, "sooner or later." Thereupon Borcan would ride no farther, and turning back toward the palace, declared he would abide no longer in this evil world.

That night he stole secretly from the palace and somehow climbed the mountain of which I have spoken. There he lived a life of great hardship and sanctity, so that he became very holy. When he died his father caused an image to be made of his beloved son, and ordered the people to adore it. This they did readily enough, for they thought Borcan a god who had condescended to dwell among them for a time as a man.

"As I see it," said Ulrich von Lichtenstein, "your hero had a grievous fault in that he appeared to be the enemy of women. There are plenty of philosophers present who will prove to you—and to him

—the folly of extremes. I know that folly myself, for I loved women too well."

"Your Sagamoni," said Dafydd ab Gwilym, "would have found a match in one of my countrywomen. It seems to me interesting to speculate on the results of their encounter, could they have met."

"To whom do you allude?" asked Iolo Goch.

"I will tell you," answered Dafydd.

"Tell it in prose," said Andrew Boorde.

"For the benefit of prosaic minds, I will," answered the Welshman.

81. DWYNWEN VERCH BRYCHAN AND MAELON DAFODRILL
Dafydd ab Gwilym

Maelon Dafodrill, and Dwynwen, the daughter of Saint Brychan, mutually loved each other. Maelon sought her in inappropriate union, and was rejected. For this reason he left her in animosity, and aspersed her, which caused her extreme sorrow and anguish. One night when she was alone in a wood, she prayed that God would cure her of her love, and the Almighty appearing to her while she was asleep, gave her a delicious liquor, which quite fulfilled her desire. And she saw the same draught administered to Maelon, who thereupon became a frozen lump of ice. The Almighty also deigned to give her three choices. First she desired that Maelon should be unfrozen; next, that her supplications in favour of all true-hearted lovers should be granted, so that they should either obtain the objects of their affection or be cured of their passion; thirdly that thenceforth she should never wish to be married. The three requests were conceded to her, whereupon she took the veil and became a saint. Subsequently, every faithful lover who invoked her was either relieved from his passion, or obtained the object of his affection.

"I can imagine no good resulting from the meeting of two such people," objected Andrew the Chaplain; "it would have been nugatory in the highest degree."

"The question has often intrigued me," said John Skelton, "whether or not a love affair between Jeanne Darc and Savonarola might not have saved both their lives."

"Such of mésalliance was fortunately prevented by Father Time," put in Guicciardini.

"Speaking of mésalliances," said Roger of Wendover, "I recall what in my opinion is a classic illustration."

82. THE YOUNG MAN MARRIED TO A STATUE
Roger of Wendover

Pope Stephen IX was succeeded, as you know, by Benedict X. At that time a certain youth, a citizen of Rome, and of senatorial dignity, married a noble virgin, and in honour of the occasion made a feast to his companions for many days. One day, being satiated with delicacies, they went out into the plain to strengthen their stomachs with exercise, and spent a great part of the day in playing at ball. In order not to lose his nuptial ring, the youth, unobserved by his companions, put it on the extended finger of a certain brazen statue; after which he joined in the game. But becoming heated with violent running, he was the first to give up the play, and on coming to the statue he found the finger on which he had placed the ring bent against the palm, and the ring firmly held on it. After many vain attempts to break the finger, or get off the ring by any means, finding that all was of no avail, he retired in great confusion, concealing what had happened from his companions lest they should laugh at him. Returning at night to the statue with his servants, he was amazed at finding the finger extended and the ring taken off. He said nothing about his loss and returned home.

The following night, as he lay down by the side of his bride, he was sensible of the presence of some misty though dense substance interposed between him and her, which might be felt, though not seen. Prevented by this obstacle from embracing his wife, he heard a voice addressing him: "Embrace me, for you wedded me today. I am Venus, on whose finger you placed the ring; I have it, and I will not give it up." Terrified at such a prodigy, the young man had neither the courage nor the ability to reply, and passed a sleepless night in silent reflection on the matter.

A considerable space of time elapsed in this way, so that as often as he sought the embraces of his wife, the same circumstance occurred. In other respects, however, he was strong and daring, as well in the forum as in military exercise. At length, urged by the complaints of his bride, he revealed the matter to her parents, and they, after holding council, communicated the matter to a priest named Palumbas living near the city. This man was skilled in necromancy, could raise magical apparitions, call up devils and compel them to do any work he pleased. Making an agreement that he should fill his purse most plentifully provided he succeeded in recovering the ring and making the lovers happy, he called up all the power of his art. Then he gave the young man a letter which he had prepared and said: "Go to the cross-roads at such an hour of the night, and stand there awaiting in silence what will happen. There will pass by figures of both sexes, of every rank, age and condition; some on horseback, some on foot, some with downcast looks, others with heads erect and haughty mien. If they address you, make no reply. This company will be followed by a person more handsome and larger than the rest, sitting in a chariot. Speak not, but give him the letter to read, and if only you have courage, your desire will be immediately accomplished."

The young man eagerly set about the enterprise and boldly took his stand at the cross-ways to test the truth of the priest's words. He saw the company, as the priest had said. Among the other passing figures he beheld a woman in the attire of a harlot, riding on a mule, her hair flowing loosely over her shoulders; in her hand she held a golden rod, with which she managed her steed, and as she went she exhibited wanton gestures, her garments being so thin that she was all but naked. At last came he who seemed to be the chief, riding in a chariot adorned with emeralds and pearls. He fixed his eyes sternly on the young man and demanded the cause of his presence. The youth made no reply, but stretching out his hand gave him the letter. The demon, who did not dare to slight the well-known seal, read it, and then extending his arms to heaven exclaimed: "O God, in whose sight every transgression is a noisome smell, how long wilt thou endure the wickedness of the priest Palumbas?" He then dispatched his servants to take the ring from Venus, and after much evasion she was at length compelled to relinquish it.

The happy youth then without any obstacle attained the enjoyment of his bride for which she had so long sighed. But the priest Palumbas, on hearing the demon's complaints of him unto the Lord, perceived that the end of his days was at hand; wherefor he cut off all his members with a knife, and died in this astonishing act of penance, after making public confession to the pope of unparallelled acts of wickedness.

"I have heard that story too," said William of Malmesbury.

"It is well known," said John of Fordun, "and portrays a situation somewhat worse than merely being in love with a statue."

"Well," remarked the Knight of La Tour Landry, "I am sure such an adventure is likely to happen to few, and will not be desired by any, for God knows, mortal wives are difficult enough to deal with.

Though I have written at length on the subject of wifely obedience—or rather my library hack has done so—I will illustrate by a single tale."

83. THREE MERCHANTS AND THEIR INOBEDIENT WIVES
Knight of La Tour Landry

It happened once that there were three merchants going homeward from a fair, and as they were riding along the way, they fell to talking, and one of them said: "It is a splendid thing for a man to have a good wife who obeys and does his bidding at all times." "By my troth," said another, "my wife obeys me truly." "By God," said the third, "I think my wife obeys her husband best of all." Then the first merchant said: "Let us lay a wager of a dinner, and he whose wife obeys worst shall pay for it." Thereupon they arranged between them how they should test their wives, and the scheme was that each should bid his wife jump into a basin that he would place before her; and they took oath that none of them would let his wife know about the wager, but each should simply say: "Look now, wife, let what I command be done."

Afterwards, then, one of the merchants bade his wife jump into the basin which he had set on the ground before her. She asked: "Why?" and he answered: "Because it pleases me, and I will that you do it." "By God," said she, "first will I know the reason." Nor would she do as she had been bidden on any other condition, so her husband up with his fist and gave her two or three good blows.

Now they went to the second merchant's house. After a little he bade his wife jump into the basin that was before her on the floor. She asked: "What for?" and said she would not do it. So her husband took a staff and beat her soundly.

Thereafter they went to the house of the third merchant, where they found food ready on the table, so the goodman whispered that he would put his wife to the test after dinner; and so they sat down. Thereupon the host said to his wife: "Whatever I bid, look to it that it be done, no matter what." And the goodwife, who loved and feared her husband, hearkened and took heed of his words, though she knew not what he meant.

Now it happened that they had soft-boiled eggs for their dinner and there was no salt. The goodman said: "Wife, *seyle sus table*," which in French means "jump on the table." She, who was afraid to disobey, jumped up on the table, throwing down food and drink, breaking the dishes and spilling all there was there. "How now!"

said the goodman, "don't you know any games but this?" "Be not wroth," said she, "for I have done your bidding in so far as I could, as you bade me, though it is to your harm and mine. But I should rather both of us suffered damage than disobey your command. What else should happen when you said: *Seyle sus table?*" "Nay," said the husband, "I said *sele sus table,* that is, put some salt on the table so that we might season our eggs." "By my troth," said the wife, "I understood you to bid me jump on the table." Then there was much mirth and laughter.

The other two merchants now said there was no need to bid her leap into the basin, for she had obeyed readily enough; and they agreed that they had lost the wager, and that their companion had won. Thereupon the wife was greatly praised for her obedience, and was not beaten as were the other two wives who refused to obey their husbands' orders.

Thus men of low station can teach their wives with fear and blows, but a gentlewoman should teach herself with fairness, for no otherwise can she be taught. And the more fairly a gentlewoman is dealt with, the more fearful should she be to displease or disobey her husband. For the good wife trusts and loves her husband; and every good woman ought to obey her man, be it in good or ill, for if he bid her do a thing which she ought not to do, then the disgrace is his.

"What a shameful story!" cried Christine de Pisan.

"In my opinion," said Jean Charlier Gerson, "it is a silly one. There are sufficient number of difficult things in life which it is necessary to do: What good purpose is served by forcing a woman to do folly?"

"You miss the point," said the Clerk of Oxenford. "Jumping into a basin is in itself of no value whatsoever to anyone, but the willingness and ability to obey orders is a virtue of the highest possible consequence. That he who is bidden should always understand the reason of the bidder does not enter into the problem at all. In any given instance, or moment, there must be one who commands and one who obeys, as Aristotle says. The beauty of this exemplum lies in this: that the merchants agreed to demand some apparently foolish thing; if they had bidden some simple and consuetudinary task, the wives would have obeyed without question, and there would have been no test. As it was, the wives of the first two were guilty of contumacy. I think Robert Mannyng will bear me out."

"Unbuxomness and disobedience," said Mannyng, "are the offspring of Pride. The good Chancellor knows that as well as I do. Did the angel provide Adam and Eve with explanations why they should not eat the fruit of a certain tree in Paradise?"

"As the Clerk says," spoke up Colin Clout, "there must be one who gives orders and one who executes them. Did you ever see a horse riding in his own saddle? Perhaps some of you recall the story of the lazy servant. One night his master said: 'Go and shut the door.' The servant replied that the door was shut. Later the master told him to get up and see if it was raining. The man was loath to leave his bed, though he pretended to do so; instead, he called the dog that was ranging about outside the house, and finding that its hair was damp answered: 'Master, it is raining.' Another time the master said: 'Rise and see if the fire is still burning.' This time the man called the cat who customarily slept on the hearth, and feeling that her fur was warm, he said: 'Master, there is plenty of fire.' On the morrow when the goodman rose, he found that the house-door had been open all night, whereupon he asked his servant why he had not closed it. 'Why should I close it,' replied the man, 'when I should only have to open it again in the morning?'"

"A man with such servants in his employ," said Camden, "would never build up an empire, as did Cyrus the Great."

"Discipline," said Cormac of Cashel, "is good for everybody, and particularly for women, who, of all animals are the most indocile. It is better to beat them than to coddle them, better to beware of them than to trust them. A wise man of my nation once said: Do not give your wife authority over you, for if she stamp on your foot today she will stamp on your head tomorrow."

"There may be something in what you say," conceded the Knight; "but must we go to extremes? I would call attention to what I said at the end of my story—that if it is shameful for a woman to disobey her husband, it is no less shameful for him to bid her do an unworthy thing—as I will illustrate by an anecdote: A young man who was newly married thought it would be good policy to get the maistrie of his wife at the very beginning. So when the pot was boiling on the fire he went to her, and though the meat had not yet boiled enough, he said she should take it off. His wife replied that the pottage was not yet ready to eat. But he said: 'I will have the pot taken off because it is my pleasure.' So the goodwife, loath to offend him so early in their marriage, set the pot beside the fire. When she had done this he ordered her to set the pot behind the door. 'You are not wise therein,' said she. But he replied severely that it should be as he bade; so the wife again did his bidding with good humour. But the young man was not yet satisfied, and commanded her to set the pot high up on the hen-roost. 'What!' said the goodwife, 'I think you must be mad.' Then the husband fiercely ordered her to place the pot where he had said, otherwise she should repent. The wife was somewhat afraid to try his patience now, so she took a ladder and set it against the roost, and went up with the pot in her hand, praying her husband to hold the ladder lest it slip; and so he did. At last, when the young man looked up and saw the pot standing on the hen-roost, he said: 'Lo, now the pot stands where I would have it.' But at that moment the ladder shook, the pot was upset, and the hot pottage lodged on the young man's head. 'And now,' said the goodwife, 'the pottage is where I would have it.'"

"If I may be so bold as to disagree with the king and bishop of Cashel," said Dr. Boorde, "I would give it as my opinion that every man ought to please his wife in all matters and not displease her; he should let her have her own will, for that she will have, whosoever say nay. And this arises from an evil education and bringing up, and a perverse mind, not fearing God nor worldly shame. Nowadays women are so that they think themselves greatly abused unless they can both hunt with the hounds and run with the hare."

"There is much truth in that remark," said Polydore Vergil, "for properly educated people understand that they ought to obey him who takes wiser thought for their interests than they themselves are able to do."

"It is a matter of common knowledge," said Barbour, "that thraldom is hard, but that marriage constitutes the hardest bonds that a man can assume."

"How true are your words, O learned Scot," cried the Goodman of Bath, "and what a heavy penalty we men pay for the dubious honour of being husbands. One time when I was in France I saw a handsome tapestry. The verses which accompanied the figures were so apposite that I made a copy of them. They are not inappropriate to this present discussion."

84. BYCORNE AND CHICHEVACHE

The Goodman of Bath

First there is represented the figure of a man dressed like a poet, who says: "O good people, give ear and remember the following tale of husbands and their wives as long as you live; call to mind how they agreed and how they quarrelled in life, and how death came to them through these two beasts. One of them, Bycorne, is of such a nature that he feeds only on subservient husbands, and the only food which Chichevache can eat is patient wives. One is as fat as can be, the other scrawny, for one finds great abundance of his natural food, and the other hardly any."

Now are portrayed two beasts, the one fat and flourishing, the other weak and thin. And the legend says: "These fearful beasts, Bycorne and Chichevache, according to their nature, can eat only patient husbands or sweet-tempered wives."

After this is pictured a great beast called Bycorne of Bicorny, who says: "I am Bycorne of Bycorny, fat and sleek, and I am bound to Chichevache by the bonds and sacraments of marriage—Chichevache who on land or sea eats no food save wives who are mild and gentle and who never vex their husbands. But her fare is very meagre, for she finds very few patient wives. The tongues of most clack all day in strife and jangling. For my part, I curse those wives who are unable, whether at bed or board, to keep their husbands from saying a word, because my proper food and my great delight consists, in a word, in those dolts who dare not gainsay their wives, who dare not stand upon their rights, who never venture to raise their voices. I swallow down all such."

Then there is shown a picture of a goodman kneeling before Bycorne to whom he says: "O sweet lord, I cry you mercy! I would have you know that I have come here to ask for your compassion, for I have a very devil of a wife, who disputes with me constantly, beats and slanders me, and never gives me a moment's peace. On the contrary, as though I were tied to a lead rope, she makes me carry out her every whim. In great dis-ease do patient husbands live."

Bycorne: Just a moment, my good fellow, while I finish swallowing this bit here—it is a savoury one, I assure you—and then I will give you my undivided attention and reply willingly to your suit. I must say that you have come at the right moment; a man who weeps and wails as furiously as you do cannot be very happy, and much weeping is bad for the eyes.

Goodman: And well may I tremble and sigh, for nowhere in the world would it be possible to find a wife worse than the one I have. If I say "Nuf," she says "Naf"; if I say "Buf," she says "Baf." She lacks no kind of malice in abundance, and so adept is she in every kind of evil that she does nothing day or night but scold. Nothing is more vexatious to a patient man.

Bycorne: Now really you are a silly fellow to suppose that you alone could get a good wife. All women are of one and the same consistency, and since they are so bad-tempered and contentious, my wife Chichevache is like to die of hunger. Still, it is not my fault if I am constrained to act in accordance with their behaviour. No long-suffering husband can escape me.

Now there is pictured a group of men approaching Bycorne, and underneath is this legend: "My friends, if you will pay attention, you can see how Bycorne devours all patient husbands—you and me both—for nothing can save us. A curse on all those husbands everywhere who allow their wives to be mistress over them! Bycorne here, according to law, will rend and devour him who leaves the sovereignty to his wife. That is the fearful fate of all patient ones, and of us, for we also have allowed our wives to become our masters. Well indeed may we admit that we have conceded the sovereignty to them, for we are slaves and they are free. Consequently this cruel beast Bycorne will eat us right down, to the last one. However, who or where is he who is master enough to teach and chasten his wife in such wise that she shall neither jangle nor disobey in some way? If such a man exists, I assure you he is safe from Bycorne."

Here, now, is represented a great beast with horns and long teeth, scrawny and lean, wasted away to skin and bones, who says: "My name is Chichevache, so wasted away by hunger, as you can see, that I am ashamed to show myself. How I suffer with hunger! There is not a bit of fat on me, for I can find nothing to eat; that is why I am nothing but skin and bones. For, you see, I am allowed to eat only sweet-natured wives who resemble Griselda in patience, or even surpass her in goodness. I have to look long before I can find anything on which to break my fast. It seems to me that patient wives are scarce this year. It must be that wives who are admonished by their husbands know too well how to defend themselves from such verbal attacks, for in searching from country to country, I have not found a single Griselda in the last thirty months. In fact, I never found but one in all my life, and she has been gone this long time. My supply of sustenance seems to be exhausted."

Then is portrayed Chichevache in the act of swallowing a wife, who cries out to all the women: "O noble ladies, be prudent and take example of me, otherwise you will not be able to escape death, I promise you. Take good care not to be meek and submissive, for if you are, Chichevache will not fail to swallow you down."

After Chichevache there is pictured an old man with a club who menaces her for having devoured his wife, and says: "Alas! my wife has been eaten! So patient was she and so humble! She never talked back to me, and this horrible beast has eaten her. Consequently, since it is impossible to find another woman like her, I am doomed to live alone all my life. Nowadays women have agreed among themselves to banish patience forever, and thus prevent Chichevache from finding anything to eat. Chichevache will have to fast for a long time now, and eventually die as the reward of her cruelty, for women in these days have grown so strong as to be able to tread humility under foot, and you will be pretty unhappy, you who have not sufficient patience to endure your wives' violence. And if you endure it, you are dead men, for this ferocious Bycorne is lying in wait for you. You tremble with fear to reply a single word to your wives, and thus, bound with a double chain, you hang between life and death."

The company laughed heartily at the Goodman's tale.

"I am glad to observe," said he, "that you have a sense of humour; my wife had not. When I read these verses to her she snatched them out of my hand and threw them into the fire. Fortunately, I was able to re-write them from memory. And though for once she said nothing, she sulked for a week. Probably she talked enough with her gossips, however; women do; and the devil himself knows what they are saying when no man is within ear-shot."

"Though I am no devil," said Dunbar, "I could tell you that. Once I stumbled by chance upon some direct evidence of the esteem in which men are held by the opposite sex. . . ."

85. THE TWO MARRIED WOMEN AND THE WIDOW
William Dunbar

On Midsummer evening, merriest of nights, I walked forth alone just after midnight beside a goodly green garth full of gay flowers hedged high with hawthorn trees. A bird burst forth with song such that no blither bird was ever heard on bough. Induced by the sugared sound of her glad song and by the sanative savour of the sweet flowers, I drew quietly to the dyke to wait for any amusement that might occur.

The dew dampened the dale and hushed the songsters. Near at hand, under a splendid green holly tree I heard high speech and haughty words; thereupon I thrust myself into the hedge so deeply that I was concealed by the hawthorn and sheltering leaves. Presently I looked through the prickles of the tangled thorn to see if anyone were approaching that pleasant garden; and as I looked I saw three gay ladies sitting in a green arbor, all adorned with garlands of goodly fresh flowers; their glorious yellow tresses glittered like gold, so that the very grasses gleamed with the reflection thereof. Their hair was combed and neatly parted, falling right down to their shoulders; above, they wore kerchiefs of fine clear lawn; their mantles were as green as the grass of May, gathered to their fair sides with their white fingers. Of wondrous fine favour were their gentle faces, as abundant in blooming fairness as the flowers of June, white, seemly and tender as the sweet lilies and like the rose new-blown upon the branch.

Before those three ladies was a marble table on which stood royal cups full of rich wines. And of those fair ladies two were wedded to lords, and one was a widow, wanton of late. As they talked at the table, turning over many bits of gossip, they drank the strong wine and overflowed with words, becoming so effusive that they avoided no subject at all.

Said the widow: "Come now, you wedded women, show what mirth you have found in marriage since you were men's wives. If you rue that unreasonable state, reveal it. Have you, perhaps, loved any man more than him to whom you have fastened your faith forever? Do you think, if you had your choice now, that you could choose better? Do you not think it a blessed bond that binds you so tightly that none may say adieu to it except through death?"

Then a lusty young woman with sprightly manners spoke up quickly: "That which you call the blessed bond which binds us so fast is baleful and bare of bliss, and causes great vexation. You ask, had I free choice, would I choose a better? Chains are ever to be avoided, and change is sweet. If I once had my choice to avoid such a cursed chance, I would escape forever out of the chains of a churl. Would to God that matrimony were only intercourse for a year! It is monstrous to be more, unless our minds agree thereto. It is against the law of love, of man and of nature, to strain together hearts that strive one with the other. Birds have a much better law than men, for every year they enter upon new joy with a new mate; they take a fresh lover, constant and still vigorous, and let their exhausted companions fly where they please. Would to Christ that such a custom were in effect among men! Then it would be well with us women! In that case we should be able to give every workman his leave to go when worn out. As for myself—I should be seemly arrayed in silk, neat, jolly, pretty, joyous, genteel, and I should be found at fairs, on the watch for new faces. And I should be found at plays, at preachings, and on great pilgrimages, to show my style royally wherever there was great press of folk. I would manifest my comeliness to a multitude of people, and blow my beauty abroad where men were many, so that I might choose and be chosen, and change when it pleased me. Then should I be very well able to select from among those of the realm one who would enjoy my feminine charms throughout the long winter night. And when I had got a handsome young man, eager to draw in the yoke for a year, and when I had proved his pith for the first pleasant month, then I would take pains to look about quietly in church and market, at the king's court and in all the country round about, in order to discover a gallant for the next year to keep up the good work when the other failed. I would look for an able-bodied man, enterprising, energetic in the traces, neither feeble nor faint nor exhausted, but fresh as May; and I would take all the fruit of his flower.

"As it is, I have a sloven, a worm, a feeble old churl, a wasted blackguard, a good-for-nothing able only to chatter words, a driveller, a drone, a bag of phlegm, a scabby cormorant, a scorpion, a scuttard. It fills me with loathing to see him scratch himself. When that wretch kisses me my sorrow begins: his beard is as stiff as the bristles of a fierce bear, but he is supple as silk otherwise. His two grim eyes are bloodshot and besmeared all round, and gorged like two puddles stopped up with slime. When that stark-staring ghost grips me, then I think hideous Mahound has me in his arms; no blessing can then save me from that old Satan, for though I cross me clean from the crown down, he will embrace my whole body and clasp me to his breast. When the old knave has shaved with a sharp razor, he pushes his wry mouth at me and splits my lips, and so hackles my cheeks with his hard hedgehog skin that my chaps glow like a gleaming coal. I shrink from the sharp pain, but dare not cry out by reason of the old shrew's threats, may shame betide him! The love-looks which that goblin casts at me from his bleary eyes abase my spirit as though Beelzebub had glanced at me; and when the sneak comes smirking at me with his feeble smolet he blubbers with his lips like a mangy old horse that has got the wind of a young filly. When the sound of his voice sinks into my ears, then is my annoy renewed, even before he approaches. When I hear his name mentioned I make nine crosses to ward off distress from that silly churl full of anger and jealousy and evil customs.

"Not a single look can I give to my lover on account of that lean cat, so full of jealousy and false deceit is he. Always is he imagining evil things in his mind, devising a thousand methods of catching me in a tryst with another man. I dare not glance at the boy who fills the cup because of the suspicions of that old shrew. And yet he himself is not worth a bean. He thinks that I yearn for young folk to pay me when he is gone. As for him, never yet have I allowed that lubber to defoul my flesh save for a great fee; and though his pen pays me poorly, his purse makes me rich reward afterwards. Before that useless old carcass climbs on my body I set up as a condition a new kerchief of the finest lawn, or a gown of cloth of grain gaily furred, or a ring with royal stone, or some other rich jewel; otherwise he may keep quiet, though he should go mad with frustration. Even so it seems to me that my favour is sold too cheap. Thus I sell him solace, though it seems sour to me. From such a lord God keep you safe, dear sisters!"

When the lovely lady had said her say to the end, then they all laughed loud and merrily, and reached round the cup full of rich wine, and jested long with riotous words before they ceased. Afterwards the widow addressed the other matron: "Now, fair sister, it falls to you to tell how you have fared since you were married in church. Tell us truly—which do you think most fitting, to bless or to curse that bond? How do you like the life of faithful wifehood? Afterwards you may examine me in the same wise, and I will tell the truth without dissimulation."

Said that gay lady: "I protest that if I reveal the truth you must be true of tongue." The other two promised, and therewith her spirit was greatly cheered. "I will not spare in what I have to say," she said, "for there is no spy near. I will pronounce a discourse from the bottom of my heart, and give voice to feelings so rank that they make me belch; now all the bile that has been so long gathering will burst out. It has been a heavy burden to bear it in my breast, but I shall void the venom with a large vent, and get some relief from the tumour that has swollen so large.

"My husband," said that lady, "was a wencher, the worst in the world, wherefor I hate him in my heart, so help me God! He is a young man and right eager, but not in the flower of youth, for he has faded much and become enfeebled in the last few years. He had been a lecher so long that he has lost his manhood. He was wasted by women before he chose me for his wife, and even in my time I have often taken him in adultery. And yet he is as showy with his bonnet on the side of his head, making eyes at the brightest in the burg, courtly in his clothes and in the dressing of his hair as is anyone who is really valiant in Venus' room. Though he is a cipher in bower, he gives the appearance of being really worth something, and looks as though he might merit loving. But he has form without force, and fashion without virtue; and he can give no effect to his fair words. For ladies in love he is as lusty as a shadow. She who has an old man as her mate is not ill used in comparison with me, for such a one is no worse at Venus' sport than he seems. But I thought I was going to enjoy a gem, and I got only a piece of jet; he shone like gold, but proved to be only glass. It seems to me that when men have lost their vigour there remains nothing but anger and jealousy in their hearts.

"You speak of birds on a bough: They may indeed sing of bliss who every year on St Valentine's day are searching for a mate. Had I that pleasant privilege, to part when I liked, to change and ever to choose again—then chastity adieu! Then I should always have a fresh lover to hold in my arms; but holding a man till he faint may be called folly. Many a time I muse on such matters at midnight, and mourn so in my mind that I murder myself. I lie awake for woe, and toss about cursing my wicked kin who cast me away on such a craven without courage—joined him to my beauty when there are so many keen knights in the kingdom. And often I dream of a seemlier man who is worth seven of my lord, and therewith I sigh. Thereupon he turns his empty carcass to me and clasps me in his arms. 'My darling, my sweeting,' says he, 'why do you not sleep better? It seems that you have a fever, as though you were distressed by sorrow or care.' Then I reply: 'My honey boy, restrain yourself and do not handle me so roughly; a pain has seized me at the root of my heart.' Then I seem to swoon, as though overcome. Thus do I deceive that swain with sweet words and gain some respite. When day has come, I look at him crabbedly, but pretend it is a love-look when he glances at me; I turn it into a tender look and regard him homely and smilingly, though in my heart I curse in secret rage. I wish a timorous young girl might have my goodman for her guest; she would not need to fear any fleshly hurt, nor budge the breadth of a straw for his stroke; and then I wish that that bond which you call blessed might bind them together."

When that amiable lady had ended her speech, the others, loudly laughing, allowed that she had much right on her side. Then those gay wives sported among the green leaves and put away care under the shadowy boughs. They drank heartily of the sweet wine, those fair-faced ladies, so that they spoke all the more briskly.

Then said the widow: "Now I cannot get out of it; I shall have to speak, for my tale is next. God inspire me and quicken my speech so that my preaching may pierce your hearts and make you meeker in manners to men.

"Sisters, I show you in shrift that I was ever a shrew, though I was beautiful in my clothes, and put on an innocent appearance. I was haughty and despiteful and bold, yet I dissembled subtly in the likeness of a saint. I seemed sober and sweet and simple, and without guile, but I could get the better of sixty who were considered cleverer. Listen to my lesson and learn wit from me if you do not wish to be deserted by faithless deceivers. Counterfeit good manners and be constant in your behaviour, even though you be keen, inconstant and cruel of mind in very truth. Though you be as fierce as beasts, be tractable in love. Be like doves in your talk, though you have temperaments easily yielding to temptation. Be dragon and dove both, and note the strength of both, and make use of one or the other as need arises. Put on a meek face like an angel, and be amiable, but sting like an adder with your tail. And take care to be expensively clothed in courtly dress: your husband will meet the bill.

"As for me, I have had two husbands, both of whom loved me. Though I, for my part, was despiteful towards them, they perceived it not. One was a hoary fellow who coughed up phlegm. I hated him like a hound, but kept my aversion well concealed. By kissing and clipping I made the old man dote on me. I knew well how to scratch his crooked back and comb his bald pate, and behind his back make fun of him with my tongue in my cheek; I knew how to kiss his shrunken chaps with a pleasant countenance, in my mind making mock of that old grandad who thought I was treating him so nicely because of true love. I was able to do this without trouble or distress, and yet be merry in mind and mirthful of cheer, for I had a more lovesome lad for the slaking of my thirst—one who could be secret and sure and save my honour, and who made his demands only at certain times and in sure places. When my old man angered me with awkward words, I got back my good temper by looking at a gallant. My wit was such that I wept but little for any vexation, and let the sweet temper the sour. If the old simpleton were to chide me with gaping jaws, then I would chuck him under the chin and coddle him so much that he assigned his chief mansion to my son, though not by him. I always behaved like a prudent woman and not like a mad fool, so that I won more by wiles than with strength of hands.

"Afterwards I married a merchant rich in goods, a man of middle age and medium stature. But we were not equals in friendship nor in blood, in largesse nor in outward appearance, nor in fairness of person. So often did I recall to his mind the disparity between us that his heart was angered. At other times I raised my voice and called him a 'pedlar.' I could be right smart in talk, for I had been married before: my innocence ended with my old husband. I made the merchant obey—there was no way out of it for him. When he understood my rights—for there was great difference between his bastard blood and my noble birth—he made me very good reverence. The fellow never once presumed to be my peer. But pity made him some concession, for gentle hearts are moved to compassion, and mercy is a great virtue in a woman. I kept it fresh in his mind that I had accepted him as a favour. I courteously taught him to know himself. If I summoned him, he dared not remain sitting, and was ready to run before the second charge, so afraid was he of blame. But, womanlike, my will was always the worse; the more he louted for my love, the less I esteemed him. It is an extraordinary thing that before I married that fellow I liked him, but have had nothing but ill will for him ever since.

"When I had got the full power, and had fully overcome him, I crew over that craven like a victorious cock. When I saw him subject and compliant to my bidding, I despised him as a loon and loathed him. Then I became so unmerciful that I schemed to martyr him: I made him do boy's work, like a beast. I would have ridden him to Rome with a rope on his head had it not been for the people's talk and the spoiling of my good name. I hid my hatred in my heart and never unstoppered my wide throat completely so long as I lacked something. But when I had taken his worldly property from that man, and got his houses and burg-lands for my child, then the stopper started out of my throat with a bang, and he was as astounded from the shock as from a steel weapon. Then I became as fierce as a dragon in my scolding. When the documents securing the heritages to my son were sealed, then I would no longer obey the bridle, but tossed up my head; no bit could make me quiet or hold my mouth in. Also, I made that effeminate zany do all sorts of women's work, and utterly abased whatever manhood he had. Whereupon I said to my gossips: See how I reined in yon colt with a keen bridle; the cappul that used to overthrow the panniers on the dungheap for skittishness, now draws the cart gently without bucking or baulking. Thus he escaped neither the harm nor the scorn of it.

"I must say too that he was no gladsome guest for a gay lady, though he tried to gain my favour by his many gifts. He decked me in gay silk and goodly array, in gowns of engrained cloth and great golden chains, with rings royally set with rich rubies, till my renown among the rude people rose high. But I gave him no *quid pro quo*, and cunningly kept those courtly adornments till after the death of that droop. He had the expense of buying me clothes, but the man who enjoys me after him shall have the worship thereof. I used to prank myself out gaily in rich attire so that lovers and lusty young gallants might look at me. I plundered him out of hand and then snubbed him, for he was stupid in the head. I scorned him and made him a cuckold, for I thought myself a papingo, and him a plucked heron. Thus did he fortify his foe and make a stout staff wherewith to strike himself down. In chamber I was loath to be leaped on by such a lubberly old horse, and reined him so tight that he nearly went mad, for a year at a time. I so despised him that I spat when I saw that bankrupt evil sprite; for you ladies know well that he who lacks riches as well as valiance in Venus' play is held to be vile.

"When I had taken all from that man, both of goods and of nature, it seemed to me that he was graceless to look at, so help me God. I decked out my children like barons' sons, and made only fools of the children he had by his first wife. I banished every one of his brothers from my presence, and held his friends in feud as my foes, nor did I like better any man who was blood-kin to him.

"That bankrupt fellow is now dead and buried in the earth, and with him died all my dool and dreary thought; my sorrowful night is now finished and my day has dawned. Adieu, dolour, adieu! My delight now begins. Now I am a widow and well at ease. I weep as though I were sorry, but well is me forever. I dress as though sad, but my heart is blithe. My mouth makes mourning, but my mind laughs. My cloaks may be sable-coloured to betoken care, but my body is white and tender underneath. When I go to the kirk clad in my weeds of care, I lay my book open on my knee and draw my cloak forward about my white face so that unespied I may spy out who is near me. Frequently I interrupt my devotion to look past my book and see what man is best of brawn or forged best for furnishing a feast. Like the new moon, all pale and oppressed with change, showing her white face through dark clouds, so do I peep through my cloak, and cast kind looks to knights and clerks and courtly persons. When my husband's friends see me from afar, then I take a sponge full of water which I have under my mantle, and wring it wilily and wet my cheeks; therewith my eyes water and the tears drop down. Then all who sit by say: 'Alas! behold how loyally yonder listless lady loved her husband. It is a pity that such a pearl of pleasure should bear such pain.' Then I sain myself as though I were a saint and assume angelic looks.

"In order that people may not find out the truth, I put on manners befitting my dark clothes, for true it is that we women set ourselves to keep the facts concealed from men. We grieve for no evil deed, providing it is kept secret. Wise women have wonderful devices wherewith to jape their husbands, and so quietly and craftily do we order our affairs that no creature under Christ knows of our doings. Other women there are, however, who mis-cook a mess, and have no colours wherewith to cover their natural mistakes. Such are those damsels who take delight in worthless persons with doting love, and deal with them so long that all the country-side knows their kindness and loyalty. Faith has a fair name, but falsehood fares better. Fie on her who is unable to dissimulate in order to save her reputation! Though I turn a deaf ear to language of lechery as though I were offended, I am wise in such matters, and have been so all my life. I may want wit in worldliness, but I have as clever wiles in love as any high-born dame. I have a privy servant and discreet who supplies certain needs of mine when I give the sign. Though he be simple in appearance, he has a sure tongue; many a more seemly man does worse service. If I have care under my cloak all day, yet I have solace under my smock till sunrise.

"Nevertheless, the whole shire considers me a devout woman. I am charitable to the poor more for the people's praise than for any grace I may gain. But it seems to me the best joke of all when barons and knights and other bachelors, blithe and blooming with youth, all my loyal lovers, frequent my lodging and wantonly fill me with wine, pleasure and joy. Some whisper, some jest, some read ballads, some burst forth rudely with riotous speech; some complain, some beseech; some praise my beauty; some kiss and clip me; some offer to do me a kindness; some carve for me courteously; some hand me the cup; some hand me one thing, some another. Some who sit far away and cannot speed as they wish, nevertheless look towards the head of the room with meaning looks. All of these I comfort with my pleasant manners. Him who sits next to me I nip on the finger, and serve him who sits on the other side in the same way. I lean hard on the one who sits behind me, and press the foot of him who sits before; and to those who are farther off I cast sweet looks. So wisely and so femininely do I speak special words to every man that the hearts of all are warmed. I am so tender-hearted that no man, howsoever low his degree, shall love me unloved. If it is merely my white body which lies between him and death, he shall not lose his life. I am so merciful to all men that my soul shall be safe on the day of judgment.

"Ladies, learn these lessons and do not make the mistake of acting like ingenuous lasses. This is the legend of my life, though not in Latin."

When this eloquent widow had finished her pretty speech, all the rest laughed loudly and made much of her. They said they would take example of her superior teaching and act according to the words of so prudent a woman. Then they cooled their mouths with comforting drinks, and chattered amicably with the cup going round. They put the night behind them with graceful dances till the day dawned and dew drenched the flowers. The morrow was mild and soft; the mist disappeared and the mavis sang. The gold-glittering gleam of the sunshine so gladdened the birds that they made glorious glee among the green boughs. The soft breeze, the sound of the stream, the sweet odour of the sward and the singing of the birds might comfort any creature of Adam's kin, and kindle his courage again though it were cold extinguished. Then those royal roses in their rich dresses got to their feet and went home to their rest through the hedge blooms. As for me, I passed privily into a pleasant arbor and wrote down a report of their merry pastime.

Now, O most honourable auditors, who have given ear to this uncouth adventure that happened to me not long ago, tell me—which of these ladies would you choose for your wife if you were to wed one of them?

"Happily that is a choice which we are not at present obliged to make," replied the Goodman of Bath.

Sir John Harington roused himself with an effort. "The bees have been booming in my ears," he said. "What a command you have of coarse consonants! You have even spoiled my own speech with your drasty drone."

"It is an art," answered Dunbar, "called alliteration."

"An art it may be," conceded John Stow, "yet if so, it seems to me an art elaborated to no fruitful end, since its creation must entail no less weariness in the mind of the poet than distress in the soul of the listener."

Dunbar shrugged and took a drink.

"Your widow," said John Skelton, "appears to have been almost unbelievably shameless; and yet I know little good of that class of women either."

"In my younger days," remarked the Curtal Friar, "while I still used to travel about the country, I met widows of one sort and another. Most of them were unexceptionable, but two have remained in my memory."

86. THE PROVIDENT MATRON

Curtal Friar

There was once a woman who had had four husbands. The fourth husband died and was brought to church on his bier. After him followed the widow making such great moan for sorrow that her gossips thought she would die. One of them approached and whispered in her ear that she should take comfort, for God's sake, and restrain her lamentation, else it would injure her greatly, and perhaps put her in jeopardy of her life. To this exhortation the woman replied: "Indeed, good gossip, if you only knew the circumstances you would admit that I have good reason to mourn. Besides this man I have buried three husbands; but I have never been in such a case as at present, for heretofore, whenever I went to a burying, I was always sure of another husband before the corpse left the house. This time, however, I am not sure of another husband, and so you see that I have good reason to be sad and heavy."

If this widow was in a bad plight, there was another of whom I heard who managed things better. As she was kneeling at the mass of requiem while the corpse of her husband was lying on the bier in church, a young man came up to her and whispered in her ear as though on a matter concerning the funeral. Howbeit, he spoke of no such thing, but ardently wooed her to be his wife. The widow answered and said: "Sir, by my troth, I am sorry you come so late, for I am already bestowed: I was made sure yesterday to another man."

"A woman must look after her interests with all the wit at her disposal," said Christine de Pisan somewhat shrilly; "otherwise she will find herself elbowed into the gutters of life."

"Everyone must look to his own interest," conceded Colin Clout; "but in this matter it strikes me that few women act wisely. By following the violent precepts of Dunbar's widow, for example, a woman defeats her own ends. Force is neither a weapon nor a tool which a woman can employ to her complete advantage. Even ladies should know that no cock will tolerate a rival on his own dung-heap. A woman should employ ways and means proper to her own nature rather than try to usurp the manners of men. Women who really understand men advance their happiness by making themselves lovable and desirable. A man in love may not be able to pluck down the stars from heaven to adorn his lady's hair, but he will try."

"Your position is well taken," agreed Hallarstein the Skald. "An apposite illustration comes to mind. Snaefrith, the daughter of Svasi, was the fairest of women. When, as hostess in her father's house, she handed a cup of honey-mead to Harald Harfagr, he took both the cup and the hand that offered it. With such passion did Harald love her afterwards that people seemed to think he neglected his realm and kingly honour for her sake. And when she died, the king sat three winters by her bier in bitter grief."

"Witchcraft," muttered Helinandus.

"Nay," protested Hallarstein. "You were born too late in a world too old if you cannot read the language of your own times. The drink in this case, as in that of Tristan and Iseult, was no more than a simulacrum of the love which sometimes exists between a man and a woman, and as such a literary device was so understood by all."

"The death of a woman's husband," remarked Snorri Sturlason, "seems to work some strange alchemy in her nature. My mother, Gudny Bodvar's daughter, was steady enough while my father lived to keep an eye on her; but after his death there was no limit to her carelessness, so that my inheritance, along with most of her own, was dissipated by her extravagance."

"Of widows," said Matheolus, "I know something, and in my opinion there are very few women whether rich or poor, ugly or handsome, wanton or chaste, churl, bourgeoise or noble, damsel, dame or widow who love their men loyally."

"You remind me of a story," said Colin Clout, "of a woman who certainly went the wrong way to work."

87. SIR NORBERT LOSES A CORPSE AND REFUSES A WIFE

Colin Clout

There was a knight, a rich reeve of a shire. He had a young and pretty wife whom he loved as the apple of his eye, and she loved him, so far as anyone could judge. One day while the knight was whittling a stick with a new sharp knife, his lady got in the way and was accidentally wounded. Though the hurt was a small one, the lady fainted at the sight of her own blood. So great was the knight's grief at this mishap that he died, and on the morrow was richly buried, as beseemed him. For her part the young wife said that since her lord had died through love for her she would on no account survive him. Her friends remonstrated with her, indeed, but when they found that their words were in vain, they built a booth by the knight's grave, and left the widow mourning there alone.

Now that same day three thieves had been taken and hanged, according to the law, in a field near the churchyard. It was the duty of a knight of the country-side to guard such felons upon the gallows for a certain time, and he held his fief in return for this service. On this occasion when the knight rode up in his steel accoutrement the weather was sharp and cold, and he was chilled to the bone. As he looked about him, he perceived the light of the fire burning in the widow's lodge in the cemetery, and went thither in the hope of warming himself.

"Who's there?" asked Dame Alis when she heard Sir Norbert's knock. "Have you any idea how cold it is outside?" queried the knight. "You seem to be cosy enough in there. For God's sake, let me in! I will do you no harm, as I am a true knight."

When the widow learned that it was a gentle knight who implored her hospitality, she opened the door readily enough. Sir Norbert tied his horse outside, and while he warmed himself at the fire, the widow returned to her weeping, to his great astonishment. When she had told him her story, he said: "Lady, you're a fool to mourn for the dead; you can't bring him back nor do him any good; pluck up your spirits lest this excess of grief do you harm. Instead of wailing here, you ought to love some good knight who could comfort you. You are young and handsome, and there is every reason to think that you may marry a lord richer than he who lies here dead." "Nay," replied the lady, "I can never love anyone else."

When Sir Norbert had warmed both his body and his wits, he bethought him of the gallows-birds. He excused himself, and rode back to the field where they were strung up. Alas! One of them had been stolen away in his absence. Now he had something over which to lament, for unless he found a corpse to take the missing felon's place, he would not only lose his fief, but hang in place of him. Probably he did not remember the old saw which says that women's rede is evil to trust, for, thinking that the weeping widow might give him some advice, he rode back to her and explained that he must now become an exile in a strange land in order to avoid punishment for his neglect.

"Sir," said Dame Alis, "if you will marry me, I will help you." "I agree to that," said Sir Norbert. Thereupon the widow bade farewell to her woe and said: "Darling," said she, "come help me dig up my lord here; he was buried only yesterday and isn't much spoiled yet. We will hang him in the place of the other." So they dug up the dead man and bore him to the gallows on the knight's horse.

"Now," said Sir Norbert, "who is going to hang him up? Not I, for he was a knight like myself." "Well," answered the woman, "I'll pull him up." Therewith she put the rope round her husband's neck and hoisted him onto the gibbet.

"Does he hang to suit you?" queried the widow. "Dame," said Sir Norbert, "the other had a wound in his head; everyone knew it, and he could be recognized by it; unless this one has a similar wound our trick will be for naught." "Sir," said the widow, "take your sword and give my husband a wound like the other's." "Nay," answered Sir Norbert; "not for anything will I strike a dead knight." "Well, give me the sword, then," said the woman, "and I'll show him how God's wrath came to town." Therewith she gave her dead lord a mighty stroke right in the middle of the crown.

By this time Sir Norbert began to understand that the lady was of light and fickle temper, and he said: "He isn't quite right yet; the other man's front teeth were broken out." "Well," said Dame Alis, "smite out my husband's." "Not I," replied the knight. "Then I will," said she; and taking up a stone she knocked out every one of her lord's teeth with a single blow.

"Will he do now?" asked the widow. "Well," said Sir Norbert, "the other corpse lacked an eye." "La! la!" said the woman; "that's a matter soon mended"; and with her bodkin she gouged out one of her husband's eyes. Sir Norbert shuddered.

When the substitute corpse had finally been arranged in a satisfactory manner Dame Alis said: "Now, sir, I have won your love." "By God in heaven," replied Sir Norbert, "I wouldn't marry a false shrew like you for gold, silver, land or house. You would serve me as you did your first lord. You shall have no husband in me. If you had your deserts it is a fire you would get. I advise you to clear out; and take good care that I never set eyes on you again."

And therewith, to the wrath and astonishment of the lady, Sir Norbert rode away.

"That tale," said John of Salisbury, "has a very familiar sound. I recall having read something like it in Petronius Arbiter."

"I know that story too," said Matheolus, "but I was afraid to tell it."

"I heard of a widow who did not escape the fire so easily," remarked Roger of Hoveden. "Perhaps you know the report about Robert Guiscard's wife?"

"No," said Matheolus; "what about her?"

"I will tell you," answered Roger.

88. ROBERT GUISCARD'S VENOMOUS WIFE

Roger of Hoveden

You must know that Robert Guiscard was born in Normandy. After he had become a knight he served the king of England for a long time; but though he was an excellent soldier in arms, still he advanced his fortunes very little in that monarch's service. For this reason he left Normandy with his wife and sons, and in company with his brother took his way to Rome. There, when the pontiff had granted him permission to attempt the conquest of barbarous peoples, a great number of knights and men-at-arms flocked to his standard. First he entered Apulia, and noting that it was a fertile country, and that the inhabitants were unskilled in the use of arms, he attacked them vigorously, conquered them, and made himself master over all the land. Indeed, he subjected all Apulia, Calabria, and the principality of Capua to his sway, and gave these lands to his son Roger.

After this Robert collected a great number of ships, proposing to attack the empire of Constantinople itself, and subject it to his rule. During the time that his ships were assembling he, together with

Tancred and Bohemund, his sons, attacked the domains of the pope, the emperor of Rome and the emperor of Constantinople in one and the same day, and got the victory over them.

When all was ready, Robert set out with his navy, his wife accompanying him. He conquered the islands of Corfu, Crete and Rhodes, as well as many other islands, wresting them from the grasp of the Eastern emperor. After these exploits he made port at a place which ever since has been known as Portus Wiscardi.

However, when Robert was about to proceed farther into Roman territory, the emperor of Constantinople, who feared him greatly, sent a message to Robert's wife to this effect: If she would bring about the death of the said Robert, and thus free his land from the invader, he, the emperor, would marry her and raise her to the rank of empress of Constantinople.

The woman agreed to the monarch's proposal, and seizing opportunity of time and place, gave her husband poison in his drink, so that he died. He is buried there in the island. Hereupon his army and navy melted away. His wife, however, fled to the emperor of Constantinople, who straightway fulfilled all his covenants, married her and crowned her empress.

When all due ceremonies of betrothal, marriage and coronation had been solemnized, the woman said to the emperor: "My lord, you have well and truly fulfilled all the articles of our agreement." Hereupon the emperor imposed silence on his court, and revealed to all the compact which he had made with her, and how she had compassed the death of her former husband. Then he asked the barons of his household to pass judgment on her action, and their doom was that she deserved death. So, from the scene of marriage and festivity she was borne to the place of execution, thrown into the blazing fire and reduced to ashes.

"If your account is a true one," said Arnaldus of Villanova, "Robert was indeed unfortunate in his wife. But then, poison and women go together, as I have indicated in a book of mine."

"As has already been remarked," said Bartholomew Anglicus, "poison is a dubious expedient, and those who have recourse to it should know how to handle it. Constantine of Africa tells of a blind man's wife who wished to kill her husband, and to that end gave him, not an eel, but an adder boiled with garlic. The husband ate it, and after he had sweat copiously, recovered his sight."

"There may really be some hope for us," said Blind Harry to Ossian. "My eyesight, too, has been failing of late."

"That remedy never did me any good, in spite of the authority of Constantine," said the Lochmaben Harper; "nor John of Gaddesden's simples, either."

"Widows or maids," said Jean de Meung, returning to the topic, "there is little to choose between them, in my opinion."

"Have you ever heard," asked Machiavelli, "how the devil took a wife?"

"Pray tell us," invited Jean de Montreuil.

89. BELFAGOR'S BARGAIN

Niccolò Machiavelli

In the ancient memorials of the city of Florence we read that a certain very holy man, while saying his orisons one day, had a vision. He seemed to see an infinite number of miserable mortals who, dying denied of God's grace, dwelt in Inferno, and who raised their voices in lamentation over nothing except that they had been reduced to such unhappiness through having taken a wife. Radamanthus and Minos, and other infernal judges, were greatly astonished by this, and being unable to credit the calumnies wherewith the souls loaded the female sex, and the recriminations growing in volume day by day, made due report of everything to Pluto. Wherefor it was decided that this matter should be gravely weighed by all the infernal princes so that they might take whatever action should be considered best, either to uncover the fallacy, or to learn the whole truth of the matter.

A council was accordingly summoned and Pluto spoke to this effect: "O well beloved, though it is true that I, by heavenly disposition and irrevocable fate, possess all this kingdom, wherefor I cannot be constrained to take notice of any opinion, whether mundane or celestial, nevertheless, I have taken thought that I will be counselled by you as to how I should act regarding a certain matter which might have the gravest consequences for our empire; for since all the souls who come to our kingdom declare that the cause of their coming is the wife, and since this seems impossible to us, we fear lest, in passing judgment on this relationship we might be calumniated as too cruel, and in not doing so as lacking in both severity and justice. And inasmuch as one fault is that of light-minded men, and the other that of unjust ones, and wishing to avoid the consequences which might inhere in either indictment, but not finding the means thereto, we have summoned you so that you may aid us with counsel, and so ensure that this kingdom may continue to exist with unspotted fame in the future as it has in the past."

All those assembled princes deemed the matter to be of the highest importance, and worthy of the gravest consideration; all concurred that it was necessary to discover the truth, though there was dissidence as to the means. Some suggested that one, some that more, be sent in man's guise to the world to learn the truth by personal experience. Others thought the business could be handled without so much inconvenience by constraining several souls with varied torments to confess the true circumstances. But since the majority thought that a representation should be sent to the world, they adopted that measure. And when they found that no one would volunteer for this errand, they chose one of their number by lot.

The choice fell upon Belfagor, the arch-devil, who, before he had fallen from heaven, had been an archangel. Even though he undertook the commission unwillingly, he dared not oppose the imperial will of Pluto, and made ready to comply with the resolutions of the council.

These resolutions were that to him who undertook the errand should be given a sum of 100,000 ducats; with this money he should return to earth, and under man's form take a wife and live with her ten years. Afterwards, feigning death, he should return to hell, and from his own experience give to his superiors a faithful account of the burdens and inconveniences of matrimony. It was further provided that during that period he should be subject to all the ills and tribulations to which mortal men are subject, involving poverty, prison and disease, and every other misfortune which men suffer, and that he was not to evade these conditions by craft or guile.

So Belfagor acknowledged the conditions and accepted the money, and providing horses and companions from his household, made a splendid entry into Florence. This city he selected as being the one most fitted above all others to maintain such as exercised their money in the art of usury, so that if funds became necessary he might borrow. He assumed the name Roderigo di Castiglia, and took a house in the Borgo Ognissanti. In accordance with the conditions imposed upon him he gave out that he had left Spain not long since, had travelled to Syria and made his money at Aleppo; thence he had come to Italy to seek for a wife in quarters more civilized and agreeable both to cultured life and his own taste. Roderigo took the form of a very handsome gentleman about thirty years old.

In a few days he had made it clear that he was not only a rich man, but a liberal one, so that many noble citizens, with few pence and many marriageable daughters, soon offered him a plentiful market. From among these Roderigo chose a very beautiful girl called Onesta, the daughter of Amerigo Donati, who, though noble and highly esteemed in Florence, was, by reason of his large family, very poor, for he had also three other daughters and three full-grown sons.

Roderigo ordered a splendid wedding, omitting nothing which pertains to such an occasion, since, by the infernal edict, he had become subject to all human passions. Forthwith he began to take pleasure in the pomp and show of the world, and to lay value on the praise and flattery of men—which cost him considerable outlay of money.

Now Roderigo had not lived long with Monna Onesta till he fell so violently in love with her that he thought he would die whenever he saw her sad or out of humour. Onesta, for her part, together with her noble blood and beauty, had brought to Roderigo's house more pride than ever Lucifer had had. Roderigo, who had sampled both, considered that of his wife to be far superior. But Onesta's pride became still greater as soon as she perceived how madly her husband was in love with her. And since it seemed to her that she could domineer over him in all things, she bullied him without pity or respect; nor did she hesitate, when he refused her something or other, to bite him with churlish and insulting words.

His wife's behaviour was the cause of considerable vexation to Roderigo. However, consideration for his father-in-law, his brothers-in-law and the family connections constrained him to patience. I say nothing of the great sums which he expended in dressing his wife to her satisfaction in the new modes and fashions which our city, in its customary manner, varies continually. In order to be at peace with her it was also necessary for him to aid his father-in-law in marrying off his other daughters—which cost him a great sum of money. After this, wishing to be on good terms with Onesta, he had to send one of her brothers to the Levant with stuffs, another to the West with silks, and set up the third in Florence as a goldsmith. In so doing he spent the greater part of his fortune. In addition to this, during the festivals of Carnival and San Giovanni, when the whole city indulges in celebration, and many noble and rich citizens honour each other with entertainments, Monna Onesta, that she might not be thought inferior to other ladies, would be content with nothing except that Roderigo must excel all others in the splendour of his fêtes.

These things were endured by him for the reasons I have mentioned, nor would he have thought them too heavy, even though they were burdensome, if he had thereby been able to obtain quiet at home, and been allowed to look forward to the day of his ruin in peace. But the result was just the contrary, for together with the crushing expenses, his wife's insolence brought him infinite vexations. In his house there was neither servant nor lacquey who could endure her presence for more than a few days, let alone a long period. This circumstance caused Roderigo the worst kind of trouble and inconvenience, for he was thus unable to retain any servant who was faithful to his interests; and this was true not alone of humans: even those devils whom he had brought with him in the rôle of household retainers chose to return to hell and dwell in fire rather than live in the world under the domination of his wife.

Now in the midst of this tumultuous and unquiet existence Roderigo, having spent his reserve in extravagant outlay, was forced to live mainly on his expectations from his investments in Western and Eastern markets, of which we have spoken. And since his credit was still good, he borrowed money on notes in order not to lower his station and manner of life. But he had signed so many notes of hand that the money-lenders began to watch him closely. Then, when his own affairs had reached an acute condition, news came from the East and West that one of Monna Onesta's brothers had lost all Roderigo's goods at play, and that the other, returning with a ship loaded with rich wares, had been lost at sea with all goods, none of which had been insured.

As soon as these circumstances became known, Roderigo's creditors put their heads together. They deemed that he was ruined; but since the notes were not yet due for payment, they dared do nothing, and decided only to keep a close watch on him, so that he should not flee.

Roderigo, for his part, seeing no remedy for his ills, and remembering the conditions of the infernal edict which constrained him, decided upon flight at all hazards. One morning he mounted his horse and rode out through the Porta al Prato. No one observed his absence till his watchful creditors began to raise a clamour. They provided themselves with the magistrates' authority and set out in pursuit. At the beginning of the chase Roderigo was not more than a mile from the city, so, seeing that he was in a tight corner, he decided to leave the road and cut cross-lots at random. But the many ditches which traversed the fields thereabouts impeded his going on horseback, wherefor he left his mount on the highway and proceeded on foot over field after field covered with vines and reeds.

In this manner he arrived above Peretola, at the house of Gian Matteo del Bricca, one of Giovanni del Bene's workmen. By good fortune he found Gian Matteo on his way home from ploughing, and threw himself on his mercy, promising that if he saved him from the hands of his enemies—who were pursuing him to put him to death in prison—he would make him very rich.

Now Gian Matteo, though a peasant, was sharp enough, and considering that he could lose nothing by taking the fugitive's part, promised to shield him. Forthwith he thrust him into a pile of manure in front of his house and covered him over with stalks and other rubbish which he had gathered for burning. Roderigo had hardly hidden himself when his persecutors arrived on the scene; and in spite of anything they could do to intimidate him, they could not get Gian Matteo to say that he had seen any fugitive. So the pursuers went farther, and having searched vainly for their quarry that day and the next, returned, worn out, to Florence.

When the uproar had subsided, Gian Matteo drew Roderigo from his hiding-place, and demanded that he keep his promise. "Brother mine," said Roderigo, "I am infinitely obliged to you, and I will certainly content you; and that you may believe I am able to do so, I will tell you who I am."

Thereupon Belfagor revealed to Gian Matteo his real identity, told him of the decree passed in hell, and of his marriage. He also explained to him the manner whereby he proposed to enrich him, which, in short, was this: When Gian Matteo should hear of any woman being possessed he could be sure that he, Roderigo, was the author of her madness, and that he would never leave her till Gian Matteo came to exorcize him, for which service he could exact whatever payment he pleased from the woman's kin. After saying this, Roderigo disappeared.

Not many days after this the news spread abroad in Florence that a daughter of Messer Ambrogio Amidei, betrothed to Buonaiuto Tebalducci, was possessed by a demon. The relatives did not fail to apply all the remedies which are usual in such cases—placing on her head the skull of San Zanobi and the mantle of San Giovanni Gualberlo—which specifics were laughed to scorn by Roderigo. And in order to make it plain that the young woman suffered from a demon, and not from a disordered brain, he made her speak in Latin, and dispute on problems of philosophy; and he revealed the sins of many, as, for example, that a certain friar had kept a woman dressed as a novice in his cell for more than four years. Such things aroused everybody's wonder. Messer Ambrogio, however, was much vexed, and having vainly tried all remedies, had finally abandoned all hope of curing his daughter.

At that moment Gian Matteo came to him and promised to cure the girl in return for five hundred florins wherewith to purchase a farm at Peretola. Messer Ambrogio accepted the terms. Then Gian Matteo, first having certain masses said, and having performed certain ceremonies in order to embellish the proceeding, came up to the girl and whispered: "Roderigo, I have come, so that you may keep your word." To which Roderigo replied: "I am ready to do so. But this affair is not enough to make you rich; so, when I have

BELFAGOR'S BARGAIN 415

left here, I will enter the daughter of King Charles of Naples, nor will I leave her till you come. Name a handsome reward for yourself, and do not trouble me after that." So saying, Roderigo issued from the girl, to the rejoicing and astonishment of all Florence.

It was not long after this when all Italy heard of the terrible misfortune which had befallen King Charles' daughter. When all remedies had failed, King Charles, who had heard about Gian Matteo, sent to Florence for him. Gian Matteo proceeded to Naples, and after some bogus ceremonies, cured the girl of her madness. But Roderigo, before he left her, said: "Look you, now, Gian Matteo, I have fulfilled the promise I made when I said I would make you rich; and so, having discharged my obligation, I am no longer indebted to you in any way. Be content never to appear before me again, for if you do, whereas in the past I have benefited you, in the future I will do you ill."

Gian Matteo returned to Florence a rich man—for the king had given him better than fifty thousand ducats—and thought he would enjoy his wealth quietly, having no suspicion that Roderigo would do him injury. But his plans were soon upset by the news that the daughter of Louis VII, king of France, was possessed. When Gian Matteo remembered Roderigo's last words and called to mind also the great authority of the king of France, he had food for thought.

Now when the French king could find no cure for his daughter, someone told him about Gian Matteo's skill. First the king simply sent for him by a courier. Gian Matteo sent back reply that he was ailing and could not make the journey. Thereupon Louis addressed himself to the Signoria, who forced Gian Matteo to accede to the king's wish.

So Gian Matteo went to Paris against his will, and there he told the king frankly that in the past he had had some success in casting out devils, but that he had no reason to believe that he could cure all and sundry, for some demons were so spiteful and recalcitrant that they feared neither threats nor incantations nor religion. However, he would try his best, and if he did not succeed, he could only ask to be pardoned and excused.

To this King Louis replied shortly that if he did not effect the cure of his daughter, he would hang him on the gibbet. This blunt statement occasioned Gian Matteo great distress of mind; but plucking up his spirits, he caused the demoniac to be brought in. He went up to her and greeted Roderigo humbly, recalling the good turn he had done him, and what a great piece of ingratitude it would be were he, Roderigo, to abandon him now in his present plight. "Ha!" said Roderigo. "Vile traitor! How have you the face to come before me? Are you going to boast of growing rich with my help? Now I am going to show you and everyone that I know how to give and take according to my pleasure. Before you go away from here I will get you hanged."

Seeing that there was no remedy in this quarter, Gian Matteo thought he would tempt Fortune by another expedient, and dismissing the demoniac he said to the king: "Sire, as I told you, there are many spirits so malicious that one cannot come to any terms with them, and such is this one. However, I am going to try an experiment, and if it succeeds, your majesty and myself will both be very well pleased; if it fails, I shall still be in your power, and I hope you will show me such mercy as my innocence merits. The plan is this: Have a great scaffolding, capable of accommodating all your barons and the clergy of Paris, erected in the Place Notre Dame, with an altar in the middle. On Sunday morning, come with your clergy, princes and barons, in royal pomp and style, and take your places on the stage. Then, when a mass has been said, bring forth the demoniac. But at one corner of the square I want a score of persons with trumpets, horns, tabours, bagpipes, cymbals, flageolets and every kind of noisy instrument. When I raise my hat they are to begin playing their instruments, and come towards the stage. I think these things, together with certain others which I must keep secret, will cause the demon to take to his heels." The king at once gave orders that everything should be done as Gian Matteo wished.

On Sunday morning the stage was filled with high dignitaries, and the square with people. After mass had been said, the possessed girl was led upon the platform by two bishops and several gentlemen. When Roderigo saw such paraphernalia and such a crowd of people he was astounded, and said to himself: "What is this rascally peasant loon up to? Does he think he is going to frighten me with this mummery? Does he not know that I am accustomed to look upon the splendours of heaven and the furies of hell? I'll teach him a lesson once for all time." When Gian Matteo drew near and begged Roderigo to leave the girl, the latter said: "What fine ideas you have! What do you think you are going to gain by all this nonsensical show? Do you think this is going to help you elude my power and escape the king's wrath? Imbecilic churl, I shall certainly get you hanged."

Thus, the one begging, the other replying with insults, it seemed to Gian Matteo that no more time was to be lost, and making the signal with his hat, all those who had been deputed to make a clamour began to sound their instruments, and moved up towards the stage with an uproar that reached the sky.

At the sound of the noise Roderigo pricked up his ears; not knowing what it portended, he was taken aback, and like one stunned asked what the noise meant. Gian Matteo, as though greatly exercised, replied: "Alas, Roderigo, that is your wife coming for you."

It was extraordinary what an alteration his wife's name made in Roderigo's mind. Such was his perturbation that without considering whether Gian Matteo's statement were possible or reasonable, and without replying a single word, he fled in a terrible fright, preferring to return to hell to cast himself on the mercy of his masters rather than submit once more to the anxieties, vexations and despites of the matrimonial yoke.

Thus Belfagor, arrived once more in hell, confirmed the report of the ills for which a wife in the house is responsible; and Gian Matteo, who knew more about it than the devil, returned home rejoicing.

"To my mind," remarked the Goodman of Bath, "the discussion seems to have wandered far afield. If it is convenient, I should like to bring it back to the subject of wayward husbands, for it seems to me that something not only can, but should be said on the other side."

"Yes, I think so," said Bonvesin da Riva. "Not all husbands are forever chasing other women or other men's wives. One of my countrymen, Tommasino di Circlaria laid it down specifically in his book that a husband shall not allow himself to care for another man's wife, for he who has one woman may do without another."

"Of course," said Sir David Lindsay, "it is not impossible for husbands to be chaste. Magnus Erlendson of Orkney was so holy that he lived with his wife, a Scots noblewoman, for ten years free from the defilements of carnal lust."

"That was probably a unique case," suggested Henry Knighton.

"As the Knight of La Tour Landry remarked," went on the Goodman of Bath, "we need not be guided by extremes; and while it is probably true that most men run after women—and always will—is it not also true that you prize a stallion or a cock above a gelding or a capon? I think most of you will admit, too, that women run after men—and always will. But do any of you gentlemen resent or repulse the attentions of a pretty lady? In my opinion the woman-lust of men is no more excessive than the man-lust of women. The matter could be illustrated by hundreds of examples."

"Something may be said in support of your view," agreed Sturla the Lawman. "Among the women of the North I recall Ragnhild, who played a baneful rôle in the lives of many men, though only the most public of her acts are recorded by history."

"What have you in mind?" asked Matthew Paris.

"The circumstances go back to the time of Eric Bloodaxe, to whom your historian Henry of Huntingdon gives a few lines in his chronicle. Eric, as you know, was the son of Harald Harfagr. After his father's death he reigned in Norway for a time, but the people preferred a man of milder mood, namely, his brother Hákon, and Eric was forced to flee the land with his wife Gunhild. Eric fell in battle in England, whereupon Gunhild went to the Orkneys with her children, and took possession of them. After a time she and her sons sailed away to Denmark, but first she married her daughter Ragnhild to Arnfinn. This Arnfinn was the youngest son of Thorfinn Skullsplitter, earl of the Orkneys.

"Not long after her mother's departure Ragnhild killed her husband at Myrkhol in Caithness, and then married his brother, Earl Thorfinn's eldest son Hávard Arsaeli. But Hávard also proved to be somehow deficient, or else another man had caught Ragnhild's fancy. Howbeit, at one of Hávard's feasts there was present his nephew, Einar Klíning, and he and Ragnhild talked much together. Einar was a great chief and a successful viking. Ragnhild said that it was fitting that he, and not Hávard, should be earl of the Orkneys, and that the woman who had him for a husband would be well matched. Einar at first rejected the proposal, but greed, ambition and Ragnhild's beauty at last won him over. Einar killed Hávard at Steinsness, and was held to be a great nithing for the deed. Moreover, he had his labour for his pains, for Ragnhild denied that she had promised him anything, and would have nothing more to do with him. Either she had taken a dislike to Einar, or else her eye had fallen again upon another handsome young man. At all events, she said to Einar Hardkjöpt, another nephew of Hávard's, that it was a pity Hávard's slayer should walk abroad, and egged him on to avenge his uncle's death; in so doing he might win both the earldom and the esteem of the people. Hardkjöpt replied that Ragnhild had the reputation for speaking differently than she thought. Nevertheless, he killed Einar Klíning. Once more Ragnhild, instead of rewarding him with her hand, married Liót, a brother of her two former husbands. Liót became earl of the Orkneys and had Hardkjöpt slain. So far as I know, or the records state, Liót proved a satisfactory husband for Ragnhild, or else she had at last met her match.

"But perhaps we must not censure Ragnhild too severely, for her mother before her, Gunhild, was a woman equally imperious and variable in her affections. After Eric Bloodaxe had fallen in battle against Anlaf Cuaran in Northumbria in the year 954, Gunhild, as I have said, went to the Orkneys, and later to Denmark, and finally to Norway, where her son Harald Grayfell became king in place of his uncle Hákon. They established their dwelling at King's Crag. Now one summer Hrut Herjolfsson came out of Iceland and laid up his ship. Gunhild, as was her custom, sent men of hers to look over the strangers, and when they had given their opinion, she invited Hrut to court. 'You shall be in the upper chamber with me tonight,' she said to Hrut, 'and there shall be just the two of us.' 'You shall have your way,' he answered. To the other men present she said: 'You shall lose nothing except your lives if you divulge a word about my affair and Hrut's.'

"After a time Hrut yearned for Iceland, and there was no gainsaying him. At parting Gunhild gave him a gold ring. 'Many good gifts have I had from you,' said Hrut. But he spoke too soon, for Gunhild was not a woman whose will or desire might lightly be thwarted; and another gift she gave him at parting, namely, that he should never have any pleasure in living with the woman he should marry in Iceland. Then she drew her mantle over her head and left him. Unna, Mord's daughter, learned the truth of that prophecy, to her sorrow.

"It was not long after this till another ship came east from Iceland, and in it was Olaf, called the Peacock, the son—by an Irish princess—of Hauskuld, Hrut's half-brother. Olaf was the handsomest of men. King Harald received him well, and Gunhild, when she learned that he was Hrut's brother's son, paid great attention to him. Some people said that she took pleasure in talking to Olaf for himself alone irrespective of others' recommendation. At this time Olaf was eighteen years old and Gunhild forty-seven.

"Even while Eric Bloodaxe was alive men said that there was great affection between Gunhild and Thorolf Skalagrimson. And Bergonund, son of Thorgeir Thornfoot, too, boasted suggestively of the esteem in which he was held by the queen-mother. It was a friendship not many men would have enjoyed, and which few were fitted to endure, for the people said of her that though she was a beautiful woman and easy of speech, so was she also guileful of heart and grim of mood. Cunning in witchcraft she was, too, as Hrut and Unna found to their sorrow. Still, it must be admitted that that was no part of her character, but rather an acquired trait, for she had early been sent to learn wizardry in Finnmark."

"You surprise me," said Ralph Higden; "what was she doing among the Finns? I thought she was a daughter of Gorm the Old of Denmark."

"Nay," interposed Snorri Sturlason. "Her father was Osur Toti, who dwelt in Halogaland, the northwestern littoral of Norway, which, as you know, has Finnmark at its northeastern end. Stretching south from the old Finn*mark,* which was the land of the Lapps, not Finns, is the modern Fin*land,* bounded by the Gulf of Bothnia and Lake Ladoga."

"Thank you," replied Higden; "I am not unversed in geography. But I am still puzzled about Finnish wizardry."

"No need to remain so," said Mac Conglinne. "Finnmark has for centuries been one of the most eminent colleges of magic and witchcraft. It is well known that Queen Meave of Connaught, in planning her revenge on Cuchulain, sent the three sons and the three daughters of Calatin (who had fallen by his hand on the Cattle Raid of Cooley), to study at her expense under all the most famous wizards of the Eastern and the Western worlds. In Alba they studied, in Babylon, in Lochlann and in Finnmark. And before their time it was in Finnmark that the Tuatha De Danann learned their arts."

"I confess," said Higden, "that I was better acquainted with Toledo as a seat of necromancy. But can you tell us more about Gunhild?" he asked, addressing the Icelandic historian.

"I will tell what I know," replied Snorri. "It is only a little, and that little preserved, I daresay, only because of its connection with Eric Bloodaxe."

90. ERIC BLOODAXE TAKES A WIFE

Snorri Sturlason

Eric was the most beloved of all King Harald's sons. When he was twelve years old the king gave him five long-ships, wherewith he made his first expedition, sailing into the Baltic, then south to Denmark, Friesland and Saxland. At the end of four years he sailed out into the western sea, plundering Scotland, Wales, Ireland and Normandy, and in this way he passed four more years.

Afterwards he sailed north to Finnmark and as far as Archangel, where he had many a battle and won many a victory. When he turned west again toward Finnmark, his men found a girl in a Lapland hut, whose equal for beauty they had never seen. She said her name was Gunhild, that her father dwelt in Halogaland and was called Osur Toti. "I am here," she said, "to learn Lapland art from two of the most knowing Laplanders in all Finnmark. Both of them want me in marriage. They are so skilful that they can distinguish tracks either upon the frozen or upon the thawed earth, like dogs; and they can run so swiftly on ski that neither man nor beast can come near them in speed. They hit whatever they aim at and thus kill every man who comes near them. When they are angry the very earth turns away in terror, and whatever living thing they look upon falls dead. They are out hunting now; you must not come in their way when they return, so I will hide you here in the hut, and you must try to get them killed."

The men agreed to her plan and she hid them. Then she took a leather bag in which there seemed to be ashes, and strewed both inside and outside of the hut. Shortly thereafter the Laplanders came home and asked who had been there. But Gunhild answered: "Nobody has been here." "That is wonderful," said they, "for we followed tracks right up to the hut, though we can find none round about it." Then they kindled a fire and prepared their food, and Gunhild made ready her bed.

It had so happened that Gunhild had slept the three nights before, but the Laplanders had remained awake, one being jealous of the other. "Now," said she to the wizards, "come here and lie down, one on each side of me." They were very glad to do as she bade. Gunhild laid an arm about the neck of each and they fell asleep immediately. She roused them, but they fell asleep again at once; again she roused them, but they fell asleep again instantly. Then she raised them up in bed, but they still slept. Thereupon she took two great sealskin bags which she put over their heads, tying them fast under their arms. When this was done she gave a sign to Eric's men, who ran forth with their weapons, killed the two Laplanders, and dragged them out of the hut. Following this there came such a dreadful thunderstorm that they could not stir out. But next morning they went back to the ship, taking Gunhild with them, and they presented her to Eric.

Thereafter Eric and his followers sailed south to Halogaland; he sent word to Osur Toti, the girl's father, to meet him, saying that he would take his daughter in marriage. Osur consented to this, and Eric took Gunhild and sailed south with her.

"That," said Henry Castide, "seems to me to have been an inauspicious beginning for any marriage. As every husband here knows, marriage is difficult enough even under the most favourable circumstances. I used to consider myself the unhappiest of husbands, but I can see now that my wife had one virtue, and that was her ignorance of witchcraft."

"We all know what happened to Eric," broke in Christine de Pisan impatiently, "but what happened to Gunhild?"

"Well," replied Snorri, "her end was perhaps justified by her life. It is a long story, and not a pretty one, and I will tell only a part of it. The bad earl, Hákon Sigurdson, comes into it. For a time

Hákon was able to hold his own against Gunhild and Harald Grayfell, but in the end he was forced to flee to Denmark. There he persuaded Gold Harald, the king's nephew, to kill Harald of Norway; then he himself slew Gold Harald, and seized the Norse throne. Thereafter he sought out Gunhild, and gaining her confidence by saying that he had avenged her son's death, told her that he was the bearer of a message from the king of Denmark, namely, that if she would come to visit him, he would make her his wife.

"Gunhild was flattered by the offer, for she considered herself to be still a very beautiful and important woman. She set sail with three ships. On landing in Jutland she was met by Harald Gormsson's men, who, she expected, were to conduct her to the bridal feast. However, as they were passing a morass, they seized her, staked her out hand and foot in the bog, and then went their ways. This place was afterwards called Gunhild's Moss."

"Retribution is not always inevitable," remarked Blaise the Hermit. "I recall the case of another pupil in necromancy who learned too much for her master's comfort, but I have not heard that she ever paid any penalty for her treachery."

"How was that?" asked Melior.

91. MERLIN AND VIVIAN

Blaise the Hermit

Living in the kingdom of Benoyk there was a vavasour of right high lineage named Dionas. He married the niece of the Duke of Burgundy, and had a daughter named Vivian, a fair and delightsome maiden. His dwelling was in a valley under a mountain beside the forest of Briok, of which he owned one half, and King Ban the other half.

The goddess Diana came often to talk to Dionas, for he was her godson, and stayed with him many days. One time as she was taking her departure she gave him a gift that pleased him well. "Dionas," said she, "I grant you that the first maid child you have shall be so much desired by the wisest of all men of mould, under the reign of King Vortiger, that he shall teach her the greatest part of his craft and skill in necromancy; for when he has once seen her he shall covet her so hugely that he shall have no power to do anything against her will, and he shall tell her everything she wishes to know."

Now Merlin used to repair to the forest to hunt the hart and the hind, the buck and the boar; it chanced that he saw that fair and lovely maiden Vivian there, and fell deeply in love with her, even as Diana had foretold. Many times, when Merlin could get away from court, he went to spend a few days with her. She always received him pleasantly and made much of him, for she in her turn loved him on account of his learning and mansuetude; and well she might, for in order to please her he taught her many things which he would have betrayed to no living man.

Little by little, under Merlin's tutelage, Vivian improved her knowledge of necromancy, but there were still many things which she craved to know. So, one day when the enchanter sought her out at Benoyk, she took great pains to show him every courtesy, and did all that she could to please him. She served him with excellent food and drink, and they lay together in one bed. But Vivian had learned so much magic that she conjured a pillow, and Merlin fell asleep with the pillow, not Vivian, in his arms. Merlin never knew any woman carnally, and yet he loved the sex better than anything in the world.

In this wise Merlin abode with his love for a long time, and every day she inquired more deeply into his art and its secret mysteries. The necromancer replied to every question, and Vivian wrote down the answers, for she was well skilled in clergy. At last, when it came time for him to leave, each tenderly commended the other to God, and Merlin said he should not return before the year's end.

At the close of the year Merlin took leave of Arthur, saying: "Sir, this is the last time I shall come to you, and so I commend you to God." At this news the king was sad and much abashed. But Merlin went his ways and came to me; he told me all the news and I diligently wrote it down in my book. And when he had rehearsed all Arthur's doings he said to me:

"Blaise, this is the last time I shall speak to you forever, for henceforth I shall sojourn with my love, nor shall I ever have power to leave her, to come or go." "If that is true," said I, "why do you go to her now? It would be better to shun her." "That I cannot do," replied Merlin, "for I have given her my word; and moreover, I am so overcome by love for her that I cannot loose myself from its toils. I have taught her everything she knows about magic and necromancy, and yet she shall learn more, for I cannot avoid the destiny that is in store for me."

So Merlin left me and went to his love. Vivian rejoiced greatly at his coming, and fondled and caressed him, doing everything she could for his pleasure and comfort. Day by day she inquired more deeply into the mysteries of his art, and Merlin answered her questions. One day, when Vivian had learned well-nigh everything, she began to consider how she might keep her lover with her always, and she began to cajole and caress him more than ever before. Said she: "There is still one matter that I would learn, and I entreat you to teach me this as you have the other things." Merlin knew what she had in mind, but he said: "And what is that?" "Merlin," said Vivian, "I would fain know how I might be able, by means of enchantment, to shut a person up in a tower without walls or enclosure in such fashion that he might never be able to issue forth without my leave." When Merlin heard this request he bowed his head and began to sigh deeply. "Why do you sigh?" asked the girl. "Vivian," he answered, "I know very well what is in your mind, and that I am the person whom you wish to enclose; but I am so besotted with love for you that I must needs do your pleasure."

Then Vivian threw her arms about his neck and kissed him many times, saying that he ought well to be hers since she was all his. "You know well," she said, "that my great love for you has made me forsake all others in order to hold you in my arms day and night; you are my sole thought and desire, for without you I have neither joy nor well-being. I have placed all my hope in you, and I expect no happiness save from and with you. Since I love you and you love me, is it not just that I should do your will and you mine?" "So it is," answered Merlin. "Now ask what you wish." "I wish," said Vivian, "that you choose a fair and proper place which I may enclose by art in such wise that the enchantment can never be undone; we shall be there together, you and I, in joy and gladness whensoever it pleases you." "Well," said Merlin, "I will make such a place." "No," answered Vivian; "not you; teach me how to do it so that I may accomplish it at my pleasure."

So Merlin taught her how to fulfil this wish, and she wrote down the instructions very carefully. Thereupon she renewed her caresses, and Merlin sank ever more deeply in love.

In such wise they lived for a long time till on a day as they were going through the forest of Broceliande hand in hand, amusing themselves with sport and play, they came upon a tall hawthorn bush white with blossoms. There they sat in the shade to rest, and Merlin laid his head in the damsel's lap. When Vivian was assured that her lover was asleep, she rose softly and made a circle round the bush and Merlin with her wimple, and then began the incantations which Merlin had taught her. Nine times she drew the circle and made the spells nine times. Then she sat down and took Merlin's head in her lap, and so held him till he awoke.

Now Merlin looked about him, and it seemed to him that he was in the fairest and strongest tower in the world, and that he was at rest in the fairest place in which he had ever lain. Said he: "Lady, you have duped me; but I pray you stay with me, for none but you can undo this enchantment." "Fair sweet friend," answered Vivian, "I shall often come and go; but you shall have me in your arms, and I you, and henceforth you may do all your pleasure." And she abode by this covenant, for there were few hours of the day or night when she was not with him. And never afterwards did Merlin come out of the tower wherein Vivian had placed him, though she came and went as she pleased.

There is little more to add except to say that Arthur was so heavy at Merlin's absence that he besought Gawain to search for him. Accordingly Gawain and Yvain, Agravain and others set out on their quest. Gawain separated from his fellows and, as it chanced, reached the forest of Broceliande. As he was riding along there in deep thought he heard a voice addressing him: it was that of the invisible Merlin. The necromancer related what had happened to him. "How can it be true," asked Gawain, "that anyone can restrain you against your will, and you the wisest man in the world?" "Nay," answered Merlin, "not the wisest man, but the biggest fool. Now go your ways, for after you no man shall speak to me again."

Thereupon Gawain sadly took his way back to Arthur at Cardoel. The king was much grieved to learn of Merlin's fate, but since they could do nothing about it, king and court turned their minds to other matters. And Merlin's last prophecy was as true as the others, for since that day no one has ever spoken to him nor heard him speak.

"Merlin was indeed a fool," said Melior with a flash of black eyes; "and Vivian still a bigger one. Fie on the woman who must have recourse to sorcery in order to hold her man! I knew something of necromancy too, but I gained my knowledge decently. My father found me cunning clerks, and I had more than a hundred at one time or another. God endowed me with the ability to learn, and my masters provided the instruction. First I learned the seven arts from one end to the other. Then I took up medicine and learned the virtues of herb, root and spice. I learned about hot and cold humours, and what was the cure for every kind of disease that is curable, as well as the astrological hour and figure appropriate to it. Afterwards I studied divinity and made great strides into it, whether the old law or the new, so that before I was fifteen years old I had surpassed my professors. Then I studied divination, necromancy and enchantment with such assiduity that there were very few who were my equals in these arts.

"Many a time, when my father wanted a little recreation, he would send for me at midnight, and I would go to him along with my teachers. Then, by means of my knowledge and art, the room would seem to them to grow big enough to hold the whole district; and though it was midnight, I would cause a brightness as of mid-day in summer. Thereupon I would conjure up armed knights on their destriers, a thousand or two, as seemed good to me, and cause them to begin an engagement. So then they would fight as long as I pleased, whereupon I would dismiss them into nothing. Then elephants and lions would do battle with each other, or whatever other beasts I might choose. Thus also, by means of the skill which God had given me, I could conceal the inhabitants of a castle or a village from one another so that one would not sense the presence of his fellow. Thus did I learn, by waking and fasting, and assiduous application. But I never played any scurvy tricks on my lover. He learned his lesson, it is true, but his own bitter folly was a stronger master than any art of mine."

"Lady," said the Clerk of Oxenford, "I salute you. I do not know whether to admire most your beauty or your learning, for I am truly astonished by both. But whereas I have met many beautiful women, I have known few intelligent ones."

"Sir Clerk," replied Melior, "I accept the compliment with the spirit in which it was offered. But as I said, God gave me an eager and receptive curiosity as well as a beautiful body; and my father gave me good masters, whose concern was to impress upon my mind the facts of knowledge rather than stupefy or dazzle it by a parade of their own egos. In my time instruction did not consist simply in mouthing and posturing before a group of stupid, indifferent or bewildered adolescents. I learned most from those professors who considered that teaching does not consist either in coaxing the student to express an individuality which he does not possess, nor in begging the question by striding up and down the platform and damning one's opponent for a fool."

"I am still amazed that one so young could have learned so much without prejudice to her womanly charm. Were you not lonely?"

"It happens that I was. But how do you mean?"

"Did your learning not set you apart from the society of other ladies?"

"Oh, as to that," answered Melior, "no. Naturally I have always found men more interesting than women, but when I was in the company of ladies I chattered as much as they about dress, disease and domestics, and the other inconsequential trifles which form the staple of their conversation. Of course, I should not advise every father to spend as much for his daughter in the way of masters as mine did for me. And please observe that I make no claim to have advanced or increased knowledge—only to have acquired it. I had the sense not to make a show of it in soller or bower. I used it for practical purposes, such as bringing Partonopeus to beguile the tedium of a purely female environment."

"If women must study the arts," grumbled Helinandus, "let the magic arts not form an item of the curriculum."

"But, sir," protested Melior, "will you not reckon my studies in divinity as a counterbalance and corrective? Is it not true that in order to defeat your enemy you must know as much about him as you can?"

"I will concede the divinity," said the Clerk, "and sometime I should like to discuss that subject—and others—with you."

"Madam," said Thormod Kolbrunarskald, "I share the admiration of the Clerk of Oxenford for your parts, for which reason I am the more anxious to point out that the North also produced remarkable women of a stamp different from both yourself on the one hand and Gunhild and her daughter on the other. I should be sorry if the ladies and gentlemen here gathered were to believe them fair or typical representatives of our women. Everyone recalls how true and loyal was Queen Thyri to Olaf Tryggvison—who could not bear to outlive his disappearance. Great heroes are not born of ignoble mothers, and if the men of our nation have made any stir on the world's stage, it is because they spring, not from such women as Ragnhild and Gunhild, but rather from such as Gyda. With your permission I will tell you about her."

92. HARALD HARFAGR AND GYDA

Thormod Kolbrunarskald

After King Harald had subdued the whole northern part of Vingulmark, and had taken King Gandalf's realm as far south as the Glommen, he sent his men to a girl called Gyda, a daughter of King Eric of Hordaland, who was brought up as a foster-child in the house of a great bonder in Valders. The king wanted her for his mistress, for she was a remarkably handsome girl, but of high spirit withal.

Now when the messengers came there and delivered their errand to the girl, she answered that she would not throw herself away by taking for her husband a king who had no greater kingdom to rule over than a few counties. "And it seems to me," she said, "a wonderful thing that no king here in Norway will make the whole country subject to him in the same way as Gorm the Old did in Denmark, or Eric at Uppsala."

The messengers thought her reply was exceedingly haughty, and asked her what she thought would come of such an answer, for Harald was so mighty a man that his invitation was good enough for such as she. But though she had replied to their errand differently from what they wished, they saw no chance on this occasion of taking her with them against her will; so they prepared to return. As they were going Gyda said to the messengers: "Now tell King Harald these words of mine. I will agree to be his lawful wife upon the condition that he shall first, for my sake, subject to himself the whole of Norway, so that he may rule over that kingdom as freely and fully as King Eric over the Swedish dominions, or King Gorm over Denmark; for only then, it seems to me, can he be called the king of a people."

Now the messengers came back to King Harald, bringing him the girl's words, and saying that she was so bold and foolish that she would well deserve it if the king were to send a greater troop of people for her, and inflict some disgrace on her. Then answered the king: "This young woman has not spoken or done so much amiss that she should be punished, but rather should she be thanked for her words. She has put into my mind something which it appears to me wonderful I did not think of before. And now I make a solemn vow that never will I clip or comb my hair until I have subdued the whole of Norway with scat and duties and domains, or have died in the attempt."

After this Harald went about fighting many bitterly contested battles in Norway until the great battle of Hafrsfjord in 872. After this battle King Harald met no opposition in Norway, for all his opponents and greatest enemies were cut off. But some, and they were a great multitude, fled out of the country, and thereby great uninhabited districts were peopled. The out countries of Iceland and the Faroë Islands were discovered and colonized, as you know.

When King Harald had now become sole king over all Norway, he remembered what the proud girl Gyda had said to him. So he sent to her, and had her brought to him, and married her.

"If the company will permit," said Cormac of Cashel, "I should like to go back a step or two. You, Master Blaise," he said, turning to the hermit, "make it quite clear in the account you gave of Vivian that she was an adept in necromancy, but it did not appear that she was particularly lustful. In the case of Caier's wife recourse to thaumaturgy was had only as a means to a more fleshly end."

93. CAIER'S WIFE AND NEPHEW

Cormac of Cashel

There was in former times a king of Connaught named Caier, the son of Guthar. His brother had a son named Nede, who was a skilful poet and satirist. Caier adopted Nede as his own son because he himself was childless.

Now Caier's wife could not get Nede out of her thoughts. She gave him an apple of silver for his love, but when Nede would not consent, she promised him the kingdom after Caier if he would go in unto her. "How can this come about?" asked Nede. "That is not difficult," answered the woman. "You shall make a satire on him so that a blemish come upon him; then the man with the blemish, as you are aware, shall no longer be king." "This is not easy for me," said Nede, "for Caier will refuse nothing I ask of him. There is nothing in the world in his possession which he will not give me, wherefor there will be no excuse for a satire." "I know a thing which he will not give you," replied Caier's wife, "namely the dagger which was brought him as a present from Scotland, for it is a tabu of his to part with it."

So Nede asked Caier for that dagger. "Woe is me," said Caier, "for I am forbidden to part with it." Thereupon Nede made a satire upon him so that three blisters came forth on his cheeks. The next morning when Caier rose and went to the well to wash, he put his hand over his face and thereon found three blisters which the satire had caused, namely, Stain, Blemish and Defect, to wit, red, green and white. On perceiving that Caier fled, so that none might see the disgrace, and he went till he was in Dun Cermnai, with Cacher, the son of Eitirscele.

Nede took the kingdom of Connaught after him, and was in it till the end of a year, while Caier abode in torment. Then Nede went after him to Dun Cermnai, seated in Caier's chariot, and Caier's wife and his greyhound were with him.

"Alas!" said Caier, "'twas we who used to ride thus." And he fled out of the house till he was on the flagstone behind the dun. Nede went into the dun in his chariot, and the dogs followed Caier's tracks till they found him under the flagstone behind the fort.

When Caier beheld Nede, he died for shame. Then the rock, at Caier's death, flamed with fire, and a fragment of the rock flew up under Nede's eye and pierced into his head. Before he died Nede said: "Not unjust was that decree."

"Nede," said Cuan O Lochan, "was nithing, as the Sasanachs say, and he got a nithing's death. I could tell you of a young man who was similarly tempted, but who proved to be better endowed with the qualities of virtue and decency."

"Give us the story," cried several.

"It is not a happy one," answered Cuan.

"Tell it anyway."

"I will, then," said the poet.

94. THE DEATH OF MAELFOTHARTAIG MAC RONAN

Cuan O Lochan

A famous king was over Leinster, even Ronan, the son of Aed; and Ethne, the daughter of Cumascach of the Deisi of Munster, was by his side. She bore a son to him, Maelfothartaig, a son the most famous that ever came into Leinster. Before him they would rise at gatherings and fairs, at fights and shooting matches. He was the desire of all the maidens, and the darling of all the young women.

Ethne died, and for a long time Ronan was without a wife. "Why do you not take a wife?" asked his son. "You would be better with a wife by your side." "I am told," answered Ronan, "that Eochaid, the king of Dunseverick in the north, has a fair daughter." "Truly, you are not a mate for a girl," replied Maelfothartaig. "Will you not take a mature woman? It appears to me that such would be more seemly for you than a little skittish thing of a girl."

But Ronan had made up his mind, and would not be dissuaded. He went and slept with the girl in the north, and then brought her home with him. At that time Maelfothartaig was from home on a journey in the south of Leinster. "Where is your son?" asked Eochaid's daughter. "I am told you have a good son." "I have indeed," answered Ronan, "the best son there is in Leinster." "Then let him be summoned to me that he may receive me and my people and my jewels," said the girl. "He shall come," said Ronan.

Now Maelfothartaig came to his stepmother and made great welcome for her. "You shall have our love," said the youth. "Whatever we obtain of jewels and treasures shall go to you for loving Ronan." "It pleases me much," she replied, "that you act to my advantage."

Among her women Eochaid's daughter had a fair young maid, and on a day she sent her to solicit Maelfothartaig. But the young woman durst not speak her message lest the youth slay her. Then the queen vowed that she would strike off her head unless the message were delivered. So the maid drew near to Maelfothartaig as he was playing *fidchell* with Dond and Congal, his two foster-brothers. She attempted to speak, but could not, and blushed. When Maelfothartaig had left Congal asked: "What is it that you want to say?" "It is not I who want it," replied the damsel, "but the daughter of Eochaid, who would like to have Maelfothartaig as her lover." "O woman," said Congal, "say nothing of this, for you will be dead if it comes to Maelfothartaig's ears. However, if you wish it, I will deal with the prince for your own behoof."

The maid told the queen how matters had gone. Eochaid's daughter said she was well pleased. "For, if you lie with him yourself," she said, "you will be able to give him my message, and deal with him on my behalf afterwards." And so it was done, yet the queen's business was not advanced thereby. "Well, now," said she, "I see that you do not plead with the prince for me. You prefer to have the man for yourself alone, so you shall die by me."

One day after this the maidservant, weeping, approached Maelfothartaig. "What ails you?" he asked. "Eochaid's daughter is threatening to kill me," she replied, "because I have not pleaded with you to lie with her." "Woman," said he, "if I were thrust into a fiery coal pit that could make ashes and dust of me three times, I would not go to a meeting with the wife of Ronan, though all should blame me. In order to avoid her I will go away." Thereupon Maelfothartaig took fifty warriors and went to Scotland. In Alba he coursed his hounds and routed the king's foes in every battle.

"What is this, O Ronan," said the men of Leinster; "have you sent Maelfothartaig out of the land? You shall die by us unless he return." This was related to the prince, so he came back from the east. The men of Leinster made great welcome for him. He resumed his old habits, and the same maidservant slept with him.

"I want the man from you," said the queen; "otherwise it is death on your head." This she told to the prince. "O Congal," said Maelfothartaig, "what shall I do in this matter?" "Give me a guerdon for it," answered Congal, "and I will keep the woman off you so that she shall think of you no longer." "You shall have my two hounds, Doilin and Daithland," answered Maelfothartaig. "Tomorrow, then," said Congal, "go to hunt at Buaib Aife. Thither shall the maid send the queen to tryst with you, and I will put her from you." When this was told to the queen, she agreed, but it seemed to her a long time till morning.

On the morrow maid and mistress went to the tryst, and when they arrived they saw only Congal. "Whither away, harlot?" said Congal. "You can be after no good walking about here. Probably you are coming to a tryst with a man. Go home," he said, "and take a curse." And therewith Congal accompanied the queen to her house. But no sooner had he returned to Buaib Aife when he saw her coming towards him once more. "Is it thus," asked Congal, "that you wish to disgrace the king of Leinster, vile woman? If I see you again, I will take your head and put it on a stake before Ronan's face. A bad woman to disgrace him in brakes and ditches alone to meet a lad!" Therewith he laid a horse-whip on her and left her once more in her house. "I will spout a jet of blood in your face," said the queen before he left her.

That night it happened that Ronan inquired: "Where is Maelfothartaig tonight?" he asked. "He is without," answered Congal. "It is indeed too bad," said Ronan, "that my son should be abroad alone, considering the number of men to whom he gives good gifts." "You deafen us with your talk about your son," said the queen. "It is right to talk about him," answered Ronan, "for there is not in Ireland a son better according to the wish of his father, for his concern for my honour is as great as my own, so that there is ease for me and for you, O woman," said Ronan. "As for ease," replied Eochaid's daughter, "he shall indeed not get from me the ease which he wishes, even to meet with me to your shame. I shall not be alive withstanding him any longer. Three times since morning has Congal taken me to him, and it was only with difficulty that I escaped from his hands." "Malediction on your lips, foul woman, that is false!" cried Ronan. "You will see a proof of it, then," she replied: "I will sing half a quatrain, and you will see whether it fits with what he will sing."

I must tell you that Maelfothartaig used to do this every night to please her. He would sing one half quatrain, and she would match it with the other half. But Ronan was unaware of this custom.

At last Maelfothartaig came home from the hunt and was drying his feet at the fire with Congal by his side. His jester, Mac Glass, was at his games on the floor of the house, and seeing him Maelfothartaig sang:

> It is cold against the whirlwind
> For anyone herding the cows of Aife ...

for the day was indeed cold.

"Do you hear, O Ronan?" asked Eochaid's daughter. Then she sang:
> It is a vain herding indeed
> Not to meet with kine or lover.

"Alas!" said Ronan, "it is true!"

Now there was a warrior by Ronan's side, Aedan, son of Fiachna

Lara. "O Aedan," said the king, "a spear into Maelfothartaig and another into Congal." And when he turned his back Aedan hurled a spear into the prince so that he put its points through him as he was in his seat. And when Congal rose, Aedan thrust a spear into him so that it passed through his heart. Then the jester jumped up, and Aedan sent a spear after him so that it brought out his bowels.

"Enough on the men, Ó Aedan," said Maelfothartaig from his seat. "It was their luck," said Ronan, "that you found no woman to solicit but my wife." "Vile is that falsehood, O Ronan," said the prince, "which has been put on you to induce you to kill your only son without guilt. By your kingship, and by the tryst to which I go —the tryst with death—not greater is my guilt to think of meeting with her than that I should meet with my own mother. But it is she who has been soliciting me since she came into this land, and Congal took her back three times today so that she might not be alone with me. There was no guilt in Congal that you should kill him."

Thereafter the three men died and were taken into a house apart. And Ronan sat at his son's head for three days and three nights.

Dond, Congal's brother and Maelfothartaig's foster-brother, now took men and went to Dunseverick. They decoyed Eochaid to the border of the land, and there they took his head and the heads of his son and wife. But Ronan sat by the corpse of his son and sang:

> It is cold against the whirlwind
> For anyone herding the cows of Aife.
> That is a vain herding,
> With no cows, with no one to love.

And Eochaid's daughter sang:

> Woe is me, O corpse in the corner
> Who wast the mark for many eyes.

Therewith came Dond and cast the head of her father on her breast, and her mother's head, and the head of her brother. At that the queen rose and threw herself on her knife so that it went up through her back. After this the Leinstermen came about Ronan at the keening and threw him down on his back; and they went in pursuit of Aedan, and Maelfothartaig's son slew him. Thereupon Ronan sang:

> A great deed it was for Aedan,
> Son of a churl, to slay a king's son:
> That was clear on his death-day
> To Aedan, son of Fiachna Lara.

"Maelfothartaig was a prince and a young man," objected Sordello; "moreover, he was not only his father's darling, if I understand you, but the people's also. Ronan was an old man married to a young wife. For these reasons there may have been some excuse for Eochaid's daughter. But what shall we say of a woman who is properly and adequately matched, but who none the less casts her love on a base and unworthy object? You will probably admit that I know something about love, and that I was always catholic in my opinions, but I can hardly condone the conduct of Berengar's wife, about whom I am going to tell you."

95. THE BASE AMOUR OF BERENGAR'S WIFE WILLA

Sordello

About the time of the death of King Hugh of Provence, Willa, wife of Berengar of Ivrea, incurred the charge of adultery. Her levity was known not only to the household servants, but was the common knowledge of merchants and townsmen.

Willa had as her chaplain a priestling called Dominic, short of stature, swarthy, churlish, bristly, indocile, irritable, barbarous, dour, uncouth, blockish, dirty, quarrelsome, truculent and venal. To this master Willa confided her two daughters, Gisla and Giberga, in order that he might drench them with the art and science of letters. When the hirsute, unwashed priest was giving lessons to the girls, their mother took advantage of the opportunity to gain his favour by gifts of dainty dishes and costly garments. Everyone who knew this woman to be habitually hard and grasping was surprised that she should show herself so generous all of a sudden. But since the Word which says: "There is nothing covered up that is not going to be uncovered, nor secret that is not going to be made known," is true indeed, people were not long left in their astonishment.

One night when Berengar was absent from home the hairy fellow, as was his habit, was making his way to his mistress' chamber; a dog appeared unexpectedly on the scene, and succeeded in giving Dominic several severe bites before the sleepers in the near-by chambers were roused by its furious barking. The household rushed to the spot and seized the intruder. When they asked him whither he was bound, Willa anticipated his reply, and cut short any excuse he might have made by crying out: "The wretch was after my maids." Hereupon the miserable priest, thinking that it would go easier with him if he supported his mistress' statement, said: "So it was."

Willa was no fool, and after this incident she put her wits to work.

She began to plot against Dominic's life, offering a handsome reward to whomsoever would kill him. But the members of her familia were all God-fearing men, and refused to undertake the business. It appears that some rumour of the matter also reached Berengar's ears, though he took no action at the moment.

When Willa saw that bribery and intimidation were unavailing to gain her ends, she had recourse to the services of wizards and soothsayers, hoping that she might succeed in her design through their incantations. Whether or not Berengar's mood was affected by the charms and spells, I cannot say, but true it is that he agreed to do as Willa wished. The miserable priestling who had whinnied after his mistress' maids was forced to undergo an operation, and was ignominiously dismissed from service. Those who effected his disgrace reported afterwards that from a certain point of view it might be considered that the lady's love was worthily bestowed, for they had found Dominic to be a man of splendid development.

"I know some words to that music," said Ariosto. "If the company is interested, perhaps Sir John will again be good enough to serve as my interpreter."

"With pleasure," said Sir John Harington; "to what do you allude?"

"Possibly I should not have mentioned the subject," answered Ariosto, "for that particular canto of my *Orlando* procured you several years' banishment from court."

Sir John laughed. "That was not banishment," he said, "but a pleasant relief from the caprices of a captious queen. Besides, I was finally rewarded with a knighthood."

"Then you have no objection to rehearsing the story of Jocundo and King Astolfo?"

"None at all," replied the Englishman.

"Before Sir John proceeds," continued the Italian poet, "I must explain that this tale was told to Rodomonte the Saracen by his quondam host as they sat with others at the inn. And for the sake of the ladies present I would add that they must not attribute to me the sentiments or attitudes expressed in the story. All ladies know my love for them, and that I would serve them in every possible way. Like Chrétien de Troyes and Étienne de Bourbon, I merely set down what I found in my author's book, and must not be blamed for his opinions. And if his aspersions of the sex offend you, pay the story no heed, and dismiss it as an idle fable."

At these words Christine de Pisan and Fenice drew nearer, and Sir John began the tale . . .

96. HOW ASTOLFO, KING OF THE LOMBARDS, LEARNED ABOUT WOMEN

Sir John Harington

Astolfo, whilom king of Lumbardy,
To whom his elder brother left his raigne,
Was in his youth so fresh and faire to see,
As few to such perfection could attaine;
Apelles match, or Zeuces he might be
That such a shape could paint without much paine;
Great was his grace, and all the world so deem'd it,
But yet himself of all men most esteem'd it.

He did not of his sceptre take such pride,
Nor that degree that common men are under,
Nor wealth, nor friends, nor meaner kings beside,
That thereabout dwelt neare or far asunder;
But of his beauty, which he would not hide,
At whose rare worth he thought the world did wonder—
This was his joy, and all that he intended,
To heare his comely face and shape commended.

Among his courtiers, one above the rest,
Fausto by name, by birth a Romane knight,
Who hearing oft so prais'd, as they knew best,
His face and hands, and all that praise he might,
The king did bid him tell, at his request,
Neare or farre off if he had seen that wight
That in all parts so perfectly was wrought:
But he was answer'd as he little thought.

My Liege, quoth Fausto, plainly to declare
Both what my selfe doth see and others say,
But few with your rare beauty can compare,
And that same few were none, were one away:
Jocundo hight, a man of beauty rare,
And brother mine, excepting whom, I may
Prefer Your Grace before all other creatures,
But he doth match or pass you in his features.

The king to heare such tidings strange it thought,
As having still till that day kept the prize;

And with a deep desire straightwayes he sought
To know this man, and see him with his eyes.
In fine, with Fausto so far forth he wrought,
To bring him to his court he must devise.
Although, quoth he, to bring my brother to it,
I shall be sure of work enough to do it.

The cause is this: my brother never went
Forth of the gates of Rome scant all his life,
And such small goods as Fortune hath him lent,
He hath enjoy'd in quiet, free from strife,
Left by our sire, and them he hath not spent,
Nor yet increast, his gaines are not so rife;
And he will think it more to go to Pavy
Than some would think to th' Indies in a navy.

But I shall find it hardest when I prove
To draw him from his loving wife away,
To whom he is so link'd in chaines of love
That all is vaine, if once his wife say nay.
But yet Your Grace is so far all above,
You shall command me, certes, all I may.
Thanks, quoth the king, and addeth such reward
As might have movéd any to regard.

Away he posts, arriving in few dayes
At Rome, and to his brother's house he went,
And with such earnest words his brother prayes
That to return with him he doth consent.
Also his sister's love he so allayes
That she doth hold her peace as halfe content,
Beside great thanks, laying before her eyes
Preferments large that hereof might arise.

Jocundo now resolv'd to go his way,
Gets men and horse against he should depart,
Sets forth himself with new and rich array,
As still we see nature adorn'd by art.
His wife at night in bed, at board by day
With watry eyes to shew a sorie heart
Complaines his absence will so sore her grieve,
Till his return she doubts she shall not live.

Ay me, the thought, quoth she, makes me so fraid
That scant the breath abideth in my brest.
Peace, my sweet love and life, Jocundo said,
And weeps as fast, and comforts her his best;
So may good fortune ay my journey aid,
As I return in threescore days at least,
Nor will I change the day I set thee down—
No, though the king would grant me half his crown.

All this might not asswage this woman's paine:
Two moneths were long, yea, too too long, she cries;
Needs must I die before you come againe,
Nor how to keep my life can I devise;
The dolefull days and nights I shall sustaine—
From meat my mouth, from sleep will keep mine eyes.
Now was Jocundo ready to repent
That to his brother he had giv'n consent.

About her neck a jewell rich she ware,
A cross all set with stone in gold well tride.
This relick late a Boëm pilgrim bare,
And gave her father other things beside,
Which costly things she kept with no small care,
Till comming from Jerusalem he di'd,
And her of all his goods his heire he makes.
This precious crosse to her goodman she takes,

And prayes him for her sake to weare that token
And think on her. The man, that was most kind,
Receiv'd it with more joy than can be spoken,
Although he needed not be put in mind,
For why no time, nor no state sound nor broken,
Nor absence long, a mean should ever find
To quaile his love, not onely while his breath
Maintaines his life, but neither after death.

That very night that went before the morrow
That they had pointed surely to depart,
Jocundo's wife was sick, and swounds for sorrow
Amid his arms, so heavy was her heart.
All night they wake, and now they bid Godmorrow,
And give their last farewell, and so they part:
Jocundo on his way with all his traine,
His loving wife doth go to bed againe.

Scant had Jocundo rode two mile forthright
But as his cross now came into his mind
Which on his pillow he had laid last night,
And now for hast had left the same behind.
He would devise to scuse it if he might,
But no excuse sufficient could he find:
But that his love must needs be much suspected
To find the precious jewell so neglected.

When no excuse within his mind could frame
But that all seeméd frivolous and vaine,
To send his man he counted it a shame,
To go himself it was but little paine.
He staid, and when his brother did the same:
Ride soft, quoth he, till I return againe,
For home againe I must, there is no nay;
But I will overtake you on the way.

Th' affaire is such as none can do but I,
But doubt you not, I will return as fast.
Away he spurres as hard as he could hie,
Alone, without or man or page, for hast.
Now had the sun's new rising clear'd the skie
With brightest beames, ere he the streame had past.
He hies him home and finds his wife in bed
Full sound asleep, such cares were in her head.

He drawes the curtaine softly without sound,
And saw that he would little have suspected:
His chast and faithfull yokefellow he found
Yok'd with a knave, all honesty neglected.
Th' adulterer, though sleeping very sound,
Yet by his face was easily detected:
A beggar's brat, bred by him from his cradle,
And now was riding on his master's saddle.

Now if he stood amaz'd and discontent,
Believe it ye to trie that would be loth,
For he that tries it doubtlesse will repent,
As poore Jocundo did, who was so wroth
That out he drew his sword, with just intent
For their ungratefull act to kill them both.
But lo, the love he bare her did withstand
Against his heart to make him hold his hand.

O ribald love, that such a slave couldst make
Of one that now was subject to thy force:
He could not break her sleep for pitie's sake
That brake all bonds of faith without remorse;
But back he goes before they did awake,
And from his house he gets him to his horse.
Love so pricks him, and he so pricks his steed,
He overtakes his company with speed.

His look is sad, all changéd is his cheare;
Full heavy was his heart they well perceiv'd;
They see no cause of grief nor guesse they neare,
And they that guesse most likely are deceiv'd.
They thought he went to Rome, but you do heare
How at Corneto he his hurt receiv'd.
Each man espi'd that love procur'd that passion,
But none descri'd the manner nor the fashion.

His brother deems that all his griefe doth grow
Because his loving wife is left alone;
But he a cleane contrary cause doth know—
Her too much company did cause his mone.
He bends his brows, his looks he casts alow,
With powting lips and many a grievous grone.
In vaine doth Faustus comfort seek to bring him,
For why he knowes not where the shoe doth wring him.

He gives a salve afore the sore is found,
His plaisters are as poison to the smart;
He seeks to heale, and wider makes the wound;
He names his wife, but her name kils his heart.
Gone was his tast, his sleeps do grow unsound,
Nature decayth, and little helpeth art,
And that faire face that erst was of such fame,
Is now so chang'd it seemeth not the same.

His eyes are sunk so deep into his head
It made his nose seem bigger then it should;
His flesh doth shrink, his bones do seem to spread:
He was so chang'd as more cannot be told.
At last an ague makes him keep his bed
And bait at innes more often then he would.
His faire complexion now is pale and witheréd,
Much like the rose that yesterday was gatheréd.

With this mishap was Faustus sore agriev'd,
Not onely for his brother's wofull state,
But fearing of his prince to be reprov'd
Unto whose grace he undertook so late
To shew the goodliest man, as he believ'd,
Now growne uncouth by force of inward bate.
Yet as they could, their way they so contriv'd
That at the last in Pavie they arriv'd.

He would not straightway shew him to the king
Lest ev'ry one might deem his judgement small,
But sent by letters notice of the thing,
And what mishap his brother did befall—
How scant alive he could him thither bring,
A secret grief so greatly did him gall,
And with an ague pul'd him down so sore
He seem'd not now the man he was before.

And yet, behold, this noble king is glad
That he is come, and meanes to make him cheare
As if he were the dearest friend he had,
So sore he had desir'd to see him here;
Nor would the worthy natur'd prince be sad,
In praise of beauty to have found a peere.
He knew Jocundo's beauty had excel'd
But that by this disease it was expel'd.

He placeth him to his own lodging nigh;
He visits him each day and ev'ry houre;
Great plenty of provision he doth buy—
To welcome him he bendeth all his power.
But still Jocundo languishing doth lie—
His wife's misdeeds makes all his sweet seem sowre.
No songs, no sights, which oft he heard or saw
One dram of this his dolour could withdraw.

Fast by his lodging was, amongst the rest,
A faire large room which very few did use.
Here would he walk as one that did detest
All pleasing sights, and comforts all refuse.
Here the wide wound he bare within his brest
With thousand thoughts unpleasant he renewes.
Yet here he found, which few would have believ'd,
A remedy for that which had him griev'd.

For at the upper end of this old hall
There was a place of windows void, and light,
Save that the lime, new molten from the wall
Let in a little beame that shinéd bright.
Here did he see—which some may think a tale—
A very strange and unexpected sight.
He heard it not, but saw it in his view,
Yet could he scant believe it should be true.

For at the chink was plainly to be seen
A chamber hang'd with faire and rich array,
Where none might come but such as trusty been.
The princesse here in part doth spend the day,
And here he saw a dwarf embrace the queen
And strive a while; and after homely play
His skill was such that ere they went asunder
The dwarf was got aloft, and she lay under.

Jocundo standeth still as one amaz'd,
Supposing sure that he had seen a vision.
But seeing plain, when he a while had gaz'd,
It was an act, and not an apparition.
Good God! said he, are this queene's eyes so daz'd,
To love a dwarf, more worthy of derision?
Whose husband is a prince of worthy fame,
So brave a man, such love? Now fie for shame!

He now began to hold his wife excus'd,
His anger now a little was relented;
And though that she her body had abus'd,
And to her servant had so soon consented,
Not her for this, but he the sex accus'd
That never can with one man be contented.
If all, quoth he, with one like staine are spotted,
Yet on a monster mine was not besotted.

The day ensuing he returnéd thither,
And saw the dwarfe couragious still and jolly.
Eke he another day repairéd hither,
And still he found the queen committing folly,
He oft returnes, he finds them oft together:
They cease not work on dayes prophane nor holy—
Yea, which was strange, the goodly queen complain'd
That of the dwarfe she found she was disdain'd.

One day when in the corner he had staid
He sees her come all sad and malecontent,
Because the dwarfe his comming still delaid,
For whom of purpose twice before she sent.
Once more she sends: This answer brings the maid:
Forsooth unto his play he is so bent
That for mistrust at chesse to leese a shilling
To come to you the ape's face is not willing.

Jocundo, who before had still been sad,
Upon this sight became of better cheare.
The paines, the plaints, the cloudy stormes he had
Away were blown, the coast began to cleare:
Most ruddie faire and chearful grew and glad
That angell-like his beauty did appeare,
So as the king and others thought it strange
In so short time to find so great a change.

Now as the king desiréd much to know
The mean whereby his hurt so soon was heal'd,
No lesse Jocundo did desire to show,
And would not have the thing from him conceal'd,
So as his choler might no greater grow
Than his had been, when as it were reveal'd.
But first he made him sweare on his salvation,
Upon the parties to use no castigation.

He made him sweare for ought he heard or saw,
Wherewith his mind might fortune be diseas'd,
Yet from his choler so much to withdraw
As that in shew he may not seem displeas'd,
Nor punish it by might nor yet by law,
Nor first nor last, but hold himself appeas'd,
So as th' offenders might not have suspected
That their misdeeds were to his grace detected.

The king so sure, by oth so solemne bound,
As one that little thought his queene so stain'd,
Jocundo first his own griefe doth expound
Why he so long so dolefull had remain'd,
And in whose armes his own wife he had found,
And how the griefe thereof so sore him pain'd;
Had not the salve unlook'd for been applied,
Of that conceit no doubt he should have died.

But lying in your highnesse house forlorn
I saw, quoth he, that minisht much my mone;
For though it grievéd me to weare a horn,
It pleas'd me well I ware it not alone.
This said he brought him where that wall was torn,
And shew'd him that that made his heart to grone:
For why the dwarfe did manage with such skill,
Though she curvets, he keeps his styrup still.

Much did the king this foule prospect mislike:
Believe my words I say, I need not sweare.
Horn wood he was, he was about to strike
All those he met, and his own flesh to teare.
His promise to have broken he was like,
If of his oath he had not had some feare.
But unrevengéd all must now be born,
For on his *agnus dei* he had sworn.

Now to Jocundo gently he doth speak:
Good brother mine, advise me what to do.
Sith I am bound by oath, I may not wreak
The fact with such revenge as longs thereto.
Forsooth, let's trie if others be as weak,
Jocundo said, and make no more ado.
This was the counsel he did give the king,
Into their order other men to bring.

We both are yong, and of such pleasing hew
Not to be matcht with such another paire.
What she will be so obstinately true
But will be won with youth and being faire?
If youth and beauty both do misse their due,
The want herein our purses shall repaire.
Let us not spare our beauty, youth and treasure
Till of a thousand we have had our pleasure.

To see strange countries placéd farre apart,
Of other women eke to make some triall
Will ease the paine that whilom pierc'd our heart,
And salve our sore, there can be no deniall.
The king, that long'd to ease his new-found smart
Consented straight, and to avoid espiall,
Himselfe, the knight, two pages and no mo,
Out of the realm forthwith disguiséd go.

Away they past through Italy and France,
And through the Flemish and the English land;
And those whose beauties highest did advance,
Those still they found most ready to their hand.
They give, they take, so luckie is their chance,
To see their stock at one stay still to stand.
Some must be woo'd, forsooth, they were so chast,
And some there were that wooéd them as fast.

In countries some a moneth or two they taried,
In some a week, in others but a day.
In all of them they find the women maried
Like to their wives—too gentle to say nay.
At last, because they doubt to have miscaried,
They mean to leave this sport and go their way:
They found it full of danger and debate
To keep their standings in another's gate.

They do agree to take, by common voice,
Someone whose shape and face may please them both,
In whom without suspect they may rejoyce.
For wherefor, quoth the king, should I be loth
To have yourselfe a partner in my choice?
I must have one, and I believe, for troth,
Among all women kind there is not one
That can content herselfe with one alone.

But of some one we two might take our pleasure,
And not inforce ourselves beyond our ease,
But, as they say, take meat and drink and leasure,
And by our doings others not displease;
Well might that woman think she had a treasure
That had us two her appetite to please.
And though to one man faithful none remaine,
No doubt but faithfull they would be to twaine.

The Roman youth much prais'd the prince's mind,
And to perform it seeméd very faine.
Away they posted, as they had assign'd,
By town and city, over hill and plaine,
Till at the last a prettie peece they find—
The daughter of an innkeeper in Spaine,
A gyrle of person tall and faire of favour,
Of comely presence and of good behaviour.

She was new entring in the flower and pride
Of those well pleasing youthfull yeares and tender;
Her father many children had beside,
And poverty had made his portion slender,
And for them all unable to provide,
It made him soon content away to send her.
The price agreed, away the strangers carie her,
Because the father money wants to marie her.

In concord great she did with them remaine,
Who took their pleasure one and one by turn
As bellowes do, where Vulcan's wonted paine
By mutuall blast doth make the metall burn.
Their meaning is, now they had travel'd Spaine,
By Siphax realme to make their home return;
And having left Valenza out of sight,
At faire Zativa they did lodge at night.

The masters go abroad to view the town,
And first the churches for devotion's sake,
And then the monuments of most renown,
As travellers a common custom take.
The gyrle within the chamber sate her down;
The men are busied, some the beds do make,
Some care to dresse their wearied horse, and some
Make ready meat against their masters come.

In this same house the gyrle a Greeke had spi'd
That in her father's house a boy had been,
And slept full often sweetly by her side,
And much good sport had passéd them between;
Yet fearing lest their love should be descri'd,
In open talk they durst not to be seen,
But when by hap the pages down were gone,
Old love renew'd, and thus they talk thereon.

The Greeke damands her whither she was going,
And which of these two great estates she keeps.
She told him all—she needs no further woing—
And how a-night between them both she sleeps.
Ah, quoth the Greek, thou tellest my undoing,
My deare Fiametta; and with that he weeps.
With these two lords wilt thou from Spaine be banish'd?
Are all my hopes thus into nothing vanish'd?

HOW ASTOLFO LEARNED ABOUT WOMEN

My sweet designements turnéd are to sowre,
My service long finds little recompence.
I made a stock according to my power,
By hoarding up my wages, and the pence
That guests did give, that came in luckie houre.
I meant ere long to have departed hence,
And to have ask'd thy sire's good will to marie thee,
And that obtain'd, unto a house to carie thee.

The wench of her hard fortune doth complaine,
And saith that now she doubts he sues too late.
The Greek doth sigh and sob, and part doth faine.
And shall I die, quoth he, in this estate?
Let me enjoy thy sweetnesse once againe,
Before my dayes draw to their dolefull date,
One small refreshing ere we quite depart
Will make me die with more contented heart.

The gyrle with pity movéd thus replies:
Think not, quoth she, but I desire the same,
But hard it is among so many eyes,
Without incurring punishment and shame.
Ah, quoth the Greeke, some meanes thou would'st devise,
If thou but felt a quarter of my flame,
To meet this night in some convenient place
And be together but a little space.

Tush, answer'd she, you sue now out of season,
For ev'ry night I lie betwix them two;
And they will quickly feare, and find the treason,
Sith still with one of them I have to do.
Well, quoth the Greek, I could refute that reason
If you would put your helping hand thereto.
You must, said he, some pretie sense devise,
And find occasion from them both to rise.

She first bethinks herselfe, and after bad
He should return when all were sound asleep,
And learnéd him, who was thereof right glad,
To go and come, what order he should keep.
Now came the Greeke, as he his lesson had,
When all was husht, as soft as he could creep,
First to the doore, which open'd when he push'd,
Then to the chamber, which was softly rush'd.

He takes a long and leisurable stride,
And longest on the hinder foot he staid.
So soft he treads, although his steps were wide,
As though to tread on eggs he were afraid;
And as he goes, he gropes on either side
To find the bed, with both hands broad displaid;
And having found the bottom of the bed,
He creepeth in, and forward go'th his head.

* * * *

Jocundo and the king do both perceive
The bed to rock, as oft it comes to passe,
And both of them one errour did deceive,
For either thought it his companion was.
Now hath the Greeke taken his latter leave,
And as he came he back againe doth passe;
And Phoebus' beames did now to shine begin:
Fiametta rose and let the pages in.

Now with Jocundo gan the king to jest:
Brother, quoth he, I doubt we do you wrong;
It were more time for you to take your rest,
That have this night a journey rode so long.
Jocundo answers him againe in jest:
O sir, you do mistake, you sing my song;
Take you your ease, and much good do your grace
That all this night have rid a hunting pace.

I? quoth the king, I would in faith, I swear,
Have lent my dog a course among the rest,
But that I found yourself so busie were,
And rode so hard you could not spare the beast.
Well, said the knight, it seemeth me to beare,
Although you brake your promise and behest;
Yet privy quips and taunts here needed none:
You might have bid me let the wench alone.

One urg'd so farre, the tother so repli'd
That unto bitter words their tongues were moov'd,
Scarce one forbare to say the other li'd;
And plaine to trie whose truth should be reproov'd,
They cal'd the gyrle the matter to decide,
Who was afraid, as well it her behoov'd.

And she must tell, they standing face to face,
Which of them two deservéd this disgrace.

Tell, quoth the king, with grim and angry sight,
Nor feare not him nor me, but tell us true,
Which of us two it was that all this night
So gallantly perforḿed all his due.
Thus, either deeming he did hold the right,
They lookéd both which should be found untrue.
Fiametta lowly laid herselfe on ground,
Doubting to die because her fault was found.

She humbly pardon craves for her offence,
And that they pitie would her wofull case,
That she with pitie mov'd to recompence
His love that lasted had so little space;
And who it was she told them, and of whence,
Had this ill luck in this unluckie place;
How she had hop'd that though they hapt to wake,
Yet for his partner either would it take.

The king and his companion greatly mus'd,
When they had heard the practice so detected,
And their conceits not little were confus'd,
To heare a hap so strange and unexpected;
And though no two were ev'r so abus'd,
Yet had they so all wrathfull mind rejected,
That down they lay and fell in such a laughter,
They could not see nor speak an houre after.

And when at last their stomacks and their eyes
Water'd and ak'd, they laughéd had so much—
Such shifts, quoth they, these women will devise,
Do what we can, their chastity is such.
If both our cares could not for one suffice
That lay betwixt us both and did us touch,—
If all our haires were eyes, yet sure, they said,
We husbands of our wives should be betraid.

We had a thousand women prov'd before,
And none of them deniéd our request,
Nor would and if we tri'd ten thousand more;
But this one trial passeth all the rest.

Let us not then condemn our wives so sore,
That are as chast and honest as the best;
Sith they be as all other women be,
Let us turn home, and well with them agree.

When on this point they both were thus resolv'd,
They gave the Greeke Fiametta for his wife,
And ti'd the knot that cannot be dissolv'd,
With portion large, to keep them all their life.
Themselves went home, and had their sins absolv'd,
And take againe their wives, and end all strife.
And thus mine host the prettie storie ended,
With which he pray'd them not to be offended.

"Your somewhat lengthy recital probably is, as Messer Ariosto says, only a poet's fable," remarked Fynes Moryson. "Now I can tell you something in the same category that is vouched for not only by history, but by a brass tablet."

"We are always glad to learn," said Sir John; "but keep the horsemeat, batzen, groshen and the coachman's dinner out of it."

"My tale shall at least have the virtue of brevity," rejoined Fynes stiffly.

"Well, tell on," said Sir John, taking a sip of sack.

97. MARGARET, COUNTESS OF HENNEBERGE AND HER THREE HUNDRED AND SIXTY-FIVE CHILDREN

Fynes Moryson

When I was staying at the Hague I once walked out half an hour's space to the village of Lausdune. There I saw a wonderful monument, the history whereof it is said the Earl of Leicester carried home with him to England written in a manuscript. Affixed to the wall were two brass basins, and between them a bronze tablet whereon was inscribed the following history:

> So strange and monstrous thing I tell
> As from the world's frame ne'er befell:
> He parts amazed who marks it well.

Margaret, wife to Hermanus, Count of Henneberge, daughter to Florence, Count of Holland and Zealand, sister to William, King of the Romans and Caesar of the Empire: This most noble countess, being about forty-two years old, on the very day of preparation called Parascene, about nine of the clock, in the year 1276, brought forth at one birth three hundred and sixty-five children, which, being baptized in two basins of brass by Guido, suffragan of Utrecht, all the males were called John, and all the females Elizabeth; but all of them together with the mother, died in one and the same day, and lie buried here in the church of Lausdune. And this happened to her in that a poor woman, bearing in her arms two twins, the countess wondering at it, said she could not have them both by one man, and so rejected her with scorn; whereupon the woman, sore troubled, wished that the countess might have as many children at a birth as there be days in the whole year; which, contrary to the course of nature, by miracle fell out, as in this table is briefly set down for perpetual memory, out of old chronicles as well written as printed. Almighty God must be in this beheld and honoured and extolled with praises for ever and ever. Amen.

"In my opinion," said John Gower, "the countess got her deserts. Since the story is inscribed on brass, it is, of course, true. But many of you here will recall that Marie de France had already worked up this motif in the *Lay of the Ash*."

"Whether true or false," said John Mirk, "the moral seems plain enough. As for adultery itself, I remember having read somewhere an account of punishment even more fearful than that meted out to the Countess of Henneberge for scepticism."

98. THE MIDNIGHT RIDER

John Mirk

There was a charcoal-burner who followed his trade in a great lord's park, and when he had made a big fire it was his custom to lie beside it all night. Now on one occasion, a little before midnight, there came a half-naked woman, running as fast as she could, behaving as though she were out of her wits; and after her came a knight with a drawn sword, riding as fast as he could prick on a great black horse, who hunted her all about the coal fire. Afterwards, the knight slew the woman, hewed her to bits, cast the pieces into the fire, and rode away again as fast as he was able.

The charcoal-burner saw this happen night after night until he finally went to his lord and told him the whole matter. The lord was a man of courage, and replied that he would inquire into those circumstances. The following night he went to the park and saw everything just as the man had related. At the moment when the knight had slain the woman and cast her into the fire the lord conjured him to tell who he was, and why he did these things. The other replied that not long ago he had been a retainer of this same lord's, and that the woman was another knight's wife; and since he had lain with her in her husband's despite, they had both had this penance put upon them. He explained that he was forced to hew her in pieces and burn her every night, that the horse whereon he rode was a fiend who burned him a hundredfold hotter than any earthly fire, and that they had to suffer that penance until they had been helped by certain masses and almsdeeds. The lord asked him what was to be done, and when informed, helped him out of his penance by the mercy of God.

"Probably you had been reading my novels," suggested Boccaccio, "the fifty-eighth of my *Decameron*. I myself got the story from Jacopo Passavanti's book."

"No," replied Mirk, "I regret to say that your *Decameron* was not known in England in my day. I must have read it in Vincent of Beauvais' *Speculum,* which has almost everything in it."

"That's where I read it," growled Caesar of Heisterbach.

"Well, Vincent got it from me," said Helinandus.

"And where did you get it?" asked Peter Bell.

Helinandus was saved considerable embarrassment by Hallarstein the Skald who said: "I know nothing about storiology, but I know that long ago the poets of the North related how Odin, on horseback, pursued a woman of the wood."

"Need we take it any farther back?" queried Sir John Harington. "I am much relieved to learn that the story was not brought to Europe through the crusades."

"Unless we change the subject," said the Clerk of Oxenford, "someone will prove that the Scandinavians brought it from India."

"Alas!" sighed Paul the Deacon, "alas for the frailty of the flesh! Tonight I have listened to things which I never thought were possible. In view of what has already been said, I no longer have much hesitancy in relating what happened to the Duchess of Friuli."

"What was that?" inquired Andrea Dandolo.

"Like Gunhild, she was a widow, and widows, I suppose, are like tigers," answered Paul.

99. THE INORDINATE LUST OF ROMILDA, DUCHESS OF FRIULI

Paul the Deacon

Not long after the death of the emperor Phocas it happened that the king of the Avars, whom they call Cagan in their language,

THE INORDINATE LUST OF ROMILDA 453

violently invaded the province of Friuli with a mighty army. Of this province, anciently named Forum Julii, a Lombard called Gisulf was the duke. On learning of Cagan's entry into his territory he boldly went to meet him with all the Lombard soldiery he could get together. There was a cruel and stubbornly contested battle, wherein streams of blood flowed, and many fell on both sides. And though Gisulf with his few fought with indomitable courage against Cagan and his immense multitude, nevertheless, he was surrounded on every side, and killed with nearly all his followers.

The wife of this Gisulf, Romilda by name, fortified herself within the stronghold of Forum Julii together with those Lombards who had escaped, and the wives and children of those who had perished in battle. With her were her four sons: Taso and Caco were growing into manhood, while Raduald and Grimuald were still young boys. She also had four daughters, Appa, Gaila—and the names of the other two I have forgotten.

Cagan, as I said, lost heavily in the battle, and yet after the victory he had sufficient troops to ride through the country, burning and pillaging, and otherwise impressing his barbarian cruelty on every age and sex. Finally he sat down before the fortress of Forum Julii with the intention of taking it. For this design his troops outnumbered his hopes, inasmuch as the fortress was exceptionally strong, both by nature and by art, was well defended by a sufficient number of hardy soldiers, and was well stocked with provisions. Cagan almost despaired of taking the place by storm or siege. Another thing that worried him was the report that a fresh Lombard army was approaching. He was, indeed, on the point of returning to his own country when Fortune enabled him to achieve what Force could not.

One day, as the Avar king was riding about the walls with a company of horsemen in order to discover some point at which the city might prove vulnerable, he was observed by Romilda from the walls. When the duchess saw him to be a man in the bloom of youth, she at once fell so violently in love with him that until she could clasp him in amorous embrace one hour seemed to her a thousand years. Forgetting that the barbarian had slain her husband, and casting to the winds every consideration of duty to her people, or love for her children, she straightway sent word to Cagan by messenger that if he would marry her she would deliver to him the fortress and all who were in it. On hearing this message the barbarian king, who desired nothing in the world so much as to take that stronghold, promised her with wicked cunning that he would accede to her conditions, and vowed to take her in marriage. The following night Romilda opened the gates of Forum Julii, and let in the enemy, to her own ruin and that of all who were there. Her sons succeeded in fleeing, but that is another story.

The Avars, having entered the fortress with their king, laid waste with their plunderings everything on which they could lay their hands, consumed the city with fire, carried away as captives everyone they found, promising to settle them in the territories of Pannonia whence they themselves had come. However, instead of so doing, they slew with the sword all Lombard males who had reached the age of manhood, and consigned women and children to the yoke of captivity.

Romilda, indeed, who had been the cause and source of all this evil, Cagan, in accordance with his oath, kept for one night as if in marriage. On the following morning he turned her over to twelve of his sturdiest soldiers who, succeeding each other by turns, abused her through the whole day and night without giving her a moment's rest. Afterwards, ordering a stake to be fixed in the open field, Cagan commanded that Romilda be impaled upon it, saying to her in scorn: "This is the husband you deserve."

By such a death perished the cursed betrayer of her country, more swayed by her detestable lust than by feelings of duty and obligation to her fellow citizens or her children.

"Reverend sir," said Sir John Harington, "doubtless your tale is as veracious as that about the Countess of Henneberge; but if I may say so, it smells just as badly. Somehow, I prefer Moryson's dirty hills of corn."

"'Gens irritabile vatum,'" answered the traveller. "Pay no attention to him. But to show you that our genius is not confined to dirty ways, whether of countries or people, I will tell another story of a different sort such as ought to appeal to all sentimentalists."

100. TWO LOYAL LOVERS OF FLORENCE

Fynes Moryson

In the year 1594, being at Pisa, and finding myself short of cash, I decided to pay a visit to my bankers at Florence. Therefore, hiring a horse for four giulii, I rode forty miles to Florence through the pleasant valley of Arno, partly tilled after the manner of Lombardy, where one and the same field yields corn, wine and wood, partly divided into sweet pastures.

Florence is a most sweet city, and abounding in wealth, and the citizens are much commended for their courtesy, modesty, gravity, purity of language, and many virtues. The city is of round form, and upon the walls thereof lie eight forts. The far greater part of the city is on the north side of the river, and lies in a plain; but in the lesser part, on the south side of the river, the houses are built upon the sides of mountains, and the dwellings are more scattered, having many and large gardens. And in that part there is a place vulgarly called Le Ruinate, that is, the ruins, because the houses had been cast down by earthquakes. Near that place lies a lane, unpaved, in memory of a maid who dwelt there. She was loved by a young man whose family adhered to a faction contrary to that supported by hers, for which reason many cruelties had been exercised between them. But they, mutually loving each other, and despairing to get their friends' consent for marriage, and at last being impatient of delay, resolved with whatever danger to meet together. But it happened that the young man, as he was on the point of ascending into the maiden's chamber by a ladder, was surprised; and to save the girl's reputation he confessed that he had come to rob the house. Thereupon he was condemned to die, and being led to execution near the house where the maid dwelt, she, laying aside all shame, came running out with her hair loose about her ears, and embracing him, publicly confessed the truth.

The parents of both young people were so moved by this circumstance that, laying aside all former malice, they contracted affinity; and the young man, delivered from the bonds of the hangman, was tied to her in the sweet bond of marriage. And of this wonderful event the Florentines thought good to keep this memorial for posterity.

"That was a good story," said the Knight of La Tour Landry, "even though brief."

"You must understand," said Sir John Harington, "that unless he restricted the space which he devotes to really important things, he would have no room for hills of corn and coachmen's dinners."

"Well, long or short," said Ulrich von Lichtenstein, "it nicely turns the subject, and I, for one, am rather weary of looking at the unlovely side of female character such as has been displayed for us during the last few moments."

"I agree with you there," said Andrea Dandolo. "And since the womanhood of Friuli has been placed in a somewhat invidious light, I propose to relate to you how a certain lady of Aquileia behaved for the sake of her honour and virtue. It is an incident which shines like a jewel amid the dung wherewith Attila overspread the world in the middle of the fifth century.—For my part, I have never been able to understand the fame which later centuries attached to his name. It seems to me that he was not strong, but that both the Eastern and the Western empires lay prostrate with a variety of maladies; that he was not great, but that he was something between an unchastised brat and a blustering buffoon. Sick as they were, it is to the vestiges of strength and virtue which remained in the civilized peoples that we owe whatever we have achieved since his time. The most hopeful reflection which can come to the minds of thoughtful men today is that the Attilas and Genghis Khans of the world shall not prevail, but shall be trodden under foot to make room for the clean wheat. However, I was going to tell you about . . ."

101. DIGNA OF AQUILEIA

Andrea Dandolo

Frightened away from Paris by Saint Genovefa, from Orléans by Bishop Anianus, from Troyes by Bishop Lupus, and beaten on the Mauriac Plains by Aetius and Theodoric the Goth, Attila returned in bewildered rage to Pannonia. There reinforcements of men flowed into his camp till he was ready to take his revenge, not on the Visigoths of Gaul—it was the Italians of Italy who were to pay for his shame.

The barbarian marched against Aquileia, a strong and important city situated at the head of the Italian kingdom. Three years he besieged it in vain, always bitterly opposed by the citizens, until finally his soldiers began to murmur. Then one day as he was walking round the city searching for some practicable means of entry, he observed that the storks, which had built their nests on the roofs of the houses, were migrating in a flock, and that some were attempting to bear away their unfledged young with them. "Behold those birds," said he to his men; "warned by instinct of the city's imminent fall, they are hastening to leave it."

The augury seemed good to his soldiers. They pushed up their engines to the walls, and employed their slings and catapults with new energy. The city capitulated almost at once. Rushing in, the barbarians looted and pillaged, killed and captured, and set fire to what remained. As you know, the city of the North Wind never recovered: the Hunnish heel had sunk too deep.

Now there was in that city a most noble woman by the name of Digna, beautiful in face and figure, but still more handsomely endowed with the whiteness of modesty. Her dwelling was upon the walls, and close to it rose a high tower, under which glided the glassy waters of the Natiso. That she might not become the victim of the lust of those filthiest of foes, and that the purity of her soul and body might not be smirched upon the entry of the lecherous host, when she heard of the city's fall, she muffled her head in her mantle, and leaped from the top of that same tower, thus by a memorable death putting an end to both life and the fear of shame.

"Your tale illustrates your argument," said Sir Thomas Elyot, "and fits with some observations lately made by Thormod Kolbrunarskald: Ignoble mothers do not breed heroes. That lady was indeed worthy of her name. Had there been more such at that time, Rome might have survived not only the shock of the barbarians, but even the rapacity of patrician landlords and the stupidities of the fisc."

"It is a mistake to think that she did not survive," said Machiavelli quietly, "though it is true that she was sick unto death for a long time. Did not your own Venerable Bede say: 'As long as the Coliseum stands, Rome shall stand; when the Coliseum falls, Rome shall fall; when Rome falls, the world shall fall'?"

"What should one do at Rome?" asked Neckam, "unless he is a skilful liar."

"Is it you who speaks or Juvenal?" asked the Clerk of Oxenford.

"For my part," said Adam Usk, "I found Rome a place of hovels, thieves, wolves, worms and desert wastes."

"That does not surprise me," said Camden, "for in order to see certain elements of the truth a man must have within him a mirror, as it were, to reflect them. Some minds are like those sieves which allow both the corn and the tares to pass through without distinction. But in spite of your opinion, and Neckam's, the Italian historian is right. What he means, and what Bede meant is that wherever the Romans were victorious they brought them whom they conquered to civility; neither was there verily in any place else throughout Europe any civility, learning and elegance but where they ruled."

"I would lend my support to the defence of Rome," said Fynes Moryson. "There you may see fair meadows, plains, mountains, woods, groves, fountains, rivers, villages, castles, cities, baths, amphitheatres, playhouses, temples, pillars, statues, triumphal arches, pyramids, gardens, water conduits, and men both good and evil."

"Until now," said the Clerk, "I have always been well disposed towards Rome. If that is a praise of Rome, give me leave to censure it."

"Gentlemen," interrupted Machiavelli, "if I may, I would finish what I started to say. Rome was sick; but as Dandolo pointed out, she had within herself reserves of strength which enabled her to rise again. And so far as women are concerned, I think that even ancient Rome can hardly point to as many noble and illustrious ladies as graced the life of Italy in my time."

"I should be inclined to agree with you," said Guicciardini. "I call to mind, among others, Vittoria Colonna. If not a poetess of the first rank, she was the tenderest of wives, who, after her husband's death could find in her heart nothing more for Michelangelo than a calm friendship—which made a man of him."

"I had in mind a more spectacular and public kind of virtue," replied Machiavelli—"Caterina Sforza, the Lady of Forlì. When the insensate and rebellious mob threatened to execute her children before her very eyes in order to force her to an impious deed, she said to them: 'I will breed up others.' And true it is that she was the mother of Giovanni delle Bande Nere, the most brilliant and redoubted captain of his day. I knew her personally, and the effect of that encounter was never afterwards effaced."

"If it is examples of heroic virtue and chastity that you want," said John of Fordun, "may I remind you of a woman of my race? Those of you who have read Plutarch recall the beautiful Chiomara, wife of the Gallic chief Orgiago or Ortiago. If the lustful Roman centurion robbed her of her honour, she deprived him of his head. And if that was long ago, I could tell you of a lady who died in my father's time who, it seems to me, was quite as admirable an example of female and wifely nobility. Even Southrons must be acquainted with the name of Marion Braidfute."

"Ay," said Skelton. "Personally I always preferred her to the allegorical abstractions with wire hair and pearly teeth under which our poets conceal either their ignorance of the sex or their inability to portray it honestly."

"Neither women nor the literary treatment of them can in a day win free from the shackles imposed by the authority of Jerome in his Letter against Jovinianus," said the Clerk of Oxenford. "But will you tell us about Marion?"

"Blind Harry has told the story better than I could," replied the historian.

"Thank you," said the minstrel. "I will repeat it in prose."

102. WALLACE AND THE MAID OF LANARK

Blind Harry

You have heard how Wallace fought with the ghost of Fawdoun at Gask Hall and how his men disappeared mysteriously. Left alone he made his way to Cambuskenneth and swam the Forth there. He rested at the castle three days and then went on to Gilbank, near Lanark, where he lodged with his uncle Auchinleck, brother of Sir Ronald, Sheriff of Ayr. The English thought he had fled the country, or been slain or drowned, and so dismissed him from their thoughts.

The hero remained with his uncle at Gilbank during Christmas, though he often went into Lanark for amusement. There dwelt Hesilrig, the English Sheriff, that cursed knight, haughty, fierce and cruel of deed.

Now in Lanark lived a gentlewoman, a mild maid about eighteen years old, named Marion Braidfute. Her father, Hugh Braidfute of Lamington, was a man of worship and renown, and descended from gentle stock. But Hugh and his wife were dead, and Marion had inherited the property. She knew not what to do save to continue living in town on tribute, and so she purchased King Edward's protection. She had servants at need, and many friends, and so she lived quietly. I mean that she lived as quietly as she could in war-time, for Hesilrig had done her much harm: he had slain her brother, eldest of the family and heir to the estate. But she suffered all with humble demeanour. She was amiable, kind, reserved, prudent, courteous, sweet and well-mannered; she spoke neither too much nor too little, and was fresh and hale. She lived humbly and virtuously, and had a good name from everyone. Decent people esteemed her highly.

One day when Marion went to the kirk Wallace saw her as he was looking about, and by reason of the maid's beauty love pierced him to the quick so sharply that he could hardly contain himself. He knew her kindred and family, and also that she was leading a good and honest life. At one moment he thought he loved her more than life itself, and then again he thought of the deceit that had been practised upon him aforetime, and how his men had been brought to confusion at Saint Johnston because of his love for the lady there; and when he remembered that affair, he thought he would let things slide. However, that idea refused to remain long in his mind.

Wallace confided this new torment to his man Kerle, and asked for his honest opinion. "Master," said Kerle, "so far as I have understanding, the matter has every appearance of weal. Since you love her so, take her in marriage; she is a girl of fine character and, moreover, possesses property. What though you once went amiss in love? God forbid that this should turn out similarly!" To this Wallace replied: "I cannot marry yet; I would see the end of the war first. Could I abandon the war now? And what is love? Nothing but folly, for it deprives a man of both wit and steadfastness." At other times Wallace would say: "Perhaps the truth is that if I were fortunate and happy in my love I should be of better proof in deeds. On the other hand, I know that a passionate preoccupation hinders the prudent conduct of war. It is true, of course, that a lover may excel brilliantly in single deeds of prowess, thinking thereby to speed his fortune. But the present circumstances are different: a great kingdom is beset by many foes, and it would be right hard for anyone who serves Love and all his fickle chance to get amends from those foes in a single attempt. I have had a sample of that, which is one of the reasons why I am now so undecided. I trust to God there will be no more such traps. I will visit my love alone no more. Keep watch over me lest something untoward happen. Still, I know that this is a true maid, and I am acquainted with her kin, whereas I knew nothing about the other woman, wherefor I lost that gage."

In such wise would Wallace argue with Kerle, and yet he could not overcome the desire to visit and see that sweet maid. He did, for a while, leave off going to town, and busied his thought with other things in the attempt to see if he could abate his passion. When Kerle saw how he suffered he said: "Dear sir, you live in sluggardy. Go see your love, and then you will have some comfort."

The knight took Kerle's advice and walked into Lanark, where Marion had her residence beside the kirk. Marion recognized him well enough, but dared not say anything to him directly lest the Southrons mark him. At this time Hesilrig had a new project on foot: he desired her in marriage for his son.

Marion sent a message to Wallace by her maid, asking him to come to her, and the girl brought him secretly through a new-made garden so that the English knew nothing about their meeting. Wallace kissed Marion courteously, and earnestly besought her friendship. "If my friendship is of any value to you," she answered modestly, "you shall have it, as God save my soul; but it seems to me it can be of little worth to you inasmuch as we are so outrageously oppressed by the English and their partisans that nearly all our family is destroyed."

When Wallace heard this simple and pitiful statement he was fiercely grieved at heart. Both wrath and love put him in a rage, but his courage was not diminished thereby. He told Marion how sorely Love constrained him. She replied calmly: "I am ready to serve you with all my heart in any honest way, and I trust you will not jeopardize your worship by doing dishonour to a simple girl who is already taxed to the full extent of her strength in protecting her womanhood from the English. And this is true in spite of the fact that I have been at considerable expense in buying immunity from them. I will not willingly be a leman to any man born; so I think you should not desire me unless it be decently. Perhaps you think I am too low to be your lawful wife? But I, so far as I am concerned, would gladly spend all my life in your service. But I beseech you, for the sake of your worship in arms, that you harm me not, but rather defend me for your honour's sake."

Wallace thanked her for her straightforward reply and said: "If it were God's will that our kingdom should be free, I would joyfully marry you; but at this time I cannot take the risk, and so I crave nothing at the moment. A man in war may not have every pleasure."

What else they said, or what agreement they made, I do not know. In Wallace's heart there was still strife between love for Marion and grief for the loss of his men at Saint Johnston. At all events, they went to dinner, and afterwards Wallace took his leave.

I will now pass over how the knight shaved young Clifford of Lochmaben with his broadsword, and how he took Crawford castle and slew the castellan thereof. February passed, and March, and when April brought in the new year, it also brought back to Wallace his lusty pain, and he returned to Lanark. There he abode for a while, taking up again the struggle between love and war in his heart. But argue as he would, it appeared plainly that Wallace was determined to love Marion best of any woman in the world. In the end they reached an agreement, and therewith the turmoil in his breast ceased. In the presence of witnesses Marion became Wallace's wife. Now may they live in peace and good concord, in bliss and perfect joy, for she has gained her choice of both lord and lover. Wallace, too, thought that love improved him greatly now that he was able to hold Marion in his arms at will. For her part, she thanked God for the happy chance, for in his time Wallace was the flower of the profession of arms. I do not know how long Marion and Wallace lived thus happily together, but true it is that they got a child between them, a fine girl, who later married a squire named Shaw.

The hero's courage was now so keen that he could not choose but continue the war. Rejoicing in his love for Marion, he thought that his days of adversity were past, and he glowed with the desire to prove his manhood upon the broad stage of his country's struggle. But Fortune showed him her false double face as she had done so often before. Fie on Fortune and her inconstant wheel who tricked him out of happiness when he thought he should continue therein! Her favour to him was but a jest, for the furious course of her wheel, that moves unceasingly, threw him out of his pleasant joy into travail and woe.

In the year 1297 it chanced that Wallace one day went into Lanark and mingled with his mortal foes. Cruel Heselrig and a felon knight named Robert Thorn schemed how they might lure him into a broil as he came from the kirk.

Sir John the Graham had followed Wallace into town with fifteen men, and the knight himself had nine. As they were coming through the burg after paying their devotions in church, one of Hesilrig's men, the stoutest the Sheriff could find, and bitter of tongue, saluted Wallace and his company in contemptuous fashion.

"Good day, Signor, and good morning," he said.

"Whom are you mocking?" asked Wallace. "Who was your teacher?"

"Why," said the man, "are you not newly come overseas? Pardon me; I thought you were an ambassador conducting a foreign quean."

"Such pardon as we are accustomed to give," said Wallace, "you shall not want."

"Well," said the man, "since you are Scots, you shall be greeted in Scots: Gud deyn, dawch Lard, bach lowch banȝoch a de." [Good day, lazy squire, the blessing of God be upon the fierce fighter.]

By this time more Southron men had joined Hesilrig's group, and so Wallace was loath to create a disturbance. But one of the Englishmen made an obscene gesture and a quick motion at his longsword.

"Hold your hand," said Wallace, "and say what you have to say."

"You are a valiant swordsman with your longsword," said the man.

"Your dame made little objection to that," answered Wallace.

"What reason have you to wear the goodly green?" asked another.

"My best reason is that it vexes you."

"What should a Scot be doing with such a fine knife?" asked a third.

"So asked the priest who last made love to your wife," answered Wallace; "she treated him so handsomely that his child became your heir."

"It seems to me," said the fellow, "that you are insulting me."

"Your dame," answered Wallace, "was wanton before you were born."

By this time the English faction which had gathered about the knight and his band numbered close onto two hundred stout men in armour, with Hesilrig and Sir Robert Thorn in command. The Scots did not hang back, but laid about them manfully. The fracas lasted a long time, but the Scots were forced from the field at last; they made for Wallace's house as quickly as they could, while Wallace and Sir John the Graham defended the rear.

Marion, roused by the din and clash of arms, raised the gate and let them in, and they passed through to a stronghold at the back; fifty Southrons lay dead in the street. As the rest of the English came up, fair Marion succeeded in holding them in check by a trick until the Scots had gained the wood.

When Hesilrig saw that Wallace and his men had escaped to Cart-lane Crags, he returned with his force and put Marion to death—I will not tell you how; where there is great dool that cannot be relieved, only pain is gained by dwelling on it. A faithful servant made her way to Wallace and told him of this deed. The sorrow pierced to his heart so that he would have sunk to the ground had it not been for the presence of his men. Sir John the Graham and all the company wept with compassion. On seeing them so bestead with grief Wallace concealed his own pain so that they might turn their thoughts to other matters. "Cease, men," he said; "this is bootless bale; we cannot bring her to life again." More he could not say because of the bitter tears which burst from his eyes. Then, after a little: "No man shall ever see me take rest or ease till this deed, this sackless slaughter of that fair and blithe creature be avenged. I swear to God that henceforth I will have no mercy on any man of that nation, young or old, save women and priests. Sir John," said he, "let be this mourning now; ten thousand shall die for her sake. Man's courage is the less for weeping—it relaxes wrath for the wrong that should be redressed."

That night Wallace and his men returned to Lanark. The watch never expected them, and they passed in without difficulty. Sir John and his band went in search of Sir Robert Thorn, while Wallace betook himself to the tall house where Hesilrig lay asleep. He kicked the door free from bar and braces so that it fell to the floor. The Sheriff cried: "Who is making that uproar?" "Even he whom you have been seeking all day," answered Wallace. "God willing, you shall pay dearly for the death of my wife."

Hesilrig thought it was no time to be lying in bed—he was eager to get out of that house. The night was dark, and yet Wallace perceived him, and as he came past in a great hurry, struck him fairly on the head. The sword burst through flesh and skull, and sheared right down to the collar-bone, and he tumbled over the stair into the thick of the men below. Good Auchinleck thought he was still alive, and thrust him through thrice with his knife. Then Wallace encountered young Hesilrig, and set a sure stroke on him, and danged him down off the stair to his death. The outcry rose rudely in the street, and many of Hesilrig's men were trodden under foot.

Many a man did Wallace's fellows slay that night in Lanark town; among others, Sir Robert Thorn was burned to ashes in his own house by Sir John the Graham. After that night's work there remained none alive in Lanark save Scots.

"The argument about ladies and lovers, wives and husbands, will probably never be settled to the satisfaction of all in this world," said the Goodman of Paris with a cough. "But as additional evidence in favour of the ladies, I should like to tell you about a gentlewoman of my acquaintance. Her behaviour I know you will all applaud; that of her husband is perhaps best passed over lightly."

103. THE RAVISHED WIFE

The Goodman of Paris

In one of the great cities of the realm of France there dwelt an honest young wife whose husband, along with other burghers, had been thrown into prison for a communal uprising. Every day the authorities chopped off the heads of two or three of these rebels. Every day, too, the young wife of whom I speak, with the wives of the other prisoners, knelt before the lords and implored them, weeping and with joined hands, to have pity and undertake the deliverance of their men.

One of the lords about the king's person, who feared neither God nor His justice, but was a cruel and felon tyrant, gave the young woman to understand that if she would do all his will, he would cause her husband to be freed without fail. The bourgeoise gave no reply to this, but besought the messenger to induce her husband's guards to allow her speech with him. Her request was granted; she was introduced into her husband's prison. There, dissolved in tears, she told him what she knew or what she had seen regarding the other rebels, how it stood regarding his own deliverance, and the vile request which had been made of her.

In reply the young man commanded her that however the matter might stand, she should do whatever was necessary to deliver him from death, and that she should spare neither her body nor her honour, nor anything else in order to save his life. Hereupon they parted one from the other, each weeping bitterly.

After this a number of the other prisoners were beheaded, but the young wife's husband was freed. The woman was blamed by some for having received the company of a great lord; but by God, men and women who know the circumstances, even those who hate this sin, say that she should have no blame, inasmuch as she acted in accordance with her husband's orders.

"The situation in which your heroine was placed was a difficult one," said Saxo Grammaticus. "I mean to say, her predicament was ugly, or rather that the choice she had to make was bitter, if I make myself clear. Now I have recollected the case of another wife who was called upon to show magnanimity of another sort, or perhaps it was just pertinacity. The circumstances to which I allude are among those which cluster about the name of Amleth, whom the English call Hamlet. I should like to take this opportunity and make use of this occasion to point out, if I may, that Amleth never studied at Wittenberg or Pavia, though he was a bright boy. I never studied at either place myself—which makes me nothing inferior to Amleth save in the matter of wives, which brings me to the case I had in mind."

"Indeed, are you there?" asked Sir John Harington politely.

"Ah," said Saxo, "you haven't been paying attention. As I was saying . . ."

"O Lord!" groaned Sir John.

"Have you a story to tell?" asked Hákon Hákonson.

"Yes, my liege."

"Then tell it."

104. HAMLET IN SCOTLAND

Saxo Grammaticus

There was a king of Jutland named Horvendil. Gerutha was his wife, and Feng his brother. You know that Feng slew Horvendil and married his brother's queen. You know too that Horvendil's son, Amleth, took vengeance for this double crime of murder and incest.

But if Amleth played the fool in order to gain his ends, Feng was no fool, and after the mysterious disappearance of a spy set to watch his stepson's actions, he began to have doubts as to the security of his position. He would have killed Amleth himself had he not feared the displeasure of Gerutha and the vengeance of the young man's grandfather, Roric. But another means was at his disposal: There was a king in Britain who was not only his friend, but his sworn brother. To him he would entrust the important and disagreeable task of removing this obstacle to his continued prosperity. Accordingly Prince Amleth was sent to the English court accompanied by two of Feng's henchmen. These men bore a letter written on wood with runes instructing the English king to put to death the youth who should come to him.

One day while his companions slept Amleth searched their effects and found the letter. He whittled away the writing, all but Feng's signature, and substituted another message to the effect that the king should give his daughter in marriage to the wise youth who was coming to visit him.

When the party reached Britain the messengers delivered their letter. The king understood it, but gave no sign; he welcomed them kindly and entertained them with great hospitality. Amleth, however, held himself aloof from the festivities, patently showing that he disdained both the food and the drink. Such unusual conduct aroused the wonder of all, and particularly of the king; so, when the guests had retired for the night, he sent a man to the strangers' chamber to listen secretly to their conversation. Of course Amleth's companions asked him why he had not partaken of the banquet. The prince replied:

"The bread was leavened with blood; in the liquor was a taste of iron; the baked meats were permeated by the stench of a human cadaver, and had, moreover, a rotten smell of the grave. I might still have eaten and drunk out of courtesy," he said, "if my hosts had been worthy. But the king has the eyes of a thrall, and the so-called queen showed in three ways the behaviour of a bondwoman."

Amleth's companions reminded him of his former weak head, suggesting with great mirth and no little scorn that he must have had a violent relapse, since no man in the full possession of his wits would think of casting such opprobrium on estimable and high-born people and their splendid provision.

When the spy reported to him these apparently insulting judgments of himself, his queen and his hospitality, the English king declared that his princely visitor must be more than humanly wise, or foolish with more than mortal folly. However, he himself had the wisdom to set on foot an investigation. He summoned the steward and asked him where he had got the bread. The man replied that it had been baked by the king's own baker. When asked whence the corn had been procured, he said that it had grown near a field covered with the old bones of men slain in battle. The king needed no further evidence for the bloody savour of the bread. He then inquired about the source of the meat. The steward replied that some hogs of his, through negligence of their herd, had gone astray and battened on the decaying carcass of an unburied robber. This explained adequately why the pork had acquired a taint of corruption. Next the king asked about the brewing of the drink. He was told that it had been brewed of water and honey, as usual. But when the well was investigated, several rusted swords were found at the bottom of it, which had tainted the water.

Now that the king had found Amleth to be right in these matters he had the courage to investigate the slur which had been cast upon his birth. He questioned his mother on the matter. At first she said that she had submitted to the embraces of no man but the king; but when he threatened her with torture, she confessed that he had been begotten by a slave. Finally the king himself asked Amleth in what way his queen had betrayed her servile origin. "Because," replied Amleth, "she wrapped her mantle about her head as slave women do; then she gathered up the skirts of her dress as she walked; and finally, she extracted the remnants of food from the crevices between her teeth with a splinter of wood, and chewed them up."

The king of England was so amazed at Amleth's wisdom that he readily gave him his daughter to wife, and had his two companions hanged on the gallows, thus executing the instructions of the forged letter.

At the end of a year spent with his father-in-law Amleth asked and obtained leave to return home for a visit. He reached Jutland without mishap, and there carried to fulfilment the revenge he had so long planned, stabbing Feng in his bed, and burning his drunken followers in the palace as they slept. Next morning, standing beside the smoking ruins of the hall, Amleth harangued the people so eloquently, and to such good purpose, that some were moved even to tears; lamentation for the dead fratricide was quenched before it had fairly arisen, and Amleth, by universal acclaim, was chosen king.

When this tedious business had at length been brought to a satisfactory conclusion, Amleth richly equipped three vessels of men, and returned to England to see his wife and father-in-law. The king received Amleth and his warriors very kindly, and entertained them with all pomp and circumstance. During the banquet he asked many questions about Feng, and whether he still enjoyed life and prosperity. Amleth replied that his stepfather had perished by the sword, and his answer was phrased in such a way as to leave no doubt in the king's mind that his friend had fallen at Amleth's hands. This placed him in a grave difficulty, for by the terms of his sworn brotherhood with Feng it now devolved upon him to avenge his sworn brother's death. Such an oath it was impious to violate, and so the king found himself torn between his duty on the one hand, and his love for his daughter and son-in-law on the other. At last duty won; he put the sanctity of his obligation before family considerations, and determined to slay Amleth. But since he was the son of a slave, he decided to execute his crime by the hand of another; and being a man of little invention, he could hit upon no better expedient than that whereby Feng had formerly attempted to rid himself of his stepson.

It happened that the king's wife had lately died, and he represented to Amleth that he, by reason of his shrewdness, was the very man to woo another wife for him. The lady of his choice, said the king, was the young queen of Scotland. Would Amleth be good enough to bear a letter suing for her hand?

Amleth would, and started north on his journey. He did not know that the Scots queen, in her pride and arrogance, had heretofore put to death every suitor or would-be lover; but the king of England knew it, and expected that she would serve Amleth as she had served others.

The prince crossed the border into Scotland, and when he had come quite near the royal residence, turned aside into a meadow to rest his horses; he himself lay down to sleep while his companions amused themselves at some distance. The queen had heard of Amleth's approach and had sent out spies to observe him and his men. One of them slipped past the prince's guard as he slept, filched his shield from beneath his head, and the letter from his pouch.

Now I must tell you that on this shield Amleth had had depicted by the hand of a skilled artist the whole story of his family tragedy, beginning with the slaying of his father, and ending with the death of his murderer. The Scots queen was clever, and when she had studied the shield, easily made out the whole affair. As for the letter—she rubbed out the old king's proposal of marriage and substituted for it a request, purporting to come from him, that she would marry the man who brought the message. To this she added a summary of the events portrayed on the shield, and sent both letter and buckler back by the man who had stolen them.

In the meantime Amleth had wakened and missed his property; but he gave no sign, and when the spy approached the second time, he feigned to be still asleep. But as soon as the man had replaced the letter and the shield, Amleth seized him and had him placed in fetters. Then he continued on his way to the queen's palace.

Queen Hermutrude received the prince very graciously. When she had read the message which he handed to her, she proceeded to commend his shrewdness in dealing with Feng. She thought it strange, however, that such a valiant man as he had made the mistake of contracting an unworthy marriage, for it was well known that the parents of his present wife had been slaves who had stumbled into royalty. A really wise man, she said, ought to choose a woman for her illustrious birth rather than for her accidental beauty. Now if Amleth would only look about him he would see, not far distant, a woman who was his equal in birth, in wealth and in temporal possessions; and if he married her, he would gain not only the woman herself, but the sceptre which she wielded as well. Indeed, he might consider himself very lucky to receive a proposal from that woman, for hitherto she had always refused lovers, and had punctuated her refusal with the sword.

So saying, Hermutrude seized the prince in a violent embrace. Amleth returned kiss for kiss, protesting that her wish was his own. Forthwith guests were bidden, the nobles assembled, and the marriage rites celebrated.

After the banquet and the feasting Amleth set his face toward England, having a strong band of Scots at his heels as a rear-guard. As he drew near to English territory his earlier wife, daughter of the king of Britain, came to meet him. She complained that she had been insulted and wronged by having a paramour set over her; and yet she could not find in her heart so much hate for the adulterer as to cease loving the husband. Her son and Amleth's, she said, might some day hate his father's leman, but she, for her part, would love her. "So far as I am concerned," said the British princess, "no calamity will ever put out the flame of my love for you, nor any malice extinguish it. As proof of what I say I will reveal the treacherous designs which have been planned against you."

Thereupon she told Amleth to beware of her father, whose rage had known no bounds when he learned how both his schemes had been foiled. While she was speaking the English king rode up to meet his son-in-law. He embraced him, but with little love in his heart; then they went on together towards the palace.

As Amleth and the king were about to ride under the porch of the hall the old man attacked him, but the coat of mail which the prince was wearing under his clothes turned aside the point of the javelin. You may be sure that Amleth now lost no time in assembling his Scots warriors. The two forces joined battle. At first the fortunes of war went against the Dane, but by a clever ruse he gained the day and put the Britons to flight. The old king was killed while attempting to escape.

Amleth followed his victory by a minute and systematic plundering foray, and enriched with the spoils of Britain, he returned with his two wives to his own land.

"Your narrative, Master Saxo, limps rather badly," said Sir John Harington. "If the Scots queen was accustomed to slay her suitors, why should she kill Amleth, who was not a suitor, but an ambassador? The repetition of that trick of the substituted messages is awkward, too."

"And as for playing the fool to gain political ends," put in John Stow, "Lucius Junius Brutus antedated your Danish hero by many centuries."

Saxo moved uncomfortably on his settle.

"Well," remarked Camden, "history often repeats itself, as Thucydides said. Your tale, Master Saxo, reminds me of an adventure which happened to the Graf von Gleichen in the year 1228. At Erfurt in Germany there is a monument, which Fynes Moryson has probably seen, representing the count placed between two wives. One is adorned with a marble crown, the other is represented naked with children at her feet."

"And what is the meaning of that?" asked Peter Bell.

"I defer to my colleague Moryson," replied Camden, "for I was never in Germany."

"I did not see the monument to which you allude," admitted Fynes.

"In that case I will tell the story.—The Graf von Gleichen was one of those who followed Frederic II's crusade. In a battle against the infidel he was taken and carried to Turkey, where he suffered a long and hard captivity, being put to ploughing the ground with a rope through his shoulder. One day the daughter of the ruling potentate, while out walking, came up to him and asked him several questions. His excellent manner and address so pleased the princess that she promised to set him free and follow him, provided he would marry her. The count answered that he already had a wife and children. 'That is no argument,' replied the princess, 'for the custom of the Turks allows one man to have several wives.' The Graf von Gleichen was not stubborn, but allowed himself to be moved by her reasons, whereupon the princess employed herself so industriously to get him out of bondage that they were soon in readiness to board a vessel. They arrived happily at Venice. There the count met one of his men, who had been travelling everywhere to get news of him. The man told him that the countess and his children were alive and in good health. From Venice Graf von Gleichen went to Rome, and after he had frankly related what he had done, the Pope granted him a solemn dispensation to keep his two wives. If the court of Rome showed itself so easy on this occasion, the count's wife was not less so, for she received very kindly the Turkish lady by whose means she had recovered her dear husband, and showed her every consideration. The Moslem princess returned these civilities very handsomely, and though she herself proved barren, she tenderly loved the children which the German wife bore in abundance."

"I thought I should never have to go back to Germany," said Moryson, "but now it seems I must."

"Such occurrences have been by no means rare," remarked Lord Burleigh. "There is a ballet on the subject, and the author of the

Fifteen Joys of Marriage has used such incidents in his thirteenth chapter."

"When I was in Flanders," said Adam Usk, "finding time hang heavy on my hands, I used to rummage about among the manuscripts in the monastery of Eeckhout, near Bruges. There I discovered a sprightly satire on the defeat of the French by the Flemings at Courtrai, among other things. But I found, too, a story, not about two wives, indeed, but one which presents a pretty problem, as well in the conflict of laws as of loyalties."

"I suppose you will have to tell it," said Sir Thomas Gray.

"Thank you," replied the historian, "I will."

105. THE BASTARS' WIFE OF BUILLON
Adam Usk

You recall that overseas in Jerusalem ruled Baudouin, the second of that name, and with him was his wife Margalie. They had a son named Ourri. But our story has to do with an illegitimate son of Baudouin's, the fruit of an intrigue with the Saracen princess Sinamonde. The child was named Baudouin after his father, though he was also referred to as Li Bastars de Buillon.

Young Baudouin was brought up by his mother's people, but when he had reached suitable age, he was sent to Jerusalem to live with his father. He and his half-brother Ourri did not get on well together, but then Ourri never got on well with anyone. One day Ourri proposed to Li Bastars that they should poison their father and share the kingdom between them. Young Baudouin's only reply to this was to plunge his hunting knife into Ourri's breast. Baudouin senior was much annoyed by this deed, and condemned his younger son to death. Hugh de Tabarie, however, persuaded him to commute the sentence into one of exile. Li Bastars bore his fate as well as he could, and from that out attached himself to Hugh. Together they left Jerusalem and rode for Tabarie.

Hardly had Duke Hugh reached his domains when he was informed by a spy of his that the lord of Orbrie was on the point of invading his lands with the assistance of Corsabrin of Mont Oscur; he tarried only to afford Corsabrin time to solemnize his nuptials with his daughter Ludie, the most beautiful female as far as Brindisi. This news vexed Hugh. "By God!" he said, "Corsabrin shall never enjoy her; Li Bastars de Buillon shall have her, and his land to boot, as well as the city of Orbrie." "My lord," said young Baudouin, "I thank you. I will take the girl willingly, for I confess that I am already deeply in love with her by reason of the praises I have heard, and I shall never have an easy moment till I behold her sweet countenance."

So said Baudouin—but very often a man sets his heart on a woman who isn't worth it.

From now on Li Bastars was so preoccupied with love for Ludie that he could neither eat nor drink. Hugh perceived that he was in the dumps and said: "Stop your mooning about, for you shall have the girl, do not fear." "Lord," answered Li Bastars, "I am on pins and needles. I do hope that you will lend your aid to a poor young knight who has nothing but his good sword, his good horse, his good hauberk and his good helm. You know that I am the miserable victim of my father's injustice on account of his wife's son. I do not think that Ourri could really have been a child of his—the traitorous dog!" "Never mind that now," said Hugh. "I am going to help you win a kingdom. First of all we shall besiege Orbrie."

Duke Hugh got together ten thousand men and made Li Bastars his master gonfalonier. They took ship and went till they reached a city boasting at least two hundred towers, whether before or behind. All the towers were covered with latten, and flashed in the sun. "By God!" cried young Baudouin, "what a lot of towers this city has! Jerusalem isn't worth a sou in comparison with it. It's Babylon, isn't it?" "Pfui!" said Hugh; "this is Orbrie, over which I am going to place you as lord, and Ludie shall be your wife." "Sir," said Li Bastars, "if I get that girl I'll love you forever."

Now four thousand Christians put out in small boats and landed under the city. The inhabitants were thrown into terror by their approach, and fled to the king, saying that the city had been betrayed to 100,000 Christians. "That is not true," said a Saracen spy; "it is only Li Bastars de Buillon who has been sent by Hugh de Tabarie to take your city and marry your daughter." At this news the king flushed red with rage. "By Mahoun!" he cried, "I'll give a good reception to this bastard who makes war on me wrongfully!" Then he caught sight of Ludie, who was a pretty girl. "Daughter," he said, "I'm sorry that I didn't send you to Corsabrin a long time ago; war is now beginning on account of your person, which same is coveted by Li Bastars de Buillon, may Mahoun curse him. He has taken an oath in the hearing of his men that he will never abandon my city till you are his wife." "Father," replied Ludie, "he shall never have me. So long as I live, I will never love a Christian. Corsabrin, the handsomest man in Pagandom shall get me. May it not please Mahoun that I should ever be the mistress of any felon Bastars." Thus it is evident that Ludie was in love with Corsabrin.

Now the Saracen king lost no time, but sallied out. Young Baudouin and his four thousand drove them in again. In the course of the fighting the Saracen lord was severely wounded. A second sortie likewise ended in discomfiture for the Moslems.

When Corsabrin, in his fortress Mont Oscur, heard of the Bastars' wonderful prowess, he hesitated to respond to the emir's frantic appeals for aid; it was only the bitter thought that Ludie might pass into young Baudouin's hands which at last brought him on the scene. The two hosts engaged: Corsabrin and his men were forced back to the city walls. There the Saracen challenged Li Bastars to single combat. The upshot thereof was that he was both unhorsed and unnerved. Baudouin spared his rival's life only on condition that he renounce all pretensions to Ludie. Corsabrin indignantly rejected these terms, and taking advantage of the press of men about them, slipped through Baudouin's fingers, and made good his escape. Hugh de Tabarie now came up, and Corsabrin continued his flight to Mont Oscur. This unchivalric conduct made Baudouin very peevish, and he set out after the fugitive to settle the question about Ludie once for all. But again, at the decisive moment, Corsabrin evaded him in most unorthodox manner.

The siege of Orbrie continued on into the winter. The emir was at last so reduced by famine that he was forced to try a ruse: He sent word that he would surrender Ludie to Baudouin if the Christian knight would come and get her, and then raise the siege. His real intention, however, was to kill the youth, and then flee to Mont Oscur. At this seemingly fortunate turn of events Baudouin was all agog, not so much at winning the city as of getting possession of Ludie. He put on his best clothes, and under them a good suit of armour, and hurried off to the emir's castle with fifteen companions.

The Saracen received Li Bastars with every courtesy and presented his daughter. "Here is Ludie," he said, "but before she can be fully yours you must renounce your faith and accept Islam. Indeed, you have no other choice, for I have you here at my mercy."

This statement so enraged Li Bastars that he drew his sword and aimed a blow at the old man, but so blinded was he by wrath that he split the skull of the emir's nephew by mistake. Thereupon he and his companions fought their way to the gate, where they were joined in the nick of time by Duke Hugh. With such reinforcements Li Bastars retraced his steps and caught up with the emir. This time his aim was better, and he left the lord of Orbrie in two halves on the pavement. Thereafter, with three hundred companions, the young knight penetrated the castle, seized Ludie, gave her in charge to thirty knights for safe-keeping, and dashed off to help Hugh complete the capture of the city.

When the fortress had fallen, there was great rejoicing among the Christians, especially on the part of young Baudouin, in spite of his many wounds. Ludie, as fair as any flower, was now brought to him, and he feasted his eyes upon her person at his leisure. "Ludie," said he, "you shall be washed and baptized, and afterwards married to me, for I intend to make you a crowned queen." To this speech Ludie replied with some heat: "Death would suit me better than being either your wife or your mistress. How can you, who have brutally slain my father, expect to have my love?"

On hearing this unwelcome reply Baudouin changed colour for ire: He had her baptized in consecrated water by main force, and carried out the various rites pertaining to marriage with equal vehemence. In so doing he acted like a fool, and Ludie swore she would pay him out.

Subsequent to these joyful events the Christian leaders extended their conquests on all sides as far as Mont Oscur, but that strong castle they could not take. When this was clear to them, they decided to go to Babylon and worry the Saracens there. They met Salehadin, but that redoubtable prince, learning the strength of the Christian army, withdrew beyond their reach. After some profitless skirmishing Hugh and Baudouin set their faces toward Orbrie, where Ludie was waiting for Li Bastars—so he thought.

During the absence of her lord Ludie had not been idle. She sent word to Corsabrin that she was coming to visit him, and purchasing the services of a sailor and his boat for a sack full of besants, she slipped out of Orbie by night, and made for Mont Oscur. Corsabrin came down to the shore to meet her, and welcomed her with loud praise of her spirited action. He led her to his palace, and there, in accordance with the Mohammedan religion, married her. Ludie complained bitterly of Li Bastars, saying that in spite of herself she had had to share his bed, and that she hated no man in the world with equal violence.

Baudouin arrived at Orbrie and immediately asked for his wife. When he heard that she had taken leave without saying good-bye, he almost went out of his head with rage. "May I give you a word of advice?" asked Duke Hugh. "Say on," replied Baudouin. "Very well, then, my advice is that you should calm down; let the baggage go, and a curse with her. Find some other woman who is more amenable to our ways." "I should be a fool to follow that counsel," said Baudouin, "for I am sure that if we were to come together again she would never misbehave in the future." So said the knight: but the truth of the matter is that if a husband recovers his wife who has eloped with another man he can never love her properly again. It is against reason.

However, young Baudouin would not be appeased, and he took oath that he would be avenged on Corsabrin, who, of course, was not to blame. "Let us go and besiege Mont Oscur," he said to Duke Hugh. "Very well," answered the baron; "but it will cost us something, for the place is strong."

The Christian host landed near Mont Oscur and proceeded on horseback through the surrounding forest. On the way Baudouin caught sight of a charcoal-burner walking beside his laden nag. He inquired whither the man was bound, and learned that it was to the castle to sell his coals. This information gave the Christian knight an idea: He drew his sword and cut the charcoal-burner in two; then he put on the man's dress and smudged his face with coal dust. He explained to Hugh that in this disguise he would go to the castle and find out about his wife. Hugh blamed this plan, but could not dissuade him; off he went.

"There," said Hugh to his companions, "you see one of the bravest soldiers since Alexander, and yet a man besotted on his wife. Still, it is no wonder, for a woman got the wise Aristotle to let her ride him round the garden with saddle and bridle; and the good clerk Vergil hung half a night in a basket from a tower at Rome through the wiles of a woman. I swear to God that if I ever lay hands on Ludie she shall never put another valiant man to shame."

When Li Bastars got to the castle he threw down his coals and looked about him. Corsabrin, he was told, was not at home, but out by the river flying a falcon. That pleased the young man well. He loitered about here and there till all at once he saw Ludie, fresh and fair, coming out of a chamber; that pleased him even more. He took her by the waist: "Lady," said he, "greet your lord, who has ventured here in disguise for love of you." Ludie thought quickly. "My lord," said she, "welcome to this house. I would rather have a sight of you than possess all Pharaoh's gold, and I humbly pray your pardon for the wrong I have done you. I will go away with you now if you will promise not to harm me." "Lady," answered Baudouin, "set your mind at rest, for from this out you shall have nothing but good at my hands."

Thereupon Ludie took the knight into her chamber. A bath was prepared; Baudouin undressed and went into it without delay. In the meantime Ludie said to her maid: "Hurry to Corsabrin, for I have something of the utmost urgency to say to him." Then she returned to Baudouin and gave her attention to entertaining him handsomely, and even accorded him the rights and privileges of a husband. After that they entered the hot bath and took their pleasure.

Now lo and behold! in came Corsabrin, and sixty fully armed scoundrels with him. The Saracen walked up to the bath and bawled out: "So and so thinks he is going to bathe at his ease, whereas he is really going to be tubbed in his own bad luck." "Corsabrin," said Ludie, "you ought to esteem me more highly than all the Saracens in your domain, for alone and single-handed I have captured Li Bastars de Buillon."

When Baudouin saw Corsabrin and his armed men, and he naked in the bath-tub, he said angrily to his wife: "To think that I came here for the pleasure of seeing you! I never saw a husband worse served by his wife than I am. I have certainly made a mistake in loving you, for it is rather hate that you deserve." And to Corsabrin he said: "I must admit that I regret my visit to your castle; but don't kill me in this bath, for that would be a dastardly deed."

"Bastars," said Corsabrin, "put on your clothes, for I am going to judge you to a shameful death." Ludie went to her room to lie down, but before going she said that if Corsabrin ever hoped to lie by her side again he should make Baudouin die the bitterest of deaths. "Have no fear," said the Saracen; "I will make an example of him for other Christians. I don't like to have people coming to visit me in this unceremonious fashion. I shall put a good end to a bad beginning."

Baudouin began to dress. His filthy charcoal-burner's outfit caused Corsabrin much amusement, but since he was a gentleman, he sent him a cendal robe. Then he said: "Tell me now, sir knight, if the rôles were reversed, how would you put me to death?" "I will not hide anything from you," replied Baudouin. "I give you my word that if you were in my power I would take you to the forest and hang you from the highest tree I could find." "By Mahoun," answered Corsabrin, "that is an excellent idea, and I will follow your suggestion."

A rope was put about Baudouin's neck as though he had been a common murderer, and he was led away to the forest by two serfs, who kept a sharp look-out for the tallest tree. Finally they stopped at a silver poplar. "This will do," said Corsabrin. Li Bastars looked about him, but saw none of Hugh's men, as he had expected to do. "Alas!" said he, "am I really going to die such a death? Ah, Ludie, I hope God bursts you to bits. He who trusts a woman has small amends. That is clear to me now, to my shame."

A Saracen looped his rope and jerked Baudouin off his feet so rudely that he almost strangled him. "Easy, there, you brute," cried Baudouin. "If I only had a horn, now," he said to himself, "my men would hear and rescue me. Corsabrin," said he to the Saracen, "I am a man of great lineage, allied to kings and nobles on both sides of my family. It seems inevitable that I be done to death, but by the faith you owe Mahoun and Termagant, I conjure you to execute me as people of my nation execute a French gentleman." "How is that?" asked the Saracen. "Sir," answered the knight, "he is given a horn so that he may blow on it five or six times to summon the angels to come for his soul. Then, when he has trumpeted a while, he says a prayer; afterwards the executioners either strangle him or cut off his head." "By Mahoun," said Corsabrin, "as between gentlemen, I will grant your request."

Well, now, you can guess what happened: Baudouin blew for all he was worth—he got nose-bleed from it in fact—and Hugh heard him. And while he was making a prayer in fifty lines of mono-rhymed alexandrines, Hugh rode to the rescue. As soon as the young man saw his brothers-in-arms on the ground below him, he turned upon the hangman and gave him such a clout that he fell to the earth with his brains oozing out of his skull. You may be sure that Hugh, for his part, lost no time. He cut his way through several Saracens until he reached Corsabrin, and him he pierced, heart, liver and lungs, with his lance.

Baudouin descended from the tree, and with a thousand men at his back rode away to Mont Oscur. The gates were open and the castle unguarded. He searched the chambers here and there till he found Ludie, whom he did not greet with a kiss. Baudouin turned his wife over to his men, and then slew all the inmates of the castle, not excepting women and children. Then he flew the Christian banners from the walls. When Hugh saw that he said to his barons: "Let us go and lodge in Mont Oscur, for it is now ours."

Li Bastars de Buillon came out to meet the duke and handed him the keys of the castle. "My lord," said he, "I owe you much thanks for the promptitude with which you saved my life." "If you are really grateful," answered Hugh, "grant me a boon." "I will refuse you nothing," said Baudouin. "In that case, I demand Ludie as my share of the spoil." "Very well," said the Bastars somewhat reluctantly; "but for God's sake, do her no harm; she is not so bad but that she would do very well in a house of religion." "By God!" answered the duke, "we'll put her there, but we'll make the convent of firewood and coals." This was not at all to Baudouin's mind, but he dared say nothing.

Accordingly, the fifteen barons to whom Baudouin had confided her brought Ludie forward. She was taken out into the fields and there burned without delay, for Hugh of Tabarie had the heart of a lion.

When Adam had finished his story there was an angry murmur in the corner where Christine de Pisan and other ladies were sitting with Jean Charlier, called Gerson, and Ulrich von Lichtenstein.

"Why should she be burned?" expostulated Fenice. "The woman was married against her will. Well do I know the bitterness of that!"

As attention was drawn in their direction men saw, apparently for the first time, a handsome lady dressed in white satin. Her hair was black and plentiful, and her complexion white and pink. Her dark eyes seemed to glow like misty stars as she spoke . . .

"You remember me; I am Pia. Siena made, and Maremma unmade me. He knows it well who wedded me with his ring and then, urged by the desire of mending his broken fortunes with the dowry of a richer wife, with simulated jealousy plotted to remove me from his path. Some of you know how his minion stole upon me in the half dark room as I was watching the sunset from my window, seized me by the feet and plunged me into the deep valley below. I, too, was married against my will, and such was my reward. How many, think you, have had no such quick release as mine, but have borne the intolerable burden in silence till all was made silent by the grave? Perhaps I should have held my peace still were it not that Messer Bandello, here present, has misstated the facts to my shame. I also have heard of Chiomara. Would that I had been cast in her mould! But Siena made me—molles Senae. .·. ."

On this there was deep silence. Bandello's conflicting emotions drove the colour to his face and then left it deathly pale. Jean de Meung's eyes shifted here and there. Matheolus took refuge in his tankard. Adam Usk fidgeted in bewilderment.

Finally Jacques de Vitry broke the tension: "No one, I suppose, would be so bold as to assert that Madonna Pia nor Ingeborg of Denmark were fortunate in their husbands," said he, "or that young Baudouin de Buillon or Berengar were happy in the choice of a wife. Quid nunc? Let me tell you how the problem of marriage was settled long ago by two young people of Auvergne."

106. THE WEDDED LIFE OF INJURIOSUS

Jacques de Vitry

I have read that in former times there lived in Auvergne a wealthy man of senatorial family by the name of Injuriosus. He wooed in marriage a girl of his own station and was accepted. Each of the young people was an only child.

When the solemnities of marriage had been celebrated, the couple, as was the custom, were placed in one bed. Thereupon the girl, weighed down with grief, turned to the wall and wept bitterly. Said the bridegroom: "Tell me, I pray you, what afflicts you?" And when she remained silent he continued: "I adjure you by Jesus Christ the Son of God, be sensible and explain to me the cause of your grief."

Then the bride turned towards him and said: "If I were to weep all the days of my life I could never shed enough tears to wash away the boundless sorrow in my breast. Know that I had resolved to keep my wretched body for Christ, unstained by the contact of man. But woe is me! who am in such wise abandoned by Him that I am unable to accomplish my wish, and that on this day—which I would that I had not lived to see—I have lost that which I have kept intact from my earliest age. Behold, forsaken by immortal Christ, who promised me Paradise for my dower, it has been my lot to become the consort of a mortal man. And whereas I would have put on the dress of purity, I have assumed the bridal regalia of shame, not of honour. But what is the use of talking? Wretched one that I am! If this is what the future had in store for me, why was not the first day of my life also the last? Instead of accepting the nourishment of life, would that I had entered the gate of death! In me the precious things of this world excite only loathing. I spurn your great and far-reaching lands, for it is the joys of Paradise for which I yearn."

As the girl, with copious tears, poured forth these and many other similar plaints, the youth was moved to pity and said: "We are the only children of parents, who are among the noblest of Auvergne, wherefor they desired our union so that our line might be perpetuated, and our estate not fall into strangers' hands after their death." Said she: "The world is naught, riches are naught, secular pomp is naught, and even the life we live is naught, for we should rather seek that more splendid life which is not terminated by death, which is not dissolved by disease nor ended by accident. In that life man abides in eternal blessedness, dwells in a light that does not wane, and, what is still better, having been advanced to the state of angels, in the very presence of the Lord enjoys ever fresh contemplation of His glory, rejoicing with indissoluble joy."

To this the young husband answered: "Through your most sweet eloquence the glory of the eternal life has illumined me as with a mighty splendour; and if it is your wish to abstain from indulgence in carnal desires, I will share your resolve. The bride answered: "It is hard for men to grant this thing to women. However, if you will take measures to insure that we remain unspotted in the world, I will share with you the dower promised me by my spouse, my Lord Jesus Christ, to whom I vowed myself a servant and a bride." Thereupon the young man, armed with the sign of the cross, replied: "I will do as you urge." Then they took each other by the hand and went to sleep.

For many years after that they lay together in one bed, observing ever a praiseworthy chastity.

When Injuriosus' wife died, he did all things that were needful, and soon afterwards himself followed her to the grave. As it happened, their respective tombs were placed far apart beside different walls of the church. But when the people entered the church on the morning after Injuriosus' funeral, they beheld, indeed, a miracle, for the tombs were found side by side, as though to show that they who are united in heaven cannot be kept apart by the material circumstances of earthly sepulture.

"Nay," protested Marsiglio of Padua, "that was not a settlement, but an evasion. We shall not improve much over the ways of our ancestors till it becomes clear that while in the world we must live according to the laws established for the world; and that by so doing we shall reach heaven, where we shall live according to the heavenly law."

"It is and has been an error," said Sir Thomas Elyot, "to believe that men can live like angels. An attempt to mix the two worlds causes the loss of both. 'Render unto Caesar that which is Caesar's.'"

"There are two kinds of marriage," spoke up Wiclif. "Spiritual, as between Christ and the Church; bodily as between man and woman. This bodily matrimony is a sacrament, and a figure of the spiritual wedlock between Christ and Holy Church, as St Paul says. Moreover, this bodily marriage is needful to save mankind through generation till the day of doom, and to restore and fulfil the number of the angels, and those damned for pride, and to save men and women from fornication. God ordained this kind of wedlock when he married Adam and Eve in Paradise."

"Sir Thomas has mentioned two worlds," said Huchown of the Awle Ryale. "I should like to speak of a third."

These words diverted Ossian's interest from a venison pasty. "'Tis long since I heard tidings of Tir na nOg," he said with a sigh. "Huchown, my friend, you make me feel years younger."

"I know no such third world save hell," said Wiclif severely.

"Pay him no heed, Huchown, man. Patrick would not listen to my stories, either; but I told them anyway. Tell on."

"I will do," answered Huchown. "What I have to say concerns Thomas of Erceldoune and an adventure of his. I will relate it as he told it."

107. THE FAIRY LADY OF ELDON HILL
Huchown of the Awle Ryale

As I was going one Endres day
Full fast in mind making my mone,
On a merry morning of May,
By Huntly Banks, myself alone,

I heard the jay and the throstle-cock;
The mavis called to mind her song,
The woodwale sounded like a bell,
That all the wood about me rung.

In that longing thereas I lay
Underneath a seemly tree,
I was aware of a lady gay
Come riding over a lovely lee.

Though I should sit until Doomsday
To sing and warble with my tongue,
Certainly her bright array
Could never be described by me.

Her palfrey was of dapple grey,
The fairest formed that e'er could be;
Her saddle bright as any day,
Set with pure pearls to the knee;

And furthermore of her array—
Resplendent clothes she had upon,
And like the sun on summer's day
Forsooth the lady herself shone.

Her saddle was of royal bone—
Such one I never saw with ee—
Set with many a precious stone,
And compassed all with crapoty;

With stones of orioles great plenty,
Diamonds thick about her hung;
She bore a horn of gold seemly—
One while she blew, another sung.

Her girths of noble silk they were,
The buckles were of beryl stone;
Her stirrups were of crystal clear,
And all with pearl over-begone.

Her poitrel was of royal fine,
Her crupper was of orfery,
And clear with gold her bridle shone,
On either side there hung bells three.

She led three greyhounds in a leash,
Eight brachets by her feet they ran;
To speak with her I would not cease—
Her neck was white as that of swan.

Forsooth, my lords, as I you tell
This was a lady fair begone.

Thomas lay and saw that sight
Underneath a seemly tree.
He said: Yon is Mary, most of might,
Who bore the Child who died for me.

Unless I speak to her so bright,
I hope my heart will burst in three;
Now will I go with all my might
To meet with her at Eldon tree.

Then Thomas quickly up he rose,
And ran across that mountain high;
And truly, as the story says
He met with her at Eldon tree.

He knelt him down upon his knee
Beneath that lovely greenwood spray:
Said, lovely lady, rue on me,
O Queen of Heaven, as well you may.

Then spoke that lady mild of thought:
O Thomas, let such greetings be;

Queen of Heaven am I not,
For I reached ne'er so high degree.

I am a lady of other countree,
Though I be apparelled much in price,
And here I hunt the wildwood fee,
My brachets running at my device.

If thou art 'parelled much in price,
And ridest here in foolish gree,
O lovely lady, as thou art wise,
Give me then leave to lie by thee.

She said, O man, that were folly;
I pray thee Thomas let me be
For I say to you sikerly,
That would destroy all my beauty.

O lovely lady, rue on me,
And I will ever with thee dwell,
Here my troth I plight to thee,
Whether thou be of heav'n or hell.

O man of mould, thou wilt me mar,
However, you shall have your will.
Believe me well, your choice is bad,
For all my beauty you will spill.

Down alighted that lady bright,
Underneath the greenwood spray,

* * *

She said, O man, you like your play;
What bird in bower may dwell with thee?
You mar me all this livelong day:
I pray thee Thomas, let me be.

Thomas stood up in that stead
And looked upon that lady gay;
Her hair hung scattered on her head,
Her eyes seemed out, that were so grey;

And all the rich clothes were away
That he before saw in that stead;
Her one shank black, the other grey,
Her body blue like beaten lead.

Then Thomas said, Alas! Alas!
This is in faith a doleful sight;
How art thou faded in thy face
That shone before like sun so bright!

Thomas, she said, this is bad rede,
For fiend of hell, that am I none;
For thee I am in great dis-ease,
And suffer tortures many a one.

These twelve months you shall with me go
And see the manner of my life,
And by the troth thou owest me,
Against that mayst thou make no strife.

Take leave, she said, of sun and moon,
And of the leaf that springs on tree;
These twelve months thou must with me go
And Middle-earth thou shalt not see.

He kneeled him down upon his knee,
To Mary mild he made his moan:
Lovely lady, rue on me,
For all my play is from me gone.

Alas! he said, and woe is me!
I trow my deeds will work me care.
O Christ, I give my soul to thee,
Wherever that my bones may fare.

She led him in at Eldon hill,
Underneath a secret lee,
Where it was dark as midnight mirk—
The water was ever to his knee.

Thus fared they on; for day-tides three
He heard but swowing of the flood.
Alas, he said, full woe is me,
Almost I die for lack of food.

She brought him to an orchard fair
Of many fruits in great plenty;
Pears and apples ripe were they,
The date and also damson tree;

The fig and also the wine-berry.
The nightingale there built her nest,
The popinjays about did fly,
The throstle sang with little rest.

He rushed to pluck fruits with his hand
As one who long has lacked his meat.
She said: Thomas, let thou them stand,
Or else the fiend will seize on thee.

If thou dost pluck, the sooth to say,
Thy soul goes to the fire of hell,
Nor comes thereout until Doomsday,
But there in pain will ever dwell.

Now Thomas soothly I thee hight,
Come lay thy head down on my knee,
And thou shalt see the fairest sight
Saw ever man of thy countree.

He acted quickly as she bade;
Upon her knee his head he laid,
For her to please he was full glad;
And then that lady to him said:

Seest thou yonder pleasant way
That lies upon yonder mountain?
That is the road to heaven for aye
When sinful souls have borne their pain.

Seest thou, Thomas, yonder way
That lies low under that fair rise?
That is the way, the sooth to say,
Into the joys of Paradise.

Seest thou yonder other way
That passes over yonder plain?
That is the road, the sooth to say,
Where sinful souls shall walk in pain.

Dost thou see now a fourth highway
That passes over yonder fell?
That is the road, the sooth to say,
Into the burning fire of hell.

And seest thou now yon fair castell
That stands upon that pleasant hill?
Of town and tower it bears the bell,
And none on earth is like there-till.

In faith, Thomas, it is mine own,
And the king's abode of this countree;
But I had rather be hanged and drawn
Than he should know thou layest by me.

When thou dost reach yon castle gay,
I beg, a courteous man thou be,
And whatso any man may say,
Forbear to answer all but me.

My lord is served at every mass
By thirty knights, handsome and free;
I shall say, sitting at the dais,
I took thy speech beyond the sea.

As still as stone then Thomas stood,
And gazed upon that lady gay,
For she was now as fair and good
As when she rode on her palfrey.

Said Thomas: Lady, joy to me
It is that I abode this day,
For now you are so fair and white—
Before you were so black and grey.

I pray you that to me you say,
O lady, if your will it be,
Why you were so black and grey:
You said it was because of me.

Forsooth, and I had not been so—
The very truth to thee I'll tell—
It had behooved me straight to go
Unto the burning fire of hell.

My lord he is so fierce and fell—
He who is king of this countree—
Full soon he would have sensed the smell
Of the default I did with thee.

Her greyhounds gathered by her side,
Her brachets fell in at her heel,
She blew her horn with might and main
And to the castle took her way.

Into the hall she proudly went
And Thomas followed at her hand.
Came ladies many, fair and gent,
And knelt before her in a band.

Harp and fiddle they demand,
Gitterns and the psaltery gay;
With lute and ribibe others stand,
To make all manner of minstrelsy.

Knights came dancing three by three,
There was revel, game and play;
Lovely ladies, fair and free
Sat there and sang, in rich array.

Now Thomas tarried in that place
Much longer than I say, pardee,
Till one day, as I hope for grace,
Up spoke that lovely lady free:

Busk thee, Thomas, turn again,
For here no longer mayst thou be.
Hie thee fast with might and main;
I'll bring thee safe to Eldon tree.

Then Thomas said, with heavy cheer:
O lovely lady, let me be,
For certes, lady, I have been here
No longer time than day-tides three.

Forsooth, O Thomas, as I thee tell,
Thou hast been here three years and more;
But longer now thou mayst not dwell,
And reason I will say wherefor:

Tomorrow morn the fiend of hell
Will come with folk to fetch his fee;
Thou art a handsome man and strong,
And well I know that he'll choose thee.

> For all the gold that e'er may be
> From heaven unto mid-earth's end,
> Thou shalt not be betrayed by me;
> Wherefor I rede thou with me wend.
>
> She brought him then to Eldon tree,
> And set him 'neath that greenwood spray.
> On Huntly Banks 'twas fair to be
> Where birds rejoice both night and day.
>
> Far out in yonder mountain grey
> My falcon, Thomas, builds a nest;
> The falcon is the heron's prey—
> Wherefor in no place may he rest.
>
> Thomas, farewell, I wend my way,
> I may no longer bide with thee,
> Give me some token, lady gay,
> That I may say I spake with thee.
>
> Wherever thou fare, by frith or fell
> I pray thee speak no ill of me.
> O Thomas, Thomas, now farewell
> I may no longer dwell with thee.

"I came back alone, too," said Ossian; "and I am still alone," he added, biting viciously into an Essex cheese.

"Pardon me," said Alexander Neckam, "there is a point on which I am not quite clear. Thomas thought he had been away for three days, but the fairy lady said it had been more than three years. That seems to me to be a considerable discrepancy."

"That is easily explained," answered Huchown: "Thomas was the victim of what is called the supernatural lapse of time. What is Time? Who but a usurer knows the answer to that? And a usurer would have made small profit in dealing with the third world. Even Joseph of Arimathia, who was in prison forty-three years, thought it only from Friday till Monday."

"In my travels," remarked the Sieur de Joinville, "I came upon a similar marvel. When I was in the East I heard of a certain Tatar prince to whom three months seemed only a single night."

"You astonish me," said Neckam.

"It was like this," said Joinville.

108. THE TATAR PRINCE AND THE KING OF KINGS
Joinville

As you know, the great emperor, Prester John, had many kings under him, and many tribes and nations were subject to his rule. Among these subject peoples were the Tatars, whom Prester John and other princes held in abhorrence. When they brought their tribute the emperor's ministers would not receive it in their presence, but turned their backs on them. Such insulting treatment aroused the indignation of one of their wise old men, who, after having had himself elected king, resolved to make war on Prester John. Indeed, he won a signal victory over him in a battle that lasted three days and three nights.

It was after this battle that a wonderful thing happened. A great prince of one of the Tatar tribes was missing for three months without anything being known of him. On his return to his people he related that at the close of the battle he had ascended an exceedingly high hill. There he beheld an assembly of the finest dressed and handsomest men he had ever seen in his life. On the highest eminence was placed a throne of gold, and seated thereon was a king who surpassed all others in beauty and in dress. On his right were six crowned kings richly adorned with jewels, and a like number sat at his left. At his right hand knelt a beautiful queen, and at his left a handsome youth with two wings as brilliant as the sun; and round about the throne were great numbers of handsome winged attendants.

The king called to the prince and said: "You have come from the host of the Tatars." "Sire," replied the prince, "that is so." "You will return, then," said the king, "and report that you have seen me, who am the lord of heaven and earth; and say that I command your king to render me thanks and praise for the victory which I have granted him over the forces of Prester John. You shall tell him also that I give him power to subdue the whole earth." "Sire," answered the prince, "how will my lord believe me?" "He will believe you from the following circumstance," replied the potentate. "With no more than three hundred men-at-arms you shall advance to combat the emperor of Persia; and though the emperor have three hundred thousand men, you shall vanquish him." "Sire," said the prince, "I shall never find my way back to my people unless you cause me to be conducted."

Then the potentate turned to one of his attendants: "Come hither, George," said he, "and lead this man back to his quarters in safety." Instantly the prince was restored to his people. After telling them his adventures he was very much surprised to learn that he had been absent three months, for it seemed to him only a single night, and he had suffered neither hunger nor thirst.

"We cannot all be illustrious princes or famous prophets," said the Goodman of Bath, "and such rare adventures as theirs, whether in this world or any other are closed to us humbler men. I find little consolation in Master Huchown's tale."

"Small blame to you," remarked the Clerk of Oxenford. "The remedies of love so far set forth have little to commend them, for they either humiliate the husband, brutalize the wife, or avoid the issue by asceticism, pusillanimity or compromise. Such, at all events, is the view of a layman in amatory matters. But there is one among us who can speak with more authority, not only by reason of his close communion with the best minds of other ages, but, unlike Andrew the Chaplain, from his own experience. I should be glad to listen were Giovanni Boccaccio to speak."

"Thank you," said the Florentine, "for your courteous words. It is true that I have had some experience of the sex . . ."

"And of onions?" asked Christine de Pisan.

"And I suppose I know as much good and evil of women as any man, for some treated me well, others shabbily, according to their nature. If you like, I will lay my opinions before you in the form of a story."

109. TAROLFO'S UNSEASONABLE GARDEN

Giovanni Boccaccio

I call to mind in the land of my birth a rich and noble knight, who, loving a noble lady of the same country with perfect love, took her to wife. Another knight, named Tarolfo, likewise fell in love with that most beautiful lady, and so passionately did he love her that he could see nothing but her, nor did he wish for anything but her; and in many ways, whether by passing frequently before her house, or by jousting or tourneying, and by many other deeds, he exerted himself to gain her affection. Often he sent her messengers, promising her handsome gifts, in order that he might know her mind.

All these things the lady permitted in silence, giving neither sign nor favourable reply to the knight, saying to herself: When he is sensible that he can gain neither agreeable response nor gesture from me, perhaps he will cease his suit and abandon his attempts to rouse me. However, Tarolfo, following the teaching of Ovid, who says: Not on account of the lady's hard-heartedness should the lover cease to persevere, for by continual dropping the soft water wears away the hard stone—did not give over his attentions. The lady, fearing lest news of these matters come to the ears of her husband, and that he might think they had happened with her consent, took thought that she would reveal them to him herself; but later, actuated by better counsel, she said: If I told him I might bring to pass something between them on account of which I should never again live happily. There must be some other way of extricating myself from this difficulty. Then she thought of a cunning scheme. She sent a message to Tarolfo to the effect that if he loved her as much as he seemed to do, she wished him to prove it by making her a present; and when she had received it, she swore by her gods and by the loyalty of a gentlewoman, that she would do all his pleasure; and if he were unable to give her what she wished, he should make up his mind not to urge her further, if he did not wish her to reveal the matter to her husband. The gift which she demanded was this: She said she wished a large garden of herbs, of flowers, of trees and abundant fruit to be made for her in her land, in the month of January, just as though it were the month of May. And she said to herself: This is impossible, and in this way I shall get rid of the fellow.

When Tarolfo heard this request, even though it seemed to him impossible of fulfilment, and though he knew why the lady asked it, he replied that he would never rest nor seek her presence again until he had procured the stipulated gift for her. He left the country, with what household train it pleased him to take, and searched all the western world for advice as to how he might arrive at his desire; and not having found it, he sought the warmer regions, and finally arrived in Thessaly, whither he had been sent by a wise man for such need. There he remained for a number of days without finding that for which he searched. One morning he rose before the sun and began to wander through the wretched plain which once was drenched with Roman blood. He had walked considerable distance when he saw before him, at the foot of a mountain, a man, bearded, but neither young nor too advanced in age, whom, by his garments, he deemed to be very poor. He was small of person, and very thin; he was gathering herbs, digging up various roots with a small knife, whereof a fold of his gown was already full. When Tarolfo saw him he was in considerable doubt as to his nature, but since judgment told him that it was a man, he approached and saluted him, asking who he was, whence he came, and what he was doing in that place at such an hour.

The oldster replied: "I am from Thebes, and Thebano is my name; and I search this plain culling herbs so that by making from their juices certain things necessary and useful for divers ills I may gain the wherewithal to live; and necessity, not pleasure constrains me to come at this hour. But who are you—who by your appearance seem to be some nobleman—who wander here all alone?" Tarolfo replied: "I come from the far west, I am a knight sufficiently wealthy, and overcome and pricked by the thought of a certain project of mine which I am unable to accomplish, I go wandering here alone that I may the better indulge my regrets without hindrance."

Said Thebano: "Are you ignorant of the nature of this place? Why did you not take your way on the other side? Here you might very well suffer harm from furious spirits." Tarolfo replied: "God is powerful everywhere; here as well as elsewhere He has my life and my honour in his hand; let him do therewith as He pleases; indeed, death would be to me a rich treasure." Then said Thebano: "What is the undertaking whose ill success causes you so much grief?" "It is such," replied Tarolfo, "that its accomplishment seems to me quite impossible, for I have not found any advice even in this land." "Can it be told?" asked Thebano. "Yes," said Tarolfo, "but to what good end? Probably none." "But to what harm?" countered Thebano.

Then said Tarolfo: "I am looking for instruction as to how, in the coldest month, one might produce a garden full of flowers, fruits and herbs, and as beautiful as though it were the month of May; but I find no one who can give me counsel in this matter." Thebano was silent for a while, then he said: "You, like others, judge men by their clothes. If my dress had been like yours, or if you had found me in the company of rich princes, instead of culling herbs, you would not have taken so much trouble to tell me your need. But many times vile habiliments conceal a rich treasure of knowledge; wherefor, none should conceal his necessity from any who offers advice and aid unless its revelation be prejudicial to him. But what would you give him who should accomplish that which you desire?"

At these words Tarolfo looked the man in the face, doubting lest he were making sport of him, for it seemed to him incredible that he could put the matter into effect unless he were a god. However, he replied: "In my country I am the lord of a number of castles and of considerable treasure therewith, half of which I would share with him who would do me this favour." "Indeed," replied Thebano, "if you would do so with me, I should no longer go culling simples." "On my word," answered Tarolfo, "if you are he who can do as you say, you shall never more have to struggle to become rich. But how and when will you do this for me?" Said Thebano: "The when lies with you, and do not concern yourself about the how. I will go with you, trusting in your word that you will keep your promise; and when we have arrived where you wish, ask what you please, and I will perform everything without fail."

Tarolfo was so pleased by this circumstance that he would have had scarcely more pleasure if he had had his lady in his arms at that moment. "Friend," said he, "the time seems long to me till you have accomplished what you have promised, so let us depart without delay, and repair to the place where it is to be done." Thebano threw away his herbs, collected his books and other things necessary to his art, and took the road with Tarolfo. In a short time they reached the destined city at about the season of the year for which the garden had been ordered. There they remained quietly and unobtrusively until the term had arrived. But when the month of January came, Tarolfo commanded that the garden should be laid out, so that he could present it to his lady.

Now Thebano waited for night, and when it came he saw that the horns of the moon had turned to complete rotundity, and that it shone in full refulgence over the bare earth. Then, quite alone, he issued from the city, barefoot and leaving his clothes behind, with hair streaming over his naked shoulders. The gentle hours of the night passed one another, the birds, the beasts and men reposed without a murmur, and overhead the unfallen leaves adorned the trees without a movement; the moist air was quiet, and only the stars gleamed. When he had circled about several times, at last he came to the place, beside a stream, which he chose for the site of the garden. There he stopped, stretched his arms toward the stars thrice, and as many times bathed his white hair in the running water of the stream, turning ever back to the stars and imploring them in a loud voice for their aid. Then he knelt upon the earth and said: "O night, securest shrine of high matters, and you, O stars, who with the moon succeed resplendent day; and you, O sovereign Hecate, who bear aid to the matters which we undertake, and you, O holy Ceres, renewer of the broad face of the earth; and you, O tropes, or arts or herbs, and you virtuous plants, whatever you are, that the earth produces; and you, O breezes, winds, mountains, streams, lakes, and every god of the woods and of the secret night, by whose aid I have in former times repulsed the flowing streams, turning them back to their sources, and made moving things stand firm and firm things move—you who once gave to my charms power to dry up the seas and search their bottoms without fear, to dissipate cloudy weather, and then again fill the clear sky with black clouds, making the winds cease or come as I wished, and with those same charms breaking the jaws of terrible dragons, and making the standing forests move, the lofty mountains tremble, the shades return from the Stygian lake to their dead bodies and the living to issue from the tomb; and sometime to draw you, O moon, to your full rotundity, whereto in the past the sounding basins lent their aid, sometimes dimming the clear face of the sun—be present now and lend me your aid. For the present business I have need of juices of herbs such as will cause the arid earth, spoiled of its flowers and fruits by bitter winter, to return partly flowery, with the appearance that spring has come before its time."

Having said this he silently added many other things to his prayer, and then became quiet. The stars did not shed their light in vain: A chariot, drawn by two dragons more quickly than the flight of any bird stopped before him; he mounted thereon, and taking up the reins, guided the dragons into the upper air. Taking his way through the high regions, he left Spain and all Africa, seeking the island of Crete; thence he examined Pelion, Otris and Ossa, Mount Neretus, Pachynus, Pelorus and Appenine. In a brief circuit he searched them all, uprooting and cutting with his sharp sickle those roots and herbs which he needed; nor did he forget those which he had unearthed when Tarolfo found him in Thessaly. He culled virtuous stones on Mount Caucasus, and sand from the Ganges, and from Lybia he brought back the tongues of venomous serpents. He saw the banks of the Rhône and of the Seine of Paris, of the great Po and the Arno and the imperial Tiber, of Nifeus, of Tanais [Don] and the Danube, culling from them still those herbs which seemed to him necessary, and adding to them those plucked on the summits of wild mountains. He sought the islands of Lesbos and of Colchos and Patmos, and whatever other he had heard might provide anything useful to his purpose.

On the third morning he returned to the place whence he had started. The dragons, who merely smelled the odour of the gathered herbs, threw off the ancient slough of many years and were rejuvenated. Thebano descended, and of two grassy turves constructed an altar, that of Hecate on the right, that of the goddess of regeneration [Ceres] on the left, after which he lighted votive fires on each, and, his ancient locks spread over his shoulders, he began, with a subdued murmur, to circle about them, frequently dipping the glowing embers into gathered blood, and now and then sprinkling the ground which he destined for the garden, then replacing them on the altars. Afterwards he scattered the ground three times with fire and water and sulphur. Then he placed upon the glowing flames a mighty vase filled with blood, milk and water, letting it boil for a long time while he added the roots and herbs culled in strange places, mixing with them various seeds and flowers of peregrine plants, adding also stones found in the far East, and hoar-frost gathered in the preceding nights, together with the flesh of starved vampires, with the ... scales of the cinifes, the shell of a marine turtle, and finally the liver and lights of a superannuated stag; and with these he mixed a thousand other things so strange that memory cannot recall them. Then he took a dry olive branch and stirred all these things together. In doing so the dry branch began to turn green, and in a short time put forth leaves, and not long after was laden with black olives. When Thebano observed this, he took the bubbling liquor and began to sprinkle it upon the chosen ground, wherein he had planted staves like trees, as many as he wished. Hardly had the ground felt this when it began to bloom, bringing forth new and beautiful greenery, and all the dry staves became fruitful trees.

This done, Thebano returned home to Tarolfo, whom he found very melancholy, for Thebano's long absence had caused him to fear that the magician was playing a trick on him. "Tarolfo," he said, "everything you asked has been done according to your pleasure." Tarolfo rejoiced greatly at this news. The next day, which was the occasion of a great feast, he presented himself to his lady, whom he had not seen for a long time, and thus he said: "My lady, after great effort and exertion I have accomplished what you commanded: it is at your pleasure whenever you wish to take possession thereof." The lady marvelled much at seeing him, and more so at his words. She did not believe him, and replied: "I am charmed; you shall show it to me tomorrow."

On the morrow Tarolfo waited upon the lady and said: "My lady, be pleased to walk into the garden which you commanded I should provide for you in the cold month." The lady rose, and accompanied by a numerous train, went to the garden, which they entered by a beautiful gate; and within it was not cold, as it was outside, but permeated by a temperate air. The lady went everywhere, looking and gathering plants and flowers which she saw growing in abundance. And the sprinkled liquor had been so powerful that the fruits which only August brings forth here adorned their trees in the midst of the bitter season, and many of the lady's companions ate thereof. The lady thought this a most beautiful and marvellous thing, such as she had never seen. And when she realized from many evidences that this was a real garden, and that the knight had fulfilled her command, she turned to Tarolfo and said: "Indeed, sir knight, you have earned my love, and I am ready to grant you what I promised. However, I should like a boon from you, namely, that you would delay enforcing your claim till my lord goes to the hunt or is engaged elsewhere in the city, so that you may more prudently and safely take your pleasure."

Tarolfo was agreeable to this request, and, more or less content, he took his departure, leaving her in possession of the garden. All the people of the district knew of this garden, though none of them, except much later, knew how it had come into existence. The noble lady to whom it had been presented departed sorrowfully therefrom and returned to her chamber cast down and melancholy; taking thought how she might withdraw her promise, and finding no reasonable excuse, her sorrow increased. Her husband observed her distress and wondered at it, asking what troubled her. The lady was ashamed to reveal the matter and replied that there was nothing amiss, fearing lest her husband be angry with her. But finally, unable to resist her husband's constant urgings that she tell him the cause of her distemper, she disclosed the circumstances from beginning to end.

On hearing this the husband was thoughtful for a long time, but conscious that his wife had had only the purest of intentions, he said: "Go and fulfil your promise, and discharge your obligation fully to Tarolfo, for he has won his reward reasonably and with great effort." At this the lady wept and replied: "May the gods remove such sin far from me. In no wise will I do it. I will kill myself rather than cause you dishonour or displeasure." The knight answered: "Lady, I should certainly not want you to kill yourself for a matter of this sort, or even that you should worry about it; it is no displeasure to me; go and do as you promised, and I shall hold you no less dear. But when this is done, take care about making such promises in the future, however impossible it might seem that your wish should be fulfilled."

When the lady heard her husband's will, she adorned herself and made herself beautiful, and taking companions, repaired to Tarolfo's hostel, where she presented herself to him, red with shame. Tarolfo rose from beside Thebano and advanced toward her, filled with wonder and joy. He received her with all honour, and asked the occasion of her visit. The lady replied: "I have come to subject myself to all your will; do as you please with me." Then said Tarolfo: "You fill me with immeasurable astonishment, when I observe at what hour and with what company you have come. This could not have happened without the knowledge of your husband."

Then the lady told Tarolfo from beginning to end how things had turned out. Afterwards Tarolfo was more amazed than ever. When he took thought, he realized the great generosity of the husband who had sent her to him, and he said to himself that whoever thought of putting shame upon so generous a man was worthy of the greatest reprehension; and he said to the lady: "Gentle lady, you have observed your pledge loyally and like a worthy woman, wherefor I consider as received that whereof I besought you, and whenever you please you may return to your husband; and thank him from me for his great indulgence, and excuse me to him for my past folly, with the assurance that in the future I shall attempt no repetition of such things." The lady thanked Tarolfo for his exceeding courtesy, and, having returned to her husband, related to him how things had gone with her.

Now Thebano sought out Tarolfo and asked him how he had sped. Tarolfo told him. "Then," said Thebano, "I have in this wise lost what you promised me?" Said Tarolfo: "No; whenever it pleases you, take the half of my castles and the half of my treasure just as I promised you, for I consider that you have served me at all points." To this Thebano answered: "Since the knight was generous to you with his wife, and you did not act like a churl to him, may it never please the gods that I should be less courteous. More than anything in the world I am pleased in having served you, and it is my will that what I should have received from you in recompense for the service remain as it always was." Nor would he accept anything from Tarolfo . . . and he went home as poor as he had ever been.

"Ser Giovanni," said Helinandus, "I could have wished there had been less necromancy in your tale. The times are evil enough without reminder. Once students used to flock to Paris for liberal arts, to Orléans for letters, to Bologna for law, to Salerno for medicine; but now all go to Toledo to learn necromancy, and nowhere for good manners."

"Sir," said the Bachelor of Salamanca, "though what you say may in a large measure be true, yet I hope you will bear in mind that Toledo was for ages a chief city of the Moorish Caliphate, and that if the Moors brought with them necromancy to our land, they brought also Aristotle, to your behoof and mine. And to show you that the study of the magic art is neither a simple matter nor one unattended by shame and danger, I will tell you a story which lately came to my ears."

110. THE NECROMANCER AND THE DEAN

The Bachelor of Salamanca

There was once a dean of Santiago who craved to learn the art of necromancy, and hearing that Don Illan of Toledo was more adept therein than anyone else far or near, he went to Toledo for the purpose of studying that science under his direction.

No sooner had the dean arrived at Toledo than he proceeded to the house of Don Illan, whom he found reading in a retired chamber. Don Illan received the dean very graciously, but requested him not to disclose the purpose of his visit till they had broken their fast. When they had eaten, the dean informed his host why he had come to see him, begging him very earnestly to instruct him in the art wherein he was so skilled. In reply Don Illan pointed out that his guest was already a dean, and that he would doubtless rise to positions of still greater eminence. He also observed that when men arrive at great place and have accomplished the objects of their ambition, they easily forget what others have done for them in the past, and that as the star of their success rises, their sense of gratitude wanes. The dean assured Don Illan that such would not be the case with him, and that if he would only do him this favour, he would be completely at his orders. Such matters engaged their conversation till supper time, and they finally reached an agreement.

Don Illan informed the dean that the art which he desired to learn could not be taught save in a very privy apartment, and taking him by the hand, led him away. As they were leaving the room he gave orders to his housekeeper that she should procure some partridges for their repast, but should not cook them till he gave the word. Then he conducted the dean down a beautifully carved stone staircase, descending so far that it seemed the river Tagus must flow over their heads. At the bottom of the steps they entered a well-appointed chamber, wherein were collected the books necessary for the study of magic, and there made themselves at ease.

As Don Illan seemed to be making up his mind which book to begin with, two men entered the chamber and gave the clergyman a letter from his uncle the archbishop. The letter informed him that his relative was dangerously ill, and that if he wished to see him alive, he should come immediately. The dean was much disturbed by this news, partly because of his uncle's illness, but more so because he was reluctant to abandon the study of magic before he had fairly begun it. He decided that he would not be hindered so easily, and so, instead of going to his uncle, sent him a letter.

At the end of three or four days other messengers appeared. They brought news that the archbishop was dead, and that the magnates were considering the dean's election to his uncle's dignity. They said that it was expected that all would go well, but that he should stay where he was, for it would be easier to secure his election if he were not present.

Now when seven or eight days had passed there arrived two richly dressed squires who kissed the dean's hand, informing him that he had been chosen archbishop. When Don Illan heard this, he expressed his pleasure that the good news had arrived while the dean was a guest in his house; and, as God had been so gracious to him, he begged that the now vacant deanery might be given to his son. The archbishop-elect replied that he hoped Don Illan would excuse him and allow him to name his own brother to fill the vacancy, adding that he would present his son with some office in his own church wherewith he should be contented. And he invited Don Illan and his son to accompany him to Santiago.

They had resided at Santiago for some time when one day there came messengers from the pope naming the former dean metropolitan of Tolosa, and he might consult his own pleasure in choosing someone to succeed him in the vacant see. Don Illan now reminded the archbishop of his promise, urging him to confer the archbishopric on his son. But the archbishop again begged that Don Illan would allow him to discharge a family obligation by naming one of his paternal uncles to fill the vacancy. Don Illan replied that he felt very unjustly treated, but that he would expect the new metropolitan to make good his promise at the first possible opportunity. The archbishop thanked him and renewed his assurance that he would favour his son at some future time; and inviting Don Illan and his son to accompany him, they all set out for Tolosa.

At Tolosa they were well received by the counts and the great men of the country. They had resided there about two years when letters came from the pope to the effect that the metropolitan had been made cardinal. He should select his own successor at Tolosa. On this occasion Don Illan went to the metropolitan and reminded him that several vacancies had occurred in church offices, but that, contrary to his promise, Don Illan's son had been appointed to none of them. Now, he said, he hoped the new cardinal would confer the see of Tolosa on his son. But once more the cardinal begged to be forgiven for bestowing the vacancy on one of his maternal uncles, a very good old man whom he wished to oblige. In Rome, however, doubtless many opportunities would arise for rewarding him with all his son could desire. Don Illan complained bitterly, but none the less accompanied the cardinal to Rome. They were well received and resided there a long time. Don Illan daily besought the cardinal to bestow some office on his son, but the prelate always found some excuse for not doing so.

While they were at Rome the pope died, and the cardinals, assembled in conclave, elected the Spanish cardinal to the throne of St Peter. After congratulating him on his new dignity Don Illan said: "You now have no excuse for not fulfilling the promises you have made me hitherto." But the new pope told him not to be so impatient, but to give him time to think of some fitting post for his son. At this reply Don Illan lost patience, and recalled to the pope how at their first meeting he had promised to do all he could to advance his interests. "In all this time you have done nothing," he said, "and have shown that ingratitude which I expected from the first. Do you imagine that I am imposed upon by this new evasion? Disabuse yourself of that idea, for henceforth I shall put no faith in your words."

These expressions angered the pope. "You forget yourself," he said. "If you persist in taking such a tone with me, I will have you thrown into prison. Perhaps you do not remember that you are a heretic and a sorcerer; but I remember it. I know that at Toledo you had no other means of livelihood than your cursed necromancy. Woe to you if you continue to importune me!"

Don Illan now had no choice but to leave Rome, and he informed the pope of his intention. The pontiff, however, would grant him no provision wherewith to support himself on the road. "In that case," said Don Illan, "since I have nothing to eat, I must needs depend upon the partridges which I ordered for tonight's refection." Then he called out to his housekeeper and gave her directions about cooking the birds for his supper.

No sooner had the necromancer spoken than the dean found himself once more in Toledo, still dean of Santiago, as he had been on his first arrival, and so overwhelmed with shame that he knew not what to say. But Don Illan said: "It is fortunate for me that I made trial of your good faith before proceeding to instruct you. Under the circumstances I find that I shall be able to eat these partridges without your assistance."

"Partridges, is it?" asked Ossian wonderingly. "In my time sparrows were larger than any partridges I have eaten lately. Woe it is that I am for the hunger that is on me in this land!" Then his glance lighted upon half a dozen roast hams ranged on a table dormant. "What might these be?" he asked Geoffrey Keating, returning to his seat and piling the lot before him on the table.

"My friend," said Giraldus Cambrensis before Keating could answer, "those are pig hams."

"Is it so, now?" exclaimed Ossian. "The thighs of ravens were larger in my day," he added as he bit into a ham.

"Why," said Giraldus, "the Chase of Slieve Cullin must be a thousand years behind you!"

"It seems only yesterday," replied Ossian through a mouthful of ham.

"Distance, of time as well as of space," observed Roger Bacon, "lends enchantment. And that is a fact which the critics of romance might profitably take into their consideration. If critics must rationalize romance, they would do well to prepare themselves for the task by a good stiff course of physics. As it is, they are almost as ignorant as doctors of medicine."

"Messer Giovanni," said the Clerk of Oxenford, "the Goodman of Bath and I—and Matheolus and Christine and Andrew—are still in some doubt as to the manner in which we should interpret your tale."

"Well," answered the Florentine, "I thought the point was clear enough—that man and wife should treat each other with mutual trust and forbearance."

"I never expected to find truth in the mouth of a story-teller," said Wiclif, "but I heartily approve of that text."

"And for those who find this beyond their strength or will," went on Boccaccio, "I have one other pill, or rather I borrow it from an eminent countryman of mine: Leave women and study mathematics. But this really applies only to men past the age of sixty."

"Now that the question pertaining to the relation of the sexes has been unsatisfactorily answered," said Hallarstein the Skald, "I should like to revert to a matter which caused considerable perturbation a while back. The exemplary characters of a cat, a horse and a fly were held up for your admiration, with the result that Dr. Keating got into a state which has caused him to neglect his drink all evening. To me, a foreigner, it seems that the learned historian might allow Adamnan's story of the horse to cancel Gerald's; but if not, I will throw a dog into the balance, and an Irish dog at that."

Keating looked at the speaker with a countenance visibly brighter as he prepared to listen to the tale of . . .

III. THE DOG VIGI

Hallarstein

After Olaf Tryggvison had married the lady Gyda he continued to reside in England for the most part, though he occasionally made business trips to the neighbouring islands. Once it happened that he lay off the coast of Ireland with a large fleet. Provisions had run short, so that a land foray was necessary to obtain supplies. The foragers collected a great number of sheep and cattle, and drove them down to the strand where their boats lay. As they did so, they were followed by a certain Irish farmer or *bó-aire,* who begged Olaf to give him back the cows that belonged to him from among those the men were driving off. Olaf told him to take his cows if he could pick them out and separate them from the others, if he could do so without delaying the men. "But I think that neither you nor any man can perform that feat," he said, "considering that there are many hundred cattle in the drove."

With the Irishman was his cattle-dog. On hearing the king's reply, he sent his dog among the cattle as they were being driven away, one man's with another's. The dog ran into the herd and drove out exactly the number which the farmer said he wanted. They were all branded with one and the same mark, which showed that the dog did indeed know the right beasts.

"O man," said the king, "your dog is extraordinarily clever; will you give him to me?" For the king always coveted any object of superior quality or value. "I will give him," replied the Irishman. In return, Olaf made the farmer a present of a gold ring, and promised him his friendship in future. This excellent dog was called Vigi. King Olaf owned him a long time after that.

One summer a man named Grim went out to Iceland. He was a member of King Olaf's body-guard, and at one time had been a forecastle man. That winter he stayed in Iceland, and in the summer attended the Thing. Also present at the Thing was an Icelander named Thorkel Fringe. During the procession to the law rock he happened to stumble, and fell, and on account of the crowd, was trodden under foot. When Thorkel got to his feet again, he was very wroth. He recognized Grim as the man whose foot had been heaviest.

With Thorkel at the Thing was a young man named Sigurd, noted for his strength and athletic prowess. Thorkel bade him take vengeance on Grim for the shame he had suffered. Late that evening, while Grim was preparing for bed, Sigurd strode into his booth and killed him. Grim's kinsmen naturally started a suit for manslaughter, and the upshot of it was that Sigurd was outlawed. Thorkel Fringe assisted him to get away. Late in autumn, passing under an assumed name, Sigurd arrived in Norway in company of some merchants.

When King Olaf learned that his man Grim had been slain, and that the slayer was probably not far away, he became very angry, and caused the merchants' ship to be searched. Sigurd was discovered and put in fetters. A Thing was summoned. Then the king ordered the prisoner to be stripped of his clothes, and gave judgment that he should bate the dogs till he was dead. On the pronouncement of this doom one of Olaf's body-guard spoke in Sigurd's behalf, but without avail. "He shall die," said Olaf, "so that other men may be afraid to kill my people without provocation." The bishop was asked to intercede, and he bade the king set the man free. "The bishop is not better able to judge a man than I," said Olaf. "Strip off his clothes at once!"

So it was done. A ring of men formed round the prisoner, and the dogs were let loose upon him as he stood before them, naked and with hands bound. But so keen was the flash of his eyes, it is said, that the dogs all turned back, and not one was so grim that it dared approach him when he turned his glance on it. Thereupon Olaf called his dog Vigi, and stroking him gently, pointed out the naked man. Vigi was somewhat hesitant, yet he stood up obediently, with hair bristling. Then he sprang at Sigurd and tore him, and then he came back and lay down at the king's feet. When Sigurd felt the bitter pain, he gave a great leap over and beyond the ring of men, and fell down dead.

There were two friends, Raud of Godeys, and Thori, surnamed the Hart, of Vaga. They were both heathen men, and Raud in particular was very skilful in witchcraft.

When Raud and Thori learned that King Olaf was sailing from the south with a great force to Halogaland, they gathered an army against him. They met the king's fleet, and at once joined battle. A great fight was there, and a great fall of men; but at last the heathen men were beaten down and their ships disabled. Raud fled out to sea with the aid of a magically induced wind. Thori Hart made for land and leaped ashore with his men. Olaf was hard at his heels, and with him was his dog Vigi. When the king saw whither Thori was running, he ran after him, and to Vigi he said: "Catch the hart, Vigi!" The dog ran in upon the fugitive, whereupon Thori made a stand. Olaf threw his spear at him, while Thori thrust at the dog with his sword and gave him a great wound. At the same moment the king's spear went in under Thori's arm, and came out on the other side of his body. Thori left his life there. Vigi was borne to the ships; Olaf let send for a skilled leech, and he recovered from his wound.

In the island of Moster there dwelt an old blind man who had a reputation for second sight. Not long before the battle of Svold, King Olaf and his fleet stopped at the island. The king and some of his men went to the old man's house, giving out that they were merchants, and asked for tidings. "Alas!" said the seer, "in one venture the men of Norway shall lose the four noblest things of their kind that ever came into the land. First is King Olaf Tryggvison; second is Queen Thyri; third is Olaf's ship, the *Long Serpent;* and fourth is the king's dog, Vigi."

We know that King Olaf disappeared from the *Long Serpent* when Earl Eric boarded her; but whether or not he went to his death is a matter upon which authorities do not agree. We know that Queen Thyri died of grief at his loss. And we know that the *Long Serpent,* after the battle of Svold, fell to Eric's share of the spoil, but that she proved unamenable to the helm, and that the earl had her broken up after he reached the Vík. On that voyage to Norway Einar Thambarskelf, the mighty archer, was aboard, along with other men to whom Earl Eric had given quarter; and in the fore-room at the front of the ship lay Vigi, who had not stirred from that place during the entire time of the battle.

When the earl finally brought the *Long Serpent* into the Vík, Einar Thambarskelf, before going ashore, went to the dog as he lay there and said: "We are masterless now, Vigi." At these words the dog sprang up growling, and then with a loud howl, as though stricken to the heart, ran ashore with Einar. He went to a mound not far away and lay down there. He would accept food from no man's hand, though he drove away birds, beasts and other dogs from his ration. Tears welled from his eyes, and lamenting the loss of his master in this way, he lay there till he died.

"That was indeed a dog of admirable character," said Alexander Neckam when Hallfred had finished, "the more so since he served a hard master."

"Pliny," remarked Sir Thomas Elyot, "cites many cases of dogs that have faithfully served and loved their masters. He says, for example, that a certain Titus Habinius and his companions were sentenced to execution. One of these men had a dog which could never be driven away from the prison. Nor, later, would he leave his master's body when it was taken from the place of execution, but howled most lamentably. One of the bystanders threw a piece of meat to the dog, and he brought it and laid it at his master's mouth. And when the corpse was thrown into the Tiber, the dog swam after it as long as he could, and even tried to bear it up to keep it from sinking."

"Some men there are," said Roger of Wendover, "who seem to inspire great loyalty, whether of humans or of dogs. The famous Ragnar Lothbroc was no less faithfully loved by his dog than the famous Olaf."

"Well," said the Goodman of Paris, "I think French dogs are no less sagacious and faithful than others. I recall Macaire . . ." But at this point the Goodman was checked by a fit of coughing.

"You should do something for that cough," advised John of Gaddesden. "I recommend—without charge—an ointment composed of honey and your wife's spittle. That was a medicament frequently employed by Lucius Vitellius, the father of the emperor."

"I have enough recipes of my own," coughed the Goodman.

"When I was travelling in Wales with the archbishop Baldwin," said Gerald, "I heard of a dog belonging to Owen . . ."

Gerald would have said more but was prevented by a burst of laughter. It was Roaring Dick, who thus gave voice to some inner amusement. "The subject of dogs," he said in reply to inquiry, "reminds me of a curious story."

"Let us hear it," said Elyot, "perhaps it will amuse us also."

112. SHEEP INTO DOG

Roaring Dick

Once upon a time I heard about a poor old man who was carrying a lamb to market to sell. As he walked along on his way he was observed by a certain practical joker, who perceived that he was old and simple. He said to some of his companions: "Do as I tell you and we shall get that sheep from the old fellow for nothing." Thereupon he stationed his friends one by one at various points where the old man was likely to pass. As he came up to the first trickster the fellow said: "O man, will you sell me that dog of yours?" The old man only looked at him askance and went on his way. When he came to the second joker the latter said: "Brother, will you sell me that hound? I will give you a penny for him." To this the old man replied: "Do not be making fun of me. It is a lamb, not a dog." When the third hooligan asked him if he would sell his dog for a penny, the old man was wroth and answered: "This is a poor joke."

He continued on his way till he met the fourth joker, who also offered him a penny for his dog. The old man was abashed and said nothing. But when the fifth rascal also offered to buy his hound, the old fellow began to wonder why so many people should want to buy a dog when it was no dog, but a sheep. He turned the matter over in his mind and finally came to a decision. "God knows I thought it was a lamb," he said to himself, "but since it really seems to be a dog, I will carry it no farther." Therewith he threw down his burden and went his ways. And when he had gone, the practical joker and his fellows came along, caught the lamb, and ate it.

When Dick had finished he looked about somewhat fatuously as though expecting applause, or at least approval; but nobody laughed, not even John the Reeve.
"Your tale," said the Clerk of Oxenford, "illustrates a principle which I have always supported, namely, that the educated man is he who not only can see things, but who knows what he is looking at when he sees it."
"Speaking of sheep," said Henry Castide, "I once heard somewhere about a man who stole one of his neighbour's sheep and ate it. The owner went to a saintly preacher who dwelt near by and complained of his loss. Speaking before his congregation the preacher many times commanded that whoever had the sheep should return it to its rightful owner, but no one would admit having taken it. Finally, one holy day when all the people were gathered in the church the preacher commanded that by the grace of God the stolen sheep should bleat in the belly of the man who had stolen and eaten it, so that all men might hear. And so it did, and the thief was known, and forced to make amends for his trespass. And all others who were present at that miracle were ever afterwards afraid to steal."
"That was one of Patrick's minor miracles," remarked John Colgan. "It would have been more instructive to tell how he contended with King Loegaire and his druids."
"Will you tell it?" asked John Capgrave.
"Willingly," replied Colgan, "on another occasion."
"Your hero, or rather your villain, got off easily," said Froissart to Castide. "At the court of Sultan Bajazet the execution of justice was less haphazard and uncertain, especially when it was suspected that the thief had eaten his loot.
"I recall," continued the historian, "that one time when the Lord of Nevers and other French barons were with the sultan, a poor woman came to him in tears to demand justice against one of his servants, and said: 'Sultan, I address myself to you as my sovereign, and complain of one of the servants attached to your person. This morning he entered my house and seized by force the goat milk which I had provided for myself and children, and drank it against

my will. I told him that I would complain to you of this outrage, but I had no sooner uttered the words than he gave me two great buffets, and would not desist, though I ordered him to do so in your name. O Sultan, do me justice, as you have sworn to your people that you would do, so that I may be satisfied, this injury punished, and everyone know that even the meanest of your subjects may obtain his rights.' Now the sultan was determined that all crimes committed within his dominions should be severely punished; he therefore listened attentively to her words, and said that he would do her justice. He ordered the varlet to be brought and confronted with the woman, who repeated her complaint. The fellow, who dreaded Bajazet, began to make excuses, saying that the accusation was false. But the woman told a plain tale, and persisted in asserting its truth. Finally the sultan stopped her and said: 'Woman, consider your accusation well, for if I find that you have told a lie, you shall suffer death.' 'My lord,' replied the woman, 'I consent to that, for if what I say were not true, I could have no reason to come before you; all I ask is justice.' 'Justice you shall have,' replied the sultan.

"Then he ordered the servant to be seized and his belly opened, for otherwise he would not have known whether he had drunk the milk or not. The milk was found in the man's stomach, for it had not yet had time to be digested. When the sultan saw this evidence he said to the woman: 'You had just cause of complaint. Now go your way, for the injury done you has been punished.' Then the woman was compensated for her loss, and she went home. This judgment of Bajazet was witnessed by the French lords who were in his country at the time."

"That was rigorous justice, indeed," commented Sir John Fortescue.

"Possibly too rigorous," ventured William Langland.

"Unless," said Thomas Linacre, "they had the criminal sewed up again. When I was in Paris one of my colleagues told me about an interesting case. There was a certain franc-archer confined in the prisons of the Châtelet for divers robberies and sacrilege. For these crimes he was condemned to be hanged at Montfaucon, but he appealed to the court of parliament, whither he was led for trial. The court dismissed the appeal and confirmed the sentence of the provost of Paris, to whom he was remanded for execution. But the surgeons and physicians of Paris petitioned the king that, as a variety of persons were afflicted with the stone and other internal disorders, and that as this franc-archer had complaints similar to those of which the lord of Bouchage now lay dangerously ill, it was requisite that the internal parts of a living man should be examined, and that no better subject could have offered than this franc-archer under sentence of death.

"The physicians and surgeons, in consequence of the king's permission, opened his body, and having examined his bowels, replaced them, and sewed up the body. By the king's orders, every care was taken of him, and within fifteen days he was perfectly cured, and not only pardoned for his crimes, but a sum of money was given to him. This was in the year 1474."

"The same anatomical curiosity, or shall we say, spirit of research, animated the emperor Nero," said Gilbertus Anglicus. "According to an authority whom I will not name, the emperor had his own mother cut open to find out how he lived and was fed before birth."

"Nero had a nasty mind," said the Clerk of Oxenford, "and if I might say so, *simile gaudet simili.*"

Gilbertus flushed and would have replied, but stopped, fascinated as it were, by the shaking hand and quivering jaw of the monk of St Evroult, who was obviously struggling to speak.

"I gather," said Ordericus Vitalis finally, addressing Henry Castide, "that the miracle which you related took place in Ireland, particularly since Colgan has ascribed it to St Patrick. Now strange as it may seem, I have never been in Ireland, but . . ."

"A similar miracle took place at Santo Domingo," interrupted Andrew Boorde, "if one can believe the townsmen who asseverate that a boiled cock crew in their mayor's dish."

"I do not doubt you, doctor," replied Orderic; "but it was a miracle of a somewhat different nature that came into my mind, and has nothing to do with roosters, though it does touch briefly on sheep."

"Don't quibble," said William of Newburgh; "what came into your mind?"

Orderic gave a deprecating cough and then told the anecdote of . . .

113. THE NUT-CRACKING THIEF AND THE CRIPPLE

Ordericus Vitalis

In a certain district of Normandy there stands a church outside the town upon a hill. One evening two thieves met there and made agreement that one of them should go steal a lamb, and the other should go and steal nuts; and he who finished his business first should come back to the church and wait for his companion in the porch.

He who had been appointed to steal nuts got through with his job quickly and returned to the porch and sat down. While waiting for the return of his friend he passed the time cracking his stolen nuts and eating them. Now it happened that the clerk came to the church to ring curfew. As he drew near to the porch and heard the noise of the nuts being cracked, he thought it was the devil, and in a great fright ran home to the priest's house as fast as he could. "The devil," said he, "is in the church porch."

In the priest's house there was an old man and lame, and he scoffed at the clerk, saying that he was not afraid of devils in porches. And he said to a young hind also present in the room, a strong fellow, that if he would carry him to the church on his back, he would make sure whether or not the devil was in the porch. The young man was agreeable, so the cripple climbed onto his back, and they set out.

When the thief who was in the church porch saw someone coming bearing something on his back, he thought it was his friend with a lamb on his neck, and cried out: "Is he fat?" On hearing this the young labourer who had the cripple on his back answered: "Whether he be fat or lean, I will leave him with you." And with that he threw the man to the ground, and fled home as fast as he could. For his part, the old man gathered his strength and courage together and ran also, and reached home before the young man who had borne him. And from that time, though he had been a cripple for seven years, he went about on his feet as well as any man.

"I, too, have heard that story," said John Bromyard, "though the details were somewhat different."

"Who hasn't heard it?" asked John Skelton. "In the version known to me the two thieves were a miller and a tailor."

"*Furtum celari non potest,*" observed Fra Cipolla, "as I always say when I am preaching among the people. I have often told the exemplum related by Roaring Dick as well as the tale to which we have just listened. But when I found a congregation more than usually hard-hearted, and whose money-pouches were suffering from quinsy, there was one story I told which never failed to have a lenitive effect."

"What was that?" asked Robert Mannyng.

"It was the story," answered Fra Cipolla, "of . . ."

114. THE THIEVES WHO WENT IN SEARCH OF DEATH

Fra Cipolla

One day a certain hermit travelling through a wooded place happened upon a spacious grotto which lay in a retired position, and, since he was very weary, he decided to rest therein. As he drew near the grotto, he saw something gleaming brightly, and there indeed, was a heap of gold. As soon as the hermit realized what he had found, he went away with all haste, fleeing to the desert as fast as he could. As he fled he encountered three rascally brigands who dwelt in the forest for the purpose of robbing any who passed through. Now they, who lay in ambush, seeing the hermit in such a hurry, though no one seemed to be pursuing him, were somewhat uneasy. None the less they stopped him to ask why he fled, for they marvelled greatly thereat.

Said the hermit: "My brothers, I am fleeing from Death, who is following close on my heels." The robbers, seeing neither man nor beast, replied: "Show us the one who is pursuing you; lead us to the place where he is." "Come with me, if you will," said the hermit, "and I will show you, though it would be far better for you to flee also." But the robbers wanted to find Death and see what he looked like, and repeated their command. Thereupon the hermit, seeing that he could do no otherwise, and standing in fear of them, led them to the grotto which he had just left and said, pointing to the heap of gold: "Here is Death who was pursuing me."

The robbers at once recognized the gold for what it was, and began to rejoice greatly. They gave the good man leave to go where he would, and he went about his business, while the robbers mocked him as a simpleton.

Now the bandits took stock of the treasure and began to discuss what they should do. One said: "It seems to me that since God has given us such good luck we should not leave without taking this treasure with us." Said another: "Not so. Let one of us take some of the gold, sell it in the city and buy bread and wine and other things whereof we stand in need; let him do as he pleases, provided only that he bring provisions back to us." All agreed to this proposal.

The devil, who is sly and cunning in effecting all the evil he can, put an idea into the head of him who went to town for provisions. "When I arrive in town," said he to himself, "I will eat and drink my fill: then I will buy certain things which I need just now; afterwards I will put poison in the provisions and carry them back to my companions. Then, when they are both dead, I shall be lord of all that treasure. And if I reckon correctly, there is so much of it that I shall be the richest man in all this district." And as he thought, so he did. He ate as much as he wished, and then poisoned all the remainder of the food, and so brought it to his fellows.

In the meantime, while he was on his way to town scheming how to kill the others and obtain all the gold for himself, those who remained behind thought no better of him than he of them, and they said, one to the other: "As soon as our fellow comes back with the bread and wine and other things, we will kill him; then all this great treasure can be divided between the two of us; and since there will be fewer to share with, each will get a larger portion."

Now the first man returned, and when the two perceived him, they set upon him with knife and spear and killed him. When he was quite dead, they sat down to eat the provisions he had brought. As soon as they had eaten their fill they fell over dead. Now all three had got their death.

Thus does God reward traitors. They went in search of Death, and thus did they find him, in a manner which befitted them. But the wise man prudently fled, and the gold remained unpossessed as before.

When Father Onion had finished his exemplum old Unibos stirred uneasily, and Martin Scabby shrank into his cloak. Peter Bell shivered. "How did we get onto this subject?" he queried.

"If I might be so bold," said Henry Castide, "I should like to return to the matter which lately caused Doctor Keating so much annoyance, now that the historian of St David's is no longer within earshot."

As a matter of fact, Giraldus Cambrensis was explaining the nature of dogs to an audience composed of Paul the Deacon, Bartholomew Anglicus, Sordello and Alexander Neckam, while Ossian gave ear with every evidence of great interest.

"There may be something in Gerald's account of the horse," continued Henry, "at least if one can put any belief in a story I heard while living in Ériu."

"Let us hear it," invited Froissart.

115. THE SECRET OF LOWRY LORC'S EARS

Henry Castide

It is related of Labraidh Loinsech that his ears were shaped like those of a horse; on which account every person who cut his hair was instantly put to death in order that neither he nor anybody else alive should be aware of that blemish.

Now it was the habit of this king to have his hair cut once every year, that is, he was wont to get all the hair that had grown below his ears clipped off. Lots were cast in order to determine the man who should perform this service, because the person upon whom the lot fell was put to death.

One time the lot fell upon the only son of an aged widow who dwelt near the king's residence. Upon hearing thereof she instantly betook herself to the king's presence, and besought him not to put her only son to death, as he was the only child she had. The king then promised to spare her son provided he would keep secret whatever he might see, and would never disclose it to anyone till the hour of his death. After this, when the youth had cut the king's hair, the burden of that secret so operated upon his mind and body that he had to lie down on the bed of sickness, and no medicine could have any salutary effect on him.

When the youth had been thus wasting away for a long time, a certain learned druid came to see him, and told his mother that the burden of a secret was the cause of her son's disease, and that he could never recover until he had told it to something. He then told the boy that though he was bound not to discover the secret to any human being, he might, nevertheless, go to the meeting of four roads, and when there, turn to his right and address the first tree he met, and tell his story to it.

The first tree the lad met with was a large willow, and to it he declared his secret. Hereupon the disease brought on by brooding over his burdensome secret was immediately dissipated, and he returned perfectly well to his mother's house.

Soon after that it happened that Craftini broke his harp, and had to go to look for materials for another. He chanced to hit upon the very tree to which the widow's son had told his secret, and from it he made him a harp. But when this harp was finished and put in order, and when Craftini commenced to play thereupon, it gave forth sounds which caused all who heard it to think that it uttered the words: "Dá o fill for Labraidh Lorc," that is, "Two horse's ears on Lowry Lorc." And as often as the harp was played upon, it gave forth the same sounds.

Now when the king heard of this he repented him of the numbers he had put to death in order to conceal his deformity; and he forthwith exposed his ears to his household, and never afterwards concealed them.

"That is just a romantic tale," said John Gower, "which some Irish shannachie adapted from the anecdote about Midas."

"Possibly," admitted Harington, "but if I remember correctly, Midas had ass's, not horse's, ears."

"Speaking of intelligent brute beasts," said John Mirk, "I have read somewhere a story which not only illustrates the perspicacity of animals, but which might serve as an example of gratitude to men themselves."

116. THE KNIGHT AND THE LION

John Mirk

Once upon a time a knight was seeking adventures in a far country. It fell out that as he was riding through a great forest he heard lamentations of some animal that seemed to be in distress. He rode in the direction whence the noise came, and saw how a long and thick serpent had entwined a lion, binding him to a tree with his coils as he leaned there to sleep. When the lion had awakened and found himself fast and helpless he made a hideous noise. And when he perceived the knight, he made a still greater noise, as though beseeching help from him.

The knight had compassion on the lion, it is true, and yet he feared that if he freed him, the lion might fall upon him. However, since he was a true knight, and saw that the lion, king of all beasts, was in distress, he drew his sword and cut the serpent in two. As soon as the lion felt himself loosed, he fell down at the knight's feet as meek as a spaniel. And from that hour, night and day, he followed this knight wherever he went, and lay at his feet at night.

In tournament and battle the beast gave such assistance to his master that this knight and his lion were the subject of all men's talk. Nevertheless, by reason of certain men's counsel, he held the lion in some suspicion; wherefor, when he was ready to return to his own country, he got into a ship secretly while the lion slept, and so sailed away. And when the lion awoke and missed his master, he gave a great roar and went after him down to the sea, and swam after the ship as far and as long as he could. Finally his strength failed and he drowned.

"I have always felt sorry for that lion," concluded Mirk.

"Certainly," said Gower, "as you pointed out, the knight himself might have learned something about behaviour from his brute companion."

"My experience of lions has not been so exemplary," put in Gerald. "At Paris I saw a lion which some cardinal had presented to Philip, the son of King Louis, when it was a cub. The lion was in the habit of frequenting the society of a silly girl, named Joan. If, by any chance, it became unruly and infuriated to the extent that no one else could approach it, Joan was called, and the sight and smell of her immediately pacified its rage. Soothed by female allurements, it followed her where she pleased, and immediately changed its fury to love. These brutes, both girl and beast, deserved death according to Leviticus XX, 16. Then, too, I knew of a goat, and a woman who had seduced it to her love. Both the goat and the woman belonged to Ruaidhri, king of Connaught . . ."

At this point Michael O Cleirigh and Geoffrey Keating rose as one man; each seized Gerald by an arm and led him gently but firmly away through the door giving onto the western wall. It was only a moment or two till Geoffrey and Michael came back.

"How is the night outside?" asked someone.

"Wet," said Geoffrey, "very wet."

"And muddy," added Michael.

"That is what I call dirty weather," said Roaring Dick, but nobody laughed at his joke but himself and John the Reeve.

"Master Jehan," said the Minstrel of Reims, "I recollect you said there was tale-telling at the house of the brewy where Lancelot took lodging after slaying the wild cats."

"That is so," answered Jehan.

"Sir knight," said the minstrel, turning to Lancelot, "do you remember any of those tales?"

"Only vaguely," replied Lancelot, wiping his moustaches with the back of his hand. "You must understand that I was forwearied. But the misfortune of the knight who had lost his eye reminded someone of a similar incident in connection with Cranat. Then, too, there was an account of a certain Blái Briuga, and another person related a story about Queen Meave of Connaught. After that I excused myself and went to bed."

"Does anyone here know those tales?" asked the Minstrel.

"I recall the miracle of Cranat's eyes," said Eices ind Righ.

117. THE EYES OF LOVE

Eices ind Righ

About the time when Ida was king of Bernicia, and Gildas was writing his famous Epistle, Cairbre Crom, the son of Crimthann Srem, was king of Munster. In Fermoy Finan was king, and his royal residence was Dun Tulcha Aird. The daughter of his mother was Cranat, and she had her ascetic retreat in the heart of the Black Wood.

Now on a time Cairbre the Crooked came to Dun Tulcha Aird to ask for Cranat's hand in marriage. The suit was pleasing to Finan, and he sent two servants, Cuanir and his brother, to bid Cranat come to speak with Cairbre.

With Cranat were her two novices, Maelbracha and Laithche. They had gone but a short distance with the men when Cranat asked them what was wanted with her at Dun Tulcha Aird. "It will be a long time till you hear that from me," said the one man. "May there be none of your race able to ask tidings," said Cranat, whereupon the man went on ahead in wrath. "What is wanted with me at Dun Tulcha Aird?" she asked Cuanir. Cuanir thought he had better tell her.

They went on after that. In her heart Cranat resolved that she would never violate her virginity, nor come near a man; and she appealed to heaven for aid in this case. In the meantime she herself would do what she could. What she did was this: she tore out both her eyes; one of them she gave into the keeping of Maelbracha, and the other of Laithche. Maelbracha laid up the eye in the bosom of her smock, next to her body; but Laithche put the eye which had been entrusted to her into the fork of a tree, and covered it over with moss.

Cuanir told all this to Finan as he was sitting down to play *fidchell* with Cairbre. The king went to meet Cranat, and saw that Cuanir had told the truth. When the king of Munster was told how things had turned out, he was very angry, and said that Finan should lose his kingdom. Then he went away to Cashel, and asked entertainment from Culcan, the saint of the church there. Culcan offered him a sprig of cress. Cairbre said he would rather fast. "It shall be a perpetual fast," said Culcan. And Cairbre died at Cashel that night.

As for Finan, he humbled himself to Cranat, and gave her his kingdom, in return for which she bestowed great excellences upon him. Then she went till she was at the place now called Scathderc. "Here," said Maelbracha, "your eyes were plucked out." "I need them now," said Cranat. "I have one by me," said Maelbracha. "Put it in my head," said Cranat. Maelbracha put it into her head, and it fitted there as well as it had ever done. "Give me the other eye now," she said to Laithche. The girl took it out of the tree and put it into her head. But the dirt and detritus of the tree adhered to the eye; wherefor, from that out, one of Cranat's eyes always had a fierce look. "Henceforth," said Cranat to Laithche, "your dwelling shall be under leaves and rubbish; but you, Maelbracha, shall be with me both on earth and in heaven."

After this Cranat went back to the Black Wood where she had her hermitage.

"If I knew anything more of the life of Cranat, I would tell it," said Eices.

"That tale has a familiar ring," said John Colgan. "It would seem that your invention is thin, for Brigit, long before Cranat, had recourse to the same expedient when her father Dubthach, and her brothers, wished to marry her to a certain wealthy neighbour of theirs."

"I have heard a similar story," said Étienne de Bourbon, "but with different characters."

"How was that?" asked Colgan.

"They say," answered Étienne, "that one time King Richard of England was much attracted by the looks of a very beautiful nun in the cloister of Fontevrault, but since he could in no manner bend her to the satisfaction of his desire, he threatened to destroy the cloister and bear her away by force. When the nun learned his purpose she was led to inquire what there was about her that so excited his love. Richard replied that above all he was in love with her beautiful eyes. Thereupon the nun, wishing rather to lose her eyes than her virginity, herself tore them out of her head and sent them to Richard on a platter, with the message that he should sate himself with their beauty and leave her in peace."

"Nay," objected King Richard, "Brother Étienne defames me. But, alas! the French never loved me!"

"You must confess, Sire, that you gave them small reason to do so," said William Marshal.

"Perhaps not. However, I never needed to invade the cloister in order to find a bit of amorous interlude," went on Richard. "The good preacher has probably confused me with my brother John."

"Your taste ran rather to secular princesses, did it not?" suggested Higden, "whether Greek, Spanish or German."

"Well," answered Richard, "the German affair was not a matter of choice. I was caught at a disadvantage."

"Indeed?" asked the chronicler. "How was that?"

"Blondel knows the story; perhaps he will tell it and do me more justice than the good Dominican."

"Why should I?" asked Blondel. "You still owe me wages. Let Ambroise tell it."

"Willingly," said Ambroise. "Though Richard owes me wages too...."

"Like father, like son," observed Wace. "Henry still owes me for the *Geste des Bretons* and the *Geste des Normanz*."

"But I have long since learned to expect no reward save in heaven."

Whereupon Ambroise told . . .

118. HOW KING RICHARD WON THE HEART OF MARGERY OF ALMAIN

Ambroise

It is not generally known that before King Richard entered upon the third crusade with the knights of his realm, he had already made a pilgrimage to the Holy Land to spy out the situation from the point of view of military strategy. He and his two fellow palmers, Sir Thomas Multon and Sir Fulk Doyly, had traversed the territory in length and breadth, and were on their way home through Germany. There befell them an adventure from which arose mickle woe.

One night at an inn they were breaking their fast on a pair of roast geese when a minstrel came in and asked if they would be pleased to hear any of his art. For some reason Richard was not in the mood for music, and told the minstrel in vigorous terms to take himself off. "O ye men," said the minstrel, "you are unkind; you badly need a lesson in manners. Do you not know that the courtly bred should offer food and drink to wandering singers? For the fame of the gentleman is in the mouth of the minstrel. I shall remember that you gave me neither meat nor drink."

The gleeman was English, and well he knew by speech, hide and hair that the palmers were English also. He took his way to the castle of the king of Almain, and there he said to the porter: "Go in and tell your king that three of the strongest men of Christendom have come to this land in the guise of palmers. They are King Richard, Sir Fulk Doyly and Sir Thomas Multon."

When King Modard heard this news he was glad indeed. "Ha!" said he, "King Richard is my deadly enemy, and he shall have reason for regret before he leaves my land, so help me God!" Then he sent knights to the hostelry to fetch the palmers. "You must come," said they, "to speak with our king, for he would fain hear tidings of overseas."

"Richard," said the king of Almain, "what are you doing in my lands? It must be that you have come to spy upon me so that you may work me some foul treason." Richard replied mildly that he and his companions were palmers passing through Germany on a pious pilgrimage. But Modard only called him "taylard" and other shameful names, and threatened him with foul imprisonment. "That is not right nor reasonable," objected Richard; "you should do no harm to palmers on their pious journey. I pray you, sir king, of your courtesy, do us no shame. It may chance that you yourself shall someday walk in a strange country." But the German king commanded that they should be thrown into prison, and the sergeant led them away.

Now the king of Germany had a son, named Ardour, who considered himself the best and strongest man in all Germany, and he thought overweeningly that he could put Richard to shame. The next morning he asked the keeper to show him the prisoners. When Richard came out he said: "Are you Richard, the fame of whose strength is in every land? If so, will you stand a buffet from my fist? I give you leave to strike me a blow in return." Richard agreed without hesitation. What else could he do? Then the king's son, keen and proud, gave Richard such a clout that he saw stars. "By Saint Helen!" said the king, "I will pay my buffet tomorrow." Ardour only laughed, but bade the porter give him his fill of meat and drink so that he might not grow too feeble in the meantime.

The next morning Richard rose early, took some wax, and melting it at the fire, waxed his hand thoroughly. Soon came the king's son, like a true man, and stood before Richard to keep his agreement. "Come on, Richard," said he, "as you are a true knight, strike with all your strength; and if I stoop or budge, I hope I may never more bear shield." Thereupon the king laid a buffet on the German prince's cheek such that he brought away skin and flesh and broke the jaw; and Ardour fell down dead as a stone.

A knight hurried off to King Modard and told him these tidings. "Alas!" cried the king, "now I have no son," and fell to the ground in a swoon. "Let be," said the knight; "there is no help for it now." The noise attracted the queen. "Well, now," said she, "what is all this to-do? What is the reason for your sorrow and care?" "Dame," said he, "your fair son has been killed. In all my life I never had such grief. Indeed, I will kill myself, so heavy is my woe." When the queen understood the import of these words, she almost went mad. She gashed herself on the face like a wild woman till it foamed with blood; she tore her robe to strips and wrung her hands. "Alas!" she cried, "and how was my son killed?" "There stands the knight who brought the news," answered Modard; "let him tell."

The knight brought the warden, and he explained the circumstances fully and truly. "Ach!" said the king fiercely, "keep them straitly in prison; and it would be best to put them in fetters, too. If I have my way, Richard shall die for killing my son." The man did as he was commanded, and that day Richard and his companions got neither meat nor drink.

In the meantime the news of Richard's mighty single blow had penetrated to the ladies' bower where the princess Margery was lying at ease among her maids of honour. "Mein Gott!" said Margery;

"what a man! I must have a look at him; if only for silencing an overweening fool—he was always going round flexing his biceps—I must show him some sign of gratitude. If he could floor Ardour with a single blow, he must indeed be a man of excellent parts."

Forthwith she went off to the donjon, and three maids with her. "Warden," said she, "let me see your prisoners at once." "Surely, my lady," said he, and opened the door. Richard was lying on his back, hands behind head, ankles crossed; far be it from me to say what his thoughts were, but he was humming a tune, and seemed unconscious of the presence of visitors. Margery stood in silence for several long moments, letting her eyes wander over his manly form. Finally Richard turned to one side and saw the lady. Immediately he sprang to his feet. Whatever he had been thinking about, it was not about a buxom wench with two thick braids of pale hair dangling to her knees. Margery was tall and straight and high-bosomed, but a little thicker in the waist than our Norman and Gascon maids. Whatever truth there may be in the story about the nun of Fontevrault, it must have been Margery's eyes which brought him to his senses; they were blue, but pale, like her hair, like the ice I have sometimes seen in the fjords of Norway.

"Lady," said Richard, "what is your will with me?" Margery's pale eyes regarded him calmly. "Richard," said she, "save God above I love you most of all things." "Alas!" said Richard; "I am in no position or condition to talk about love. In me you see a poor prisoner, unjustly put under restraint; for two days neither food nor drink has passed our lips." "I will mend all that," replied Margery. "Sergeant," said she, "take the irons off him and his companions and bring him food. After supper dress him up in the garb of a squire and bring him to my chamber. I will take care of him from then on."

The porter did as he was ordered, and brought Richard to Margery's chamber. For a sennight he played that game, coming and going privily, until, on one occasion, a certain knight happened to catch sight of him as he entered Margery's bower. Straightway he hurried to the king with the news that his daughter was forlain. "Ha!" said the king, "and who has done that foul deed?" "Sire," said the knight, "I saw Richard both go and come."

As soon as Modard could speak he summoned clerks and bade them send for his council. In a fortnight the counsellors had assembled, and then King Modard asked them to pass judgment on the traitor Richard, explaining how he had killed his son and forlain his daughter. "I would fain have him dead," said Modard, "but in these days the law says that a king may not be done to death."

The council spent three days wrangling, but could come to no agreement, and they told Modard they could pass no judgment. Then stepped forward Eldrid, a wily knight, and said: "Sire, if you will do according to my judgment, you will neither hang Richard nor draw him, for that is against the law. But take that lion of yours, keep him without food for three days till he is properly hungry, then put him and Richard together in the same room. Thus you shall be rid of your enemy without breaking the law."

Now it came to Margery's ears, through her maid Hildegund, that a treacherous death had been planned for her king. She sent for him at once and laid bare the whole scheme. "Sweetheart," said she, "tonight we will gather together all the treasure in the castle, gold and silver enough to last us for our lifetime, and flee the land." "Nay," said Richard, "it would be discourteous to leave without the king's permission, and I will not so insult him. And as regards th lion, I don't value him as much as a clove of garlic, for I have plan how to kill him. I will make you a present of his heart before prime on the third day. Take supper with me this evening in the tower, and bring forty kerchiefs of white silk with you. Have no care for anything save that the silk be of the best quality."

That night Margery and her two maids went to Richard's tower and supped richly. As the night drew on Sir Fulk and Sir Thomas and the two maids seemed to have mingled with the deeper shadows of the room. But Richard and that sweet bird dwelt together all that night.

In the morning Richard prayed her to wend her way. "Nay," said Margery, "I shall die for my love. If you are killed, I'll wait for my own death right here." "Lady," said the king, "if you do not go away quickly now you will vex me so sorely that I shall never love you more." "Ach! I could not bear that," said Margery; "God be with you and save you if He will."

Richard now took the handkerchiefs and wound them round his right arm, and dressed only in a kirtle, he stood in the middle of the chamber waiting for that fierce mad lion. He had not long to wait. The porter and two others let the lion in to him; its claws were sharp and long. With a roar it sprang upon the man as though it would have swallowed him at a bite. But Richard feinted to one side, and with his left hand gave the lion such a knock on the breast that it spun him around. The lion was lean and hungry and lashed his tail furiously, to whip up his courage. He crouched on all four paws and roared, and as he gaped, Richard thrust his right arm down his throat, rent out the lights, liver and heart, and anything else he could get hold of. The lion's hunger was gone.

Richard was without scratch or wound, and knelt down and thanked God for his delivery. Then he took the heart, warm and still palpitating, and walked unchallenged into the hall where the king had gathered his men. On a dais the king sat at meat with dukes and earls to right and left, in high good humour at the anticipated news of Richard's accident. Before the king stood the salt cellar. There Richard paused, pressed the blood out of the lion's heart, wet the heart in the salt, and ate it down without so much as a crust of bread. Modard and his dukes gaped in wonder. "By God!" said the king, "this man is a devil and no man, though his name be Richard. Since he has eaten my lion's heart, let him be called Richard of the Lion-heart."

While the king and his company sat as though turned to stone, Margery took Richard by the hand and led him out of the hall. Who was a sorry man now but King Modard?

"Well," said Guilhem de Poictiers, "is that all? Don't leave us hanging in mid-air. Richard had given the king of Germany three very bad quarter hours, it is true; but he was still inside the castle, very much a prisoner, if I follow you."

Richard gave a belly laugh. "Prisoner I was indeed," he said; "Lion-heart I may have been; but it was Modard who had the tiger, or rather the lion, by the tail. I was getting plenty of food now, and had a warm fire in my chamber; and Margery was always attentive, though I must confess those pale eyes of hers were beginning to get on my nerves—there was no life in them, if you know what I mean; and her forehead was always shiny. But I had gained every gage so far, and I had no worries about the future. Do you know why? Some time before the affair of the lion I happened to be looking through a loop-hole of the tower, when whom should I see but that rascal Blondel walking beyond the curtain wall. We made ourselves known to each other— But that is another story; perhaps he will condescend to tell that tale, since it is something to his own credit. Hey, Blondel!"

But the trouvère did not reply, and with good reason. In the embrasure of one of the north windows he and Jehan Madot were throwing dice, while John the Reeve, Roaring Dick, Unibos, Beryn and Richard Sheale looked on with interest. Already he had lost his coat and mantle in pledge to Martin Scabby for some ready money, and the sweat stood out on his forehead in spite of the brisk air.

"Hey, Blondel!" bellowed Richard. And at that moment the unhappy poet threw "hasart"!

"With your permission, Sire, I will tell the tale," said the Minstrel of Reims.

"As you will," answered Richard; "nothing can be expected from Blondel in the present circumstances."

119. HOW BLONDEL FOUND KING RICHARD IN GERMANY

The Minstrel of Reims

After a reasonable length of silence the barons of England and the families of Sir Fulk and Sir Thomas began to be uneasy as to the whereabouts of Richard and his two companions. No news had been heard of them since they had left Tripoli. Now, as you know, Richard had reared up in his household a minstrel named Blondel. This man determined to wander through all lands in search of his king until he should get sure news of him; and he was helped to this decision not so much by patriotism and affection as by the fact that Richard owed him wages.

Blondel took to the road and travelled hither and yon through the countries of Europe for a year and a half without hearing the slightest news of the king. Finally Fortune brought him to Germany, and as chance would have it, he went to the very castle wherein the king was imprisoned, though he was, of course, ignorant of that fact. He took lodgings with a widow dwelling near by and inquired who was lord of that strong and well-placed castle. His hostess replied that it belonged to the king of Germany, and that the present châtelain was the duke of Austria. "Good hostess," asked Blondel, "are there any prisoners lodged in it just now?" "Certes," said the good woman, "yes; there has been one there for four years, but we could never find out his identity, for you must know that he is very carefully guarded. We have come to the conclusion that he is a gentleman or a great lord."

When Blondel heard this his heart was marvellously lightened, for it seemed to him probable that he had at last found what he was looking for; but he was careful not to allow the hostess to observe his joy. That night he slept well for the first time in many days, and when the watch cried the hour of daybreak, he went to the church to pray God to aid him. Afterwards he strolled to the castle and struck up an acquaintance with the châtelain, saying that he was a minstrel and would gladly remain with him for a time, if he wished. The châtelain was a gay young blade, and answered that he would willingly retain him. You may be sure that Blondel was well pleased at this, and he went off to fetch his viol and other gear. So well and so long did he serve the châtelain and the others within the castle that he was well regarded by all the meiny.

Blondel spent the winter in this way without hearing so much as a whisper concerning the identity of the prisoner in the tower. One day, about Easter, he was walking up and down in the inner ward near the tower, looking about him sharply if he might by chance catch a glimpse of the prisoner. It happened by the greatest good fortune that at that very moment King Richard looked out through an archer's loop-hole, and saw his minstrel walking up and down. Blondel could not, of course, see his master behind the narrow slit, and the king bethought himself how he might make known his presence and identity. Then he recalled the words and tune of a *canso* which he and Blondel had composed together, and which was known to no one but the two of them; so he sang the first stanza loud and clear, for he had a good singing voice. When Blondel heard that song, he knew for a surety that his lord was behind the wall, and his heart was flooded with joy to think that he might get his back wages after all. He returned quickly to his chamber, took his viol and began to play the music of the song Richard had sung. Thus things remained till Pentecost, and so well did Blondel bear himself that no one perceived anything of the matter.

Finally, when the weather had cleared somewhat and the roads were again fit for travelling, Blondel went to the châtelain and said: "Lord, if you would give me leave, I should very much like to be on my way, for it is a long time since I saw my own country." "Blondel, my good fellow," replied the baron, "don't be in a hurry; wait a little yet, and it shall be to your profit." "Indeed, my lord," said Blondel, "I certainly will not stay." When the duke saw that he could not retain him, he gave him permission to go, and presented him with a rouncy and a new robe.

Blondel travelled with what speed he was able to make till he reached England, and told the friends and barons of the king how he had found him in prison in Germany. This news was an occasion for great rejoicing—save on the part of Prince John. In council the magnates decided to send ambassadors to treat with the German king about the ransom.

When the messengers reached the castle of the Duke of Austria they said: "My lord, news has reached us that you hold King Richard prisoner, and we beg that your royal master may be pleased to accept ransom for him; and he may make his own terms." The duke said he would seek counsel.

In the course of a few days the duke returned to the ambassadors and said: "Gentlemen, if you want the king's body, you shall pay a ransom of 200,000 marks sterling. Take it or leave it." The Englishmen held council with the barons at home, and in due time the money was collected and turned over to the duke. After subtracting a middleman's fee of twenty per cent the duke turned the ransom money over to his royal master, and delivered King Richard to his friends. I daresay Richard was glad to have a change of scene, for he had never remained in one place so long before.

"It is true," said Richard, "that the ransom amounted to 200,000 marks in money, but when Modard was informed of the ambassadors' petition he spoke in other terms.—'That strong traitor Richard has wrought me mickle woe,' he said [Richard chuckled], 'but since I may not do him to death, I will take ransom for his body, and indemnity for the shame he has done my daughter. And this shall be his ransom: From every church in England where there are two chalices, I shall have one of them; and if there be more than two, the half shall come to me. When I get that, Richard shall be delivered.'"

At the mention of money Martin Scabby had drawn near. "Two hundred thousand marks sterling!" he exclaimed. "If I had been your broker in the matter, I could have saved you something and died a richer man myself."

"It is obvious," said Giovanni Villani, "that you know not the ways of kings. The Bardi and Peruzzi, Florentine bankers, once loaned Edward III the sum of 1,365,000 gold florins, each twenty-four carats fine. I would not venture to estimate the equivalent of this sum in English money—some say £4,000,000; at all events, the worth of a kingdom. After the battle of Crécy they had good hopes of recovering their money, but King Edward had other ideas. Later, I understand, he was able to make a present of 21,868 large pearls to Alice Perrers. However, the king's nonchalance in money matters ruined not only the Bardi and Peruzzi, but their depositors as well; and the fall of these two columns of mercantile credit crushed all the smaller houses, and imposed great hardships on the commune of Florence."

Martin Scabby's eyes glistened. "What a pleasure just to try to imagine such amounts of money!" he said.

"Of course Edward surpassed me," admitted Richard, "but wealth had increased by his day. My own £300,000 was a tidy sum for those times, and was a delicate testimony of the esteem in which I was held by both friends and enemies. St Louis of France never brought half that price to the Saracens of Egypt, I am told. Best of all, I got the money back again, for as soon as I could collect men, I went to Cologne and had a heart to heart talk with Modard. He was glad to make restitution—and something more."

"Did you see Margery again at Cologne?" asked Christine de Pisan.

"Oh, yes," replied Richard; "we had a rendezvous. But my favorite falcon fell sick and I could not go. Blondel went. I have never been in Germany since."

"An irresistible attraction for the ladies seems to be an hereditary trait in our family," remarked Guilhem de Poictiers. "I suppose you also inherit some of my grand-daughter's sex appeal as well as my own virility. Margery had you at considerable disadvantage, I must admit. But what was the aftermath of the meeting at Cologne? I believe that I handled things better in my day."

"We should be glad to hear," said the Goodman of Bath.

120. TWO LUSTY LADIES OF AUVERGNE AND THEIR CAT
Guilhem IX

One day I was riding quietly along in Auvergne, beyond Limousin, when I met the wife of Sir Garin and the wife of Sir Bernard. They greeted me courteously in the name of St Leonard, and one of them said in her dialect: "God save you, sir pilgrim; you seem to me to be a proper kind of man, and yet one can never tell, for the world is full of fools."

Now what did I say to this? I replied neither *but* nor *bat,* but only babbled *babariol, babariol, babarian.* Then said Agnes to Hermessen: "Ha! we have found just the fellow for whom we have been looking. For the love of God, sister mine, let us offer him our hospitality, for he is certainly a deaf-mute, and will never be able to report the matter."

Thereupon one of them threw her mantle over me and led me into her chamber where a cheery blaze was going in the fire-place. That was indeed a welcome change from the drizzle outside. By the time I had well warmed myself they had prepared a meal of fat capons, more than a brace. There was neither cook nor scullion present—only the three of us. The bread was white, the wine strong, and there was pepper in abundance.

All seemed to be going as well as a man could hope when one of the ladies said: "Sister mine, perhaps this man is fooling us, and only pretends he is unable to speak. Fetch our red cat: he'll make him talk, if, indeed, he is only feigning." So Agnes brought in the huge foul creature with long moustaches. When I saw him my intention faltered, and I almost lost my courage. However, after we had eaten and drunk, I took off my jerkin, as they bade me; and while I was not looking, one of them seized the wicked creature by the tail and dragged him across my naked back from the nape to the heel. In that moment I got a hundred wounds, you may be sure; but I would not have uttered a sound if they had killed me. "Sister," said Agnes to Hermessen, "he really is dumb. Let us make the bath ready now and enjoy ourselves."

For a whole week I remained with the charming ladies to our mutual satisfaction multiplied by 188. The wounds inflicted by the wretched cat healed, but not the memory of them. Back in Poictiers again, I made a poem about the whole affair and sent it to the ladies with the compliments of the Duke of Aquitaine. Love, as you know, was always a joy to me.

"Your Grace," said Ralph Higden, "though it happened long before the time with which I am most familiar, I cannot say that I am surprised at your adventure, for I have read some curious things about Auvergne. Among other matters one of my authorities says that Auvergne was the district which principally harboured and suffered from a great company of men-at-arms of divers nationalities; and though they were called a host without a head, their chiefs, I am sorry to say, were frequently Englishmen. These companies, says my author, wasted France greatly, and occupied many towns and castles in it, in spite of the efforts of the king of France and others to expel them."

"What you say is true," said Froissart. "But Auvergne and Limousin were not the only districts ravaged by those men, nor were the leaders always English. There were, of course, such captains as Ruffin the Welshman, Sir Robert Knolles and Sir John Hawkwood. But probably you refer to the circumstances which prevailed toward the close of Pope Innocent IV's pontificate at Avignon. At that time there was a certain knight, Sir Arnold de Cervole by name, who caused the pope much alarm by his reiving in Provence. In the north there was another company of men-at-arms—robbers collected from all parts—who stationed themselves between the Loire and the Seine so that no one dared to travel between Paris and Orléans. This company had chosen as their leader the Welshman Ruffin or Griffin, whom they knighted, and who by his depredations acquired such immense riches as could not be counted.

"On the sea coast of Normandy there was a still greater number of English and Navarrois, plunderers and robbers. Their leader was Sir Robert Knolles, who conquered every town and castle he came to, as there was none to oppose him. Sir Robert followed this trade for some time, and by it he gained upwards of 100,000 crowns.

"However, if you are interested, I will tell you something about these Free Companies, as they were called, and also relate an incident concerning one of their captains who operated in the district alluded to by Higden."

"Pray do so," cried King Richard and his father in unison.

121. THE FREEBOOTERS OF AUVERGNE

Jean Froissart

After the Peace of Brétigny and the return of Jean le Bon to France, the king, according to the articles of peace, dispatched commissioners ordering all men-at-arms who were garrisoned in the different castles and forts of France, to evacuate and surrender them to the king of France under pain of confiscation and death. Some of the knights and squires of the English side obeyed, but there were others, partisans of the king of Navarre, who would not surrender. There were also some from various lands who would not on any account leave the country: such as Germans, Brabanters, Flemings, Hainaulters, Gascons and bad Frenchmen, who had been impoverished by the war. These persons persevered in their wickedness, and afterwards did much mischief to the kingdom.

When the captains of the forts, in accordance with the king's orders, delivered them up and dismissed their men, these others, knowing well that their return home would not be advantageous to them, and that they might perhaps suffer for the bad actions they had committed, assembled together and chose new leaders from the worst-disposed among them.

They made their first stand in Champagne, using the castle of Joinville as their headquarters. From here they scoured the country and got together about 100,000 francs. Then they entered Burgundy, plundering and despoiling the land everywhere. Their numbers were continually increasing, for those who quitted the castles and towns on their being surrendered, and those who were disbanded by their captains, came to those parts, so that by Lent these companies numbered at least 16,000 combatants. When they found their numbers so great, they appointed many captains, all of whom they obeyed implicitly. Among these captains were Tallabaton, Guyot du Pin, Le Petit Mechin, Le Bourg de l'Espare, Le Bourg de la Salle, Robert Briquet, Abrethoury the Scot, Carnelle, Bourdonnelle the German, Aimenon d'Ortige, L'Ortingo de la Salle, and many others.

When the king of France, Jean le Bon, heard how these freebooting troops overran and pillaged his kingdom, he was mightily enraged. The council informed his majesty that unless these bands were repressed they would multiply so greatly, and do so much mischief that France would suffer as much from them as during the war with the English. Accordingly the king commissioned Lord James de Bourbon to proceed against the freebooters. This my lord James did with good will, for he had always served the king faithfully. However, he made the mistake of attacking the companies when they were in a strong position at the top of a flinty hill. Without making a long story of it, the French were completely worsted, and Lord James was so severely wounded that he died on the third day following the battle. This was the Battle of Brignais, fought on the Friday after Easter in the year 1361.

The freebooters of course rejoiced at the fortunate issue of the engagement. They had been great gainers, as well by what they had seized on the spot, as from the ransoms of their wealthy prisoners. They now separated into two divisions, the smaller being commanded by Sir Seguin de Bastefol. He devoted his attention to the region between Lyons and Nevers. The other division, under the command of Carnelle, Robert Briquet, Ortingo and Bernard de la Salle, Le Bourg de l'Esparre, and many others, said they would go to Avignon to visit the pope and cardinals, and have some of their money; otherwise they should be well vexed.

On their way south the companions got information that very great wealth had been assembled at the castle of Pont du St Esprit, seven leagues from Avignon. They thought the possession of this town would make them masters of the Rhône as well as of Avignon, so Guyot du Pin and Le Petit Mechin set off with their companies. After riding fifteen leagues they came at break of day to St Esprit, which they took, and all those of both sexes who were therein. It was a pitiful sight, for they plundered many a decent man, and violated many a virgin. After this they collected their companies and continued their march toward Avignon.

Pope Innocent VI and the Roman College now saw themselves threatened by these accursed people. They were exceedingly alarmed, and ordered a crusade to be published against those wicked Christians who were doing everything in their power to destroy Christianity by ruining all the countries whither they resorted, by robbing wherever they could find anything, by violating women both young and old without pity, and by killing men, women and children without mercy, who had done no ill to them; for he was reckoned the bravest and most honoured who could boast of the most villainous actions.

Now it happened that the pope and cardinals cast their eyes upon a very accomplished knight and a good warrior, that is to say, upon the Marquis of Montferrat, who for a long time had been engaged in war against the lords of Milan, and was at this time so employed. With him they entered into a treaty whereby, in exchange for a considerable sum of money, he engaged to free the district of these freebooting companies, and lead them into Lombardy. The marquis negotiated with the captains of the companies, and managed so well that by means of the sixty thousand florins which he divided among them, and the high pay he promised them, they consented to follow him into Lombardy. But they also insisted on receiving pardon and absolution from all crimes and sin. When these articles were fulfilled, they gave up the town of St Esprit, quitted the territory of Avignon, and marched away with the Marquis of Montferrat.

Among these leaders was the right valiant English knight Sir John Hawkwood, who received for himself and his troops ten of the sixty thousand florins. At the time of the Peace of Brétigny he had been a poor knight who thought there would be no advantage in returning home. When he saw that by the treaties all men-at-arms would be forced to leave France, he put himself at the head of those free companies called "late-comers," and marched into Burgundy. Hawkwood was one of the principal leaders, with Briquet and Carnelle, by whom the battle of Brignais had been fought, and who had aided Bernard de la Salle to take the Pont du St Esprit. When the war against Milan had been concluded, Sir John Hawkwood remained in Italy, where he performed many most gallant deeds of arms.

The agreement between the pope and the Marquis of Montferrat did not, however, empty France entirely of these pillagers; many still remained to harry and devastate the country. Among these was a Breton called Geoffrey Tête Noire. This Geoffrey was a wicked man; he showed mercy to none, and would just as soon put to death a knight or a squire as a peasant. His headquarters was the castle of Ventadour, one of the strongest castles in the world, on the borders of Auvergne and the Bourbonnais, from which he had evicted the old Count Montpensier de Ventadour. In this stronghold he maintained fully four hundred men, whom he paid regularly every month. The whole country was under such subjection and awe of him that none dared to ride over his lands. His castle of Ventadour was more largely supplied with every sort of stores than that of any other lord. There were warehouses of Brussels and Normandy cloths, of furs, of merceries and other articles, which he sold to his people, deducting the price from their pay. He had stores of steel, iron, wax, spices and every necessity, in as great plenty as could be found at Paris. Sometimes he made war on the English as well as on the French, in order to be the more dreaded. And his castle of Ventadour was always provided for a siege of seven years.

With Geoffrey Tête Noire there were other captains, who performed many excellent deeds of arms, such as Aymerigot Marcel, a Limousin squire attached to the English party, who took the strong castle of Cassuriel, situated in the bishopric of Clermont in Auvergne. From there he and his companions overran the country at their pleasure. It is about the fate of this Aymerigot that I intend to tell you.

In 1388, as you know, a truce of three years was arranged between France and England. This was a godsend to the peasants and small folk; but for the knights and squires, whose opportunities for engaging in adventures and splendid feats of arms were thus abolished by law, time passed wearily. Under such circumstances you can imagine the eagerness with which the knights of France, England and some other countries accepted the invitation of the Genoese to undertake an expedition against the kingdom of Barbary. Fourteen hundred knights and squires set out in galleys on St John's day, 1390.

During the time of the assembly of this body of men-at-arms in France for the expedition to extend the Christian faith and gain renown, there were another sort of men-at-arms wholly given up to plunder in Limousin, Auvergne and Rouergue, who, in spite of the truce, were continually doing mischief in these districts. The king of France had caused the truce to be publicly notified to the captains of the freebooters, particularly to Perrot le Béarnois, governor of Chalucet, Olim Barbe, captain of Donzac in Auvergne, and Aymerigot Marcel, who were personally named in the act; and they were assured that if the truce were in the smallest way infringed, those guilty should be corporally punished without hope of mercy. This was done that there might not be any excuse made from ignorance of the treaty.

Some of the captains kept the peace well; others did not. John, Count of Armagnac, and the Dauphin of Auvergne laboured hard to win over these captains so that the country might be at peace; and to this end a sum of 200,000 francs had been assessed in Auvergne, Cahorsin and Limousin. The tax pressed so hard on rich and poor that men were forced to sell their inheritance to obtain peace. They imagined that having paid such sums they would remain unmolested by these robbers; but it was not so in many places, more especially in those parts where Aymerigot Marcel had his garrison. Notwithstanding the fact that he had surrendered his castle of Aloise in the heart of Auvergne, he continued to do much mischief to the inhabitants. He was so rich as to be able to pay down 100,000 francs for his ransom, if necessary, which sum he had gained by plunder during the ten years he had carried on his trade.

But it was not long till Aymerigot repented that he had parted with the castle of Aloise, for by its loss he felt that the respect and dread which the country cherished for him was diminished. At times he used to repine with his companions something in this manner: "There is no pleasure or glory in the world similar to that which such men-at-arms as ourselves enjoyed. How happy we were, when riding out in search of adventures, to meet a rich abbot, a merchant or a string of mules well laden with draperies, furs or spices. All was our own, or at least ransomed according to our will. The peasants of Auvergne and Limousin loved us, and provided our castle with corn, meal, baked bread, litter for our horses, oats, hay, good wine, fat beeves, sheep and all sorts of poultry. We lived like kings, and when we rode abroad the country trembled. Everything was ours, both in going and returning. By my troth, this was a profitable and pleasant life."

Among his companions there were those who were ready enough to return to the old way of life, and by their advice and with their assistance that is what Aymerigot did. He and his companions took possession of a dismantled fort called La Roche de Vendais, a mesne fief on Limoges, and by degrees restored it to good repair. When they had made it sufficiently strong, they began to overrun the immediate neighbourhood, making prisoners and ransoming them. They laid in stores of flesh and wine, iron, steel and other necessaries; nothing, indeed, came amiss to them that was not too hot or too heavy.

The inhabitants of the country were astonished at this turn of events, for they had considered themselves secure on account of the truce. But the robbers seized whatever they pleased in their houses or in the fields, calling themselves "The Adventurers." When the disbanded men, who were now out of pay, heard of these doings, they rejoiced greatly and flocked to Aymerigot's standard in such numbers that he soon had more than he wanted. Nothing was talked of in Auvergne and Limousin but the robbers of La Roche de Vendais, and greatly was the country terrorized by them.

But the good people did not bear this burden quietly. They sent a deputation to Paris to complain to the king, the Duke of Berry and Sir Oliver de Clisson. The king and his council did not delay in attending to the business, and to the Viscount of Meaux was assigned the task of chastising Aymerigot.

Whether from pilgrims, spies or others, Aymerigot learned that a large body of men was marching against him, and he repented of what he had done. He knew that if he was taken no ransom would be accepted for his life. "I have taken bad advice," he said, "and avarice will be my ruin." But he took care to send the greater part of his wealth to another fort near by, Saint Soupery, where his wife resided.

The siege of La Roche Vendais lasted nine weeks. During this time Aymerigot, who was a vassal of the English king, determined to seek English mediation so that at least La Roche might be preserved to him. His messenger did, indeed, reach England, and spoke to such purpose that both the king and the Duke of Lancaster promised to intercede. Letters from both the king and his uncle were returned by Aymerigot's messenger to the Viscount of Meaux and the Duke of Berry, complaining that the viscount was wrongfully occupying English territory and molesting an English subject, and bidding the viscount raise the siege at once.

These letters made no impression on the viscount, so the messengers took their way to the Duke of Berry. The duke's affection for his English cousins was such that he was persuaded to comply with their request, and he wrote to the Viscount of Meaux, bidding him raise the siege. When the viscount had read the duke's letter he said: "Gentlemen, the duke commands me to raise the siege, but by my faith, I will do no such thing, for if the duke supports Aymerigot, we shall never have peace."

Finding that his plan had failed, Aymerigot now set out secretly to try to get aid in Périgord and other places, leaving his uncle Guyot du Sel in command of La Roche. Before going he laid particular strictures on his uncle never to sally out or open the barriers. "It shall be so," said Guyot. "I will remain shut up here till you return."

La Roche continued to be assaulted as usual, and one day Guyot, forgetful of his promise, sallied forth, was surprised by an ambuscade, and obliged to surrender the castle. News of the loss of La Roche was carried to Aymerigot as he was raising troops to break up the siege. On learning that the castle had been lost through the imprudence of Guyot du Sel he exclaimed: "Ah, the old traitor! By Saint Marcel! if I had him here I would slay him. He has shamed me and all my companions. This loss can never be recovered, nor do I know whither to make my retreat. Considering all things, I am in a distressing situation. I have too greatly angered the king of

France, the Duke of Berry and the barons of Auvergne to expect any favour, for I have made war on them during the truce, thinking to gain; but now I am more likely to lose everything. I wish my wife, myself and my fortune were at this moment in England, where we should be safe. But how the devil to get there? I have forfeited my life, that is clear; and if I am taken and sent to Paris, I shall be punished accordingly, and lose my all. My safest plan will be to make for Bordeaux, and have my wealth conveyed there little by little, and then remain there as long as the truce holds; for I am in hopes that after these truces—a curse on them!—the war will be renewed with more vigour than ever between France and England."

If Aymerigot had followed this plan he would have done well, but he acted otherwise, and, as the events will show, suffered for it. It is thus that Fortune treats her favourites: when she has raised them to the highest point of her wheel, she then suddenly plunges them in the dirt. In one day the foolish Aymerigot lost both his hundred thousand francs and his life. So I say that Dame Fortune played him one of her tricks, such as she had played on others before, and she will do the same for many after him.

In the midst of his tribulation the thought came to Aymerigot that he would go to his cousin-german, a squire called Tournemine, and ask his advice. He thought to be well received on account of the relationship, but he was disappointed. Tournemine was hated by the Duke of Berry, as he well knew; so when Aymerigot entered his castle and laid aside his arms, Tournemine arrested him as a traitor who had broken the truce, alleging that it was on his account that the Duke of Berry hated him. Aymerigot was seized, fetters were placed on his legs, and he was confined under safe guard in a strong tower.

Tournemine wrote the duke, offering him the person of Aymerigot in return for his amity. The duke laid the matter before the king and his council, who decided that Aymerigot should be brought to Paris and delivered over to the provost of the Châtelet, who would take good care of him. And so it was done.

Aymerigot offered sixty thousand francs for his pardon, but no one would have anything to do with him; he was told that the king was rich enough and wanted not his money.

There was no delay in his trial, and he was condemned to a shameful death as a traitor to the crown of France. First he was carried in a cart to the pillory in the market-place, and turned round within it several times. His different crimes, for which he was to receive death, were read aloud. Then his head was cut off, and his four quarters were hung over four different gates of Paris.

Such was the end of Aymerigot Marcel; but I know not what became of his wife or his wealth.

"A rich widow does not go begging," observed the Goodman of Paris, "and I think you need be under no apprehension as to her fate."

"Thank you, Sir Jean," said Higden. "I had but a vague idea of these matters, and of course most of what you have related occurred after my time."

"Outrages by such strong-armed ruffians were not unknown in my country," said Sir David Lindsay, "at least up to the time of James I. No king ever loved his country and his people as did he, and the reforms he instituted were designed for the lasting benefit of the kingdom. No sooner had James accepted the crown when he made firm peace everywhere. Neither the magnates nor the smaller folk dared to rage among themselves as they had been wont to do —like the Clan Quhele and the Clan Kay. Everywhere, to the farthest bounds of the kingdom, tumults and disorders were put down, for there was no malefactor so high-hearted as to dare to ignore James' commands. If anyone proved obstinate, he suffered punishment without delay."

"I remember very well," said Hector Boëce, "an incident which illustrates what you say; it happened soon after James came to the throne, and proved that the tender lover could also be a stern man of justice. If the company please I will tell about it."

"Pray do so," said Thomas Gascoigne.

122. THE WIDOW WHO WORE HORSESHOES

Hector Boëce

Beyond the mountains, in Ross, there dwelt a famous cateran named MacDonald, the greatest oppressor of his time, whether of rich or poor, in despite of any law. Near the field of his operations there lived a poor widow who had the courage to withstand him. From her he reived two cows. She, lamenting her loss and being refused restitution, swore she would never wear shoes again till she had laid her complaint before the king. "You lie," said MacDonald; "I will help you on your way to the king by having you well shod." Forthwith he took a hammer and nails, and to the soles of the woman's feet he affixed two horseshoes, driving the nails through flesh and bone and clinching them. "Now," said he, "these shoes will protect your feet from bruises as you go along, whether by road or street."

The widow somehow made her way to the king and related

the facts all in order, showing the wounds in her feet as evidence. James straightway sent a message to the sheriff in whose district the ruffian lived, and he, with nine or ten of his fellows, was brought in bonds to Perth. The king flung him into prison, where he remained a good while, until the widow's feet were completely healed and she was able to walk again without pain. Then, convicted of robbery and malfeasance, the king ordered that MacDonald should be dressed in a tunic whereon was painted a picture of himself nailing the horseshoes to the woman's feet, and thus dressed, he and his fellows be led with tongs and pincers through the streets of the city as a spectacle for the people. Afterwards he should be dragged at the tail of a horse. When this had been done, MacDonald was brought to the market-place and hanged on the gallows; or, as some say, beheaded, and his head set on a pole. Afterwards, with the approbation of all, his companions were strung up on gibbets. Such was the swift justice of the poet-king James I.

"A dastard's blood," said John Major, "would never have been allowed to stain steel. It was a rope that met MacDonald's neck, not a sword. Moreover, it was not a picture of his horseshoeing prowess which he carried up and down the streets of Perth, but the very horseshoes which he had nailed to the widow's feet, now nailed to his own."

"Your cateran," spoke up Caesar of Heisterbach, "probably received due punishment, whether by rope or steel, according to the requirements of the temporal law; but I have no doubt that his soul went to hell, where it received its real or adequate punishment—if we can draw any inferences from the case of Elias of Rheinbeck. That knight, who had been burgrave of Horst, was seen in the abode of pain by a certain usurer named Gottschalk. He was seated, facing the tail, upon a mad heifer that plunged and reared and dashed here and there, pausing now and then to throw up her head and gore knight Elias in the kidneys. 'Why are you tormented thus?' asked Gottschalk. 'Because,' answered Elias, 'I had no pity on the poor widow from from I wrested this beast, and now I must pitilessly endure these thrusts from her horns.'"

"Right you are," agreed the Curtal Friar, "and yet it is not always necessary for justice to be done in hell, or even on the scaffold. The weak often have a weapon with which to defend themselves; force frequently finds itself at a disadvantage in a contest with wit, as Monk Eustace has already shown. An exercise of wit, for example, may save the owner his property, and the would-be aggressor from sin, as I will show by the tale of . . ."

123. THE CRAFTY FARMER

The Curtal Friar

The song that I'm going to sing—
I hope it will give you content—
Concerning a silly old man,
That was going to pay his rent.

As he was riding along,
Along all on the highway,
A gentleman thief overtook him,
And thus to him did say.

"Well overtaken," said the thief,
"Well overtaken," said he;
And "Well overtaken," said the old man,
"If thou be good company."

"How far are you going this way?"
Which made the old man for to smile;
"By my faith," said the old man,
"I'm just going two mile.

"I am a poor farmer," he said,
"And I farm a piece of ground,
And my half year's rent, kind sir,
Just comes to forty pound.

"And my landlord has not been at home,
I've not seen him this twelvemonth or more,
Which makes my rent be large—
I've to pay him just four score."

"Thou shouldst not have told any body,
For thieves there's ganging many;
If any should light on thee,
They'll rob thee of thy money."

"Oh, never mind," said the old man,
"Thieves I fear on no side,
For the money is safe in my bags,
On the saddle on which I ride."

As they were riding along,
The old man was thinking no ill;

THE CRAFTY FARMER

The thief he pulled out a pistol,
And bid the old man stand still.

But the old man prov'd crafty,
As in the world there's many;
He threw his saddle o'er the hedge,
Saying, "Fetch it if thou'lt have any."

The thief got off his horse,
With courage stout and bold,
To search for the old man's bag,
And gave him his horse to hold.

The old man put's foot i' the stirrup,
And he got on astride;
To its side he clapped his spur up,
You need not bid the old man ride.

"Oh, stay!" said the thief, "Oh, stay!
And half the share thou shalt have."
"Nay, by my faith!" said the old man,
"For once I have bitten a knave."

This thief he was not content,
But he thought there must be bags;
He out with his rusty old sword,
And chopt the old saddle in rags.

When he came to the landlord's house,
This old man he was almost spent;
Saying, "Come, show me a private room,
And I'll pay you a whole year's rent.

"I've met a fond fool by the way,
I swapt horses and gave him no boot;
But never mind," said the old man,
"For I got the fond fool by the foot."

He open'd this rogue's portmantle,
It was glorious to behold;
There were three hundred pounds in silver,
And three hundred pounds in gold.

And as he was riding home,
And down a narrow lane,

He espied his mare tied to a hedge,
Saying, "Prithee, Tib, wilt thou gang hame?"

When he got home to his wife
And told her what he had done,
Up she rose and put on her clothes,
And about the house did run.

She sung and she sung and she sung,
She sung with a merry devotion,
Saying: "If ever our daughter gets wed,
It will help to enlarge her portion."

"Ach! my friend," exclaimed Unibos, "you are right. Always I have thought that it is the clever man who comes out. From a boy even have I tried to have brains, for my father used to say: 'Hans,' said he, 'it is brains that makes the mare go round.'"

This speech was not entirely intelligible to some members of the audience till Fynes Moryson, who had been in Germany, came to the rescue. "He means, I think, that the destiny of the world is in the end shaped by ideas."

"Yes, yes, that is it," cried Unibos. "Of the world I know nothing, but of myself, yes."

Harington: Perhaps that is not an unmixed blessing, or even definitely a blessing. We cannot tell yet what the destiny of the world will be. The year 1,000 passed, and nothing happened except that King Olaf lost the battle of Svold, and Pope Sylvester acknowledged Duke Stephen to be king of Hungary. John Ball and Wat Tyler had some ideas; but we want no more of that kind, I think.

Machiavelli: True enough. Cola di Rienzo had an idea, but after a time the people of Rome had a different one, and he lost his life in a street riot.

Fortescue: Jeanne Darc's idea led her no farther than the stake.

Machiavelli: Savonarola followed an equally selfless idea, of which today the only commemoration is a brass medallion in the Piazza della Signoria.

Harington: I myself once had an idea about Ireland, but it came to nothing. Prince Henry of Portugal and Cristóbal Colón had ideas, and who can say that in the end they will not prove as disastrous —for the destiny of the world—as those of Guy Fawkes might have been?

Roger Bacon: It is obvious that ideas have to be tried before it can be determined whether they are good or bad.

Langland: Perhaps the difficulty lies not so much with ideas as with men.

Machiavelli: One must confess that if the world was not ready for Cola di Rienzo's idea, no more was he fit to execute it.

"William Wallace had an idea," said John of Fordun quietly, "which in the end contributed largely toward the liberation of Scotland from the heel of the invader."

Sir Thomas Gray would have said something in reply to this, but was stopped by a faint smile in Snorri Sturlason's eyes.

"I was only thinking," said Snorri, "that ages ago the mythologists of my race had the best idea of all."

"What was that?" asked Thomas Gascoigne.

"Ragnarök."

"That seems very terrible," said Adamnan.

"And yet in your vision you saw the alternative," answered Snorri.

"Your poets may prove to be right," said Marsiglio of Padua, "unless in the meantime we can improve the quality both of men and their ideas, as Langland said."

"What is your experience of the matter, Herr Meier?" inquired Fynes Moryson.

"Of the world I know nothing," replied Unibos, "but of myself, yes. I tell you how I come out, no?"

This proposal aroused consternation among some of the guests, and there was many an anxious glance till Fynes Moryson again came to the rescue. With the traveller acting in the rôle of interpreter Unibos was understood to tell . . .

124. THE STORY OF A SELF-MADE MAN

Unibos

My real name is Mistmeier, but people call me Unibos, that is, One-ox; and I will tell you why. When I started out in life I used to plough my fields with oxen, but jealous Fortune, who interferes in the affairs of small men as well as of great, denied me the privilege of possessing more than one ox at a time. However many I bought, one of two always died, or was killed by wild beasts. Hence my good neighbours jeered at me with the name Unibos.

One time when an ox had died on me, I took the hide to market to try to get something for it; no one would offer me more than eight pence, so I took that. On my way home I tarried a while in the forest. On rising to go, I stretched out my hand to one side, but instead of leaves or grass, my hand fell upon three pots of gold. I had no idea of the extent of my good fortune, so when I arrived home I sent my boy to the burgomaster to borrow his official measure, so that I might make an exact reckoning of my money.

My request aroused no little surprise in the burgomaster's mind, and he wondered how a man who had always been so poor should suddenly need a peck measure for estimating his wealth. He brought the measure himself, and when he saw my gold he accused me of having stolen it. His attitude and his suspicion did not please me particularly; moreover, he had always been among those who had laughed the loudest when an ox of mine had died; so I told him that the gold was the proceeds from the sale of an oxhide at the market. The mayor was apparently not quite convinced of the truth of this statement, for he went off to confer with his cronies, the steward and the parish priest.

What talk these three had I do not know, but the upshot of it was that all three decided to slaughter their cattle and sell the hides, so that they might become as rich as I was. Off they went to market with their load of hides, and spent a great part of the day waiting unsuccessfully for buyers. Finally a dirty cobbler came up and cautiously priced their wares. Three pounds per hide, said they. The cobbler laughed in their faces and asked if they were drunk. Now these respectable personages were not accustomed to such an attitude on the part of an inferior, and some words passed back and forth. The bystanders took the cobbler's part, and scoffed at the merchants derisively. They grew angry, and words passed into deeds, with the result that the three were haled into court. There the judges asserted their ancient prerogative of interpreting the law in a manner most profitable to themselves, and whatever loose money my estimable co-villagers had about them was transferred from their pouches to those of the court. In a towering rage they abandoned their hides in the market-place and went home with empty pockets, swearing that my death should wipe out the ignominy they had suffered.

My boy, who had kept watch on them, told me all this, so that by the time they had reached my cottage I was prepared for them. I made my wife smear herself with pig's blood and lie down on the floor as if dead. When the three furious men burst in they were somewhat taken aback by the sight of what seemed to be a dead woman; recovering themselves, they forthwith accused me of murder. "No," said I, "the woman is not dead; and if she is, I can bring her to life again quickly enough, as you will see." Then I walked about the corpse, blowing a certain horn as I did so, and repeating the service for the Resurrection. On completing the third circuit I commanded my wife to stand up, whereupon she rose and washed herself.

Imagine the amazement of the three good men to see a young and beautiful woman in the person of one who had a moment ago seemed a wrinkled old hag! They determined to buy my horn, whether I wanted to sell it or not. No sooner had the purchase —at a good price—been effected when they fell into a heated argument as to which of them should first kill his old wife and restore her in the form of a beautiful young woman. However, the priest slew his old woman first, and then the others killed their wives. They walked about the corpses blowing and chanting. But in vain! The women remained dead. My boy was watching and listening, and he reported that they cursed me roundly. They swore to be the death of me this time. But the boy ran home before them, and when they arrived I was ready.

In the stable I had a mare which, with a bushel of corn, was all my father had been able to bequeath me when he died. She was blind of one eye, lame and afflicted with both the botts and the heaves. I took some of my gold pieces and stuffed them into certain natural apertures of her body, and then covered her carefully with a blanket. As the three furious dignitaries rushed up they found me rubbing the mare down. Seizing a moment when their attention was fixed on my movements, I extracted the gold pieces coin by coin, with appropriate exclamations of delight. They were so astonished at this marvel that they forgot their revenge. They purchased my mare for fifteen pounds and led her home as fast as she could hobble. When they failed to get any gold out of the old nag, their rage knew no bounds, and they spent some little time in discussing what death would be the most painful kind to inflict on me. They did, indeed, lay hold of me, and I offered no resistance; and since they could still not agree on how to make an end of me, I offered a suggestion. "Tie me up," I said, "and put me into a barrel; bind it round with hoops and throw it into the sea."

The three cronies thought this was an excellent idea, and thanking me for the suggestion, they did as I had said. When they had rolled me, with considerable panting and puffing, as far as the strand, I bade them stop. "Here," said I, "are twelve shillings; and since you are hot and uncomfortable with your labour, pray take them and refresh yourselves at the tavern for a while. There will be plenty of time to finish your work when you have had a drink or two." This proposal also met with their hearty approval, and they went away to the inn.

While the mayor, the steward and the priest were getting drunk on my money, I saw through the bung-hole a peasant driving a herd of pigs, and began to bawl. He came up and knocked on the barrel with his staff: "Hey! what are you doing in there?" he asked. "You would never believe me," I replied, "but the villagers wanted to elect me mayor, and when I refused such a great honour, they shut me up here, and intend to drown me in the sea." "Well," said the herd, "you may not, as you say, be worthy; but I have no doubts about my own ability to fill that post. I'll change places with you." Thereupon he liberated me and got into the barrel himself. I fastened the hoops again and hurried away, driving the fattest of the swine with me.

Sometime later the three eminent men returned to the barrel and rolled it a little farther down the shore. "Stop!" cried the pig-herd; "I will be your mayor if you like." But befuddled with drink as they were, they paid him no heed, and sank the barrel in the deepest part of the sea. Then they staggered home in high glee, confident that they had seen the last of Unibos.

But I bided my time, and what was their astonishment, three days later, to see me driving a herd of swine through the town! Could that really be Unibos whom they had packed in a barrel and drowned? They approached me cautiously. I let them wrangle and wonder for a while. "Gentlemen," I said finally, "I am indeed Unibos, and that drenching you gave me in the sea was the best turn you ever did me, for at the bottom of the ocean are innumerable herds of swine like these. I drove away as many of the best ones as I could."

Once more the cupidity of the three eminent citizens was aroused. Away they dashed into the sea to get themselves herds of pigs as fine as mine. Of course, they never came back. From that out I was able to live in peace. I converted my movable property into money, and that I have loaned out at usury these past two score years.

"Brother," said Martin Scabby, "that was an exemplary tale. I, too, can prove the rightness of your contention in my own person. When I started life I had not the advantage of even a bushel of corn, for my mother, who was wanted by the sheriff, was forced to drop me in a gutter as she hurried through the town of Cahors. I knocked about the streets for a while as a waif, and so scurvy was my appearance that people called me Scabiosus. When I was a little older, I earned my bread by delivering meat for a butcher. I, myself, ate with the dogs, like St Alexis, and saved my money. Thus did I get together a few pence, which I loaned out at usury. As my goods increased, I began to dress more respectably. My fame as a usurer grew, and I accumulated so much money that people called me

Martin Scabiosus. When I had become rich I was called Master Martin. Eventually I was numbered among the richest men in the city and was addressed as Sir Martin. At last, when the practice of usury had made me the city's wealthiest man, I was honoured by the title of My Lord Martin. Thus did the scabby waif and foundling rise to be the friend of kings."

"By the legs of God!" roared Richard the Lion-heart, "you lie in your throat."

"Sit down," said Henry II. "You were always too violent. You have your mother's temper."

"How did these people get into this company, anyway?" inquired Wiclif.

"Your Reverence," answered the Clerk of Oxenford, "usurers are everywhere."

"Gentlemen," spoke up Matteo Bandello, "whatever we may say, and keep on saying, it will still be necessary to say that this blind greed for money is a potent cause of many evils. Not only does it render a man ill-famed, and cause him to be pointed out with scorn by all decent people, but in his own house he is frequently ridden, body and soul, by thirty pairs of devils. Wherefor I should like to tell you a tale of mine, which is a true story, and shows how excessively greedy men grow impudent and careless of God."

125. TOMASONE GRASSO, USURER OF MILAN, DOES A SHREWD STROKE OF BUSINESS

Matteo Bandello

In our city of Milan there lived not long ago a usurer named Tomasone Grasso, who, in his time, profited as much in lending out money at usury as had ever any money-lender before him, wherefor he became immeasurably rich. Nevertheless, in order to conceal his sin, he was always the first to enter the church, and with his own hand he distributed large sums of money to whatever poor were within; he heard two or three masses, and made other similar demonstrations of piety, so that anyone who did not know better would have considered him the most holy and Catholic man in Milan. When there was preaching, he never missed a sermon, but took his place directly in front of the preacher, and listened with the closest attention.

Now Fra Bernardino da Siena, a famous preacher of those times, came to preach at Milan; later, as you know, the Church placed him among the number of the saints. But as he was of advanced age, and already a saint in the opinion of many, the whole city crowded to hear his sermons, wherefor he very soon acquired the respectful esteem of both high and low.

Tomasone let no day pass without hearing Bernardino, and having listened to twelve or more sermons, and observing that the preacher said nothing against usurers, decided that he would pay him a visit. Tomasone was a man of venerable appearance and authoritative bearing, and he dressed very well, though soberly. Fra Bernardino received him very graciously, and sat talking with him on matters of virtue and decency for a while. Tomasone assumed the Ser Ciappelletto rôle, showing himself religious and zealous for the honour of God and the salvation of his soul. After considerable talk he said to the holy man as follows: "Reverend Father, we Milanese are deeply thankful to our Redeemer, Messer Jesu Christo, for having inspired Your Saintliness to preach in our city, for by the grace of the Saviour I hope that your sermons will yield good fruit and cause many, who live most dishonestly, to mend their ways. Our city is smirched with sins and vices aplenty, but more prevalent and worse than any is the cursed and abominable sin of usury, for many of our citizens follow no other profession. I, now, moved by a charitable impulse, have come to suggest that you reprove this foul vice in these most salutary sermons of yours, and thus uproot it from our city."

The holy man, who had no suspicion that Tomasone was other than the decent gentleman he seemed to be, thanked him heartily for his suggestion. Thereafter Fra Bernardino preached most fervently against the vice of usury in such wise that in all his sermons he did nothing but blame and reprehend all who lent money at interest. This aroused no little disgust among his audience, with the result that he was visited by several honest gentlemen, who begged him not to labour so much at usurers, but to follow his usual manner of preaching. "You must not take this amiss," said the holy friar, "for I was urged on by one of your citizens; he dresses in violet, and sits immediately in front of me every day when I speak." From this and other indications everyone knew at once that it was Tomasone to whom he referred. "Alas!" cried one of the gentlemen, "what do I hear? That man, O Reverend Father, is the worst usurer in all Italy, and in all Milan you can't find anyone from whom to borrow money save him. I myself, constrained by necessity, have borrowed money from him more than once at tremendous rates of interest."

When Fra Bernardino heard this he was greatly shocked, and wishing to be assured in his own mind, he sent for Tomasone, who came at once. The holy friar said it had come to his ears that he was a great usurer, wherefor he was much amazed that he had so earnestly besought him to preach against usury. "I did so," replied Tomasone, "because I wish to be the only one to follow that profession in this city, so that I may make more money. Whoever told you that there are no others who lend out money on interest deceives himself, for I have observed for some time past that my income is not what it used to be; for which reason I am convinced that there are others as shrewd as myself who practise money-lending. I assure you, O Father mine, that he who has not money, and plenty of it, is a fool. You—pardon me—are little versed in the ways of the world; your way of life is one, and ours is another. The sum of the whole matter is this—that he who wishes to be honoured and esteemed by the folk must have money. Even were a man most nobly born, were he of the house of the Visconti—which is the house of our lord duke—he would be held to be of no account unless he had money. You must not think I am made of gold, but I do possess a few pence, and if I go to the castle to talk to the duke, I am admitted at once, even if he is in bed, for the reason that, on certain occasions when he needed two hundred thousand ducats, or three hundred thousand ducats, I served him readily, and with a profit for myself which was agreed upon between us in advance. Moreover, there is not a gentleman nor a merchant nor a burgher nor a poor man in all this city who does not show me honour, for I give my services to all. Now you will tell me that I ought to lend my money without charging interest: Father mine, this manner of lending money is not in style, nor will it be made so by me. I want the pledge in my hand, and I want my money to return home bringing a profit with it. I force and constrain no one to borrow from me. And since the possession of money is something which immeasurably rejoices the heart so that the more one has, the greater one's joy, therefore did I pray you to preach against usurers, so that I alone might get all the business and profit."

The saintly friar made a vigorous effort with true and holy words to remove this fantasy from Tomasone's mind, but he cited civil and canon law, the Old Testament and the New in vain. Tomasone retained his point of view. The friar shrugged his shoulders with compassion, and when the usurer had gone prayed God that He would unseal the eyes of his mind.

Now since I have spoken of Tomasone at such length, I will add one more gem—a circumstance which took place a few days before the conversation reported above. The usurer went, as I said, to hear the sermons every day. Once when Fra Bernardino had preached valiantly against money-lenders, a poor shoe-maker, who had intended to borrow money from Messer Grasso, took fright on hearing the friar condemn such transactions so severely. As Tomasone was returning home from the sermon, he dared not approach him, but followed hesitantly at a discreet distance. Messer Grasso perceived him, and turning round said: "My good fellow, do you want something from me?" "I should indeed like something," replied the cobbler, "but since the friar has cried down money-lending so fiercely, I dare not ask you. I'm afraid you may have been converted, and be unwilling to lend me any money." "My good man," replied Tomasone, "what trade do you follow?" "I am a shoe-maker," replied the other. "Good," said Tomasone; "you have listened to the sermon, and now you are going home to your shop. What do you intend to do there?" "I am going to make shoes," answered the poor fellow, "for I don't know how to do anything else." "And I," said Tomasone, "have also heard the sermon, and I am going home to be a money-lender, for that is my business." And he lent the man what money he wanted.

This was the same Tomasone, I should add, who later became converted, and restored all his ill-gotten gains, both in cases where he was sure, and in cases where he was not sure, and bequeathed such a sum for alms and pious works that the end of it has not yet been reached in Milan; and who, if he lived evilly, at least died a good Christian, so far as we can judge.

"I once heard," said Robert Mannyng in a quiet voice, of a usurer who was labouring at the point of death, but was unwilling to part with his money. Wherefor he called his wife and children and made them promise on their oaths that after his decease they would divide his wealth into three equal parts: one part should be for his wife, so that she might marry again, another part for his children, and the third part they should tie in a sack round his neck, and bury it with him. After the man had been buried the family went to the cemetery to recover that immense sum of money, but fled in terror when, on opening the grave, they beheld demons stuffing red-hot coins into the corpse's mouth."

Herr Meier's rotundity seemed to have grown suddenly flabby, and Martin's face was several shades paler behind his fur collar.

"But there is hope even for usurers," continued Robert, "as you may learn by the tale of . . ."

126. PIERS THE TOLLER

Robert Mannyng

Saint John the Almoner says that Piers was a usurer, a niggard, exceedingly covetous and avaricious, and that he heaped up money in a store, as is the practice of usurers everywhere.

It happened one day that poor men were sitting by the road-side warming themselves in the sunshine, and they fell to talking about those houses where they had received alms, and those where they had received none, praising the one and blaming the others. While they were talking of this and that, they saw Piers coming along the road, and each of the beggars said: "Here comes Piers, who never did a good deed in his life." Each asked the other whether or not he had ever received any good at Piers's hand. They all said they had not, and that no poor man would ever get anything from him, no matter how cleverly he begged.

Then one of the mendicants spoke up. "I lay you a wager," he said, "that I shall get an alms from him, however fierce and grim he be." The rest of the company thought it highly unlikely that Piers would give him anything, but each promised to make him a gift should he succeed. So he of whom I speak got up and went to the gate of Piers's house. As he stood there quietly waiting for the evil fellow to come home, a servant approached leading an ass loaded with loaves of bread which Piers had bought. And when he saw Piers following along behind the beggar thought: Now I will ask him for something. "For charity's sake, Piers," said he, "give me some alms, if you please." Piers stood very still for a moment, and looked at him angrily with grim eyes. Then he bent down to look for a stone, but as it chanced, he could find none. So instead of a stone he took a loaf of bread from the ass's load and hurled it violently at the poor beggar.

The poor man took the loaf up quickly and was very glad thereat. He ran back to his fellows and cried: "See what Piers has given me!" "Nay," said the others, "Piers never gave anyone a gift like that." But he replied: "On the contrary, I assure you that I had it from Piers's own hand; I will swear to it on the holy relics in the presence of all of you." The rest of the beggars were marvellously astonished that he should have had such luck.

Now on the third day after this, as I find it written, Piers fell grievously ill, and as he lay in his bed it seemed to him that a messenger came to lead him off to his doom. He was brought before the judge to give an account of his deeds. Piers stood there in great dread, abashed and bemused. On one side he saw a fiend who was accusing him violently. His whole life since his birth was shown there before him, and particularly every wicked deed whereof he had been guilty since he had assumed charge of his affairs; and he was called upon to give a reason why he did them, and to what end. On the other side were standing shining figures of men who would have saved him if they could; but they were unable to find any good deed that would rescue or release him. The fair men said: "What shall we do? In his whole life we find that he has done no deed pleasing God except that once he let fly a loaf of bread at a poor beggar; and even that he did not give with good will, but hurled it at him wrathfully. Not for the love of God or as an alms did he give it. Nevertheless, it is true that the poor man got the loaf." Now the fiend laid Piers's wicked works in the balance, and the fair men, since they had nothing else, laid the loaf in the other balance, and we are told that the one balanced the other. Then the fair men said to Piers: "Thus you can see, if you are wise, how this loaf teaches you to tend your soul with almsdeed."

Thereupon Piers woke out of sleep and began to think earnestly about his dream, sighing, and with mournful cheer, like a man in great distress. He recalled how many fiends had accused him of his trespasses, and how they would have damned him had it not been for the mercy of Jesus Christ. These matters he turned over in his mind and at last he said to himself: "Since a single loaf of bread given in ill will helped me out of my extreme peril, almsdeed performed with good will would be even more salutary."

From that time forward Piers became a man of such fair manners that no one could observe but that he was meek and kind to poor men. A milder man, or one who gave alms more freely to the poor, could not be found anywhere. And he was compassionate also, as you shall hear.

One day on the road Piers met a poor man, naked as he was born, for he had lost all his goods in the sea. He begged an alms and some clothing. Piers pitied him, and took off his kirtle at once and put it on the other man, and bade him wear it for his love. The man took it gratefully and went and sold it at once. Piers watched him do this, and was exceedingly wroth; he could not endure it, and went home grieving sorely. It seemed to him that it was an evil sign which indicated that he, Piers, was not worthy of the beggar's prayers, and that for that reason he would not wear the kirtle.

When he had wept for a long time a part of his grief was assuaged and he fell asleep, for after tears it is usual for sleep to come quickly. As he slept Piers had a fair dream. It seemed to him that he was in bright heaven, and there he saw God sitting clad in the kirtle which he had given to the poor man. "Why do you weep and lament?" He asked. "Behold, Piers, this is your garment, which you gave to the beggar for my sake. Whatever you gave him in charity, every bit thereof have you given to me."

Piers woke and was much amazed. "Blessed be all poor men," said he, "since God loves them. Well off are they who are poor in this world since they are dear to God. Wherefor I shall strive night and day to become poor, if I can."

Thereupon Piers gathered together his goods and gave all he had to the poor. Then he called his clerk, who was a notary, and bade him give heed. "I am going to confide to you a very secret matter," he said, "and take care that you divulge it to no man. You shall take my body and sell it into bondage to some man so that I shall live in servitude. Unless you do this, I shall be wroth, and you and yours shall be loathly to me. But if you do it, you shall have ten pounds of gold, which I give you here. I do not care to whom you sell me, except only that he be a Christian. And the price which you receive for me you shall divide, withholding not so much as a farthing of it, among poor men." The clerk was loath to do that deed, and consented only because of fear and Piers's threat.

When the clerk had taken an oath to carry out his master's instructions, Piers put on a foul garment, and both took their way to the church to transact the business. The clerk thought to himself: "Lord, whom can I find willing to buy this man?" Finally he remembered an acquaintance of his who had once been rich, but who had lost much of his property through misfortune. His name was Zoilus. The clerk went to him, and Zoilus told him how it stood with him. "Well," said the clerk, "my advice is that you buy a bondman through whose service you may recoup your fortune." "I would willingly employ my silver in such a deal," said Zoilus. Said the clerk: "Lo, here is a true and well-mannered man who will serve you to your pleasure scrupulously in every way that he can. His name is Piers; you will profit much through him; God will bless you and give you increase." So Zoilus paid over the price for Piers, and the clerk distributed the money among the poor of the town without keeping back a single farthing.

Not long after this it happened that the emperor sent his messengers to look for Piers, but nowhere could they get news of rich Piers the Toller, nor learn what had become of him.

Now Piers, who was once stout and rich, had come to low estate. Whatever any man bade him do, that he did gladly. He became so mild and meek that a milder man could not have been found anywhere, for his humility went so far that he willingly swilled the pots and dishes. He performed great penance, fasting much and sleeping little. He was patient and forbearing to rich and poor, high and low; he performed everyone's bidding with humble subservience. And since he assumed such a soft demeanour, shrews did him evil often, considering that his meekness was a sign of folly or madness. Even his fellows spoke ill of him. But he suffered their scorn and contempt without ever saying anything against them. Zoilus, his master, readily perceived that his good fortune and improved circumstances were due to Piers. One day he summoned him and said: "Piers, you are far more worthy of respect than I, for Jesus loves you well; He shows forth great virtue in you; wherefor I will set you free, and you shall be my fellow."

Piers did not agree to this proposition, for he wished to remain always for ever more in servitude, but he thanked his lord mildly for his great courtesy. Afterwards Jesus appeared to Piers in a vision, so that he might remain steadfast in his intention. "Let it not grieve you to do penance," He said, "for I am with you in any chance that may befall. I have you in mind, Piers. Lo, here is the kirtle which you gave for my sake; and for that I will grant you the grace to make an end in all goodness."

It happened now that sergeants and squires who were formerly wont to serve Piers went on a pilgrimage to the country where he dwelt as a bondsman. Zoilus invited them home to his hall; and Piers, who was there, knew each of them very well. He, who was wont to have their service, now served them. They did not recognize him at once, for penance had changed his hue. However, when they regarded him closely, one said to the other: "This fellow here is very like Piers the Toller." Piers concealed his visage as much as he could, but as they looked at him more and more, they knew him well at last, and said: "Zoilus, is yonder fellow your page? A rich man is in your service. Him whom we find here has been sought far and near by the emperor."

Piers heard what they said and went quietly to the porter. The porter had been deaf and dumb since birth, but by the grace of Christ a miracle was shown through Piers. "Let me out," he said to the porter; and he who was deaf and dumb replied: "Yea."

Piers went out the gate and wandered where it pleased God that he should go. The porter entered the hall and related the marvellous thing that had happened to him. "When he spoke to me," said the man, "it seemed to me that a clear flame of fire broke from his mouth, and that flame made me both hear and speak. Blessed be God and Piers."

The lord and all the guests in the hall were astonished at that miracle. They quickly set out in search for Piers, but their seeking came to naught, for they never found him anywhere, night or day. For He who took up Enoch and Ely, through His mercy received Piers for his meekness and good deeds into everlasting rest.

Take example of Piers, you usurers, for you shall never have joy until you abandon that sin and distribute as alms what you have gained by usury.

"Don't go—yet—" said the Clerk of Oxenford as Martin Scabby was helping Unibos to his feet. "I want you both to hear a fine tale, which I read somewhere, which well illustrates the wit of the weak."

127. THE CHURL AND THE BIRD
The Clerk of Oxenford

One time, more than a hundred years ago, there lived a rich villein or churl. I do not know his name, but I do know that he was very well provided with meadows, woods and plough-land, and whatever else constitutes wealth. His manor was so handsome and delightful that it had no peer in burg or village anywhere in the world; the description of it would probably seem to you like a fable. Nevertheless, I think no one will ever build such a donjon nor such a high tower as he had. Round about ran a river enclosing the domain. The beautiful orchard was likewise enclosed by water. The man who originally planned and executed this homestead was no fool—indeed, he was a well-born knight. But after the father the son succeeded to the property, and he it was who sold it to the villein of whom I speak. Thus it passed from hand to hand, for well you know that burgs and manors decay by reason of bad heirs.

But to return to the manor: The garden or park was as excellent as one could wish. Many kinds of herbs, whose names I do not know, grew there. There too were sweet-smelling flowers and such spices that anyone lying ill in a litter would come away whole and sound if he passed a night in the garden. It was circular in form and very spacious. In the middle was a clear and wholesome fountain which bubbled up copiously, as cold as marble. Near by, shading it, was a lofty tree with beautiful spreading branches. It was so thickly leafy that in the month of May no beam of the sun could penetrate its foliage. This tree was held in great esteem, for such was its nature that its leaves lasted always: neither wind nor storm was ever strong enough to detach a single leaf or a piece of bark.

Now I must tell you that morning and evening, twice a day and no more, a bird came to sing in this pine tree. The bird was so beautiful that one would be hard put to it to describe him. He was smaller than a sparrow and somewhat larger than a wren. He sang so well and sweetly that the song of the lark or the chalendre was not so pleasing to hear. He was particularly adept in singing lays and new songs, rotrouenges and chansons. It seems to me that in comparison with him neither gigue nor harp nor viol, neither merle, mavis, nightingale nor starling was worth a haw. You should know, too, that his song had a marvellous quality, the like of which has never been known, for its virtue was such that no matter how sorrowful a man might be, he would straightway forget his griefs and rejoice if he heard the song of the little bird. And if he had never been in love before, he would straightway become enamoured, and consider himself as good as a king or an emperor. Moreover, if he were a hundred years old or more, whether churl or noble, if he heard the bird's song he would be so rejuvenated as to seem a youth, and think himself well worthy to be loved by maids and ladies.

But I must tell you another marvel, too: The garden could endure only so long as the bird came to sing his sweet songs there; for from the songs arose the virtue whereby the flowers and the tree and all the demesne remained in vigour. If the bird should ever cease to come, the garden would wither, and the fountain cease to flow.

Now the villein to whom the property belonged was in the habit of coming every day to listen to the bird's sweet song. One morning he came to the fountain under the pine tree to wash his face in its water, and as he did so the bird in the tree began to sing a delightful lay. And this is what the bird said in his language: "O layman, clerk or knight, and all you who have regard to love and suffer from its ills, listen to my lay. I also sing for you sweet maids who delight in worldly pleasure. I tell you truly that first you must love God and obey His commands; go willingly to church and listen to the service, for no ill can ever come to you from so doing. Indeed, God and love are one, for God loves honour and courtoisie, nor does He frown upon true love at all. God loves honour and bounty, and above all He approves largesse. God listens to a fervent prayer, and love in no wise hinders it. But the avaricious are greedy for gain, the spiteful are envious, churls are base and rascals are wicked. Love is maintained by sense, courtoisie, honour and loyalty, and if you practise these you may win both God and the world."

So sang the bird; and when he saw the churl sitting under the tree, he sang again, but in a different strain: "Stop your course, O river, perish donjon, decay, O tower, fade flowers, wither trees! O tree, cease your office. Clerks, knights and ladies who cherished the fountain,

THE CHURL AND THE BIRD

who lived longer and loved more amorously by virtue thereof, who were adept in courtoisie and prowess, who sustained chivalry and gave largesse willingly—such used to come to listen to me here. But now the one who listens to my song is a villein stuffed with envy, a churl who loves a penny better than gentle behaviour. My song has had no power to raise him from the slough of covetousness wherein he lies. Gentlefolk used to listen to me for delight and for greater love and solace, but this fellow's only concern is that he may eat more and better."

So saying the bird flew away. The churl sat still and considered that if he were able to snare the bird he could sell it for a good price; and if he couldn't sell it, he would put it in a cage where it might sing to him early and late. Accordingly he prepared his snare, observed carefully what branches the bird usually perched upon, and there he set it skilfully. At vespers the bird returned to the garden, and flying to the pine was caught in the net. Alas! the wretched one! He attempted to fly, but stuck fast. Such is the reward of him who serves a churl!

"It seems to me," said the bird, "that you have done ill to snare me, for I shall bring you small ransom." "On the contrary," replied the churl, "for I shall now hear many a song; you shall sing for me more frequently. In the past you served me as you pleased; now you shall serve me as I please." "The parts in this cantata are badly assigned," answered the bird, "and I've got the worse one. Once I had country, riverside, wood and meadow at my pleasure; now I am locked up in a cage. Never more shall I rejoice. I used to live on what I could find; now I shall be fed by another, like any other prisoner. Let me go, good friend, for I assure you I will never sing in prison."

"By my faith," cried the churl, "in that case I will eat you; you will not get out any other way." "It seems to me I should make you a poor meal," replied the bird. "Your reputation would not be much enhanced by killing so poor a thing as myself. If you let me go, I will do a good deed; kill me and it will be a sin."

Churl: You're wasting words; the more you beseech me, the less inclined I shall be to grant your prayer.

Bird: Alas, you speak truly. You yourself have often heard it said that rational arguments make a churl wroth. But another proverb instructs us that necessity forces one to do many an unwonted and difficult thing. My puny strength avails me nothing, but if you let me go, I will give you three precious articles of wisdom such as were never known by any man of your breed, and which will be of great profit to you.

Churl: Well, if you will give me surety, I will do as you ask.
Bird: I loyally pledge you my faith.

So the peasant let him go. The bird flew up to the tree. He was soiled and ruffled, for he had been shamefully handled. He rearranged his feathers with his bill as well as he could, while the churl impatiently waited to be informed of the three articles of knowledge. The bird was cunning and said: "If you pay attention you will learn something to your advantage. The first point is: *Do not believe everything you hear.*"

The churl scowled. "I knew that well enough already," he said. "Cherish that knowledge carefully, then," said the bird, "and don't forget it." "Certainly, I am well on the road to hearing great wisdom," answered the man. "You talk like a fool to bid me bear such things in mind. I wish I had you here! But if you really intend to keep your bargain, tell me the next item, and I will give heed."

"If you are able to understand what I say you will now learn something of great significance," answered the bird: *"Never lament for the loss of something you never possessed."*

The villein was not a fool and exclaimed violently: "You have broken your faith. I understood you to say that you would teach me three choice bits of wisdom such as none of my blood ever posssessed. But what you have just told me is the common property of all the world. No one is or has been such a dolt as to bewail what he never had. You have lied to me atrociously."

"Shall I continue?" asked the bird. "I very much fear that you will forget this point. You are so ready for dispute that I doubt if you will be able to retain what I have to say."

Churl: I know such things better than you do, and have done this long time. Curse anyone for thanking you for telling him what he already knows. By my head! I'm not such a simpleton as you take me to be. But since you have escaped me and I can no longer constrain you, tell on. But no more jokes.

Bird: Listen well. The third item of knowledge is such that whoever possesses it will never be poor.

Churl: Now that is a thing I should dearly like to know, for it has a bearing on business. But it is dinner time now, so tell me quickly.

"Very well," replied the bird. *"I instruct you, O churl, not to throw to your feet what you hold in your hand."*

The villein snorted with rage when he heard this, but after a moment he said: "Is that all? These instructions are child's prattle. You have lied and tricked me. I have been fully aware of all you have told me this long time."

Bird: If you are so wise, you would never have let me go when you had me in your hands.

Churl: True enough; but I certainly knew the other two points.

Bird: But this one is worth a hundred times more than the others.

Churl: How do you mean?

Bird: I'll tell you, thick-skull. You really don't know what has happened to you. If you had killed me, as you intended, by my eyes! you would have been the better off for it all the days of your life.

Churl: Pshaw! what good are you?

Bird: Well, base-born one, I will tell you. In my body there is a dear and precious stone weighing three ounces. Its virtue is so great that whoever possesses it shall never wish or ask for anything but that it will be his at once.

When the villein heard this he lamented his fault, rent his clothes with rage and tore his face with his nails, calling himself a miserable wretch, while from his perch on the pine the bird looked on with pleasure. He waited till the man's face was a mass of lacerations and then said: "Wretched oaf, when you held me in your hands just now I was lighter than a sparrow or a tomtit or a finch, which do not weigh half an ounce." "You are right," replied the churl wrathfully.

Bird: Well, then, O man, you must realize that I lied to you about the precious stone.

Churl: I know it well enough now, though I did believe you.

Bird: O churl, now I have surely proved to you that you really did not possess the three articles of wisdom, and by your own words I have demonstrated that there is no greater fool than he who laments over something which he never had, for right now it seems to me you are blubbering for something you never had and never shall have. My three articles of wisdom have astounded you. Dear friend, take care to learn them well.

Therewith the bird flew away and never returned to the garden. The foliage fell from the tree, the park decayed and withered, the fountain dried up and the churl lost his pleasant domain. True is the proverb which says: He who covets everything shall lose all.

"Before the conversation turned to these commonplace and churlish themes," said Peter Bell, "something was said about Queen Eleanor's sex appeal. Had it anything to do with her sixteen years' imprisonment?"

"I know nothing about that," said the Minstrel of Reims, "but I know what happened at Tyre between her and Salah ad-Dîn."

"We all know," answered Richard of Devizes, "but we haven't all told it."

"There is no harm in it—now—" replied the Minstrel.

128. QUEEN ELEANOR AND SALAH AD-DÎN

The Minstrel of Reims

My lords, as you know, Louis le Gros had two sons. Robert, the elder, knew nothing, and Louis, the younger, had very little wit. But choosing the lesser of two evils, the magnates of France selected the younger son to succeed his father as king of France.

One day Louis decided that he would go to the Holy Land and liberate the sepulchre of Christ from the hands of the infidels. Now this was an enterprise requiring considerable capital—much more than Louis had at his disposal. In vain did his barons try to dissuade him; the more they argued against it the more stubbornly set became his mind—or what there was of it. Finally one of the wise peers thought of an excellent expedient: "Sire," said he, "you must marry. There is Eleanor, daughter of Count Guilhem of Poictiers. She holds not only Poitou, but Limoges as well, and altogether more than three times the amount of your land." "That's the very thing!" said Louis.

Eleanor was not much dazzled by the crown of France, but she had a taste for travel, which was considerably impeded by her single state, and so, expecting to reap some benefit herself, she consented to the match.

On St John's day the king and queen of France set sail, and in the course of a month they arrived with the army at Tyre. There the king rested all winter, recovering from the effects of seasickness, and spending Eleanor's money. Many times Salah ad-Dîn challenged the king to battle, but Louis always put him off with some excuse—it was too rainy, or he had a headache, or he was feeling liverish.

Time, you may be sure, hung heavily on Eleanor's hands. Near by, the Orient seemed less colourful than when viewed through the glass of her imagination. But when she heard stories of the worth, the prowess, the wit, the generosity and breeding of Salah ad-Dîn, life took on a new interest for her. It was not long before she loved him passionately, though she had never seen him. With Eleanor to think, or rather to feel, was to act. Through an interpreter she sent a message of greeting to the Saracen, saying that if he were able to arrange the matter, she would renounce her faith and take him for her lord.

When Salah ad-Dîn understood the import of the Frank queen's letter, he rejoiced greatly, for he had long heard of Eleanor as the noblest and richest lady of Christendom. Forthwith he armed a galley and sent it from Ascalon to Tyre, where it arrived about midnight. By means of a false postern the interpreter insinuated himself into Eleanor's chamber. "What news?" cried the queen. "Lady," answered the other, "behold the galley of Salah ad-Dîn all ready and waiting for you. Make haste, now, before we are perceived." "By my faith," said the queen, "this is well and expeditiously done." Then she bade two of her damsels pack some coffers with gold and silver as quickly as they could, and was about to send them to the galley when another of her maids caught the drift of what was going forward. She sneaked out of the chamber quietly and made her way to the bed of the sleeping Louis. "Sire," she said, "evil is afoot. My lady is on the point of going to Ascalon with Salah ad-Dîn; the galley is even now riding in the port. For God's sake, Sire, hurry up!" "Mon Dieu!" exclaimed Louis, "is she taking her gold too?" "Two chests full, Sire," replied the maid.

This information stung Louis into action. A party of armed men under the command of his marshal found Eleanor at the port with one foot already on the galley. The marshal took her by the hand and led her back to the king's chamber, while the men-at-arms seized the galley and those within it, for the Saracens were too surprised to offer resistance.

"Eleanor," said the king, "I am shocked and hurt. Tell me, now, why did you want to do this thing to me?" "Why?" repeated Eleanor with a nasty laugh. "That's easily answered: because of your cursed pusillanimity, for you aren't worth a rotten apple. I have heard such reports of Salah ad-Dîn that I consider him a man worthy of being loved by a woman like me. And let me tell you another thing: After this you shall never more enjoy possession of me."

These few words amply answered Louis' question. He had no desire to hear more, and sent his wife away under heavy guard.

Not long after this, acting on the advice of his council, Louis decided to go back to France, for his money was running low, and he had gained nothing at Tyre but shame. At Paris Louis assembled his barons, related the escapade at Tyre, and asked counsel what he should do with Eleanor. "By God!" exclaimed the astonished barons, "the best advice we can give you is that you get rid of her. She seems to be a devil, and if you keep her by you much longer, she will find some way of murdering you." Louis turned pale. "Moreover," said another baron, "you have no male child by her." "That is probably not Eleanor's fault," muttered the Count of Dreux under his breath.

The king accepted the advice of his barons, and in so doing he acted like a fool. He should have walled her up, and then her extensive lands would have belonged to him during her lifetime, and the great evils which followed would have been averted.

No sooner had Louis divorced Eleanor—on the grounds of consanguinity, the clerks said—than she sent for Henry of Anjou, whom she had met through his father Geoffrey, and who was attracting much attention to himself on the borders of her domains. Henry, disregarding his father's warning, married her, and two years later made her queen of England.

"As you say," agreed Peter Bell, "there is no harm in it. Englishman that I am, I cannt blame Eleanor much, considering that Louis was such a poor stick. But so far as I know, she never gave her second husband similar cause for complaint after she had become queen of England."

"If she had done," replied the Minstrel, "it would have been sauce for the goose. Probably you recall how Henry treated Alix of France, the betrothed of his own son, and how Henry Courtmantle died of shame and a broken heart as a result."

"You journalists," said John Stow with a shake of his head, "possess an uncanny faculty for twisting the straightest story almost beyond recognition. Though it is true that King Henry debauched his ward Alix at the age of twelve years, it was not to Henry Courtmantle—who was already married to Margaret—that she was betrothed, but to Richard. And the prince died of dysentery, not a broken heart."

"As for Salah ad-Dîn," remarked Conrad of Montferrat, "at the time Eleanor was amusing herself at Antioch—not at Tyre—the Saracen was only ten years old, and was still memorizing the Koran in his father's house at Damascus."

"Well, it makes a good story," muttered the Minstrel.

"And truth makes even a better one. The man who looked at the eggs but took the bacon was merely cross-eyed; but you journalists can plead no excuse other than an inveterate lust for sensationalism."

"It seems to me," said Lord Burleigh, "that some of you read too much and others too little. It is the light and unconsidered trifles which often preserve the real truth. Peter Bell has apparently never heard the ballet called 'Queen Eleanor's Confession.' I see John de Rampaigne over there by the fire-place; he ought to know it."

"I do, indeed," said John with a smile, "though Norman-French comes more readily to my tongue than English."

However, he picked up a handsome rote, and after strumming a few bars, sang as follows:

129. QUEEN ELEANOR'S CONFESSION
John de Rampaigne

  Queene Elianor was a sike woman,
   And afraid that she should dye;
 Then she sent for two fryars of France
   To speke with her speedilye.

  The king calld downe his nobles all,
   By one, by two, by three:
 "Earl Marshall, I'le goe shrive the queene,
   And thou shalt wend with mee."

  "A boone, a boone," quoth Earl Marshall,
   And fell on his bended knee,
 "That whatsoever Queene Elianor saye,
   No harme thereof may bee."

  "I'le pawne my landes," the king then cryd,
   "My sceptre, crowne and all,
 That whatsoere Queen Elianor sayes,
   No harme thereof shall fall.

  "Do thou put on a fryar's coat,
   And I'le put on another,
 And we will to Queen Elianor goe
   Like fryar and his brother."

  Thus both attired then they goe.
   When they came to Whitehall
 The bells did ring and the quiristers sing,
   And the torches did light them all.

  When that they came before the queene,
   They fell on their bended knee:
 "A boone, a boone, our gracious queene,
   That you sent so hastilee."

  "Are you two fryars of France," she sayd,
   "As I suppose you bee?
 But if you are two English fryars,
   You shall hang on the gallowes tree."

"We are two fryars of France," they sayd,
  "As you suppose we bee;
We have not been at any masse
  Sith we came from the sea."

"The first vile thing that ever I did
  I will to you unfolde:
Earl Marshall had my maidenhed
  Beneath this cloth of gold."

"That's a vile sinne," then sayd the king;
  "May God forgive it thee!"
"Amen, amen!" quoth Earl Marshall—
  With a heavye heart spake hee.

"The next vile thing that ever I did,
  To you I'le not denye—
I made a box of poyson strong,
  To poison King Henrye."

"That's a vile sinne," then sayd the king,
  "May God forgive it thee!"
"Amen, amen," quoth Earl Marshall,
  "And I wish it so may bee."

"The next vile thing that ever I did,
  To you I will discover:
I poisonéd fair Rosamonde,
  All in fair Woodstocke bower."

"That's a vile sinne," then sayd the king,
  "May God forgive it thee!"
"Amen, amen," quoth Earl Marshall,
  "And I wish it so may bee."

"Do you see yonders little boye
  A-tossing of the balle?
That is Earl Marshall's eldest sonne,
  And I love him best of all.

"Do you see yonders little boye
  A-catching of the balle?
That is King Henrye's youngest sonne,
  And I love him worst of all.

"His head is fashyon'd like a bull,
   His nose is like a boare."
"No matter for that," King Henrye cryd,
   "I love him better therfore."

The king pulled off his fryar's coat
   And appeared all in redde.
She shrieked and cryd and wrung her hands,
   And sayd she was betrayde.

The king lookt over his left shoulder,
   And a grimme look looked hee:
"Earl Marshall," he sayd, "but for my oathe,
   A hanged man thou shouldst bee."

"Now," said William of Wykeham, "it begins to be clear why Eleanor had sixteen years in which to study prison architecture. But I am somewhat surprised by the conduct of our host, Earl Marshal."

The earl glanced under his brows at Countess Isabel, who was regarding her lord with more attention than she had bestowed on him for some time past. "If you only knew," said the earl sadly, "how that woman chased me! We met at Lusignan, where I attempted to take vengeance for the murder of my uncle Patrick. I gave a good account of myself, and Eleanor looked on during the affray. But, as you know, I was made prisoner through treachery. Eleanor paid my ransom, and after that she would not take 'no' for an answer. I was twenty-three years old, and she was forty-five!"

"Do not be blaming the man, now," said Ossian to Wykeham. "There are women and there are women. Some are like Eleanor and some are not. No fault could be found with Emer, Cuchulain's wife, for example, nor with Etaine. But with one whose character is such as Eleanor's, a man is but like a mouse under the cat's claw. Take Celtchar's wife, for instance."

"I have heard something about Celtchar," said Henry Castide, "but never the whole story. Did he not have a famous spear?"

"He did so," answered Ossian, "but that is another tale, and first I will tell you about Celtchar's wife and Blái Briuga."

"You will not," said Senchan Torpeist.

"Indeed?" queried Ossian.

"Not without the permission of the Great Bardic Association, of which I am head and professor."

"But you will give the permission?" asked Henry.

"I will not," replied Senchan.

"Very well," conceded Ossian, "I will keep Blái Briuga and Brig Brethach out of it. But I will tell about the spear; the Great Bardic Association has no monopoly of that."

130. THE DEATH OF CELTCHAR MAC UTHECHAIR

Ossian

Marvellous indeed were the qualities of that spear. No one who was struck with it escaped death or disfigurement. When its coverings were removed, it emitted fiery flashes, and its blade was constantly overspread with a dew of poison. Originally it belonged to Pezar, king of the Persians, and was called the Slaughterer. The three sons of Bicrenn obtained that spear as part of the eric-fine which they owed to Lugaid for the slaying of his father. Lugaid called it the Yew. When it later came into Celtchar's possession it was named the Luin Celtchair. One day Celtchar slew a pestiferous hound named Dóelchú with it, and as he raised the *luin* aloft after that deed, a drop of the dog's blood ran along the shaft and went through him into the ground so that he got his death. After the hero's death the *luin* was owned by Cet mac Magach, the famous champion of Connaught, who slew Cumscraigh Menn, Conchobar's son with it. Two hundred and fifty years later, in my time, it belonged to King Cormac mac Art, who called it the Blood-spotted. Unfortunately, one of Cormac's eyes was injured by that spear, for which reason one of Ireland's wisest kings was forced to abdicate, since no blemished king might rule over Ériu. After this it was called the Poison Spear.

Few people know what happened to the *luin* after that, but I know. It came into the hands of Guaire Aidne mac Colman, who was king of Connaught during the high kingship of Tuathal Maol Garbh. Guaire, most generous of men, gave it to his brother Marvan.

Now you recall that Senchan Torpeist once quartered himself on Guaire, hoping for an occasion to satirize him, and that Marvan came to Guaire's aid in meeting the professor's outrageous demands. One of those demands had necessitated the slaying of Marvan's white boar. This was very grievous to him, for that boar was his herdsman and his physician, his messenger and his musician.

One day Marvan said to himself: "It is a long time since I proposed going to be avenged on the Great Bardic Institution for the loss of the white boar." In the course of time he came to the abode of the Great Bardic Order, and he brought the Luin Celtchair with him. When Marvan arrived at the bardic mansion, it was not to the open door that he came, but to the best closed door of the building, and the door rose open before him. The manner by which he entered was thus, having the skirt of his mantle full with wind, and there was not a person within doors that a portion of the wind did not blow into his bosom. The Great Bardic Association rose as one man; Senchan rose too, and inquired who it was who came to him against the wind. "You are in error there," said Marvan; "it was with the wind I came, and in proof thereof I have brought much of it along with me." "What is your pleasure?" asked Senchan. "I have heard," answered Marvan, "that every person gets his choice of music or of arts from you, and I have come to ask my choice." "You shall obtain that," said Senchan, "if you can show your relationship to the arts." "That is easy," answered Marvan: "the grandmother of my servant's wife was descended from poets." "You shall obtain your choice," said Senchan, "though your connection with the arts is very remote. What art is it that you prefer?" "At present I desire no better than as much *cronan* as will content me," replied Marvan. "The professors here present can perform that art for you more easily than any other," said Senchan.

Now as you know, the *cronan* is something like a lullaby, something like the buzzing of a bee, something like the purring of a cat, and something like a bass obbligato. Musicians came to Marvan, thrice nine of them, and they wished to perform the regular *cronan*. That, however, was not what Marvan wanted; it was the bass *cronan* that he desired, in the hope that they might break their heads, feet and necks, and that their breathing might the sooner be exhausted by it.

The three nines were singing the bass *cronan* after that, and whenever they wished to stop Marvan would say: "Give us as much of the *cronan* as we desire, in accordance with your promise." The three nines soon became exhausted, but Marvan desired that more of the *cronan* should be sung for him; only nine responded to his call, and they poor singers. They lasted a shorter time than the others. "Let me have as much *cronan* as I desire," said Marvan. But there was no one to answer him. Three times he called for the music, and three times he did not obtain it.

Hereupon Marvan brought his spear, the Luin Celtchair, into a more favourable position, and took off its coverings. Then Senchan said that he himself would perform the *cronan* for Marvan. "It will be more melodious to me from yourself than from any other person," said Marvan.

Senchan raised his white beard up high and would have performed the regular *cronan*, but Marvan would have no other from him than the bass. Whenever Senchan would wish to stop, then Marvan would say: "Give me my fill of *cronan*. It seems to me that you are an indifferent performer." Senchan was ashamed of that. He exerted himself to his utmost to content Marvan, and so much did he strain himself that one of his eyes started out of its socket and lay on his cheek. "That is enough *cronan*," said Marvan. And picking up his spear, he went his ways.

Thus it seems that an accident to Senchan's physical eye impaired the perspicuity of his intellect.

"I am well satisfied with the information about Celtchar's spear," said Henry Castide; "but I confess that my curiosity is now aroused concerning his wife."

"Under the circumstances," said John Bromyard, "you will probably have to remain curious.—Senchan's misfortune, however, reminds me of King Evelak's clerk, who wished to dispute on religious matters with Joseph of Arimathia. When he attempted to speak it seemed to him that someone or some thing had hold of his tongue, and so violently did he force himself to give voice that both his eyes flew out of his head and fell at his feet."

"I daresay that silenced him," said Adam Usk.

"If," said Mac Conglinne to the soldier, "you will come to me privately, I will tell you all about Celtchar's wife."

"Thank you," said Henry Castide.

"Sir minstrel," said Fynes Moryson, turning to the Minstrel of Reims, "if I understood you correctly, you disapproved of the way in which Louis VII treated his queen."

Minstrel: Well, it would not have been my way.

Moryson: You said something about walling her up, I believe.

Minstrel: I only meant that she should have been put in prison earlier.

Moryson: Ah, yes. It happens that a gentleman of whom I heard on one of my travels held the same opinion in regard to his wife, and actually put it into practice.

Goodman of Bath: How was that?

"I was in Germany," answered Moryson, "on my way to Bamberg . . ."

131. THE LADY IN THE WALL

Fynes Moryson

After leaving Emden I and my English consorts hired a coach for thirty dollars to take us to Nürnberg, forty-eight miles distant, and the coachman paid for his own horse-meat. On the first day we passed through fruitful hills of corn and came to Rauchell, where each of us paid for ours and the coachman's supper, five silver groshen. On the morrow we passed through fruitful hills of corn, and arrived at Emersleben, where we paid three groshen for ours and the coachman's supper. In the afternoon we passed over a dirty way of pleasant hills fruitful of corn, but having no woods, to Mansfield. Here each of us paid a quarter of a dollar for our own and the coachman's dinner. On the fourth day we passed through pleasant hills of corn over a dirty way, and to our supper had a pudding as big as a man's leg, for which we jointly paid fourteen grosh. On the fifth day we reached Erfurt where, with our coachman, we paid a dollar and twenty-one grosh for our dinner, with sour wine. This is a free city, and large, being a Dutch mile in compass, and pays some tribute to the Duke of Wineberg. Of old there was a university here, but Time hath dissolved it.

After dinner we passed by Armstadt where the Count of Schwartzburg keeps his court, and arriving at Blaw we paid fourteen grosh for our supper. On the sixth day we passed into the wood of Thuring, that is, Thuring Forest, vulgarly called Thuringwald. This forest hath many lords, that is, the Elector of Saxony, the Duke of Wineberg, the Duke of Coburg, and the Count of Schwartzburg. The Duke of Coburg has a fair castle in this place, and here we paid sixty-four grosh for our supper and breakfast. The seventh day . . .

"God," said Colin Clout, "created the whole world in six days and rested on the seventh. Will you not do as much for us?"

The seventh day, in the morning, we passed three miles over dirty mountains, but fruitful in corn, to Coburg, which is seated in the province of Franconia. They say that of old this city was called Cotburg, that is, the city of dirt, and the dirty streets well deserve the name. Here one of the dukes of Saxony, called von Coburg, kept his court. And our host told us that his duchess, for adultery, was there bricked up in a wall, the place being so narrow that she could only stand; it had no door, but only a hole through which they gave her food. Here we paid sixteen grosh for our dinner. In the afternoon we rode two miles to the town of Clawsen, through fruitful hills of corn, and over a most dirty way, where we paid forty-nine grosh for our supper. . . .

"Fair coz," said Sir John Harington lazily, "a pox on your dirty ways and your supper. I thought you were going to tell us a story—not give an insulting imitation of William Camden. Have done with your dollars, groshen, Dutch miles, Wineberg, Schwartzburg, Nürnberg, Coburg, horse-meat and the coachman's dinner. Come to the point, will you? What about the Duchess von or zu Sachsen and Coburg?"

"I told you," replied Fynes, "the duke bricked her up in a wall."

"It would take a thick wall to accommodate my wife," snickered John the Reeve.

"Is that all you know about the affair?" asked Sir John.

"That is all," answered Moryson sourly.

"Ah! what a romancer English literature was spared in you! Pray continue on your way to Bamberg while we remain here."

"I am sure that what he said was enough," said Christine de Pisan. "It was a disagreeable story any way you look at it. Sir minstrel," she asked, turning to John de Rampaigne, "who was the Rosamund you mentioned in your song? Have you her history in a ballet, too?"

"Lady," answered the poet, "I have indeed; but my colleague, Richard Sheale, has a better one, and to him I yield the honour."

"Come up, Richard, and let us hear," invited Lord Burleigh.

"Gentlemen," said the minstrel, "it has been a long time—a very long time—since anyone besought me to sing. I thank your lordships. I will do what I can."

132. THE POISON CUP

Richard Sheale

When as King Henry rulde this land,
The second of that name,
Besides the queene he dearly lovde
A faire and comely dame.

Most peerlesse was her beautye founde,
Her favour and her face;
A sweeter creature in this worlde
Could never prince embrace.

Her crispéd lockes, like threads of golde
Appeard to each man's sight;
Her sparkling eyes, like Orient pearles,
Did cast a heavenlye light.

The blood within her crystal cheekes
Did such a colour drive
As though the lillye and the rose
For mastership did strive.

THE POISON CUP

Yea Rosamonde, fair Rosamonde,
Her name was calléd so,
To whom our queene, Dame Ellinor,
Was known a deadlye foe.

The king therefore, for her defence,
Against the furious queene,
At Woodstocke builded such a bower
The like was never seene.

Most curiously that bower was built
Of stone and timber strong;
An hundered and fifty doors
Did to this bower belong,

And they so cunningly contriv'd
With turnings round about,
That none but with a clue of thread
Could enter in or out.

And for his love and ladye's sake,
That was so fair and brighte,
The keeping of this bower he gave
Unto a valiant knighte.

But Fortune that doth often frowne
Where she before did smile,
The king's delight and ladye's joy
Full soon shee did beguile.

For why? The kinge's ungracious sonne,
Whom he did high advance,
Against his father raiséd wars
Within the realme of France.

But yet before our comelye king
The English land forsooke,
Of Rosamonde, his lady faire,
His farewelle thus he tooke:

"My Rosamonde, my only Rose,
That pleasest best mine eye,
The fairest flower in all the world
To feed my fantasye;

"The flower of mine affected heart,
Whose sweetness doth excelle,
My royal Rose, a thousand times
I bid thee now farewelle!

"For I must leave my fairest flower,
My sweetest Rose, a space,
And cross the seas to famous France,
Proud rebelles to abase.

"But yet, my Rose, be sure thou shalt
My coming shortlye see;
And in my heart, when hence I am,
I'le bear my Rose with mee."

When Rosamonde, that ladye brighte,
Did heare the king saye soe,
The sorrow of her grievéd heart
Her outward lookes did showe,

And from her clear and crystall eyes
The teares gusht out apace,
Which like the silver-pearléd dew
Ran downe her comely face.

Her lippes, erst like corall redde,
Did wax both wan and pale,
And for the sorrow she conceivde,
Her vitall spirits faile;

And falling down all in a swoone
Before King Henrye's face,
Full oft he in his princelye armes
Her bodye did embrace,

And twentye times, with watery eyes,
He kist her tender cheeke,
Until he had revivde again
Her senses milde and meeke.

"Why grieves my Rose, my sweetest Rose?"
The king did often say.
"Because," quoth shee, "to bloodye warres
My lord must part awaye.

THE POISON CUP

"But since your grace on forrayne coastes
Among your foes unkinde
Must goe to hazard life and limbe,
Why should I staye behind?

"Nay, rather let me, like a page,
Your sword and target beare,
That on my breast the blowes may lighte
Which would offend you there.

"Or let mee, in your royal tent,
Prepare your bed at nighte,
And with sweete baths refresh your grace
At your returne from fighte.

"So I your presence may enjoye,
No toil I will refuse;
But wanting you, my life is death—
Nay, death I'ld rather chuse!"

"Content thyself, my dearest love,
Thy rest at home shall bee
In England's sweet and pleasant isle,
For travell fits not thee.

"Faire ladies brooke not bloodye warres,
Soft peace their sexe delightes,
Not rugged campes, but courtlye bowers—
Gay feastes, not cruell fightes.

"My Rose shall safely here abide,
With musicke passe the daye,
Whilst I, amonge the piercing pikes
My foes seeke, far awaye.

"My Rose shall shine in pearle and golde,
Whilst I'me in armour dighte;
Gay galliards here my love shall dance,
Whilst I my foes goe fighte.

"And you, Sir Thomas, whom I truste
To bee my love's defence,
Bee carefull of my gallant Rose
When I am parted hence."

And therewithall he fetcht a sigh
As though his heart would breake,
And Rosamonde, for very griefe,
Not one plaine word could speake.

And at their parting well they mighte
In heart be grieved sore:
After that day faire Rosamonde
The king did see no more.

Now when His Grace had past the seas,
And into France was gone,
With envious heart Queene Ellinor
To Woodstocke came anone.

And forth she calles this trustye knighte,
In an unhappy houre,
Who with his clue of twinéd thread
Came from this famous bower.

And when that they had wounded him,
The queene this thread did gette,
And went where Ladye Rosamonde
Was like an angell sette.

But when the queene with stedfast eye
Beheld her beauteous face,
She was amazéd in her minde
At her exceeding grace.

"Cast off from thee those robes," she said,
"That riche and costlye bee,
And drinke thou up this deadlye draught
Which I have brought to thee."

Then presentlye upon her knees
Sweet Rosamonde did falle,
And pardon of the queene she crav'd
For her offences all.

"Take pity on my youthfull yeares,"
Faire Rosamonde did crye,
"And lett mee not with poison stronge
Enforcéd be to dye.

"I will renounce my sinfull life,
And in some cloyster bide,
Or else be banisht, if you please,
To range the world soe wide.

"And for the fault which I have done,
Though I was forc'd theretoe,
Preserve my life, and punish mee
As you thinke meet to doe."

And with these words her lillie handes
She wrunge full often there,
And downe along her lovely face
Did trickle many a teare.

But nothing could this furious queene
There with appeaséd bee;
The cup of deadlye poyson stronge,
As she knelt on her knee,

Shee gave this comelye dame to drinke,
Who tooke it in her hand,
And from her bended knee arose,
And on her feet did stand;

And casting up her eyes to heaven,
She did for mercy calle,
And drinking up the poyson stronge,
Her life she lost withalle.

And when that death through every limbe
Had showde its greatest spite,
Her chiefest foes did plaine confesse
Shee was a glorious wighte.

Her body then they did entomb,
When life was fled away,
At Godstowe, neare to Oxford towne,
As may be seene this day.

"That was a sad tale," said Huchown, clearing his throat.
John Skelton shivered.
"Jealousy is a fearful sin," said Robert Mannyng, "and entails consequences quite as fearful."

"That is so," said Ossian, who had listened attentively. "Have you ever heard the story of the first jealousy of the Western World?"

"Have you the tale?" queried Christine de Pisan.

"I have, indeed," replied Finn's son and poet.

"And will you tell it?" asked the Goodman of Bath.

"I will not," answered Ossian, "tell it on an empty stomach."

"I will tell it," offered Cuan O Lochan.

133. THE UNTIMELY DEATH OF SAMHER THE LAP-DOG

Cuan O Lochan

For about three hundred years after the Deluge Ireland remained a desert place until Partholon, the son of Sera, the son of Sru, *et reliqua*, came and took possession of it.

Upon his coming to Ériu Partholon fixed his dwelling on an island near Erni, a spot altogether delightful, abounding in flowers, fruit and fish. One day he went fishing along the shore, leaving his wife Delgnat and his attendant Topa alone in the island. When they were thus together it was not long till Delgnat began to solicit Topa, for he was young, handsome and well made. At first Topa said nothing in reply; but that did not satisfy Delgnat, so she stripped herself before him, and they went together to the bed. Afterwards the two of them were seized with a great thirst.

Now there was with Partholon a vessel of delicious drink, and the manner of it was such that no one could drink from it save through a tube of red gold. The tube was brought, and the man and woman drank their fill.

When Partholon returned from fishing he asked for some drink. As soon as he had tasted the liquor he sensed the savour of Topa's mouth and Delgnat's mouth on the tube, and a familiar spirit who used to accompany him revealed the shameful deed which the two had committed. Said Partholon to Delgnat: "Why am I not far from you? You have put me into a vexatious situation. The two of you have sullied the face of your lord, and I must have compensation from you for your misdeed."

"Nay," replied Delgnat, "the fault is yours, and it is fitting that I should pass a judgment upon it. You know very well that it is not right to leave together two people who desire each other, as all the world will tell you. It is like leaving honey with a woman, milk with a boy, flesh with a cat, food with a generous man, a cutting tool with a wright; for when a woman is with a man, the one will go to the other when the desire—hard to be resisted—comes upon them. It is you who owe compensation to me by reason of your neglect."

While Partholon was digesting this judicial pronouncement Samher, Delgnat's lap-dog ran in. Partholon gave him a slap with the palm of his hand so that he died. And that was the first jealousy in Ériu.

"What a filthy business!" exclaimed Robert Mannyng when the poet had finished.

"Illogical, too," remarked Matheolus. "It was pure casuistry on the woman's part."

"I wish Partholon had been more of a man," sighed the Goodman of Bath. "His evil example has fostered evil consequences."

"Amen!" said Henry Castide.

"King Henry, at least," spoke up Peter Bell, "seems to have had little regard for ancient tradition, for it is a fact that Eleanor was in various prisons during sixteen years for some reason or other."

"Something may be said for both Rosamund and Delgnat," protested Fenice, "for those who have had experience know that the urge of real love is hard to thwart."

"Rosamund should have put more faith in the clergy," said Iolo Goch. "I once read of a holy cleric who had the proper way with poison cups."

"How was that?" asked Fenice.

134. SAMSON'S ADVENTURES AT THE COURT OF KING HILDEBERT

Iolo Goch

In the time of St Illtyd of Llanilltyd Vawr, which the English call Lantwit Major, there was a young man, his pupil, living on an island of the Severn Sea. His name was Samson. One day, on the eve of the Resurrection of Our Lord, an angel appeared to him and commanded him to pass beyond the sea to Brittany. Nothing more is told of him till he came to Dol.

In those days Count Commotus, a cruel and tyrannical person, governed all Brittany, having slain Jonas, the native count of the Bretons. Judual, Jonas' son, he delivered up to King Hildebert and his queen to be kept in captivity.

On hearing an account of these matters, Samson was grieved at the misery of the people, and went quickly to King Hildebert, desiring him to release Judual from confinement, and deliver the people from a foreign ruler.

When Samson entered the king's palace he found there a certain count who was a demoniac; him he anointed on the face and breast with holy oil, and thereby liberated him from the devil. As soon as the king heard this, and also that Samson had come to intercede for Judual, he received the cleric with suitable honour and invited him to dine. It was Hildebert's queen, however, who held Judual in captivity. Not only would she not release him, but she abused Samson with shameful expressions, which vexed him greatly. And also, that she might destroy the holy man, she prepared for him a deadly drink.

Now when the king and the archbishop sat down to dinner, the queen, at the instigation of the devil, mixed poison with wine in a glass, and sent it to Samson by a servant of hers. Thereupon, being divinely inspired, Samson made the sign of the cross over the glass, which immediately broke into four parts, spilling its contents upon the hand of him who held it; and wonderful to relate! in the sight of all present, the flesh and skin were corroded to the very bone. "This drink," said Samson, "is not fit to be drunk." The king was abashed, and all the people wondered. But Samson marked the hand of him who had been hurt and completely restored it.

After they had dined, Samson, with Hildebert's permission, made ready to visit the place wherein Judual was confined. The queen, whose animosity had been in no wise diminished, again tried to destroy him, for she sent a furious and unmanageable horse for him to ride on. But the archbishop marked him with the cross, and when he mounted, the horse became as mild as though he had been tamed by the King of Heaven.

But the queen's heart was still hardened, and she ordered a fierce lion to be let loose upon the holy man. However, instead of seizing him, the lion took to flight. And Samson said: "I command thee in the name of Jesus Christ to hurt no one any more, and that thou speedily die. Thereupon the lion immediately leaped headlong into the air and expired."

The king, beholding such marvellous miracles, released Judual from chains and delivered him over to Samson. And now the queen, too, with her companions, fell prostrate at his feet, imploring his pardon. And Samson granted it.

Afterwards the king said to Samson: "In this province there is a serpent which grievously afflicts all who dwell in the vicinity of his lair; and because we see thee shine with such miracles, we beseech thee to deliver us from it." "Find me a guide for the way," replied the archbishop, "and in the power of God I will expel the serpent from your parts."

A guide was found, and taking with him his two brethren, Samson set out for the serpent's lair. When he came to the cave he bent his knees and prayed to the Lord, and taking the serpent by the neck, brought it out and commanded it to swim beyond the river called Sigona, and there remain under a certain stone. The serpent dared not disobey, and hid itself under the rock; and soon afterwards, by his word alone, Samson drowned it in the sea.

King Hildebert now loved Samson greatly for his miracles, and freely gave him valuable gifts, and commended himself to his prayers.

"You see," added Iolo, "Rosamund should have had a soul-friend upon whom she might have depended in emergencies."

"That may be so," conceded Mannyng; "but it would have been far simpler for Henry to have left Rosamund alone, and to have been content with Eleanor. A man should cleave to one, and a woman take none."

"Was that the rule you followed at Sempringham?" inquired the Minstrel of Reims. "I have heard queer tales. Besides, life in the world is seldom simple."

"Gentlemen," hastily interposed John Stow, "let us face the facts. All this about Eleanor and William Marshal, Rosamund and the poison cup, is mere literature."

Sir William atte Pole snorted.

"The truth is," went on the historian, "that the king imprisoned his queen because she was furious with him for neglecting her—she was ten-twelve years older than he—wherefor she fomented rebellion among his sons in France. Henry got wind of her machinations and arrested her as she was on the point of fleeing over to them in man's apparel."

"You may be right," conceded Higden. "However, I have read that Hugh de St Maur and the queen's uncle, Ralph de Fay, had already begun to stir up the Young King against his father while Henry was in Ireland in 1172, whereas Eleanor was not incarcerated till 1173. Sire," said he, turning to King Henry, "why did you put your queen behind bars?"

"She kept on talking about her first husband," answered Henry.

"Sir Minstrel," said John Skelton, turning to Richard Sheale, "do you really think that Rosamund had pearly eyes, crystal cheeks and lily hands? How could a man love a woman like that? He might get himself one made at the goldsmith's shop. In my younger days I loved a lady, but I would not describe her as you have portrayed Rosamund."

"How would you describe her?" asked Ariosto.

"As follows," answered Skelton.

135. A SATIRICAL DESCRIPTION OF HIS LADY

John Skelton

My fayr lady, so fressh of hewe,
Good thryft come to your goodly face,
Of colourys like the noble newe,
As bryght as bugyl or ellys bolace.
So weel were he that myght purchace
At good leyser with hire to been,
Hire semly cors for to embrace,
Whan she hath on hire hood of green.

For yif I shuld hire al discrye,
Fro the heed to the novyl, and so forth down—
I trowe there is noon suych alyve;
For to begynne at hire motle crown,
The whyght flekkyd with the brown,
Shoorn as a sheep with sherys keen:
There is noon so fayr in all our town,
Whan she hath on hire hood of green.

The kryspe skyn of hyr forheed
Is drawyn up and ontrustily bownde,
Of colowrys dunne, yelewe, pale and reed,
And therwithal hire cheekys been rownde;
A reynbowe hew so fayr she is fownde,
For whan the sunne shyneth sheen,
Allas! she gevith myn herte a wownde,
Whan she hath on hire hood of green.

Here smothe browys, blake and fyn,
Arn soft and tendir for to fele
As been the bruskelys of a swyn;
Here jowys been rownde as purs or bele;
What though hire herte were made of stele,
And I ne myght hire nevir seen,
Yit must I love hire evir wele,
Whan she hath on hire hood of green.

Here greet shulderys, square and brood;
Here breestys up bere hire bely so large,
For upon hire is a greet carte lood—
She is no bot, she is a barge;

A stouthe that no man may charge,
Whoos boody may not suffysed been,
And evir abrood she beryth hire targe,
Undir hire daggyd hood of green.

This fayr floure of womanheed
Hath too pappys also smalle,
Bolsteryd out of lenghth and breed,
Lyche a large campyng balle;
There is no bagpipe halff so talle,
Nor no cormyse, for sothe as I ween,
Whan they been ful of wynde at alle,
And she have on hire hood of green.

And forth to speke of hire entraylle,
Liche a cow hire wombe is gret—
Rympled liche a nunnys veylle,
And smothe berdyd liche a gete.
Hire teeth been whight as ony jete,
And lych a seergecloth hire nekke is clene,
And for to kepe hire froom the heete,
She weryth a daggyd hood of grene.

Hire skyn is tendyr for to towche
As of an hownd-fyssh or of an hake,
Whoos tewhyng hath coost many a crowche,
Hire pylche souple for to make;
Wheer ovir many an hed hath ake
In skorn whan she lyth on the splene;
And yit she shal hym clene out shake,
Undir hire daggid hood of grene.

Hire buttokys ar not lowe sunke,
But brood as is a Spaynych stede;
For febylnesse she is nat shrunke,
Men may that se thorugh out hire wede:
Hire crowpe doth the semys shrede
Whan they so streyght lasyd been.
Now good thryfft have he for hys mede,
That best can shakyn hire hood of green.

Hire lemys not smal, but liche a spere,
But jumbelyd lyke as is an olyvaunt,
The greet clocher up for to bere,

A belfrey for the bodyfaunt;
Or ellys for to pley at dé,
Or for an hasard of heightene,
So weel were he that had a graunt
To towche hire daggyd hood of grene.

This is the lady that I serve,
That hath so many men on honde;
For of hire can no man thank deserve,
That trottyth on the drye londe,
But on them she wyl have a bonde,
As weel of bayard as of brende,
And yit for sorelle she wyl stonde,
Though men hire daggyd hood wolde rende.

In cherysshyng of the yemanry
She hath weykyd many a bowe,
But moost she lovith specially
Hym that can shote bothe styffe and lowe;
And but the deer be ovir-throwe,
The arwe was nat fyled kene,
And to the deth she can weel blowe
Whan she hath on hire hood of grene.

Hire watir lyme is maad ful weel,
Bothe for the cormeraunt and the snyte;
The botoore that etith the greet eel
Is cause yif he wyl his rochys byte;
The se-mewe with his fetherys whyte,
Nor the caldmawe, nouthir fat nor lene,
Gooth nat from hire panteer quyght,
Whan she hath on hire hood of grene.

Of huntyng she beryth the greet pryse,
For buk or do, bothe hert and hynde;
But whan she dotyth and wyl be nyse,
Maale deer to chaase and to fynde,
That can hym feede on bark or rynde,
And in hire park pasturyd been,
That weel can beere with a tynde,
Undir hire daggyd hood of green.

This sovereyn lady moost enteer,
On hobyng what she lyst to fare,
With hire brood serkelys hire behynde,
To make the larke for to dare,
That fro hir gravys and hir snare,
Goth not awey that comyth between,
The thruschylcok nor the feld fare,
Whan she hath on hire hood of green.

It is deynty of this flowyr,
That is so boold upon hire braunche,
And wyl abyde every showyr,
Whoos thruste may noo stormys staunche;
But the flood wyl ovir launche,
That no man may wade, it is so kene,
It wyl not palle in hire haunche,
Whan she hath on hire hood of grene.

Now what she beryth I wyl yow telle,
Although I can not armys blase,
Nor to the fulle rynge hire belle,
That is so wrymplyd as a mase;
So longe a man may loke and gase,
To telle what shuld hire baggys been,
Whoos fenestralle were hard to glase,
Whan she hath on hire hood of green.

Hire cote armure is duskyd reed,
With a boordure as blak as sabyl,
A pavys or a terget for a sperys heed,
Wyde as a chirche that hath a gabyl;
For who shalle justyn in that stabyl,
But he be shodde he is not sene,
Litel Morelle were not abyl,
Whan she hath on hire hood of grene.

Hire cote armure, though it be rente,
Yit hernyd she nevir the bak,
Though many a robe hath be shente
On hire sarpelere and on hire sak;
Evir moore she stood for al the wrak,
And for shot she lyst not to fleen—
A castyng dart took no tak
Undir hire daggyd hood of green.

> Now fareweel hert, and have good dey,
> Of yow me lyst nat moore to endight,
> Colowryd lyche a rotyn eey,
> In morwe among your pylwys whight;
> The blak crowe moote yow byght,
> Your byl clothyd thirke and onclene,
> A froward velym upon to wryt,
> Whan she hath on hire hood of grene.
>
> Now fareweel fayr and fressh so cleer,
> For whoom I may noo mone take,
> Thowh I se yow not of alle this yeere,
> I can not moorne for your sake,
> Tyl every foul chesyth hys make,
> And the nytynggale that syngeth so sheen,
> And that the cokkow me awake,
> To look upon your hood of green.

"If that is your conception of female beauty," said Ariosto, "I think you would find kindred spirits in Francesco Berni and Antonfrancesco Doni."

"Musha!" exclaimed Mac Conglinne, "I prefer the Old Woman of Beare, myself. . . ."

"Or the Gyre Carling," said Blind Harry.

"But the portraits drawn by Berni and Doni were never displayed on canvas, to my knowledge," went on Ariosto. "Rather it was the ideas and ideals of womanly beauty advanced by such writers as Francesco da Barberino, Agnolo Firenzuola and Giangiorgio Trissino that found reproduction in painting, as in the canvases of Sandro Botticelli and Bernardo Luini. Giovanni Nevizano in his *Silva Nuptialis* reduced the beauties of woman to thirty-four: three white, three black, three rosy, three long, three short, three slender, three large, three small, three narrow, three wide, in addition to white skin, white teeth, flaxen hair and black eyes. But this is a slavish and mechanical elenchus. I much prefer my own portrait of Alcina, even though it was reprobated by Roger Ascham and Luis Vives."

"Well," said Skelton, "neither Ascham nor Vives is present, so let us hear; and it would make no difference if they were."

"Still," answered Ariosto, "since there was an objection to Alcina, I will draw for you instead the portrait of Olimpia, mistress of the faithless Bireno.—

> "Olimpia's beauties are of those most rare,
> Nor is the forehead's beauteous curve alone

Excellent, and her eyes and cheeks and hair,
Mouth, nose and throat, and shoulders; but, so down
Descending from the lady's bosom fair,
Parts which are wont to be concealed by gown
Are such as haply should be placed before
Whate'er this ample world contains in store.

"In whiteness they surpassed unsullied snow,
Smooth ivory to the touch; above were seen
Two rounding breasts, like new-pressed milk in show,
Fresh taken from its crate of rushes green:
The space betwixt was like the valley low
Which oftentimes we see small hills between,
Sweet in its season; and now such as when
Winter with snows had newly filled the glen.

"The swelling hips and haunches' symmetry,
The waist more clear than mirror's polished grain,
And members seem of Phidias' turnery,
Or work of better hand and nicer pain.
As well to you of other parts should I
Relate, which she to hide desired in vain.
To sum the beauteous whole from head to feet—
In her all loveliness is found complete."

"I see nothing to cavil at there," said Skelton, "or nothing much. You go no further in your enthusiasm than is justified by poetic licence. I am a poet of sorts myself, but my genius has a matter-of-fact strain in it. To call a lady's eyes diamonds, her teeth pearls, and her breasts two snowballs seems to me to do her a monstrous disservice, and to admit a lamentable barrenness of invention. On second thoughts, I am not so sure about the cheese in that picture of yours; you would have done better to have followed the lead of Theocritus. There is a certain *oaristys* of his . . ."

"Good, now," interrupted Mac Conglinne somewhat impatiently. "Since even the most exacting lover or artist must be satisfied with either Ariosto's or Skelton's recommendations, we will leave the matter. I should like to comment on certain aspects of Iolo's story. If it was any skill in thaumaturgy that Samson had, sure now, it is from the Irish he must have learned it. You mind how the poison offered to Patrick on one occasion turned to curds and fell out of the cup; and as for quelling dragons, it was Mac Creiche, alive in Ireland when Samson visited Ériu, who was the champion dragon-queller."

"Since you hold no high opinion of my skill as a slayer of dragons," said Fulk Fitzwarin, "I am naturally eager to hear about anyone who elicits your approval. Pray tell us about Mac Creiche."

"I will do so," answered the Illustrious Scholar, "by the leave of Michael O Cleirigh."

136. HOW MAC CREICHE SLEW THE YELLOW PEST

Mac Conglinne

Mac Creiche, son of Pesslan, went into his place of ascetic devotion between Formael and the river Eidnech. His hermitage was of four stones, that is, a stone at the back, a stone at the front, and a stone on either side. He took no food with him into his hermitage save a loaf of bread and four sprigs of cress, and of these he ate nothing save on Sunday. Great was his age from his birth till his death, namely, nine score years.

In the time when great pestilences attacked all Ireland, and Wales too, for that matter, Mac Creiche performed many illustrious miracles. In his early days he reduced the Crom Chonaill to dust and ashes by raising against it the Finnfaidech, his melodious bell. Later he gave his attention to the Gribh Ingnech, the Buide Connuil, the Bolg Sighi, and the Broichsech of Loch Broicsige in Cinel Fermaic. This last was a monster most vehement, strong, malignant and unwearied with its bestial rage upon it, and it wreaked great slaughter throughout the land generally. When it assailed the land its thunderous race was like the thunder-beat of fifty horses on the strand. What it would do was this: it would open its ravenous raging maw like a mad dog, with its jaws all on fire, and emit a broad terrifying stream of harsh magical breath; and every man whom that poisonous breath touched, and every animal, died a premature and sudden death. It would come out of the loch with the dappled clouds of dawn and continue its rapine till its yellow hue spread over the sun; then it would return to the loch in the last third of the day. Wherefor the land was stripped of good men, whether by death or voluntary exile.

Seeing the devastation of their land, the Cinel Fermaic assembled their sages, their seniors and their saints to know what should be done. The clerks rang their bells and smote their pastoral staffs, and all the people shouted. But the monster only waxed more fierce, so that the clerks were abashed at the helpless distress of the country.

Now when Saint Blathmac was in his sleep the angel Victor came to him, and directed that he seek assistance from Mac Creiche on the brink of Loch Lein. "How will the land be protected till he comes?" asked Blathmac. "Easy to say," replied Victor; "I will sing a lullaby in its ear so that it will sleep for three days and three nights." Thereupon Victor drove the monster into the loch and laid him asleep there.

With twelve hundred in his company Blathmac went till he found Mac Creiche. With the cleric were only Mainchin, his disciple, and the Finnfaidech, his sweet-tongued bell. Blathmac implored him to deliver the Cinel Fermaic from the rage of the Broichsech. "What shall I have for this?" asked Mac Creiche. "Thy tribute to be fulfilled to thee every third year," said Blathmac, "and two scruples for ever and for ever from every hearth, and the tax of thy bell every year."

After this Blathmac returned and found that the Broichsech had awakened and was pursuing the people and slaughtering them. Mac Creiche came on the third day. When the people saw him approaching, they came to him on their knees; they commended themselves to him in servile rent of service, and to his monks after him.

They had not been there long when they saw the monster approaching, and they fled for refuge behind the saint. The monster came as far as the weir of Cell Subulaig, and as it came it kept discharging balls of fire through its ravenous raging maw. Great fear seized Mac Creiche, even though Mainchin was behind him with the Finnfaidech. "Reach me my bell, O Mainchin," said Mac Creiche. Mainchin gave it to him, and the saint struck the bell fiercely, so that the monster halted and stared. It reared itself on its hind legs till it was higher than a bushy tall-topped eminent tree, or a round tower on a hill. The numerous claws and talons growing out of it were horrible, and great fear seized the cleric at the thing which he saw. He prayed, and while he was making his prayer the Broichsech stood still. Afterwards it hurled itself onto the weir with dreadful, horrible, unnatural fury; and with such rage did it discharge its balls of fire through its ravening maw and through its nostrils, and so violent was its bestial wrath upon it, that all its bristles could be seen standing on end, with a drop of red blood on every hair of its body from ear to tail.

Hereupon Mac Creiche smote his bell, while the monster was traversing the weir. At the third stroke a ball of fire shot from the bell into the monster's maw, and its gullet caught fire. When the Broichsech perceived that its maw was on fire it let out a horrible scream and screech, while the host of the Cinel Fermaic and the host of the cleric set up a shout of triumph.

Now Mac Creiche began to drive the pest with his crooked staff.

He was behind the monster, Blathmac and the saints were behind him, and the people of the land were behind them, raising continuous shouts and cries. In this wise they reached the loch, and the monster dived into its depths.

But they had not been there long when they saw the loch breaking in fierce red streams over its banks, and behold! the monster rose to the surface and stood erect as before. At this the hosts raised shouts of reproach, insulting the cleric. Mac Creiche was ashamed that the monster should reappear, and his heart bounded in his breast. He looked here and he looked there, but he found nothing with which to smite the Broichsech except one thing. He laid hand on the head covering of his tonsure, that is, his skull-cap, and he flung it against the monster. As he did so his tonsure-cap grew and extended so that it appeared to all the people like a cowl of smelted iron enveloping the beast. After that they saw the monster curling itself in twisted coils under the skull-cap which pressed it down to the bottom of the loch; thence it should never rise again till the brink and doom of life.

Then both hosts raised shouts of joy and gladness. Men, women and children offered themselves in servile labour to Mac Creiche and his monks, and all their stocks and tributes were driven towards him from every quarter; and the freeman who owned nothing but his arms placed himself at the saint's disposal. And Mac Creiche gave thanks to God.

"What!" exclaimed Fulk Fitzwarin. "He took tribute and reward for a deed of Christian charity?"

"Cyrus, king of the Persians," remarked John Stow, "refused to take pay from the Armenians for doing good. But Cyrus was a great man."

"If I remember correctly," rejoined Mac Conglinne, "there was a hero named Beowulf who accepted reward for ridding Hrothgar's court of a demon."

"True enough," agreed John Leland, "but he said nothing about it, nor did Hrothgar. And anyway, Mac Creiche's job was too easy: Beowulf had to use his bare hands."

"It seems to me cleverer," answered the Illustrious Scholar, "to abate a demon by means of one's wits."

"Sir," said Froissart, addressing Cuan O Lochan, "you lately referred to a demoniacal spirit that accompanied Partholon everywhere and betrayed Delgnat to him. The demons of your day—or Partholon's —seem to have been much more malicious than those of ours. The

Lord of Corasse, at all events, had a familiar spirit of a somewhat milder nature."

"Would you tell us the tale?" asked the poet.

"If you wish," answered Froissart.

137. ORTHON, FAMILIAR SPIRIT OF THE LORD DE CORASSE
Jean Froissart

About twenty years ago there lived in southern France a baron called Raymond, who had a suit before the pope at Avignon for the tithes of his church against a priest of Catalonia. The priest who claimed these tithes was very learned, and proved his case so clearly that Pope Urban gave definitive judgment in his favour. But the Lord de Corasse was doubtful, refused to part with his inheritance, and bade the priest begone. The clerk, who knew Raymond to be a hard man, dared not persist, but he said: "I am not so powerful in this land as you are, but since you deprive me of the rights of my church, I will send you, very soon, a champion of whom you will be more afraid than you are of me." Raymond was not alarmed, and the clerk departed.

Some three months after this, when the Lord de Corasse was peacefully sleeping in bed with his lady in his castle of Corasse, there came invisible messengers, who made such a noise, knocking about everything they encountered in the castle, that it seemed they were determined to destroy everything within it; and they gave such loud raps at the door of the knight's chamber that his lady was exceedingly frightened. The knight heard it all, but did not say a word, since he would not have it thought that he was frightened, for he was a man of courage sufficient for any adventure.

On the morrow the servants assembled and went to Raymond, saying: "My lord, did you not hear what we all heard last night?" "What was that?" asked Raymond. When they related to him the circumstances you have heard, the knight laughed and said: "It was nothing; you dreamed it, or it was the wind." "By God!" said the lady, "I heard it well enough." On the following night the noises and rioting were renewed, and much louder than before; and there were such blows struck against the door and windows of the knight's chamber that it seemed they would be broken down.

Now Raymond could stand it no longer. He leaped out of bed and cried: "Who is it who thus knocks at my chamber door at this unseemly hour?" Immediately he was answered: "It is I." "And who sends you hither?" asked the knight. "The clerk of Catalonia whom you have wronged," answered the voice, "for you have deprived him of the rights of his benefice, and I will never leave you in quiet till you have rendered him a just account, and such as will content him." "What are you called," inquired the knight, "who are so good a messenger?" "My name," said the voice, "is Orthon." "Orthon," said the knight, "serving a clerk will not be much advantage to you, for if you put trust in him, he will cause you great trouble. I beg, therefore, that you leave him and serve me, and I will think myself very much obliged."

Orthon was ready with his answer, for he had taken a liking to the knight. "Do you really wish it?" he asked. "Yes, indeed," answered Raymond; "but no harm must be done to anyone within these walls." "Very well," answered Orthon. "I have no power to do ill to anyone—only to awaken you and disturb your rest, and that of other persons." "Do what I tell you," urged the knight; "leave this worthless priest and serve me." "Well, since you will have it so, I consent," replied the voice.

Orthon took such a fancy to the Lord of Corasse that he often came to see him in the night-time; and when he found him sleeping, pulled his pillow from under his head, or made great noises at the doors or windows. On waking the knight would say: "Orthon, let me sleep." "I will not," replied the other, "till I have told you some news." This so frightened the knight's lady that the hairs of her head stood on end, and she hid herself under the bed-clothes. "Well," replied Raymond, "what news have you brought me?" Orthon replied: "I have come from England, Hungary—or some other place, as it might be—which I left yesterday, and such and such things have happened."

Thus did the Lord of Corasse, by means of Orthon, know all things that were passing in different parts of the world. This connection continued for five years till at last the knight could not keep the matter to himself any longer, and discovered it to the Count of Foix, as I shall tell you.

The first year the Lord de Corasse came to the Count of Foix, perhaps at Orthès, and said to him: "My lord, such and such an event has happened in England,"—Scotland, Germany, or some other country. And the Count of Foix, who found that this intelligence proved true, marvelled greatly how he could have acquired such early information. He entreated him so earnestly that the Lord de Corasse finally told him how he came by his news and the manner of its communication. Hereupon the Count of Foix said: "Raymond, nourish the love of your intelligencer. I wish I had such an informant. He costs you nothing, and yet you are truly apprised of everything that passes in the world." "My lord," answered Raymond, "I will do so."

Thus Orthon served the Lord of Corasse for a long time. I do not know whether Orthon had more than one master, but true it is that two or three times every week he visited Raymond and told him all the news of the countries he had frequented. This Raymond immediately sent to the Count of Foix, who was greatly delighted therewith.

Once when the count and Raymond were talking the former said: "Raymond, have you ever caught sight of your messenger?" "No, my lord," said the knight; "I have never pressed him in this matter." "I wonder at that," replied the count, "for had he been so much attached to me, I should have begged him to show himself in his proper form. I urge that you do so, in order that you may tell how he is made, and what he is like." "Since you request it, I will do all I can to see him," replied the Lord of Corasse.

It fell out that one night when the Lord de Corasse was in bed with his lady—who was now so accustomed to hearing the demon that she was no longer frightened—that Orthon arrived and shook the knight's pillow. "Where have you come from?" asked Raymond. "From Prague in Bohemia," he replied. "How far is it hence?" "Sixty days' journey," said Orthon. "And have you returned thence in so short a time?" inquired the knight. "Yes, so help me God; I travel as fast as the wind, or faster." "Have you wings?" asked Raymond. "Oh, no," said the other. "Then how can you fly so fast?" "That is no business of yours," said Orthon. "Perhaps not, yet I should like to see what form you have, and how you are made." "That does not concern you either," answered the other; "be satisfied that you may hear me, and that I bring you intelligence upon which you can depend." "By God!" answered the Lord de Corasse, "I should love you better if I had seen you." "Well," said Orthon, "since you desire it so vehemently, the first thing you shall see tomorrow morning on quitting your bed will be myself." "That suits me," said Raymond.

When morning came the knight arose, but his lady was so much frightened that she pretended to be sick, and said she would never leave her bed the whole day. "Sir," she said, "if I do get up, I shall see Orthon, and if it please God, I would neither see nor meet him." "Well," replied Raymond, "I am determined to see him." And leaping out of bed he seated himself on the bedstead, thinking that he should see Orthon in his own shape; but he saw nothing that could persuade him that he had done so.

The following night Orthon came and began to talk in his usual manner. "Go away," said Raymond; "you are a liar; you were to have shown yourself to me this morning. and you did not." "Oh, yes," said Orthon, "but I did." "No, I say." "Did you see nothing at all when you got out of bed?" Raymond considered for a while, and finally he said: "Yes, as I was sitting there thinking about you, I saw two straws turning and playing together on the floor." "That was myself," said Orthon, "for I had taken that form." "That will not satisfy me," replied the Lord de Corasse. "I beg you to assume some other shape, so that I may see and know you." "You ask too much," replied Orthon; "if I comply with your request, you will ruin me and force me away from you." "You shall not quit me," said Raymond. "If I had seen you once, I should not wish it again." "Well," said Orthon, "you shall see me tomorrow if you will pay attention to the first thing you catch sight of on leaving your chamber." "I am content," said the knight. "Now go your ways, for I want to sleep."

On the morrow, about the hour of eight, the knight had risen and dressed. On leaving his apartment he went to a window and looked into the court of the castle. The first thing he observed there was an immensely large sow, all spotted, with long, hanging ears, and a sharp-pointed, lean snout; but she was so lean that she seemed to be only skin and bones. The Lord de Corasse was disgusted at such a sight, and calling his servants he ordered them to loose the dogs on the sow so that she might be killed and devoured. When the dogs were loosed on her the sow looked up at the Lord de Corasse leaning on the balcony, uttered a loud cry, and was never seen afterwards; she vanished so suddenly that no one knew what had become of her.

The knight returned very pensive to his chamber, for he now recollected that Orthon had told him that if he ever angered him, he should lose him forever. And Orthon kept his word, for never did he return to the Hôtel de Corasse, and Raymond died in the following year.

When the chronicler had finished there was silence for several moments. Finally a sombre voice spoke from the half-shadow: "A great deal of time has been spent, and a great deal of sympathy wasted, it seems to me, on the imprisonment of Eleanor of Aquitaine," said Bernardo del Carpio. "After all, she got what she deserved, if the anecdotes related by her biographers here present have any truth in them."

"The worst fault of Henry's gesture," said Ulrich von Lichtenstein, "was the bad example it afforded Philippe Auguste. His treatment of

Ingeborg of Denmark will hardly be mentioned by the tongues of gentlemen."

"To what do you refer?" asked Peter Bell.

Ulrich remained silent.

"Perhaps a simple monk may speak at certain times when a gentleman must hold his peace," said Ralph Higden. "I will tell enough of the story to satisfy your curiosity.—The chroniclers write that in the year 1200 Philippe II of France married Ingeborg, sister of Cnut VI of Denmark, but that on the morning after the wedding he shut her up in prison. He asserted that her breath stank, and when this was proved to be a shameless lie, he said that he had been kept from his wife by the arts of necromancy. And so powerful was Philippe at home and abroad that neither Ingeborg nor her friends were able to effect her release."

"The treatment my father received at the hands of Alfonso the Chaste," continued Bernardo, "was much more bitter and shameful, and constitutes one of the darkest blots on the pages of Asturian annals."

"How was that?" asked Giovanni da Procida.

"You must excuse me," said Bernardo huskily.

"By your leave," said the Bachelor of Salamanca, "I will tell the story."

138. THE LOVE, IMPRISONMENT AND TREACHEROUS SLAYING OF SANCHO DIAZ, AND WHAT BERNARDO DEL CARPIO DID ABOUT IT

The Bachelor of Salamanca

When Alfonso the Chaste sat upon the throne of the Asturias there lived a young noble called Sancho Diaz, Count of Saldaña. One day at the court he had seen Ximena, the sister of the king, and loved her. She, in return, loved Sancho with an ardour equal to his. Many times they evaded the eyes of the curious to meet in some hidden recess of the palace until Alfonso dismissed the cortes. Then, instead of returning to her own lands, Doña Ximena accompanied Sancho to Saldaña. In the course of time a child was born of their love, and they called him Bernardo.

The news of these matters, on reaching the ears of King Alfonso, oppressed his heart as though with a weight of lead. Not for nothing was he called "the chaste." He was outraged, not so much by the alliance, irregular as it seemed to be, for the count was of as good birth as Ximena, but by the fact that one of his blood had been defiled by the pleasures of the flesh. His militant chastity was shocked. In some respects he resembled his great contemporary, Charlemagne, who, though not chaste, always opposed the mating of any of his female kin. Well did Alfonso illustrate the old proverb that the dog, though he can eat no corn himself, can keep the oxen from the manger.

For many days the king brooded in silence. Finally he commanded his cortes to assemble at León, and addressed the barons as follows: "My friends, I marvel greatly that Sancho Diaz does not come, or that he is so tardy. Under the circumstances it seems to me desirable that he should be fetched. Let two knights go and greet him from me, and say that we have need of him, and will do nothing without him."

In the court were two nobles of high rank, Orios Godos and Count Tiobalte. They said they would bear the king's message to Sancho. "Take no equipage with you," said the king, "save what is indispensable."

At Saldaña the knights delivered their message. Sancho greeted them well, though he thought it strange that if they wished to show him honour they should have come with so small a retinue.

As the count and his companions rode into León no one came to greet them, for the king had forbidden it. This grieved the count deeply, and it seemed to him an omen of evil. On learning that Sancho had arrived, the king caused certain men to stand armed, and instructed them to lay hold on the count in such a way that he could not escape. When the count entered the palace, greeting everyone as he advanced, no one returned his salutation nor said a word. The king saw that all stood in some awe of him and cried out: "Why do you delay? Why do you not seize him?" The men now understood that his command had been in earnest, so they seized Sancho and bound his hands so that the blood gushed from beneath the finger-nails.

"Alas! my lord the king," exclaimed Count Sancho, "why do I receive such treatment? I do not think I have deserved it." "You have indeed deserved it," replied King Alfonso, "for we know the whole story of your affair with Doña Ximena." "Ah, my lord," answered Sancho, "if you are really determined to ruin me because I love your sister, I pray and beseech that you will at least rear up our son Bernardo."

After this Alfonso caused the count's eyes to be put out, loaded him with irons, and threw him into prison in the castle of Luna. Later he seized Ximena and put her willy-nilly into a cloister, where she was closely guarded.

As regards the boy Bernardo—the king had him educated at court, where he grew to young manhood, handsome of face and figure, intelligent and well mannered. Above all he was skilful in the use of arms, and a splendid cavalier.

News of his son's prowess and brilliant career from time to time penetrated to Sancho Diaz in prison. He had been a youth when he had entered Luna, but now his beard was long and white. The tears of his sightless eyes brought no relief to his mind, and served only to deepen the rust which shackled his hands, feet and waist. "Alas! my son," he would cry, "you were born in an evil hour—are you for that reason unfilial and forgetful? To what end your splendid feats, your courage and daring, if not that one day you should set me free?"

But Bernardo was neither undutiful nor forgetful. When he learned the story of his father's imprisonment, his blood seemed to curdle in his veins; and he put on mourning dress, swearing never to lay it aside while his father remained in durance.

Many times Bernardo had implored King Alfonso to release Sancho, but the king had always put him off with ill words and dark looks. Once, when closely pressed by the Moors of Merida, he had unwillingly consented to free the count in return for Bernardo's services. But, the danger past, the memory of his promise passed with it, and to rid himself of a gloomy and importunate suitor, he banished Bernardo from the court.

This was an unwise move on the part of the king, for Bernardo now fortified the castle of Carpio on the confines of Salamanca, and gathering about him a group of friends, raided and harried Alfonso's kingdom. It was a situation which the temper of Alfonso the Chaste was not calculated to endure. In royal wrath he sent letters to Bernardo, summoning him to a cortes at León. Bernardo threw the letters into the fire and gathered his men.

When the knights and men-at-arms had assembled Bernardo said: "Four hundred friends I see about me—friends and men-at-arms who have eaten my bread and salt. Never before have you been separated one from the other; but today one hundred shall remain in Carpio to defend the castle; one hundred shall guard the roads so that none can pass; two hundred shall go with me to speak with the king. If he gives me evil, worse shall he receive."

Arrived at León Bernardo posted one hundred men to guard the city gate; fifty he left at the door of the castle so that none might pass; thirty he distributed up and down the staircase; with twenty retainers he went to hold audience with Alfonso the Chaste.

"God preserve you, mighty king," said the knight, "and your court with you." "Bernardo," said Alfonso, "in an evil hour have you come, traitor that you are, and son of a traitor!" "O king," answered Bernardo, "you lie in your teeth! No traitor am I, nor is there traitorous blood in all my line. You should remember Encinal—when your enemies hedged you so closely about that they slew your horse. Was he a traitor who then put them to flight with his lance, covered you with his shield, and plucked you from their midst? That day you gave me Carpio as a reward, to hold as my fief; and you promised me the liberty of my father—and broke your kingly oath."

"Seize him, men," cried the king, "and stop his foul insulting tongue!" But all looked on and dared not lift a hand, while Bernardo, winding his mantle about his arm, drew his sword. "To me! To me! my valiant men-at-arms," he shouted, "you who eat my bread and salt, for the day has come when you may pay for it."

As Bernardo's men crowded about him Alfonso flushed and paled. "Ah, my dear nephew, what ill manners you have! Can you not give them up for a moment? What a man says in jest you should not take in earnest. I give you Carpio, Bernardo, by my oath, for your hereditary fief." "Evil are your jests, O king," replied the knight, "and such as ill beseem you. And as for Carpio, no one can give me what is already mine, and I know well how to disappoint anyone who seeks to take it from me." And with that Bernardo rode away with his men, while the king's guard stood still in their tracks.

Now it happened that since Alfonso had no heir of his body, he made an agreement with Charles of France that after his death the French king should succeed him. The nobles of Spain, however, refused to accede to what they considered treason on the part of their sovereign, and calling upon Marssil, king of Saragossa, they forced Alfonso to meet Charles in battle array when he crossed the Pyrenees to solemnize the agreement. It was due primarily to the heroic valour of Bernardo—whose personal wrong could not yet make him the enemy of his native land—and of Marssil, that the French were beaten and driven back with dreadful loss that day at Roncesvalles. In that battle fell Don Roldan, Count Anselm, Guiralte, and many another noble man of France.

After the victorious battle at Roncesvalles, in which he had several times saved the life of his uncle, it seemed to Bernardo that he had well earned pardon for any crime of which his father might have been guilty, as well as the thanks and gratitude of his sovereign.

One day a handsome knight, lance tilted, shield on arm, rode through the streets of León on a spirited roan charger. All León admired him, and the king, too, looked from his balcony. "That," said he, "is Musa of Granada or else Bernardo del Carpio." "O king," said Bernardo, pausing before the balcony, "though I am the son of your sister, I am called Bastard. It is you and your people who say it, for no one else would dare. But I tell you that those who call me by that name lie in their beards: never was my father a traitor, nor my mother a whore, for at my birth my mother had been duly married. My father you threw into chains; my mother you encloistered; Spain you would have sold to the king of the Franks—a treason which cost the blood of many a noble Spaniard. At Roncesvalles I saved your life and I saved your kingdom. Now I have come, not to ask, but to demand, nay, to exact the liberty of my sire."

Bernardo had ridden alone into the square without a single squire. But now there was a group of men-at-arms gathering at his back whose numbers were growing swiftly. Alfonso looked about him covertly and saw only scowling faces, and neither beside nor behind him did he see anyone save Count Tiobalte. "Ha!" said the king. "You still preserve your bad manners, O Bernardo. Carpio I gave you once, but I will surrender to you Don Sancho's person if you will now give it back to me." "I ask no more," replied Bernardo, and therewith rode out of the square. "Quick!" said Alfonso to Tiobalte; "off to Luna"; and whispered in his ear.

That night Don Sancho ate and drank well. Alas! he drank too well of the king's spiced wine. They bathed his corpse so that almost all the stains of the rusted fetters were washed away; in rich robes they clad him, of cendal and scarlet. And then they set him, with a face like wax, upon a horse, and brought him riding to the palace of the king. Bernardo rushed to meet Don Sancho, and took his hand to kiss it. But at the touch of the cold flesh he looked up at the pallid face and perceived the truth. "Ay! Don Sancho Diaz," he cried. "Evil was the hour in which you begot me! Evil was the hour in which I sought to free you from your chains! Of all men I am the most unfavoured by Fortune in this world. Since you are dead, and since Carpio is lost to me, happiness also is forever lost, and refuge there is none. What happens to me now I care not. But one duty I still have, and that I will fulfil."

Bernardo sent his men to the convent where his mother dwelt, and they forcibly brought out Doña Ximena. She was led to the palace, and there laying her hand in that of the dead Count of Saldaña, her former secret marriage with him was now publicly confirmed. No longer should Bernardo be called Bastard.

Of the further history of Bernardo del Carpio I know nothing save that with ten of his men he passed into the service of Musa of Granada, seeking on the field of battle a wound to quench the bitter sorrow of his heart.

The company were silent. The fire had burned low. The Curtal Friar threw on an armful of fresh logs, and as it blazed up brightly again the tension lessened.

"I have been wondering," said Conrad of Montferrat, "I have been wondering why Bernardo, so powerful, with so many good men at his back, did not storm Luna and liberate his father by force?"

"Bernardo was—and is—" replied the Bachelor, "a man of honour. By such a deed of violence Don Sancho's name would not have been cleared; only a voluntary act of the king could have done that."

"One aspect of your tale," said Dick O the Cow, "reminds me of an incident that took place in Leicester in my time. A tragedy, indeed, and yet not without its amusing side."

"How was that?" asked John the Reeve.

139. FUN WITH A CORPSE

Dick O the Cow

In the town of Leicester there was once a very famous abbey of monks. One among them, whose name was Dan Hugh, was more famous than the others. He was young and lusty, and had a fancy for fair women, and was forever on the watch for them.

Now in Leicester there dwelt a tailor, wedded to a fair and good woman, whom he loved and she him. For seven years Dan Hugh had sighed sorely after the tailor's wife, and was always pondering how he might find her alone in order to have either "yes" or "no" from her own lips. One day he said to her: "Fair dame, unless I have some pleasure of you I am like to go out of my wits." "Sir," she replied, "I have many a shrewd fit from my husband every day." "Dame," said Hugh, "do not refuse me, for I must have you, whatever it may cost me." Said the wife: "If that's the way it is, come tomorrow; I shall be ready to do your will, for my husband will be out of town; we shall have a good time. But first, Dan Hugh, tell me what my reward shall be." "Dame," said the monk, "by my faith, you shall have twenty nobles of good money, and we shall make good cheer to boot." Then they kissed, and each went about his business.

When the tailor came home that evening his wife told him the whole story of Dan Hugh's proposal, how she had agreed to receive him the next morning, and how she was to have twenty nobles. "What! dame," said the tailor, "will you make me a cuckold's hood? That would grieve me sorely." "Nay, sir," said she; "I will keep myself a good woman, and yet keep the money too. Before Dan Hugh arrives tomorrow morning I will hide you in the chest; when he comes, about five o'clock, as he said, I shall call out for you, and then take care that you come quickly."

Early the next morning Dan Hugh took his way to the tailor's house in great haste, fearing lest he be late for his appointment. The goodwife answered his knock and bade him enter, and Hugh immediately took her in his arms. "Sir," said the wife, "let be, for shame. First I wish to see what I shall have, for when I have it, I shall not crave it; give me the twenty nobles first, and then do as you please." "By my troth," answered Hugh, "you shall have the gold and silver at once, and ask it of me no more. Lo, mistress, here are the nobles." And therewith he threw them into her lap. "Gramercy," said she.

Dan Hugh thought that sufficient time had been spent on accidents, and now wished to attack the substance of the matter; but the goodwife said: "Sir, wait a moment till I have laid up the money." She went to the chest and opened it, as if to put the coin in safe-keeping, and out sprang the tailor her husband. "Sir monk," said the tailor, "stand where you are, and I will give you such a stroke with my brand that you will have little lust to meddle with my wife now or at any future time." And therewith he hit Dan Hugh upon the crown so that he fell down stark dead. "Alas!" cried the tailor's wife; "you have killed this monk; what shall we do now?" "Well," answered the tailor, "we must get rid of him; have you any suggestion?" "Yea, sir," said the wife. "Leave him here till evening; then carry him to the abbey when it is dark, and set him up straight by the wall; then come away home as quickly as you can." And so it was done.

Now the abbot had been seeking Dan Hugh, and when he learned that he was out of the cloister, he became angry, and swore he would never rest till Hugh had been found. He sent a servant to seek him, with the message that Hugh should come to speak with him. The man went out and looked here and there till he happened to see Hugh leaning, as he thought, against the wall. "Dan Hugh," said he, "I suppose you don't know that I have been looking for you this long while?" But Hugh said nothing. Said the servant: "Well, you must come to the abbot now, or you will be blamed." But when Hugh answered nothing at all, the man thought he would seek counsel, and returned to the abbot. "Sir," said he, "come and see where Hugh stands by the wall, staring at one spot like a man out of grace; and he will not answer a word to what I say." "Ha!" said the abbot; "give me a staff, and I shall see whether or not he will answer me."

The abbot came up to the wall where Dan Hugh was standing and addressed him in this wise: "Ho, false rascal, why do you not attend to your services properly and like a true man? Come here; you shall smart for your negligence." But Hugh said never a word. "What!

whoreson," cried the abbot; "you say nothing? Speak up now, or by God! I will give you such a tap on your skull as will stretch you dead." And with that he gave Hugh such a rap that he fell down forthwith. And thus was Dan Hugh slain the second time.

"Sir," said the abbot's man, "you have killed the monk, and for that crime you will be suspended from this place, I have no doubt." "Can you save my honour?" cried the abbot. "If so, you shall have forty shillings." "Well," said the fellow, "you must know that he was always hanging about a certain tailor's house to woo his pretty wife. I will take him there and set him up standing so that no one shall see or know it; and everyone will say that the tailor has slain him in anger for coming to see his wife so often."

The abbot thought this was good counsel, so the servant took up Dan Hugh and set him at the tailor's door, and came away again as fast as he could. In the meantime the tailor and his wife had gone to bed, very uneasy lest some harm come to them on account of the monk.

In the morning the tailor said to his wife: "All last night I dreamed that that miserable wretch came back to our door." "Jesus!" said his wife, "what a man you are to be so afraid of a corpse; you killed him dead, or so it seems to me." "Well," said the tailor, "I'll go and see, anyway"; and he caught up a pole-axe as he went to the door. When he saw Dan Hugh standing there, you may be sure he was like one bereft of his wit. After a little he called to his wife: "Dame, I am a dead man unless I kill this fellow first." And with that he hit Dan Hugh such a crack on the head with his pole-axe that he fell down dead. Thus was Dan Hugh three times slain.

"Alas!" said the tailor's wife, "this wretch is certainly too bold." "Dame," said the tailor, "what shall we do now?" "Sir," answered the woman, "lay the monk up in the corner till tomorrow's dawn; then take him in a sack and cast him into the mill-dam."

In the grey morning, therefore, the tailor put Hugh into a sack and hastened off to the mill-dam. As he approached, he saw two men, thieves for the nonce, who were hurrying towards him from the mill. When they caught sight of the tailor, they were very much frightened, for in the dim light of the morning they mistook him for the miller. They hastily laid down their sack and drew away to one side. When the tailor came upon the sack, he laid down his own burden and looked into it; it was full of bacon which the thieves had stolen. So he left Dan Hugh where he was and went away home as fast as he could with the thieves' sack.

The scoundrels now returned, took up the sack lying on the ground, and went away home. One of the thieves said to his wife: "Dame," said he, "look in this sack; it is full of fine bacon to make us good cheer." When the woman unbound the sack and found the dead monk therein she cried out: "Alas! you have slain Dan Hugh, and you shall be hanged, if it come to be known." "Nay, good dame," said the thieves; "it was the rascally miller who killed him." Thereupon they took Dan Hugh and carried him back to the mill, and hung him up on the beams whence they had stolen the bacon.

Now when it was fully morning the miller's wife rose to fetch some bacon for breakfast, but when she looked up and saw the monk hanging there, she was aghast. "By cock's bones," said she, "here hangs the knavish monk who was always dallying with men's wives; somebody, probably the devil of hell, has paid him out amply. Moreover, our bacon is stolen. I call this sharp practice. I don't know what we shall eat this winter."

"Never mind the bacon," said the miller; "give me some good suggestions as to how to get rid of this corpse." "Sir," said the wife, "lay him in a dark corner till nightfall. Near by is the abbot's close, and a good horse roaming at his will therein. When it is dark, go fetch him. We will bind Dan Hugh upon his back, and tie a long pole under his arm as though he were armed against enemies. In the morning when the abbot rides abroad on his mare to oversee his workmen, the horse will run to her."

The miller thought his wife's advice was good, and did as she had suggested. He bound Dan Hugh securely on the horse's back so that he could not slip off, took him by the halter and led him where he could get wind of the mare. As the miller's wife had foreseen, the horse made for the mare at more than a pace when the abbot rode out in the morning. When that worthy man saw Dan Hugh riding toward him at a great rate, lance couched, he was frightened almost out of his wits. "Help!" he cried, "for the sake of the Trinity. Dan Hugh is seeking vengeance. I am a dead man!" And therewith he slipped off his mount and ran. At his outcry the abbot's men ran up to Dan Hugh, and laid on thick and fast with staves and clubs till they had cast him to the ground. Thus they killed him once again.

Such is my story how Dan Hugh was once hanged and four times slain, and finally buried. I pray God send us all good rest.

"Sir," said Sighvat Skald, ignoring Dick and turning to Bernardo, "your sad story reminds me in some measure of the vengeance taken by a son of the North. In spite of the climate, to which the poet of Troyes has so bluntly, and I might say ignorantly, referred, our sense of right and wrong is no less keen than that of more southern peoples. With the permission of the company I will tell . . ."

140. HOW OLAF TRYGGVISON PAID A DEBT

Sighvat Skald

As you know, King Trygve Olafson was set upon and killed at Vegger by the men of King Gudrod Björnson. Now King Trygve had married a woman called Astrid, the daughter of a great man who dwelt at Ofrostad. After Trygve's death Astrid fled, taking with her all the loose property she could find. Her foster-father, Thorolf Lusiskiaeg, accompanied her and never left her, and others of her faithful followers spied about to discover her enemies, and where they were.

Astrid was pregnant with a child of King Trygve, and she went to a lake and concealed herself in a holm in it with a few men. Here her child was born. It was a boy; water was poured over it, and it was called Olaf after the grandfather. Here Astrid remained all summer, but when the weather began to be cold, she was obliged to return to the mainland with Thorolf and a few other men. She went to her father Eric, and when she had been there a short time, her attendants left her, so that she was alone save for her two servant girls, her son Olaf, and Thorolf Lusiskiaeg with his son Thorgils.

Now in the spring Astrid's enemies began to hunt for her, and when her father Eric got wind of this, he sent her to Hákon the Old of Sweden. The Swedish king received her with honour and respect, and with him she remained for two years.

Astrid had a brother called Sigurd who had long been abroad with King Valdemar in Russia, and was held in great esteem by him. Her circumstances being such as they were, Astrid thought she might well seek out her brother in Russia. Hákon the Old gave her good attendants and what was needful for the journey, and she set out in the company of some merchants. As they were sailing out into the Baltic they were captured by Esthonian vikings, who made booty of both the people and the goods, killing some and dividing others as slaves.

In this affray Olaf was separated from his mother. An Esthonian called Klerkon got him as his share of the spoils, along with Thoralf Lusiskiaeg and his son Thorgils. Klerkon thought that Thoralf was too old to be much good as a slave, and that there was not much work to be got out of him, so he killed him. Later he sold the boys, and eventually Olaf was purchased for a good cloak by a man called Reas. With him Olaf remained for a long time, and was well treated.

After this it happened that Sigurd, Astrid's brother, came into Esthonia from Novgorod to collect taxes for King Valdemar. In the market-place he happened to observe a very handsome boy, and know-

HOW OLAF TRYGGVISON PAID A DEBT

ing that he was a foreigner, asked his name and family. The boy, Olaf, told him the circumstances of his life, whereupon Sigurd arranged to buy him and Thorgils from Reas. He took them back to Novgorod with him.

One day Olaf Tryggvison was in the market-place of Novgorod, where a great number of people had gathered. Among them he recognized Klerkon, who had killed his foster-father, Thoralf Lusiskiaeg. At the moment Olaf had a little axe in his hand: Therewith he clove Klerkon's skull down to the brain and ran home to his lodging, where he told his friend Sigurd what he had done. Sigurd immediately took Olaf to Queen Olga's house, related to her what had happened, and begged her to protect the boy. The queen replied that the lad was far too comely to be slain, and ordered her people to get under arms.

At that time it was the law in Novgorod that whoever was responsible for the death of a man, save by judgment of law, should be put to death. By reason of this law and usage the whole people rose in tumult and sought after the boy who had slain Klerkon. When it was reported to the king that the slayer was in the queen's house and under her protection, he went there with his suite and would allow no bloodshed. At last it was peaceably settled that the king should name a fine for the murder, and the queen paid it. Olaf afterwards remained with Queen Olga and was much loved.

After these events Sigurd told the queen of what family Olaf was, and for what reason he had come to Russia, namely, because he could not remain safely in his own country; and he asked her to speak to the king about the matter. The queen did so, and begged the king to help a king's son whose fate had been so hard. In consequence of her entreaty Valdemar promised to assist Olaf. He received the youth into his court and treated him nobly, like a king's son.

Olaf was nine years old when he came to Russia, and he remained nine years more with King Valdemar. He was the handsomest of men, very robust and strong, and in all bodily exercises he excelled every Northman who was ever heard of.

"A remarkable feat, indeed, to be performed by one so young," said King Richard. "I wish I might have known Olaf as a man," he added with a sigh.

"It seems incontestable that he was a man's man, as the saying goes," remarked Matthew Paris, "but I have read that he was not always equally successful with women."

"To what do you refer?" asked Hallfred Vandraethaskald.

"Probably," interrupted Einar Rattlescale, "he is thinking of the affair with Iron Skeggi's daughter."

141. JARNSKEGGI'S DAUGHTER
Einar Rattlescale

There was a man from Ophaug in Yriar. His name was Jarnskeggi. During the famous battle between Earl Hákon and the Jomsberg vikings in Hjörungvag, Jarnskeggi had shared with Svein Hákonson and Rognvald the leadership of the earl's left wing.

Towards summer Olaf Tryggvison collected men and sailed north to Nidaros in the Thrandheim country. He called a Thing at Froste and exhorted the assembled chiefs and bonders to accept Christianity. The bonders, however, told him to be quiet, and Jarnskeggi was foremost in speaking against the new religion. Olaf saw that the men were in a nasty temper and that his force was outnumbered; so he temporized, saying that he would attend their sacrifice festival. This apparently mild attitude appeased the bonders, and the festival was set for midsummer at Maere.

Now when the time appointed for the festival of sacrifice drew near, Olaf held a great feast at Lade. On the morning after the carouse, the king made an announcement to his assembled guests— the great men of the district—to the effect that he himself would provide for the forthcoming blood-sacrifice; on this occasion, however, the sacrificial victims should not be slaves or malefactors, as in the past, but they should be noble men worthy of the gods. Thereupon he named eleven of the greatest chiefs present, ordering that they should be seized forthwith. It was now the bonders' turn to give ground. Seeing themselves in the minority, they sued for peace and accepted baptism.

Elated with this success, Olaf now went to Maere in Thrandheim, where the chiefs and great bonders who opposed Christianity were assembled. He summoned a Thing, and harangued the men, urging them to accept the Christian faith. Again Jarnskeggi replied on behalf of the bonders, saying that they were still of the same mind as formerly, namely, that Olaf should not break their laws. The bonders applauded this speech, and agreed that they would have things as Jarnskeggi had said, and that Olaf should offer sacrifice as kings before him had done. "Well," said Olaf, "I will go into the temple and see how things are done." Inside the temple sat an image of Thor adorned with gold and silver. Olaf lifted his axe and struck Thor so that the image rolled to the ground. At the same time Olaf's men threw down all the other gods from their seats.

When Olaf went into the temple, Jarnskeggi waited outside at the temple door. As soon as the violence broke out within, the king's men outside struck down Jarnskeggi and killed him. Olaf now offered the bonders the choice of two things: either that they should fight with him, or that they should accept Christianity. Since Jarnskeggi was dead, and the bonders were thus left without a leader, they agreed to the second condition, and were baptized.

Hereafter, as a matter of policy, Olaf appointed a meeting with Jarnskeggi's kin, and offered them the compensation which was due for his death. Many bold men had an interest in the business, on one side as well as on the other, and it was a long time before any satisfactory conclusion could be reached. However, Jarnskeggi had a daughter named Gudrun, and it was finally agreed between the parties that the king should take her in marriage. The girl's wishes in the matter were not consulted.

When the wedding-day came, King Olaf and Gudrun went to bed together. As soon as Gudrun thought the king was asleep, she drew a knife, with which she intended to run him through. But the king saw it and took the knife from her, whereupon he got out of bed and went to tell his men what had happened. Gudrun, for her part, took her clothes, and went away with all the men who had followed her thither. Gudrun never came into the king's bed again.

"That was the story I had in mind," said Matthew Paris, "but I never heard the rights of it before."

In the group of guests composed of John Capgrave, Paul the Deacon, John Wiclif and William of Wykeham there was considerable hum of talk about the ethics of this situation.

"Well," broke in Snorri Sturlason, "you could not really blame the girl, could you, for giving expression to a natural resentment against him who was at least indirectly the cause of her father's death? We admit that according to certain standards the homicide would have been deplorable had Gudrun succeeded. But all this company knows, as Gudrun did not know, that there are always some who are trodden down and crushed by the march of events. Jarnskeggi could not avoid, and Gudrun could not correct or repair: the blind force of circumstance is always stronger than the hearts of men."

No one contested Snorri's words.

"Good, now," said Mac Conglinne, "you have heard how a lad avenged his foster-father, and how a daughter attempted to take vengeance for her father's murder. In the ancient histories of my country I have read how a son avenged the murder of his mother. With the permission of Doctor Keating I will relate the circumstances."

And without waiting for leave from Keating or anyone else, Mac Conglinne told the story of . . .

142. QUEEN MEAVE'S LAST BATH
Mac Conglinne

Eochaid Feidlech, the son of Finn and king of Ireland, had three sons, Bres, Nar and Lothur, and three daughters, Eithne Uathach, Meave of Cruachan, and Clothru of Cruachan.

When Eochaid's three sons would have wrested the kingship from him, their sister Clothru met them and tried to put them off. "Do you realize that it is your father against whom you are preparing this outrage?" she asked. "If you were to succeed, it would be a great wrong." "Nevertheless, it cannot be helped," replied the young men. "Well, then, since you shall lose your own lives there, probably you have children to come after you," said Clothru. "None to speak of," replied the brothers. "Come in to me then," said their sister, "for my time is upon me, and we shall see if you may have offspring by me." And so it was done; they lay with her one after the other. Good came of that, for Clothru bore Lugaid of the Red Stripes, son of the three Findemna. Thereafter Clothru said: "Abandon this hosting against your father now; you have been guilty of sufficient unrighteousness in lying with your sister; do not increase it by bearing arms against your sire." But those three brothers would not be hindered; they fought that battle at Druim Criad, and fell in it because of their sin.

Now it was in Inis Clothrand in Loch Rí that Clothru administered the laws of Connaught. It is said that her sister Meave killed her, and that the child with which she was pregnant, namely, Furbaide mac Conchobuir, was taken from her side with swords. Thereupon Meave seized the lordship of Connaught and took Ailill to be her consort.

In respect of Meave I must tell you that she was under a *geis* or injunction to bathe every morning in a spring at the head of the island. One day Furbaide, Clothru's son, went to Inis Clothrand and set up a pole at the spot where Meave was accustomed to bathe, and the pole was as tall as Meave; and he stretched a cord from the top of the pole across Loch Rí from east to west; then he took that rope home with him. When the other youths of Ulster were at play Furbaide's game was this: By means of his rope he would measure the distance between two poles, and practise slinging between them; nor did he leave off till he was so expert that he could hit the apple that was on the head of the one pole.

On a day there was a great gathering round Loch Rí of the men of Connaught from the one side, and of the men of Ulster from the other. Early in the morning Meave went to bathe in the spring above the loch, as she was bound to do. "How beautiful is yonder figure!" said everyone. "Who is it?" asked Furbaide. "It is your mother's sister," said all. At that time Furbaide was eating a piece of cheese. He did not delay to pick up a stone; he put the cheese into his sling, and when Meave's forehead was turned toward them, he slung the piece of cheese and lodged it in her head. By a single cast he killed her, and thus avenged his mother.

"You have added several unnecessary details," said Geoffrey Keating. "A picture must have a setting," answered Mac Conglinne.

"Among the old heroic legends of the North," spoke up Thormod Kolbrunarskald, there is one which I think will compare favourably with any of its kind. Some of our critics, such as Chrétien de Troyes, have reproached us with what seems to them sluggishness, or even stolidity. Nothing could be farther from the truth than such an opinion, which is voiced only by those who, like Chrétien, know nothing of us by actual contact, whether in the flesh or in our literature. A certain callousness or seeming indifference was merely an assumed shell of protection for those whom Wyrd never allowed any rest. Under correction from Snorri Sturlason, it seems to me that Gudrun, Sigurd's wife, had lived long enough to realize the hopelessness of her struggle, but not long enough to become reconciled to it. Hamther, Sörli and Erp sensed impending disaster too; Randver and Svanhild died young, but none the less heroically. Wyrd always won, but over victims who never fully acknowledged themselves beaten. Therein lies the heroism of the North. Oedipus, Antigone, Orestes, were vanquished from the start. But—I am not going to give you a lecture, but tell you the story of . . ."

143. SVANHILD AND RANDVER

Thormod Kolbrunarskald

After the murder of Sigurd the Volsung, Gudrun, as you know, was married to King Atli. You remember how Atli slew Gunnar and Högni, and how Gudrun took revenge for that deed—first by slaying the two small sons she had by Atli, serving him their blood in his mead-cup, setting their roasted hearts before him to eat, and finally by slaying Atli himself. Thereafter she set fire to the hall and went her ways down to the strand.

When Gudrun came to the seashore, she took stones in her arms and waded out into the sea, for she had no desire to live longer after the sorrows she had borne. But the billows upheld her, and drove her along over the sea till she was borne to King Jonakr's land. The king took her and wedded her, and they had three sons called Hamther, Sörli and Erp.

With King Jonakr, too, was reared Svanhild, Gudrun's daughter by Sigurd. Of all women she was the fairest, and, like her father, so eager-eyed that few could abide her glance. King Jörmunrek the Mighty heard of her beauty, and he called to him his son Randver and said: "You and my counsellor Bikki shall go on an errand of mine to King Jonakr; for with him is Svanhild, daughter of Sigurd Fafnir's-bane, and I know indeed that she is the fairest maid under the sun. Rather than all others would I have her for my wife, and you shall go and woo her for me." "My lord," replied Randver, "it is fitting that I should go on your errands."

The prince and Bikki set forth on their journey. At the abode of King Jonakr they saw Svanhild, and marvelled greatly at her beauty. One day Randver approached the king and said: "King Jörmunrek the Mighty would fain be your son-in-law; he has heard tell of Svanhild, and it is his desire to have her to wife. I hardly think she could be given to a mightier man than he." King Jonakr replied that the alliance did him honour. Gudrun was against the match, but through the king's favour and approval the wooing was accomplished.

Svanhild was taken to ship with a goodly company, and took her place in the stern beside Randver. Bikki watched them as they sat and talked together, and finally he said to the prince: "It would be right and good if you, rather than your father, who is an old man, were to take such a lovely woman for your wife, for you are both young." That counsel was very pleasing to Randver, and he spoke sweet words to Svanhild, and she to him likewise.

So the voyage wore on till at last they came to land and went home to King Jörmunrek. Then said Bikki: "My lord, even though the telling be hard, it is proper that you should know what has fallen out, for it concerns your beguiling by your son. He has obtained the full love of Svanhild, and she is no other than his mistress. Let not that deed of treachery remain unavenged."

Now Bikki had given the king many an evil counsel before this, but of all his ill reports this stung him most. In quick wrath he cried out that Randver should be taken and tied up to the gibbet.

As the prince was being led away to the gallows, he took his hawk and plucked off all its feathers, and bade his guards show it thus to his father. When the king saw it he said: "Now all men can see very well that Randver thinks all my honour is gone from me, just as the feathers are gone from this hawk." And therewith he ordered the execution to proceed.

When Randver was dead Bikki approached the king and said: "You have still greater cause for resentment against Svanhild; let her die a shameful death." "Yea," answered the king; "I will do as you advise." Accordingly Svanhild was bound in the gate of the burg, and horses were driven at her to tread her down; but when she looked at them with her flashing eyes, the horses durst not trample her. Bikki saw how it went, and he ordered that a bag should be drawn over her head. They did that, and thereupon Gudrun's daughter lost her life.

"I heard the matter somewhat differently," interrupted Snorri. "It was related to me that when Jörmunrek saw the featherless hawk he realized that, just as the bird was now powerless and useless without its feathers, so he, the king, was shorn of his might, since by his own act he had made himself childless. After this, when he was riding home from the hunt, he happened to see Svanhild washing her hair outside the house; and as he looked at her, it seemed to him that she was the cause of all his woe; so he and his men rode her down under their horses' hooves."

"However that may be," continued Thormod . . .

When the slaying of Svanhild was reported to Gudrun she spoke to her sons and said: "Why do you sit here in peace and idle pleasure when Jörmunrek has slain your sister, trampling her under the hooves of horses in shameful wise? My blood runs thin in you: Gunnar and Högni would long since have avenged their kinswoman." Hamther answered that it would be a good thing to kill Jörmunrek. Then Gudrun laughed. She provided her three sons with good byrnies, and helmets so strong that iron would not bite on them, and other needful implements of combat. And she told them that when they came to King Jörmunrek they should go to him as he slept, that Sörli and Hamther should hew off his hands and his feet, and that Erp should smite off his head. And she warned them not to use stones or other heavy materials, for it would be to their scathe if they did so. Then said Hamther: "This is our last parting, for when you hear tidings of us again, you will be able to drink one death-ale over us and Svanhild."

The brothers went their ways. The two of them asked Erp what help they might expect of him, and he answered: "Even such aid as the hand gives the hand, or the foot the foot." Hamther and Sörli said that the help which the foot received from the hand was altogether nothing; and they were wroth with their mother for sending him with them on this errand. So they killed Erp, for him their mother loved best.

Now it was not long before Hamther stumbled, and he put down his hand to steady himself. "It appears that Erp spoke nothing but the truth," he said, "for I should have fallen just now had my hand not steadied me." A little afterward Sörli stumbled, but he turned about on his feet and succeeded in keeping his balance. "Yea, now had I fallen too," he said, "if I had not supported myself with both feet." Both agreed that they had done evilly by their brother Erp.

Thus they went their ways till they came to the abode of King Jörmunrek. They set upon him at once: Hamther cut off his hands, and Sörli cut off both his feet. The king called out to his men. Said Hamther: "The head would be off by now if Erp were alive." Jörmunrek's men attacked them, but they defended themselves in manly wise, and were the scathe of many a warrior, for no iron would bite on their armour.

Then there came a certain aged and one-eyed man who said: "Do you call yourselves men and cannot bring these two to their end?" "Perhaps you can give us some good advice?" suggested Jörmunrek. "I can indeed," replied the old man: "Smite them to death with stones." They did that. The stones flew thick and fast, and that was the end of their life-days.

When Gudrun heard these tidings she retired to her chamber, her heart swollen with sorrow. "O Sigurd," she cried, "do you not remember the time when we sat together on the bed, and you promised that you would come again, even from hell, to meet me? Come now." And to her men she said: "O ye earls, rear the pyre of oak-boughs now, and make it the highest that ever a hero had. Then let the fire burn and melt away the sorrows of my grief-filled breast." And so it was done.

"What a woman!" murmured Andrea Dandolo.

"What a woman indeed!" exclaimed Paul the Deacon. "Did she by blood achieve the alleviation of her sorrow, or restore her daughter to life? And you, O Illustrious Scholar, what did Furbaide gain? Did he win the kingdom of Connaught, or even the rule of Inis Clothrand? Did he secure the health of his own soul? In my view, vengeance is often a two-edged sword. If you like, I will illustrate my belief by telling how a daughter avenged her father."

"Tell on," invited John Gower.

144. ROSMUNDA'S REVENGE

Paul the Deacon

During that dark period of human history subsequent to the death of the great emperor Justinian there dwelt in Pannonia, a plain at the junction of the Danube and the Mur, a people called Gepidae. Beyond them on the banks of the Theiss to the east lived the Langobards, or Lombards, and north of them a terrible Hunnish race—the Avars.

Alboin was king of the Langobards, and he said to the Khan of the Avars: "Let us unite our strength and crush these Gepidae; your part of the spoil will be my present lands, and Pannonia too; I, with my people, will pass on into Italy."

When Cunimund, king of the Gepidae, learned that this coalition had been formed against him, he was in despair. "Let us fight first," he said, "against our more inveterate foes; if we vanquish them, we shall doubtless also be able to drive the Huns beyond our borders."

Cunimund and his warriors marched to meet Alboin. Both sides fought stubbornly; but at the close of day there was hardly a single man of the Gepid race alive to tell the story of his people's defeat. In this battle Alboin slew King Cunimund—an old man—in hand to hand combat, and with the taste which has rightly been characterized as barbarian, cut off his head. From the skull of his fallen foe the Langobard made a drinking goblet, and thinking no doubt to dignify the object and palliate the deed, adorned it with silver and pearls. Ever afterwards, on solemn festivals, that gruesome goblet, handed to the king full of wine, recalled to his savage heart the triumph of that bloody day. But something more precious he carried away from battle—Rosmunda, Cunimund's daughter; and since his former wife, Chlotsuinda, had died, he married her.

Rosmunda was a king's daughter, and with sturdy fortitude she bore for nearly four years the fortunes thrust upon her by war and defeat. Then one day at Verona, when Alboin sat unduly long at the feast, and the recollection of his former mighty deeds had been refreshed by copious libations, the memory of the battle with Cunimund and its ghastly souvenir came distortedly to his mind. "Bear," said he to his attendant, "this goblet of wine to my wife, and bid her from me to drink merrily with her sire."

Rosmunda gave no sign and spoke no word, though her mind was torn with anguish. In her heart she planned that Alboin should pay dearly for the shame done her father, and for the gratuitous insult now offered to herself. But whom could she, a foreigner in a strange land, enlist in her aid? Who among the king's retainers had ready access to her husband's person? Fortune favoured her. There was a young man, Helmechis, the king's shield-bearer and foster-brother. To him she offered her hand and the Lombard crown if he would compass Alboin's death.

Helmechis was prouder of his looks than of his strength, and though he was willing to accept the lady and the kingdom, he preferred that someone else should actually commit the murder. "Who?" asked Rosmunda. "Peredeus the chamberlain," replied Helmechis, "for he is very strong of arm."

Peredeus was also, as rarely happens, strong of mind, for he refused to enter into the plot. But where is the man whom a woman cannot beguile or trick into doing her will? Was it not a woman who deceived Solomon and ruined Samson, and made a saddled and bridled fool of the wise Aristotle? Why say more? It happened that Peredeus was in love with one of Rosmunda's chambermaids. One night the queen substituted herself in the maid's bed, and when Peredeus had lain with her she said: "Whom do you take me to be?" "Why, are you not Addua?" asked the chamberlain. "It is not as you think," replied Rosmunda. "I am the queen; and now you must either kill Alboin or he will put you to the sword on my representation."

Peredeus well understood the weakness of his position. One day while Alboin was enjoying his noonday siesta Rosmunda removed all the arms from his chamber except the sword at the head of his bed; that she left, so as not to arouse suspicion, but she tied it so fast that it could not be removed nor the blade withdrawn. Helmechis, for his part, secured quiet by dismissing the usual guards. When all was ready, Peredeus entered. Alboin sensed danger and awoke; since he could not draw his sword, he defended himself for a long while with a footstool, but at last sank beneath the assassin's stroke. They buried him under the palace steps. Cunimund was avenged.

But should not Alboin be avenged? His subjects thought so. Only by flight were Helmechis and Rosmunda able to save themselves from the fury of the Lombards, going by night to Longinus, the Prefect at Ravenna, and not forgetting to take with them the Lombard treasure.

But a lion's den is scarcely a safe retreat from a pack of wolves. "You," said Longinus the Prefect to Rosmunda, "are beautiful, and though a barbarian, move me strangely. Moreover, you are rich, and your gold will go far to help me wipe out the shame of my many administrative failures. Get rid of this milksop husband of yours, and I will make you lady of Ravenna. Accede to my wishes, or I will kill Helmechis myself, and deliver you over to the Lombards."

What could Rosmunda do? While Helmechis was relaxing in the frigidarium after the bath, Rosmunda handed him a cooling drink, which she said would do much for his health. The unfortunate youth had drunk no more than half of it when he felt the fiery poison coursing through his veins. "Alas!" said he; "I forget my manners. Ladies should be served first. Do not hesitate to drink. I insist at the point of this sword."

"Truly," concluded Paul, "vengeance is a matter wherewith mortals should not meddle."

"To that opinion, reverend sir, I cannot wholly subscribe," countered Froissart, "though by profession I also am a man of peace."

"Which adequately explains, I suppose, why you spent most of your life writing about wars and what you call gallant deeds of arms," said Wiclif.

"And as you are a man of justice," went on Froissart, "I think you will admit that the case I am going to lay before you was one in which revenge was well bestowed. At least such was the judgment of heaven."

145. HOW SIR JOHN DE CAROUGES AVENGED THE HONOUR OF HIS WIFE

Jean Froissart

In the household of Peter, Count d'Alençon, were two young men, a squire called James le Gris, and a knight, Sir John de Carouges. Both men were highly esteemed by the count, but particularly James le Gris, whom he loved above all others, placing his entire confidence in him.

It chanced that Sir John de Carouges took it into his head that his fame would be enhanced if he undertook a pilgrimage to the Holy Land, whither he had long desired to go. He took leave of his lord, the Count d'Alençon, and of his wife, who was then a young and handsome lady, and left her in his castle, called Argenteil, on the borders of Perche. There she remained with her household, living in the most decent and virtuous manner.

Now it happened that the devil entered the body of James le Gris, and, by divers and perverse temptations, induced him to commit a crime. He cast his thoughts on the lady of Sir John de Carouges, whom he knew to be residing with her attendants at Castle Argenteil. One day, therefore, he set out, mounted on the finest of the count's horses, and arrived, full gallop, at the castle. The servants received him cordially, for they knew he was a particular friend, and attached to the same lord as their master. The lady, thinking no ill, welcomed him with pleasure, led him to her apartment, and showed him many specimens of her handiwork. Then James, fully intent on accomplishing his wickedness, begged her to conduct him to the donjon, since his visit was partly to examine it. The lady instantly complied and led him thither; and, as she had the utmost confidence in his honour, she was not accompanied by maid or valet.

As soon as they had entered the donjon James le Gris fastened the door unnoticed by the châtelaine, who was preceding him; she, as indeed James gave her to understand, thought the wind had blown it shut. When they were alone thus the squire embraced her and discovered what his intentions were. The lady was much astonished, and would have escaped had she been able, but the door was fastened. James, who was a strong man, held her tight in his arms, flung her down on the floor and had his will of her. Immediately afterward he opened the door of the donjon and made ready to depart. The lady, exasperated with rage at what had happened, wept silently. But as the squire was going she said: "James, you have not done well in thus forcing me. The blame, however, shall not be mine, but the whole of it shall be laid on you if it please God that my husband ever return."

James laughed and mounted his horse, and made such good speed that he was present to attend the rising of his lord the Count d'Alençon at nine o'clock. I should say that he had been seen in the count's hôtel at four o'clock that morning. I am thus particular because such circumstances were inquired into and examined by the commissioners of parliament when the case came before them.

On the day when this unfortunate event befell her, the Lady de Carouges remained in her castle and passed it off as well as she could, without mentioning a word of it to valet or chambermaid, for she thought she would have more shame than honour by making the matter public. But she retained in her memory the day and hour when James le Gris had come to the castle.

The Lord de Carouges returned from his voyage and was joyfully received by his lady and household, who feasted him well. When night came Sir John went to bed, but his lady excused herself, and on his gently pressing her to come to him, only walked pensively up and down the chamber. At last, when the household were in bed, she flung herself on her knees at his bedside and bitterly bewailed the outrage she had suffered. Sir John could not believe the thing had happened, but at length, so strongly did she urge it, he did believe her and said: "Lady, if the matter has happened as you say, I forgive you, certainly, but the squire shall die. I will consult your relatives and mine on the subject: should you have told me a falsehood, never more shall you live with me. The châtelaine again and again assured him that what she had said was the pure truth.

On the morrow the knight asked his friends to assemble at Argenteil. When they had gathered he led them to his apartment and told them the reasons for summoning them, and made his lady relate most minutely everything that had happened during his absence. When the friends and kinsmen had recovered from their astonishment, he asked their advice how he should act. They replied that he should wait upon his lord, the Count d'Alençon, and apprise him of the facts.

As Sir John had been advised, so he did, but the count, who much loved James le Gris, disbelieved the story. However, he appointed a day for the parties to come before him, and desired the lady might attend to give her evidence against the man whom she thus accused. Lady de Carouges attended, as desired, accompanied by a great number of her kinsmen, and the examinations and pleadings were carried on at great length before the count.

James le Gris boldly denied the charge, declared it was false, and wondered much how he could have incurred such mortal hatred from the lady. He proved by the count's household that he had been seen in the castle at four o'clock in the morning. The count said that he was in his bedchamber at nine o'clock, and that it was quite impossible for anyone to have ridden twenty-three leagues and back again, and do what he was charged with, in four hours and a half. The count told the Lady de Carouges that he would support his squire, and that she must have been dreaming. He commanded that henceforward all should be buried in oblivion, and under pain of incurring his displeasure, nothing further done in the business.

Sir John, being a man of courage, and believing what his wife had told him, would not submit to this, but went to Paris and appealed to the parliament. The parliament summoned James le Gris, who replied, and gave pledges to abide by whatever judgment the parliament should give. The case lasted upwards of a year, and they could not in any way compromise it, for Sir John, from his wife's information, was positive of the fact, and declared that since it was now so public, he would pursue it till death. For this reason the Count d'Alençon conceived the greatest hatred against the knight, and would have compassed his death had he not placed himself under the safeguard of the parliament.

The pleadings dragged on, and the parliament at last, because they could not produce other evidence than the lady herself against James le Gris, judged that the case should be decided in the tilt-yard by a duel for life or death. The knight, the squire and the lady were instantly put under arrest until the day of this mortal combat, which, by the order of parliament, was fixed for Monday ensuing in the year 1387.

At this time the king of France and his barons were at Sluys intending to invade England. When he heard about the duel he declared that he would be present at it, and sent orders to Paris to postpone the day thereof till he should arrive.

When King Charles had returned to Paris the lists were made for the champions in St Catherine's Square behind the Temple. The two contestants entered the lists armed at all points, and each was seated in a chair opposite the other. The Count de Saint Pol had charge of Sir John de Carouges, and the retainers of the Count d'Alençon stood by James le Gris. On entering the field the knight went to his lady, who was dressed in black and seated in a chair, and said: "Lady, upon your accusation, and in your quarrel am I thus adventuring my life to combat James le Gris. You know whether my cause be just and true." "My lord," she replied, "it is so, and you may fight securely, for your cause is good."

Seated there in her chair the Lady de Carouges made fervent prayers to God and the Virgin, humbly entreating that through her grace and intercession she might gain the victory according to her right. Her affliction was profound, for her life depended on the event: Should her husband lose the battle, she would be burned and her husband hanged.

The two champions mounted their horses and made a handsome appearance, for they were both expert men-at-arms. They ran their first course without hurt to either. Thereafter they dismounted and prepared to continue the fight on foot. Both fought with courage and address; but Sir John, in the first onset, was wounded in the thigh, which alarmed all his friends. Still, in spite of his wound, the Lord de Carouges fought so desperately that he struck down his adversary, and thrusting his sword through the body, caused his instant death. Turning to the spectators the knight asked if he had done his duty, and they replied that he had. Then Sir John approached the king and fell on his knees. The king bade him rise and ordered one thousand francs to be paid him that very day. He also retained him as a gentleman of his household, with a pension of two hundred livres a year, which he received as long as he lived. After thanking the king and his lords, Sir John went to his lady and kissed her. They went together to make their offering in the church of Notre Dame and then returned home.

The body of James le Gris was delivered to the hangman, who dragged it to Montfaucon and there hanged it.

"The Count d'Alençon's legal adviser—if he had one—was clever," remarked Adam Usk. "He called no witnesses from among the servants of Castle Argenteil."

"In this instance," conceded John Major, "an appeal to arms seems to have been justified. The verdict was sharp and neat, and invested with a finality seldom achieved by the slow and equivocal processes of verbal or statute law."

"Feudalism was not all bad, you see," said Earl Marshal. "It was not afraid to make decisions, nor to abide by the consequences of them once made. It may have unintentionally caused the death of a number of innocent persons, but it did not condone crime, nor connive at the evasion of criminals. Such things were reserved for a later age, though even in yours, Master Chronicler, we may see, in the attitude of Pierre d'Alençon, the beginnings of that failure of nerve to which Bernardo del Carpio has alluded."

"I," said Blind Harry, "hold with Froissart. To my mediocre mind it seems that there may at times be circumstances which extenuate revenge. There are some injustices so bitter, some acts of treachery so black, some deeds of blood so cruel that they inevitably generate another deed of blood. I should be ashamed to own myself a Scot if my countrymen had not on one occasion retaliated with equal violence upon their violent oppressors."

"Two wrongs do not make a right," said Paul.

"But they cancel each other and clear the field," answered the poet, "as you will see if you give ear to my tale."

146. THE BARNS OF AYR

Blind Harry

In February of the year 1297 the English made a truce with William Wallace, and it was kept faithfully till the end of March. In the interval the English employed all their wits and subtlety to find some means whereby they might confound the Scots.

When April had come the king of England summoned a council at Carlisle. The Scots had no reason to be pleased at that. Many an English captain came there to his king, but no Scot was summoned to attend save Sir Aymer, that ancient traitor. Of him they inquired how they might go about it to scour the faithful blood out of Scotland. Said Sir Aymer: "Their chief is a mighty man in war, and he has great power at his back; and their boldness is increased by this truce. But if you were to follow my advice, I could tell you how to make this present peace cost them dear." Then he and the false Southrons debated and deliberated how they might best hang the Scots barons.

At that time there were great barns standing in Ayr, which had been built for the king when he had had his quarters there. They were so constructed that only one man at a time could enter, and that without seeing or being seen. And there it was that the Southrons decided the Scots lords should be slain.

The result of their deliberations was laid before Lord Percy, but he replied stoutly that he would not himself see hanged the men who had kept faith with him so long, but that since he was their foe he would not warn them; and he said he would retire to Glasgow. Under these circumstances they appointed a sturdy Justice fierce and fell, named Arnulf, a very high magistrate of Southampton; and he undertook to make the Scots stretch rope. Also, they ordered a similar court to be held at Glasgow on the same day for the Clydesdale men; and they charged that court earnestly not to let Wallace escape by any means, for they knew that if his men were beaten or dispersed they might enjoy Scotland as their own.

When these matters had been thus arranged at Carlisle, they put their seals to the order, and King Edward went south again. Lord Percy, as he had declared, betook himself to Glasgow, and the new Justice took up his quarters in Ayr. The court was set for June 18. Inasmuch as there was peace in the land, the Scots marvelled what reason the English could have for setting this business on foot.

On the day before the assembly Wallace's uncle, Sir Reginald, appointed a meeting with his friends at Monkton Kirk. There came Wallace and paid his devotions at the church, after which he had a wonderful vision. Then he rode home to Corsby with his uncle and passed the night there. The next morning they prepared to attend the Justice's court, and rode on their way as far as Kingace. Suddenly Wallace felt a pang of apprehension, and he asked Sir Reginald if he had the charter of peace with him. "Nephew," replied the knight, "it is at Corsby in the chest where you yourself put it, and no one else knows about it." "If the English prove to be treacherous," said Wallace, "they would not be able to beat us down if we had the charter to show as evidence." "Son," answered Sir Reginald, "only you and I know where the charter is; do not send, but go back for it yourself."

Wallace turned about, taking three of his men with him, Kerle, Kneeland and Baird—stout fellows. Sir Reginald continued on his way to town, all unaware that treachery was brewing. Alas, the mis-

THE BARNS OF AYR

chance that led him on so that he tarried not for Wallace and the charter! Alas that Saturn was in ascendancy at this time!

Sir Reginald rode on to the designated building. Such a toll-booth had never been seen before, for therein was a beam with stout ropes hanging therefrom. Stern men were set to guard the entry; no one might pass in before he was called. Sir Reginald went in first to do homage for his land. They did not keep him standing long: they slipped a running cord over his head and hanged him dead from the beam. Sir Brice Blair passed in next, and him also they quickly hoisted to his death—his head was in the snare as soon as he entered, and he was strung up tight to the beam. The third who went in, alas! was Sir Neill of Montgomery, and after him many other landed men of the country-side.

Many went in, but no Scots came out. Many a Crawford came to his end there; Kennedys also they slew, and Campbells, who had never been false; never had they rebelled against their rightful lord, and therefore the Southrons ruined them. Berkeleys, Boyds, Stuarts—all good families—the English brought to their end there. No Scot who entered the barn escaped, and when they had hanged them from the beam, they cast the bodies into the nook beside the other dead. Since the beginning of the war the Saxons had not brought to their death so many Scots in a single day. Eighteen score bold barons and worthy knights they put to a shameful death on that occasion.

When the Southrons had killed the worthiest they made no further inquiry about the lowly. The bodies they cast into a yard, despoiled of clothes and as naked as they were born.

In the meantime Robert Boyd, who had been left in command, gathered twenty of Wallace's doughty and fierce warriors in a tavern. One of them, Stephen of Ireland, happened to walk into the street. There he met a true Scotswoman and asked her what had happened at the Justice's court. "Sorrow is there and nothing else," she replied. "Where," she asked, trembling, "is Wallace?" "He left us, and turned back at Kingace," said Stephen. "Go warn his men," said the women, "and urge them to get out of Ayr. I myself will warn Wallace." Stephen returned to his companions at the inn and related the dire misfortune that had occurred. Thereupon they lost no time in going to Laglane Wood.

Now Wallace was returning as fast as he might, for he stood in great fear for his friends. He hastened on to the barn, ignorant of the tragedy that had taken place there. The woman of whom I spoke called out to him: "O brave Wallace, a cruel tempest has raged during your absence. Our countrymen have been slain so that it is a pity to see, hanged over a beam like brute dogs, one by one as they entered the barn." Wallace reined in his horse to inquire more closely into the matter. "Dear niece," said he, "tell me if you know: is my uncle dead?" "I saw him carried out of yonder barn," answered the woman, "and cast naked onto the cold earth; there I kissed the frosty mouth of him who a moment before had been a noble figure of a man, now despoiled and dead. I covered his corpse with a cloth: I could do no less for him who never shamed a woman in all his life. You are his sister's son, noble and brave. Avenge that deed if you can, for God's sake; and as I am a true and loyal Scotswoman, I will help you."

Wallace wept for the death of his kinsman. "If you know Robert Boyd," he said, "and William Crawford, and Adam Wallace, for Mary's sake, bid them come to me. I pray God they are all alive! Also, spy out the Justice's lodging and tell me what his circumstances are. Then we will concert our plans in Laglane Wood, which has so often been our refuge."

Wallace turned his horse and rode away, and such mourning did he make for his kinsman that it seemed his heart would break. As he rode off in sorrow and wrath fifteen Englishmen, brave and sturdy men, rode after him with a mace-bearer to bring the Scot before the law. Wallace turned about angrily and went among them with his sword. One he cut nearly in two in the middle; another he banged on the head; another he cleft through the side; the fourth he drove violently to the ground; the fifth he dinged with great ire; and in this wise he left all five dead. In the interval his three men had slain another five, whereupon the remaining five fled to their lord and told him what had happened.

The Southrons were astonished at this tale of ten dead men, and guessed that it was Wallace who had slain them. Said an old knight: "If he has escaped this court your recent activities will serve only to increase our trouble." The Justice was wroth. "How fearful you would be of many foes," he said, "you who flee from one man, though you do not know whether it be Wallace or another! And even though it be he, I take little account of him. Whoever bides here will be a knight, for tomorrow I intend to divide the Scots' property among English-born."

The Southrons retired to their lodgings without more ado; four thousand of them stopped that night in Ayr; the Justice lay in the barns outside the town with many bold barons, and he caused to be proclaimed everywhere that no Scot should remain among them. Provisions were brought to them from the sea, along with Irish ale, the strongest that could be brewed. No watch was set, for they had no fear of Scotsmen dwelling round about. They indulged copiously in wine and ale, observing no restraint, like beasts. Soon slothful sleep slid into their limbs, and they lay stupefied like swine in their gluttony. Bacchus had taken over the command.

Wallace's men assembled in Laglane Wood. The knight drew his sword and took oath that he would neither eat nor sleep till he had avenged the death of his uncle and the other noble men who had perished in the barn. "Since they are drunk," he said, "it seems to me best to visit them with fire." He had chalk brought, and ordered his niece to mark the doors of the houses where the English lay. Twenty men he bade gather withes, a pair to each man.

The woman went to the town and chalked the doors; the men came after and fastened the doors securely, binding withes to staple and hasp. Boyd was dispatched to the castle, with fifty men under his command, to seize it if the garrison made a sortie on seeing the fire. The rest of the men-at-arms went with Wallace to the barns. There they set brisk blazes in every single nook. The knight commanded his men that they should allow no Southron to break out; if anyone, whoever he might be, were to rescue anyone from the red fire, he himself should be cast into it.

Soon the flashing flames roared high. "This," said Wallace, "is a cheery sight, and should bring some comfort to our hearts. When these are done for, the power of the remaining English will be less in the land." And to the Justice he called out: "We will bail our men, those who escaped alive from your court and your false law. You shall not apportion their lands to any followers of yours, as you will presently be convinced by the fate that hangs over you."

Keen and fearful cries arose as the fierce fire burned up brightly; that wakening was not sweet to sleeping men. From outside the sight was awful to see. Nowhere save in purgatory or in hell could there be greater pain than that which those within were forced to endure. Mad folk were hampered in many a hold as the buildings burned; none got away, captain, knave or knight. When the brands from the burning rafters fell among them, some leaped violently into the air with the strong bitter pain; some, all naked, burned to an ash; some never rose, but smothered where they lay; some rushed wildly here and there, seeking to escape to the town, but blinded by fire their movements were futile. Like wild beasts the men raged against the walls, emitting many a grisly groan; some shrieked till their life was snuffed out. Some sought to force the doors, but the Scots beset them so shrewdly that if any happened to break out he was soon cut down with the sword, or forced back into the fire. None escaped —all were burned up, bone and flesh. The reek of the carrion was foully noisome; the stench spread so thick and wide that the Scots were forced to retire to windward till the fire had finally extinguished all that false blood.

While the barns of Ayr were burning the Prior of Ayr was not idle. Seven score had taken lodging in his hostel that night. When he saw the red fire he armed himself and his seven brothers; with drawn swords they went two by two to each of the houses where the Southrons were sleeping, and set upon them with sore heavy blows. Many a man those friars dinged to death there. Some, dazed with sleep, fled naked to the water to escape; they fell into the deep, dark ford, plunged to the bottom and died without grace. All who lodged with that prior were drowned or slain. People still call it "The Friar of Ayr's Blessing."

In the castle, which had been made over to Earl Arnulf on Lord Percy's departure, there remained but few important men. When those left within saw the red fire blazing merrily, they made a sortie. Robert Boyd, who lay in ambush, paid them no heed, but passed on to the castle and won the gate. He entered and quickly slew the nine or ten men he found there. Then he posted twenty of his men and went to Ayr to see what further orders Wallace might have.

By this time the town was a mass of smouldering ruins. By sword or fire five thousand likely men of England had lost their lives there that night.

During Blind Harry's recital most of the Englishmen present had maintained a stony immobility, and only Henry Knighton, when he had finished, was heard to mutter something about "base-born ruffian," "sacrilegious thief," and "scurvy traitor."

"Nay," protested Robert Mannyng, "even King Edward was forced to admire the steadfast spirit and tireless courage of the man who could defend his country so well. And traitor he was not, for he had never sworn allegiance to the English crown. If you apply such terms to a patriot, what names have you left for Sir John Menteith, who betrayed him for a hundred pounds? It is un-English to contemn the gallant foe."

Paul the Deacon was shivering and looked sick. "Five thousand men burned like rats in a trap!" he sighed.

"Every war," said John Major, "must give occasion for excesses of all kinds, and this was no exception. I approve of violence and bloodshed as little as you, reverend sir, except when the cause is just. We men are imperfect, and have only imperfect means at our disposal wherewith to adjust our differences. Until the means be improved, let us not judge Wallace more harshly than he was judged by his contemporaries. In this connection our chroniclers relate that an English hermit was vouchsafed a vision of several souls taking flight from purgatory to heaven, and one of them was Wallace. When he marvelled how this could be, seeing that Wallace had shed men's blood, a voice answered him that it was in a just cause, and while fighting for his country's freedom that he had slain men."

"Ah!" exclaimed Barbour, "Freedom is a noble thing! Only freedom guarantees to man the peaceful and unhampered pursuit of his destiny. Only freedom enables a man to live as God intended he should—like a man, and not like a beast or a slave. The usufruct of thraldom is heart-break and misery for men and women, waste and frustration for the State. Anyone who has experienced thraldom knows well that there is no price too great to pay for freedom. In the free air your ripe corn ripples in wave after wave under the generous sun: but what virtuous living thing can you find under a stone?"

"A moment ago," said Master Wace, "the reverend deacon inquired what was gained by revenge. I am one of those who believe that revenge is sometimes appropriate, especially if it brings material rewards—as I will illustrate by the story of Gwendolen and Estrildis."

147. GWENDOLEN OF CORNWALL

Master Wace

When Brutus had cleared the island of Albion, or Britain, of giants, and had founded the city of Trinovant, now called London, he died, and his kingdom was divided between his three sons. Locrine, the eldest, held the middle region, which was called Logres or Loegria after him; Camber had that part which lies beyond the river Severn and was called Cambria, now Wales from Queen Galaes; Albanac, the youngest son, took a wooded land to the north and gave it the name of Albania from his own name, though we now call it Scotland. For a long time the three brothers ruled in peace over their respective lands.

Now in these days Humber was king of the Huns. He was greatly dreaded, for he went about wasting the isles and ravaging the sea coasts. With a great party of warriors he landed on the coast of Scotland and engaged Albanac in battle. When Albanac was killed, along with the greater part of his men, the survivors fled for protection to Locrine in Britain, and Locrine and Camber united their forces to avenge their brother. In the interval Humber went about pillaging the coast of Scotland till he was brought to bay at a certain river which has been called Humber after him; there he was wrecked and killed, as Ralph Higden can testify.

Previous to this Humber had been in Germany, where he had robbed and plundered; thence he had borne off three young girls, and kept them in his ships. One of them, Estrildis by name, was the daughter of a king; she was so beautiful that her peer was hardly to be found anywhere. When Humber was drowned, Locrine and Camber rushed to the boats to seize the booty, and there found the three girls. Locrine was much impressed by Estrildis' loveliness: no ivory, no new-fallen snow, no lily could exceed the whiteness of her skin, and though of Teutonic blood, no fault could be found with her shape. Locrine ordered her to be well guarded, for he intended to marry her, and averred, indeed, that he would take no other woman to wife.

These matrimonial plans of the king's reached the ears of Corineus and displeased him greatly, for Locrine had already entered into an engagement to marry his daughter Gwendolen.—Corineus will be remembered as that companion of Brutus who distinguished himself in a contest with Gogmagog. One day when the Roman leader was observing due religious rites in port, his party was attacked by the giant and twenty of his associates. The giants were, of course, worsted and killed, all save their leader. This fellow was twelve cubits long, and him Brutus saved in order to see him fight with Corineus. The warrior was also very eager for the match. He and the giant laid hands on each other and wrestled. Gogmagog, with a mighty heave, threw Corineus to the ground and broke three of his ribs, two on the right side and one on the left. This so annoyed Corineus that he hoisted the giant to his shoulder, ran with him to the top of the neighbouring cliff and flung him into the sea at a place which is still known as "Gogmagog's Leap."

But as I was saying, Corineus, with battle-axe in hand, sought out Locrine and addressed him angrily and haughtily. "Locrine," said he, "low-born felon, base fool, no man can now guarantee you against death, for you have refused my daughter, to whom you were affianced. What is the meaning of this repudiation? Is this my reward for serving your father? Is this the recompense for the great ills which I suffered, and the wide wounds which I gained in battle against foreign peoples? In order to aggrandize your father's honour I suffered many a sorrow and tribulation; and the thanks I get for it is that you cast aside my daughter Gwendolen in favour of I do not know what foreign wench. But you will not do so with impunity, for if I still have any strength left in the arm which you see raised here, you will be cut to pieces first."

Therewith Corineus advanced towards Locrine as though he intended to kill him; and he would have done so had not their friends interposed and separated them. They calmed Corineus and besought Locrine to abide by his covenant rather than precipitate disaster.

Yielding to persuasion Locrine did indeed marry Gwendolen; but he did not on that account forget Estrildis; so deep was his love for the girl that he made her his mistress. He caused one of his very privy servants to make an underground chamber at London, and there Estrildis resided a long time. Seven years, indeed, she lived in that subterranean apartment, honourably served by trusted attendants of the king's household. When Locrine wished to visit her he caused Gwendolen to believe that he was sacrificing to the gods, and that the rites proper thereto must be performed with the utmost secrecy.

In the course of time Estrildis bore a child, a daughter whom she named Sabrina; and she was even more beautiful than her mother. In the same year Gwendolen also bore a child, a boy, who was called Madan. When he could walk and speak he was sent to his grandfather Corineus to be reared.

Finally the time came when Corineus had to die. After his death Locrine's fear was abated: He repudiated Gwendolen and raised Estrildis to be queen beside him. The furious Gwendolen retired to her father's estate in Cornwall, where she assembled the youth of the country and began to harry Locrine's kingdom. Then, when her army had been increased by foreign warriors eager for booty, she faced her husband's forces near the river Stour in Dorset. The fortune of war was such that Locrine was wounded to death by an arrow, and after he fell, his people fled.

Thereupon the victorious Gwendolen took all the kingdom into her hand. Being her father's daughter, one of the first things she did on assuming the power over Britain was to drown Estrildis and her daughter in a river. And thinking to reflect shame on Locrine as well, she commanded that the river should henceforth be called by the name of his daughter Sabrina. Today this has been corrupted into Severn, and is the river which flows from Cirencester to the sea.

After this Gwendolen reigned over Britain for fifteen years; and when she saw that her son Madan had arrived at maturity, she invested him with the kingdom and herself retired into Cornwall, where she passed the rest of her life.

"Do you not," objected Colin Clout, "view the situation almost entirely from the side of Gwendolen and her son? What of Estrildis? Was she to blame if Locrine loved her? Could she help herself, being a captive? Was Locrine to blame if he loved her? Even the gods themselves, says some old writer, cannot act wisely when it comes to love. And what of Sabrina, whose only guilt lay in having Locrine for her father and Estrildis for her mother? Justice is like Janus: it looks in two directions, towards plaintiff and defendant, and tries to effect a balance between right and wrong, or reconcile a conflict of two wrongs."

"I agree with you there," said Marsiglio of Padua. "We all know, or should know, that one of the most important contributions to social progress made by the modern world is the growth of the consciousness that there cannot be one justice for the mighty and another for the weak."

"You are right," agreed William of Wykeham, "and I would add that if the Christian Church had done nothing else, its glory would have been sufficiently great in having done that. Who will deny that such a concept represents an advance over the old law of an eye for an eye and a tooth for a tooth?"

"The times of which I speak were pagan times," said Wace.

"Ills grow by what they feed on," observed Sir John Fortescue. "Neither Locrine nor Estrildis, nor, in a measure, Gwendolen, were to blame; Corineus was to blame, and the barons of Locrine's household."

"But when ills have not been smothered in their infancy," said Keating, "and have at last grown so big that they overspread a whole land, like the dragon of which Mac Conglinne has told, what then? I agree with Master Wace, but more particularly with Blind Harry. If you have failed to cut off an infected finger, there may still be time to save the arm by cutting it off at the elbow. In the hearts of my countrymen there has never been any censure of the heroism displayed by Maoilseachlainn of Meath and his daughter. I will tell you the circumstances so that the candid minds of those present may judge for themselves."

148. TURGESIUS KEEPS A TRYST

Geoffrey Keating

The thraldom of the Gaels under the yoke of the Scandinavian foreigners or Lochlannaigh was such that great weariness thereof came upon the men of Ireland. The few of the clergy that had survived the destruction of their monasteries fled to the forests and the wildernesses, where they prayed fervently to God to deliver them from the tyranny of Turgesius, king of the Lochlannaigh. And God heard their supplications.

While Turgesius was in possession of his usurped authority, and

TURGESIUS KEEPS A TRYST

while the Gaels were yielding him an involuntary obedience, he had built himself a fortified residence not far from the dun-liss of Maoilseachlainn, son of Maolruanaidh, king of Meath. Now on a certain day when he had come to the dwelling of Maoilseachlainn, he chanced to see a beautiful, marriageable maiden, who was the daughter of the king of Meath. The usurper, though now grown old, was still inveterate in the indulgence of his lusts, and he demanded the maid from her father with the intention of making her his mistress. "My lord," said Maoilseachlainn, "I know well that you do not mean to take my daughter as your married wife, but that what you desire is to possess her for a while as your mistress. I therefore beseech you not to demand my child of me in public, lest she be prevented from getting a husband. But since your fortress is near this liss where I live, I will send the maiden privately to your dwelling; and she shall be accompanied by fifteen of the most beautiful and most lovely women in all Meath; and I know that when you have seen those women you will feel neither love nor desire for my own daughter, so much do they exceed her in beauty."

This plan was pleasing to Turgesius, and between them they fixed upon a particular night when the maiden and her attendant train of beautiful women were to be brought into the fortress of the tyrant.

About this time there was a gathering and general assembly with Turgesius at Ath Cliath, and all that there was then in Ireland of Lochlannach chieftains were gathered thereat, for the purpose of taking counsel as to how they might best guard the country and maintain their own possession thereof. And while they were there Turgesius communicated the arrangement made between himself and Maoilseachlainn to some of the assembled chieftains; and he promised women to some whom he asked to accompany him. He then set out with fifteen of the boldest and most lascivious of those lords, and they made neither stop nor stay until they had reached his fortress in Meath.

During the same time Maoilseachlainn had privately brought together fifteen of the most comely youths, without beards, that could be found in Meath. He caused them to put on female attire, under which each of them carried a sharp sword at his girdle. Thus did he prepare to send these youths, instead of women, to meet Turgesius, in company with his daughter. When the night appointed had come, the maiden set out with her band of counterfeit women; and when she and they had come close to the fortress, a message was sent to Turgesius saying that she and her female companions were ready to meet him. Upon receiving this message the tyrant commanded the warriors in his company to withdraw to their chambers, and he would send the women to them. So they did, and made a pile of their arms upon the table which stood in the hall.

While this was taking place Maoilseachlainn joined his daughter with an armed band. Some of the disguised youths he ordered to lay hold upon Turgesius as soon as he might attempt to lay hand upon the girl in order to detain her with him; others he commanded to seize the arms, and to fall upon the chieftains who were in the house; then he himself would dash in with his men in order to aid them in dispatching the foreigners.

Now the girl and her companions entered the fortress through a postern, and came to the room where Turgesius was awaiting her. He sharply scrutinized the lady and her attendants, but none of them was pleasing to him except herself, and he laid his hand upon her in order to keep her with him. As soon as the youths saw this, some seized him with violence and held him captive, while others seized upon the discarded arms. Maoilseachlainn and his armed men now broke in, and together they fell upon all of the Lochlannaigh who were in the fortress; of them they spared neither chief nor serf, with the exception of Turgesius himself. Then, having sacked the fortress, they took Turgesius to Maoilseachlainn's dun-liss, where they held him for a time in chains.

Now when the rest of the Lochlannaigh throughout Ireland learned that their principal chiefs had been slaughtered, and that their leader had been captured in Meath by Maoilseachlainn, there fell a great terror and loss of confidence upon them all, so that those of them who were stationed in the country stole away by night to the seaports; and those who were at the seaports fled to their ships to avoid the onslaught of the Gaels who were in pursuit of them. In this manner were all the Lochlannaigh driven out of Ireland at that time, with the exception of a small remnant that remained therein under subjection to the Gaels.

Afterwards Maoilseachlainn drowned Turgesius in Loch Aninn; and from that deed it resulted that the Gaelic nobles, with one accord, elected him High King of all Ireland, for it was he who had freed their country from bondage to the men of Lochlainn. This was in the year 845.

"Justice," said Giovanni da Procida, "is in heaven—and mercy and charity. But we mortals live in the world, not in heaven. And being of the earth, our habits and manners are coloured by our substance and our habitation. I will leave it to John Wiclif, or Thomas Gascoigne or John Major to explain how it is that there can be any nexus between the mortal and the heavenly world and its denizens. Perhaps the golden cord is that subtile sense of truth and beauty and honour, and love of freedom and decency which somehow illumines the minds of those of us who are least gross. But mortals that we are, gross and fine, we must live together, and that means that we must contend, one with the other until such time as the differences between one extreme and the other shall have been effaced. It is not with demons or angels that we strive; our quarrel is with men; and we cannot look for aid to heaven: the angel with the flaming sword —and St Augustine after him—made that sufficiently clear. But we must do what we can, even though we fail. We have one weapon, if we know how to use it—the proterity itself of our enemy: hoist him with his own petard. What is right for me? What is right for you? Turgesius thought he was right in plundering and oppressing the Gaels; Maoilseachlainn thought he was wrong. Charles of Anjou thought he was right in treating the Italians of the two Sicilies worse than slaves. I, and Alaimo di Lentini, thought he was wrong. The drunken libertine of Naples thought he had a right to steal away my daughter for himself, and my wife for his stable grooms. My son thought he had no right, and paid for his opinion with his life. How many broken bodies of sons and brothers, how many dishonoured bodies of wives and daughters had been calling out for vengeance for their shame since the disasters at Benevento and Tagliacozzo? I took that vengeance, and who here will say that I was wrong?"

"I," said Sir John Harington, "have engaged in some questionable enterprises—the destiny of empire has always lain heavy upon the sons of England—but I should be loath to accept that challenge."

"We should be glad, Ser Giovanni," said Bernardo del Carpio, "to know more of the matters to which you allude so darkly."

"My rôle was that of an actor in the drama," answered the physician. "The circumstances can be better related by one whose part it was to view events in perspective. Giovanni Villani has told the story once, and though the Florentines fought against us, he himself is a fair-minded man whom I have no hesitation in asking to tell it again."

"It is regrettable," said the historian, "that Brunetto Latino is not present, for he has some valuable notes on the subject. However, I will relate the facts as I know them."

149. THE VESPERS OF MONREALE

Giovanni Villani

In the year of Our Lord 1279 King Charles of Anjou, by reason of his victories at Benevento and Tagliacozzo, had become the most powerful and redoubted ruler of Christendom on land or sea. So swollen was his pride that he held all men save those of his nation in contempt, and if he had had his will, he would have placed all the world under the heel of the French. The Apulians and Sicilians particularly did he treat worse than slaves; and the lords whom he placed over them, emulating the presumption of their master, forced and ravished the wives and daughters of the citizens at their pleasure. The protests and just complaints of husbands and fathers were unheard by Charles, but God heard them. It has been well said that pride goes before and shame follows after; when pride is in the saddle, shame and mischief are on the crupper. Pride, envy and wrath are pitfalls set by the devil for weak minds, and of these God hates pride worst of all.

In his overweening arrogance Charles of Anjou conceived the idea of conquering the empire of Constantinople for his kinsman, Baldwin II, whose son was betrothed to his daughter Beatrice, for Baldwin had been expelled from Constantinople by the emperor, Michael Palaeologus VIII. To this end he prepared a mighty armament against the Greek empire; nor did his dream of conquest stop with that, for it seemed to him that when he was once in possession of it, the conquest of Jerusalem and the Holy Land would follow as an easy and natural consequence. So he equipped more than 100 swift sailing galleys, 20 great ships, and caused to be constructed 200 transports for horses, besides a great number of other ships for the transport of troops. Seconded by the approval of Philippe III le Hardi of France, and depending upon his own mighty treasure, increased by money aids from Rome, to defray expenses, he invited all the worthy knights of France and Italy to participate in that enterprise. By facile promises the Venetians, too, were easily persuaded to lend their assistance. Thus, with the said navy, 40 counts and 10,000 knights, the king intended to embark upon his expedition in the following year. He would have succeeded in all this without difficulty or opposition, for Palaeologus had no power on land or sea capable of offering resistance to his forces, and, moreover, a great part of Greece had risen in rebellion.

However, in order to abate the presumption of the French, God in His providence brought Charles' enterprise to naught. By reason

THE VESPERS OF MONREALE 627

of his misrule of the Two Sicilies many of the worthiest men of the kingdom had rebelled or departed into voluntary exile. Among such exiles was an intelligent and learned knight, Giovanni, Lord of the island of Procida. He was a physician by profession, and had been in the service of Emperor Frederic of Suabia. His wife and daughter had been outraged by one of Charles' great barons, and his son killed in defence of them. He remonstrated to Charles, but when his sovereign paid him no heed, and when he had become convinced that he was losing his time and abasing his honour in appealing to a graceless king, Messer Gianni resolved to employ his own wits to compensate himself for the injury he had received. And so, through his wisdom and energy, and by the grace of God, he effected such things that the power and pride of King Charles and his adherents were brought low.

First of all Messer Gianni went secretly to Constantinople to talk to the emperor Michael Palaeologus. He informed him of the coalition which had been made against him by King Charles, the former emperor Baldwin, and the Church of Rome. Then he said that if the emperor were willing to put faith in him, and to part with some of his treasure, he, Giovanni da Procida, would subvert the proposed expedition. This he would do by causing the lords of Sicily, who loved neither Charles nor the French, to rebel; in their aid he would enlist the forces of the king of Aragón, who would certainly be disposed to engage in the venture by reason of the fact that Sicily was the legal heritage of his wife, King Manfred's daughter.

To Palaeologus all this seemed impossible, for he was well aware of King Charles' power, and understood that he was more feared than any other lord of the West. But, on the other hand, he realized his peril, and as though in despair of any other remedy or assistance, he acceded to Messer Gianni's proposal. He consented to send with him to the West ambassadors who should represent his interests, and these bore with them a great treasure in jewels and money.

Messer Gianni and the Greek ambassadors arrived secretly in Sicily. There he revealed the nature of his negotiations at the Eastern capital to Messer Alaimo di Lentini, Messer Palmerio Abate and Messer Gualtieri di Caltagirone. These were the most important and influential barons of the island, and they loved neither Charles nor his sway. At first the barons viewed Messer Gianni's plan with diffidence. Considering the severity of King Charles' rule in the island it did not seem probable to them that a rebellion of the citizens had much chance of success. "If you will only have faith in me," said Messer Gianni, "I am confident that we shall bring it off." In the end the barons allowed themselves to be persuaded, and to Messer Gianni they gave letters to the king of Aragón in which they implored him for God's sake to free them from bondage. If he could do that, they would accept him as their lord.

Armed with credentials in the form of these letters, Messer Gianni set out on his journey. On his way he stopped at Rome and visited Pope Nicholas III at a castle of his called Soriana. He told him what agreement he had made with the emperor of the East, and presented to him and his treasurer Orso the rich gifts and jewels which Palaeologus had sent. The pope was pleased, and now listened readily as Messer Gianni proceeded to urge his interests. Among other things, he reminded the pope how Charles had refused to contract an alliance with the Orsini family, tearing up the pope's letter with contempt.

This was an argument which could not fail to influence Niccolò Romano degli Orsini, and as long as he continued to occupy the throne of Peter, he worked both openly and secretly against King Charles. In that very year he succeeded in hindering the expedition to Constantinople by withholding money and other aid which had been promised to Charles by the Church. Moreover, His Holiness was good enough to write letters to King Pedro of Aragón, sealing them with his private seal, wherein he promised the lordship of Sicily to the Spanish monarch if he would come and conquer the island. This was in the year 1280.

Giovanni da Procida now continued on his way to the court of Pedro of Aragón in Catalonia. When the king had read the letters from the emperor, the pope and the Sicilian barons, promising money, support and material assistance, he secretly agreed with Messer Gianni to undertake the conquest of Sicily; and he instructed him and the other ambassadors to return so that the necessary arrangements might be completed.

At this moment, however, the knight's plans received a temporary check due to the death of the pope. In the month of August in the year 1281 Pope Nicholas III of the Orsini passed from this life in the city of Viterbo. King Charles was very elated thereat—not because he had uncovered the plot which Giovanni da Procida had concerted with Palaeologus and the pontiff, but because he realized that the pope was inimical to him in all things, and had but recently interfered grievously with his expedition to Constantinople. Wherefor, since he was in Tuscany when the pope died, he proceeded straightway to Viterbo so that he might secure the election of a friend of his to the papal see. When, by the orders of King Charles, two of the dissentient cardinals of the Orsini faction had been put in prison, the remaining cardinals agreed to elect a French cardinal named Simon de Brion. The new pope took the name Martin IV.

In the meantime Messer Gianni had been busy with the furtherance of his scheme. At Trapani he met the Sicilian barons and encouraged them with news of his progress. Thence he took ship for Constantinople, where he brought his negotiations with Palaeologus to a successful termination.

The year 1281 saw Giovanni da Procida, accompanied by ambassadors from Michael Palaeologus, again at the court of Pedro of Aragón in Catalonia. The death of Pope Nicholas had somewhat cooled the Spanish king's enthusiasm for the Sicilian undertaking, for he felt less sure of success against the powerful Charles without the support of a friendly pontiff. But Messer Gianni spoke wisely and to the point. "My lord," he said, "fear nothing. If the new pope is our friend, well and good; if not, let us enter upon the struggle none the less so that we may not fail now, having already accomplished so much." He reminded Pedro that the house of France had killed his grandfather, that Charles himself had killed his father-in-law Manfred, and Manfred's nephew Conradin. He pointed out further that Sicily belonged rightfully to Pedro as the inheritance of his wife Costanza, heir and daughter of King Manfred. Furthermore, by promising to rouse the island to rebellion against Charles, the Sicilians had given proof of their desire to accept him as their lord.

When, in addition to these arguments, Pedro saw the great treasure brought by the ambassadors of Palaeologus, his fears and scruples vanished; his heart was once more fired with a lust for power and land. So he pledged himself with the emperor's ambassadors and with Giovanni da Procida to undertake the expedition, assuring them of his faith, and telling them to return to Sicily so that they might ·ve the signal for the rebellion when he should have assembled and placed his armada. And this was done.

Pedro of Aragón now had at his disposal 30,000 ounces of Greek gold, and had the assurance that more would be provided once he had landed in Sicily. He therefore set about equipping galleys and ships, assigning good wages to sailors and men-at-arms, and giving ' ∶ he had raised his standard against the Saracens.

News of these preparations spread abroad. King Philippe of France, who had married King Pedro's sister Isabella, sent messengers to learn against what Saracens he intended to proceed, and in what country, offering him aid in men and money. King Pedro replied merely that he was certainly arming against the Saracens of a place which he did not care to name at the moment, for it would soon be known to all. However, he asked aid to the extent of 40,000 livres tournois, which Philippe sent him at once. But knowing that Pedro, though a bold and courageous man, was also a Catalan, and so of perfidious temper, he immediately sent word to his uncle in Apulia that he should have an eye to his lands.

King Charles brought word of this matter to Martin IV. The pope was somewhat perturbed and sent a legate, a Dominican by the name of Friar Jacopo, to inquire more fully into Pedro's intentions. It was a matter, he said, which touched the Church closely, and though Pedro might count on his support in any righteous cause, he should under no circumstances take up arms against any Christian people. King Pedro thanked the legate, but refused to divulge his plans. And he said also something which sounded very suspicious, namely, that if one of his hands were to reveal his destination to the other, he would cut it off.

Pope Martin was highly displeased with this reply. But Charles, who was so high-hearted, and who considered himself so puissant, paid little or no attention to the matter, saying scornfully: "Have I not always told you that Pedro of Aragón is a mad rascal?" But Charles did not bear in mind the popular proverb, which says: "If you are told your nose is shortened, take hold of it to make sure." Rather did he remain indifferent, and took no measures whereby he might have learned of the activities of Messer Gianni and the other barons of Sicily. A ready executioner is always found for him whom God intends to judge.

In the year of Our Lord 1282, on the Monday of Easter Resurrection, which fell on March 30, in conformity with Messer Giovanni da Procida's arrangements, all the barons and chiefs who had the uprising of Sicily in hand were gathered in Palermo to celebrate Easter. The citizens of Palermo, men and women, went to observe the festival at Monreale, a short distance outside the city. So also went the French, and a certain Drouet, one of King Charles' favourite captains among them. It chanced, by the machinations of the enemy of God, that the captain approached Ninfa, the beautiful young daughter of Roberto Mastrangelo, a nobleman of Palermo, as she was walking with her father, her brothers and household servants. From her he solicited those favours which modesty and good manners forbid me to name; and when she shrank back from him, he laid violent hold upon her with intent to force her, as the French were accustomed to do. The lady cried out, and the people rushed up; among them was a young man, her betrothed, one of Messer Palmerio Abate's retainers. He said nothing, but snatching Drouet's sword from the scabbard, disemboweled him on the spot.

Hereupon ensued a great battle between the French soldiers and the Sicilians, and many were killed and wounded on both sides. The Palermitanians, being unarmed, got the worst of this encounter; but fleeing to the city, they began to arm themselves, crying out: "Death to the French!" As the leaders of the uprising had ordered, they assembled in the square. King Charles' regent, attracted by the uproar, met them there. Him they took and killed, as well as whatsoever French were found in the city, whether in houses or in churches. Whomsoever they found speaking French, them they slew without mercy.

After this initial revolt the barons left the city, and each in his own barony or county repeated the slaughter of Palermo, with the purpose of slaying every Frenchman in the island. Only the people of Messina delayed somewhat in joining the rebellion. But the Palermitanians reminded them of their miseries, urging them to throw in their lot with them on the side of liberty and fraternity; so they also finally rose in revolt, and did even worse execution upon the French than those of Palermo had done. The number of dead in Sicily amounted to 4,000, or, as some say, to 6,500. No one dared to shield a Frenchman, if he loved his life, no matter how great a friend he might be; and if he had hidden any, he had to tell where he was or kill him himself. Indeed, only one Frenchman escaped, a certain De Porcellet.

At this time King Charles was at the papal court. When he received information of the Sicilian rebellion, brought him by the messengers of the archbishop of Monreale, he grew very wroth in mind and manner. The pope and cardinals lamented with him over his loss, but encouraged him, too, saying that he should take immediate steps to regain the island, by peaceful means, if possible, otherwise by war; and both the pope and the cardinals promised him whatever aid, spiritual or temporal, the Church could command. And as a preliminary step the pope sent a legate to Sicily to treat for terms. The legate's name was Messer Gherardo da Parma, and he was a man of great good sense and ability.

Charles, by means of letters and ambassadors, made representations to his nephew, the king of France; and he commanded his son Charles, Prince of Salerno, who was in Provence, to go at once to King Philippe, to the Count of Artois, and to other barons, and beseech them to come to his aid. The prince was well received by King Philippe, who said: "I fear very much that this Sicilian rebellion has been the work of Pedro of Aragón. If he has been guilty of perfidiousness against the Church and the house of France, may I never wear crown if I do not take condign vengeance therefor." And he kept that vow well.

When news of the great preparations which King Charles was making against the island was spread abroad, it seemed to the Palermitanians and other Sicilians that they had done ill, and to Pope Martin they sent envoys—friars and priests—asking mercy. The terms of their message were only: "Agnus Dei, qui tollis peccata mundi, miserere nobis; Agnus Dei, qui tollis peccata mundi, miserere nobis; Agnus Dei, qui tollis peccata mundi, dona nobis pacem." The pope in full consistory replied with the words of the Passio Domini: "Ave, rex Iudeorum, et dabant ei alapam; Ave, rex Iudeorum, et dabant ei alapam; Ave, rex Iudeorum, et dabant ei alapam." With this answer the envoys departed, much discomfited.

Now King Charles assembled at Brindisi the ships with which he had intended to sail to Constantinople, and proceeded with them to Pagliare, outside Messina. With him were 5,000 French, Provençal and Italian knights, and an innumerable host of men-at-arms. This manoeuvre so alarmed the Messinese that they sued for peace. But in them and the other Sicilians Charles saw a people without a leader and without means of defence, and so was little inclined towards mercy. He denounced them as traitors to the Church and the crown, and bade them defend themselves if they could. In adopting this attitude the king sinned greatly against God, and acted much to his own harm. But him to whom God wishes ill He deprives of sense and judgment. For their part the Messinese deliberated four days whether they should defend themselves or surrender.

During this time Charles' troops took the castle of Melazzo, near Messina, and a number of Messinese were killed in the engagement. This casualty alarmed the people of Messina greatly, and they invited the cardinal legate to come to them and intercede for them with the king. The legate had the greatest good will to effect a reconciliation, and in order to help matters along he presented the pope's letter wherein Martin threatened to excommunicate the Sicilians unless they submitted to King Charles. Hereupon the citizens chose thirty wise men from among their number to frame terms of peace; and the terms were these: If the king would pardon their offence, they would yield the land and pay him such dues as their ancestors had paid King William; but for their lord they would accept neither Frenchman nor Provençal, but a Latin only.

The legate forwarded these terms to King Charles, urging him to accept them. But when the king read the Messinese proposal he cried wrathfully: "Is it possible that our subjects, who have deserved death at our hands, have the temerity to make terms? Would they deprive me of my signory? And they will pay me dues such as were paid King William, whose part in the island was hardly any thing at all? I will certainly not agree to this. But since the legate is anxious to make peace, I will pardon them in this wise: They must surrender to me eight hundred hostages to do with as I choose; they shall have such governance as I, their lord, am pleased to give them; and they shall pay the customary dues and imposts. If they will agree to this, let them do it; if not, let them defend themselves." Wise men blamed Charles greatly for this reply of his; but him whom the sin of pride and wrath has overcome is never able to act prudently in any circumstance.

When the thirty Messinese received Charles' outrageous answer they communicated it to the assembled citizens. Thereupon all cried out in desperation: "We will eat our children rather than surrender. Each one of us would be among those eight hundred hostages. We will die within the walls of our city with our wives and children rather than die in strange lands in prison and by torture."

The legate, seeing that the Messinese were determined not to yield, became very wroth, and before he took his departure he excommunicated and interdicted them, commanding all the clergy to leave the island within three days.

On their part, too, the barons of Charles' host were angry that he had refused the citizens' terms; but so powerful was the king, and so greatly feared by all, that none dared withstand him. So they gave it as their advice that he should attack the city on one side where there was no wall, but only a rampart of miscellaneous timbers and stones. Charles replied that he would not destroy the city which had yielded him such good income, nor did he wish to kill the innocent children. He said he would starve the citizens into surrender.

But the Messinese were not caught napping. With their wives and children they sallied out and erected a wall opposite the king's camp in three days. A song was made about this—

> Alas! is 't not a shame
> To see how lime and stone
> Are borne by maid and dame
> With hair untressed?
> God grant them grief and woe
> Who seek the city's wrack . . .

This defence they were able to maintain for a good two months.

In July 1282 King Pedro of Aragón left Catalonia with his armada, which numbered fifty galleys, with eight hundred knights and a great number of transports. As admiral of his fleet he appointed a valiant knight of Calabria, a rebel against King Charles named Ruggero di Lauria. They arrived at the kingdom of Tunis on the coast of Barbary, and there feigned a siege of Alcoyll for two weeks, awaiting news from Sicily. Here King Pedro was joined by Messer Giovanni da Procida, Messer Guglielmo di Messina and two other envoys. These bore letters patent from all the districts of Sicily, wherein the citizens besought the king to assume the sovereignty of the island, imploring him to hasten to the succour of Messina, now being hard pressed by King Charles and his host.

On learning the great number of Charles' troops and his power, in comparison with which his own forces seemed as nothing, King Pedro was loath to advance. But Messer Gianni encouraged and reassured him; whereupon, seeing that the whole island was disposed to obey him, and that the citizens had so far transgressed against Charles that he might well be sure of them, Pedro said that he would indeed go to the assistance of Messina.

The King of Aragón now abandoned the siege of Alcoyll and sailed for Trapani, arriving there at the beginning of August. At Trapani Messer Gianni and the other barons advised him to ride forthwith to Palermo, sending the fleet thither by sea. On August 10 Pedro rode into Palermo where, with great honour and enthusiasm, he was received by the citizens as their lord. He was made king by popular acclamation. He was not crowned by the archbishop of Monreale, as was the custom, for the archbishop had fled to Rome; but the bishop of Cefalù, a small city not far distant, crowned him.

Following this solemnity King Pedro summoned a parliament to deliberate on what was to be done, and all the barons of the island were present. Messer Palmerio Abate spoke for them. He thanked King Pedro for his coming and said that it would have been better had he come with a greater force of armed men, inasmuch as King Charles had five thousand knights and innumerable men at arms. "We fear," he said, "that Messina may have capitulated already, for it has been greatly reduced by lack of provisions." Messer Palmerio concluded by urging that every effort be made to enlist their friends everywhere for the defence of the other cities of the island.

The effect of the barons' counsel on King Pedro was to persuade him that he had got into a bad situation, and he seriously considered retiring from the island in the event that Charles showed any intention of moving towards Palermo with his host.

While parliament was in session there came a swift galley from Messina with letters saying that the city was so reduced that it could not hold out for more than another week; unless the king were pleased to succour the citizens, they would have to surrender to

Charles. The king laid this information before the barons, and asked their advice. Messer Gualtieri di Caltagirone rose and besought him for God's sake to go to the assistance of Messina, for if that city fell, the whole island, and they themselves, would be in the greatest danger. It was his opinion that Pedro and his forces should ride towards Messina to a point about fifty miles from the city: when King Charles heard of his approach, it was possible that he might raise the siege.

In reply to this Messer Gianni rose and said that King Charles was no raw youth to be easily frightened away, and that he would raise the siege when time and circumstances seemed to him to require it. "It seems to me," said Messer Gianni, "that the king should send messengers to Charles demanding his departure from the island, which same falls to King Pedro rightfully as his wife's inheritance, wherein he has been confirmed by the Church of Rome and Pope Nicholas. And if he will not withdraw, let him be defied. At the same time, swift galleys should be made ready, and the admiral Ruggero di Lauria should proceed to Faro to seize the small vessels and vessels of burden which may be bringing supplies to the besiegers. Thus, with little trouble or effort we can annoy King Charles and his troops so that he will have to abandon his position; for if he remains, he and his men will die of hunger."

The king and the barons at once accepted Messer Gianni's advice, and two Catalan knights were sent by Pedro on the suggested embassy.

It would be hard to say whether King Charles' barons were more overcome by rage or astonishment when they heard the terms of King Pedro's message. They contented themselves with sending a return message to the effect that he and his should quit the island immediately. "My liege," said Messer Gianni to the king and the assembly of barons, "for God's sake, now send your galleys quickly to Bocca del Faro and cause the ships bringing supplies to the enemy to be seized. If you do this, you have won the war. If Charles dares to remain, he will be caught and will perish with all his people."

Messer Gianni's advice was followed. The admiral, Messer Ruggero di Lauria, a man of great daring and valour, and one of the most fortunate in battle on land or sea, prepared sixty swift galleys, manning them with Catalans and Sicilians. A spy in the employ of Messer Arrighino de Mari, King Charles' admiral, learned these preparations and reported them to his master. "By God!" said Messer Arrighino to King Charles and his council, "let us take thought to pass over to Calabria with our people without delay, for I have received certain news that the king of Aragón's admiral is even now approaching with armed war galleys. I, on the contrary, have no armed galleys, but only unarmed ships of burden. If we do not decamp, we shall be taken, and our entire navy burned in spite of anything we can do; and you, O king, will perish for want of victuals. Ruggero di Lauria will be here in three days; we have not a moment to lose. Reflect, too, that winter is approaching, and that you have no port wherein your ships can pass the winter season; if you delay, they will be dashed to pieces on the coast. Hence you must withdraw to terra firma where you can receive supplies from the cities of the kingdom."

In no battle or other adversity had King Charles ever been afraid, but when he learned these circumstances, he was frightened indeed. Sighing, he said: "Would to God that I were dead, since Fortune is so contrary to me that I have lost my realm in spite of my great power on land and sea. I do not know why I have lost it, for it is wrested from me by people whom I never harmed in my life. I now greatly regret that I did not take Messina on terms when I had the chance. However, since I have no other choice, raise the siege, and let us go. But whoever is responsible for this treachery, be he layman or cleric, I swear that I will wreak great vengeance upon him."

On the first day the queen, the artisans, and much of the equipment were sent over; on the second day the king went with his suite. But as a measure of war he left behind in ambush two captains with a thousand knights each, so that if the Messinese, after their departure, were to sally out to loot the camp, they might fall upon them and win the city. The trick was well planned, but it was met by equally good thinking, for the Messinese discovered the ambush, and issued orders that no one should leave the city on pain of death. When the French saw that they had been discovered, they succeeded in passing over to Calabria on the third day. The announcement of their failure made Charles wroth and sorrowful, for he had placed considerable faith in the scheme.

Thus was the siege raised from the city, and the people, in the last extremities for lack of food—they had victuals for only three more days—were liberated on September 27, 1282.

The next day Ruggero di Lauria arrived at Faro with every manifestation of joy and triumph. He seized twenty-nine ships, galleys and others, among them five Pisan galleys in the service of the French king. Thence he proceeded to Catona and Reggio di Calabria, and burned eighty of Charles' transports which lay disarmed at the strand. Charles and his people saw this without being able to render any assistance, and the king's rage and grief were doubled. At this time the king had in his hand a small wand which he was wont to carry, and which for very rage he now began to gnaw. "O God!" he said, "You have allowed me to rise high indeed. I pray Thee that the descent may be gradual and easy!"

As though dead and prostrated with amazement and grief, King Charles held a parliament at Reggio and dismissed all those of his army who were not his feudatories. Then he took his way sorrowfully towards Naples.

Upon receiving news of Charles' departure from Messina, and of the operations of Ruggero di Lauria, King Pedro was very happy, and proceeded with all his barons and knights to the city, where he arrived on October 10. With feasts and processions the men and women of Messina received him as their new lord and as their emancipator from the tyranny of Charles of Anjou. Thus it is evident that neither human wit nor force of men provides any protection against the judgment of God.

"Mine was a personal vengeance," said Bernardo del Carpio, "and compared with yours, Messer Giovanni, it seems almost petty. The world must indeed be growing old and asthenic when justice requires for its operation a stage extending from the Golden Horn to the Gates of Hercules."

"In my day," replied Giovanni da Procida, "the State was already beginning to take form, and the difference between your effort and mine is as the difference between the individual and the commonwealth. In the process of time the statesman succeeds the hero on the scene of public action."

"The truth of that," agreed Lord Burleigh, "is well attested by the figure of Louis XI of France."

John Gower fidgeted irritably. "Those who stir up war," he said, "are cursed by the people, and God curses them too."

"I am a lover of justice as much as any man," said Sir Thomas Elyot, "and yet I deplore the fearful slaughter which seemed necessary to effect your end. The shedding of all that blood did not restore your wife or son or daughter."

"Admitted," answered Giovanni da Procida, "but it saved other sons from death, and other wives and daughters from shame. Are you perhaps equally tender-hearted towards the wolves that ravage your sheep-fold?"

"As someone remarked not long ago," said Sir John Fortescue, "the march of events is inevitable and irresistible, and whether or not we mortals approve of the direction of that march, we can do nothing about it. As long as we have what is called civilization, that is, differing degrees of excellence among human kind, we shall have preponderating ideas vesting themselves in institutions; and those institutions will clash, the old with the new, while the new struggle among themselves for supremacy. No man or woman can go through life without some beating and buffeting—that is normal."

"But he escapes with least battering who swims with the tide instead of against it," observed Fynes Moryson.

"If everyone followed that advice," protested John of Salisbury, "grades and degrees of difference would soon disappear, and civilization likewise."

"That is so," agreed Peire Cardenal, "and when we realize it we begin to understand a part of the meaning of the old fable which portrayed the sons of the dragons' teeth fighting with each other."

"The implication of your remark is terrible to contemplate," said John Major with a gesture of deprecation.

"As I hinted earlier," said Snorri, "we of the North had the same idea more or less concealed under the poetic fiction of Ragnarök. The conceit of cleanliness or catharsis has always appealed to neat minds."

"Civilization!" exclaimed Colin Clout. "What is civilization save an interminable series of maladjustments between man and his environment, each error carrying him farther and farther from the possibility of contentment and quiet than the last? Civilization is a race between man and his follies. Where does your philosophy lead you save into the misery of unanswerable questioning? All the philosophers that have ever been have fallen into the pit of one fallacy or the other —either that man is a beast, or a damned soul, or an outcast angel. He is neither the one nor the other. He is an animal, but a human animal, who rejoices in the sun on his back, the cool earth under his naked feet, the taste of fresh water on his tongue, the smell of wood smoke in his nostrils, and the song of birds. You ask: 'What is happiness?' The answer is simple: Each man his woman, each woman her man. After that, food and drink, work and play until such time as the earth once more claims its own. But man doesn't deserve happiness. Once he had the chance to enjoy it in the Garden of Eden—but he chose to be a philosopher."

"In my opinion," said Thomas Gascoigne, "man has not yet had sufficient time to adjust himself to his environment, nor learn how to live, one man with another. I do not know whether such adjustment between man and man, and between man and his milieu can ultimately be achieved. There seem to me to be three possibilities: Gradual but continual improvement, leading to heaven; maintenance of the status quo of mutually destructive and nugatory forces; or, as Snorri says, Ragnarök."

"The concept of Ragnarök is not peculiar to the Scandinavians, nor original with them," said the Clerk of Oxenford. "Most peoples have had the idea of a great cleansing flood, whether of fire or water. But I question the inevitability of any of the alternatives you offer. If man is made of clay, it follows from your premiss that you cannot wash away the dirt without washing away the man."

John Wiclif made an impatient gesture. "You go too high," he said, "and Colin Clout too low, though perhaps you may meet at some point eventually. That is all very well as regards absolute ends; but in the meanwhile, pilgrims on the earth that we are, we must have a way of life."

"I could suggest one," said Peire Cardenal.

"Pray do so," came a chorus of voices.

150. THE RAIN OF FOLLY

Peire Cardenal

There was a city—its name I do not know—
To which there came a storm of rain
Such that all the citizens on which it fell
Were changed into madmen.
Indeed, all lost their wits save one;
He escaped the wetting because,
When the rain came down,
He was lying asleep in his house.
Now when the storm had passed,
This man rose from his sleep and went out,
To mingle with the people, whom he found,
All of them, engaged in acts of folly:
One man had dressed himself in a flowing gown,
While another went about naked;
One was spitting at the sky, another
Throwing stones or sticks at random,
And another was tearing his clothes to shreds.
One went about striking all he met;
Another thought himself a king,
And swung along with a stately air,
And others were jumping over benches.
One man threatened, another cursed;
One swore, another laughed at nothing at all;
Some mouthed gibberish or made ugly faces.

Now the man who was in his right mind
Gazed at these strange antics in astonishment
Until he understood that his fellows were mad.
He looked up and down the street to see
Whether or not there were a single sane man
Anywhere. There was not one.

If the rational man marvelled at these fools,
They were even more greatly astonished at him
Whom they saw behaving himself quietly.
Since they did not see him doing as they did,
They concluded that he had lost his mind.
Each citizen considers himself sane and sensible,
But him they believe to be out of his wits.
Therefore one strikes him on the cheek,
Another gives him a clout on the neck
So that he stumbles here and there.
As he strives to get out of the crowd,
One plucks him and another punches him.
One pushes him this way, another drags him back,
And others pound him whether he is up or down.

At last he freed himself and fled at great speed
To the safety of his house, befouled, bruised
And half dead, glad enough to have escaped
Even half alive from his tormentors.

Peire paused. "Need I go on?" he asked. "The moral seems obvious."

"It is far from evident to me," said Peter Bell.

"What is evident is that you lack the benefits of a classical education," said Fynes Moryson.

"Granted," replied Peter, "but you must admit that I am always willing, and even eager, to be instructed. Perhaps you will be so kind?"

"Gladly," said Moryson. "The man of whom our poet speaks was forced to pray unto Jupiter for another like shower, wherein he wetted himself also, choosing rather to have the love of his foolish neighbours, being a fool, than to be despised by them because he alone was wise. And no doubt in many things it is prudent to follow the opinion of the commonalty, with whom it is better to be foolish, than wise in isolation."

Hereupon there ensued so much and such vociferous discussion that Seithenyn ab Seithyn Saidi and Senchan Torpeist each opened an inquiring eye. Some would not agree that all the world was mad, some would not concede that one man was wiser than another, some would not admit that they had ever been fools, and all were dissatisfied with Peire Cardenal's "way of life."

Finally—"This conversation is becoming too sombre," said Sir John Harington. "We all know that serious discussions on a large scale never lead to anything. Let us keep the talk on a lower plane."

TO WHAT LOW LEVELS the conversation sank thereafter I cannot report, for something hit me a fearful blow in the ribs. It was the elbow of Mac Conglinne putting on his pointed shoes of seven-fold leather.

"A blessing on the new day," said Mac Conglinne cheerfully, "and a blessing on you."

"Is it day, then?" I asked, peering into the cheerless mirk between earth and sky.

"It is so," answered my companion.

"Then take a blessing for yourself, O Illustrious Scholar," said I, and put on my own shoes.

Acknowledgments

TO LEARNED FRIENDS living and dead I owe a debt of gratitude which can be paid only in part. Some have given me counsel and advice, which has been absorbed and so has left no tangible trace; to some others my obligations are obvious. To them and to the publishers who have printed their works I herewith render acknowledgment and thanks.—To Miss Antonie Meyer, who has allowed me to make use of Kuno Meyer's English versions of Irish stories printed in *The Celtic Magazine*, XII, 1887 (Aided Meidbe) and in the *Revue Celtique*, XIII, 1892 (Fingal Rónáin); to Miss Mary Catherine Welborn for leave to use parts of her translation of Roger Bacon's "De Erroribus Medicorum" in *Isis*, XVIII, 1932. To the Delegates of the Clarendon Press, Oxford, who have graciously allowed me to use extracts from Thomas Arnold, *Select English Works of John Wyclif;* Thomas Gascoigne, *Loci e Libro Veritatum*, edited by J. E. T. Rogers; Charles Plummer, *Bethada Náem nErenn;* and to translate passages from Dante Alighieri, *Opere*, edited by Edward Moore; Benedeit, *Voyage de St. Brandan*, edited by E. G. R. Waters; and from G. Vigfússon, *Sturlunga Saga*. To the officers of the Early English Text Society, who have given me permission to make modern renderings from the Society's volumes 19, 20, 21, 28, 33, 36, 37, 38, 61, 91, 119, 126, 127, 191, x, lxxiv, lxxxviii, xcvi, and cv. To Humphrey Milford, London, for allowing me to use extracts from Charles Plummer's "On the Colophons and Marginalia of Irish Scribes," *Proceedings of the British Academy*, Volume XII, and to translate from *The Seven Sages of Rome*, edited by K. Brunner for the Early English Text Society. To Colonel Sir John Murray, who has very kindly permitted me to retell portions of *The Book of Ser Marco Polo*, translated by Colonel Sir Henry Yule. To the Max Niemeyer Verlag, Halle, for permission to translate from *Wistasse le Moine*, edited by W. Foerster and J. Trost; *Beiträge zur Romanischen und Englischen Philologie: Festgabe für Wendelin Foerster;* Chrétien de Troyes, *Cligès*, edited by W. Foerster; *Jaufre*, ed. H. Breuer; and *Les Mervelles de Rigomer*, edited by W. Foerster and H. Breuer. To the Secretary of the Scottish History Society, who has generously permitted me to make use of A. Constable's edition of John Major's *Historia Majoris Britanniae*. To Father Paul Grosjean and the Société des Bollandistes, Brussels, for permission to retell legends from Charles Plummer's *Miscellanea Hagiographica Hibernica*. And to Messrs. Williams and Norgate, who have allowed me to quote from W. Stokes, *Three Irish Glossaries,* E. O'Curry, *On the Manners and Customs of the Ancient Irish,* and S. H. O'Grady, *Silva Gadelica.*

BIBLIOGRAPHY

Philippe d'Alcrippe, *Fabrique des excellens Traits de Verité*, Paris, 1853

Dante Alighieri, *Tutte le Opere*, ed. E. Moore, Clarendon Press, Oxford, 1894

Anonimo Fiorentino, *Commento alla Divina Commedia*, Bologna, 1866-74

L. Ariosto, *Orlando Furioso*, tr. W. S. Rose, London, 1858

T. Arnold, *Select English Works of John Wyclif*, Clarendon Press, Oxford, 1869-71

V. Ásmundarson, *Fornaldarsögur Norðrlanda*, Reykjavík, 1891

T. Austin, *Two Fifteenth Century Cookery Books*, EETS, 1888

Roger Bacon, *De Erroribus Medicorum*, ed. tr. M. C. Welborn, *Isis*, XVIII

Matteo Bandello, *Novelle*, Firenze, 1833

M. M. Banks, *An Alphabet of Tales*, EETS, 1904-05

E. de Barbazon et M. Méon, *Fabliaux et Contes*, Paris, 1808

Bartholomaeus Anglicus, *De Proprietatibus Rerum*, (Wynkyn de Worde), 1495

K. Bartsch, *Chrestomathie Provençale*, Elberfeld, 1880

Pierre Bayle, *Dictionnaire Historique et Critique*

Benvenuto da Imola, *Comentum super Dantis Aldigherij Comoediam*, Florentiae, 1887

Berthold von Regensburg, *Vollständige Ausgabe seiner Predigten*, Wien, 1862

Giovanni Boccaccio, *Opere*, ed. Ignazio Moutier, Firenze, 1827-34

Hector Boëce, *The Buik of the Croniclis of Scotland*, Rolls Series, London, 1858

J. Bongars, *Gesta Dei per Francos*, Hannoviae, 1611

A. Boorde, *The Fyrst Boke of the Introduction of Knowledge*, EETS, 1870

Sir John Bourchier, *The Boke of Duke Huon of Burdeux*, EETS, 1882-87

BIBLIOGRAPHY

J. D. Bruce, *Le Morte Arthur*, EETS, 1903

K. Brunner, *The Seven Sages of Rome*, EETS, Oxford University Press, London, 1933

Sir Samuel E. Brydges, *Restituta, or Titles, Extracts and Characters*, London, 1814-16

Caesarius Heisterbacensis, *Dialogus Miraculorum*, ed. J. Strange, Köln, 1851

William Camden, *Britannia, etc.*, ed. R. Gough, London, 1806

Luis Camoës, *Os Lusiadas*, ed. C. von Reinhardstoettner, Strassburg, 1874

J. F. Campbell, *Popular Tales of the West Highlands*, Edinburgh, 1860-62

Willima Caxton, *The Golden Legand*, Temple Classics, London, 1900

Cento Novelle Antiche, (Giunti), Fiorenza, 1572

Chrétien de Troyes, *Cligès*, ed. W. Foerster, Halle, 1910

Chronique anonyme, Paris, 1855

T. O. Cockayne, *Leechdoms, Wortcunning and Starcraft*, Rolls Series London, 1865

Philippe de Commines, *Memoirs*, tr. A. R. Scoble, London, 1855

O. Connellan, *Imtheacht na Tromdhaimhe*, Dublin, 1860

T. F. Crane, *The Exempla of Jacques de Vitry*, London, 1890

G. W. Dasent, *The Story of Burnt Njal*, Edinburgh, 1861

E. G. Duff, *Solomon and Marcolphus*, London, 1892

William Dunbar, *Poems*, ed. D. Laing, Edinburgh, 1834

Sir Thomas Elyot, *The Boke Named the Governour*, ed. H. H. S. Croft, London, 1880

España Sagrada, Madrid, 1763

Étienne de Bourbon, *Liber de Donis*, ed. Lecoy de la Marche, Paris, 1877

Eulogium Historiarum, ed. F. S. Haydon, Rolls Series, London, 1858-63

Flateyjarbók: En Samling af Norske Konge-sagaer, Christiania, 1860-68

Fornmanna Sögur eptir Gömlum Handritum, Kaupmannahöfn, 1825, 1826, 1827

Historia Francorum per Fredegarium Scholasticum, Paris, 1869

Jean Froissart, *The Chronicles of England, France and Spain*, tr T. Johnes, London, 1839

Fulk Fitzwarin, ed. J. Stevenson in R. Coggeshall's *Chronicum Anglicanum*, Rolls Series, London, 1875

Thomas Gascoigne, ed. J. E. T. Rogers, *Loci e Libro Veritatum*, Clarendon Press, Oxford, 1881

P. de Gayangos, *Mohammedan Dynasties in Spain*, London, 1840

Geoffrey of Monmouth, *Historia Regum Britanniae*, tr. J. A. Giles, London, 1848

Edward Gibbon, *The Decline and Fall of the Roman Empire*, London, 1806

Giraldus Cambrensis, *Topographia Hibernica*, tr. Sir R. Colt Hoare, London, 1881

W. Goodall, *Joannis Forduni Scotichronicon, etc.*, Edinburgh, 1759

Gregorius Turonensis, *Historiae Francorum*, ed. H. Omont, Paris, 1886

J. Grimm und A. Schmeller, *Lateinische Gedichte des X. und XI. Jahrhunderts*, Göttingen, 1838

G. Gröber, *Beiträge zur Romanischen und Englischen Philologie*, Halle, 1902

Francesco Guicciardini, *Storia d'Italia*, (G. A. Bertano), Venetia, 1580

Guillaume de Nangis, *Gesta Philippi Tertii Francorum*, Paris, 1840

K. Halm, *Fabulae Aesopicae*, Leipzig, 1852

Sir John Harington, *Orlando Furioso in English . . . Verse*, London, 1634

W. C. Hazlitt, *A C. Mery Talys*, London, 1887

W. C. Hazlitt, *Remains of Early Popular Poetry of England*, London, 1864

Henry of Huntingdon, *Chronicle*, tr. T. Forester, London, 1853

Herodotus, *History*, tr. H. Cary, London, 1882

Antonio de Herrera y Tordesillas, *Historia General de los Hechos de los Castellanos en las Islas, etc.* [Madrid], 1726-30

Ralph Higden, *Polychronicon*, ed. C. Babington and C. R. Lumby, Rolls Series, London, 1865-86

K. Hildebrand, *Die Lieder der älteren Edda*, Paderborn, 1876

J. A. Hjaltalin and G. Goudie, *Orkneyinga Saga*, Edinburgh, 1873

W. Holland und A. Keller, *Die Lieder Guillem's von Peitieu*, Tübingen, 1850

Sancti Isidori Hispalensis . . . Opera, ed. F. Arevalo, Romae, 1797-1803

Islendinga Sögur, Reykjavík, 1892, 1895

J. Jamieson, *The Bruce and the Wallace*, Edinburgh and London, 1820

Jaufre, ed. H. Breuer, Göttingen (Halle), 1925

Jocelin of Brakelond, *Chronica*, ed. J. G. Rokewode, London, 1840

Jocelin of Furness, *Vita Kentigerni*, ed. A. P. Forbes, Edinburgh, 1874

John of Salisbury, *Opera*, ed. J. A. Giles, Oxford, 1848

Joinville, *Histoire de Saint Louis*, ed. N. de Wailly, Paris, 1868

A. Jubinal, *Nouveau Recueil de Contes, etc.*, Paris, 1839-42

Geoffrey Keating, *Foras Feasa ar Éirinn*, tr. J. O'Mahony, New York, 1866

Henry Knighton, *Leycestrensis Chronicon*, ed. J. R. Lumby, Rolls Series, London, 1889

D. Laing, *Early Scottish Metrical Tales*, London, 1889

William Langland, *The Vision of William concerning Piers and Plowman*, ed. W. W. Skeat, EETS, 1867-73

The Life of Brother Juniper, tr. T. W. Arnold, Tempie Classics, London, 1926

Robert Lindsay of Pitscottie, *Cronicles of Scotland*, ed. J. G. Dalyell, Edinburgh, 1814

Sir David Lindesay, *Ane Satyre of the Three Estaitis*, EETS, n.d., reprint of Edinburgh, 1602

Liudprand of Cremona, *Antapodoseos*, in J. P. Migne, *Patrologia Latina*, Paris, 1881

H. Lizeray et W. O'Dwyer, *Leabar Gabala: Livre des Invasions*, Paris, 1884

J. G. Lockhart, *Ancient Spanish Ballads*, Boston, 1857

W. H. Logan, *A Pedlar's Pack of Songs and Ballads*, Edinburgh, 1869

V. Luzarche, *La Vie du Pape Grégoire le Grand*, Tours, 1857

Niccolò Machiavelli, *Opere*, Milano, 1820

Sir Frederick Madden, *Syr Gawayne*, London, 1839

John Major, *Historia Majoris Britanniae*, ed. A. Constable, Edinburgh, 1892

John Mandeville's Travels, ed. P. Hamelius, EETS, 1919

Robert Mannyng of Brunne, *Handlyng Synne*, ed. F. J. Furnivall, EETS, 1901

Juan Manuel, *El Conde Lucanor*, ed. A. Keller, Stuttgart, 1839

Manuscript Bibliothèque nationale, f. fr. 375
Manuscript Bibliothèque nationale, nouv. acq. 1943
Manuscript Royal Irish Academy, 23.P.16 (Lebor Brecc)
Walter Map, *De Nugis Curialium*, ed. T. Wright, London, 1850
Juan de Mariana, *Histoire générale d'Espagne*, Paris, 1725
K. Meyer, *Aided Medba, The Celtic Magazine*, 1887
K. Meyer, *Aided Maelfothartaig maic Rónain, Revue Celtique*, 1892
Les Mervelles de Rigomer, ed. W. Foerster, H. Breuer, Dresden (Halle), 1908
John Mirk, *The Festial*, ed. T. Erbe, EETS, 1905
Enguerrand de Monstrelet, *Chronicles*, tr. T. Johnes, London, 1867
A. de Montaiglon, *Recueil de Poésies françoises, etc.*, Paris, 1855
A. de Montaiglon et G. Raynaud, *Recueil général et complet de Fabliaux*, Paris, 1872-90
Fynes Moryson, *An Itinerary, etc.*, (J. Beale), London, 1617
L. Muratori, *Rerum Italicarum Scriptores*, Mediolani, 1723-51
J. A. H. Murray, *Thomas of Erceldoune*, EETS, 1875
Martín Fernandez de Navarrete, *Colleccion de los Viages y Descubrimientos que hicieron por mar los Españoles, etc.*, Madrid, 1825
Joannes Nevizanus, *Silva Nuptialis*, Lugduni, 1556
E. O'Curry, *Manners and Customs of the Ancient Irish*, London, 1873
J. O'Donovan, *The Banquet of Dun na nGedh, etc.*, Dublin, 1842
S. H. O'Grady, *Silva Gadelica*, London, 1892
Ordericus Vitalis, *Historia ecclesiastica*, tr. T. Forester, London, 1853
Partonopeus de Blois, (G. Crapelet), Paris, 1834
Paulus Diaconus, *Historia Langobardorum, Monumenta Germaniae Historica: Scriptores*, Hannoviae, 1878
Percy's Reliques of Ancient English Poetry, Everyman's Library, London, 1910
J. Pichon, *Le Ménagier de Paris*, Paris, 1846
J. Pinkerton, *A General Collection of . . . Voyages, etc.*, London, 1808-
Charles Plummer, *Bethada Náem nErenn*, Clarendon Press, Oxford, 1922
Charles Plummer, *Colophons and Marginalia of Irish Scribes, Proceedings of the British Academy*, XII, Oxford University Press, London, 1926

Charles Plummer, *Miscellanea Hagiographica Hibernica,* Société des Bollandistes, Bruxelles, 1925

Plutarch, *Opera,* ed. T. Doehner and F. Dübner, Paris, 1877-

Marco Polo, *Travels,* tr. Sir Henry Yule, London, 1871

M. A. C. Press, *The Laxdaela Saga,* Temple Classics, London, 1906

Récits d'un Ménestrel de Reims, ed. N. de Wailly, Paris, 1877

W. J. Rees, *Liber Landavensis,* Llandovery, 1840

W. Reeves, *The Life of Saint Columba . . . by Adamnan,* Edinburgh, 1874

Richard of Devizes, *De rebus gestis Ricardi Primi,* tr. J. A. Giles, London, 1848

Roger of Hoveden, *Chronica,* ed. W. Stubbs, Rolls Series, London, 1868-71

Roger of Wendover, *Flores Historiarum,* tr. J. A. Giles, London, 1849

Le Roman des Aventures de Fregus, ed. F. Michel, Edinburgh, 1841

Saxo Grammaticus, *Gesta Danorum,* ed. A. Holder, Strassburg, 1886

A. Scheler, *Li Bastars de Buillon,* Bruxelles, 1877

Sir Walter Scott, *Minstrelsy of the Scottish Border,* Edinburgh, 1810

Selection from the Minor Poems of Lydgate, Percy Society, London, 1840

J. C. L. Simonde de Sismondi, *Histoire des Français,* Paris, 1826

W. F. Skene, *Celtic Scotland,* Edinburgh, 1876-80

W. Stokes, *Three Irish Glossaries,* London, 1862

W. Stokes, *Cath Maige Tured, Revue Celtique,* 1891

G. F. Straparola, *Tredici piacevoli notti,* tr. J. Louveau et P. de Larivey, Paris, 1882

Snorri Sturlason, *The Heimskringla,* Everyman's Library, London, 1915

The Tale of Beryn, ed. F. J. Furnivall and W. G. Stone, EETS, 1909

W. J. Thoms, *Early English Prose Romances,* London, 1858

G. Vigfússon, *Sturlunga Saga,* Clarendon Press, Oxford, 1878

Giovanni Villani, *Cronica,* (Giunti), Firenze, 1587

Wace, *Roman de Brut,* ed. Leroux de Lincy, Rouen, 1838

Wace, *Roman de Rou,* ed. F. Pluquet, Rouen, 1827

E. G. R. Waters, *Benedeit: Voyage de Saint Brandan,* Clarendon Press, Oxford, 1928

H. W. Weber, *Metrical Romances, etc.,* Edinburgh, 1810

H. W. Weber, R. Jamieson, Sir W. Scott, *Northern Antiquities,* London, 1814

H. B. Wheatley, *Merlin,* EETS, 1869

E. Wilken, *Die Prosaische Edda* . . . *nebst Volsunga Saga,* Paderborn, 1877

William of Malmesbury, *De Gestis regum Anglorum,* tr. J. A. Giles, London, 1847

T. Williams, *Iolo Manuscripts,* Llandovery, 1848

E. Windisch, *Irische Texte,* Leipzig, 1880

T. Wright, *The Book of the Knight of La Tour Landry,* EETS, 1906

Wistasse le Moine, ed. W. Foerster und J. Trost, Halle, 1891

James Yonge, *The Governance of Prynces,* ed. R. Steele, EETS, 1898

INDEX OF PERSONS AND TITLES

In those cases where the second component of a personal name is not a true surname, but indicates a place, profession, quality, etc., entry is made under the letter which begins the given name; *e.g., Roger* of Wendover, *Clerk* of Oxenford; *John* the Reeve, *Blaise* the Hermit; *Richard* sans Peur, *Lambert* li Tort.

An attempt has been made to give the approximate life dates of historical personages: *b.* = born, *c.* = circa, *d.* = died, *fl.* = flourished.

Adamnan, *c. 624-704*, 246, 372, 501, 539
Adventures of Saint Brandan in the Western Sea, The, 246
Ambroise, *fl. 1175-1200*, 33, 36, 516
Anastasius Buried Alive, 239
Andrew the Chapelain, *fl. 1196-1220*, 361, 362, 367, 386, 490, 501
Archebald, Master, *15th century*, 331, 336
Arderne, John, *c. 1306-c. 1390*, 185
Ariosto, Lodovico, *1474-1533*, 197, 198, 361, 435, 450, 575, 580, 581
Arnaldus de Villanova, *c. 1235-1311*, 180, 182, 186, 361, 362, 409
Asmund's Sepulchral Adventure, 226

Bachelor of Salamanca, 309, 314, 497, 589, 594
Bacon, Roger, *c. 1214-1292*, 186, 501, 538
Bandello, Matteo, *1480-1562*, 14, 20, 25, 240, 314, 317, 478, 543
Barbour, John, *1316-1395*, 33, 35, 40, 180, 181, 392, 619
Barns of Ayr, The, 613
Bartholomaeus Anglicus, *fl. 1250*, 40, 41, 53, 62, 120, 146, 148, 195, 197, 246, 260, 351, 376, 409, 511
Base Amour of Berengar's Wife Willa, The, 434
Bastars' Wife of Buillon, The, 471
Belfagor's Bargain, 410
Bell, Peter, 33, 36, 62, 120, 121, 133, 158, 161, 162, 183, 197, 210, 211, 212, 272, 280, 292, 309, 372, 373, 375, 452, 470, 511, 555, 558, 589, 640
Benvenuto da Imola, *d. 1390*, 159, 161, 168
Bernardo del Carpio, *9th century*, 68, 103, 309, 588, 589, 594, 597, 613, 625, 637
Beryn, 14, 25, 169
Beryn at the Bar, 169
Blaise the Hermit, 103, 153, 158, 167, 168, 173, 372, 422, 428
Blind Harry, *fl. 1470-1492*, 52, 68, 94, 103, 105, 409, 458, 580, 613, 618, 622
Blondel, *12th century*, 516, 521
Blood-lust of Albina and What Came of It, The, 90
Boccaccio, Giovanni, *1313-1375*, 336, 361, 362, 452, 490, 497, 501

INDEX OF PERSONS AND TITLES

Boëce, Hector, *c. 1465-1563*, 52, 53, 54, 70, 373, 534
Bonvesin da Riva, *c. 1240-1315*, 41, 45, 52, 55, 62, 64, 68, 153, 240, 299, 417
Boorde, Andrew, *c. 1490-1549*, 35, 104, 105, 120, 121, 128, 152, 166, 180, 197, 261, 272, 386, 392, 508
Bourchier, Sir John, *1467-1533*, 182, 183, 378
Boy Ignorant of Women, The, 337
Brestison, Sigmund, *10th century*, 281, 292, 373
Bromyard, John, *d. 1390*, 25, 148, 509, 564
Brother Juniper's Hospitality, 43
Buondelmonte de' Buondelmonti Falls into a Trap, 314
Burleigh, Lord, *see* Cecil, William
Bycorne and Chichevache, 392

Caesarius Heisterbacensis, *d. 1240/50*, 71, 103, 120, 148, 150, 368, 369, 452, 535
Caier's Wife and Nephew, 429
Camden, William, *1551-1623*, 26, 62, 65, 94, 104, 153, 261, 273, 314, 373, 391, 457, 470, 565
Capgrave, John, *1393-1464*, 14, 186, 339, 506, 601
Cardenal, Peire, *d. c. 1274*, 103, 340, 638, 639, 640, 641
Carle of the Drab Coat, The, 4
Castide, Henry, *14th century*, 52, 71, 73, 421, 506, 508, 511, 561, 564, 573
Cecil, William, Lord Burleigh, *1520-1598*, 50, 314, 340, 358, 470, 558, 566, 637
Chrétien de Troyes, *d. c. 1180*, 153, 188, 197, 230, 231, 273, 435, 597, 603
Christine de Pisan, *c. 1363-1440*, 52, 103, 159, 390, 405, 421, 435, 478, 490, 501, 525, 566, 572
Churl and the Bird, The, 551

Cipolla, Fra, 167, 168, 509, 511
Clerk of Oxenford, 26, 27, 36, 54, 103, 168, 182, 273, 351, 362, 367, 368, 369, 390, 391, 426, 427, 452, 457, 458, 490, 501, 506, 508, 543, 551, 639
Clidna's Wave, 373
Clout, Colin, 62, 73, 177, 391, 405, 406, 565, 621, 638, 639
Cobbler of Constantinople, The, 376
Colgan, John, *d. c. 1657*, 52, 372, 506, 508, 515, 516
Columcille, *521-597*, 52, 151, 372
Columcille's Garron, 151
Conall Gulban and the Amhuish, 109
Conrad of Montferrat, *see* Montferrat, Conrad of
Cormac of Cashel, *d. 908*, 103, 373, 375, 378, 391, 392, 428
Crafty Farmer, The, 536
Cucuimne, *c. 746*, 12, 13, 147
Curtal Friar, 33, 36, 40, 51, 52, 94, 146, 404, 535, 594

Dafydd ab Gwilym, *c. 1340-c. 1400*, 261, 386
Dandolo, Andrea, *1304-1354*, 452, 455, 457, 606
Death of Celtchar mac Uthechair, The, 562
Death of Maelfothartaig mac Ronan, The, 430
Devils' Conclave, The, 285
Dick O the Cow, 48, 50, 51, 285, 594, 597
Dicuil, *fl. 800-825*, 260
Digna of Aquileia, 456
Divorce by Death, 231
Dog Vigi, The, 501
Douglas, James, *1286-1330*, 33, 384
Dunbar, William, *c. 1460-c. 1520*, 5, 55, 161, 187, 188, 395, 404

INDEX OF PERSONS AND TITLES 655

Dwynwen verch Brychan and Maelon Dafodril, 386

Earl Richard, 358
Eices ind Righ, 62, 514, 515
Einar Rattlescale, *10th century*, 65, 71, 599
Eindridi Broadsole Shoots at a Mark, 295
Elevation of Pierre de la Brosse, The, 159
Elyot, Sir Thomas, *1490-1546*, 14, 20, 25, 103, 147, 152, 304, 378, 384, 457, 504, 505, 637
Empress of Rome and Her Maids Who Were Men, The, 154
Eric Bloodaxe Takes a Wife, 420
Espaign du Lion, *14th century*, 241
Étienne de Bourbon, *d. c. 1261*, 73, 165, 182, 362, 368, 369, 435, 516
Eustace the Monk, *d. 1217*, 162, 165, 281, 295, 299, 300, 535
Eyes of Love, The, 514
Eyjolf's Last Fight, 86

Faidit, Gaucelm, *d. c. 1220*, 114, 120, 121, 339
Fairy Lady of Eldon Hill, The, 481
Fenice, 435, 478, 573
Ferreira de Vasconcellos, Jorge, *d. 1585*, 69
Fight on the Inch of Perth, The, 68
Fight for the Marrowbone, The, 62
Fitzwarin, Fulk, *c. 1180-c. 1257*, 88, 90, 287, 294, 373, 582, 584
Florinda, 310
Fly with the Wooden Leg, The, 150
Fongasso, Lorenzo, *14th century*, 306
Fortescue, Sir John, *c. 1394-1476*, 151, 173, 179, 180, 317, 340, 507, 538, 622, 637

Fountain of Youth and the Island of Bimini, The, 183
Freebooters of Auvergne, The, 527
Friars of Berwick, The, 55
Froissart, Jean, *1337-1410*, 33, 35, 70, 188, 241, 317, 321, 506, 511, 526, 584, 585, 609, 613
Fulk Fitzwarin's Seafaring, 212
Fun with a Corpse, 594

Gascoigne, Thomas, *1403-1458*, 173, 179, 188, 534, 539, 624, 638
Gautier de Coinci, *1177-1236*, 368
Geoffrey of Monmouth, *c. 1100-c. 1154*, 43, 133, 197, 261
Gerald de Barry, *see* Giraldus Cambrensis
Gerson, Jean Charlier, *1363-1429*, 390, 478
Ghost of Fawdoun, The, 94
Gianni Schicchi and the Mule, 167
Gilbertus Anglicus, *fl. 1250*, 121, 195, 508
Giovanni da Procida, *c. 1210-c. 1299*, 589, 624, 637
Giraldus Cambrensis, *c. 1146-c. 1220*, 35, 36, 62, 71, 109, 133, 152, 153, 260, 261, 373, 375, 376, 501, 505, 511, 513
Gogmagog, 94
Goodman of Bath, 392, 395, 404, 417, 490, 501, 525, 564, 572, 573
Goodman of Paris, *fl. 1358-1393*, 41, 45, 52, 55, 338, 340, 362, 464, 505, 534
Gower, John, *1330-1408*, 129, 169, 173, 179, 342, 362, 451, 512, 513, 606, 637
Gray, Sir Thomas, *d. 1369*, 261, 272, 273, 373, 471, 539
Gregory's Petrine Penance, 261
Guicciardini, Francesco, *1483-1540*, 70, 306, 336, 386, 458

Guilhem IX, *1071-1127*, 40, 86, 115, 521, 525
Guillaume de Nangis, *d. c. 1303*, 51, 159, 161, 238
Gwendolen of Cornwall, 619

Hákon Hákonson, *1204-1263*, 86, 114, 198, 241, 299, 465
Haliday, Walter, *fl. 1400-1425*, 42, 167, 272, 322
Hallarstein, *11th century*, 405, 452, 501, 504
Hallfred Vandraethaskald, *fl. early 11th century*, 228, 284, 287, 299, 305, 599
Hamlet in Scotland, 465
Hanging of Marcolf, The, 162
Harald Harfagr and Gyda, 427
Hard Judge, The, 178
Harington, Sir John, *1561-1612*, 61, 105, 120, 121, 129, 133, 153, 198, 210, 272, 404, 465, 469, 512, 538, 565, 625, 641
Harry, *see* Blind Harry
Harsley, William de, *14th century*, 188
Hartmann von Aue, *c. 1170-c. 1220*, 120
Hawkins, Sir John, *1532-1595*, 26, 183, 185, 246, 260, 287
Heart of King Robert, The, 33
Helinandus, *d. 1237*, 405, 427, 452, 497
Henry II, *1133-1189*, 40, 543, 573, 575, 588
Henry of Huntingdon, *1080-c. 1154*, 291, 418
Hermit and the Outlaw, The, 276
Higden, Ralph, *c. 1299-c. 1363*, 54, 148, 149, 181, 246, 419, 420, 516, 526, 534, 575, 589, 620
How Amadas Fought with the Fiend at the Tomb of Ydoine, 96
How Astolfo, King of the Lombards, Learned About Women, 436
How Beryn Was Ruined by Dice-play, 14
How Blondel Found King Richard in Germany, 522
How Bödvar Improved Table-manners at the Court of King Hrolf, 65
How Columcille Freed Scanlann from Salt Bacon and Beer, 46
How Duke Astolfo of England Found Orlando's Wits on the Moon, 198
How Eledus Slew His Host, 105
How Eustace Sold Pots, 300
How Jeffrey Longed to Sleep at Castle Monbrun, 121
How the Jongleur of Sens Threw Dice with Saint Peter, 27
How King Richard Won the Heart of Margery of Almain, 517
How Lancelot Fought with the Demon Cats, 130
How Mac Creiche Slew the Yellow Pest, 582
How Olaf Haraldson Gathered Scat in the Faroës, 292
How Olaf Tryggvison Paid a Debt, 598
How Sir John de Carouges Avenged the Honour of His Wife, 609
Huchown of the Awle Ryale, *d. c. 1376*, 342, 480, 481, 488, 490, 571

Initiation of a King, The, 152
Inordinate Lust of Romilda, Duchess of Friuli, The, 452
Illustrious Scholar, *see* Mac Conglinne
Iolo Goch, *fl. 1328-c. 1412*, 35, 43, 103, 168, 272, 281, 386, 573, 575, 581
Isabel, Countess of Pembroke, *b. 1173*, 42, 561

Jacques de Vitry, *c. 1178-1240*, 216, 478
Jarnskeggi's Daughter, 600

INDEX OF PERSONS AND TITLES

Jean de Meung, *c. 1250-c. 1305*, 27, 188, 410, 478
Jean de Montreuil, *fl. 1400*, 410
Jean d'Outremeuse, *fl. 1350-1375*, 73, 180, 181, 182, 185, 373
Jeffrey's Fight with the Giant Mezel, 115
Jehan, Master, *c. 1200-1250*, 12, 13, 129, 133, 219, 342, 514
Jocelin of Brakelond, *fl. 1200*, 178, 180
John of Fordun, *d. c. 1384*, 373, 388, 458, 539
John of Gaddesden, *1280-1361*, 105, 121, 188, 195, 339, 410, 505
John de Rampaigne, *see* Rampaigne
John the Reeve, 25, 26, 33, 351, 358, 361, 378, 506, 514, 521, 566, 594
John of Salisbury, *1115-1180*, 13, 14, 230, 304, 361, 362, 408, 638
Joinville, Jean, Sieur de, *c. 1224-1317*, 103, 120, 210, 228, 488

Keating, Geoffrey, *c. 1570-c. 1644*, 45, 62, 64, 104, 153, 373, 500, 501, 511, 514, 601, 603, 622
King Edward III Reckons Without His Hostess, 318
King Fernando and the Wife of Lorenzo d'Acunha, 307
King Henry's Guest, 48
King Richard Entertains Saracen Ambassadors at Lunch, 36
Kinmont Willie, 379
Knight of La Tour Landry, *c. 1371*, 27, 362, 388, 391, 417, 455
Knight and the Lion, The, 513
Knighton, Henry, *fl. 1363*, 35, 69, 304, 417, 618

Lady of Lango, The, 73
Lady in the Wall, The, 564
Lambert li Tort, *fl. 1160-1200*, 180, 182

Lancelot, Sir, 129, 133, 219, 228, 246, 342, 346, 514
Lanfranc of Milan, *fl. c. 1295*, 120, 317
Langland, William, *d. c. 1400*, 148, 168, 173, 177, 179, 186, 294, 300, 351, 507, 539
Lefèvre, Raoul, *fl. 1454-1464*, 54, 105, 152
Leland, John, *1506-1552*, 103, 188, 211, 216, 226, 246, 287, 317, 346, 361, 584
Linacre, Thomas, *1460-1524*, 120, 195, 507
Lindsay, Sir David, *1490-1555*, 172, 179, 273, 534
Lochmaben Harper, 35, 103, 378, 384, 410
Lopez de Ayala, Pedro, 104, 158, 309, 314
Love, Imprisonment and Treacherous Slaying of Sancho Diaz, The, 589

Mac Conglinne, 3, 4, 11, 12, 33, 40, 43, 47, 61, 109, 120, 129, 219, 420, 564, 580, 581, 582, 584, 601, 603, 606, 622, 641
Machiavelli, Niccolò, *1469-1527*, 104, 317, 338, 339, 340, 410, 457, 458, 538, 539
Mad Lover, The, 189
Madot, Jehan, *c. 1275*, 13, 14, 27, 95, 103, 189, 195, 197, 521
Maid of Astolat, The, 342
Major, John, *1470-1550*, 26, 35, 54, 71, 73, 94, 153, 197, 300, 304, 322, 535, 613, 618, 624, 638
Malgherita Spolatina and Her Paramour, 369
Man-eating Maiden of Dundee, The, 53
Mannyng of Brunne, Robert, *fl. 1288-1338*, 26, 70, 158, 177, 260, 261, 276, 287, 331, 390, 509, 546, 571, 573, 575, 618

Map, Walter, *d. c. 1209*, 43, 103, 120, 261, 299, 376, 378
Margaret, Countess of Henneberge and Her Three Hundred and Sixty-five Children, 450
Marion de la Bruère, 347
Marshal, Earl William, *1146-1219*, 40, 41, 294, 516, 561, 575, 613
Marsiglio of Padua, *c. 1270-1343*, 68, 294, 300, 480, 539, 622
Matheolus, 406, 408, 478, 501, 573
Melior, 422, 425, 426, 427
Merlin and Vivian, 422
Midnight Rider, The, 451
Minstrel of Reims, *c. 1260*, 36, 129, 514, 522, 555, 556, 558, 564, 575
Miracle, The, 363
Mirk, John, *fl. c. 1400*, 54, 120, 178, 179, 451, 452, 512, 513
Mochua, *c. 580-637*, 149, 151, 152
Monster of Male Gaudine, The, 219
Montferrat, Conrad of, *d. 1192*, 103, 180, 558, 594
Moryson, Fynes, *1566-1630*, 36, 43, 61, 133, 153, 185, 373, 450, 454, 457, 470, 538, 539, 564, 566, 638, 640
Murder in the Jewish Quarter, 174

Neckam, Alexander, *1157-1217*, 120, 152, 195, 260, 376, 457, 488, 504, 511
Necromancer and the Dean, The, 498
Nut-cracking Thief and the Cripple, The, 508

O Cleirigh, Michael, *1575-1643*, 514, 582
O Lochan, Cuan, *d. 1024*, 47, 141, 145, 430, 572, 584
Ordericus Vitalis, *1075-1142*, 133, 508
Orthon, Familiar Spirit of the Lord de Corasse, 585
Ossian, *3d century*, 47, 61, 62, 103, 121, 409, 480, 488, 500, 501, 511, 561, 562, 572
Outlawing of Thorkel Dryfrost, The, 281

Pangur Ban, 147
Pardoner and the Barmaid, The, 352
Paris, Matthew, *d. 1259*, 65, 71, 295, 418, 599, 601
Paulus Diaconus, *c. 720-c. 800*, 150, 452, 511, 601, 606, 609, 613, 618
Payn Peverel's Adventure with Gogmagog, 89
Piers the Toller, 547
Poison Cup, The, 566
Pole, Sir William atte, *d. 1366*, 26, 284, 575
Polo, Marco, *c. 1254-1324*, 336, 378, 384
Ponce de Leon, Juan, *c. 1460-1521*, 103, 183, 185, 246, 260, 287
Prioress and Her Three Suitors, The, 135
Provident Matron, The, 404

Queen Eleanor's Confession, 559
Queen Eleanor and Salah ad-Din, 556
Queen Languoreth's Ring, 273
Queen Meave's Last Bath, 602

Rain of Folly, The, 639
Rampaigne, John de, *13th century*, 558, 566
Ravished Wife, The, 464
Return of Viga Hrapp, The, 229
Richard I, Cœur de Lion, *1157-1199*, 33, 36, 40, 86, 103, 165, 185, 186, 294, 516, 521, 522, 524, 525, 527, 543, 558, 599
Richard of Devizes, *fl. 1191*, 172, 173, 373, 555
Richard de Haldingham, *fl. 1283-1314*, 183, 260, 373

INDEX OF PERSONS AND TITLES 659

Richard sans Peur and the Unquiet Corpse, 134
Roaring Dick, 165, 358, 361, 505, 506, 509, 514, 521
Robert I, the Bruce, 1274-1329, 33, 35
Robert Guiscard's Venomous Wife, 408
Roger of Hoveden, fl. 1174-1201, 71, 376, 408
Roger of Wendover, d. 1237, 386, 505
Rosmunda's Revenge, 607

Sacrilegious Caroller, 35, 42, 272
Sad End of Peter the Dicer, The, 20
Sagamoni Borcan, the Virtuous Prince, 384
Samson's Adventures at the Court of King Hildebert, 573
Satirical Description of His Lady, A, 576
Saxo Grammaticus, d. c. 1220, 103, 226, 228, 238, 464, 465, 469, 470
Scabby, Martin, 165, 373, 511, 521, 524, 542, 546
Scrivener, Adam, 14, 25, 75, 169
Second Priest's Tale of Peblis, The, 331
Secret of Lowry Lorc's Ears, The, 511
Seithenyn ab Seithyn Saidi, 43, 47, 105, 260, 261, 641
Senchan Torpeist and the King of the Cats, 142
Sheale, Richard, 16th century, 521, 566, 575
Sheep into Dog, 505
Sighvat Skald, fl. 998-1042, 292, 597
Sir Norbert Loses a Corpse and Refuses a Wife, 406
Skelton, John, c. 1460-1529, 135, 141, 386, 404, 458, 509, 571, 575, 580, 581
Sordello di Goito, c. 1200-c. 1269, 43, 45, 434, 511
Spenser, Edmund, 1552-1599, 361
Story of a Self-made Man, The, 539

Stow, John, c. 1525-1605, 54, 291, 404, 469, 558, 575, 584
Sturla the Lawman, 1214-1284, 86, 88, 280, 281, 299, 300, 417
Sturlason, Snorri, 1178-1241, 26, 51, 65, 103, 230, 295, 405, 419, 420, 421, 539, 601, 603, 605, 638
Svanhild and Randver, 603

Tarolfo's Unseasonable Garden, 490
Tatar Prince and the King of Kings, The, 489
Thieves Who Went in Search of Death, The, 509
Thormod Kolbrunarskald, 997-1030, 304, 305, 427, 457, 603, 605
Three Merchants and Their Inobedient Wives, 389
Tolomei, Pia de', d. c. 1300, 103, 478
Tomasone Grasso, Usurer of Milan, Does a Shrewd Stroke of Business, 543
Torpeist, Senchan, 7th century, 40, 135, 141, 142, 561, 564, 641
Tournament of Totenham, The, 322
Tragic Death of the Young Count of Foix, The, 241
Turgesius Keeps a Tryst, 622
Turkish Doctor, The, 187
Two Loyal Lovers of Florence, 454
Two Lusty Ladies of Auvergne and Their Cat, 525
Two Married Women and the Widow, The, 395

Ulrich von Lichtenstein, 1200-1276, 385, 455, 478, 588, 589
Unibos, 162, 373, 521, 538, 539, 546, 551
Untimely Death of Samher the Lapdog, The, 572
Usk, Adam, c. 1352-1430, 35, 103, 168, 457, 471, 478, 564, 613

Vergil, Polydore, c. 1470-1555, 26, 54, 104, 182, 210, 216, 317, 392
Vespers of Monreale, The, 626
Villani, Giovanni, c. 1275-1348, 524, 625

Wace, Master, d. c. 1175, 26, 133, 135, 182, 287, 516, 619, 622
Wallace and the Maid of Lanark, 458
Wedded Life of Injuriosus, The, 478
Wedding of Sir Gawain and Dame Ragnell, The, 75
Wench of Santo Domingo, The, 166
Werwolves of Meath, The, 71
White Ship, The, 287

Wiclif, John, c. 1320-1384, 25, 71, 292, 480, 501, 543, 601, 609, 624, 639
Widow Who Wore Horseshoes, The, 534
William de Harsley, *see* Harsley
William of Malmesbury, c. 1080-c. 1143, 64, 65, 388
William of Newburgh, d. c. 1198, 133, 153, 292, 508
William of Wykeham, 1324-1404, 261, 276, 280, 285, 339, 340, 561, 601, 622

Yonge, James, fl. 1423, 103, 177, 179, 306
Young Man Married to a Statue, The, 387